OXFORD READINGS IN C

The series provides students and schol
tion of the best and most influential articles on a particular author, work, or subject. No single school or style of approach is privileged: the aim is to give a broad overview of scholarship, to cover a wide variety of topics, and to illustrate a diversity of critical methods. The collections are particularly valuable for their inclusion of many important essays which are normally difficult to obtain and for the first-ever translations of some of the pieces. Many articles are thoroughly revised and updated by their authors or are provided with addenda taking account of recent work. Each volume includes an authoritative and wide-ranging introduction by the editor surveying the scholarly tradition and considering alternative approaches. This pulls the individual articles together, setting all the pieces included in their historical and cultural contexts and exploring significant connections between them from the perspective of contemporary scholarship. All foreign languages (including Greek and Latin) are translated to make the texts easily accessible to those without detailed linguistic knowledge.

# OXFORD READINGS IN CLASSICAL STUDIES

**Aeschylus**
Edited by Michael Lloyd

**Ovid**
Edited by Peter E. Knox

**The Attic Orators**
Edited by Edwin Carawan

**Lucretius**
Edited by Monica R. Gale

**Catullus**
Edited by Julia Haig Gaisser

**Seneca**
Edited by John G. Fitch

**Vergil's *Eclogues***
Edited by Katharina Volk

**Vergil's *Georgics***
Edited by Katharina Volk

**Homer's *Odyssey***
Edited by Lillian E. Doherty

**Livy**
Edited by Jane D. Chaplin and Christina S. Kraus

**Persius and Juvenal**
Edited by Maria Plaza

**Horace: *Odes* and *Epodes***
Edited by Michèle Lowrie

**Horace: *Satires* and *Epistles***
Edited by Kirk Freudenburg

**Thucydides**
Edited by Jeffrey S. Rusten

**Lucan**
Edited by Charles Tesoriero, with Frances Muecke and Tamara Neal

**Xenophon**
Edited by Vivienne J. Gray

**The Religious History of the Roman Empire**
*Pagans, Jews, and Christians*
J. A. North, S. R. F. Price

**Greek and Roman Historiography**
Edited by John Marincola

**Tacitus**
Edited by Rhiannon Ash

**Latin Panegyric**
Edited by Roger Rees

*All available in paperback*

# *Propertius*

Edited by
ELLEN GREENE AND TARA S. WELCH

OXFORD
UNIVERSITY PRESS

# OXFORD
## UNIVERSITY PRESS

Great Clarendon Street, Oxford, OX2 6DP,
United Kingdom

Oxford University Press is a department of the University of Oxford.
It furthers the University's objective of excellence in research, scholarship,
and education by publishing worldwide. Oxford is a registered trade mark of
Oxford University Press in the UK and in certain other countries

© Oxford University Press 2012

The moral rights of the authors have been asserted

First Edition published in 2012
Impression: 1

All rights reserved. No part of this publication may be reproduced, stored in
a retrieval system, or transmitted, in any form or by any means, without the
prior permission in writing of Oxford University Press, or as expressly permitted
by law, by licence or under terms agreed with the appropriate reprographics
rights organization. Enquiries concerning reproduction outside the scope of the
above should be sent to the Rights Department, Oxford University Press, at the
address above

You must not circulate this work in any other form
and you must impose this same condition on any acquirer

Published in the United States of America by Oxford University Press
198 Madison Avenue, New York, NY 10016, United States of America

British Library Cataloguing in Publication Data
Data available

ISBN 978–0–19–956303–6 (hbk)
978–0–19–956304–3 (pbk)

Printed and bound by
CPI Group (UK) Ltd, Croydon, CR0 4YY

Links to third party websites are provided by Oxford in good faith and
for information only. Oxford disclaims any responsibility for the materials
contained in any third party website referenced in this work.

# *Preface*

This book is the first to bring together some of the best and most influential scholarship written during what is, arguably, the most productive period in modern Propertius studies. The study of Propertius was, until relatively recently, largely confined to specialists. The reason for this is twofold. First, the unsettled nature of Propertius' manuscripts has made it difficult for scholars to reach a consensus about the text. Second, the highly allusive, sometimes obscure character of Propertius' poetic style has led some readers of Propertius to consider him one of the most difficult Latin authors. Thus, much of the modern scholarship on Propertius has focused almost exclusively on textual reconstruction and biography. Beginning in the 1970s, however, a tradition of interpretive scholarship emerged that has led not only to a renewed appreciation for Propertius' poetic gifts but also to the recognition of his crucial importance in informing our understanding of the larger context of Roman culture and society.

Developments in Propertius scholarship have coincided, in a number of ways, with many of the major critical approaches that have emerged in classical studies in general, approaches that deal with issues of genre, intertextuality, gender, and the social and political context of ancient poetry. Along those lines we have divided our collection into four sections: "The Text," "Poetic Contexts," "Poetry and Politics," and "Gender." These sections represent an organization of a range of positions and critical concerns that often overlap and are more diverse than such categorization might suggest. They are meant to guide the reader through the major strands in Propertius scholarship and to provide a sense of the lively debate and competing critical positions within Propertius studies.

Some of the papers in this volume are classics in the Propertian canon; others are less well known, or authored by scholars whose primary contribution to our understanding of Latin literature has been in other authors and genres. All were chosen because of the clarity of their arguments, their invitation to scholarly dialogue, and their implications for several of the broader questions that still govern Propertius studies. We have sought a balance of short papers and long, and of focused readings of select poems and broader overviews of poetic books or the whole corpus.

The selection is, we believe, as lively and quicksilver as the poetry it seeks to unfold. We are grateful to the many colleagues and friends who helped bring this book from idea to print. The editors at Oxford University Press have been ever helpful and encouraging: Hilary O'Shea, Taryn Campbell, Jenny Wagstaffe, Dorothy McCarthy, and Desiree Kellerman. Our departments at the University of Kansas and University of Oklahoma have provided support in the form of research assistants—Cara Polsley, Lauren Callahan, and Kelly Taylor —whose keen eyes helped find and correct editorial mistakes. Our colleagues also suggested and encouraged at just the right times; we single out Emma Scioli and Anthony Corbeill. Two gifted linguists translated into English the selections originally in Italian and German: Anna Talleur rendered Fedeli's and Pinotti's prose into distinct and elegant English, and Mark Preus captured Herman Tränkle's wit and precision in his translation from the German.

Most of all, we owe a debt of gratitude to all the authors represented in this collection; they are a generous and gracious bunch. It has been a pleasure to work with them and to have the opportunity to synthesize and articulate their ideas. We wish the conversation this book represents could happen in real time and space—what a meeting that would be! Which leads to our one regret: that James Butrica could not oversee his own contribution. His young death was and remains a sore loss to our field, and to his memory we dedicate this book.

On a more personal note, Ellen Greene wishes to thank Jim Hawthorne, whose technical support, companionship and love make all things possible. She dedicates this book to him. Tara Welch dedicates the book to her Oxford tutors.

## Contents

Acknowledgments     ix

1. Whose Reading of what Propertius?     1
   *Tara S. Welch*

### PART I. THE TEXT OF PROPERTIUS

2. Propertius: Between the Cult of the Transmitted Text and the Hunt for Corruption     31
   *Paolo Fedeli*

3. Editing Propertius     42
   *James Butrica*

### PART II. POETIC CONTEXTS

4. The Language of Propertius and the Stylistic Tendencies of Augustan Poetry     97
   *Herman Tränkle*

5. Propertius IV 9: Alexandrianism and Allusion     116
   *Paola Pinotti*

6. Propertius 1.4 and 1.5 and the 'Gallus' of the Monobiblos     138
   *Francis Cairns*

7. Propertius and the Unity of the Book     186
   *G. O. Hutchinson*

8. Poetic Baldness and its Cure     203
   *James E. G. Zetzel*

## PART III. POETRY AND POLITICS

9. A Farewell to Promethean Man  235
   *Hans Peter-Stahl*

10. Propertius 2.7: *Militia Amoris* and the Ironies of Elegy  273
    *Monica Gale*

11. Images of the City: Propertius' New-Old Rome  302
    *Elaine Fantham*

## PART IV. GENDER

12. Mistress and Metaphor in Augustan Elegy  323
    *Maria Wyke*

13. The Natural and Unnatural Silence of Women in the Elegies of Propertius  355
    *Barbara K. Gold*

14. Gender and Genre in Propertius 2.8 and 2.9  373
    *Ellen Greene*

15. 'Beyond Good and Evil': Tarpeia and Philosophy in the Feminine (4.4)  404
    *Micaela Janan*

16. Why Propertius is a Woman  430
    *Paul Allen Miller*

*Works Cited*  472
*Index of Propertius Poems*  507
*General Index*  508

# Acknowledgments

We thank the publishers of the original articles and papers for their permission to reprint. The original publication data for all the papers, in order of their appearance in this book, is as follows:

- Fedeli, P. 1987. "Properzio fra culto del testo tradito e caccia alla corruttela." *Bulletin de la Faculté des Lettres de Mulhouse* 15: 107–12.
- Butrica, J. 1997. "Editing Propertius." *Classical Quarterly* 47: 176–208.
- Tränkle, H. 1985. "Die Sprache des Properz und die stilistischen Tendenzen der augustustischen Dichtung." In G. Cantanzaro and F. Fantucci, eds. *Bimillenario della Morte di Properzio*,. Assisi: 155–73.
- Pinotti, P. 1977. "Properzio IV.9: Alessandrinismo e arte allusiva." *Giornale Italiano di Filologia* 29: 50–71. Reprinted in Pinotti, P. *Primus Ingredior: Studi su Properzio.* Bologna.
- Cairns, F. 1983. "Propertius 1.4 and 1.5 and the Gallus of the *Monobiblos.*" *Papers of the Liverpool Latin Seminar* 4: 61–103. Reprinted in Cairns, F. 2008. *Papers in Roman Elegy.* Bologna.
- Hutchinson, G. 1984. "Propertius and the Unity of the Book." *Journal of Roman Studies* 74: 99–106.
- Zetzel, J. 1996. "Poetic Baldness and its Cure." *Materiali e Discussioni* 36: 73–100.
- Stahl, H.-P. 1985. "A Farewell to Promethean Man." In *Propertius "Love" and "War."* Berkeley: 189–212 + 354–61.
- Gale, Monica. 1997. "Propertius 2.7: *Militia Amoris* and the Ironies of Elegy." *Journal of Roman Studies* 87: 77–91.
- Elaine Fantham, E. 1997. "Propertius' New-Old Rome." In *Roman Cultural Revolution*, eds. T. Habinek and A. Schiesaro. Cambridge: 122–35.

- Wyke, M. 2002 "Mistress and Metaphor in Augustan Elegy." *Helios* 16: 25–47. Reprinted in Miller, P. A. 2002. *Latin Elegy: An Anthology and Reader* and in Wyke, M. *The Roman Mistress.* Oxford.
- Miller, P. A. 2001. "Why Propertius is a Woman: French Feminism and Augustan Elegy." *Classical Philology* 96: 127–46.
- Gold, B. 2007. "The natural and unnatural silence of women in the *Elegies* of Propertius." *Antichthon* 41: 54–72.
- Greene, E. 2005. "Gender and Genre in Propertius 2.8 and 2.9." In W. Batstone and G. Tissol, eds. *Defining Genre and Gender in Latin Literature.* New York: 211–38.
- Janan, M. 1999. "'Beyond Good and Evil': Tarpeia and Philosophy in the Feminine." *Classical World* 92: 429–44.

# 1

## Whose Reading of what Propertius?

*Tara S. Welch*

What is an Oxford Reading? The question has arisen over the years as volumes such as this have appeared on our bookshelves and in our libraries. The stated aim of the series is to 'provide students and scholars with a representative selection of the best and most influential articles on a particular author, work, or subject. No single school or style of approach is privileged: the aim is to offer a broad overview of scholarship, to cover a wide variety of topics, and to illustrate a diversity of critical methods.' Propertius seems an ideal candidate for such a volume, for rarely has an ancient author provoked such varied responses as the love poet from Assisi. Is his love affair genuine or rhetorical, even textual? Has he abandoned his male prerogatives or does he slyly maintain them? Is he dissident or patriot? The conflict goes to the very text itself: is it reliable or not?

*Oxford Readings in Propertius* offers a panorama of these debates, and brings the views of a wide constituency of international scholars into critical and productive dialogue. Though established scholars may cherish the convenience of this volume, our ideal audience is perhaps the graduate student or advanced undergraduate seeking an overview on Propertian scholarship and, more importantly, an overview of the major critical trends in scholarship on Latin poetry.

The surfeit of work on Propertian elegy in the last decade—I count three critical editions, two commentaries, six monographs, and an edited volume[1]—is a welcome shift from the previous era, in which the

---

[1] Texts: Viarre 2005, Giardina 2005, Heyworth 2007. Commentaries: Heyworth and Morwood 2010, Hutchinson 2006. Monographs: Janan 2001, Pinotti 2004, Welch

study of Propertius was generally limited to those already expert in Latin literature. The difficulty of the text—not only its recondite allusiveness and quicksilver shifts in thought but also the very real challenge of reconstructing Propertius' words from a corrupt tradition—kept Propertius out of the undergraduate classroom. This seems to be changing, and Propertius' poetry is emerging as a fruitful lens through which to explore not only elegiac poetry, but also Roman culture and society including the role of women, the Augustan regime, and the literary milieu.

At every turn, reading Propertius' poetry complicates our understanding of these things. The poet from Assisi seems at times revolutionary in his proposal of an alternate lifestyle ('love not war'), but at other times—and sometimes at those same times—he relies on the very lifestyle he seems to reject so heartily. He defines himself vis-à-vis a mistress who is here a real woman (*matrona* or *hetaera*—again she shifts), there an article of commerce, elsewhere a metaphor for his poetry, and still elsewhere a conversation topic around which Propertius relates to other men. He rejects epic poetry yet with every rising foot he crafts it beautifully. He asserts as genuine feelings he expresses through the language of other poets. The lament of his broken heart seems simultaneously to be his greatest delight, making his attitudes all the more difficult to pin down.

This volume sees Propertius' notorious difficulty as a virtue, and as the common ground around which the included scholars enter into conversation with each other. Though they were published over a period of thirty-some years, we imagine the included essays to be a synchronous dialogue and hope our reader will treat them as such, reading if not the whole book in a sitting, at least section by section. While sectional organization facilitates editing and reading a book such as this, the reader will quickly realize that all the papers here presented could appear in some other section, and certainly engage other parts of the book. To ease the reader's approach to the included essays as an organic whole, we have endeavored to make the essays stylistically consistent—but only in matters of punctuation and citation style, never changing the words of the authors.

2005a, Cairns 2006, Keith 2008, Johnson 2009. Collection: Gunther 2006. Propertius also looms large in P. A. Miller 2003.

Our four sections, 'The Text of Propertius', 'Poetic Contexts', 'Poetry and Politics', and 'Gender' represent an organization of critical concerns that often overlap and are more diverse than such categorization might suggest. Thus cross-references abound both in the papers themselves and in our introductory contextualization of them. These sections are meant to guide the reader through the major strands in Propertius scholarship and to provide a sense of the lively debate and competing critical positions within Propertius studies, through and within which we may come to form our readings.

## THE TEXT OF PROPERTIUS

It is ironic that one of the most quoted quips about the Propertian text—Phillimore's '*quot editores, tot Propertii*' (there are as many Propertiuses as there are editors of Propertius) is itself the victim of a difficult textual tradition, having been copied and repeated in numerous contexts that do not look to Phillimore's original collocation. As Butrica points out in the article we include in our first section, Phillimore's sentiment was the apodosis of a simple condition: *if* editors are allowed to emend at will, the result is as many Propertiuses as there are editors of Propertius. The first section of our book takes up the question: which Propertius are we reading?

This question has sparked very heated debate in recent years with several new editions—Giardina's 2005 edition out of Rome, Viarre's 2005 edition for Budé, and especially the 2007 appearance of a new Oxford text of Propertius edited by Stephen Heyworth with a companion volume *Cynthia* (Heyworth 2007a and 2007b), a commentary that explains Heyworth's critical principles and shows them in action. So controversial is Heyworth's contribution to the international dialogue about the Propertian text that it spawned a seminar at the 2010 annual meeting of the American Philological Association led by luminaries of Latin poetry and of the textual tradition: Heyworth himself, Richard Tarrant, Richard Thomas, Allen Miller, Francis Cairns, and Alison Keith. The points raised at this vibrant seminar together convey why the issue of Propertius' text is so volatile:

- The manuscript tradition is complex. Recent *stemmata* include two lines from the twelfth century (problematic but popular A, cleaner but less popular N), and a third, independent line traceable to a manuscript in the possession of fifteenth-century humanist Poggio Bracciolini.[2] The manuscripts themselves are replete with gaps, corrections, and jumps. They confuse in their book divisions. Lacking divisions between poems, they leave much to the editor, especially when one considers the existence of interpolations and transpositions.[3]

- Propertius' language is difficult, peppered with archaisms, neologisms, Greek forms, obscure or arcane names, periphrases, redeployed tropes, evocations of little-known myths or variants, mixed grammatical constructions, and the like. Hermann Tränkle's book *Die Sprachkunst des Properz und die Tradition der lateinische Dichtersprache* (1960) went quite some way to demonstrating the sheer difficulty of Propertius' poetic language, which Steele Commager described as 'darkness visible.'[4]

- Propertius is highly allusive and given to creative and abrupt intertextual combinations. In addition to the long-recognized evocations, both in content and structure, of various Callimachean texts, scholars have found individual elegies rife with successive— sometimes competing, sometimes 'window'—allusions to various Hellenistic epigrams and their poetic progeny.[5]

- Ancient readers characterize Propertius as *tener* (slender, Ovid *Ars* 3.333), *blandus* (charming, Ovid *Tr.* 2.465 and 5.1.17), and *facundus* (easy, Martial 14.184.1 applied to the first book), and his style of poetry as *tersum, molle, iucundum* (refined, supple, pleasant, Pliny the Younger, *Ep.* 9.22.1). Propertius himself wishes his poetry to come softly to the lips (*veniat mollis in ora liber*, 2.1.2).

---

[2] Butrica 1984: 172, Heyworth 2007b: xiv. For the tradition, see also Butrica 2006 and Günther 1997.

[3] See the overviews in Tarrant 2006 and see Heyworth 1995 on the difficulties editors face and the tools at their disposal.

[4] Commager 1974: 3.

[5] See Hinds 1998 and Thomas 1996 on 'window allusions,' that is, allusions to a source text through an intermediary, and Thomas 2004, Keith 2008: 45–85, and Zetzel in this volume for analyses of Propertius' intertextual dexterity.

Yet it is in no way clear or straightforward what these terms signify, not least because they may describe style or content, or even the poet, or his beloved. The latter two in this list may, in a further twist, also be understood not as people but as embodiments of style and content, or of poetry itself.

- Modern sensibilities that reify the poet compromise our approach to the text. There are several dimensions to this difficulty. First, the ancient testimony does not authorize an assumption of consistency across Propertius' oeuvre. Benediktson has indeed argued that, if there is any unity to this poet, it is in his insistence on the absence of unity in any classical sense (1989, cf. Zetzel 1980 on Horace). What is more, recent work has underlined the inadequacy of 'the monological and humanist ontology of the intending subject' (P. A. Miller 2010). The speaking subject is always a hall of mirrors, such that to expect or seek a Propertius whose style is consistent is to flatten rather than read his poetry.

These difficulties give rise to a conundrum: can we discover or locate an authentic text of Propertius before we start to analyze his oeuvre, or must we use the oeuvre and what is said about it (as in Ovid's *blandus*) to try to recover an authentic text? The nineteenth century saw much of the latter, beginning with Lachmann's 1816 edition which combined a rigorous scientific approach to the text with courage to change it. Phillimore's fearful response about textual anarchy ushered in the relatively conservative twentieth century, whose editors emended words but by and large left the shape and numbering of the poems as they found them in the tradition.

The state of the question is introduced in this volume with two scholars who represent these two positions: the (textually) conservative Paolo Fedeli, and the skeptical (of the textual witness) James Butrica. It is our hope that these two articles—which speak indirectly and directly to each other—will help our readers better understand the editorial principles that form the modern textual tradition,[6] and, more importantly, appreciate the implications textual questions have on the business of interpretation.

---

[6] Viarre's text is conservative, Giardina's text is skeptical. Some would classify Heyworth's as skeptical but it is *sui generis*.

One of the foremost critics of Propertius in the twentieth century (and into the twenty-first), Fedeli has written numerous articles on Propertius' style and meaning across poems and poetic books, has authored commentaries on all four Propertian books, and is the editor of the most recent Teubner edition of Propertius. His importance in the field is demonstrated in our composite bibliography; nearly all our contributors cite Fedeli's works. 'Properzio fra culto del testo tradito e la caccia della corruttela' ('Propertius: between the text as handed down and the hunt for corruption') attempts to trace just this right path. It lies closer to cult than to hunt. Where Propertius seems abrupt or dissonant, for example, the editor must first look to Latin poetic style of the Augustan age, which delights in neologism, archaism, zeugma, and the like, and to Greek sources even beyond Hellenistic epigram, notably to tragedy and lyric. Fedeli also argues passionately for a balanced and courageous *apparatus criticus* that does more than catalogue all possibilities, but winnows them down and, like a commentary, takes a stand.

Butrica's article 'Editing Propertius' rests on the foundation that, in order to make sense of the text, one must know the history of the text. He therefore examines the earliest evidence for assuming a corrupted text (notices such as *Propertius blandus*, the Pompeii graffiti that differ from the earliest MSS), and shows how various forms of corruption—misspellings, word substitutions, morphological changes, various dislocations, duplications, interpolations, *lacunae*—can be definitively identified in the manuscript tradition. Since we know where, why, and how these corruptions occur, we can attempt to discover them elsewhere—and, moreover, we should *expect* to discover them elsewhere. Though this article appeared in print after Fedeli's (and in response to it, in part), one has the sense that Butrica's approach is what Fedeli would classify—and caution against—as *la caccia della corruttela* (the hunt for corruption).

One can tell by the length of these two articles which textual-critical position still holds the day: Fedeli's seven pages (~4000 words) are met with Butrica's 36 pages (~17,000 words). The skeptics must still defend their positions more thoroughly, especially since the conservative tradition has congealed into a sort of vulgate text. Departures from that vulgate must be chronicled and made visible. Part of the controversy of Heyworth's Oxford Classical Text

(OCT) volumes stems from the fact that his highly rearranged text (with dubious couplets removed and printed elsewhere, for example) appears as part of the OCT series, the traditional locus of the traditional (the last OCT was Barber's very conservative text of 1953 [1960]).[7] But Heyworth's preface is in English, and the companion volume *Cynthia* argues and defends his editorial choices. His edition forces the reader to contend with textual issues, like it or not. We shall see in coming years what impact these volumes will have on the 'conservative-skeptic' debate, and whether it will remain that debate or morph into something wholly different.

Which Propertius are we reading? This question goes deeper than an allegiance to an editor, text, or a set of critical principles. To a large degree, try though we might to recover an authentic text, we must all admit that we are reading our own Propertius. The reader does much to constitute the text, approaching it with a set of expectations or at the least with a set of experiences in reading poetry, Latin love poetry, Augustan literature, Greek epigram, Ezra Pound, or snippets of prose in a Latin primer to name a few, or having visited Assisi, or being in love with a woman named Cynthia, or being in any fiery and difficult romance.

## POETIC CONTEXTS

Our second section orients readers to one of the ways Propertius' readers may approach his poetry: as a text in the context of other texts. Here at the outset a distinction must be made between immersive reading and discursive or critical reading. The immersive reader (engaged in 'ludic' reading[8]) desires to get lost in a text and experience the emotions it generates. The discursive reader remains aware that a text is a discourse defined and housed in a set of discourses such as prior literary works, history, memory, etc. Of course, the immersive reader can never fully abandon discourses,

---

[7] See also Reeve 2000: 204 characterization of the OCT as having a 'narrower range and usually a selective apparatus.'
[8] Nell 1988.

nor can the discursive reader avoid an initial reaction. But these two terms are important in understanding Propertius' or any other poetry. Two recent books on Propertius demonstrate the difference between these modes of reading. W. R. Johnson's *Propertius: A Latin Lover in Rome* approaches the poet immersively. Writing for the newcomer, Johnson seeks to restore the pleasure of reading this poet rather than to replicate the tedium of traditional scholarship. Johnson's Propertius is the almost natural result of the evolution of the 'Mad Lover' type, a man who pursues the erotic at the expense of his public career. This type is an iconoclast who is a literary and cultural reaction to the imperatives of traditional Roman masculinity, imperatives which were crumbling alongside the Republic. Jason, Aeneas, Catullus, Gallus, Catulus, Sulla, and Antony all enabled the unique poetic and personal contribution of the genius from Assisi, giving him means and mission: to articulate a new way of being a Roman man. Toward the other end is Alison Keith's book *Propertius: Poet of Love and Leisure*, which does not locate Propertius' poetry as an articulation of a lifestyle but as a discourse tangled with other, sometimes opposing, discourses, such as rhetoric (a career the elegist ostensibly opposes) and leisure (dependent as it is on empire, which the elegist ostensibly opposes). Similarly Cynthia is a real or realistic woman but also a text, a way of speaking, and even a poetic manifesto. The contrast between these two excellent and insightful books is revealed in their very titles: Johnson's *Propertius Lover* and Keith's *Propertius Poet*.[9]

The irony is that critical readings help recuperate for the modern reader some of the circumstances that might have conditioned an ancient reading, offering us a pathway toward an immersion into the text that is no longer possible. To those of us who learned Latin as adults, all Latin texts are somewhat exotic. What must Propertius'

---

[9] Two other books must be mentioned here. Paul Veyne's 1988 *Roman Erotic Elegy* offers a ludic, but not immersive, reading. For Veyne, elegy is a discourse and only that—a game of poetic rules and codes not to be confused with real life. Its emotional response is delight. Duncan Kennedy's *Arts of Love* (1993) suggests that even our emotional response to the poetry is conditioned by discourses, and indeed discourse and experience cannot be severed. Whatever world elegy invents, that world is supremely implicated in discursive practices.

poetry have sounded like to a native speaker? What frames of reference were available to ancient audiences?

Though modern critics have had to work hard to uncover these poetic entanglements, they were much more readily available to Propertius' original audience, whether that audience was aware of them or not. Much scholarship of the last thirty years is devoted to locating and analyzing Propertius' nods to other authors, from Homer to Tibullus. A surfeit of superb scholarship pursues these questions with titles such as 'Propertius and—'. Such a volume as this cannot hope to present the range of debts Propertius owes to his predecessors, so we have gone in a different direction. The five papers in this section illustrate some of the ways modern scholarship can use criticism to restore immersion.

All five papers make visible to the reader various aspects of the elegies' textuality—the processes, seams, and tensions in the poetry that make it obvious that the poetry is a constructed text rather than an outpouring of sentiment. None of the papers starts from an immersive reading, though some, like Johnson, use criticism to move in that direction. Propertius asserts the textuality of his poems in three primary ways: linguistically, generically, and intertextually. Propertius' very syntax and lexicon identify him as a poet, an Augustan poet, even an Augustan elegist. Elements of language (conventional words and phrases, various aspects of content, and of course, meter) help define the poetry generically as well; that is, the presence of generic markers invites in the reader a horizon of expectations about what she will encounter and how to interpret it. Finally, Propertius' identifiable nods to specific prior or contemporary texts offer not only concrete interpretive tools to the reader, but offer a running commentary on the poetry itself. For this sort of textuality we use this broader term 'intertextuality' rather than the more traditional term 'allusion' in order to embrace the variety of ways Propertius situates himself in various poetic traditions, only one of which is direct quotation (flagged or not) of other works.[10] As the papers in this section explore, language, genre, and intertextuality overlap.

---

[10] Hinds 1998.

The linguistic approach analyzes Propertius' language itself—its morphology and syntax—in order to identify those features that make it uniquely Propertian. As mentioned above, Hermann Tränkle's 1960 book *Die Sprachkunst des Properz und die augusteischer Dichtersprache* made the greatest contribution to date toward understanding the idiosyncrasies of Propertius' style. Propertius' textuality is underscored through Grecisms in form, syntax, and lexicon, shifts in register, striking grammatical transitions, and the like. By these means, when we approach the text we know, meter and content aside, that we are not reading Cicero—or even, if we are highly in tune with nuances of style, another Augustan poet, for Propertius is 'not a man of restrained gesture' (p. 108 within). Tränkle's findings permeate commentaries and critical assessments of Propertius, but this sort of traditional philological analysis has fallen from fashion in recent decades. It should not, since it is foundational for so many other approaches to this poet. Thus, our section opens with Tränkle's own assessment of his work and its impact, the 1985 article 'The Language of Propertius and the Stylistic Tendencies of Augustan Poetry.' Like his book, this article invites us to read Propertius' poetry with an eye to his Latinity. In this respect Tränkle's work tries to reconstruct for the modern reader some of the circumstances that might accompany a more immersive reading.

Yet Tränkle acknowledges a limit to his approach: a focus on Propertius' 'Latin style' obscures the impact of the Hellenistic poetic tradition and its Roman adherents, the Neoterics. Felicitously, the greatest overall contributions of the last thirty years toward understanding Propertian intertextuality involve these two source sets. Francis Cairns, Richard Thomas, Hans-Christian Günther, Gregory Hutchinson, Adrian Hollis, and Alison Keith, to name but a few, have all explored the epigrammatic quality of Propertius' poems—both his allusions to known epigrams and the vexed questions of origins and generic identity the likeness raises.[11] One feature these studies all show is that Propertius, when he evokes specific epigrams, often blends them with others or calls to mind several epigrams in succession, even within a poem. This accounts in some instances for the

---

[11] A sampling by these scholars: Cairns 1987, Hollis 1996, Günther 1998, Hutchinson 2002, Thomas 2004, Keith 2008: 45–84, and the overview in Hollis 2006.

puzzling shifts of thought the poems display. Epigram in the background might also account for the mosaic quality of the books as a whole. A striking recent textual discovery has confirmed some speculations about the linkages between Propertian elegy and Greek elegy. The new Posidippus roll, a collection of some 100 poems likely all by the eponymous author, shows a remarkable range of topics similar to the variety seen across Propertius' four (or five) books, and it displays some motifs that Propertius seems to have adapted closely.[12]

A new text has also opened up to greater scrutiny the Neoteric influence on Propertius' poetry. The Qasr Ibrim papyrus of Gallus—a tantalizing nine lines—shows a subjective poet-speaker in love with a harsh mistress, Lycoris.[13] But it also preserves bits of two other poems: one addressed to Caesar, the other addressed to poetic critics. These three fragments show a varied collection of elegies fifteen years before Propertius entered Rome's poetic scene. Before the Qasr Ibrim papyrus was discovered, David Ross proposed that Gallus lay behind much of Propertius' poetry—particularly those poems that were least like love elegies. While the Lycoris line proves the subjective lover to be a Gallan feature as well, Ross' study nevertheless compels us to admit that the prevalent voice of the subjective lover is a Propertian innovation, not a feature inherited from Gallus or inherent in the genre.[14] Consequently, readers must come to grips with Propertius' enjambment of the subjective voice of the anguished lover and the detached, self-conscious, and highly wrought voice of the poet.[15] Though new fragments would be more than welcome in this context, there is much to be done until they resurface. In particular, work on Propertius' relationship to other poets of the Augustan age will help illuminate his relationship (and theirs) to their poetic fathers and forebears.[16]

From Tränkle's broad overview we zoom in onto one poem. Paola Pinotti's 'Propertius IV.9: Alexandrianism and *Arte Allusiva*' examines

---

[12] Hutchinson 2002, Wilson 2006.
[13] Anderson, Parsons and Nisbet 1979; see especially p.148 for the subjective voice of the poet.
[14] But see also Günther 1998.
[15] Ross 1975a with Zetzel's 1977 review.
[16] Batstone 1992, Butrica 1983, and Lyne 1998a show the range possible among unexpected source texts.

Propertius' elegy on Hercules' establishment of the *Ara Maxima*. This elegy is atypical in that it is not a subjective love elegy governed by a real or textual beloved, but rather a narrative aetion of an important urban sanctuary. Pinotti examines how this elegy draws on Alexandrian conventions of giving etymologies and embedded *aitia*, casting it in the Callimachean 'learned poem' type. Yet soon it becomes recognizable as a *paraklausithyron* (song by the closed door), a topos in the repertoire of subjective love elegy. Pinotti outlines in detail the constituent elements of this topos, locates them in Hercules' poem, and catalogues Greek and Roman examples of these elements.

Pinotti's systematization of these constituent elements and their deployment in Propertius' text reveals the work done by tradition in establishing poetic identity. The sheer number of analogues Pinotti finds for each aspect of the *paraklausithyron* or *aition* suggests the lack of specificity of the source texts in the background. We are not perhaps to note, when reading Propertius' poem, 'Of course, this is precisely what Strato, Meleager, Callimachus, Theocritus, and Asclepiades did on those five instances' but rather 'one sees this sort of thing all the time in Hellenistic poetry'. Thus the phrase *arte allusiva* is fruitfully ambiguous, and we leave it untranslated in Pinotti's title. This is not to say there are not discrete poetic echoes in this poem; Pinotti identifies several of these as well. Yet Pinotti draws attention to the ways Propertius plays with tradition in order to be original. The accretion of topical elements produces a generic reading: the reader, whether she approaches this text with a set of expectations as to its modes and manners or not, soon knows what sort of text it will turn out to be—or, let us be clearer, what sort of text it will establish itself as being. For Propertius sets up one set of expectations (erudite *aition*) only to replace it with another (*paraklausithyron*) and ends up with a generic *tour de force*, that contradiction in terms in which something recognizable as partaking of a category dismantles the very category itself. Such a paradoxical stance is eminently Alexandrian.

The paper by Francis Cairns, 'Propertius 1.4 and 1.5 and the "Gallus" of the Monobiblos,' is a thorough and detailed argument that ranges across several poems in Propertius' first book. Like Pinotti, Cairns evaluates general evocations, such as 'overall analogies of subject matter' and 'general resemblance in their (*sc.* the poems') thematic structure' as well as 'detailed verbal and conceptual coincidences' (all p. 140 *infra*) between poems, in this case, two of Propertius' own poems: 1.4 to Bassus and 1.5 to Gallus. Cairns' respect for codes and structures reveals his scholarly interests in the ways genres are formed, evoked, and defined. In both poems Propertius adopts the conventions of various subgenres, such as '*erotodidaxis/magister amoris*' and 'symptoms of love.' The recombination of these subgenres in the two poems stresses Propertius' originality in manipulating traditional elements, but also allows the poet to comment obliquely on genre—all the more so since the addressees Bassus and Gallus must evoke the famous contemporary iambist and elegist, respectively. Because Bassus is in love (with Cynthia) in 1.4, Propertius *magister* may instruct him about love—and about love poetry. The upshot—Bassus is ill-suited for both and should stay put in his own generic camp. In poem 1.5 Gallus is similarly told to butt out of Propertius' affair with Cynthia, but Gallus the elegist proves to be a more serious and threatening rival and the poet's own relationship with Cynthia seems less and less sure as 1.5 progresses. This is ironic, since Gallus does not seem, either in his own fragments nor in the evocation of him in other poets, to have been the successful lover he is in Propertius' first book. This pair of poems thus sports with the breadth of elegiac poetry (its link to iambic poetry; Callimachus had written both), and the dimensions of one of elegy's most memorable subgenres, the subjective lover. The tension between these two poems and their juxtaposed commentary on elegy as a genre animates Propertius' poetry in ways no single poem could.

The paper by Hutchinson takes this idea yet a step further. As Hutchinson asserts, 'Meaning—it will be insinuated—is not always confined within the individual poem: a part of the poet's meaning can be contained in the relations between the poems in a book.'[17] Hutchinson examines the meaning added if one reads Book 4 and Book 1 as whole books rather than as a collection of otherwise unrelated or unarranged poems. Book 4 is not a mish-mash nor a catch-all nor a cleverly designed pyramid nor a back-and-forth

---

[17] See page 187 *infra.*

struggle between the lover and the Roman. Rather, each poem responds to the last and speaks to the next, and all of them look to 4.1 in some way. The result is a collection that retains a Propertius who is as 'piquant and unpredictable' as ever (p. 195 herein). Book 1, seemingly cohesive until the tectonic rupture of tone and topic in elegies 20–22, is in fact a carefully crafted whole: 1.20 lifts urban and urbane love into the realm of myth, and 21 and 22 throw the book's characters into the atrocities of civil war. Hutchinson's article, like Cairns', has much to say about the identity of Gallus and the way this named figure colors our reading of Propertius' poetry.

Like the other authors in this section, Hutchinson sees surprise, tension, and even discomfiture as one of the hallmarks of Propertius' poetry. This notion is one of the strongest arguments against radical emendation of the Propertian text (for which see above), but the aspects to which we here wish to draw our readers' attention are the way tension, surprise, and discomfiture result from reading Propertius *against* something else, and the power the poet derives from arrangement. Scholars have teased out some of the intricacies of contemporary philosophical theories of poetry vis-à-vis arrangement. Horace's *Satires* and *Epistles* are even explicit on metathesis, the *callida iunctura*, and the relationship between *res* and *verba*. Elegy, less overtly theoretical and closely bound to the fiction of a subjective lover, lends itself less to such conversations. The papers in our section, however, suggest that such an inquiry might be very fruitful, especially in light of the Alexandrian obsession with novelty expressed as a repackaging of standard tropes and figures.

The final paper in this section examines the end-game of creative repackaging. James Zetzel's article 'Poetic Baldness and its Cure' looks back at Propertius' poetry through the lens of Ovid's poetry. The speaker of *Amores* 1.14 laments the loss of his girlfriend's hair; she has primped and dyed too much and it has all fallen out. Zetzel traces hair and its adornment as a metaphor for poetry itself. This idea leads him to Propertius 1.2 and its context, the programmatic trio of poems that opens Book 1, and thence to those poems' evocations of prior conventions and texts (Catullus, Callimachus, Meleager, Gallus, and more). The net that binds these poems all together is gossamer-subtle but strong as silk. Once again, context expands interpretation exponentially, and the net (to pursue the metaphor) not only holds poems in place but pulls them in various directions.

Zetzel's argument is that Ovid's echoes of Propertius, and Propertius' of Catullus', and so on, are not mere uses of tradition but are conscious evocations of and meditations on poetry itself. Ovid comments on Propertius the commentator. The net is so dense and extensive that everything has already appeared and been rearranged and redone. If dyed hair stands for adorned and treated poetry, then by Ovid's time the hair/poetry has been treated to destruction. Other images of overuse abound, such as the over-inscribed tree, now dead, and the failure of the poet as *medicus* and *magus* to effect any change for the better. It is no longer possible, suggests Ovid's poem, for the elegist to claim originality in traditional ways. To put it the opposite way, if the assertion of originality is itself trite, how can it be either original or trite? One of elegy's hallmark features is its candor about this conundrum, and its resolute resolution to it—to celebrate its deficiencies as its very claim to originality.


POETRY AND POLITICS

Literary texts are but one sort of 'background noise' with and against which Propertius' poetry sounds. Politics are another. In part, it is our own inability to come to grips with the upheaval of the Roman world that Propertius' era witnessed that leads modern readers to seek Propertius' commentary and stance on the events of his day. But in part it is the poet's own doing, because one of the dominant tropes of Propertian (and Roman) elegy is the elegiac lover's avowed opposition to conventional Roman *mores* and values. The Propertian lover claims to reject the traditional roles that defined a Roman male citizen, that of statesman and soldier. Yet his frequent discursive engagement with the realities of Roman politics, and with the values of militarism and conquest attendant on those realities, reveals an intimate connection between poetry and historical context.

Two axes help define Propertius' stance vis-à-vis his times. The first is the most obvious: was Propertius pro- or anti-Augustus? Note that we phrase this opposition in terms of the persons—Propertius,

Augustus—rather than the abstracts such as the poetry or the regime. Readings along this axis tend to emphasize Propertius' own family history, his movement into Maecenas' circle, the pressures and benefits brought to bear on his poetry by his new well-placed friends, and his relationship with Cynthia (or even a fictitious 'Cynthia') as an expression of real or potential passions. A recent paper by Stephen Heyworth (which, incidentally, reads Propertius as anti-Augustan) expresses the need to read a person and persons behind the poetry (2007c: 95):

> In trying to reconstruct his meaning in various poems, I assume that (though corrupted in transmission) they were originally written by a single individual, whose character and attitudes had similar incoherence and similar unity to those we experience around us, whether through personal acquaintance or other media. In his poetry he expresses a face to the world, and identifies it with the name Propertius. This provides a continuity that should radically affect our reading. The attitudes of the persona are established early on; this enables the poet to be less overt later, yet expect all he writes to be read as coming from the elegiac lover.

Whether this is the poet speaking frankly or the elegiac lover who is the poet's creation, the reader is entitled to hear the voice of a person across Propertius' four books. How does this person relate to the new regime?

At one end of this axis is the work of Francis Cairns. Cairns' substantial contributions to our understanding of Propertian poetry lie in his explorations of genre and Propertius' literary antecedents, but throughout his oeuvre Propertius emerges as Augustus' man through and through. Such, argues Cairns, is the nature of ancient patronage, which entails material benefits on the part of the poet and that of the patron. In his 2006 book, *Propertius: The Augustan Elegist* (note the emphasis on the man), Cairns traces the *princeps* himself as an evolving theme in Propertius' poetry throughout Books 2–4 as the poet–patron relationship became tighter and more focused.

At the other end is Ettore Paratore, an immensely influential scholar of Latin poetry in the twentieth century. In one of his last articles, 1985's 'Gli atteggiamenti politici di Properzio' ('The Political Attitudes of Propertius'), Paratore reprises a theme to be found throughout his life's work on the elegist: all four books of Propertius'

Whose Reading of what Propertius? 17

poetry depict a Propertius who remains, for personal and poetic reasons, distant from, and even critical of the new order. Paratore's title again assumes a hierarchy: the man before the poetry. Paratore's article, written in a conversational tone that supports its focus on artists and critics as people, also provides the most eloquent and powerful defense of the prosopographical approach: it insists that personal politics and art are entwined. In Europe of the early and mid-twentieth century, this relationship between politics and art is obvious, and Paratore discusses, in passing, the constraints of an artist or critic writing under Italy's fascist era. In recent years these constraints are less visible, but the implication of art (and/or criticism) in politics is certainly still there.

The second axis along which critics understand Propertius' relationship with his era is that which considers Propertius' poetry (or any elegiac poetry, or any poetry) as a set of rhetorical norms—a discourse—rather than as the expression of, or window into, a personality. This discourse may be understood as standing deliberately apart from the realities of production or, on the other end, as fully implicated in the ideologies in which it is created. Once again, Francis Cairns' approach exemplifies the former, and three articles illustrate this position. Cairns 1984 examines the Actium elegy (4.6) and concludes that its structure and content are hymnic. As such a devotional poem, it cannot at the same time be critical of the devotee. The poem lauds Apollo and his human protégé, Augustus. Similarly, Cairns 1992 reads Propertius 4.9 on Hercules in the komastic tradition, and this literary pedigree determines the poem's content and form, which are divorced from any contemporary meanings of Hercules and the Bona Dea. Finally, Cairns 1979a reads Propertius' reaction against the marriage law (elegy 2.7) as pro-Augustan in this way: the persona Propertius presents in this elegy is so cantankerous as to prevent the reader from taking him, or his criticism, seriously. The poem parodies such a grump, whose criticism is laughed off.

Paul Veyne in his 1988 book *Roman Erotic Elegy* urges us to read Propertius' poetry in just this way—as a textual exercise whose rules are known by poet and reader. Veyne's approach reacts against the biographical reading outlined above; he seeks to liberate modern readers from our modern poetic aesthetic, which desires to see a passionate poet behind passionate poetry. Instead we should recognize the poetry as a series of elaborate jokes, designed for the pleasure of the poet and reader alike. When we read Propertius we recognize ourselves to be entering into another world, the world of elegy in which characters do what they always do in elegy (the lover pines; the mistress eludes; the rival prods).

Against this we find Duncan Kennedy's *Arts of Love* from 1993, in which Kennedy argues that elegy, as a discourse, is always implicated in politics (broadly defined); it can never be severed from the context in which it was produced and the context in which it is consumed. His chapter 'An Irregular in Love's Army' engages Veyne's textualist reading to argue that, even when elegy beckons its reader to assume its world is discrete, and even when its reader, savvy to its generic conventions, is willing to 'play the game' (to adopt Veyne's terminology), elegiac poetry nevertheless can only assert its autonomy from the real world by invoking, assuming, and engaging that real world. This is true for the poetry *and* for the reader: 'I have presented elegy . . . as a discourse constituted by all the forces that moulded the text plus its reception, including our own, in recognition both of its "determinateness" and its "contingency"' (p.100). Propertius' fictive Cynthia arises from real possible Cynthias in his world, and ours. Because of the embeddedness of Propertius' figures and language, all his poems—whether anti-Augustan or not—serve in the end to reinforce the idea of Augustus and therefore his authority.[18]

Kennedy's exploration is highly theoretical and seeks to test the contours of reading any poetry, not just Latin love poetry. His reading, which owes much to the merger of literary critical theory and Classics scholarship in the seventies and eighties, was harbinger to a number of book-length studies of Propertius' poetry that read Propertius foremost as a discourse implicated in its cultural milieu (rather than extricated from it). Two such studies stand out from the last decade. Michaela Janan's *Politics of Desire* (2001) and P. A. Miller's *Subjecting Verses* (2004) both bring (Lacanian) psychoanalytical theory to bear on Propertius' poetry. Since Lacan's work explores the interaction between self and society, it is a productive way to grapple with Propertius' 'politics' (in the broadest sense of the word, i.e. relationships to and

---

[18] See also Kennedy 1993.

within a civic society). Janan's book focuses on Propertius' fourth book, in which the poet explicitly engages public themes. Miller's book surveys all elegy as a poetic phenomenon whose lifespan exactly matches the greatest political and social upheaval the Roman world had ever seen, the transition from Republic to Empire.

Put these two axes together and we have a grid on which to plot approaches to Propertius' politics. In this section we have chosen to present one article from each axis, and then a paper that presses what 'political' means. The section opens with Hans Peter Stahl's 'Farewell to Promethean Man.' This paper is a chapter of Stahl's 1985 book *Propertius 'Love' and 'War.' Individual and State under Augustus*. Like the titles mentioned above from the first axis, Stahl's title reveals an emphasis on the poet as a person; the word 'individual' in his title underscores just how he reads Propertius. Stahl's book traces Propertius' evolution as a poet of the new era, from the modest poet of personal themes, homelander of another town (Assisi), lover of love and of the sweet poetry it generates; to member of Maecenas' court, elbow-rubber with people of power, voice read by more than his personal circle; to man fully within the circle of power, powerless to resist its insistent if unspoken demands, yet unable in the end to capitulate to it. Propertius' poems reveal a man at odds with his station in the world, as he refuses, then resists, then succumbs, to the pressure to write poetry that flatters his emperor's milieu, before he at last falls silent. Stahl's Propertius is a bundle of contradictions not because of the flaws of the text or the complexity and inscrutability of his sources, but because he is trying to walk the fine line between his authentic inner self and the self he shows to the world.

The paper we select from Stahl's book explores a pair of elegies in which 'the gap between the poet's public concessions to the régime and his personal standpoint (sc. 'is') wider than ever before' (p. 240 below). Elegies 3.4 and 3.5 offer together the two sides of the poet's persona, intimately bound with each other through parallels in language and content. From their mutually evocative opening salvos (*arma deus Caesar,* 'God Caesar (prepares) war,' and *pacis Amor deus* 'Love is the god of peace,' 3.5.1) to the side-stepping closing thoughts of each poem, these two poems demonstrate Propertius' hierarchy of values: love above all, then the philosophy of peace (which is still antithetical to Augustan arms), then—well, not ever—arms. Stahl's essay closes with a dark reading of elegy 3.22 whose love of Rome and fear of Greek mythology must, if the reader is at all acquainted with Propertius' prior poetry, ring (in Stahl's opinion) false. The clever poet asks us to read between and around the lines.

From the other interpretive axis ('poetry as discourse') our representative is Monica Gale's 1997 article, 'Propertius 2.7: *Militia Amoris* and the Ironies of Elegy.' Here Gale addresses the debate about Propertius' pro- or anti-Augustan views by arguing that the very terms, pro-Augustan and anti-Augustan, are oversimplified and are, in themselves, problematic. Engaging with earlier readings of elegy 2.7 that focus on the poem as evidence of Propertius' attitudes toward Augustus, Gale uses 2.7 to explore a way of reading Propertius that transcends the aforementioned categories of pro- and anti-Augustan. Gale argues that the poem sets up a series of oppositions which it then collapses in various ways. This produces, in Gale's view, a duality of discourse that suggests Propertius' ambivalent identifications with both elegiac and Augustan ideals. Gale further argues that though the ambivalence in Propertius' text may allow readers to see Propertius as pro-Augustan or as anti-Augustan, an 'ironic sub-text' ultimately undermines such clearly defined oppositions.

Gale's approach is reminiscent of the influential work of J. P. Sullivan, whose book *Propertius: A Critical Introduction* (Cambridge 1976) inaugurated the current age of Propertian scholarship, which approaches the text as a cultural document rather than a purely aesthetic one. In advance of Gale, Sullivan also locates irony in Propertius' poetry. Yet Sullivan sees Propertius' irony as a hedged form of criticism of the regime, subtle so as to evade detection and censure. In a Veyne-like vein, Sullivan attributes Propertius' ironic stance to the requirements of his poetry (p.57: 'the conventional elegiac preference for love rather than war'), but he also, Stahl-like, sees an injured man behind the dissonant stance (also p.57: 'Propertius had his own personal reasons for his anti-militarist stance'). We draw in Sullivan's work here to illustrate how Propertius' difficult and ambiguous language can give rise to a number of diverse critical positions, even contrary ones. Gale's treatment of Propertius' irony in 2.7 (an assessment that is transportable to other poems) makes it not a conundrum to be resolved, but a conundrum deliberately unsolvable except by the predilection of the reader.

*Whose Reading of what Propertius?* 21

The elegist's fourth book, with its professed patriotic program (*sacra diesque canam et cognimina prisca locorum*, 4.1.69) looms large in most studies of Propertian politics; it is partly for this reason that we illustrate the axes above with papers on poems from his first three books. Thus our readers may see Propertius' political dimension as a feature that recurs in his collection rather than something new that emerges late in his poetic life. We may observe that the patriotic program of 4.1.69 is not an explicitly Augustan program (though the *princeps* appears in the Actium elegy, 4.6),[19] but scholars have demonstrated that Augustus is there nonetheless, in the imperialism that keeps Arethusa's lover away in 4.3,[20] to the presence of Livia in the background of 4.9's Bona Dea priestess,[21] to the *mores* enacted against Tarpeia in 4.4,[22] and expressed, in shadow form, by ghost Cornelia in the closing poem of his life's work.[23]

Paul Veyne had called elegy 'pastoral in city clothes,' a label that distances Rome from anything essential and overdetermines it as a discourse, in that it is a mode of communication (pastoral) cloaked in another mode of communication (clothes).[24] We close this section with a paper that deals explicitly, and literally, with *political* Propertius: Propertius as poet of the Rome-as-*polis*. Elaine Fantham's 'Propertius New-Old Rome' looks at the politics of Book 4 in panorama rather than by scrutiny of any one poem. Like Sullivan, Fantham blends the man with the discourse; Propertius was a man who lived in the newly golden capital city of the incipient empire, and thus he witnessed the transformation of the very context in which he wrote, but also a poet inspired by previous 'poetic cities' such as the ones built by Vergil in *Aeneid* 8 and Tibullus 2.5. For all the glitter and marble of the new city, Fantham demonstrates that Propertius lingers instead on the purity and possibility of the early city, not yet overbuilt and overlaid with imperial concerns. His preference for the simpler urban past is, to Fantham, a powerful expression of his lingering discontent with the new order. It also constitutes the same sort of escape Veyne saw when he likened elegy to pastoral.

---

[19] For political readings see Cairns 1984, Johnson 1973.
[20] Hallett 1971: 141–7, Wyke 1987a.    [21] Spencer 2001.
[22] See Janan in this volume, Welch 2005b.    [23] Johnson 1997.
[24] Veyne 1988: 101.

The presence of Fantham's paper in this volume allows the *Oxford Readings* reader to broaden the scope of motifs that convey Roman ideologies, but more importantly, requires the reader to recognize at once the convergence of the poet of the first (personal) axis with the poetry of the second (discursive). When the poetry refers to events, places, rituals, and persons whose existence is demonstrably external to the poetry,[25] the modes of identity are especially complex. This relationship is better theorized in the case of ekphrasis: where works of literature refer to works of art that readers can see independently, the reader is also the spectator and confronts this double role, bringing real experience and literary experience to bear on the meaning of the text and on her interaction with it.[26] Yet how much richer perhaps the theory can become in the case of monuments and rituals, which are not exclusively viewed as artworks (in the sense of being artifacts that draw attention to their own aestheticism) but as the environment and activities of one's daily business. Propertius' monuments (both included and omitted) are both a thing itself and a thing in which.

## GENDER

Text, literary texture, and political context all come together in the gender identities of the Propertian lover and his beloved. This may be one reason gender in elegy, and Propertius particularly, has been such a dominant theme in Propertian studies in the last quarter of a century. Another reason is the explosion of feminist critical theory in this period, fueled by political and social changes. After the initial political and economic gains in voting and property rights gained by the suffrage movement (called 'first wave' feminism of the late nine-

---

[25] Cynthia's ghost in 4.7, for example, does not have a demonstrable existence external to the poetry, but the rites to Juno at Lanuvium that Cynthia has visited (4.8) do.

[26] For studies of ekphrasis and the visual as a junction of the real and the poetic, see Fowler 1996. For monuments specifically as the bridge between real and literary experience in Propertius 4, see Welch 2005a for Book 4, and Pinotti 1983 and O'Neill 2000 on the Vertumnus elegy/monument. Ramsby 2007 explores inscriptions (though imagined ones) as a bridge between the durable world of stone and the literary heritage of elegy in epigram.

teenth and early twentieth centuries), the 1960s and 1970s gave rise to what is now called 'second wave' feminism, aimed at addressing social and cultural inequality. These trends in feminist studies focused on the lived experience of women claiming for themselves a new freedom from the marginalized positions they had occupied before as underpaid workers, unrepresented voters, unfulfilled lovers, and unheard voices. One goal of this long period was the achievement of gender equity, that is, closing the perceptible gap between women and men in various contexts. Thanks to the vigilance and labor of the participants in the first and second waves, this goal has largely been achieved in the West (though woefully not in other parts of the world, and even here complacency would undermine these results).

More recently, feminist critical studies have moved toward a 'third wave' concentration on the discourses that define and confine women and men. This wave resists an essentialist definition of women (and the resulting consistency of women's needs), not only because the 'essential woman' of the second wave seemed steadfastly to be white and middle class, but also because any essential understanding of 'woman' erases or underplays change, difference, conflict, or even irrationality. Third-wave women (by this, we mean the women as objects of thought *and* as authors of theory) are culturally bound rather than of a universal stamp, and resolutely individual, and so resisting description.

Propertian gender studies have followed the path of feminist criticism more broadly. The first and second waves emerged in the attempt to recover a real Cynthia (or a real Propertius, for that matter) and understand her role in society. Judith Hallett's work on Cynthia in the 1970s blazed the trail. Her article 'The Role of Women in Roman Elegy: Counter-Cultural Feminism' encapsulates the second wave, concluding thus: 'What better cause for living counter to standard *mores* than a female companion who defies the expectations of what is ultimately an inequitable, hypocritical society and affords inspiration for a simple, honest, and rewarding life?'[27] Evidence that the second wave continues to be a fruitful way of approaching Propertius is found in Sharon James' book, *Learned Girls and Male*

---

[27] Hallett 1973: 123, and see also her 1971 Harvard dissertation.

*Persuasion*,[28] which examines elegy from the point of view of the *puella*, whom James reads as a learned courtesan asserting herself within a male erotic and financial economy. Understanding the *puella* as a courtesan makes her knowable or identifiable as a real person (or character portrayed as a real person) with a stable identity, the sort who must negotiate her prescribed position in a male world.

The more recent trend, following the third wave, is toward an attempt to understand how the *puella* is and is shaped by a set of discursive practices. I note here the parallel between this development and the interpretive configurations seen in the sections above: does the text have a firm, essential identity, or are we to read its history as one of gaps and fissures? Is poetry meant to be unselfconsciously enjoyed, or does it require that we take note of its embeddedness within a tradition? Was Propertius a man reacting to his time, or a speaker using discourse to interact with his times, which are also a form of discourse?

Our last section offers five papers which display a range of third-wave approaches to the text. Their implication in and dependence on the other three large rubrics under which this collection is organized—text, literary background, and politics—will be clear from the frequency with which these final five papers cite the other papers in this volume. We open with Maria Wyke's paper, 'Mistress and Metaphor in Latin Love Elegy.' Wyke has authored several now canonical papers in which she exposes the elegiac mistress as the product of a set of discourses, even a discourse herself: she is not only a metaphor for the poetry, in a sense she *is* the poetry. In Wyke's analysis, Propertius' poetry does not seek to reveal nor elevate real women, even if they, or one, lies behind the poetry. Rather, the mistress is a way the poet explores and discusses his own role as a man in society: alienated from normative positions of power and from other men who do what is expected of men, such as fight, marry, procreate, and legislate. In this sense too Wyke's paper crests the third wave, which looks not only at femininities but masculinities as well as part of a larger, diverse, complex, even contradictory system of gender. Unfortunately, the normative man and his world

---

[28] James 2003.

still reign supreme, controlling, even writing the woman (and the non-normative man) into the contours of the masculine.

Ellen Greene's article, 'Gender and Genre in Propertuis 2.8 and 2.9,' similarly examines the role of the male poet in the larger system of gender roles. The poet of the Monobiblos had established himself as a different sort of man by refusing to participate in the normative masculine activities of fighting, marrying, procreating, and legislating. In the second book he refuses even to write about such things (which writing could itself be construed as a normative masculine activity), and Propertius' literary program is often his subject in the second book. Greene's paper focuses on what she regards as one of the most striking features of Propertian elegy: the constant interplay between epic and elegiac discourses and between conflicting images of the *amator* as both lover and poet, master and mastered. Revealing these contradictions at work in poems 2.8 and 2.9, in which Propertius laments Cynthia's infidelity and invokes several stories from the epic tradition, Greene argues that by allying the elegiac enterprise with the heroic values of epic and thus linking *amor* to images of death and glory, Propertius often collapses oppositions between the images of an effeminized lover and a masculine hero. By reconstituting the *amator*'s passivity in the context of masculine heroic achievement, Greene contends, Propertius implicitly grants heroic status both to the traditionally disempowered male lover and his putatively 'soft' poetic genre.

Masculine autonomy and control, paradoxical byproduct (or intention) of the espousal of an alternative lifestyle and the treatment of the *puella* as a metaphor, find their strongest footing in the fact that elegy is, of course, voiced by a man. This man frequently grants his female protagonist (protagonists, in Book 4) a voice—which is always tempered through the male author—but he also silences her, sometimes overtly so. In 'The natural and unnatural silence of women in the *Elegies* of Propertius', Barbara Gold takes up this feature of the elegies and asks what it means that women are silenced and silent in this collection of poems. She opens her essay with a discussion of the difference between these two forms of non-speech: 'silenced' is something that happens to one, imposed on someone who becomes a victim of this sort of control, whereas 'silence' is itself a speech act, a deliberate placement of space into communication.

Gold helps explain the role of the ventriloquized woman as a form of silencing: the one who wields the pen has all the power of speech and he can choose not to name her, to obscure her personhood by turning her into a metaphor for the book as written, and by revealing her to be a performance (through his own ventriloquism of her voice). When the woman is allowed to speak in Propertius' collection, her words are liable to get out of control—she becomes angry, hyperbolic, deceitful. These are also forms of 'silencing' in that they make a case that women should not be allowed to speak; they are only safe when silenced. These elements in the poetry reassert that very gender hierarchy that elegy on the surface professes it disrupts. Yet in Gold's analysis a further sort of silence undermines this male control. Book 4 puts on record two women who speak from beyond the grave: Cynthia, back in a dream, and Cornelia who closes the collection. These women, 'silent' speakers in the sense that their words are not of this world, linger after the poet has stopped speaking and, through the possibility that they will have the last word, reveal the poet's willingness to relinquish to them some control over his own voice. When Cynthia and Cornelia speak from the other side of life, we have a glimpse of what they might have said on this side *if allowed*. Their words thus not only constitute them as speakers but even draw attention to the flesh-and-blood silencing they endured. We thus see the danger they might have posed to the masculine world if allowed to speak, and this visible danger opens a fissure in the bedrock on which masculine authority stands.

This very fissure is the focus of the last two essays in the collection, which in very different ways bring psychoanalytical theory to bear on our understanding of the Propertian gender paradox. Michaela Janan's paper '"Beyond Good and Evil": Tarpeia and Philosophy in the Feminine' explores elegy 4.4, an extraordinarily rich poem in its blend of gendered content (a transgressive Vestal), political import (who betrays the Roman state), literary background (with Parthenius' *Erotika Pathemata* and Vergil's Dido looming in the background), and crucial textual thorns (at least three, at 4.4.3, 34, and 69). Janan traces moments of indeterminacy throughout the poem, from the poem's refusal to determine whether Tarpeia is to be our heroine or villain, to her role as (Vestal) man-hater and (erotic) man-lover, to her imagined life as Tatius' captive/lover/legitimate wife/queen.

These indeterminacies are not merely instances in the poem or indicative of Tarpeia's situation, but they are the very heart of Propertius' elegiac poetry. As in Gold's paper, when we start looking at what is *not* there, what is silenced or excluded or impossible to pin down, we begin to have a sense of the precariousness of what *is* there. Tarpeia collapses male categories of thought: 'if "manhater" and "manlover" are fundamentally so indistinguishable, if feminine margin and center of the state exchange places so readily, are "man" and "state" meaningful reference points?' (p. 419 *infra*). Tarpeia's paradox—her central marginality, her fundamental instability, her resolute indeterminacy—present themselves, in Janan's reading (via Lacan nuanced by Irigaray), as a 'feminine syntax' that resists, even undermines, the rules of discourse.

P. A. Miller reads this concept of a feminine discourse across the ouevre, particularly Books 2 and 3, and concludes that Propertius' fissures in thought do not simply reveal the feminine, they *are* the feminine. This explains to Miller, 'Why Propertius is a Woman.' Both within poems and across poems (some of which are analyzed elsewhere in this volume), the poet occupies subject positions that are at once official and subversive, pro and con, conscious and unconscious. This position is, in Lacanian terms, a feminine position—outside the Symbolic (defined as the world of rules and codes, including language and all semiotic systems, and styled as masculine) and outside the Imaginary (our construction of ourselves, which we project into the Symbolic), but necessary to both, the 'intrinsic eccentricity', the excluded thing whose exclusion must be included for the Symbolic to have meaning (p. 441 *infra*).

Miller contends, however, that Propertius' appropriation of the feminine position does not represent a new egalitarianism in amatory relations. Rather, the feminine discursive position adopted by Propertius suggests a destabilization of conventional Roman notions of masculinity. The elegist's pose of *servus amoris*, which inverts normative gender roles, thus serves to call into question a host of social and political norms concerned with gender, power, discourse, and male desire. In the decayed ruins of the Republic and the gleaming new empire, in which one man was building a new Symbolic, it could not be otherwise.

Whose reading of what Propertius? Yours.

# Part I

# The Text of Propertius

# 2

## Propertius: Between the Cult of the Transmitted Text and the Hunt for Corruption[1]

*Paolo Fedeli*

It is not purely for the love of autobiography that I take the liberty of opening this contribution with a personal memento. I had just finished my studies at the university when Eduard Fraenkel began to hold his seminars in Bari. Of course, amongst us new Ph.D.s there was a noble rivalry to submit to him our first works and the philological problems that troubled us. To all of this he responded with infinite patience, as well as with extraordinary discernment and unbeatable doctrine. I do remember, however, that when I began to consult him regarding Propertian matters, he objected, with the frankness that was his trademark, that on Propertian matters he had very little to say; in fact, the Umbrian poet was of no interest to him at all, because too obscure and contorted. In this, Fraenkel probably expressed the ancient distrust of his great teachers, Leo and Wilamowitz: the contributions made by the former regarding Propertius were merely a couple of articles[2] and a review of the first edition of Rothstein's commentary.[3] Wilamowitz also was only marginally interested in Propertius, and he never wrote directly about

---

[1] This essay was translated into English by Anna Talleur, who also translated Fedeli's quotations of Latin passages.
[2] Leo 1889: 431–7; 1898a: 469–78.
[3] The review appeared in Leo 1898b: 722–50.

him (except for a note of textual criticism).[4] Fraenkel's judgment however reflects the remaining *communis opinio* regarding Propertius, so much so that the motto with which Phillimore premised his edition (*quot editores tot Propertii*, 'there are as many Propertiuses as there are editors') is still constantly picked up and reused.

So it is not surprising that Propertius' text is fertile ground for conjectural criticism, so fertile in fact that Smyth diligently listed thousands of conjectures:[5] very few Propertian verses have been left intact. So it is truly amazing when one finds that, in appraising new editions of Propertius, ingenuous and fiery reviewers continue to reckon with the conjectures made by their editors.

In approaching such a complex author as Propertius, it is necessary now more than ever to state a few precepts at the outset. It is obvious that one must 'know' the author whose work one is examining: 'knowing' means of course having a strong sense of the manuscript tradition and of the history of the transmission of the text; it means having real intimacy with the author's style, but also with the way the author works and with his technique, with his sources and with the topoi that merge in the author's work as well as familiarity with the work of contemporary authors. These are elementary rules, necessary not only to the study of Propertius, which should be obvious. Perhaps they are not so obvious, though, if one takes into account the superficiality with which all of us approach authors without knowing them adequately. This is the reason for which we often see absurd defenses of indefensible readings, or, on the other hand, the display of 'brilliant' conjectures which are entirely gratuitous, and end up changing the text on the basis of what we would like the author to be saying.

It is worthwhile to reflect for a moment on the situation of Propertian studies in the light of the precepts stated earlier. As far as the manuscript tradition is concerned, the Neapolitanus (N) is undisputedly the main manuscript, since it is undoubtedly superior to those belonging to the secondary family. The review made by

---

[4] The note, regarding 1.12.2, was originally published in 1884 and reprinted in Wilamowitz 1935–72 *Kl. Schr.* IV: 565.
[5] Smyth 1970.

Hanslik of the inferior manuscripts did not provide any interesting results; in fact, this review made the whole apparatus of his critical edition almost unusable because of the hodgepodge of obvious copyists' interventions. Recently a noteworthy contribution to the knowledge of the manuscript tradition has been made by J.L. Butrica:[6] he found a series of codices that he believes to be akin to N, but independent from it, and that would thus allow a better definition of the secondary family.[7] The results of the soundings made by Butrica on only a few elegies must be examined scrupulously; it is foreseeable, however, even if his conclusions are confirmed, that still the result will not be a whole overturning of Propertius' text, since Butrica himself recognizes the superiority of N.

As far as the style of Propertius is concerned, recent works (especially that of Tränkle, even if it by now is weighed down by years and by an aged methodology) brought to light its composite and variegated character—in the use of archaisms and neologisms, in the influence of the *sermo communis* and of lyric style—and at the same time its extreme adaptability according to the context. His love for brusque changes, for swerves in logic, and for sudden transitions from one subject to the next, as well as for continuous variations in apostrophe, have also become more and more evident. It is ever clearer that one cannot know Propertius without placing him in relation, also in terms of style, to the work of the Alexandrians: his taste for erudition, his continuous pursuit of allusion, and his predilection for a mosaic-style composition seem to be the true trademark of Propertian poetry. Thus the logical conclusion is that one may not approach Propertius without knowing his Hellenistic sources well (and this is the most obvious limitation of the otherwise well-deserving research of Tränkle, which has too limited a conception of language and style). However, it is also necessary to approach a work such as that of Propertius with much humility in order to avoid on the one hand making the author's sentences

---

[6] Butrica 1984.
[7] It is Z (Bibl. Naz. Marciana, Fondo antico 443 [19129]) and a series of manuscripts derived from the lost codex of Poggio: v (Bibl. Vaticana, Vat. Lat. 3273), m (Paris, Bibl. Nat., Lat. 8233), r (Geneva, Bibl. Bodmeriana, Cod. Bod. 141), u (Bibl. Vaticana, Vrb. Lat. 1514), s (München, Universitätsbibl., C im 22 [Ms 8° 291]), c (Rome, Bibl. Casanatense 15 [A.V. 50]).

senseless or not even Latin (perhaps with the pretext that the author has great stylistic audacity), on the other hand changing it gratuitously because of an inadequate knowledge of his poetry and of his way of composing.

Today the tendency of the textual critic of Propertius, now that the Housmanesque furies have been put to sleep, can be defined as 'cautiously conservative:' this is a position which I wholeheartedly share, especially if by conservative tendency one does not mean a blind defense of the text as it has come down to us; because doubtlessly even in the direction of defense of the transmitted text there has been some excess. To prove this, a few examples will suffice.

In elegy 1.3 the poet comes to Cynthia's house in the middle of the night after a banquet, drunken and lusty. Upon seeing his lady placidly sleeping, he is first overwhelmed with an impulse of ecstatic admiration; but Bacchus and Amor, in an unfortunate union, push him, in several clumsy attempts, each less innocent than the previous, to approach her amorously. Propertius puts his garlands of flowers on her forehead (21–22), he fixes her hair (23), he attempts to place a few apples in her lap with disastrous results (24–26). The least that Cynthia can do, as she is disturbed in her sleep by her lover's clumsy attempts and by the sudden falling of apples, is sigh (27–30):

> *et quotiens raro duxti suspiria motu,*
> *obstipui uano credulus auspicio,*
> *ne qua tibi insolitos portarent uisa timores,*
> *neue quis inuitam cogeret esse suam.*
>
> And whenever, but rarely, you stirred and sighed, I froze, trusting in futile omen, lest anything you saw bring you strange fear, or that someone unknown might force you to be his unwillingly.

At v. 27, however, *duxti* is the correction of the minor manuscripts for *duxit* in the more authoritative codices. Although the variation is minimal, the reading given in the minor manuscripts was defended by Rothstein and subsequently by Salvatore and by Pasoli.[8] In order to solve the problem it is necessary to make one preliminary logical consideration: the presence of *tibi* in the following sentence (v. 29) and of *tuis* in v. 22 allows us to understand that this is an apostrophe

---

[8] Rothstein 1898; Salvatore 1956: 193–4; Pasoli 1957: 25.

to the beloved woman. It is supposed, although I do not understand why, that the effect of speaking directly to Cynthia would be pedantic; but it seems to me more important to note how Propertius seems generally to be very free in his use of apostrophe. And regarding the accusation of 'pedantry', here we are before one of the many cases in which personal taste is brought into a discussion of textual criticism: how often do we hear that in the choice among variants the preference is given to one of them because it is 'poetically more effective!' Rather, those who work with poetic texts should always keep in mind a sentence of the greatest Italian writer of the century, Carlo Emilio Gadda: 'It is doubtful that those poets who are labeled as sublime are able to be so in every instance both in intention and in outcome: by "outcome," I mean in the verse. They throw out verses: for they are not lacking in good intentions. Good intentions, so the saying goes, pave the road to hell. What sort of a pastiche comes out in the end, however, remains to be seen.'[9]

In this case, if one engages the discussion at this level, the fact that the apostrophe to the beloved woman occurs right at this very moment is even more significant: the fact that it breaks in on the narration right at the very moment when the rapture over Cynthia's beauty is most ecstatic. It is this apostrophe which creates a break between the primitive lascivious desires of Propertius and the end of his reverie over Cynthia's beauty (an end caused by the moonlight). This is where a discussion of style comes in: Rothstein's objection to the syncopated form appears to be more serious; such forms appear twice in fact in this same elegy (the other is at v. 37 *consumpsti*) while in the rest of Propertius' work there is only one other case (4.2.29 *est imposta*). However, this very repetition in the same elegy of a rare form, far from being strange, is actually a stylistic procedure that is dear to Propertius, for which Löfstedt has given two explanations: the repetition of rare forms within short range of each other allows Propertius to legitimate them, or to demonstrate his predilection for those forms.[10] This is a case in which the knowledge of the technique and style of the author leads one to embrace the emendation.

---

[9] Gadda 1982: 64.   [10] Löfstedt 1933 (1942): 205.

At times the defense of the transmitted text, in an attempt to avoid accepting corrections of minimal consequence, becomes almost ridiculous. In elegy 3.3 after Propertius has dreamt of being on Helicon and of trying to drink from the spring of epic, Apollo warns him to stay within the bounds of 'slender' poetry: 'Why (he asks) did your poetry leave the beaten track?' (v. 21, *cur tua praescriptos euecta est pagina gyros?*). The Propertian manuscripts concur, with only minor differences, in transmitting *cur tua praescripto seuecta est pagina gyro*, while the text that I accept is the one proposed by Lipsius. The transmitted manuscript is not lacking illustrious defenders: the acceptance of the phrase *seuecta est* means admitting the presence of a *hapax*; despite the fact that Lachmann,[11] Hertzberg,[12] and Tränkle[13] agree that a *hapax* in Propertius is nothing to be surprised at, in defense of this position they cite verbs with the same prefix, such as *segredi, secedere, secludere*, and the presence of neologisms in Propertius. It is clear that such proceedings are not only risky, but even methodically incorrect: if we were to generalize them, we would in fact end up attributing to Latin authors who knows what *monstra*, all in the defense of the text as it has been handed down. In our case in particular, it is easy to understand that the mistake lies in the erroneous division of *praescriptoseuecta* (*praescripto seuecta* in the place of *praescriptos euecta*) that dragged with it as an obvious consequence the changing of the accusative *gyros* into the ablative *gyro*. Lachmann's other objection to *euecta est* with the accusative (the impossibility in his opinion of *euehi gyros* in the place of *euehi ex gyris* or *extra gyros*) is unfounded: *Thes.* V 2.1007, 62ff. cites as examples of middle passive *euehi* used transitively in poetic examples up through Tacitus (*Culex* 107 *iam medias operum partes euectus erat sol*, Sil. 16.375 *fere medium euecti certamine campum*; cf. also Tac. *Ann.* 12.36; 14.52; Apul. *Flor.* 2, p. 2.14 Helm).

Despite everything, it is certain that in the field of Propertian studies the greatest exaggeration has occurred in the exasperated search for corruption. Often a more adequate use of the Greek sources would suffice in resolving these presumed difficulties.

---

[11] Lachmann 1816: 236.  [12] Hertzberg 1843: 260.
[13] Tränkle 1960: 62.

In the central section of elegy 1.15 Propertius makes a list of mythological heroines, with the objective of contrasting an idealized world of human affections with his tormented relationship with Cynthia. In lines 21–22 he cites the example of Evadne, Capaneus' wife who throws herself onto her husband's funeral-pyre in order to remain united with him even after death. Propertius felt the influence of the drama of Evadne in Euripides' *Suppliants*: this can easily be inferred from a series of allusions (for which you may consult my commentary on Propertius' elegy). This fact is of inestimable value to the reconstitution of the text. The codices in fact have given *miseros elata per ignes* for v. 21; but the definition of the meaning of *elata* has given many problems to critics and editors who prefer to go back to *delata* of the lesser manuscripts.

Nonetheless, even those who defend *elata* understand it to have the meaning of 'accompanied to burial,' the only exception being Giri, followed by Pasoli,[14] according to whom Evadne 'climbed up the pyre where her dead husband's body was burning. The *"per"* expresses this movement up the steps of the lofty pyre.' I think that *TLL* V 2.142.69ff. places our piece very opportunely among the cases of *efferre* '*accedente ui celeritatis, i.q. praecipitare*' (to carry out 'with violent burst of speed, that is, to rush headlong'): cf. for example Livy 3.61.9 *perruptis ordinibus elati* (sc. *milites*) *ad nouissimam aciem* (the enemy ranks broken, the soldiers swept through to the rear line), Sen. *Epist.* 40.7 *incitato corporis pondere se rapit ac longius quam uoluit effertur* (with the very weight of the body set in motion, a person rushes along and is carried farther than he wished). However, the decisive argument comes from a comparison with the *Suppliants*: if one keeps in mind the Euripidean context, the Propertian distich is made entirely clear. In Euripides the fact is mentioned more than once that Evadne is at the top of a rock that stands above her husband's pyre and is ready to jump onto it (lines 1014–17, 1045–47, 1065). Especially cf. 1014–17:

ἀλλὰ τᾶς
εὐκλείας χάριν ἔνθεν ὁρ-
μάσω τᾶσδ' ἀπὸ πέτρας πη-
δήσασα πυρὸς ἔσω.

[14] Pasoli 1957: 105.

But I rush to leap onto the fire from this stone, for the sake of my good reputation.

Euripides' πηδήσασα corresponds in fact to *elata* in the Propertian codices. Rothstein is probably right about *per ignes* in that it must have a pictorial effect: the image of the body of Evadne, which rather than falling straight onto the pyre falls through the flames until it reaches the ground, is tragically efficacious.

Sometimes the motive behind certain linguistic choices is even '*pruderie*' (the well-known *pudicitia philologorum*!). We spoke earlier of the situation of 1.3. In lines 13–18 Propertius approaches Cynthia's bed and starts to get more serious in his amorous intent:

> *et quamuis duplici correptum ardore iuberent*
>     *hac Amor hac Liber, durus uterque deus,*
> *subiecto leuiter positam temptare lacerto*
>     *osculaque admota sumere et arma manu,*
> *non tamen ausus eram dominae turbare quietem,*
>     *expertae metuens iurgia saeuitiae.*

And although Bacchus on one side and Amor on the other, both harsh gods, were bidding me to slip my arm gently underneath her as she lay and try her, and to steal kisses and, with my hand drawn near, to take up my weapon, nevertheless I did not dare to disturb my mistress' rest, fearing the insults of a spite already known.

In v. 16 it is best to construct it so: *et sumere oscula et sumere arma admota manu* (sc. *corpori*: *admota manu* is an ablative absolute) and to translate thus: 'to steal kisses and, having drawn my hand near (to her body), to pick up my weapon.'[15] The bashful philologists believe rather that Propertius, although drunken and lusty, brings his hand close to Cynthia's head in order to kiss her without making her bend her neck. The ancient interpreters, who had fewer complexes than modern ones, understood well the erotic character of the context; for Beroaldus: '*uerecunde uirilia appellauit arma. Hoc enim telum est uenereae pugnae*' (with modesty, he calls his genitalia 'arms.' For this is the weapon of Venus' battles), while for Passerat: '*sin ad*

---

[15] Editors' note: This rendition of line 16 is Fedeli's own, given in Italian in the original text of this article. We have reproduced this sense in the translation of the passage immediately above.

*arma admouetur manus, id significat obscenitatis*' (if his hand is moved toward his weapon, this means something vulgar). It is superfluous to add that military terminology, such as *arma, bellum, proelium, castra,* and such, often take on an erotic meaning. There have been many proposed corrections for *et arma.* The main cause of these interventions has been on the one hand a reluctance to give the distich an erotic meaning, and on the other the presence of the zeugma *osculaque... sumere et arma.* What is not taken into consideration, however, is that zeugma was particularly loved by Augustan poets.[16] In Propertius cf. 2.31.13–14, *altera deiectos Parnasi uertice Gallos,/altera maerebat funera Tantalidos* (one door mourned the Gauls cast down from Parnassus' height; the other mourned the funeral of the Tantalids), and 3.9.23–24, *cum tibi Romano dominas in honore secures/et liceat medio ponere iura foro* (since you have the right to set up imperial axes in Rome's honor, and laws in the middle of the Forum).

In elegy 1.21 Gallus, mortally wounded in the battle of Perugia, turns to a fellow-soldier who is fleeing to ask him to tell his sister where to find his bones (9–10):

> *et quaecumque super dispersa inuenerit ossa*
> *montibus Etruscis, haec sciat esse mea.*

> And whatever bones she might find scattered on the Etruscan hills, let her know that these are mine.

In this case too the text as it has been handed down by the most authoritative representatives of the manuscript tradition has been mistakenly corrected. According to Butler[17] the final distich tells that which the *soror* must not know, just as in lines 5–8 *sic te seruato possint gaudere parentes,/ne soror acta tuis sentiat e lacrimis:/Gallum per medios ereptum Caesaris ensis/effugere ignotas non potuisse manus* (thus may your parents rejoice, since you are safe, and may your sister not realize from your tears what has happened: that Gallus, snatched away from the swords of Caesar, was unable to escape unknown hands). Consequently he corrects *et* v. 9 into *nec* and thus translates the distich: 'nor let her never know that whatever

---

[16] Hofmann, Szantyr, *et al.* 1965: 832, and the bibliography.
[17] Butler 1905: 165–6.

bones she may find on the Tuscan hills are mine.' But Housman,[18] with his well-known sharpness, objected that the discovery that her brother had 1000 skulls, 2000 femurs, and 26,000 vertebrae would have both dealt a hard stroke to her fraternal affection and, at the same time, would have made an addition of fundamental importance to her notions of anatomy.

The *quicumque* found in the manuscripts of the D family (a conjecture made by 'one who is well in possession of his Latin and who carefully discusses the text that he has before him'[19]) proves that this text has been misunderstood since very ancient times: the end of the poem contains his message to his sister, who will take care of his burial.

However, there are also absurd interpretations in defense of the manuscripts as they have been transmitted: there are those who, like Rothstein in his commentary and W. Baehrens,[20] relate *haec* to *quaecumque* and have Gallus say: *ossa omnia quae inuenerit, sciat soror esse mea* (all the bones that she found, let my sister know that they are mine). According to Baehrens, '*soror ossa quaecumque in montibus Etruscis reperta pro suis sepeliat, orat Gallus*' (Gallus asks his sister to bury as his whatever bones she finds on the Tuscan hills): the sister, obliged to pick up bones, may end up erecting a whole sanctuary! On the other hand, setting aside other amenities, I believe Housman's interpretation[21] to be correct: he sees no relation between *quaecumque inuenerit* (sc. *licet sescenta alia inuenerit*) and *haec*, which has a normal demonstrative value here ('let her know that these bones are mine'). The sister, therefore, should be able to understand precisely which of the many bones of the fallen soldiers are Gallus' from the story told by the fugitive. Certainly Gallus is not trying to say that all of the bones found by his sister on the Etruscan mountains are his own: all emphasis is placed on *haec*. Therefore I translate thus: 'and, whatever bones she may find on the Etruscan mountains, let her know that these right here are mine!'

Freidrich Leo maintained rightly that a commentary has its own style. I would like to add to this that an edition also has its own style.

---

[18] Housman 1905: 320 (= 1972 [vol. II]: 635).
[19] La Penna 1951a: 206–7.
[20] Baehrens 1913: 270.
[21] Housman 1893: 184 (=1972 [vol. I]: 294–5).

It seems important to me to state this in the face of the increase of critical editions that are mere catalogues of variations in the codices (often not even well selected) and a crude list of conjectures, both worthy and unworthy. What is worse still is when (and this happens far too often) variants are cited without discernment—including graphics, including obvious one-off interventions of the copyists—and are followed by a mention of all or almost all of the editors who accepted them. To me, pursuing the mirage of completeness has no sense, unless one is dealing with an edition of fragments. Besides, from this point of view, a critical edition immediately ages and is fatally surpassed the moment it goes into print. And also, one must not overwhelm the unfortunate reader with an indiscriminate heap of variants and conjectures. Thus, the critical apparatus must first be selective, and must show the reader only so much as the reviewer believes to be indispensable to the constitution and understanding of the text.

But there is more. The job of an editor is not to offer an ample but illegible apparatus, but rather to make an ample but reasonable apparatus: one in which at least the most important choices made are explained. We could, in this way, break off from Housman for his hypercritical tendencies and often unnecessary conjectures; but, we will have to conclude that at least as far as this is concerned his apparatus on Lucan and Manilius, which really turn out to be commentaries, still point us in the right direction.

# 3

# Editing Propertius[1]

## James Butrica

### I

'*Quot editores, tot Propertii*' ('For every editor, a different Propertius') has been a familiar—and much misunderstood—phrase in Propertian scholarship ever since it first appeared in the preface to Phillimore's Oxford Classical Text of 1901. In its original context it described not an existing situation but rather the chaos that Phillimore alleged would result if editors began to adopt significant numbers of transpositions.[2] Such chaos, however, does characterize

---

[1] All translations of Propertian passages are from Goold's 1990 Loeb; all other translations are the editors' own. Where Butrica has extensively paraphrased whole poems (without word-for-word translation), we have not provided a translation.

[2] Phillimore 1901. The antepenultimate paragraph of the introduction denounces transpositions of the sort proposed by Housman and introduced by Postgate in his *Corpus Poetarum Latinorum* text (1893), then continues: '*sed cuinam probari potest nostri archetypum ita dilaniatum et κατακεκρεματισμένον ut disticha passim inter se locum mutaverint, omnino superfuturum fuisse? Est profecto ut peccaverint in non nullis librarii; homines enim. At non beluae. Quod si in summa re codicum fidem respuerimus, quo denique stabitur? Vnus quisque enim in quolibet argumento proprium phantasiae tenorem propriam carminis deducendi inventionem sequitur, licet non semper optimam illam nec ceteris maxime arrisuram. Quid enim est aliud ingenium? Sin autem poetae cogitationem suo cuique arbitrio resarcire licet, non interpretari, quot editores tot Propertii.*' (But can it be credible to any of us that an archetype so slashed and minced that the distichs have changed place amongst themselves would have survived at all? It is true that copyists made mistakes in some cases; they are after all human. But they are not beasts. But if at the core we completely reject the trustworthiness of the codices, where will that lead us in the end? Each one in every instance will follow his own course of fantasy, his own design of construing the poem—surely that design

the current state of Propertian studies; every interpreter seems to create a different Propertius, who in the last twenty-five years has been represented as a feminist,[3] a neurotic traumatized by the siege of Perugia,[4] an anti-Augustan iconoclast,[5] an apostle of love oppressed by a quasi-Stalinist principate,[6] a decadent pre-Raphaelite,[7] and most recently as the 'modernist poet of antiquity.'[8] There is significantly less variation among editors; Barber's 1953 (1960) OCT and Fedeli's 1984 Teubner differ only in relatively minor details involving poem-divisions or choices of reading, nearly always in the same places that editors and critics have discussed again and again throughout the past century. This similarity of editorial approach is matched by a prevailing uniformity in views of Propertius' style: he is regularly described as a difficult, idiosyncratic, and uniquely modern poet, a judgment seemingly borne out by these editions, where the text, despite much conspicuous elegance and artistry, is at times awkward almost to the point of unintelligibility and marred by banal couplets, abrupt transitions, and disconcerting shifts in tone or stylistic level. The notion that such a text could represent the work of an Augustan poet has its roots in the early nineteenth century with editors like Karl Lachmann, who consciously tried to free Propertius from an elegance which he thought earlier editors had foisted upon him through conjecture,[9] but its imposition upon the English-speaking

won't always be the best nor entirely pleasing to others. What else, after all, is expertise? If one can emend—not interpret—the thought of the poet according to one's own judgment, then there will be a different Propertius for every editor).

[3] Hallett 1973: 103–24.
[4] de Sanctis 1973.
[5] This view has been advocated or assumed in a number of articles by a variety of (especially American) scholars, but its chief exponent has perhaps been Sullivan 1976.
[6] Stahl 1985.
[7] Papanghelis 1987.
[8] Benediktson 1989.
[9] On 1.9.9 (1.10. [9.] 9 in his numbering) Lachmann (1816) says of *ducere* in that line and of *totis* in 21 that '*Immerito obtrusas Propertio elegantias hic ostentant exemplaria*' (here the exemplars reveal that refinements have been crammed undeservedly into Propertius), attributing the latter to Jan Dousa the younger, the former to Volscus' edition of 1482; he notes that '*Scripti omnes, ne uno quidem demto*' (all manuscripts, with not even one exception) have *dicere* and *totiens*, and concludes, '*Quis jure impugnet? quis tanti ducat defendere?*' (Who could reasonably argue with that? Who could even consider it worth their while to defend?). Another conjecture

world is largely due to the influence of J. P. Postgate and the introduction to his 1881 *Select Elegies of Propertius*.[10] Postgate articulated here a fascinating, even sensationalistic vision of Propertius as a poet quite unlike anything else the world had seen. He described the poetry in such terms as 'These contrasts, these extravagancies, these fluctuations and incoherencies, these half-formed or misshapen thoughts,' and he called the poet himself 'no ordinary phenomenon,' a man 'whose natural bent was towards the singular and solitary' (lxxii). This view received reinforcement when J. P. Sullivan, in discussing Ezra Pound's *Homage to Sextus Propertius*, claimed that Pound's 'versions' of Propertius showed an appreciation of a modernity that conventional scholars had missed.[11]

Most Propertian scholars now belong to one of two irreconcilable camps. One regards many of the phenomena noted by Postgate as textual corruptions to be removed through conjecture; Postgate himself quickly joined this camp, repudiated the views expressed in *Select Elegies*,[12] and produced the heavily emended text criticized by

---

that Lachmann rejected in a similar manner is *furit* at 4.6.56 (which I shall advocate later in this paper), of which he wrote, '*Nempe critici poetas ubique aut furere aut magna verba aut elegantias effundere volunt. Liceat, quaeso, Propertio nostro ita loqui, ut eum locutum esse libri veteres testantur*' (Certainly critics desire poets to be mad ubiquitously, or to drip with grand words or delicacies. I ask, please let Propertius speak how the ancient manuscripts say he did). Here Lachmann's attitude was anticipated in the commentary of C. Kuinoel (1805) and apparently in that of Vulpius as well, which is not available to me; Kuinoel first quoted Burman's note, in which *fuit* was described as '*languidius*' (a little sluggish), then continued, "*Non nego, furit exquisitius esse: neque tamen scriptores vett. huius generis elegantias quouis loco sectati sunt, et cum vulgaris lectio commodum sensum pariat: nihil sine codicum auctoritate mutandum. Nec quaerendum, ut ad h. l. notauit Vulpius, quid scriptor scribere potuerit, vel debuerit, sed quid vere scripserit*" (I don't deny, *furit* is more polished. But ancient writers did not pursue refinements of this sort all over the place, especially when the common reading provides good sense. Nothing must be changed without the authority of the codices. Nor should it be asked, as Vulpius noted *ad loc.*, what the author could have written, or ought to have written, but what he really did write). Note that the unwillingness to alter '*sine codicum auctoritate*' limits one effectively to conjectures made before the age of printing, and that both Kuinoel and Lachmann, instead of maintaining an open mind, were predisposed to assume without question that what the manuscripts gave was what Propertius wrote.

[10] Postgate 1881.
[11] Sullivan 1964.
[12] It seems to have gone unnoticed that every printing of *Select Elegies* from 1894 on contains the following 'Publishers' Note:' 'The present issue is an exact reprint of

Phillimore which attempted to bring order to what he had once called 'this chaos.' The other camp, the one that prevails today, especially in Italy and the United States, has responded to Postgate's pre-conversion vision with an 'act of critical salvation' akin to that described by Gary Taylor in *Reinventing Shakespeare*: 'If Shakespeare wrote something that appears to be awful, then in fact it must be brilliant, if only you look at it carefully enough. Blemishes need not be emended, if all blemishes can be redefined as beauty marks.'[13] In other words, the 'extravagancies' that Postgate found, which he thought were blemishes due to an immature mind in which thought was still 'crystallizing,' were not flaws at all but 'beauty marks,' according to some the signs of deep psychological penetration or of an especially inventive approach to Latinity, for others the result of imitating Hellenistic poetry, for still others the daring flashes of an innovative, modernist genius. The followers of this camp believe that they see beauty and artistry in what their excessively rational counterparts of the other camp call clumsy or illogical and corrupt; though most of them lack first-hand knowledge of the Propertian manuscripts or of textual criticism in general, they nevertheless declare the Propertian tradition a good one and pronounce themselves satisfied with Barber's or Fedeli's edition, quite unaware that even these relatively conservative texts—and one can say 'relatively' only because of editions like Rothstein's and Phillimore's—incorporate hundreds of conjectures. The process of textual criticism and correction that has gone on for at least the six and a half centuries since Petrarch brought Propertius back to Italy has been declared at an end by Giuseppe Giangrande's proclamation that the sole occupation of Propertian textual studies today should be the exercise of critical judgement within the limits of the modern vulgate represented by Barber and Fedeli.[14] But not all minds have closed completely. Margaret Hubbard has demonstrated that ancient estimates of Propertius' style contradict

---

the edition of 1884, and the Editor wishes it to be known that the book does not represent his present views on the text and interpretation of Propertius.'

[13] Taylor 1989: 408.

[14] Reviewing Fedeli's 1984 Teubner text and 1985 commentary on Book 3 (1986: 212); 'L'opera del critico del testo di Properzio, oggi, non può che consistere nell'esercizio del giudizio critico entro i limiti di quella che si può chiamare la "volgata moderna" di Properzio' (The work of the Propertian textual critic today

modern ones;[15] Goold's Loeb edition of 1990 has done more than any other since Postgate's full text to restore elegance and polish to Propertius;[16] and critics like Allen, Heyworth, and Morgan continue to propose new conjectures or to revive neglected conjectures of the past.

This paper has two purposes. It will first offer evidence to show that the discrepancy between these ancient and modern views of Propertius' style is due to the fact that the modern views are based upon a text that has been distorted from its original state by an exceptionally high degree of corruption and that more extensive emendation is therefore needed to restore it to that original state. It will then discuss some of the means through which our texts might be improved by applying sound principles of textual criticism and by acknowledging the particular vicissitudes that have always affected the transmission of poetic texts like Propertius.

II

It is clear that all existing manuscripts of the works of Propertius descend from a single *exemplar* which can for the most part be reconstructed with relatively little difficulty.[17] Where editors differ

---

can consist of nothing other than the exercise of critical judgment within the limits of what one can call the 'modern vulgate' of Propertius).

[15] Hubbard 1974 (1975).

[16] Goold has also discussed the text of Propertius in a series of articles: 1966: 59–106; 1987: 27–38; 1989: 97–119; 1992: 287–320.

[17] Butrica 1984; Heyworth 1986. The principal manuscripts that will be discussed in the following pages are N (= Wolfenbüttel Gud. lat. 224, *c.* 1200), A (= Leiden, Voss. lat. O. 38, *c.* 1240), F (= Florence, Bibl. Laurenziana pl. 36,49, *c.* 1380), L (= Oxford, Bodleian Library Holkham misc. 36, a. 1421), P (= Paris, Bibl. Nationale lat. 7989, a. 1423), and Z (= Venice, Bibl. Naz. Marciana Fondo antico 443 [1912], a. 1453); FLPZ are known collectively as the Petrarchan manuscripts because they derive from Petrarch's lost copy of A. In addition, a group of fifteenth-century manuscripts appears to derive from the archetype independently of the other primary witnesses (Butrica calls their source X and argues that it shares an intermediate source with N, while Heyworth calls their source Λ and thinks now, as he has pointed out to me, that it might have been the archetype itself); these are v (= Vat. lat. 3273, a. 1427), m (= Paris, B.N. lat. 8233, a. 1465), r (= Geneva, Bibl. Bodmeriana Cod. Bod. 141, a. 1466), u (= Urb. lat. 641, *c.* 1465–70), s (= Munich, Universitätsbibliothek Cim 22, *c.*

is on how far we should trust the text of the archetype thus reconstructed. The mainstream view, which puts a good deal of faith in that text, is best represented by Paolo Fedeli, whose 1987 article on editing Propertius depicts his approach as a 'cautiously conservative' middle way between the two extremes mentioned in his title, 'the cult of the transmitted text' and 'the hunt for corruption.'[18] He advises that an editor must 'know' his author, i.e. possess not only a sound understanding of the manuscript tradition and history of the text, but also intimate familiarity with the author's style, working method, and technique, as well as his sources, his topoi, and the work of his contemporaries.[19] These reasonable-sounding criteria, however, involve a fatal flaw. Whence does the editor acquire his knowledge of Propertius' style and working method? Fedeli has got his from the text, of course, and specifically from editions like Barber's; but that text is the document whose authenticity is supposed to be at issue in the practice of textual criticism. As an editor Fedeli is running in circles, establishing the genuineness of the text before him on the basis of its consistency with—itself, a procedure that works well if the general reliability of the text is guaranteed in advance (in which case there is little for textual criticism to do), but not if the text is seriously compromised by corruption. In a tradition like Propertius', where all copies descend from a deeply corrupted archetype, this is a prescription for disaster: corrupted passages are defended as sound by com-

---

1460–70), and c (= Rome, Bibl. Casanatense 15, a. 1470 or 1471). (Heyworth's sigla for these six manuscripts are the upper-case equivalents of those given above, except that he uses T for v. In addition, he cites three descendants of a contaminated copy of X [Λ]—Parma, Bibl. Palatina 140; Wroclaw, Bibl. Uniw. AKC 1948 197 KN; and Bibl. Vaticana Capponianus 196—as JKW, collectively Γ, but their value remains to be established; the one case that he cites of an 'apparently true, and not conjectural, reading not found in any other authoritative mss' [92] could easily be accidental if not in fact conjectural.) The agreement of all or most of the witnesses to the text is here designated by the traditional symbol O.

[18] Fedeli 1987 (in this volume). For the phrase 'cautiously conservative' see 108, where Fedeli writes, 'Oggi la tendenza della critica testuale properziana, sopiti ormai i furori di tipo housmaniano, può esser definita "accortamente conservatrice": è questa una posizione che sostanzialmente condivido' (Today the tendency of the textual critic of Propertius, now that the Housmanesque furies have been put to sleep, can be defined as 'cautiously conservative': this is a position which I wholeheartedly share).

[19] Fedeli 1987: 107

parison with other similarly corrupted passages, and scribal errors are thus elevated to the status of authorial traits, with the inevitable result that in Fedeli's edition, as in Barber's, Propertius sometimes writes less like an Augustan poet than like a corrupt and interpolated manuscript of one.

Text and interpretation are inextricably linked, and to edit Propertius one must interpret him; but one cannot produce a reliable text without knowing what sort of poet Propertius was, and one equally cannot know what sort of poet Propertius was without a reliable text. Fortunately the circularity that undermines Fedeli's approach can be avoided, for we have objective evidence, from the poet's own lifetime or shortly after, with which we can answer two questions fundamental not only to editing Propertius but to Propertian studies as a whole: what sort of poet was Propertius, and how reliable is the version of the text transmitted by the manuscripts?

First, the matter of style. As Hubbard has shown, allusions to Propertius' poetry by ancient authors indicate what sort of writing we should expect; without exception they describe qualities that can be summed up as a pleasing elegance. Ovid deemed him *tener* ('soft' or 'tender')[20] and *blandus*,[21] 'a term,' in Hubbard's words, 'suggesting an insinuating softness of style rather than the abrupt vigour more recently attributed to him.'[22] Martial called him *facundus*, 'witty' or 'eloquent.'[23] Quintilian offers no explicit description but implies that Propertius, like Tibullus, was *tersus* and *elegans*, 'polished' and 'elegant,' or at the very least not *lasciuus* ('undisciplined') like Ovid or *durus* ('rough') like Gallus.[24] Pliny the Younger wrote of a poet

---

[20] *Ars.* 3.333 *teneri possis carmen legisse Properti* (you would be able to read soft Propertius' song).

[21] *Tr.* 2.465 *inuenies eadem blandi praecepta Properti*, 5.1.17 *blandique Propertius oris* (you will find the same rules in soft Propertius; Propertius with the smooth tongue).

[22] Hubbard 1974 (1975): 2.

[23] 14.184.1 *facundi carmen iuuenale Properti* (the youthful song of agreeable Propertius).

[24] 10.1.93 *elegia quoque Graecos prouocamus, cuius mihi tersus atque elegans maxime uidetur auctor Tibullus, sunt qui Propertium malint. Ouidius utroque lasciuior, sicut durior Gallus* (we challenge the Greeks in elegy, too, of which genre Tibullus seems to me the leader in polish and elegance. There are some who prefer Propertius. Ovid is less disciplined than each, and Gallus is more severe). This important point, that Quintilian in no way implies disparagement of Propertius, was first made by Hubbard.

descended from Propertius that 'If you take up his elegies you will read a work polished, tender and agreeably amusing, one absolutely written in Propertius' family.'[25] To quote Hubbard again, 'Ancient criticism knows no dissent from this verdict; it valued in Propertius not an obscure master of the passions, but a poet of finish, grace and charm' (p.3). These qualities are in fact evident, or only a few letters away, in far more passages than one might expect of Propertius the proto-Pound; but there is also much that would scarcely have been termed *blandum, elegans, facundum, molle, tenerum*, or *tersum* by an ancient critic.

Modern accounts of Propertius' style, on the other hand, emphasize qualities like abruptness, obscurity, lack of logic or even of clear meaning which are antithetical to those praised by ancient readers.[26] Postgate dealt with the inconsistency between ancient evaluations and the 'chaos' that he observed through the condescending claim that 'the literary criticism of the Romans was essentially superficial. They had not at their disposal the keen scalpel and the polymath terminology of modern analysis. Nor had they the delicate percep-

---

[25] *Ep.* 9.22.1 *uir est* [sc. Passennus Paullus] *optimus, honestissimus, nostri amantissimus; praeterea in litteris ueteres aemulatur, exprimit, reddit, Propertium in primis, a quo genus ducit, uera suboles eoque simillima illi in quo ille praecipuus. si elegos eius in manum sumpseris, leges opus tersum, molle, iucundum et plane in Properti domo scriptum.* (he's tops, very frank, most devoted to me; moreover he emulates the old authors in his own works, he squeezes them out and gives them back, Propertius above all, from whom he derives his stock—a true scion and most similar to his ancestor in that way in which is ancestor stood out). The translation of the last sentence given in the text has been taken from Hubbard 1974 (1975): 2–3.

[26] To choose only one example from among many, I append the words of an Italian translator of Propertius: 'Egli rimane un po' come una divinità il cui linguaggio è troppo ermetico per la folla dei fedeli.... Egli è in certo modo il precursore dei nostri ermetici.... La sua oscurità non è mai fine a se stessa; attraverso le ambagi dello stile, egli mira più a suggerire che a dire: meglio che un'immagine egli vuole destare in noi una sensazione: e crea intorno a sé un alone musicale in cui non sempre si può cercare un significato preciso' (Lipparini 1970: xix; he remains a little like a god, whose language is too obscure for the crowd of the faithful... He is in a way the precursor of our hermetics... his obscurity is never an end in itself; through the wanderings of his style, he tries more to suggest than to say; better than an image, he wants to leave in us a sensation; and he creates about himself a musical aura in which one cannot always seek a precise meaning).

tion and flexibility of expression which might have supplied these deficiencies' (lviii). In other words, they were either too dull-witted to notice that what they were describing as elegant was actually misshapen and incoherent, or else insufficiently articulate to describe their true impressions. Although ancient critics like Quintilian and Longinus and Dionysius of Halicarnassus were inevitably unacquainted with such modern techniques as reader-response theory and instead discussed literature in rhetorical terms (with good reason, since rhetoric formed the basis of their literary culture), their critical judgment was certainly capable of a task so essential to their craft as distinguishing the elegant from the abrupt and the obscure. Postgate went on to argue that 'if the Roman critical resources were thus limited, Propertius must have taxed them severely' (lviii). Indeed he must, if they were so consistently driven to describe his alleged 'extravagancies', 'fluctuations', and 'incoherencies' as 'elegant', 'polished', and 'beguiling'. Quintilian termed Gallus *durior*, a judgement confirmed by the papyrus fragment;[27] but that fragment is still so much more lucid than many stretches in Book 2 of Propertius that, if Propertius really had written as the manuscripts represent him, Quintilian would surely have been forced to employ for him some epithet more severe than *durus*. The real reason for the discrepancy between ancient and modern views of Propertius' style is that 'act of critical salvation' described earlier; the casual scribal errors that created his 'incoherencies' have been accorded the exalted status of his most distinctive and admirable stylistic traits.

The second category of evidence demonstrates just how seriously our text has been affected by scribal error. Propertius was popular enough to be quoted several times by those who wrote *graffiti* on the walls of Pompeii; thanks to these vandals we have texts of six lines from within a century of the poet's lifetime which permit an instructive comparison between Propertius as he appeared in the first century and Propertius as he appeared 1200 years later in the archetype of our tradition. One thoughtful scribbler wrote out a couplet

---

[27] Note, for example, the hiatus *tum erunt* in 2, the difficulty of ascertaining the precise meaning of *legam* in 5, and the awkward double modifier *fixa . . . deiuitiora* in the same line.

that is now slightly truncated by damage but is still recognizable as a version of 2.5.9–10 (= *CIL* 4.4491):

> *nunc est ira recens nunc est disc[edere tempus*
> *si dolor afuerit crede redibit [amor.*

This correctly gives *afuerit* in 10 rather than the corruption *affuerit* offered by our manuscripts. Another (= *CIL* 4.1894) provides a version of 4.5.47–8, which are given by the manuscripts as

> *ianitor ad dantes uigilet si pulset inanis*
> *surdus in obductam somniet usque seram.*

In the *graffito*, however, they appear as

> *ianitor ad dantis uigilet si pulsat inanis*
> *surdus in obductam somniet usque seram.*

There are two differences from the version of the manuscripts. One is the *i*-stem accusative plural *dantis* where the manuscripts give *dantes*, the other the indicative form *pulsat* where the manuscripts give *pulset*. The criterion of 'Which reading is more likely to become the other?' suggests that the *graffito* is right in both cases. Medieval manuscripts frequently normalize forms like *dantis*, while *pulset* was perhaps assimilated to the preceeding *uigilet* and to the upcoming *somniet*. Stylistic considerations also favour *pulsat*, which is so much more vigorous than the subjunctive form that, if our manuscripts were divided between *pulsat* and *pulset*, editors would prefer the former without hesitation.

But the anonymous Pompeian to whom we are most indebted is the one who wrote out 3.16.13–14 (= *CIL* 4.1950) as

> *quisquis amator erit Scythiae licet ambulet oris*
> *nemo adeo ut feriat barbarus esse uolet.*

The same lines appeared in the archetype as

> *quisquis amator erit Scythicis licet ambulat oris*
> *nemo deo ut noceat barbarus esse uolet.*

Two errors, *ambulat* and *deo*, are immediately apparent. A third is probable, for in 14 editors should do as Goold does and print *feriat* rather than *noceat*.[28] One way of accounting for these two readings is to suppose that one of them has been accidentally substituted for the other; since *feriat* is the more vigorous and colourful word, we should assume that it represents Propertius' original and that *noceat* is the substitute, rather than believe that an anonymous vandal improved Propertius by substituting *feriat* for *noceat*. But a more plausible way of accounting for these readings is to suppose that Propertius' original *feriat* was glossed at some point in the tradition by *noceat* and that the gloss displaced the original reading in the archetype or at some earlier stage. The process is unlikely to have proceded in the other direction. Usually it is the general that glosses the specific, not the other way around (sometimes a glossator will indicate that a general has been used for a particular, but that situation does not apply here). Someone might indeed gloss *feriat* with *noceat* to show that Propertius means that, even in Scythia, no one would harm a lover in any way whatsoever, whereas a strict interpretation of *feriat* would not necessarily exclude the lover being jeered at, robbed, spat upon, etc.; but no one would ever gloss *noceat* with *feriat*, because this would restrict the range of meaning for *noceat* to certain specific forms of harm such as striking and wounding. A helpful parallel is available in the process of corruption that I believe produced the reading of the archetype at 3.11.51, *fugisti tamen in timidi uada flumina Nili*. Emenders usually try to correct *uada*, but I think instead that *uada* is sound and that its epithet has been lost behind *flumina*, which originated as a gloss on *uada (Nili)*. Whatever the process of corruption, it is clear that, while *flumina* can gloss *uada* to show that it means 'river' here rather than some other body of water, *uada* could never gloss *flumina*.

In the case of *Scythiae* in the *graffito* versus *Scythicis* in the manuscripts certainty is impossible, but the other indubitable errors of the manuscripts make it difficult to place much faith in them. In any case this couplet as transmitted by the archetype of our tradition contains two, or three, or four errors, while in all six lines taken together the manuscripts show three or four absolutely certain errors, with

---

[28] The first advocate of the reading, however, seems to have been Hubbard 1968: 318–19, who correctly terms it 'lively' and suggests that *noceat* might have been interpolated after the corruption of *adeo* to *deo*.

another three or four possible, for a total of between three and seven in those six lines. To put it another way, at the most conservative possible estimate, three out of the six lines—50 per cent—contain at least one corruption; at the most extreme estimate, the number of corruptions in our text could surpass the number of lines! By any objective standard a text with a corruption even in every second line has deteriorated significantly; it would seem that there could well be 2000 or so corruptions in our manuscripts rather than the approximately 600 recognized by Fedeli and Barber.[29] Fedeli himself has asked whether an edition which like his own admits hundreds of conjectures can be too conservative; to judge by these *graffiti*, the answer is a resounding 'yes'. The Pompeian *graffiti*, and especially the lines from 3.16, are a virtual textbook on editing Propertius. They confirm the predictable (and frequent) presence of simple scribal errors which, like *ambulat*, offend against grammar or, like *deo*, offend against sense; but they also alert us to others like *noceat* which are not so obviously 'wrong'. If we had only the evidence of the manuscripts for this couplet, 'cautiously conservative' critics would condemn the 'Anglo-Saxon hypercriticism' and 'Housmanitis' of anyone who dared 'improve' Propertius by conjecturing *feriat*.[30]

These then are the criteria that ought to guide the editing and interpretation of Propertius. Ancient testimonia speak unanimously of grace and elegance; ancient *graffiti* confirm that the source of our manuscripts was riddled with minor scribal errors. When faced with awkwardness or weakness in the transmitted text (especially of a kind that can be healed through slight alteration), the editor must ask whether Ovid, Martial, Pliny, and Quintilian were wrong and Propertius wrote clumsy poetry that has been preserved perfectly by those

---

[29] This figure was arrived at by counting transpositions, *lacunae*, places where an archetypal reading has been replaced by a conjecture, and obelized passages (an entire obelized line was counted as three corruptions, an obelized half-line as two, and, of course, a single obelized word as one).

[30] A comparable, though less extreme, result emerges from the lines cited by ancient grammarians: two or three of those nine lines are corrupt in the entire tradition, while two more were corrupted in one branch. (These are readily accessible in Butrica 1984: 30–2.) The lines corrupt in the entire tradition are 2.3.24 (*ardidus* for *candidus*), 3.8.37 (*tendisti* for *nexisti*), and perhaps 2.14.1 (*est* added at the end of the line); those corrupt in a single branch are 2.1.2 (*ore* in N) and 2.33.37 (*demissa... serta* in the Petrarchan manuscripts).

manuscripts, or whether an original elegance has been corrupted in an unreliable transmission; mainstream scholarship has for too long accepted the untested assumption that the first alternative is right.

### III

As to the matter of specific suggestions for improvement, a few examples will suffice to illustrate the general principles involved.

In the light of the considerations offered above, it should be clear that editors have good reason to be less tolerant of even slight awkwardness in the transmitted text and to correct more scribal errors; yet there are many places where all editions, not just Barber's and Fedeli's, yield to manuscript authority rather than restore elegance and point by the alteration of a letter or two, a process often denounced as 'rewriting' the author. Dozens and dozens of such passages were corrected by Renaissance scholars so long ago that modern scholars are largely unaware that a corruption was ever present; yet dozens more remain. A characteristic example occurs in 3.14, which purports to argue that Rome should adopt the Spartan custom of requiring women to exercise as well as men, so as to make wives and maidens alike equally accessible to seduction. Such conditions are declared vastly preferable to those at Rome, where women are surrounded in public by crowds of chaperones too dense to get a finger through, so that *nec quae sint facies nec quae sint uerba rogandi/ inuenies: caecum uersat amator iter*, 'You will find neither what are the faces nor what are the words of solicitation; the lover plies a blind road' (31–2). Not only is seduction out of the question; according to the manuscripts, Propertius says that there is no opportunity even to learn the techniques of seduction. In itself this might be an apposite, though extreme, demonstration of the lover's frustration, but there is a difficulty with *facies*. It cannot mean 'what are the faces of Roman women' without something that indicates whose faces are involved, and one is therefore compelled to construe *facies* with *rogandi* and make Propertius talk about 'faces of solicitation', whatever winks, leers, and squints those might be. The case is a typical one: the transmitted text scans and contains no grammatical errors or nonsense words, and a kind of meaning can be extorted from it as long as one takes it for granted that Propertius wrote a peculiar kind of Latin that does not always make sense; it hardly qualifies as something that an ancient critic might have called polished, witty, or elegant. But such qualities are only a few letters away if we follow Enk (1911 *ad loc.*) and adopt Gebhard's *faciles* for *facies*,[31] together with *dent... roganti* (Enk's variation of Burman's *det... roganti*) for *sint... rogandi*; these conjectures add one letter and change three (surely not an unreasonable rate of alteration for a tradition with a corruption in every second line) to produce *nec quae sint faciles nec quae dent uerba roganti/inuenies*, 'You won't find out which ones are easy and which ones prove a tease when you chat them up.' An elegant expression of an appropriate sentiment has been achieved with minimal change. Given Propertius' ancient reputation and the demonstrable inaccuracy of the manuscripts, I do not hesitate to accept this as what he wrote; needless to say, no 'cautiously conservative' editor incorporates these corrections, and most do not even mention them in the apparatus (to his credit, however, Fedeli records *faciles* and *det... roganti*).

Another example is available elsewhere in 3.14 in the description of the lover's paradise alleged to have existed in ancient Sparta. The supposed advantages of having women exercise include being at a woman's side in public (22), talking to her without a go-between (25–6), getting a good look at her without her clothes (27), and the relative indifference of athletic women to the state of their hair (28); in addition, according to the manuscripts' version of 23–4, *nec timor aut ulla est clausae tutela puellae,/nec grauis austeri poena cauenda uiri*, 'neither is there fear or any guarding of a secluded girl, nor need one beware the heavy punishment of a severe husband.' To say absolutely that 'there is not fear' is too sweeping and too vague; and if *timor* is parallel to *tutela*, one is left with 'fear of a secluded girl'—but there can be no such fear if there is also no such seclusion. In fact the couplet seems to contrast two kinds of fear (expressed by *timor* and *cauenda*) in two kinds of situation, the seduction of an

---

[31] Gebhard seems to have derived the correction from his *liber Commelinianus*, which is Paris, BN lat. 8458 (written no earlier than 1474); I have not verified the presence of the reading in that manuscript, but it certainly does appear in Rome, Bibl. Casanatense 3227, copied around 1470 by Franciscus Maturantius.

unmarried citizen girl, or *clausa puella*, and the seduction of a woman married to a *uir austerus*. Broekhuyzen saw the solution that restores balance and contrast: *nec timor est ulli clausae tutela puellae*, 'neither is the guard of a sequestered girl a source of fear to anyone' (*tutela* of course can be either the fact of guarding or the guards themselves).[32] Two possible explanations of the corruption suggest themselves. One is that *ulli* first became *ulla* through anticipation of *tutela*, then *aut* was added and the order of words changed to restore the metre; such a correction, however, must have taken place in antiquity, not in the Middle Ages, because medieval rules of scansion freely admitted the lengthening of short syllables at the principle caesura and no medieval reader would have balked at *nec timor est ulla clausae tutela puellae*. The other is that the order of *est ulli* became reversed (perhaps through the omission and incorrect replacement of one of them), and the consequent loss of a syllable was remedied by adding *aut*.

Earlier in Book 3, at 3.2.7–8, editors do Propertius another disservice by continuing to print *quin etiam, Polypheme, fera Galatea sub Aetna/ad tua rorantes carmina flexit equos*, 'and indeed, Polyphemus, Galatea at the foot of ferocious Etna turned her dripping steeds toward your songs.' There is no reason for Etna to be *fera* here; it is not erupting, nor are its past or potential eruptions at issue—it is only the backdrop for the pretty picture of Galatea deflecting the course of her chariot to hear the songs of Polyphemus. Now, other ancient accounts of the wooing of Galatea by Polyphemus emphasize the contrast between her loveliness and his monstrous brutishness; rather than believe that Propertius gave his scenery an irrelevant and needlessly dramatic epithet but failed to exploit this natural and traditional contrast, I think that Wakker was right when he proposed to replace *fera*, modifying Etna, with *ferox*, modifying Polyphemus. As well as being more elegant and to the point than the transmitted reading, the correction better suits Propertius' train of thought. The

---

[32] Broekhuyzen's own note runs, '*vix apparet quo referri debeat istud timor. tentabam ego aliquando, Nec timor est ulli clausae tutela puellae*, i.e. *nec quisquam amator timet custodes dominae suae, quo minus ad eam accedere audeat palam*' (It is scarcely apparent how this *timor* should be rendered. At one time I was trying, *Nec timor est ulli clausae tutela puellae*, i.e. no lover fears the guardians of his mistress, such that he wouldn't dare to approach her openly).

passage as a whole illustrates the power of song: the previous examples have been Orpheus taming beasts and stopping rivers (3–4) and Amphion animating the stones of Cithaeron to create Thebes (5–6). Obviously the power of song is expressed all the more effectively if it can bring a lovely nymph to hear a *hideous* Cyclops. In the other examples it was wild nature that succumbed to the power of song; in Polyphemus' case, wild nature itself wields that power, and it exerts an attraction that is even stronger than the repulsion of his *ferocitas*.

In 3.4.21–2, at the end of a poem in which Propertius wishes success for an Indian campaign while proposing to stay at home and enjoy the eventual triumph from a comfortable vantage, editors continue to print *praeda sit haec illis quorum meruere labores:/me sat erit Sacra plaudere posse Via*, 'let this booty belong to those whose efforts have earned it: it will be enough that I am able to applaud in the Sacred Way.' Since the accusative *me* can only be construed as subject of the infinitive *posse*, that is indeed what the transmitted text must mean, but it raises the question '*For whom* will it be enough that Propertius can applaud in the Sacred Way?' The answer to that question is embodied in the contrast that Propertius draws between the warriors who will go off and fight and earn their booty—the *illis* of 21—and himself, the one for whom it will suffice to join in the acclaim. But that contrast requires *mi* rather than *me*, as Pontano first saw over five hundred years ago.

Another example of a minor scribal error still uncorrected in our editions can be found in the description of *suttee* in 3.13. When the pyre is set ablaze, the wives compete to see who will follow their spouse, and not being allowed to die is accounted a disgrace. There follows the couplet 21–2, *ardent uictrices et flammae pectora praebent/ imponuntque suis ora perusta uiris*, 'the winners are afire and display their breast to the flame and lay their scorched mouths upon their husbands.' Despite the consensus of editors, *ardent* cannot be right; if it is literal we must take the line as a weak example of *hysteron proteron* (the women of course are not on fire before they have even rent their garments, much less leapt into the flames), and if it describes the 'ardor' of the victorious wives it is a sick joke thoroughly inappropriate to the context. Here the remedy, which was first seen by Stephanus and Passerat, is to be deduced from the contrast between the disgrace of those who are not permitted to join in the mass suicide (20 *pudor est non licuisse mori*) and the attitude of the *uictrices* who win the competition; the shame of defeat has as its opposite not the zeal of competition but the joy of victory, and therefore the winners do not burn—yet—but rather *gaudent*, 'rejoice,' in their right to burn. The first letter of a line is frequently detached in medieval manuscripts of Latin poetry (the corruption of *candidus* in 2.3.24 to *ardidus* involves the same phenomenon), and the proximity to *flammae*, not to mention the context as a whole, could have had a psychological effect in the transformation of *audent* to *ardent*.

Interpreters have spilled much ink over my final examples, where the failure to recognize the presence of a corruption has abetted misinterpretation of the poem as a whole. The context is 4.6, Propertius' second major treatment of the battle of Actium and the centrepiece of Book 4, cast by the poet himself as the culmination of his ambitions toward the imitation of learned Hellenistic elegy but seen by many recent scholars as hopelessly inept or subversively humorous. Propertius has cast Apollo as commander, Augustus as soldier, and the god exhorts the man very much as Augustus exhorts his own troops in Dio's account of the battle. All the fury and slaughter is reduced to 55–6, a miniature tableau of the god and his protégé wielding their weapons side by side, though with the god of course more prominent (he is a god, after all, and the elegy commemorates a temple erected in his honour): *dixerat, et pharetrae pondus consumit in arcus:/proxima post arcus Caesaris hasta fuit,* 'he had spoken, and he expends the burden of his quiver upon his bow: next after the bow was Caesar's spear.' Here some have thought that the weak *fuit* deliberately demeans Augustus' participation in the victory,[33] but it should be suspect not only because of its weakness and flatness but because a past tense is anomalous among the present tenses that Propertius uses consistently in this part of the narrative (55 *consumit*, 57 *uincit . . . dat*; 58 *uehuntur*; 59 *miratur*; 61 *prosequitur*; 63 *petit*). We should either follow such distinguished editors of the past as Broekhuyzen and Burman and read *furit*, with Guyet and Heinsius

---

[33] I had thought that this was an exclusively modern attitude until I consulted the commentary of Barth 1777, which remarks sarcastically here, '*Eximia laus fortitudinis Augusti!*' (extraordinary praise of Augustus' bravery!), but one can hardly imagine Propertius depicting the officially pious, and not yet officially deified, Augustus as greater than or even equal to a god.

(not elsewhere applied to weapons, but cf. V. Fl. 1.144 *ense furens*), or else read *ruit* (cf. V. Max. 4.7.2 *ruentibus telis*). A later couplet, 59–60, has inspired even more amusement in scholars doubtful of Propertius' serious intentions here: *at pater Idalio miratur Caesar ab astro:/ 'sum deus: est nostri sanguinis ista fides,'* 'but his father Caesar marvels from the Idalian star: "I am a god: this is the honour of our bloodline."' Julius Caesar's announcement of his divine status is banal (out of harmony with what is otherwise one of Propertius' most ambitious and highly wrought elegies), otiose (the *astrum Idalium* itself recalls both Caesar's descent from Venus and the comet that was supposed to have announced his divinity, and he had officially been *Diuus Iulius* for over a quarter of a century), and stylistically anomalous (the quoted words are not introduced by any formula that signals the quotation). I suggest that the words quoted here were not spoken by Caesar at all but by Apollo, who is otherwise the only figure to speak in the account of Actium, that the words quoted were *est uestri sanguinis ista fides,* 'that is the honour of *your* bloodline,' and that they were introduced by the phrase *cui deus,* 'to whom the god [said]' (for a similar introductory formula cf. Stat. *Theb.* 7.294 *cui senior ridens*). The additional alteration that this necessitates in reading *uestri* rather than *nostri* is no barrier to having Apollo commend Augustus to his adoptive father as the hero of Actium; these words are confused frequently, even in texts less corrupted than Propertius. One might also consider reading *haec* rather than *at* as the first word of 59; not only does it identify the object of Caesar's admiration, it also gives *ista* a more specific reference.

Our texts can also be improved through the application of sound principles of textual criticism. Lachmann's method of stemmatic reconstruction works relatively well with Propertius: there is indeed an archetype to reconstruct, and most of the doubts pertaining to its reconstruction tend to involve relatively small details. Yet conservative editors often prefer a shortcut. Instead of reconstructing the archetype first and then judging its correctness, they choose a single so-called 'best' manuscript (in this case N, which is probably the least corrupted and least corrected of surviving witnesses) and print its reading unless obviously defective. Of course 'best' is only a relative term; even the 'best' copy of an extremely corrupt archetype is, ironically, a manuscript 'worse' than its source, and it can be a thoroughly 'bad' manuscript in the quality of its text. In addition, 'cautiously conservative' editors are reluctant to accept emendations unless some glaring error compels it, but they forget that the purpose of classical textual criticism is to restore the author's original, not to correct a medieval copy of it to a merely acceptable level of grammar and syntax.[34] They also fail to appreciate that all errors do not leave obvious traces; the choice between *noceat* and *feriat* in 3.16.14 is a case in point. The text of Propertius is so corrupt that an editor must indeed suspect everything, and must go 'hunting' for corruptions rather than wait for them to present a calling card.

This optimist approach goes hand in glove with adherence to an unwritten law: if the two branches of a tradition give different readings, one of them will always be right. In fact two branches can err independently, especially when small words of similar appearance are involved, and editors should avoid the trap of accepting an error of this kind that happens to give speciously 'acceptable' sense or syntax when the reading of the other branch does not. A particularly egregious example is 1.20.1, which all editions print as *hoc pro*

---

[34] 'Sometimes editors, both of classical and of modern works, argue that the most they are justified in doing is to attempt to purge the copy-text, or archetype, or paradosis, of errors—not to try to restore what the author wrote. But this argument cannot be praised for its respect of historical evidence; rather, it confuses two kinds of edition, both legitimate, neither of which, when done properly, disregards the evidence. If one is interested in a text as it appeared at a particular time to a particular audience, a diplomatic or facsimile edition of it serves the purpose best; correcting errors in it—editing it critically—would be out of place, for the errors, though unintended, were part of what the contemporary readers saw in the text in front of them. If, on the other hand, one wishes to correct errors—to try to repair the damage done to the text in transmission, however famous or influential its corrupt form may be—then one is producing a text that differs from any now extant (probably from any that ever existed), and the aim of the alterations is obviously not the preservation of a documentary form of the text but the construction of a text as close as possible (as close, that is, as surviving evidence permits) to the one the author intended' (Tanselle 1990: 301-2). For a classicist's perspective on the same matter, see the entertaining preface to Hermann Koechly's 1857 Teubner text of Nonnus, especially vi–viii, where he contrasts fashionably conservative modern editors, who boast that by reconstructing the archetype and removing only the most obvious and most trivial errors they have 'emended, not interpolated' their text, with the practice of men like 'the ancient Hermann,' who '*codicis archetypi—si quidem fuit—scripturam pro necessario quidem erigendi aedificii fundamento, sed non pro ipso aedificio habent*' (who consider the text of the archetype manuscript—if ever it existed—as a necessary foundation for a building, but not the building itself).

*continuo te, Galle, monemus amore*, 'I give you this warning, Gallus, in recognition of your constant affection.' For the first word N and X (Λ) give *hoc*, while A has *nec*; the former makes sense, the latter does not, and therefore *hoc*, being found in N, the 'best' manuscript, is assumed to be what Propertius wrote. In fact the poet himself proves otherwise, for he has designed the poem's last hexameter (51) as an echo of its first: *his, o Galle, tuos monitus seruabis amores*, 'Warned by this, Gallus, you will preserve your love.' Nearly every word here has its equivalent in 1: *amores* takes up *amore*, *monitus* takes up *monemus*, *tuos* takes up *te*, *Galle* repeats the earlier vocative, and *his* corresponds to—certainly not *hoc*, unless someone can explain what aesthetic *frisson* we are meant to feel from this inconcinnity between singular and plural forms of a commonplace word, akin I suppose to what a modernist poet might evoke by leading us to expect 'this' and then startling us with 'these.' Of course Propertius wrote *haec*, not *hoc*, in 1, and the readings *hoc* and *nec* are independent corruptions of what the archetype must have offered: *hec*, a medieval spelling of *haec*.[35] It is worth remarking that the correct reading was apparently restored here about 600 years ago by Salutati in his corrections to F, if not by Petrarch himself.[36] To the best of my knowledge, *haec* last appeared in print in the Aldine edition of 1502.

---

[35] I would argue that *hoc* here is one of the associative errors demonstrating that N and X shared a common intermediate source; other possible examples of such errors include *obcenis* for *obscenis*, found in N and v at 1.16.10; *fletus* for *flemus*, found in N[pc] (*fletu* N[ac]) and v (in the form *fletu*⁹) and mru at 2.27.7 (note also *fle* followed by a lacuna in c); *(a)eoi* for *Coi*, found in N[2] and sc at 3.1.1; and *flamine* for *flammae*, found in N and sc at 3.13.21.

[36] F reads *nec*, but *h̄*, apparently representing *haec*, stands in the margin, written by a correcting hand attributed to Salutati (though it is not always certain which of the four hands present in F has made a particular correction). The possibility that the correction could have been made originally in Petrarch's lost manuscript, the exemplar of F and itself a copy of A (which reads *nec*), arises from the fact that other descendants of Petrarch's copy also read *h(a)ec*. It is certainly the reading of P (whose scribe, however, introduced a substantial number of improvements as he copied). L is lost for this portion of the text, but Naples, Bibl. Nazionale IV.F.19, a descendant of it (or perhaps of its exemplar, as Heyworth has argued [1986: 30–2]), reads *haec* according to my own collation; Professor Heyworth, however, informs me that according to his own collation that manuscript offers in the text a reading that might be either *Hec* or *Nec*, with *hoc* in the margin. Brussels, Bibliothèque Royale 14638, another descendant of L (or of its exemplar), reads *hoc*, but this is surely derived from v (for the suggestion that the Naples and Brussels manuscripts derive

Misplaced veneration for a so-called 'best' manuscript has perhaps led editors to foist another error upon Propertius in 3.7.43. Lamenting the death of young Paetus at sea, the poet remarks that he would be alive today, with nothing to mourn but his wealth, had he stayed at home on his ancestral estate. All editions print the line as *quod si contentus patrio boue uerteret agros*, 'But if he were contentedly turning his fields with ancestral ox.' N and X (*Λ*) have *contentus*, the Petrarchan manuscripts have *contentos*; a 'contented' Paetus makes sense, 'contented' fields do not, and therefore *contentus* is assumed to be right. Not necessarily. There is a 50 per cent chance that the archetype read *contentus* and that my next remarks are therefore irrelevant. But there is an equal chance that the archetype read *contentos* and that *contentus* in N and X (*Λ*) is an associative error of those manuscripts (or perhaps a conjecture made independently in the two sources).[37] In medieval orthography forms of *contentus* are interchangeable with those of *contemptus*; *contentos* in the archetype could therefore represent *contemptos* (P in fact reads *contemtos*, probably as a conjecture based upon *contentos*); this gives equally good sense and perhaps superior expression to the universally accepted version of the line. 'But if he were ploughing with ancestral ox the fields he scorned,' with *contemptos... agros* enclosing *patrio boue*, strikes me as more elegant, more polished, more pointed—and therefore, of course, more Propertian. Some might be tempted to dismiss *contemptos* as an unnecessary conjecture, but it is not even a conjecture, only an interpretation of an authoritative manuscript reading in the light of medieval orthography; ironically, it could be *contentus*—which those

---

from v and L, see Butrica 1984: 110–12). Thus it remains at least possible that Petrarch had already introduced *h(a)ec* in his own copy and that the careless scribe of F corrupted it back to *nec*, but small words like these are interchanged with such frequency that certainty is impossible.

[37] It needs to be remembered that X (*Λ*) would certainly have been corrected by Poggio and perhaps by Niccoli as well before the first surviving transcript (v) was made, and that half of its descendants were copied by able scholars who surely introduced corrections of their own (Panormita copied v, Poggio's son Jacopo copied s, Pomponio Leto copied c; for speculation that the common source of mru might have been a transcript made by Niccoli, see Butrica 1984: 70, with n. 16). For possible conjunctive errors of N and X, see n. 35 above.

who dismiss *contemptos* would regard as an authoritative transmitted reading—that is a conjecture.

All manuscript traditions are unique because all manuscripts are unique, and that is because all manuscripts are products of unique human individuals in unique circumstances; an editor must therefore know as much as possible about the human quirks of the people who copied them. In 3.6.22 Cynthia is complaining, 'Poor me, that man can abandon me, though I've done nothing, and can keep in his house the sort of woman I don't want to name.' The line is now always read as *et qualem nolo dicere habere domi; domi* is Heinsius' idiomatic correction of the universally transmitted *domo*, and *nolo* is a palmary emendation of Palmer for *nulla* of the archetype (N has *nullo*, but this perhaps has been influenced by *nullo* in 21 directly above); *et qualem* comes from N, Fedeli's 'best' manuscript, the other manuscripts having *(a)equalem*. Again one reading makes sense, the other does not, but giving tolerable sense is not the same thing as being what the archetype gave or what the author wrote. The scribe who copied this part of N had an interesting habit. At 1.2.18, where the archetype had *euenit* at the beginning of the line, he wrote *et uenit*, and at 2.1.44, where the archetype had *enumerat* at the beginning of the line, he wrote *et numerat*; in other words, he was prone to turn initial *e* into *et*. Our haste to adopt his speciously acceptable reading here should be tempered by the realization that it could be nothing more than the unconscious result of an ingrained habit; it is entirely possible that the archetype read *equalem*, representing *aequalem*, and that this is a corruption of *ac qualem*. The sense that this gives is precisely the same as that given by *et qualem*, but the ugliness of the clashing *k* sounds seems to me to suit even better the harsh and accusatory context. Even the scribes of 'best' manuscripts have their quirks, and accidents do not always produce ungrammatical nonsense.

The evidence of the Pompeiian *graffiti* shows that the text of Propertius has been extensively affected by verbal corruption; but the editor of Propertius also needs to be more open than recent editors have been to the possibilities of transposition and interpolation.

The first editor to introduce a significant number of transpositions was Scaliger in 1577, and he was followed by several others who reordered the text in even more disruptive ways.[38] The reaction against these drastic interventions has cast the concept of transposition into a disrepute which it does not deserve. Transpositions, of course, are necessitated by dislocations that have occurred in the transmission of a text. One major cause of dislocation is omission, since dislocation often results from the unsuccessful correction of such an omission. Omission is a widespread phenomenon; out of the approximately 150 surviving Propertius manuscripts, at least 112 contain at least one omission before or even after correction.

In addition, the process of transcription itself frequently leads to dislocation, as eyes skip from one occurrence of a word to another or from one word to another of similar appearance, or simply fail from fatigue.

Many of the surviving manuscripts contain dislocations of various kinds within a single poem, some corrected, some not. One common form of dislocation is the reversal of adjacent lines. A number of manuscripts exhibit a single example of the phenomenon:

El Escorial g.iii.12 (3.13.17/16)
Florence, Bibl. Laurenziana pl. 38,37 (2.34.93/92)
Leiden, Universiteitsbibliotheek I.Lips. F.43 (3.7.36/35$^{ac}$)[39]
Naples, Biblioteca Oratoriana dei Gerolamini M.C.F. 3–15 (4.7.85/84$^{ac}$)
Salamanca, Bibl. Universitaria 245 (3.2.14/13$^{ac}$)
Pal. lat. 910 (2.25.42/41)
Urb. lat. 641 (1.13.15/14$^{ac}$)

Often these dislocations have obvious palaeographical causes. The reversal of 4.7.84–5, for example, surely occurred because of the presence of *hic* in 83 and 85, the reversal of 3.1.13–14 because of the presence of *meas* in 12 and *Musas* in 14, the reversal of 2.25.41–2 because of the repetition of *uidistis* in 41, 42, 43, and 44, and the reversal of 1.13.14–15 because of the presence of *uidi ego* in 13 and 14. Some manuscripts offer two examples:

---

[38] Smyth 1970 offers in 'Excursus I' a conspectus of the wholesale reorderings of all four books by Gruppe, Carutti, and Richmond.

[39] In these lists of dislocations, corrections made by clearly later hands have been ignored; $^{(ac)}$ indicates a correction that at least could have been made by the scribe himself, though many even of these were undoubtedly made by later hands as well.

Hamburg, Staats- und Universitätsbibliothek Scrin. 139.4 (1.6.16/15 and 2.27.4/3)[40]
Oxford, Bodleian Library lat. class. e 3 (2.7.3/2; 4.3.53/52)
Pal. lat. 1652 (3.3.32/31$^{ac}$; 3.11.35/34$^{ac}$)
Vat. lat. 5177 (1.5.19/18$^{ac}$; 4.1.89/88$^{ac}$)

A very few have three or more examples:

Berlin, Staatsbibliothek Diez B. Sant. 52 (three examples: 2.25.36/35$^{ac}$; 2.28.39/38$^{ac}$; 4.6.55/54$^{ac}$)
Venice, Bibl. del Museo Civico Correr 549 (six examples: 2.7.3/2$^{ac}$; 2.13.20/19$^{ac}$; 2.28.40/39$^{ac}$; 3.24.9/8$^{ac}$; 4.3.70/69$^{ac}$; 4.10.9/8$^{ac}$)

Again palaeographical causes are frequently evident. For example, the reversal of 2.27.3–4 in the source from which Hamburg Scrin. 139.4 inherited it surely arose from the presence of *quaeritis* in 2 and 3 and of *quae sit* in 4, while the displacement of 2.25.35–6 arose from the presence of *quod* in 34 and 36, and that of 2.13.19–20 from the presence of *mei* in 18 and 20.

On occasion single lines have been displaced to a new location within the same elegy. Sometimes this happens because a scribe initially skips a line, then returns to it:

Brussels, Bibl. Royale 14638 (1.6.14, 16–18, 15, 19$^{ac}$)
El Escorial g.iii.12 (2.18.17, 19–20, 18$^{ac}$)
Hamburg, Staats- und Universitätsbibliothek Scrin. 139.4 (4.7.13, 15–18, 14, 19$^{ac}$)

Sometimes the scribe copies a line both in its proper place and in a later position:

Rome, Bibl. Casanatense 15 (3.6.33, 24, 34)

Sometimes the line appears out of place through anticipation:

Florence, Bibl. Laurenziana pl. 33,14 (1.18.2, 5, 3$^{ac}$)
Leiden, Universiteitsbibliotheek I.Lips. F.43 (2.21.4, 11, 5$^{ac}$)
Oxford, Bodleian Library lat. class. e 3 (4.8.73, 80, 74)

---

[40] Of these two dislocations the second is certainly inherited, either from L or from its source, and the first may be as well; 1.6.15 was lacking in A and in Petrarch's manuscript, so that the order 16/15 could have arisen from 15 being restored in an incorrect or unclear manner.

Parma, Bibl. Palatina 716 (4.9.16, 19, 17[ac])
Ravenna, Bibl. Classense 277 (4.8.39, 44, 40[ac])
Vienna, Österreichische Nationalbibliothek 224 (1.8.42, 46, 43)
Vienna, Österreichische Nationalbibliothek 3153 (2.12.15, 20, 16[ac])[41]

Of course whole couplets can be displaced as well. Nearly every case that involves the displacement of adjacent couplets can be explained easily through some palaeographical cause such as homoearchon or homoeoteleuton:

> Carpentras, Bibl. Inguimbertine 361 (2.13.19–20 and 21–2 reversed[ac] [*mei* 18,20])
> Florence, Bibl. Laurenziana pl. 33,14 (4.8.69–70 and 71–2 reversed [*Lygdam-* 68,70])
> Florence, Bibl. Riccardiana 633 (4.3.3–4 and 5–6 reversed[ac] [*meus* 2, *meis* 4])
> Padua, Bibl. Capitolare C.77 (3.11.51–2 and 53–4 reversed)
> Rome, Bibl. Vallicelliana F.93 (4.2.11–12 and 13–14 reversed[ac] [*Vertumn-* 10, 12])
> Venice, Bibl. Marciana 4208 (1.8.23–4 and 25–6 reversed[ac] [*mea est* 24,26]; 4.9.13–14 and 15–16 reversed[ac] [*boues* 12,16])
> Barb. lat. 23 (2.15.25–6 and 27–8 reversed[ac] [*dies* 24,26]; 4.11.49–50 and 51–2 reversed[ac] [*metu* 48, *meo* 50])
> Pal. lat. 910 (2.8.7–8 and 9–10 reversed[ac] [*est* 6,8])
> Vat. lat. 3188 (2.24.37–8 and 39–40 reversed[ac] [*eras* 36,38])
> Vat. lat. 5174 (2.14.5–6 and 7–8 reversed)

But displacement can extend beyond contiguous couplets. Sometimes two or more consecutive lines have been displaced to a non-contiguous site within the same elegy. This often happens through anticipation:

> Leiden, Universiteitsbibliotheek Voss. lat. O.13 (2.33.7, 10, 8–9, 11[ac])
> London, British Library Egerton 3027 (2.24.30, 33, 31–2, 34[ac])
> London, British Library Add. 10387 (3.20.14, 27–8, 15)
> Munich, Universitätsbibliothek Cim 22 (4.6.32, 37–8, 33[ac])
> Rome, Bibl. Casanatense 15 (3.17.5, 12–13, 6[ac])
> Ottob. lat. 2003 (3.2.20, 22–3, 21, 24[ac])

---

[41] In this case the intrusive line was originally written in an erasure over a version of 16 itself!

Sometimes larger groups of lines have been displaced elsewhere within the same elegy:

> Florence, Bibl. Laurenziana pl. 38,37 (3.11.51, 53–5, 52, 56$^{ac}$)
> Grenoble, Bibl. Municipale 549 (3.19.11, 14–16, 13$^{ac}$)
> Leiden, Universiteitsbibliotheek Voss. lat. Q.117 (2.3.32, 34–6, 33$^{ac}$)
> Padua, Bibl. Capitolare C.77 (3.1.14, 19–24, 15–18, 25)
> Rome, Bibl. Vallicelliana F.93 (4.9.3, 17–18, 13–16, 19–26, 4)[42]

A comparable disturbance in the text of 2.1 in Florence, Bibl. Nazionale Centrale Magliabecchi VII 1162 will be mentioned below.

Sometimes lines or couplets are repeated in the wrong location, presumably because a scribe initially returns to the wrong place in his *exempla*r:

> Genoa, Bibl. Universitaria E.III.29 (2.12.13 repeated after 16)
> Leiden, Universiteitsbibliotheek I.Lips. F.43 (2.13.19 repeated after 20)
> Paris, Bibl. Nationale lat. 8237 (2.18.28 repeated after 31$^{ac}$)
> Parma, Bibl. Palatina 716 (3.24.3–4 repeated after 20$^{ac}$)
> Rome, Bibl. Casanatense 15 (2.16.46–7 repeated after 53$^{ac}$)
> Wroclaw, Bibl. Uniwersytecka AKC 1948 197 KN (3.13.23–4 repeated after 34)

Sometimes displacement is combined with omission and/or repetition. Displacement combined with omission has occurred in:

> London, British Library Harley 2550 (2.30.14–21 = 14, 19–20, 17–18, 19, 16, 21)
> Oxford, Bodleian Library lat. class e 3 (2.20.20–7 = 20, 25, 21–4, 27)
> Venice, Bibl. Marciana 4208 (3.22.27–31 = 27, 30–1, 28$^{ac}$)

Displacement and repetition, without omission, are exhibited in:

> Berlin, Staatsbibliothek Diez B. Sant. 53 (3.22.39–42 = 39, 41, 40–1, 42)

Repetition and omission, without displacement, are exhibited in:

> Barb. lat. 23 (1.9.28–31 = 28, *lacuna*, 30, *lacuna*, 30, 31)
> Vat. lat. 3274 (2.10.18–21 = 18–19, 18, 21)

---

[42] The scribe subsequently deleted this muddled version of 4.9 and began again from scratch.

Many of the dislocations mentioned above have been corrected, either by the scribe himself or by a later hand. Such correction, however, does not guarantee that a copy of a corrected manuscript would incorporate those corrections, nor does the fact that a dislocation has been corrected guarantee that it has been corrected 'correctly' or successfully; botched correction can then lead to further disruption through additional attempts at correction. Three manuscripts illustrate this phenomenon:

> Florence, Bibl. Riccardiana 633:
> 2.9.42–7 before correction = 42, 45–6, 43–4, 47
> after correction = 42, 43, 45–6, 44, 47
> Leiden, Universiteitsbibliotheek Voss. lat. Q.117:
> 4.1.87–91 before correction = 87, 90, 89, 88, 91;
> after correction = 87, 88, 90, 89, 91
> Padua, Bibl. Capitolare C.77:
> 2.29.7–13 before correction = 7, 9, 12, 11, 10, 13
> after correction = 7, 10, 9, 12, 11, 10, 13

Sometimes dislocations have occurred between two adjacent poems, presumably because a scribe returned to the wrong point in his *exemplar*, missing the correct location by a folio or two. Most of these involve single couplets. Sometimes the lines are dislocated through anticipation:

> Pal. lat. 910 (3.5.2, 3.6.6–7, 3.5.3[ac])
> Vat. lat. 1611 (3.2.7, 3.3.8–9, 3.2.8[ac])
> Vat. lat. 5177 (1.16.15, 1.17.15–16, 1.16.16[ac])

Sometimes the lines are accidentally repeated in a new location:

> Florence, Bibl. Laurenziana Acquisti e doni 124 (4.9.6, 4.8.59–60, 4.9.7[ac])
> Florence, Bibl. Riccardiana 633 (4.9.6, 4.8.59–60, 4.9.7[ac])

Rarely the lines appear only in their new location:

> Pesaro, Bibl. Oliveriana 1167 (1.9.16, 1.8.43–4, 1.9.17[ac])

Some migrations between contiguous poems involve chunks of text rather than single couplets. In British Library Add. 23766, copied by the scholar-poet Mattia Canali, lines 2.7.13–20 appear at the end of 2.8. In Florence, Bibl. Laurenziana pl. 38, 37, elegies 3.19 and 3.20 have been shuffled together so that after 3.19.19 we find 3.20.1–26, then

# Editing Propertius 69

3.19.20–8, then 3.20.27–30. In Florence, Bibl. Nazionale Centrale II. IX.125 the order of elegies 2.4 and 2.5 has been reversed. But dislocations do not always occur between contiguous poems; for example:

> Vat. lat. 5177 (3.8.37, 3.11.34–6, 3.8.38, etc.)

The most difficult to explain are the dislocations that have occurred between books; for example:

> Florence, Bibl. Nazionale Centrale Magliabecchi VII 1162 (4.4.1, 3.1.2, 4.4.2$^{ac}$)
> Venice, Bibl. del Museo Civico Correr 549 (2.3.26, 1.16.11–13, 2.3.27$^{ac}$)
> Naples, Biblioteca Oratoriana dei Gerolamini M.C.F. 3–15 (1.5.2, 4.9.31 [in the form *huc ruit in siccam comesta puluere*], 1.5.3$^{ac}$)

Dislocations have also taken place over a series of poems within a single book:

> Leiden, Universiteitsbibliotheek Voss. lat. O.81:
> Book 2 = 1.1–14.7, 16.48–18.35, 14.8–16.14, 18.36 *ad fin.*
> Leiden, Universiteitsbibliotheek B.P.L. 133A:
> Book 1 = 1.1–6.11; 8.12–9.28; 6.12–8.11; 11.27–14.2; 9.29–11.26; 14.3 *ad fin.*
> Salamanca, Bibl. Universitaria 85:
> Book 1 = 1.1–6.20; 8.25–10.10; 6.21–8.24; 12.17–14.24; 10.11–12.16; 15.1 *ad fin.*
> Florence, Bibl. Laurenziana pl. 33,15$^{pc}$:
> Book 1 = 1.1–6.20; 7.1–8.24; 12.17–20; 8.27–10.10; 6.21–36; 11.1–14.24; 10.11–30; 15.1 *ad fin.*
> Florence, Bibl. Nazionale Magliabecchi VII 1162:
> Book 2 = 1.1–16, 65–78, 17–64; 2.2.1–6.31; a *lacuna* of one line; 20.25–22.35; 8.39–20.24; a *lacuna* of one line; 6.32–8.38; 22.39 *ad fin.*
> Cambridge, University Library 3394:
> Book 1 = 1.1–3.46; 6.1–7.26; 4.1–5.32; 9.25–11.20; 8.1–9.24 (without 8.7–8, 25–6, and 43–4$^{ac}$); 11.21 *ad fin.*
> Book 2 = 1.1–9.52; 13.1–58; 10.1–12.24; 15.29–16.30; 14.1–15.28; 16.31 *ad fin.*
> Book 4 = 1.1–7.54 (7.55–82 are omitted); 7.83–8.36; 7.31–82; 8.37 *ad fin.*

The first three examples unquestionably involve disruption in the arrangement of folios in the *exemplar* or its source. In Leiden Voss.

lat. O.81 the passage 2.16.48–18.35 totals 64 lines (including two lines as space for two titles), while 2.14.8–16.14 totals 95 (including two lines for two titles); three folios containing about 32 lines per page apparently became detached in the source of the *exemplar* and were restored in the wrong order, while the side containing the 33 lines 2.16.15–47 was somehow missed completely. An *exemplar* with 32 lines to the page also lies behind the disruptions in Leiden BPL 133A, where (including single spaces for titles) four blocks of 64 lines have been shuffled. An *exemplar* with 33 or 34 lines to the page lies behind the disruptions in Salamanca Bibl. Universitaria 85, where the four blocks of lines that have been shuffled respectively represent 68, 68, 66, and 67 lines (including a single space for titles). The disordered arrangement of lines in Laurenziana pl. 33,15 is unique in that it is not inherited from the *exemplar*. The scribe copied the lines in their normal order but used a series of signs and notes in the margins to indicate the order of lines that I have noted above; he seems to have found this arrangement in another manuscript, and here we have a scribe 'correcting' the normal order in accordance with a disordered *exemplar*—another potential source of dislocations in a manuscript. The dislocation of folios could lie behind at least some of the disorder in Magliabecchi VII 1162; lines 2.6.32–8.38 and 2.20.25–22.35 represent blocks of 69 and 72 lines respectively (again allowing for titles). The same might be true for Cambridge 3394 as well. In Book 4.7.31–82 and 7.83–4.8.36 are equal blocks of 52 lines each if two spaces are allowed for the title before 4.8.[43] In Book 2 13.1–58, 10.1–12.24, 15.29–16–30, and 14.1–15.28 are, respectively, blocks of 58, 58, 57, and 61 lines (allowing as always for titles). The lengths of the blocks in Book 1 are even more irregular but there is a remote possibility that they could still represent the contents of individual folios; 6.1–7.26, 4.1–5.32, 9.25–11.20, and 8.1–9.24 contain, respectively, 63, 61, 56, and 71 lines (allowing again a single space for titles).

There is one example of extreme disruption occurring between books.

---

[43] Heyworth 1986: 67 makes the interesting observation that 4.7.31–82 occupy a complete folio in v (his T); it might be added that 4.7.83–8.36 do as well. For the descent of Cambridge 3394 and other manuscripts from a copy of v, see Butrica 1984: 100–3; it would appear, however, that the equivalency in 4.7.31–8.36 is purely coincidental, since the other blocks of lines shifted in Cambridge 3394 do not match the contents of folios in v.

Florence, Bibl. Nazionale Centrale Magliabecchi VII 1164:
1.1.1–16.38; 2.13.1–15.8; 1.16.39–2.6.16 (with 1.16.46–7 omitted);
2.15.9–16.52; 2.6.17–12.24; 2.16.53 *ad fin.*

Here again it is possible that leaves were disrupted in the *exemplar* or an ancestor, in this case one with perhaps 25 lines to the page: the two blocks 2.13.1–15.8 and 2.15.9–16.52 represent, respectively, 100 and 99 lines (two pairs of leaves reversed); 1.16.39–2.6.16 and 2.6.17–12.24 are also close to being multiples of 25, at 395 lines and 201 lines respectively (always allowing one space for each title).

While the vast majority of dislocations are accidental, dislocation by conjecture is not to be dismissed completely, and indeed seems to have occurred in Oxford, Bodleian Library Add. B 55. Here a corrector has written the letters 'b' and 'c' respectively alongside lines 1.20.51 and 52. This apparently means that the lines are to be moved to after the line marked 'a,' namely 1.21.8. In addition, '*vacat*' has been written in the margin to remove 1.21.9–10 from their usual location, and they have been added by the same hand after 1.22.8. The resulting arrangement in 1.21 and 22 runs as follows (this version incorporates the scribal errors of the manuscript; 1.21 is run on from the end of 1.20, which I have not reproduced):

*Tu qui consortem properas euadere casum,*
    *Miles ab Etruscis saucius aggeribus,*
*Qui nostro gemitu turgentia lumina torques,*
    *Pars ego sum uestrae proxima militiae.*
*Sic te seruato ut possint gaudere parentes,*
    *Nec soror acta tuis sentiat e lacrimis:*
*Gallum per medios ereptum Caesaris enses*
    *Effugere ignotas non potuisse manus.*
*His, o Galle, tuos monitus seruabis amores,*
    *Formosum Nymphis credere uisus Hylan.*
*ad TULLUM*
*Qualis et unde genus, qui sint mihi, Tulle, Penates,*
    *Quaeris pro nostra semper amicitia.*
*Si Perusina tibi patriae sunt nota sepulcra,*
    *Italiae duris funera temporibus,*
*Cum Romana suos egit discordia ciues,*
    *Sit mihi praecipue puluis Etrusca dolor:*

*Tu protecta mei propessa es membra parentis,*[44]
*Tu nullo miseri contigis ossa solo.*
*Proxima supposito contingens Vmbria campo*
  *Me genuit terris fertilis uberibus,*
*Et quaecumque super dispersa inuenerit ossa*
  *Montibus Etruscis, haec sciet esse mea.*

These dislocations (which incorporate 1.21.1–8 within 1.20 as a single elegy and make the final couplet of 1.21 the final couplet of 1.22) are not found in any extant manuscript and therefore could be conjectural; if that is the case, however, their author has not considered what Gallus' unsuccessful escape has to do with Hylas and the Nymphs, or why Propertius in his *sphragis* to the *Cynthia* should indicate that his bones are scattered over the mountains of Etruria.

Many of the dislocations discussed above have been corrected by the scribes who created them; but the fact that many were not corrected at all, or corrected only by much later hands, shows that such correction was a matter of chance. In addition, the lines that have been displaced sometimes appear in the correct position as well as in the incorrect one, and a corrector would need to know which occurrence should be deleted. In both of these situations correction is easier if other copies are available for consultation, but this would not have been the case for most of the Middle Ages. Thus a variety of circumstances could have conspired to keep a freshly disordered text in that condition.

The dislocations in the surviving manuscripts that I have surveyed in these pages do not of course prove the validity of any of the transpositions proposed by modern critics; but they do show that the related phenomena of omission and dislocation are significantly more common than most imagine. They are so common that transposition can never be rejected out of hand as a possible remedy for a textual difficulty (any proposed transposition, however, should be explicable in terms of recognized types of dislocation), and they are sometimes so violent that even extreme transpositions cannot simply be dismissed as impossible. Some important considerations must be remembered in this regard. One is that, because the Propertian

---

[44] The manuscript originally read *propinqui*, but the hand that has introduced the transpositions discussed here has also introduced *parentis* as a correction.

tradition demonstrably depends upon a single archetype, any transpositions effected in that archetype or inherited from its ancestors will be present in all its descendants, so that arguments based upon 'the agreement of all the manuscripts' become meaningless. Moreover, as was noted above, the number of Propertian manuscripts in active existence after late antiquity must have been small indeed; this scarcity of copies would have made it difficult or even impossible for errors in the order of lines to be corrected through collation of other copies. It must also be borne in mind that these data about dislocations derive from partial collations that covered a little more than one half of the text;[45] this means that, while I have recorded all or nearly all of the more drastic dislocations that involve more than one elegy, I have surely missed a number of dislocations within the elegies that I did not collate in full. Those who express confidence in the state of the Propertian text should reflect seriously upon the consequences of these data. Lines do indeed move about within a poem; they can move from one poem to a contiguous one; they can move from one poem to a non-contiguous poem in the same book or in a different book; and whole stretches of text can be shuffled about like a deck of cards, usually within a single book but on occasion between books. Many scribes effect no dislocations at all; many effect at least a few; and some effect a good many. It may well be that one or two stages in the ancestry of our archetype were entrusted to the sort of scribe who is inclined to omit and dislocate. In any case, such dislocations happen so often that it would be naive to assume that none, or even only a few, occurred in the twelve centuries of copying that separate our earliest manuscripts from Propertius himself. It is necessary to face the possibility that the archetype or one or more of its ancestors could have been a manuscript like Cambridge 3394 or Magliabecchi VII 1164. One can only imagine what theories of Propertian composition would arise from interpreting the elegies as these manuscripts arrange them, or the arguments that would be used to refute anyone who tried to restore through transposition the order with which we are familiar.

---

[45] The poems collated were 1.1–2, 11–13, 17, 20–2; 2.1–3, 8–13, 19–20, 24–34; 3.1–5, 11, 13, 22; 4.1–2, 6–9, 11, representing 2238 lines, or about 55 per cent of the text.

Since all editions accept at least a handful of transpositions, I shall offer only two examples, both in 3.10. The first is Barber's unduly hesitant proposal to put 17–18, *et pete, qua polles, ut sit tibi forma perennis/inque meum semper stent tua regna caput*, after 12. In 11 Propertius begins to offer directions to Cynthia on the observance of her birthday. In the order of lines given by the paradosis, he tells her first to rise and pray to the gods (11–12), then to wash her face and arrange her hair (13–14), then to put on the robe in which he first saw her and to cover her head with flowers (15–16), then to 'ask that your beauty, the source of your power, should be enduring and that your dominion should stand forever over my head' (17–18), after which the instructions turn toward the celebration of an intimate *symposion* that night. But how is Cynthia to seek or ask for this enduring beauty and eternal domination over Propertius? It is surely not from the passing beauty of the flowers that are to deck her head, or from dragging out an old dress again and again, or from washing her face and arranging her hair. In fact what she is told to seek could only come from the gods, and 17–18 are surely the continuation of 12, where she is told to entreat the gods but not what she is to ask of them. Here 17–18 were originally omitted because of homoeoteleuton, the similar line-endings *pennis* 11 and *p(er)ennis* 17.

The directions for the evening's festivities also involve a dislocation. Those instructions include sacrifices at the altars that will illuminate the house with their propitious light (19–20), then dinner and a night of drinking and unguents (21–2); then they take a distinctly raucous turn, with much piping, nocturnal dances, verbal *nequitia*, late-night *conuicia*, and noise spilling out into the alley (23–6), after which the rolling of the dice in 27–8 to see which is more in love with the other seems a distinct anticlimax (*sit sors et nobis talorum interprete iactu/quem grauius* [Beroaldus: *grauibus* O] *pennis uerberet ille puer*). Surely this activity, and the lines that contain it, belong in the earlier, quieter part of the evening, with the food and drink and unguents, not with the near-riot of 23–6, and the original location of 27–8 was after 21–2: *sit mensae ratio noxque inter pocula currat/et crocino nares murreus ungat onyx,/sit sors et nobis talorum interprete iactu*, etc. With the transposition of 27–8, the final eight lines of the elegy run smoothly as well:

> tibia nocturnis succumbat rauca choreis
> et sint nequitiae libera uerba tuae
> dulciaque ingratos adimant conuiuia somnos:
> publica uicinae perstrepat aura uiae.
> cum fuerit multis exacta trientibus hora
> noctis et instituet sacra ministra Venus,
> annua soluamus thalamo sollemnia nostro
> natalisque tui sic peragamus iter.

The closing section, 'When the hour has been passed with many pints,' follows more effectively after the injunction that the party should last long and loud than it did after the suggestion to roll dice. Here it is homoearchon that explains the original omission that led to the dislocation (*sit* begins both 21 and 27).

The concept of interpolation, whose most prominent advocates have been Günther Jachmann and Ulrich Knoche, has fallen— unjustifiably—into equal or even greater disrepute. And yet interpolation has demonstrably taken place in the Propertian tradition at a prearchetypal stage; the evidence is lines 1.2.1–2, which are also printed in editions as 4.5.55–6 because an early reader of Propertius recalled them while reading 4.5 and inscribed them in the margin of a copy from which the archetype derives. Interpolation has also taken place in the Renaissance tradition. Ovid's celebrated lines at *Ars Amatoria* 2.277–8 about gold and the corruption it engenders made their way into Propertius 3.13 not only in manuscripts but even in printed editions.[46] In British Library Harley 2778 they are found after 3.13.46; in Dresden, Sächsische Landesbibliothek Dc 133 they can be found at the bottom of a page, after 3.13.48, awaiting incorporation; and in Grenoble, Bibl. Municipale 549 they are again at the bottom of a page, but the rubricator has marked them for insertion after

---

[46] An amusing reflection of this occurs in the *Patrologia Latina* edition of Petrus Cantor's *Verbum abbreviatum* at section 60 (= *PL* CCV 84–5). Here we find 'Nunc impletum est poetae illud: *aurea nunc vere sunt saecula, plurimus auro/venit honos./auro perficitur, quidquid captatur inique,/nemoque praetenso munere vana rogat*' (Now that (sc. sentiment) of the poet has been fulfilled: The times are truly golden, great honor comes with gold, whatever is captured unfairly is made perfect with gold, and no one questions baseness when a reward is on the table). The editor attributes this to 'Propert. l. III, elegia 11,' having consulted, it seems, some edition which incorporated the Ovidian lines and numbered 3.13 as 11 (the Delphin edition of 1685 is the most likely candidate; I have not, however, identified the source of *auro perficitur . . . vana rogat*).

3.13.50. Pesaro, Bibl. Oliveriana 1167 has *qui sapit in tacito gaudeat ipse sinu* (= [Tib.] 3.19.8) incorporated between 2.25.29 and 30 (presumably this had originally been adduced as a parallel passage because of its similarity to 30, *in tacito cohibe gaudia clausa sinu*). In addition, Barb. lat. 23 has a spurious couplet of unknown origin marked for insertion between 1.3.33 and 34 (*et subito aduentu palluit illa meo;/mox, ut erat, neglecta comis et pectore nudo*).[47]

Perhaps even more significant is the fact that interpolation and dislocation have demonstrably occurred in the medieval tradition of Propertius. Interpolation and dislocation are most likely to happen when an active readership annotates texts. Activity of this sort seemed unlikely so long as it was thought that Propertius was virtually unread in the Middle Ages; but, while it is true that circulation remained quite limited geographically (Orléans and Paris) and that interest was equally limited chronologically (the twelfth and thirteenth centuries), it deserves notice that every medieval witness to the text of Propertius reveals, especially through annotations, precisely the sort of scholarly interest that can lead to transpositions and interpolations.[48] The most important documentation of this activity is undoubtedly the Propertian extracts found in the thirteenth-century florilegium partially contained in Bibl. Vat. Reg. lat. 2120.[49] Not only have these extracts experienced at least two separate phases of medieval annotation; the nature of the interventions shows quite dramatically how easily transposition and interpolation can occur, and even catches the process itself in action. The interpolation involves an obviously medieval couplet that has been included between two consecutive authentic lines, 2.33.33 and 34, with no indication that it is not by Propertius: *omnis amans cecus, non est*

---

[47] Heyworth 1986: 76 indicates that v (his T) contains 'A spurious couplet, written vertically in the far margin, for insertion between I ix 26 and 27;' the lines are in fact 1.9.27 (with *tibi* rather than *ubi non* and *subcludere* rather than *seducere*, as in the version in the text) and 1.9.30 (with *assiduas* where the text has *assuduas*, corrected to *assiduas*), and it is uncertain whether they were intended as an interpolation or as corrections.

[48] For Propertius in the Middle Ages, see Butrica (above, n. 16), 20–30.

[49] See now the fine facsimile printed in Buonocore 1995 as pl. XVIII, showing f.21ʳ, the first of the two sides containing extracts from Propertius, where all the phenomena discussed here can be observed.

*amor arbiter equs,/nam deforme pecus iudicat esse decus*, 'every lover is blind, love is not a fair judge, for it deems an ugly beast to be a beauty.' Presumably these lines are now found here because they were added to the margins during an earlier stage in the transmission of this florilegium in order to confirm or comment upon a sentiment expressed in one or another of the authentic lines. But the interpolated lines also document the phenomenon of dislocation, for they do not occupy their intended position. This can be argued through logical analysis. The lines concern the power of love to warp male vision (making a *deforme pecus* appear to be a *decus*: the oenophile's equivalent of the phenomenon known colloquially in North America as beer-goggles), and therefore they do not belong tucked inside a couplet on the deleterious effects of wine upon women's beauty and sexual judgment (*uino forma perit, uino corrumpitur aetas/uino saepe suum nescit amica uirum*, 'through wine beauty withers, through wine youth is spoilt, through wine a girlfriend often doesn't know her man'). More importantly, this logical analysis is confirmed by the physical evidence of the manuscript itself, for at the end of the hexameter of the interpolated couplet the scribe has written '. *b* .' This is evidently intended to correspond to the '. *a* .' found above at the end of Propertius 2.14.18 *scilicet insano nemo in amore videt* ('of course no one in a mad love-affair can see'), a line which refers explicitly to the warped vision of those in love. The inescapable conclusion is that, in an earlier stage of transmission, the interpolated couplet originally stood as a comment on 2.14.18, then was displaced in the copying of Reg. lat. 2120 itself. It should be observed, incidentally, that this case shows that an interpolated passage that originated as a gloss need not be found in immediate proximity to the passage that it glossed, only in the general vicinity.

In this instance we have seen an interpolation and a dislocation that have already occurred; but Reg. lat. 2120 also shows several potential interpolations, of words and of an entire line, waiting to occur. Propertius 2.15.30 has been glossed with the dactylic pentameter *est in amore modus non habuisse modum*; if Reg. lat. 2120 itself was ever copied, an unwary scribe might well think that this was an additional line of Propertius and incorporate it, just as the scribe of Reg. lat. 2120 incorporated the medieval couplet. Most of the glosses that consist of a single word could not be mistaken for corrections and so would be incorporated only by the most careless or inattentive scribes (and we would detect their presence easily). But a gloss which happens to be metrically equivalent to the word that it glosses is hardly distinguishable from a correction and therefore is not only particularly liable to be incorporated but is also particularly difficult to detect; the substitution of *noceat* for *feriat* in 3.16.14 discussed earlier is a case in point. Reg. lat. 2120 contains one example, *tarde* glossing *sero* in 2.25.28. This process of glossing and citing parallel passages is of course not a medieval innovation but a continuation of a practice rooted in antiquity; if we can detect so much actual and potential interpolation and dislocation in the 43 lines of this thirteenth-century florilegium, we can hardly reject out of hand the possibility of interpolation and dislocation in all of the rolls and codices that constitute the ancestors of the archetype of our tradition.

I believe that such interpolation has substantially affected the text of Propertius only in Book 2 and, to a lesser extent, Book 3 (Book 1 is the least corrupted section of the text in any case, and Book 4, being at the end of the collection, was reached and explored thoroughly by only the hardiest of readers). There is nothing sinister or diabolical about the process, nor does it represent anyone's attempt to 'adulterate' the text of Propertius or to pass off his own work as that of Propertius; the interpolated lines were brought into the text not by those who originally wrote them in the margins but by later copyists unable to distinguish clearly between original and additional material but obviously anxious to preserve whatever might be by Propertius. These interpolations can be classified in two principal categories. One is the kind that R. J. Tarrant has called 'collaborative,' in which the interpolator vies with the author by trying his hand at the same or a similar theme or offers a comment upon the content[50] (and it must be remembered that even in the twelfth century any reader educated enough and classically oriented enough to be reading Propertius would have been capable of composing elegiac couplets). The second type comprises quotations of other authors adduced in the margin like the parallel passages of modern commentaries. Since

---

[50] Tarrant 1987: 291–8 and 1989: 121–62.

such passages naturally tend to bear some resemblance to the passage that they are glossing, they often blend in easily with their surroundings and can be difficult to detect. The degree of interpolation that I imagine need not involve any more than two stages of substantial annotation, one in antiquity, one in the Middle Ages.

Examples of 'collaborative interpolation' are apparent right from the beginning of Book 2. The opening lines give a breathless account of how everything about Cynthia, even her disordered hair, gives rise to poetry. The couplet that follows, 2.1.15–16, is less a fitting climax than a flat summary: *seu quicquid fecit siue est quodcumque locuta,/maxima de nihilo nascitur historia*, 'whether she's done anything or whether she's said anything, a great big story is born from nothing'. Moreover, two words in the pentameter cannot have been used by Propertius with the reference apparently intended here. One is *nihilo*; Cynthia's clothes and looks and sleepy eyes are far from being 'nothing' to him—they are the source of his poetic talent (2.1.4 *ingenium nobis ipsa puella facit*). This is the perspective of an outsider: Propertius' poetry is simply a big fuss about nothing, a mountain made out of an erotic molehill. The other impossible word is *historia*, which in classical Latin had no meaning that Propertius could have used to define his poetry.[51] W. R. Smyth's *Thesaurus Criticus* reports that, according to E. C. H. Heydenreich, the couplet was first deleted by O. F. Gruppe.

Four such couplets, probably all of medieval origin, can be found in 2.3.25–32. Here the chief cause of suspicion is the conspicuous incoherence of the passage. All is reasonably clear as far as 21–2, where Cynthia is said to esteem her own compositions over those of Corinna (and probably those of Erinna as well, if Propertius wrote *carminaque Erinnae non putat aequa suis*).[52] All is still well in 23–4 (which are unquestionably by Propertius since a grammarian named Macrobius cites the pentameter under his name). Here the poet wrote the lines that inspired the interpolators, asserting that Cupid sneezed a favourable omen when Cynthia's life began (*nam* [Naples, BN IV.F.19, Ayrmann: *num* X FP, *non* N] *tibi nascenti primis, mea uita, diebus/candidus argutum sternuit omen Amor*). The following three couplets then offer three completely different, incompatible,

---

[51] The word has a different sense in 1.15.24, *tu quoque fieres nobilis historia* where it means 'legend' or 'myth'.
[52] For this reading, see Butrica 1984: 77–8.

and mutually exclusive elaborations of the themes embodied in this couplet, namely Cynthia, beauty, divinity, and birth. For the author of 25–6, Cynthia's desirability is a gift from the gods and not the legacy of her mother (*haec tibi contulerint caelestia munera diui,/haec tibi ne matrem forte dedisse putes*, 'the gods conferred these heavenly gifts upon you; don't think that maybe your mother gave them to you'). Not only is the pentameter hopelessly banal; I can imagine no reason why Propertius should want to offend this woman (who is mentioned in the authentic works at 2.6.11 and 2.15.20) and perhaps her daughter as well by pointing out so emphatically that Cynthia's looks were not inherited. The author of 27–8, on the other hand, did not suggest that Cynthia's beauty was a gift of the gods but that it was not the result of normal human gestation, thus implying that her mother had slept with a god (*non, non humani partus sunt talia dona:/ista decem menses non peperere bona*, 'no, such gifts do not belong to human parentage: ten months did not give birth to that treasure'). Here a medieval origin is suggested by two features, the apparent attempt to rhyme *dona* and *bona* (possible only when classical quantities had been forgotten) and the repeated *non, non*, which reflects the use of the word's descendants in the Romance languages rather than the style of Augustan poetry (commentators offer as parallels only the colloquial Terence, *Phormio* 303 and Catullus 14.16; in both cases the reduplicated *non* modifies *sic*). The author of 29–30 (and probably of 31–2 as well, since the two couplets seem to cohere with each other though not with the context on either side) has yet a third conception, Cynthia as born to be the first Roman 'girl' to sleep with Jupiter (*gloria Romanis una es tu nata puellis:/Romana accumbes [accumbens* O] *prima puella Ioui,/nec semper nobiscum humana cubilia uises:/post Helenam haec terris forma secunda redit*, 'you have been born a unique glory to Roman girls: you will be the first Roman girl that sleeps with Jupiter, and you will not always visit human bedrooms with us: this beauty returns to earth second after Helen' [?]). Here the author has not thought through precisely how Cynthia bedding Jupiter will bring 'glory' to the other Roman girls who had not previously and still have not been thought worthy of divine fornication, or how 'this beauty' of Cynthia's can be said to 'return;' the relevance of Helen, who did not sleep with Jupiter or indeed with any god, leaves me utterly baffled, but she was no doubt suggested to the interpolator by the fact that she is the subject of 35–40.

A similar interpolation in Book 3 is 3.13.23–4, *hoc genus infidum nuptarum, hic nulla puella/nec fida Euadne nec pia Penelope*, 'this race of brides is faithless, here no girl is neither a faithful Evadne nor a devoted Penelope.' Not only is the writing distinctly flat (and problematic because of the *nec... nec* that must be taken as *aut... aut*), while it has clearly been suggested by the disappointment with Roman women expressed elsewhere in the elegy, the point that the couplet makes (that there are simply no devoted and faithful brides in Rome) is not really the same as the one that Propertius is making (that luxury has corrupted *all* women and makes them demand money for sexual favours). Moreover, the couplet stands as an irrelevant interruption between the two obviously parallel sections 15–22 and 25ff., both introduced by *felix*.

But some other passages which appear to have been interpolated into the text of Propertius seem to be indisputably ancient and must therefore have been added to an ancient copy. One of these is the much-discussed 'Virgilian' section at 2.34.65–84. But this passage must first be separated into its two component parts, of which one is the celebrated couplet 65–6, *cedite Romani scriptores, cedite Grai:/ nescioquid maius nascitur Iliade*, 'out of the way, writers of Rome and of Greece; something bigger than the *Iliad* is arising.' The lines are unquestionably by Propertius, but they do not seem to have been written to stand here. Donatus, who quotes them in his life of Virgil (and thus provides the source from which they were interpolated into the text, whether in antiquity or in the Middle Ages), implies that they were Propertius' reaction to the tremendous buzz that accompanied Virgil's reported inception of the *Aeneid: 'Aeneidos uixdum coeptae tanta exstitit fama ut Sextus Propertius non dubitauerit sic praedicare, Cedite*, etc.' 'when the *Aeneid* was scarcely begun, such talk of it arose that Sextus Propertius did not hesitate to proclaim, "Out of the way," etc.' Donatus' *praedicare* (rather than, say, *scribere*) is entirely consistent with the couplet emerging as a spontaneous utterance, no doubt in the context of some banquet or recitation. Since Virgil had only just begun the epic, Propertius could not have been appreciating the greatness or criticising the length of a poem that did not yet exist. Rather, as Donatus says, the words are a reaction to the *fama* that spread as soon as the news was out that Virgil was beginning to write it. Presumably that *fama* predicted the world's greatest masterpiece ever or something close to it, and it is to this advance publicity that Propertius responds: the predictions of its greatness are so exaggerated that, if they are true, it will surpass every work of every writer. The lines, then, are a humorous, perhaps even ironic or sarcastic, reaction to the noise—emanating surely from Maecenas' circle in the first instance and perhaps also from the general direction of the Palatine—that greeted the announcement of Virgil's first work on the *Aeneid*; they have nothing to do with the praise of the *Eclogues* and *Georgics* that follows or with the contrast of Propertius and Virgil that precedes.

But 2.34.67–84, the second component, is another matter entirely. On its own, the passage is relatively unproblematic apart from the corrupt and therefore incomprehensible final couplet:

> *tu canis umbrosi subter pineta Galaesi*
> *    Thyrsin et attritis Daphnin harundinibus*
> *utque decem possint corrumpere mala puellam*
> *    missus et impressis haedus ab uberibus.*                70
> *felix qui uiles pomis mercaris amores*
> *    (huic licet ingratae Tityrus ipse [ipsa O] canat),*
> *felix intactum Corydon qui temptat Alexin*
> *    agricolae domini carpere delicias:*
> *quamuis ille sua lassus requiescat auena,*                  75
> *    laudatur facilis inter Hamadryadas.*
> *tu canis Ascraei ueteris praecepta poetae,*
> *    quo seges in campo, quo uiret uua iugo.*
> *tale facis carmen docta testudine quale*
> *    Cynthius impositis temperat articulis.*                 80
> *non tamen haec ulli uenient ingrata legenti,*
> *    siue in amore rudis siue peritus erit.*
> *nec minor his animis aut sim minor ore canorus*
> *    anseris indocto carmine cessit olor.*

One might paraphrase, 'You sing of rustic lovers, you sing of Hesiod's precepts, you write poetry comparable to Apollo's own song; yet it will not be unpleasing to any reader, however experienced or inexperienced in love.' Virgil (who seems, in contradiction to 65–6, not yet to have begun the *Aeneid* since only the *Eclogues* and *Georgics* are cited) is being complimented in language derived from his own poetry. Though his songs are *Eclogues* and *Georgics* rather than love poetry, they will nevertheless (*tamen* 81) be read with pleasure by lovers, presumably because of their high quality and the erotic element contained in the *Eclogues* at least; the compliment in 79–80, that he sings as skilfully as Apollo, alludes through *Cynthius* to *Eclogue* 6, while the presumed compliment in 83–4 also seems to allude to a Virgilian context, this time *Eclogues* 9.35–6.

In addition, the Propertian context seems to run smoothly enough without these lines (I begin the citation at 55 in order to suggest at least some of the context for the contrast between Propertius and the other poets mentioned):

*aspice me, cui parua domi fortuna relicta est* (55)
   *nullus et antiquo Marte triumphus aui,*
*ut regnem mixtas inter conuiua puellas*
   *hoc ego quo tibi nunc eleuor ingenio.*
*me iuuet hesternis positum languere corollis,*
   *quem tetigit iactu certus ad ossa deus:* (60)
*Actia Vergilio custodis litora Phoebi*
   *Caesaris et fortes dicere posse rates,*
*qui nunc Aeneae Troiani suscitat arma*
   *iactaque Lauinis moenia litoribus.* (64)
*haec quoque perfecto ludebat Iasone Varro* (85)
   *(Varro Leucadiae maxima flamma suae),*
*haec quoque lasciui cantarunt scripta Catulli*
   *Lesbia quis ipsa notior est Helena,*
*haec etiam docti confessa est pagina Calui*
   *cum caneret miserae funera Quintiliae,* (90)
*et modo formosa quam multa Lycoride Gallus*
   *mortuus inferna uulnera lauit aqua!*
*Cynthia quin etiam uersu laudata Properti*
   *hos inter si me ponere Fama uolet.*

Here one could paraphrase, 'I'm not from a rich old consular family, but I reign supreme in banquets amid a bevy of girls thanks to this poetic talent for which you disparage me. Let me enjoy this state, since Cupid has shot me full of arrows; Actium I leave to Virgil, who is now starting his *Aeneid*. Varro also wrote this sort of thing, as did Catullus and Calvus and Gallus.' Propertius is addressing someone who seems to be disparaging him on account of the nature of his talent, the *ingenium* that causes him to write love poetry, symbolized by *puellae mixtae* and *hesternae corollae*. With 59 he begins a six-line passage contrasting his own ambitions and those of Virgil. The unity of this section is apparent in the parallelism that has been devised to emphasize the contrast. Propertius wants to be allowed the pleasure (*me iuuet*) of 'languishing' because the unerring archer Amor has shot him to the marrow (*quem tetigit*). In 61–4 he somehow associates Virgil with a narration of the battle of Actium, and does so because Virgil is now embarked upon the *Aeneid* (*qui nunc... suscitat*).[53] The descriptions of the two poets have relative clauses as their second elements. These are certainly parallel in their structure and in their function, which is to explain: first why Propertius should continue 'languishing', then why Virgil would be a good candidate for writing up Actium (a subject that Propertius in 2.1.25–36 said he would essay if he had a talent for epic poetry). One therefore expects a parallelism in the first elements as well; the transmitted text offers none, but 61 seems to be corrupt in any case, and it is probably here that we should seek the parallel to what Propertius says of himself, 'let it be my pleasure' (*me iuuet*). One way of saying 'let it be Virgil's pleasure' would be *Vergilio cordi sit*; *Vergilio*, though usually 'corrected' to *Vergilium* (with *iuuet* to be supplied), is the paradosis, and *cordi sit* perhaps lies behind the transmitted *custodis*: 'let it be dear to Virgil to speak of Apollo's Actian shores and Caesar's brave fleet,' since he has now begun his *Aeneid*.[54] The catalogue of poets in 85ff. then provides further justification for Propertius' poetic choice; Varro wrote such poetry after his *Argonautae* was finished (thus the catalogue, appropriately, starts off with another epic poet), so did Catullus, Calvus, and Gallus.

But problems begin once the 'Virgilian' passage is inserted within the Propertian context. First of all, the possibility that the *Eclogues* and

---

[53] It should be noted that, in contrast to the circumstances that (according to Donatus) led to the creation of 65–6, Virgil has by now made sufficient progress in writing the *Aeneid* that Propertius can allude to its opening lines (compare *Troiani... arma... Lauinis moenia litoribus* in Propertius 2.34.63–4 and *arma... Troiae... Lauiniaque... litora... moenia* in *Aen.* 1.1–7).

[54] A remedy adopted by some editors has been to keep *Vergilio* while altering *me iuuet* to *mi lubet* (Housman); this creates an ungainly and awkwardly long sentence, and leaves the mystifying and irrelevant *custodis* intact.

*Georgics* might make pleasurable reading for lovers has nothing to do with Propertius' own point here about how Actium is better left to Virgil, who is becoming an epic poet. Second, the present tense *canis* is entirely incompatible with the fact that Virgil has already begun 'singing' his *Aeneid* in 63–4. Third, *tu* in 67 is confusing. An attentive reader will soon figure out that it is Virgil who is being addressed, but Propertius has just spoken of him in the third person only a few lines before (61–4), and another couplet has intervened in which he has addressed all the writers of Greece and Rome; no classical poet would leave readers in such perplexity about the reference of emphatic pronouns. A fourth difficulty involves the repeated *haec quoque* of 85 and 87 and the *haec etiam* of 89. The *quoque* and *etiam* suggest that whatever *haec* refers to in 85–90 has a close connection with something else in the context, while *haec* itself suggests that this ought to be something near at hand. But what has preceded is chiefly a distorted summary of the *Eclogues* and *Georgics*; and Propertius would surely not suggest that Varro and Catullus and Calvus had written *Eclogues* and *Georgics*. Moreover, *haec* has occurred within the 'Virgilian' passage with precisely that reference in 81, *non tamen haec ulli uenient ingrata legenti*. One can hardly imagine that a reader who has seen *haec* in this sense in 81 will see *haec quoque* and *haec etiam* in 85, 87, and 89 and will then look for a reference twenty lines earlier instead of thinking that these phrases are linked with the first *haec*. To avoid this difficulty, some commentators suggest that *haec* in 81 refers to 'personal love-elegy, and more specifically the personal love-elegy of Propertius himself' (Camps on 2.34.81), but this entails difficulties of its own: even if 81–2 could somehow refer to Propertius' poetry (it seems much more natural to refer *haec* to the *tale . . . carmen* of the previous couplet), 83–4 refer to the *Eclogues* again through the images of the swan and the goose. The 'Virgilian' passage is also suspect here because of its high concentration of pentameters with polysyllabic endings, which make it look as though Propertius at the very end of Book 2 suddenly reverted to his practice in Book 1. While the 18 lines preceding the interpolation offer three scattered examples (48 *laqueis*, 58 *ingenio* and 64 *litoribus*), the 18 lines of the 'Virgilian' passage contain a cluster of five examples (68 *harundinibus*, 70 *uberibus*, 74 *delicias*, 76 *Hamadryadas*, and 80 *articulis*); the eight examples found within these 36 lines actually surpass the frequency found in 1.1, which has seven examples within 38 lines. These polysyllabic endings show that the passage can not be a medieval interpolation; it is only in the Renaissance that one again finds an appreciation of and interest in imitating this practice. There is no reason to think that these lines are Propertian at all, least of all to think that Propertius wrote them for this context, for they reflect a metrical practice that he had already in large part abandoned.[55]

Another interpolation of ancient origin can be detected in 3.13. As noted earlier, this elegy begins with a denunciation of women's venality; it then contrasts this unhappy situation at Rome with, on the one hand, the current felicity of Indian husbands, whose wives display their fidelity by leaping into the pyre, and, on the other hand, the felicity of an imaginary rural golden age of the past (note especially 25 *quondam* and the verbs *erant* [26, 27], *operibat* [35], *circumdabat* [37], *reduxit* [40], and *praebebant* [42]). Propertius returns to his theme of venality in present-day Rome with the emphatic *at nunc* of 47, but before he does, according to the manuscripts, he includes four lines spoken in the *persona* of Pan (43–6, cited here together with 41–2, as read by the archetype, to provide some of the ostensible context):

> *dique deaeque omnes quibus est tutela per agros*
>     *praebebant uestris uerba benigna focis:*
> '*et leporem, quicumque uenis, uenaberis, hospes,*
>     *et si forte meo tramite quaeris auem:*
> *et me Pana tibi comitem de rupe uocato,*
>     *siue petes calamo praemia siue cane.*'

But apparent lack of relevance is not the only difficulty here; the wording, especially in 45–6, is so close to that of an epigram of Leonidas of Tarentum (*AP* 9.337) that the lines of 'Propertius' can only be called a translation of it:

---

[55] I do not know on what grounds C. Heimreich, as reported in Smyth's *Thesaurus Criticus* (1970), proposed the deletion of 61–80 as an interpolation, but that deletion would discard part of the genuine Propertian context (61–4) as well as break up the obvious unity of the 'Virgilian' insertion by detaching 81–4. (Smyth also reports that Heimreich proposed to transpose 83–4 to after 78; it is not clear whether this is part of the same proposal to delete 61–80 or a completely independent one.)

Εὐάγρει, λαγόθηρα, καὶ εἰ πετεεινὰ διώκων
ἰξευτὴς ἥκεις, τοῦθ᾽ ὑπὸ δισσὸν ὄρος,
κἀμὲ τὸν ὑληωρὸν ἀπὸ κρημνοῖο βόασον
Πᾶνα: συναγρεύω καὶ κυσὶ καὶ καλαμοῖς.

For the choice between hare and bird as objects of the hunt (*et leporem uenaberis... et auem*) cf. λαγόθηρα, καὶ εἰ πετεεινὰ διώκων; for *uenis* cf. ἥκεις; for *et me Pana... de rupe uocato* cf. κἀμὲ τὸν ὑληωρὸν ἀπὸ κρημνοῖο βόασον Πᾶνα (*comitem* was no doubt suggested by the prefix of συναγρεύω; and for *siue... calamo... siue cane* cf. καὶ κυσὶ καὶ καλάμοις. The only substantial difference is a simple matter of variation, *meo tramite* instead of τοῦθ᾽ ὑπὸ δισσὸν ὄρος. The only thing in Propertius that is remotely comparable is the very close adaptation of *AP* 12.101.1–4 in 1.1.1–4, but that is a freer version than the version of Leonidas in 3.13 (Cynthia replaces Myiscus, for example), there is no difficulty over the lines' relevance, and it is not an entire epigram that has been included but only a part of one. In the case of 3.13 the lines are clearly irrelevant. Propertius has evoked an imaginary rural past in which lovers presented gifts like quinces, flowers, grapes, or birds (25–34), and he develops this into a more general picture of a rustic golden age, where lovers wore skins and slept on natural beds of grass, trees provided shade, goddesses could be seen naked, the sheep looked after themselves, and apparently (there is some corruption in 41–2) all the deities of the countryside had propitious words for their worshippers (35–42). Why Pan should be quoted at this point inviting hunters of birds and rabbits to invoke him in the present is anything but apparent, since hunting has not been mentioned before and is not part of Propertius' theme, the contrast between present corruption in Rome and past felicity in the countryside. In any case the lines that follow, 47–8 *at nunc desertis cessant sacraria lucis:/aurum omnes uicta iam pietate colunt*, with their reference to worshipping at shrines, follow on much more appropriately from the hearths at which the deities of the countryside are worshipped than from the words of Pan.[56] Thus several anomalies

---

[56] Given the contrast between past and present here, emphasized particularly by *at nunc* in 47, one should perhaps emend 42 by reading *ueterum* for *uestris*; i.e. 'all the deities of the countryside offered propitious words at the altars of the folk of old; but now the groves are deserted and the shrines abandoned,' etc.

88     *James Butrica*

point to interpolation here: the unlikelihood of Propertius including a translation of a complete epigram of Leonidas within his own elegy; the irrelevance of the epigram's content to the themes of the elegy; the disruption of the flow of thought within the elegy caused by the presence of the epigram. Needless to say, a translation of Leonidas can not be a medieval interpolation; we must be dealing with an anonymous ancient version that was cited in the margin of some ancient copy of Propertius as an example of *uerba benigna* associated with one of the gods *quibus est tutela per agros*, then incorporated by a later scribe.[57]

In 3.14 we seem to have an ancient and a medieval interpolation side by side. One obvious problem in the poem is how 15–16, and especially their first two words, fit the context: *et modo Taygeti, crines aspersa pruina,/sectatur patrios per iuga longa canes*, 'and now, her hair sprinkled with frost, she follows her native hounds throughout the long crests of Taygetus.' The difficulty is usually solved by transposing the couplet after 10 (with Housman and Otto) or after 12 (with Canter and Scaliger). But wherever the lines are put, the autumnal hunt fits awkwardly with the athletic and military exercises described in 11–12, which are not specified as occurring in a particular season, and with the elegant simile of bathing Amazons that precedes it in 13–14; nor has any advocate of transposition found a mechanical explanation for the dislocation. The lines are thoroughly competent, even elegant, and therefore probably not a reader's comment; in fact *et modo*, which one expects to find co-ordinated with another *modo* at least, suggests that we are dealing with a passage from some ancient author that was cited in the margin of an ancient copy of Propertius because someone was reminded of it by the hardy Spartan women at their training.

But the Amazon simile was probably the chief inspiration for the medieval reader who concocted the inept comparison in 17–20 of the Spartan women at their exercises to Castor and Pollux doing something in the presence of Helen: *qualis et Eurotae Pollux et Castor harenis,/hic uictor pugnis, ille futurus equis,/inter quos Helene nudis capere arma papillis/fertur nec fratres erubuisse deos*, 'just as Pollux

---

[57] In his *Emendationes Propertianae* (Housman 1888 = Diggle and Goodyear 1972: I.36), Housman commented laconically, 'III xiii 43–6 I fear have no business here,' but he offered no reasons for his view and apparently accepted Propertian authorship.

and Castor as well in the sands of the Eurotas, the latter destined to be victorious with his fists, the former with horses, between whom Helen is said to take up arms with bare nipples and the brother gods not to have blushed.' The comparison contains no verb. If *qualis et* means that this is a pendant to the Amazon simile, then surely we are entitled to supply the verb used there; in that case the Dioscuri are bathing too (cf. 14 *turba lauatur*), and are doing so in the 'sands of the Eurotas' (*harenis* is a Renaissance conjecture but certainly right; N and X [*Λ*] give *habenis*, while the Petrarchan manuscripts, with scant regard for geography, have *athenis*). The second couplet is additionally suspect for two reasons, first on account of the pointless variation between the present infinitive *capere* and the perfect infinitive *erubuisse*, and second because *fertur*, though initially construed with Helen as its subject, must then be taken impersonally ('it is said that') in order to accommodate the brothers as subject of the indirect statement construction *fratres erubuisse*. It is possible that the interpolator left his work here in an unfinished state, unable to decide how to complete 19. This is suggested by the split in the two branches of the tradition between *capere arma* (NX) and *armata* (FPZ); perhaps he was unable to decide whether he preferred Helen to 'take up arms bare-breasted' or to be 'armed with her bare breasts' (the weapons of course were suggested by the Amazons, while the model for 19 as a whole was 4.3.43 *felix Hippolyte nuda tulit arma papilla*; this establishes, if evidence were necessary, that the interpolator wrote *papillis* and not *capillis*, as given by the Petrarchan manuscripts). It is also possible that the interpolator never got even this far in completing the line and that he wrote only *arma*, without *capere*; L presents the line in exactly this form, and the addition of *capere* in NX and the reading *armata* in FPZ could represent two separate attempts to make the unfinished line scan. The deletion of 17–20 has already been proposed by Knoche, but the deletion of these lines together with 15–16 has a most remarkable effect upon the elegy as a whole. It leaves an elegantly structured poem of 28 lines consisting of two equal parts of 14 lines each, the first describing the exercises, the second their alleged effect upon Spartan sexuality. Both 14-line sections comprise a section of 8 lines followed by one of 6 (1–8, 9–14; 21–8, 29–34), and both are set off by the repetition of key words or concepts at beginning and end (in the first section 2 *uirginei*, 12 *uirgineum*; in the second 21 *lex... Spartana*, 33 *iura... Laconum*).

Finally, every editor has failed in his duty to question the poem-divisions given by the manuscripts, above all in Book 2.[58] Most critical editions divide about half a dozen elegies here into two or more subsections; though the unreliability of the manuscripts' divisions has long been acknowledged,[59] those who question them are invariably rebuffed by articles arguing that the poems concerned really do constitute satisfactory unities and should not be divided against the evidence of the manuscripts. Some of these articles brandish magic wands like semiotics; others simply appeal to Propertius' alleged fondness for awkward structures or difficult transitions, arguing in effect that one concatenation of unrelated lines should be read as a unity because our demonstrably unreliable manuscripts also present other groups of unrelated lines as unities, in a classic demonstration of how the corrupt state of the text can be used to victimize it further by keeping it corrupt. In fact the tradition is so unreliable that we simply do not know how many poems Book 2 contained. Editions give 34, but one branch of the tradition recognized only 32, another only 27; one branch made poems 29–32 a single elegy, while the last 138 lines of the book—what we know as poems 33 and 34—were presented by the archetype as a single poem. In the course of the fifteenth century different manuscripts altered these divisions in different ways. Some joined two originally separate poems and so created the elegy that we now know as 2.7;[60] others, by introducing new divisions, created the poems that we now call 32[61]

---

[58] This point has been made forcefully and persuasively by Heyworth 1995: 171–5.

[59] So, for example, Hubbard 1974 (1975): 44–5, 'The sad result is that of all the poems in a book of 1362 lines there are only eight, amounting in all to 276 lines, which both have a harmonious manuscript tradition about where they begin and end and which have not been linked with others or themselves split into two or more poems by editors from the fifteenth century on.'

[60] The début of 2.7 as a unified poem seems to have occurred in Salamanca, Bibl. Universitaria 85 and Florence, Bibl. Laurenziana pl. 33, 15, but only as an accident, to judge by the fact that it was 'corrected' in both places; the earliest occurrence of deliberate unification seems to be in Berlin lat. fol. 500, Pontano's copy.

[61] Some sixteen manuscripts have incorporated this new division, while a number of others have it marked by later correcting hands; its earliest occurrence seems to be among the manuscripts of shortly before the middle of the fifteenth century (London,

Editing Propertius 91

and 34.[62] But other manuscripts introduced other alterations: some formed a new elegy by combining 23 and 24,[63] and others created new poems by introducing breaks at 3.23,[64] 20.21[65] 20.23,[66] 22.43,[67] 26.29,[68] 29.23,[69] and 34.9,[70] 27,[71] and 61.[72] None of these alterations appeared in a fifteenth-century edition. Both groups of changes are equally conjectural and equally devoid of authority; but the former are now canonical and the latter, like a host of others proposed subsequently, are rejected as mere conjectures, all because of such accidents of history as the nature of the texts chosen for the two Venetian editions of 1472, from which all the others ultimately derive,[73] and the textual decisions of important early editors like Beroaldus. The poem that we call 2.34, for example, whose unity several scholars have laboured fruitlessly to demonstrate, exists in its current dimensions only because an anonymous Italian scholar working shortly before 1450 marked a new division at the line *cur quisquam faciem dominae iam credat Amori*; ever since Beroaldus

---

British Library Harley 2574; Brescia, Bibl. Civica Queriniana A. VII.7; Leiden, Universiteitsbibliotheek Voss. lat. O.13); for these manuscripts, see Butrica 1984: 132–5.

[62] This too occurs first in the ε manuscripts (see note 61 above).

[63] These include Hamburg, Staats- und Universitätsbibliothek Scrin. 139.4; Naples, Bibl. Nazionale IV.F.19; Florence, Bibl. Riccardiana 633; and Florence, Bibl. Laurenziana pl. 33,15.

[64] Leiden, Universiteitsbibliotheek Voss. lat. O.82; Salamanca, Bibl. Universitaria 245.

[65] These also include the ε manuscripts (for which see note 61 above).

[66] Leiden Voss. lat. O.82.

[67] This division, which seems to appear first in Berlin lat. fol. 500, could be another conjecture of Pontano; it is also found in some manuscripts, including the loosely related Vienna, Österreichische Nationalbibliothek 3153, Parma, Bibl. Palatina 716, and Pesaro, Bibl. Oliveriana 1167, which are loosely related to Pontano's copy.

[68] Vienna 3153 after correction.

[69] As the original reading of the manuscript in Florence, Bibl. Laurenziana pl. 38,37; Leiden, Universiteitsbibliotheek Voss. lat. O.81; and Oxford, Bodleian Library Canon. class. lat. 31. The commentary of Gaspar Manius in Vat. lat. 1612 has a note arguing against the division.

[70] In the two closely related manuscripts Bergamo, Bibl. Civica Angelo Mai Σ.2.33 and British Library Harley 5246.

[71] In a group of related manuscripts of certain or probable Ferrarese origin, former Abbey 3242; Modena, Bibl. Estense α.T.9.17; and Berlin, Staatsbibliothek Diez B. Sant. 57; also as a late correction in Vienna 3153.

[72] Laurenziana pl. 38,37; Leiden Voss. lat. O.81.

[73] For the affiliations of the incunabula, see Butrica 1984: 159–69.

introduced this division into his influential 1487 edition and commentary (followed by the equally influential first Aldine edition of 1502), subsequent editors have reproduced it mechanically, apparently unaware that it has not the slightest claim to be authentic or definitive. It is imperative that Book 2 be reread without the influence of traditional poem-breaks in order to determine where the real sense-divisions occur;[74] the next step, in my opinion, should be to identify the extraneous material—the interpolations—by which our text of Book 2 has been bloated to its present Gargantuan proportions.[75]

An analogy can be drawn between the editing of Propertius and the restoration of Michelangelo's paintings on the ceiling of the Sistine Chapel. As the work was being done, many objected that the techniques applied were improper or dangerous; similar complaints are constantly made about textual criticism itself and about individual conjectures to the text of Propertius. When the restoration was finished, one art historian declared that the result was not Michelangelo; accustomed to the paintings in their uncleaned state, he had interpreted centuries of soot and grime as part of the artist's intention. Similarly, the current mainstream of Propertian scholarship, in making beauty marks of blemishes, has become accustomed to interpret the palaeographical equivalent of soot and grime as defining features of Propertius' style. The chapel's ceiling became soiled from the ordinary burning of candles in their hundreds over the span of centuries and the respiration of thousands of visitors; similarly, the text of Propertius has been affected by the ordinary vicissitudes of copying (though now and again it seems to have gone through the hands of someone more prone to error than most) and by the 'respiration' of interpolators visiting the text, while the lack of copies for comparison probably contributed more than any other circumstance to preventing the removal of those everyday errors. Textual criticism gives us the tools for cleaning, and some will say when the job is finished that the result is not Propertius; but ancient

---

[74] Heyworth 1995: 173–5 records some instances where these divisions have been suspected.

[75] My suspicions are roused particularly by the poems late in Book 2 involving such Greek pseudonyms as Panthus, Demophoon, and Lynceus; why should such names be used only in one part of one book?

critics and Pompeian *graffiti* confirm that the dirt is there—we only need the will to remove it. Phillimore thought that a sceptical approach to editing Propertius would lead to chaos; but healthy, vigorous, original debate is in fact the only way to achieve in the long term a reliable text and therefore a sound basis for assessing Propertius' achievement as a poet.[76]

---

[76] Briefer versions of this paper were originally delivered at the annual meeting of the Atlantic Classical Association in St John's, Newfoundland in 1991 and at the annual meeting of the Classical Association of Canada in Charlottetown, Prince Edward Island in 1992. I should like to thank Dr Heyworth and the Anonymous Referee for their stimulating and constructive comments upon the original draft.

# Part II

# Poetic Contexts

# 4

## The Language of Propertius and the Stylistic Tendencies of Augustan Poetry[1]

*Herman Tränkle*

After a long period of being relegated to the background due to scholarly occupation with Horace and especially Virgil, a reinvigoration of Propertian studies began in the 1950s, which endures still today. At that time two books arose that occupied themselves with the language and style of Propertius, Shackleton Bailey's *Propertiana*, published in 1956, and my first work *Die Sprachkunst des Properz und die Tradition der lateinischen Dichtersprache*, published in 1960. While Shackleton Bailey, always proceeding from a discussion of exegetically and text-critically disputed passages, set forth a good many valuable observations, I myself sought to advance—daring youth that I was—an overall characterization of the language of Propertius. The material that has appeared since then has been richly employed both in commentaries, especially those of Enk and Fedeli, and in monographs about the poet, for instance that of La Penna; some of their claims have been corrected. What has not come out of this, however, is an extensive discussion of questions about the meaning of certain passages. Only a few essays on Propertius, out of the many in the last few decades, have dealt with them. Nevertheless one should immediately add that the situation

---

[1] This article—both Tränkle's German and the Latin and Greek passages he quotes—was translated into English by Mark Preus.

in the area of Roman literature, with a few exceptions, looks much different. Research of the aforementioned kind has for a long time not enjoyed any special favor among classical philologists. Even during my research preparing for this paper it pained me to notice that there are only a very few essays that deal with the other Augustan poets in the same manner as my book on Propertius. I became motivated by this to refer to a few collections or, in case these were lacking, to begin painstakingly to gather the material myself. This has resulted in my being able to present to you today not so much a summary of scholarly consensus produced through extensive discussion as a deconstruction of a few positions.

At the time, it was a declared concern of my book that the widespread view (virtually sanctioned in J. B. Hofmann's *Latin Syntax*) that Propertius had carelessly used numerous colloquial Latin expressions, some of which were not so erudite, was being demonstrated inappropriately. I believed I could show that the proofs set forth in favor of this assessment had partially to do with forms of expression that were common to both the language of the poet and to colloquial language, and that in other cases there were very specific stylistic trends at play—for example, Propertius' effort to make his poems appear as excerpts of exciting conversation, or his tendency to characterize his subjects and scenes in a very direct, unembellished way. It seemed to me to speak in favor of such a view that his colloquial or unpoetic expressions are often inserted in syntactical connections that are very extraordinarily or exceptionally poetic. These reformulations have found wide acceptance, so that today all talk of the 'carelessness of Propertius' may be viewed as moot. There is, however, an exception: A. Szantyr's revision of Hofmann's *Latin Syntax*. At the time my book appeared, Szantyr's work was so far advanced that the publisher did not want to commit himself to any more changes. Already in the introductory historical overview Propertius (and, by the way, Ovid) is accused again of 'insouciance'.[2] As a prime example there appears in this work the so-called deferred pluperfect. According to Szantyr this was used in accordance with the norm of colloquial language by Propertius and Ovid, but not by

---

[2] Hofmann, Szantyr, *et al.* 1965: 43; cf. also p. 321.

Virgil and Horace. Of course he is here thinking of the compound forms of the passive such as *clausus fuerat* (it had been closed) being used in the place of *clausus erat* (it was closed) in order to designate a selected instance, not a continuous condition of the past ('the temple had been closed,' not 'the temple has been closed').

Since this example is typical of the means and manner of how the aforementioned view on Propertius came about, a few responses to them may be allowed. Szantyr's claim is true as long as one limits oneself to the indicative of the pluperfect; it should of course also be added that in Virgil there are forms of the *clausus erat* type. If, however, one includes the subjunctive, it will be seen that the man from Mantua conducted himself no differently from his younger colleague from Assisi; since as the latter used *mentita fuisses* (had deceived) in a hexameter line (1.15.35), so we read in the well-known lines of the former's Aeneid, *defensa fuissent, suscepta fuisset* and *correpta fuisset* ([Pergama] would have been defended, 2.292; [if a child] had been conceived, 4.327; [I wish] she had not been swept up, 11.584), while forms with *essem* etc. are lacking completely in this same work. If one factors in examples outside of the relevant forms of the perfect subjunctive and of the second future, Horace joins himself, alongside Virgil,[3] to the two incriminated elegiac poets. His witness has lesser value only because both of the examples he offers us are found in his Satires (1.4.95; 1.9.58), whose genre allowed for special liberties. Forms of the perfect indicative of the *clausus fuit* type are not at all present in this poet.[4] Taken together, these observations indicate that even here a phenomenon appears, that generally belongs to poetic language.[5] Indeed, in this case one cannot go farther than to say that the perfect stem's passive forms were

---

[3] Aen. 6.62: *hac Troiana tenus fuerit fortuna secuta* (Trojan fortune has pursued us thus far).

[4] Hor. Sat. 2.8.6–7: *leni fuit austro captus* ( . . . was caught in a gentle South wind); cf. Heinze 1921 (1967) ad loc.

[5] It is no different with the deferred pluperfect outside of its compound forms. Prop. 1.11.28–9: *multis ista dabunt litora discidium,/litora quae fuerant castis inimica puellis* (that coast will bring discord to many,/that coast which was harmful to chaste girls). Cf. Virg. Aen. 6.166–7: *Hectoris hic magni fuerat comes, Hectora circum/et lituo pugnas insignis obibat et hasta* (he was the companion of great Hector/with Hector he went to battle, renowned for his trumpet and spear); cf. also 5.397 and 10.613.

constructed with a certain freedom a long time before the elegists, even if the constructions of the *clausus est* kind are strongly prevalent long into the age of the emperors. It was not only those writers influenced by the colloquial language who took this liberty, but also such painstakingly careful authors as Sallust and Livy.[6] Only the strictest classical prose of the first century BCE regimented its grammar so rigorously. The grammarians of modern time have made their practice the norm, and it is hard for them to deem variations from this norm appropriate.

As favorable as was my assessment of the real and supposed elements of Propertius' use of colloquialisms, there was still a rather negative response to the fact that I had treated Propertius only within the linguistic limits of Latin poetry. Primarily Italian scholars found that my book said too little of Greek poetry and that especially the name of Callimachus was too seldom mentioned. On account of this I would like to explain that, in my judgment, the role that the example of Greek (and especially Hellenistic) poetry played in the gradual arrangement of the language of Latin poetry can hardly be underestimated. In addition to this, Propertius' familiarity with Hellenistic poets (e.g. Callimachus, Theocritus and Meleager) was already thoroughly familiar to me when I wrote the book, not the least because one of my teachers was R. Pfeiffer, 'the greatest authority on Hellenistic poetry in modern times,' as another distinguished classicist of the same epoch succinctly called him.[7] I also hope that, through further research, the manner and scale of the Roman Callimachus'[8] dependence on Hellenistic poetry will become continuously better defined; I do not, however, want my impression kept secret, that a real consensus on this question has up to this point not been attained. A difficulty to which their response is bound consists in this: that very fruitful decades of literature in Rome preceded the point in time when Propertius began to write poetry. These decades were marked by a very enthusiastic reception of the achievements of

---

[6] Cf. the evidence in Kühner and Stegmann 1955, Vol. 1: 166–7.
[7] Lloyd-Jones 1984: 63.
[8] Propertius identifies himself thusly in 4.1.64, after he shared his intention to write something like Roman *Aetia*. The phrase therefore relates to the subject-matter and content of his poetry.

Hellenistic poetry. This time period involves that generation of poets, whom we take care to call *poetae novi* (the new poets), according to Cicero's expression, and to whom the oldest representatives of Augustan poetry were personally and closely bound through their basic approach towards art. Propertius named many of these men as his immediate predecessors: Calvus, Catullus, Varro Atacinus and Cornelius Gallus. But nothing but a few sparse fragments has come down to us from any of these men except Catullus. That Propertius knew his poems extremely well and received important ideas from him is indisputable, if one is viewing the influence of Catullus on the formation of his language. How would things look if the works of these predecessors who wrote in Latin had been preserved for us either in full or to a more significant extent? To what extent then would the elements of Propertius' poems prove themselves to be either Hellenistically inspired or procured from his Latin predecessors, especially considering his language and style?

Particularly in the case of Cornelius Gallus, whom the ancient critics were accustomed to call the actual founder of Roman erotic elegy, one must always reckon with close relationships, since the only work from which there is a reliable representation of his poetic style—Virgil's tenth *Eclogue*—demonstrates conspicuous correlations with Propertius' elegy 1.8a.[9] Despite the refined objections of G. Giangrande,[10] I do not doubt that the meager fragments of this poet, which come to us from a papyrus discovered in 1978 as four complete and six incomplete lines,[11] do belong to Gallus. They have confirmed the aforementioned assumption with a clarity that leaves nothing to be desired. Some poets since Catullus did deal with bad experiences of their lovers' faithlessness, but none at all qualified their behavior as *nequitia* (wickedness) except for Propertius, who followed Gallus exactly. When Propertius uses *nequitia*, it emerges in the same connection and metrical position (3.10.24). The word *historia*, which appears neither in Catullus, nor in Virgil, nor in

---

[9] Cf. especially Prop. 1.8a.7–8. with Virg. *Ecl.* 10.46–49, where Serv. *Ecl.* 10.46 should also be considered: *hi autem omnes versus Galli sunt, de ipsius translati carminibus* (These are all Gallus' lines, rendered from his poems).
[10] Giangrande 1980: 141ff.
[11] Cf. Anderson, Parsons, and Nisbet 1979: 125ff.

Tibullus, is found in Propertius no fewer than seven times, five of which are at the end of the line, just as in the new fragment. Two of these instances deserve special attention in the present context: line 3 of the fragment reads *maxima Romanae pars eris*[12] *historiae* (you will be the greatest part of Roman history); compare this with Prop. 2.1.16 *maxima de nihilo nascitur historia* (the greatest story is born out of nothing) and 3.4.10 *ite et Romanae consulite historiae* (go and look after Roman history). *Pars erit* is even found in Propertius in the same metrical position (1.6.34). Two other correlations are of lesser value, namely that the phrase *carmina facere* also shows up in Propertius (2.8.11 and 2.34.79) and that Propertius twice puts the union of *domina* and *mea* in precisely the same position in the pentameter as Gallus does. It should be added, moreover, that the Gallus fragment corresponds conspicuously to the metrical practice of Propertius' first two books. As is generally known, these books contain a great many pentameters which, in contrast to Tibullus, end with three and four syllable words, and syntactical breaks before the sixth foot of the hexameter. Also striking in these books is the habit of syntactical breaks before the sixth foot of the hexameter, after which preferably two monosyllables follow. The editors of the fragment have rightly referenced two of Propertius' line-endings, which may be paralleled with Gallus' *quom tu*: 2.18.19 *cum sis* and 2.33.23 *cum iam*. In the hexameter *et tu*, *nec tu* and the like may be compared. When considering the small amount of reference material available to us, one must concede that the convergences are surprisingly abundant. On account of these convergences, there is a very strong basis, in my opinion, for the conjecture that the young Propertius, in his effort to find language suitable to himself, did in fact take up the poems of Cornelius Gallus and that he owed to these poems some of his vital ideas.

Leaving behind these preliminary comments we may now turn ourselves to the actual problem of our paper: the position that Propertius' style takes within the generally operative trends in Augustan poetry. At first glance this might almost be too daunting, difficult and multilayered a theme, since a good variety of characters

---

[12] *eris*: Anderson, Parsons, and Nisbet 1979; *erit*: Papyrus. Against the attempt to justify the traditional wording by Giangrande 1980: 141–2 and Lee 1980: 45–6, cf. Graf 1982: 23, note 6, who rightly amended it.

and genres of literature is hidden behind the common collective term 'Augustan poetry.' Upon closer examination, however, the use of this phrase in the case of Propertius is actually uniquely benefited by the fact that two Augustan poets, Tibullus and Ovid, wrote elegies just as he did. Thus, if we are to differentiate their styles we need not ask which differences are to be credited to the literary genre and which pertain to the personal peculiarity of the poet. Above all, a comparison with Tibullus, who wrote at precisely the same time, is very instructive here, while Ovid is a little less qualified for this purpose, since his work already presupposes the works of the two older elegists and received important inspiration from them, especially from Propertius. We would like then to move a comparison between Propertius and Tibullus to the center of discussion, so that a few facts might be addressed, which to my knowledge have not yet been observed sufficiently. It is naturally understood that Virgil and Horace should also be kept in mind.

Despite all the differences in personal approach and in literary genres, there rules among the Augustan poets a type of doctrinal unity in questions of style. This unity of doctrine, modeled after the phrasing of Horace' literary epistles, may be thusly defined: the actual release of a poet's creative power into the area of language is the artistic dispensation through which common words become renewed and at the same time altered. The famous sentence of the *Ars Poetica* (47f.):

*dixeris egregie, notum si callida verbum*
*reddiderit iunctura novum.*

You will have spoken admirably,
if a clever association renders a known word new.

is virtually the highest maxim of Augustan poets in questions of style. Of course Horace soon afterwards recognizes that occasional linguistic scavenges are necessary, and these will in his opinion also gain recognition, if one employs them with a certain measure of restraint and abides by the pattern set by the Greeks. It is thereby significant that he does not exemplify this procedure by means of a word re-coined in the Greek pattern, that is, by means of what we are accustomed to call a neologism, but rather through the verb form *invideor* (*AP* 56, instead of *mihi invidetur*), which is related to the Greek $\phi\theta o\nu o\hat{u}\mu\alpha\iota$ and thus represents a very daring syntactical Grecism. In another place—not in the *Ars*

*Poetica*, but in the epistle to Florus—Horace, with firm resolution, recommends to poets the alteration of old and inconstant words, so-called archaisms, if they are suitable for their purposes (2.2.115–8):

> *obscurata diu populo bonus eruet atque*
> *proferet in lucem speciosa uocabula rerum,*
> *quae priscis memorata Catonibus atque Cethegis*
> *nunc situs informis premit et deserta uetustas.*

A good poet will dig obscurities out for the people and he will bring to light beautiful words for things, words once spoken by ancients, by Catos and Cetheguses, but now covered by homely neglect and lonely old age.

The practice of contemporary poets, even in these broader points, corresponds to the theoretical claims recorded in Horace. The neologism (which from Livius Andronicus and Naevius, through Plautus, Accius and Pacuvius, to Laevius and the great poems of Catullus had been one of the principle linguistic characteristics of the creative power of a poet), while not totally avoided, nevertheless generally fades into the background.[13] On the other hand a place opens up for Grecisms, especially syntactical Grecisms, like never before. Archaisms also held a secure place among all these poets, even if in varying degrees. Whether one talks of the vital meaning of the *callida iunctura*, which still operates with conventional words even if it alters them through syntactical context, or of the common occurrence of mostly syntactical Grecisms, or of the striking decrease of neologisms—all these point in the same direction. They all pertain collectively to an art that works with refined tools and avoids overly gaudy and brash effects. These poets deal with a public of judicious connoisseurs, who are precisely in a position to listen.

---

[13] It would not be superfluous to point out that while the term 'neologism' is easy to define, yet in certain cases it is often very difficult to determine whether a neologism actually is present. For this it is of course not enough to consult dictionaries and indexes and then to determine in which author a word first emerges. One must consider the usual use of the word, its frequency, its development, and the layers of language to which it belongs. Since our tradition is very incomplete, lexical research can very well be based on chance. Thus, within the valuable list of Horace's neologisms, which Viparelli Santangelo (1984: 62) has compiled, there are some which most probably do not fall under this term, e.g. most adverbs and the verbs *dinoscere* and *recalcitrare*.

## The Language of Propertius and the Stylistic Tendencies 105

The tendency of Tibullus toward distinguished restraint from and avoidance of loud tones is exaggerated in a genuinely striking manner. Tibullus is just as much a *poeta doctus* (learned poet) as any one of these poets. The research of the last decades has brought out more and more his eminent familiarity with Hellenistic poetry, and this to such an extent that Cairns could hyperbolically identify him as 'a Hellenistic poet at Rome.' But one needs to peer very intently to discover it, since Tibullus himself is almost scrupulously anxious to hide it. And so it is also with the linguistic form of his elegies. It almost looks as though he was using endless care, which he quite obviously applied to these λεπταὶ ῥήσεις (refined discourses), for the sole purpose of producing the easiest and smoothest flowing verses, which at the same time would not leave the reader guessing. It is a very neat and thoroughly sophisticated language, but one which almost wholly avoids the extraordinary. Of the words first or only used by Tibullus, for the most part compounds of common verbs, none, upon closer examination, gives the impression Tibullus has brought it in as a neologism. Only in individual places does it suddenly become clear that here writes a man who by all accounts has all the poetic instruments of contemporary language in his hand, or rather, it *would* be in his hand if he only wanted it. Although he only sparingly makes use of archaisms familiar to common poetry, as for instance *aequor* (sea), *cautes* (rocks), *letum* (death) or the verb *memorare* (remember, recount), there do appear scattered in Tibullus two very conspicuous adjectives of the old language: *furvus* (dark) and *sonticus* (serious, pertaining to diseases). The second, which is an old legal term, appears only in Tibullus, if one looks past a few documents of the playwrights of the second century BCE. The use of Grecisms is generally limited to the Greek accusative, common among the extant poets since Lucretius and Catullus, and to instances associated with the genuinely Latin accusative of specification (with the exception of *saucia pectus* [wounded with respect to the heart, 1.6.49]). Nevertheless, in his works one suddenly comes upon such striking diction as *serpens novus exuit annos* (the fresh snake sheds his years, 1.4.35) and *sic venias hodierne* (thus may you come today, 1.7.53). Even the *callida iunctura* he practiced masterfully when he wanted. The reader becomes conscious of this in the very beginning of Tibullus' first poem with *classica pulsa* (rhythmic war-horns). Moreover, this example is supplied in such a way—as also in other cases—that the poet's meaning immediately becomes clear, and one might ponder how the expression came into being. Precisely where Tibullus gives up his normal caution and once dares something entirely out of the ordinary, the fluidity of the linguistic expression for which he strives remains preserved.

At this point we now turn to Propertius! The basic positions, which we summarized when we spoke of the doctrinal unity that reigned in the circle of Augustan poets, were also true for him; yet in the wide spectrum of possible individual traits within this framework, he exhibits something in his style very much opposite to Tibullus. Even Propertius himself felt that the *callida iunctura* was the virtual dispensation of his creative power in the realm of language. This is so well-known that one hardly needs to mention it. There is more to say about the peculiarity of his phrases, but that will happen later. In the area of neologisms Propertius does not hold himself to the rigorous constraint to which Tibullus subjected himself, but what he offers is very different compared to Virgil and Ovid, although differences of genre naturally play a quite considerable role. Indeed, epic, next to tragedy and comedy, was since ancient time that genre of literature in which the most space was allowed for neologisms. It is most probable that Propertius formed only a few adjectives with *-fer, -ger* and *-osus* and also only a few substantives from verbs. In the area of archaisms he offers a little more than Tibullus, but in this respect he stands not only behind Virgil (which is understandable considering genre differences), but also behind Horace.

The role that Grecisms play in Propertius merits special consideration. Naturally, in contrast to Tibullus' restraint, they are very common, just as they are in Virgil and Horace. But if one peers more closely, there is a striking difference in procedure. Whoever picks up a text of Propertius, pages through it and begins to read at a random spot, can easily come under the impression that it is thoroughly littered with elements of Greek. This has partly to do with the great number of Greek proper names that come up in Propertius, but also with the fact that these proper names are preferentially declined according to the Greek. Such morphological Grecisms are also familiar

## The Language of Propertius and the Stylistic Tendencies 107

to the reader of Virgil and Horace, but there can be no doubt that Propertius goes further than both of them and, incidentally, Ovid. It is known that both of the older Augustan poets, whenever they used Greek proper names, with the exception of the dative form *Orphei*, confined themselves to using Greek inflections in the nominative, accusative and vocative, while in the genitive, dative and ablative the Latin forms prevail. In Propertius, however, the Greek inflection is additionally expanded, after the example of Catullus,[14] to include the genitive singular, i.e. forms such as *Danaes, Penelopes* and *Pallados, Thaidos* (in 3.22.5, with *Helles Athamantidos,* he joins two together). And in the story of Hylas (1.20), which is especially rich in morphological Grecisms, he also even adds the rare dative with *Adryasin, Hamadryasin* and *Thyniasin.* The fact that in his first two books he concludes no fewer than three hexameters with the four longs of *heroine*[15] (a word which in Roman literature only he uses and which stems from Hellenistic poetry) fits well into this context. The picture is not so impressive if one skips over to the syntactic and semantic Grecisms. One could naturally cite several instances of these, but Propertius' temerity here has from time to time been overestimated; and ever since Löfstedt's opinion, that there were actually traces of the Greek genitive absolute in his works, was proved wrong,[16] one can actually only cite one place in which Propertius clearly surpasses the risks taken by his contemporaries (3.9.17–8):

*est quibus Eleae concurrit palma quadrigae,*
    *est quibus in celeres gloria nata pedes.*
There are some for whom the chariot races
    for the prize at Elis,
For others glory is born into swift feet.

This corresponds to the Greek ἔστιν οἷς (some). In my knowledge this happens nowhere else. But compared to the singular daring that Horace more than anyone else has to offer, it is a modest exception. Think only on the aforementioned *invideor*, on *hora* in the sense of 'a year's time'[17] or on the use of the genitive after *abstinere, desinere,*

---

[14] Cf. Fordyce 1961 *ad* 64.2.     [15] 1.13.31; 1.19.13; 2.2.9.
[16] Against Löfstedt 1933 (1942): 235–6, cf. Tränkle 1968: 574ff.
[17] *Carm.* 1.12.16; 3.13.9; *Epist.* 1.16.16; *Ars* 302.

*invidere*, and *regnare*.[18] Likewise in Virgil one could assemble similar and substantial material. The matter does not appear different if one factors in the frequency of syntactic Grecisms, which are used in the same way by Propertius and the other two older poets, as e.g. in the use of the dative with verbs of fighting according to the example of the Greek μάχομαί τινι et al., which, after their onset with Plautus, are found first in Lucretius, Catullus, and Varro Atacinus. Propertius offers altogether five examples, two with *certare*, two with *contendere* and one with *pugnare*. While there are later examples,[19] Virgil and Horace each offer five already in the works completed before 30, works which lay ahead of the work of Propertius. The predicate vocative in the fashion of *quo moriture ruis* (where are you rushing off to die?), which we had already mentioned in context with Tibullus, is also in Propertius represented by only one example (1.7.24), in Horace by one or two, in Virgil by six, all of which are in the *Aeneid*.[20] According to my understanding these numerical proportions should hold water. Taken together, the examples which I have presented show that Propertius stands behind Virgil and Horace in the area of syntactic and semantic Grecisms, when it comes to number and temerity, but, in the view of the causal observer, he outdoes them with respect to many striking morphological Grecisms.

With that, every characteristic of the poet that fundamentally differentiates him from Tibullus and assigns him a special place among his contemporaries has now been brought into our field of vision. I mean the provocative character of his skill. In contrast to the tendencies so dominant in Augustan poetry, Propertius is not a man of restrained gesture. Soft tones are not his thing—more often he engages the reader very directly, boldly challenges him. The provocative showing off of Greek elements placed in his elegies belongs in

---

[18] *Abstinere*: *Carm.* 3.27.69; *desinere*: *Carm.* 2.9.17; *invidere*: *Sat.* 2.6.84; *regnare*: *Carm.* 3.30.11–2.

[19] Lucr. 3.6; Cat. 62.64; Varro At. fr. 30.3 Mor.; Prop. 1.7.3 and Fedeli 1980 *ad loc.*; Virg. *Ecl.* 5.8; 8.55; *Georg.* 2.96,99,138 *et al.*; Hor. *Epod.* 2.20; 11.18; *Sat.* 1.2.73; 2.5.19; 7.57 *et al.*

[20] Virg. *Aen.* 2.283; 7.425; 10.327, 811; 11.856; 12.947; Hor. *Carm.* 1.2.37; *Sat.* 2.6.20 (?). In the case of Propertius several examples are sometimes given incorrectly, such as by Rothstein 1898 *ad* 2.7.24, and Tränkle 1968: 560, note 6.

this context, but also helps his *callidae iuncturae* to maintain their own imprint. Of course the phrases constructed by Virgil and Horace are not always entirely as easily comprehensible as those for which we lauded Tibullus, and yet it is not that they directly surrender all mystery to their readers. With Propertius, however, one sometimes gets the impression that he wants to call out to his readers, 'I tormented myself with my poems through long nights. Now torment yourselves with them and see to it that you understand them!' There follow unending discussions about the exact meaning of words in individual constructions, which, as could hardly be otherwise in the awkward condition of the Propertius tradition, often lead to doubt about whether the poet himself actually wrote that which is in our text. In some cases the last decades have brought some clarity, e.g. with the phrase *sibila torquet* (it twists its hisses, 4.8.8—of the snake of Lanuvium), which is taken up by many imperial poets; in this case G. Danesi Marioni[21] was able to show that two examples, or rather, two sides of one and the same process were forced together into a very brief expression: *lingaum torquere* or *vibrare* (to twist or flash the tongue), and *sibila mittere* (to loose the tongue); i.e. *serpens sibila mittit linguam vibrando* (a hissing serpent looses his hisses by flickering the tongue). Another is still controversial and will very well remain so: *in magicis sacra piare focis* (1.1.20)[22] and *osculaque admota sumere et arma manu* (to snatch kisses and, drawing my hand near, my weapon, 1.3.16), where the traditional wording unfortunately continues to be attacked.[23] In particular the discussion about the passage just mentioned shows that even those very familiar with Propertius sometimes have to put forth a good amount of effort to show what kind of circumstances the poet put up with so that he might evoke in the reader with a few words the richest and most versatile idea from the process he portrayed. Here it is significant that one must go to Ovid and the poets who followed him to find closely similar zeugmas, while the older contemporaries of Propertius offer

---

[21] Marioni 1979: 104–5. Cf. also Langen 1896–7 on Val. Flacc. 7.525.
[22] Cf. on the one side Shackleton Bailey 1956: 4–5, and on the other side F. Cairns 1974b: 102 and Fedeli 1980 *ad loc.*
[23] As of late by Skutsch 1973: 317, and Führer 1975: 217ff. Against them, cf. Tränkle 1968: 577 ff. and Fedeli 1980 *ad loc.*, who rightly rebutted Führer's incongruous attempt to argue with the 'euphony.'

hardly anything comparable. Through his *callidae iuncturae* Propertius is simply a forerunner of the poetic style that afterward ruled in the first century CE. From these 'clever associations' it is not a distant journey to the *iuncturae acres* (keen associations) of Persius and other poets of the imperial period.

In the same context belong the often very surprising transitions from sentence to sentence and line to line, which do not allow the reader to rest. Much of that which could be mentioned here is related more to content than to the nature of the language and could only be demonstrated through in-depth interpretation. But there are also examples which belong to the area we are treating, such as the exchange of the indicative and subjunctive in parallel sentences, as, for example in 2.16.29–30:

> *aspice quid donis Eriphyla invenit amaris,*
>     *arserit et quantis nupta Creusa malis.*
>
> See what Eriphyla found in bitter gifts, and with what great evils Creusa the bride burned.

This is present in several other places, especially in indirect questions, but also in the factual *quod* clause just as in conditional and temporal clauses.[24] This phenomenon, which has more than once evoked amazement from good linguists, is to my knowledge, at least within Augustan poetry, entirely unique; but it is supported so well through steadfast examples, that in no way can the manuscript tradition be blamed. And it is precisely here that the phenomenon carries special significance; it shows that occasionally in Propertius one actually has to deal with syntactical difficulties that one would not expect with a poet of the first century BCE. Another phenomenon is less certain and disputed. At least it seems clear by now from the frequently discussed *modo-et-etiam* of book 1's introductory poem that the prevailing opinion should be that in this case the poet's desired wording has been preserved. Of course the preparer of the 1960 thesaurus article for *modo*, being under the sway of Housman's explanations, could not decide to incorporate the available passages into his article;[25]

---

[24] Cf. 2.1.51ff.; 2.30.28ff.; 2.34.33ff.; 3.5.25ff.; 4.4.10ff.; 4.6.47ff.
[25] *TLL* VIII 1312, 26ff. s.v. *modus* (G.Pfligersdorffer). Among recent editors Housman's hypothesis of a *lacuna* (1888: 1 = 1972 I: 29) has been unanimously rejected.

still, the material presented in his selection shows that, instead of a mere *modo—modo—modo* (soon—soon—soon), the possibilities for variation were from the early first century BCE quite broad. Propertius himself gives in another passage *modo—rursus et—interdum* (1.3.41ff.); Seneca in the *Phaedra*: *modo—nunc—que* (301ff.), and in *Octavia*: *modo—modo—idem* (205ff.); in Apuleius: *modo—nunc—et item* (*Plat.* 2.7.4); even the panegyrist of Messalla: *in vicem modo—seu libeat* (93f.), and finally Donatus in his commentary on Terence: *modo—vel* (*Phorm.* 485). Naturally one can assure oneself that there are no exactly comparable passages available, but one will have to concede that it is no longer a far stretch from the aforementioned examples to the 'coincidence' in Propertius; it might be added that there are not even content-related reasons for changing the traditional wording. It is indeed a difficult collocation, even on the fringe of anacoluthon, but it is nevertheless uniquely lively, even ... Propertian.

The analyses of what at that time I called 'characteristic, drastic expressions' took up a large portion of my dissertation. These are words and phrases that, in the language of sophisticated poetry, were usually avoided, but that Propertius still used in order to characterize scenes, conditions or even people as accurately as possible. Most of these are descriptive of something displeasing or repulsive, as when he represents Cleopatra in 3.11 as *mulier, meretrix regina* and as *trita inter famulos suos* (a woman, queen of whores and well-known to her own slaves). Another example is when he opens his epicedium on Paetus with lamentation about the baleful influence of money on human beings. He is not thereby ashamed to address money by its common name *pecunia*, which none of the other elegists ever used in writing, even though money desired by a lover is quite often the topic in their poems. The context of such expressions then led to the observation that these are conspicuously heaped up at certain points, sometimes in the midst of stylistically very sophisticated passages, and so I dedicated an entire chapter to the change of levels in style in Propertius. It would be hardly useful for me to present to you at this point a review of these two chapters. But I would very much like to try at the conclusion of my comments to classify their observations within the broad spectrum of stylistic tendencies of the Augustan poets.

I have already pointed out in my dissertation that the unpoetic expressions so richly represented in Propertius are almost entirely lacking in Virgil and Tibullus. The significance also ought to be understood that Tibullus is one who, when it is necessary, has a more realistic way of speaking, which is nowhere so clear as there where he speaks about a rival in love, who came as a slave to Rome and for a long time found no buyer, but now has obtained freedom (2.3.59–60):

> .....*quem saepe coegit*
> *barbara gypsatos ferre catasta pedes.*
> Whom often a foreign platform forced to endure chalked feet.

There were certainly reasons for Virgil's behavior which had to do with his standard genre, since in epic affairs poets take care to ennoble more ordinary affairs with especially choice language. But this cannot be the only reason; for he operates no differently in his *Bucolics*, even though he took for himself as an example a poet who understood how to change levels of style masterfully and let the ordinary world of herdsmen and farmers come out with refreshing straightforwardness. The situation is made clear by the fact that Virgil has nothing else at hand to use for the crude sexual suggestions of Theocritus' fifth *Idyll* than a modest aposiopesis (*Ecl.* 3.8 f):

> *novimus et qui te transversa tuentibus hircis*
> *et quo (sed faciles Nymphae risere) sacello...*
> We know both who, while the goats looked askance at you, and in what shrine (though the tolerant nymphs laughed)...

It is different with Horace. It is no coincidence that a significant portion of unpoetic expressions present in Propertius also finds a place in his works, such as *mulier, meretrix,* and *pecunia*, which we just mentioned. And this is true not only for his *Epodes, Satires* and *Epistles*, where one would expect it, but also for his *Odes*, even though there are of course fewer there. It is well known that Goethe believed that a 'terrible reality' should be imputed to these poems,[26] and it was then B. Axelson who brusquely assigned what kind of a role those words played among the sophisticated poets, which were otherwise largely avoided by them.[27] At the same time the astute Swedish

---

[26] To Riemer in November 1806 (cf. the Artemis edition Vol. 22: 423; Grumach 1949 Vol. 1: 366).
[27] Axelson 1945: 98ff.

scholar did not sufficiently take into account the metrical necessities to which the poet was subject, and still less that these words appear often enough in very unordinary contexts, and that Horace also ennobled them by means of the *callida iunctura*. But his commentaries doubtlessly possess a kernel of truth, and one has to regret that until today no competent person has made a niche for himself by expanding and completing them with a refined approach. In any case Propertius and Horace stand close to each other in the relatively rich use of unpoetic words, i.e. otherwise dominant in prose or even used in slang. There is, however, an important difference that ought not be overlooked: in Horace this stylistic characteristic emerges mostly in his early works, in his *Epodes* and *Satires* occasionally with provocative ribaldry; later, in the *Epistles* and in the fourth book of his *Odes* it appears only in a mitigated form. Propertius undergoes an almost opposite development. His third and fourth books provide the greatest number and most obvious examples. One will recognize that this ever more strongly present propensity of giving names to things so bluntly was practiced not only with the treatment of certain themes, if one once contrasts the instruction of the bawd, who occupies the middle part of 4.5, with 1.8, a poem thematically similar to Ovid.

Also with regard to the changing of levels of style Propertius comes especially close to certain works of Horace. Of course a stylistic flexibility was not lacking in those Augustan poets known to us. When Virgil in the *Georgics* speaks about a thunderstorm or the departure of a beehive, he knows how to use epic's artistic matter in extreme concentration to make the moment still more epic than usual; the effect is thus even bigger.[28] This could hardly be otherwise in a culture which had experienced the influence of Alexandrian poetry, and in which rhetoric had actually been practiced.[29] The public of the late first century BCE would not have enjoyed a uniform linguistic form of poems. But abrupt changes of the stylistic levels of the kind we find in Propertius, especially in some poems of his fourth book,[30] are found nowhere in Virgil, nor in Ovid, and in Tibullus

---

[28] Cf. 1.316ff. and 4.67ff.  [29] *Cf.* especially Cic. *Or.* 103.
[30] It concerns 4.2, 5, 7, and 8. The attempt by Fedeli 1969: 90ff. against this, to prove such alternating styles present even in 4.9, failed; the conversation cannot at all be about the colloquial character of lines 33ff. Cf. for example, 34: *pandite . . . hospita*

only very rarely. Then again, the expert reader will remember off hand in which works this type of *variatio* is practiced most skillfully: in the *Satires* and *Epistles* of Horace. Horace knew what he was doing and in the end did not thereby believe that he had overcome his predecessor Lucilius. In *Satire* 1.10 he says (11ff.):

> *et sermone opus est modo tristi, saepe iocoso,*
> *defendente vicem modo rhetoris atque poetae,*
> *interdum urbani, parcentis viribus atque*
> *extenuantis eas consulto.*

Your diction should sometimes be sad, sometimes funny, it should maintain alternately the role of the orator and the poet, sometimes of the urbane man, who is thrifty with his strength and knows how to mitigate it.

This achievement did not remain a secret to his readers, and thus the abrupt change of levels of style remained an essential characteristic of satirical poetry also in the imperial age. Several things move me to assert that Propertius too gained some crucial ideas from this, particularly that both books of *Satires* anticipate his elegiac poetry, and because one of his poems in which this alternation of levels of style is especially noticeable, 4.2, the Vertumnus elegy, contains a reminiscence of Horace *Satire* 1.8.[31]

Thus it seems that we have finally arrived at a problem about which much has been written, even with entirely conflictive meaning: the problem of the relationship between Horace and Propertius. In the past there has been much talk about the mutual aversion between the two poets, of which they must have been aware, but which they never mention, and one could even believe that it is possible to read a malicious allusion to the elegist from a passage in Horace's letter to Florus. Fortunately one hears little of this in recent times; instead speculations about literary reliance have come into fashion, which have brought hardly anything halfway certain about it that was not already known before: the just-mentioned reminiscence in the

---

*fana*; 35: *circa... sonantia lymphis;* 36: *succepto;* 39: *Herculeae... clavae, et al.* (open your welcoming sanctuary; around places resounding with waters; (with the river) taken up; the Herculean club).

[31] Compare Prop. 4.2.59–60 with Hor. *Sat.* 1.8.1–3.

elegy on Vertumnus and the conspicuous allusions to Hor. *Ode* 3.30, which both introductory poems of Book 3 entail. But this is modest compared to Propertius' allusions to Virgil and Tibullus. On the other hand, the question as to what thanks Propertius could offer to the older poets for inspiration in the arrangement of his language has not been posed at all. I believe that one should not underestimate it.

5

# Propertius IV 9: Alexandrianism and Allusion[1]

*Paola Pinotti*

Among the aetiological elegies of Propertius' IV book, the ninth (a favorite of commentators and scholars for its artistry)[2] is usually known as 'the *aition* of the Ara Maxima' or 'the *aition* of the exclusion of women from the cult of the Ara Maxima'. Unfortunately this definition, like most definitions, is too limiting and can distract both from the nonlinear composition that leads the reader to the *aition*, and from the complexity of the aetiological material that is the framework of the elegy. Our analysis starts from this last point, and from the evidence that in 4.9 there is far more than one *aition*: a first *aition* regarding the Forum Boarium is presented explicitly in vv. 19–20, the second (the main subject of the elegy) explains the cult of the *Ara Maxima* in vv. 67–70, and it is followed by the *aition* of the name *Sancus* given to Hercules by the Sabines in vv. 73–4. Alongside these, two other minor *aitia* can be seen (although less explicitly) in vv. 3 and 5–6: the expression *pecorosa Palatia* (flock-filled Palatine, 3)

---

[1] This article and its Latin were translated into English by Ann Talleur.
[2] Cf. La Penna 1951b: 75ff.; 1977: 88; Boucher 1965: 149; Pasoli 1974: 49. See also the following studies: Holleman 1977: 79ff.; Coli 1978: 298 ff.; McKeown 1979: 71ff. (77–8); Warden 1980: 106ff.; Nagore-Perez 1981: 35ff.; Taliercio 1985: 13ff.; Levi 1989: 341ff.; and, on the relationship with archaic Greek lyric and Apollonius Rhodius, Cairns 1992: 65ff.

contains the explanation of the name Palatium,[3] and the τοποθεσία of vv. 5–6 (*qua Velabra suo stagnabant flumine, quaque/nauta per urbanas velificabat aquas,* where the Velabrum was soggy with its own river, and the sailor set sail through city waters) seems to allude to the etymology of Velabrum;[4] the presence of two parallel *aitia* is confirmed by the use of the poetic plural for both place names.[5]

What is more significant, however, than the list of aetiological material is the way in which Propertius presents such material: we do not find a series of learned explanations provided by the poet, but rather two rapid allusions at the start (vv. 3; 5–6); and then the *aition* of the Forum Boarium inserted without any pretense of solemnity amongst the words tired Hercules utters to his oxen (vv. 19–20). This passage already partially exemplifies the Callimachean technique adopted by the poet: firstly by placing the *aition* in the mouth of a god, whether that be a detached narrator (like the Muses in *Aitia* frs. 7 and 43 Pf.) or one who is directly involved (like the statue of Apollo at Delos in fr. 114 Pf., or Herakles giving an *aition* for the Isthmian games in the form of a prophesy in fr. 59 Pf., which is particularly similar to ours); and secondly through the choice of a rare explanation of the

---

[3] Varro *L. Lat.* 5.53 *eundem hunc locum a pecore dictum putant quidam; itaque Naevius Balatium appellat* (some believe this place took its name from the sheep, and so Naevius calls it 'Balatium'). Cf. Rothstein 1898 *ad loc.*

[4] Camps 1965 *ad loc.* suggests an etymology derived from the *vela* (sails) of the boats, without however dealing with all of the consequences, because in this case one could see an etymological figure in the verb *velificabat*. Differently Varro (*L. Lat.* 5.43) found the origin of Velabrum in the presence of ferries (*velabrum a vehendo,* Velabrum from 'conveying'): the Propertian expression *quaque/nauta... velificabat* could also allude to such an explanation. In Propertius however one other etymology is excluded (recorded by Plut. *Rom.* 5) that sees the origin of the name in the *vela* strung up in the area on the occasion of public shows.

[5] Pillinger 1969: 178–81 sees, probably reasonably, an allusion to Hercules' ritual epithet in *invictos* (*montes*) of v. 3, and cites as a parallel elegy 4.5 in which *spinis* (thorns, v. 1) recalls the name Acanthis. On Hercules Victor cf. Paratore 1976: 432; Binder 1971: 143. On the other hand, Rothstein 1898 *ad loc.* read v. 3 *venit et ad victor pecorosa Palatia montes* (and as victor he came to the hills, the flock-filled Palatine): even setting aside the difficult construction of the hexameter, given the representation of Hercules *fessus et ipse* (himself exhausted, v. 4) it seems hard to introduce explicitly the ritual name of the god at this point. Shackleton Bailey 1956: 260 sees another probable aetiological idea in v. 38 *Alciden terra recepta vocat* (the earth he received calls him Alcides): cf. Serv. *ad Aen.* 6.392 *Alciden volunt quidam ἀπὸ τῆς ἀλκῆς dictum* (some want to call him 'Alcides' from 'might').

name of the Forum Boarium, one different from the one handed down by the other witnesses of the *aition*.[6] Also, the *aition* of the Boarian Forum, placed as it is at the end of the fight between Hercules and Cacus, is in the very place where contemporary readers would expect to find the foundation of the *Ara Maxima*, since it was connected with the killing of Cacus in all other versions of the myth, including the best known version given by Virgil.[7] In this way, Propertius frustrates the expectations of the readers by delaying to vv. 67–70 the *aition* of the *Ara* by means of an aposiopesis that is extremely functional both because it creates tension and expectation, and also because it allows the poet to give a different and more complete motive for the *aition* than other sources—that is, with the explanation of a characteristic of the cult of the *ara*, the exclusion of women, that derives from Hercules' second adventure.[8] This observation anticipates several others regarding the second of the three main *aitia*, that of the cult of the *Ara Maxima*, which acquires greater importance thanks to its delayed position. The aetiological explanation is once again put into the mouth of Hercules himself, who, through v. 67 (*Maxima quae gregibus devota est Ara repertis*, the *Ara Maxim*a, which was vowed when the flock was found), connects the foundation with the recovery of the oxen stolen by Cacus. In this manner the Propertian narration is brought back into the track of the orthodox version. At the same time, though, the words of the demigod give a last touch to his irascible and vindictive character.[9]

An invocation to the deified Hercules (vv. 71–2) comes next in the elegy and it anticipates the Sabine name of the god (*Sance, velis libro dexter inesse meo!*, Sancus, may you deign to enter my book propitiously!) for which an explanation is given as the third *aition* in the two final verses. The structure of this explanation retraces the model given in the finale of the elegy of Tarpeia (4.4.92–4) in which an apostrophe to the protagonist precedes the aetiological explanation of the name *mons Tarpeius* (Tarpeian hill). This analogy

---

[6] Varro *L. Lat.* 5.146 and Ov. *Fast.* 1.582. Cf. Frazer 1929 *ad* Ov. *Fast.* 1.581.

[7] Regarding the *aition* of the *Ara Maxima*, cf. Virg. Aen. 8.268ff.; Liv. 1.7; Ov. *Fast.* 1.579ff.; Dion. Hal. 1.39ff. Cf. Warden 1982: 228ff.

[8] George 1974: 56 and n. 3, puts forth the hypothesis that an allusion to the exclusion of women from the rite is visible in the chorus in honor of Hercules which, according to Virgil's description, is made up only of men.

[9] Cf. Becker 1971: 451f.; Galinsky 1972: 155.

speaks in favor of keeping vv. 71–4 in the order handed down by the manuscripts.[10] This is confirmed by the presence of a 'ring composition' in which the elegy opens with an apostrophe and an aetiological section (v. 1 *o Erytheia* and vv. 3, 5–6) and closes in an analogous manner. The analogy with the final clauses of the hymns of Callimachus, which is used by some editors to enforce the transposition of vv. 71–72, is not conclusive: in fact we find ourselves facing an Alexandrian 'Mischung der Gattungen' (blending of genres) adopted by Propertius to contaminate the form of the hymn with the form of aetiological elegy,[11] as is obvious given the alternation between the 'Du-Stil,' second person address (vv. 71–2) typical of the hymn, and the 'Er-Stil,' third person address of narrative poetry.[12] While the similarity to Callimachus' hymns is not conclusive in establishing the order of the final verses, it is still useful in illustrating another aspect of Propertius' Callimacheanism.[13] One can even take it farther than the editors of the *Elegies* have done, if one takes into consideration the scheme that is found at the end of Callimachus' *Hymns*: the greeting (χαῖρε with epithets)-praise-prayer[14] is perfectly applicable to vv. 71–2 of 4.9: *Sancte pater, salve* is the greeting (hail, Father Sanctus), *iam favet aspera Iuno* is the praise (implied in the recognition of Hercules' deification, 'now harsh Juno favors you'), and *Sance, velis libro dexter inesse meo* is the prayer (Sancus, may you deign to enter my book propitiously). This invocation to Hercules Sancus, followed by the aetiological explanation of his Sabine name, is the final part of the aetiological frame in which Propertius has enclosed the two adventures of Hercules: the fight with Cacus and the

---

[10] Those who maintain the order of the manuscripts are: Lachmann 1816 (who reads *Sancte- Sancte- Sancum*); Rothstein 1898 (*Sancte- Sancte- Sanctum*); Pasoli 1974 (the edition I have followed: *Sancte- Sance- Sancum*). Those who are in favor of the switching of the last two distichs, following Schneidewin, are Butler-Barber 1964 (1933) (*Sancum- Sance- Sance*); Camps 1965 (*Sanctum- Sancte- Sance*); Fedeli 1965 (*Sancum- Sance- Sance*).

[11] On the 'Mischung (Kreuzung) der Gattungen' cf. Kroll 1924: 202ff.; Deubner 1921: 375; Rossi 1971: 83ff.

[12] On the concept of 'Du' and 'Er-Stil' cf. Deubner 1921: 363–5.

[13] On the Callimacheanism of Propertius cf. Wimmel 1960; Boucher 1965: 161–204 (chap. VI); Pasoli 1974: 25–7; La Penna 1977: 85–92.

[14] Cf. George 1974: 66ff. Among Callimachus' *Hymns* cf. especially Hymn. 3.268 (*To Artemis*) and also Hymn. 5.140–2 (*The Bath of Pallas*).

episode in the sacred woods. In fact the *aitia* of the Palatium and of the Velabrum functioned as an introduction to the scene of the theft of the oxen, and the *aition* of the Forum Boarium is the transition to the scene of the *lucus* by means of the thirst which comes upon Hercules immediately after his speech and that pushes him to seek a spring. After the conversation between Hercules and the priestess and Hercules' reaction, the new words of the hero containing the *aition* of the *ara* conclude the episode of the *Bona Dea* and introduce the scene of the foundation of the *Ara Maxim*a, where the reader knows Hercules receives divine honor. Thus it is at this point and no sooner that the poet's invocation to the deified Hercules occurs, and it is in this invocation that Propertius does not resist inserting yet another aetiology that is also a further confirmation of the hero's deification.

The technique of a frame that holds together various episodes helps us again to recognize Propertius' Alexandrian influences, although he switched the functions of the two components making the *aitia* into a frame for the narrative sections rather than the other way around, as in Callimachus (where it was the author's own conversation with the muses that was the frame in which to place a series of aetiologies).[15] Virgil too followed closely this same compositional technique, and precisely in the episode of Hercules and Cacus that we are about to examine, by framing the aetiological story of the fight with the scene of the rite celebrated around the *Ara* (which came to be thanks to that very battle).[16] Also, the entire series of *aitia* of ancient Roman names and places in the VIII book of the *Aeneid* has the voyage of Aeneas and his visit to Evander as a frame. In Propertius' case, the poet, using the elegiac structure with the compositional rhythm of *aition*-narration-*aition* seen above, gave greater space to the adventure of Hercules in the *lucus* (grove) of the *Bona Dea*, since he did not wish to concede space to an epic story such as that of the battle between Hercules and Cacus that would be extraneous to the elegiac genre. The asymmetry deriving from this choice gives Propertius' story a distinctively elegiac flavor, in opposition to the compositional harmony of epic poetry:[17] Propertius

---

[15] Cf. Pfeiffer 1949 (1965): 11, and *ad* fr. 43, 12–17; George 1974: 90.
[16] Cf. Wimmel 1973: 64f.; George 1974: 36, 65.
[17] Cf. Heinze 1919 (1960): 346f.; Otis 1966: 29f.

purposefully avoids a direct comparison with Virgil's book VIII, since contemporary theories on *imitatio*[18] would accord more value to his attempt at creating an elegiac 'remake' of a famous epic episode.

The *incipit* of the elegy immediately reveals the poet's intentions through an Alexandrian-style allusion: the use of the patronymic *Amphitryoniades*,[19] which reminds the reader of *Aen.* 8.103 and 214, and so provides the term of comparison: the archaism of the first word is consistent with that of the expression *qua tempestate* (in which era).[20] Add to this the exceptionality of the hexameter made up of only four words[21] and, in the next verse, the apostrophe *o Erythea*, which is not at all necessary to the narrative development and appears to be a rhetorical device to confer solemnity to the beginning of the tale.[22] Nonetheless the following description of the *Palatium* (vv. 3–6), rich with flocks and with the marsh ploughed by small boats, a description very beautifully crafted by Propertius in a manner similar to the bucolic scene that opened the elegy of Tarpeia (4.4.2 ff.), is different from the τοποθεσίαι of epic poetry: it is one of the best examples of what Boucher calls *poèsie du dépaysement* ('poetry of disorientation'),[23] which represents, in the eyes of the Augustan reader, the primitive and picturesque appearance of the places where the city now stands. This is the backdrop against which the characters of the tale are presented: the hero Hercules just returned from one of his labors, *fessus et ipse* (v. 4) like the oxen that he brings with him, oxen who, as is immediately obvious (vv. 7–8), cannot remain *incolumis* (safe) even in this idyllic place in which rest and peace seemed assured. Obviously, in this first presentation the poet emphasizes the ἐλεεινόν (pitiable) motif rather than the δεινόν (terrible)

---

[18] Cf. Kroll 1924: 139–84.
[19] Cf. Pasoli 1974: 49f.; on allusive technique cf. Kroll 1924: 139ff.; Pasquali 1942 (1968): 275ff.; Conte 1974: 8ff. On the stylistic function of the 'mots longs' (long words) cf. Marouzeau 1935 (1970): 96–103. See also Dimundo 2000: 264 n. 84.
[20] Cf. Tränkle 1960: 37 n. 1; Pasoli 1974: 49.
[21] For example, in Catullus' *liber* there are four hexameters composed of four words, all in *c.* 64: cf. Quinn 1970, *ad* 64.15. In general cf. Cupaiuolo 1963: 10 and n. 4.
[22] The apostrophe, although a common figure in epic, does not pertain exclusively to this literary genre, as Heinze (1919 [1960]: 354f.) showed in his comparison of the *Metamorphoses* and the *Fasti*.
[23] Boucher 1965: 149.

of epic poetry.[24] This tendency to avoid the δεινόν is even more explicit in the tale at the point in which Cacus is introduced: first, through the use of the expressions of vv. 7–8 *infido... hospite Caco* and *furto polluit ille Iovem* (Cacus was a treacherous host... he polluted Jove by his thieving), Propertius makes a rapid and allusive reference to a relationship of hospitality between the thief and Hercules, which presupposes a sort of 'bourgeois' meeting between a *fessus* (exhausted) foreigner asking for a place to stay, and the *incola* (resident, v.9); the fact that this *incola* has three heads (v. 10) and is a *raptor* (thief) who comes forth *metuendo ab antro* (from a fearsome cave), seems to be told in order to give a touch more of the picturesque than of the terrifying to the episode.[25]

The treatment given by Virgil of characters and scene in which the deed takes place is very different: King Evander (*Aen.* 8.190 ff.) begins his tale by pointing out to Aeneas the remains of the cave of Cacus near the place where the sacred rite is celebrated, and this offers a pretext for a transporting description, full of 'Stimmung' (sentiment, vv. 190–7), in which epic ἔκπληξις (terror) is particularly intensified;[26] the horror of the place matches the appearance of its inhabitant, who is transformed by the poet into a monster, a son of Vulcan vomiting fire.[27] What is more, he also steals the oxen out of innate malice and with sacrilegious intent. This sort of presentation, with its tendency toward the δεινόν, enhances the *auxilium adventumque dei* (aid and help of the god) and the figure of *Hercules maximus ultor* (Hercules the greatest avenger, v. 201) who comes to free the local inhabitants of the monster:[28] there is evidently no place for the *fessus* (exhausted) hero of Propertian elegy, and the hero in Virgil is purposely not represented in non-epic attitudes (for example, asleep

---

[24] Cf. Heinze 1919 (1960): 322–7. For the validity of the reading *incolumis*, nominative plural form in -is, given in v. 8 by all authoritative humanistic codices and by the most part of the editors, cf. Pasoli 1974: 69. On problems presented by this form of the nominative plural, cf. Nosarti 1976: 55 n. 3.

[25] Cf. Galinsky 1972: 153f.; on the novelty of the representation of Cacus with three heads, cf. Rothstein 1898 *ad loc.*; Alfonsi 1971: 1–6. Cf. Paratore 1976: 438 on the epithet of Tricaranus given to Hercules (probably due to confusion); cf. also Puccioni 1970: 235ff.

[26] Cf. Heinze 1915 (1965): 397, 466, 485 n. 1; George 1974: 49f.

[27] Cf. Heinze 1915 (1965): 485 n. 1; Paratore 1976: 497. Regarding the omission of the incredible details given by Livy, cf. Ogilvie 1965: 57.

[28] Cf. Heinze 1915 (1965): 485 n. 1; George 1974: 53.

because of food and wine as Livy[29] shows him) in order to explain how the theft could occur. The Virgilian demigod is also above counting the herd to see how many animals are missing, and he discovers the theft only when it is revealed to him by the lowing of the stolen oxen (vv. 213–18).[30] Hercules' sudden anger, amplified and described repeatedly (vv. 219–21, 228–30), leads up to a dramatically animated description of the flight of Cacus, of the repeated attempts by the hero to penetrate the cave, and finally of the opening of the cave (vv. 223–40). Virgil uses the tendency of epic toward ἔκπληξις and toward ὑψηλόν (loftiness) to reach a climax, underscored by a Homeric simile (vv. 241–6)[31] that creates a pause in the tale before the description of the long and scary battle fought by these two truly supernatural enemies (vv. 247–61). In none of the other versions of this tale is so much space given to these two protagonists, nor does Virgil's finale have parallels, which effectively represents the monstrous appearance of the dead Cacus through the horrified reactions of the spectators (vv. 262–7).[32] At this point Evander concludes his tale by directing attention once again to the foundation of the *Ara Maxima* and to the rite that was the initial impetus for his speech: the Callimachean aetiological frame encloses the episode (cf. *supra* n. 16).

Just as the description of the characters in Propertius is different, so the tale as told by Propertius has an entirely different rhythm: having set aside the description of the cave in the concise expression of v. 9 *metuendo ab antro*, which seems to wish to bring to the readers' mind Virgil's virtuoso treatment of this subject, the poet concentrates the entire strategy of Cacus into two lines (11–12);[33] in the distich that follows there is an extremely rapid development in the action, given in three brief paratactic propositions: *nec sine teste deo* (not without the god as witness) and *furem sonuere iuvenci* (the

---

[29] Liv. 1.7; cf. also Ov. *Fast.* 1.547; Dion. Hal. 1.39.
[30] Cf. Heinze 1915 (1965): 485 n. 1.
[31] Cf. the commentary of Conington-Nettleship 1883 (1963) *ad Aen.* 8.244; Highet 1972: 254 n. 97; George 1974: 54.
[32] Cf. Heinze 1915 (1965): 161, 485 n. 1; George 1974: 55.
[33] These are the verses in Propertius that show a real dependency on Virgil in terms of vocabulary: cf. Becker 1971: 451 n. 3, which compares 4.9.11–12 with *Aen.* 8.209–12 and 263; Paratore 1976: 432 n. 18.

cattle shouted 'thief') bring Hercules and his stolen oxen back to the forefront. And in v. 14 the punitive action of the hero is almost impersonal (*ira diruit fores*, anger smashed the doors), as if to confirm the fact that the elegiac poet is not interested in the image of Hercules victoriously engaged in another ἆθλος (labor). The same may be said of the description of the battle, or rather the lack thereof, since after the hint given in v. 14 regarding the reaction of the hero, we only see the result of this reaction between hexameter 15 and pentameter 16, in which Hercules' address to the oxen has already begun, the first of the speeches that occupy most of the elegy.[34] In this manner Propertius has brilliantly (and briefly: since there are not even ten verses from Cacus' first appearance to his death) solved the problem of a comparison with Virgil's epic, and he does this avoiding direct emulation and instead going down the more difficult and more typically Alexandrian road of allusion, which presumes the knowledge by the readership of every detail of the story: such a readership was also able to appreciate the difficulty of transposing an epic subject to elegy.

At the same time, the poet could not ignore the symbolic value that the story of the victory of Hercules over Cacus had acquired in Augustan propaganda (Augustus had in fact celebrated his triumph over Antony on the anniversary of that mythical victory)[35] when he chose as main *aition* the foundation of the *Ara Maxima*. Add to that the fact that the episode as it is narrated in *Aen.* 8.184–275 is a mythical prefiguration of the battle of Aeneas against Turnus and of the battles of Augustus against the enemies of Rome.[36] However, this whole apparatus of symbols would have been too heavy for elegy, and Propertius got around this problem by giving the battle of Hercules and Cacus an almost introductory function with respect to the adventure in the *lucus* of the *Bona Dea*; consequently, the figure of Hercules in the first half of the elegy, after the 'pathetic' presentation in v. 4, is not characterized as strongly heroic (as is natural), but it also is not elegiac-comical, as one might expect. The anti-epic Hercules begins to take shape as soon as the necessity of a

---

[34] Cf. Boucher 1965: 149. On the hero's monologues cf. also Álvarez Hernández 1997: 301.
[35] Cf. Grimal 1951a: 51–61; 1953: 15; Iglesias Montiel 1975: 102.
[36] Cf. Bellen 1963: 23–30; Galinsky 1966: 18–51; Binder 1971.

Virgilian comparison is less strong; in fact, the apostrophe to the oxen (vv. 16–20) is not particularly solemn, and is actually given in a rather tired tone, with an accentuation of the pathetic element.[37] At v. 21 Hercules ends his speech after having given the reader not the *aition* of the *Ara Maxima* as was expected, but rather that of the Forum Boarium, and he does this in an unknown version which increases the effect of ἀπροσδόκητον (the unexpected) already highlighted before. Immediately after this, the epic formula *dixerat, et...* is openly desecrated, because instead of another heroic act, what is described is the thirst that overtakes Hercules all of a sudden.[38] Hercules' situation becomes openly absurd at this point, and the parodic effect is created by the obvious contradiction with the initial description of a land of navigable marshes and pastures: now this land *non ullas ministrat aquas* (v. 22, offers no waters), and the victor of Cacus is not capable of finding a place to drink. In this manner the poet has found a way to introduce the second adventure of Hercules, an ἄτριπτος ἱστορία (untold history),[39] a story that is rare but not unknown, according to the Callimachean precept, since it was already existent in abbreviated form in Varro.[40] The story tells of the arrival of the thirsty Hercules in the *lucus* of the *Bona Dea*, and of his attempt to get water from the priestesses. This is an episode that has been compared to a *paraklausithyron* by Anderson in an interesting article in which several analogies are found between Hercules kept outside of the sacred enclosure and the *exclusus amator*.[41]

---

[37] George 1974: 49 n. 4 sees a comic-rustic effect in the monotonous repetition of *boves, ite* and *bis*, but frankly to me such an observation seems rather problematic. On the other hand Becker 1971: 451 correctly sees in vv. 16–18 a bucolic apostrophe in the style of Verg. *Ecl.* 1.74 *ite meae, quondam felix pecus, ite capellae* (go now, my nanny goats, go, once happy herd).
[38] Cf. Pillinger 1969: 178–81.
[39] Cf. Heinze 1919 (1960): 367.
[40] Varro *apud* Macr. *Sat.* 1.12.27.
[41] Anderson 1964: 1–12. The author also recognizes (p.4) tight correspondences, both in vocabulary and in situation, between the adventures of Hercules narrated in 4.9, as if the reaction of the hero before the closed cave of Cacus anticipated his same behavior at the sanctuary of the *Bona Dea*. On the other hand Anderson, in the light of this reading of the elegy, does not accept (p. 3) the interpretation of Grimal (1953: 15 f., 34) who saw in the correspondence between the two episodes of 4.9 an allusion to Augustan politics, since this is common to both. In fact, according to Grimal, the mention of the sanctuary of the *Bona Dea* alludes to a program of restoration of

Since I agree with the interpretation given by this American scholar,[42] I set out to find Propertius' allusions to the literary genre of the *paraklausithyron* in the structure and vocabulary of the second part of the elegy. And since Anderson showed these correspondences in a nonsystematic way, I thought it advisable to make a classification of the material taken from the most important examples of *paraklausithyra* in Greek and Roman poetry, following the method given by F. Cairns in *Generic Composition in Greek and Roman Poetry*,[43] in order to detect the topical

---

ancient cults that Augustus undertook, and that in this case was realized by Livia who (according to the testimony of Ov. *Fast.* 5.157 f.) restored the temple at that time. It seems to me that the comical-elegiac representation of Hercules as *exclusus amator* is not entirely irreconcilable with the Augustan symbology seen by Grimal: already in other parts of book 4, Propertius has placed together aetiological motifs of great importance to the history of Rome with an anti-conformist or even funny representation of the protagonists of the *aition*. The same is evident in the episode of Tarpeia, who betrays Rome but makes the fusion of Romans and Sabines possible (cf. Pasoli 1974: 42–6, and my study, 1974: 70, 73 f.). It can be found also in the casual description of the 'transformations' of Vertumnus, who is nonetheless a deity and alludes to the person of the powerful Maecenas (cf. Lucot 1953: 65–80).

[42] The arguments against Anderson given by Lefèvre 1966: 92f. seem weak; cf. 93: 'Überhaupt fehlt eine offene Anspielung, die vorgetragene Hypothese beweist' (in any case an obvious reference is lacking, which proves the presented hypothesis).

[43] Cairns 1972. Examples of the classification of primary and secondary elements (topoi) are given, for example, for the genres of the *prosphonetikon* (21–3), of the *syntaktikon* (38f.), for the *renuntatio amoris* (80f.), and for the *epibaterion* (212f.). Our scheme is based, without any pretense of being definitive or exhaustive, on several suggestions made by Cairns (6, 85–9, 146, 201ff., 209ff., using nonetheless the denomination of *paraklausithyron* in the place of *komos* used by Cairns 6) as well as on the general bibliography of the *paraklausithyron* (P. Maas in *RE*); Pasquali 1920 (1964): 419–40; Canter 1920: 355–68; La Penna 1951b: 149–52; Copley 1956; and the aforementioned article by Anderson. See also Yardley 1978: 19ff. The examples of poetry from which the topoi are taken are not only *paraklausithyra* that are immediately recognizable as such, but sometimes are components of other literary genres that contain allusions to our genre: Alc. *C.* 65 D.; Arist. *Ecl* 960–75; Theocr. *Id.* 3.6.6–41. 7.96–127, 11.19–79; *Corpus Theocr.* 23.17–63; *A. P.* 5.23; 92; 145; 164; 167; 189; 191; *A. P.* 12,72; 118; 252; *Fragm. Grenf.* (Powell, *Coll. Alex.* 177ff.); Plaut. *Curc.* 147–55; Lucr. 4.1177–82; Hor. *Epod.* 11.20–2; *Carm.* 1.25; 3.7.3,10; Tibull. 1.2 and *passim*; Prop. 1.16; 3.25 and *passim*; Ov. *Am.* 1.6 and *passim*; Pers. 5.164–6; Mart. 10.13.7–8. For the relative bibliography cf. particularly: for Arist. *Eccl.* Bowra 1958: 376–91; for Theocr., the commentary of Gow 1950 (1965) and Cairns 1972 (General index 324–7); for *Fragm. Grenf.*, Wilamowitz 1935–72 vol II: 95ff., and Canter 1920: 359f. and n. 18; for Hor. *Carm.*, Pasquali 1920 (1964): 419–40, and Cairns 1972 (Index 300–3); for Tibull. 1.2, the commentary of Smith 1913 (1971), and Copley 1956: 92–107; for Prop. 1.16, LaPenna 1951b: 144ff., and 1977: 40f.; for Ov. *Am.* 1.6, Copley 1956: 125–34, and

motifs that Propertius has resumed, varied, overturned, or omitted in 4.9 operating in the spirit of the Alexandrian literary *lusus* that exists thanks to the expectations of an audience that can foresee the development of the topoi and enjoy the *variationes in imitando*.

The *paraklausithyron*, in order to be recognized as such by ancient readers, usually had some 'primary or logically necessary elements' (A) and some 'secondary elements' (B); the primary ones are:

A1: The *exclusus amator*.
A2: The beloved.
A3: The attempts of the former to reach the latter (usually expressed through a plaintive monologue).
A4: The appropriate environment (i.e., a city street, with the closed door of the loved one, and the *komos*, or procession of youths that comes to the door after a banquet).

Each of these 'primary elements' is present in Propertius, but some change is made to each: in fact, first of all the *exclusus amator* is played by Hercules, who is deified at the end of the elegy, and is a mythological character rather than a common lover; also, he prays to enter to satisfy his thirst, not his love.[44] The effect of this 'speaker variation'[45] is to give a comic and humorous image of the protagonist of the elegy[46] who is represented at a moment when his heroic dignity as killer of monsters is not on display and *iacit ante fores verba minora deo* (at the doorstep he lets fly words lesser than the god, v. 32); the topical situation of the κωμαστής, the reveler who comes drunk to the door of his beloved and acts under the effects of wine, is

---

Cairns 1972: 225f. See also Dimundo 2000, 'The lover's lament and the inflexible *custos*', ch. V, 95ff.

[44] Anderson 1964: 12 notes the ambiguity of the expressions *torquet sitis* (thirst tortures him, v. 21) and *aestus* (feverishness, v. 63) that also belong to erotic vocabulary.

[45] Cf. Cairns 1972: 177ff.

[46] Cf. Lefèvre 1966: 92–4; Anderson 1964: 1–3 remembers the interpretations that Heinze 1919 (1960): 368, and Rothstein 1898 *ad* 4.9.63 gave, who only took into account the pathetic element of elegy. This element has also been highlighted by Pasoli 1974: 49f., who however recognizes signs of the topical situation of the *paraklausithyron*. This mixture of pathetic passages and humorous ones in the representation of Hercules' behavior and story is an element of the 'Mischung' (mixing) typical of Propertian Alexandrianism in this elegy as elsewhere.

turned on its head:[47] instead poor Hercules not only has not touched a single drop of wine, but has not touched even a drop of water, and this fact will nonetheless not keep him from a violent reaction in the end. There is also a *variatio* in the way in which Propertius presents the second element (A2): the place of the beloved is taken by a group of girls who never appear on the scene, not out of cruelty toward the lover or because they are guarded, but because they are celebrating the rite of the *Bona Dea*, from which men are excluded (vv. 23–6); beyond this 'addressee-variation'[48] with respect to the standards of the *paraklausithyron*, there is also a swerve from the norm in the description of religious rites, because here the women who participate are defined as *puellae*, just as in erotic elegy,[49] and they laugh and joke (v. 23 *audit ridere puellas*, he hears girls laughing; v. 33 *vos... quae luditis*, you who are playing). Propertius' game of allusions may be read in both ways: the sacred rite has been adapted to the situation of the *paraklausithyron*, and the *paraklausithyron* has been inserted into the context of a sacred rite.

The third of the primary elements (A3), the lament of the *exclusus amator*, will be analyzed in depth soon, according to each of the topoi that it is made up of: at the moment it is adequate to notice that the poet inserts it into a narrative-dramatic development that also contains the answer of the old priestess and the violent reaction of Hercules, and thus goes beyond the borders of the *paraklausithyron*, in which a 'reaction'[50] of the *exclusus amator* is sometimes given at the end of his song, but is purely verbal and never includes other speaking characters.

The scenery that is background to Propertius' characters constitutes yet another *variatio* with respect to the topical scheme of the genre, with a move from the city to the country, similar to that in Theocritus' *Idyll* 3,[51] which creates a comically unlikely situation; in fact the place that corresponds to the 'home of the beloved' is a

---

[47] Cf. A. P. 5, 167 (Ascl.), 2; A. P. 12, 118 (Call.), 3f.: Tibull. 1.2.1–4; Prop. 1.16.5; Ov. Am. 1.6.59f.; Pers. 5.166.

[48] Cf. Cairns 1972: 218ff.

[49] Cf. Anderson 1964: 7. For *ludere* in amorous vocabulary, cf. for example, Catull. 61.204 and Ov. Ars. 1.91; 3.62; cf. Pichon 1902 (1966) s.v.

[50] Cf. Cairns 1972: 138ff. For the reaction at the end of a *paraklausithyron* cf. Theocr. Id. 7.122f.; Hor. Carm. 3.10. 19f.; Ov. Am. 1.6.53f.

[51] Cf. the comment of Gow 1965 (1950) vol. II: 64; Rossi 1971: 85.

dilapidated shack within the enclosure of the sacred wood (vv. 24–30), and the description is such that it leads the reader to believe that the door that everyone speaks of (v. 32 *ante fores*, in front of the doors; 54 *limina*, threshold; 61 f. *postes, ianua clausa*, doors, closed doors) is purely a literary convention made necessary by the *paraklausithyron*: what sort of door can a *lucus* have if the poet himself seems to enjoy playing with the misunderstanding and speaks of *postes opacos* (v. 61, shaded doors), which reminds the reader of the opening scene (v. 24 *ab umbroso orbe*, in a shady circle; v. 30 *multa umbra*, much shade)? The description of the *lucus* (grove, vv. 24–30), beyond the 'town-to-country transference,'[52] allows Propertius to insert yet another virtuoso piece similar to that of the τοποθεσία seen in the beginning: the pretty picture of the rustic sanctuary near a spring, in the shade of the poplars,[53] where the only sounds are the murmur of water (cf. v. 35) and birdsong, is also an homage to the style of the time and to the taste of his readership, since the stylized scenes with a little temple and a rustic spring in the country are a tried and true cliché in Greek literature from the fourth century on[54] and had been picked up by Latin literature;[55] one finds

---

[52] Cf. Cairns 1972: 144f. and 194.
[53] According to the interpretation given by Iglesias Montiel 1975: 101 and n. 16, Hercules would be confident of being welcomed thanks to the poplars that shade the temple; effectively, these trees are sacred to the god, as Serv. says *ad Aen.* 8.276 *Herculea populus: Herculi consacrata. Qui cum inferos discendens fatigaretur labore, dicitur de hac arbore corona facta caput velasse: unde foliorum pars temporibus cohaerens et capiti albuit sudore, pars vero exterior propter inferorum colorem nigra permansit.* (The Herculean poplar—i.e. dedicated to Hercules. Who, when he was exhausted from the labor of descending to the dead, is said to have covered his head with a crown made from this tree: whence part of the foliage stuck to his temples and turned white with the sweat of his brow, while the part on the outside remained black because of the color of the dead). Thus probably the allusion to poplar in v. 29 is not casual.
[54] Cf. Pasquali 1920 (1964): 533ff.
[55] It came to the point that Horace (*A.P.* 14–18) made fun of the habit of inopportunely sticking in descriptions of the *lucus et ara Dianae/et properantis aquae per amoenos ambitus agros* (the grove and altar of Diana and the path of the scurrying water through pleasant meadows). Regarding the derision of the ekphrastic descriptions that were pragmatic elements in the study of poetic composition (and descriptions of the sort also were part of the rhetorical curriculum: cf. Frassinetti 1949: 252–60), cf. Pers. 1.70–5 with the commentary of Scivoletto 1961 *ad loc*. An example of the hypertrophic expansion of these ekphrases occurs in certain *Silvae* of Statius and in some *Epistulae* of the Younger Pliny.

the same subject in Roman and Pompeian paintings of the second style, and Pliny *Nat.* 35.116 speaks of a painter (Studius or Ludius) of the Augustan age *qui primus instituit amoenissimam parietum picturam, villas et porticus ac topiaria opera, lucos, nemora, colles, piscinas, euripos, amnes, litora* (who first introduced the most appealing painting on walls: (images of) villas and porticoes and trimmed hedges, groves, glades, hills, pools, channels, rivers, shorelines).[56] So it is that a thirsty Hercules breaks into this idyllic and stylized scene: here we find the recherché use of the word *pulvis* (dust, v. 31) in feminine form according to the Ennian model,[57] and the allusive function of the two expressions *ante fores* (before the doors), which turns the following speech of Hercules[58] into a *paraklausithyron*,[59] and *verba minora deo* (words lesser than the god) which prepares the reader to hear a god speak using the *sermo communis* (common parlance).[60]

Hercules' speech from v. 33 to v. 50 constitutes the real *paraklausithyron*. For ease of analysis let us go back to a scheme taken from literary examples of the genre, and expressly the part of it that regards the 'secondary elements,' the topoi commonly (but not necessarily) included in the examples examined before.

They are:

B1: Plea to open the door.

B2: Accusations of cruelty (hardness, sleepiness, deafness, with eventual comparisons) against the beloved woman, the door, or the doorkeeper.

B3: The *exclusus amator's* laments: a) tears; b) pain, shame, desperation; c) suicide plans.

B4: Bad weather: a) nighttime; b) rain; c) wind; d) cold (often such factors appear together in pairs).

B5: Long vigil on the part of the *exclusus amator* (or else sleep on the threshold).

B6: Attempts at the *captatio benevolentiae* ('securing goodwill,' made toward the woman/the door/the doorkeeper): a) serenades, verses;

---

[56] Cf. Strong 1929: 220–2.   [57] Cf. Tränkle 1960: 31.
[58] Cf. Anderson 1964: 6.   [59] Cf. Anderson 1964: 6.
[60] Cf. Fedeli 1969: 91f., who shows how the 'Callimachean' sections of the elegy maintain an elevated tone, while the style lowers in Hercules' *paraklausithyron*.

b) valuable gifts; c) adoration (directed at the door): offerings of wine, unguents, kisses, and garlands.
B7: Momentary hopefulness (that the door might open, or that the beloved might be moved).
B8: a) Bragging about the lover's own virtues, riches, etc.; b) fear of appearing ugly.
B9: Appeal to a deity (Venus, or other gods).[61]
B10: Mention of a rival (often with insults).
B11: Threats: a) of making an assault on the door; b) of going away; c) that in the future the roles will be reversed, so that the beloved will eventually be *exclusa* herself; d) of the rapid decline of beauty/ youth; e) of divine anger that strikes those who do not love.
B12: Physical assault on the door (or brawl with other lovers in the street).
B13: Arrival of the dawn (announced by the crowing of the rooster or of other birds) which puts an end to the *paraklausithyron*.

Naturally the topoi above never occur in so schematic a form, nor in a fixed order, and the ability of the one who uses them lies precisely in varying and weaving them together according to the circumstance, as well as in choosing the elements that are most suitable to the creation of a particular poetic situation: it is exactly what Propertius does in this case.

The prayer that the door be opened (B1) is the 'Leitmotiv' of the entire speech given by Hercules, and is anticipated by *verba minora deo* (words lesser than the god, v. 32), since it is a lowering of the hero's dignity, in a gracefully comical light: especially vv. 33ff. *Vos precor... pandite hospita fana* (I beg you, open your sanctuary as a shelter) show from the beginning that Hercules is stooping to entreat the *puellae*.[62] The accusations of cruelty and hardness (B2) instead are present in the allusive form of the comparison to a notoriously cruel character, in this case Juno, whose hostility Hercules has already experienced; it takes the topical form of the negative comparison: not

---

[61] Cairns 1972: 203 sees the invocation of Pan and of the Amores in Theocr. *Id.* 7.103 and 117 as an 'addressee-variation,' but I would not say that the appeal to the gods always belongs to this category, and so I prefer to insert it amongst the other topoi. In general for the criteria for the classification of these by Cairns cf. pp. 6, 21, 202.

[62] For examples of B1 cf. Alc. 65 D.; Arist. *Eccl.* 961–3; Theocr. *Id.* 11.42 and 63; *Fragm. Grenf.* 27ff.; Plaut. *Curc.* 147–51; Tibull. 1.2.9f. and 15f.; Prop. 1.16.19f.; Ov. *Am.* 1.6.1–4 and 24/32/40/48 (refrain) and 61.

even the *amara noverca* (ruthless stepmother, vv. 43–4) would deny Hercules drinking-water.[63] This comparison fits well with the general 'Stimmung' of Hercules' words, in which the plaintive tone creates the already noted parodic contrast with the figure of the hero victorious over Cacus. In such a context the use of topos B3—the lamentation of the *exclusus amator*—is not out of place, naturally not in the form of suicidal plans (which would be unfitting to a hero about to be deified), nor in the form of tears pouring down like rain or rivers (which would introduce an amount of water inconsistent with the situation), but rather through Hercules' insistence on his own unhappy condition (B3b): at v. 34 *defessis viris* (exhausted men) he generalizes the situation, while with *me mea fata trahentem* and *fesso mihi* in vv. 65f. (me dragging out my fate, weary me)[64] the hero speaks of himself pathetically, picking up the *fessus et ipse* of v. 4 (himself exhausted).[65] Nonetheless, here and there the topoi of the *paraklausithyron* are picked up and switched in a less explicit form as in the case of inclement weather (B4), present in 4.9 in a way that is exactly the opposite of the cliché of night-rain-wind-cold. The scene takes place in full daylight (and the insistence on the pleasing coolness of the *lucus* makes one imagine dazzling sunshine outside the sacred enclosure), and the *exclusus* Hercules is not tormented by rain nor winter wind, but by the dryness of the climate and landscape, as well as by the heat.[66]

---

[63] For this sort of a comparison cf. especially Hor. *Carm.* 3.10, 1–4, and 17f.; Prop. 1.16.29ff. In general for accusations of cruelty (B2) cf. Theocr. *Id.* 3.24, 27, 33, 52, 54; 11.29; *Corpus Theocr.* 23.17–19; *A.P.* 5.23 (Call.), 3–5; 92 (Ruf.), 3f.; 164 (Ascl.), 2f.; *Fragm. Grenf.* 17–22; Plaut. *Curc.* 155ff.; Lucr. 4.1178f.; Hor. *Epod.* 11.20–2; *Carm.* 1.25.7f.; 3.7.31f., Tibull. 1.1.56; 1.2.5f.; 2.6.47; Prop. 1.16.9, 11f., 17f., 25f., 29f., 35, 43; 4.5.48; Ov. *Am.* 1.6.17, 27f., 41f., 54, 62, 72–4; 3.1.53; *Rem. am.* 35; Mart. 10.13.7f.

[64] For the placement of vv. 65–6 I follow the editions of Camps 1965 and Pasoli 1974, who place them between vv. 41 and 43, eliminating v. 42.

[65] Lamentations of the *exclusus amator*: B3a (tears): cf. *A.P.* 5.145 (Ascl.), 3 and 6; 191 (Mel.), 5f.; *A.P.* 12.72 (Mel.), 6; Lucr. 4.1177; Tibull. 1.2.75 s.; Prop. 1.16.48; 3.25.9; Ov. *Am.* 1.6.18; Pers. 5.165f.; Mart. 10.13.8. B3b (pain, shame, etc.): cf. Arist. *Eccl.* 969f., 972, 975; Theocr. *Id.* 3.12, 17, 52; 11.51–3, 69; *A.P.* 5.189 (Ascl.), 3f.; *A.P.* 12.72 (Mel.), 2–6; *Fragm. Grenf.* 3, 15, 23, 29; Plaut. *Curc.* 152; Hor. *Carm.* 1.25.7; 3.10.14; Tibull. 1.2.9; Prop. 1.16.13, 21, 35, 39; Ov. *Am.* 1.6.5f. B3c (suicide plan): cf. Arist. *Eccl.* 963; Theocr. *Id.* 3.9.25f, 52f.

[66] Inclement weather: B4a (nighttime): cf. *A.P.* 5.167 (Ascl.), 1; 189 (Ascl.) 1; 191 (Mel.), 1f.; *Fragm. Grenf.* 11; Hor. *Carm.* 1.25.7; Tibull. 1.2.25; Prop. 1.16.23; Ov. *Am.*

## Propertius IV 9: Alexandrianism and Allusion 133

On the other hand, the topos of the long wait of the lover on the *limen* of the beloved (B5) must have seemed far from productive to the poet: Hercules is in fact portrayed as having very little patience, and his references to his tiredness fit best with the 'lamentations' since the *exclusus amator* who spends hours at the door usually does not describe himself as 'tired' so much as 'sleepless', 'waiting', etc.[67] Similarly the motif of hope of obtaining the desired result (B7), inserted in long laments for variety by introducing a possible 'reaction' (cf. *supra*, n.49) from the beloved,[68] would be nonproductive or even unfitting to the situation of this elegy, since the eventual reaction coming from behind the door is represented in a concrete manner by the answer of the priestess in vv. 51–60.

Now we return to the motif of the *captatio benevolentiae* momentarily set aside: we observe that while the serenades, gifts, and kisses to the doors are not present because they are not fitting to a demigod, who, although he is seen with irony, does not degrade himself beyond a certain point,[69] an allusion is made to garlands hung on the door (B6c) in vv. 27–9, in which the leafy branches of the poplars and the *puniceae vittae* (dark red bands) that cover the threshold are the bucolic and ritual equivalent of the *coronae* (crowns) and *serta* (garlands) that adorn the *limina* (thresholds) in erotic poetry: Propertius' use of allusion is even more functional since the detail of the leafy branches is at the beginning of the scene as if to tell the reader

---

2.9.22; *Am.* 1.6 (refrain), 24, etc.; *Ars.* 3.70. B4b (rain): cf. *A.P.* 5.167 (Ascl.) 2; Hor. *Carm.* 3.10.19f.; Tibull. 1.2.30. B4d (cold): cf. *A.P.* 5.23 (Call.) 2; 167 (Ascl.) 2; 189 (Ascl.) 1; Hor. *Carm.* 3.10.7f.; Tibull. 1.2.29; Prop. 1.16.24; Ov. *Am.* 2.19.22; *Ars.* 3.70. For the text of Prop. 1.16.23–24 cf. Giardina 2003: 39ff.

[67] Long waiting at the door (B5): cf. Theocr. *Id.* 3.39; *A.P.* 12.72 (Mel.), 1f.; Hor. *Epod.* 11.22; Tibull. 2.4.22; Prop. 1.16.14 and 40; 2.6.2; 2.17.13–15; Ov. *Am.* 2.19.21f.; *Ars.* 3.70; Mart. 10.13.7. (Sleep on the threshold in Prop. 1.16.22f.).

[68] For B6 cf. n. 69. Momentary and immediately frustrated hope: B7: cf. Theocr. *Id.* 3.39; Tibull. 1.2.31f.; Prop. 1.16.27 and 31f.; Ov. *Am.* 1.6.49f.

[69] *Captationes benevolentiae* (B6): a (verses, serenades): cf. *A.P.* 5.191 (Mel.) 7ff. Lucr. 4.1182; Hor. *Carm.* 3.7.29ff.; Tibull. 1.5.67; Prop. 1.16.41; Ov. *Am.* 3.1.45f.; Pers. 5.166. B6b (valuable gifts): cf. Theocr. *Id.* 3.10 and 34; 11.40f.; Hor. *Carm.* 3.10.13; Tibull. 1.5.68; 2.4.21; Prop. 1.16.36, 4.5.7. B6c (offerings left before the door): cf. for wine Plaut. *Curc.* 80 (parody); for unguents Lucr. 4.1179; for kisses *Corpus Theocr.* 23.18; *A.P.* 12.118 (Call.) 6; Lucr. 4.1179; Prop. 1.16.42; for the garlands Theocr. *Id.* 3.21–3; *A.P.* 5.92 (Ruf.) 3; 145 (Ascl.) 1f.; 191 (Mel.) 5f.; Catull. 63.66; Lucr. 4.1178; Tibull. 1.2.14; Prop. 1.16.7; Ov. *Am.* 1.6.67; *Ars.* 3.72; *Rem. am.* 32.

that what follows is a *paraklausithyron*.[70] A different treatment is reserved for the topical motif (B8a) of the *exclusus amator*'s boasting of his own worth, as well as for his preoccupation about appearing ugly to the beloved (B8b): both of these elements occur in examples of the genre with the intent of making the *amator* a comical character,[71] and clearly this is how they are used by Propertius in vv. 37–41, where Hercules boasts in a self-satisfied tone of his glorious deeds,[72] and in vv. 45f. where the hero appears to be worried that his wild looks might scare the women, and so he hastens to add a further list of his own virtues (vv. 47–9), giving particular attention to the domestic tasks that might be most appreciated by the *puellae*. The characteristics of Propertius' characters render the topos of the appeal to a deity (B9) for help or for revenge useless;[73] and the same is true of the topos of insulting a rival who has been successful in breaching the door (B10):[74] Hercules can get himself out of this mess on his own, since he himself is about to become a god; and as far as the *puellae* are concerned, they exclude men from their rites indiscriminately, as is repeated more than once (vv. 25ff., 55f., 59f.), and so there is no reason for accusations of partiality.

At a certain point in the topical development of a *paraklausithyron*, even the most plaintive *exclusus amator*, having obtained nothing with his tears, moves on to threats (B11); Hercules does not use words in this case, but realizes the topical motif physically[75] in the

---

[70] This announcement of theme should be added to those given by Anderson 1964, 6: v. 23 *inclusas puellae* (closed-in girls); v.25 *loca clausa* (enclosed places); v. 32 *ante fores* (at the doorstep).

[71] See particularly the presentation of Polyphemus in Theocr. *Id.* 11.34–40 and 48; Hor. *Carm.* 3.7.23–8; cf. Cairns 1972: 210. For B8b (fear of appearing ugly, etc.) cf. Theocr. *Id.* 3.8f.; 6.34ff.; 11.30–3.

[72] Cf. Anderson 1964: 8.

[73] Appeal to a divinity (B9): cf. Arist. *Eccl.* 966; Theocr. *Id.* 7.103 and 119; *A.P.* 5.167 (Ascl.) 5f.; 191 (Mel.) 7f.

[74] Mention of a rival (B10): cf. Theocr. *Id.* 7.125; *A.P.* 5.191 (Mel.) 5; Prop. 1.16.33; Ov. *Am.* 1.6.45 (topos applied to the *ianitor*, doorkeeper).

[75] Threats: B11a (of assaulting the door): cf. Ov. *Am.* 1.6.57f.; (*A.P.* 12.252 [Strato] 1: later payback). B11b (of going away): cf. Hor. *Carm.* 3.10.19f.; a threat realized in Theocr. *Id.* 7.122f.; 11.75ff.; *A.P.* 12.252 (Strato) 4, see a. B11c (of a future reversal of roles): cf. Theocr. *Id.* 7.119f.; *Corpus Theocr.* 23.33f.; *A.P.* 5.23 (Call.) 3f.; 16 (Ascl.) 3f.; 167 (Ascl.) 3f.; Hor. *Carm.* 3.10.10; Prop. 3.25.15f. B11d (of the decline of beauty/youth): cf. Theocr. *Id.* 7.121; *Corpus Theocr.* 23.28–32; *A.P.* 5.23 (Call.) 5f.; 92 (Ruf.)

action that follows and in the foundation of the *Ara Maxima* (vv. 61–70). In this way Propertius is able to extend his allusions to the *paraklausithyron* even beyond the speech of the hero and into the development of the episode to include the *aition* of the cult; in fact the assault on the door is not just threatened by the protagonist, but is put into action after the negative response of the priestess (v. 61f.), and similarly there are no threatening future predictions of a reversal of roles unfavorable to the *puellae* (B11c), nor of divine punishment (B11e), but both misfortunes come true immediately in Hercules' *tristia iura* (sad regulations, vv. 64ff.): *haec (Ara) nullis umquam pateat veneranda puellis* (may this altar never be open to women for their worship). So the *puellae* will now be excluded from the cult of the *Ara*, and it is significant that Hercules does not give up the terminology of the *paraklausithyron* even while he solemnly gives the *aition* of his altar (cf. v. 69 *pateat* and *puellis*): the punishment of the god will always perpetuate the memory of the refusal that he received (cf. *umquam*, ever, v. 69; *aeternum*, eternal, v. 70). The disproportion between the penalty and the crime and the excessively vindictive character of Hercules add new elements to the parodic characterization of the god, to which Greek comedy made a contribution.[76]

A more complex section must be set aside for the topos of the threat that old age will drive lovers away from the woman (B11d), which is apparently extraneous to Propertius' elaboration of the *paraklausithyron*; the figure of the old woman who repels Hercules from the *lucus* (vv. 51ff.) is interpreted by Anderson as the equivalent of the hated *lena*, who usually watches over the *puellae* of erotic elegy,[77] but the definition *alma sacerdos* (caring priest)[78] and the presence of Augustan symbols, according to which the priestess is a prefiguration of Livia, guardian of the most ancient cults,[79] are an argument against the American scholar's interpretation. The old

---

5f.; Hor. *Carm.* 1.25 (realization); Prop. 3.5.11–14; Ov. *Ars.* 3.69–72. B11e (of divine anger): cf. *Corpus Theocr.* 23.54ff. (realization); Hor. *Carm.* 3.10.9.

[76] The thirst that can dry up a stream is also a comic motif: cf. Anderson 1964: 11; Galinsky 1972: 81ff. and 154f.
[77] Cf. Anderson 1964: 9.
[78] At v. 51: cf. Rothstein 1898 *ad loc.*     [79] Cf. Grimal 1953: 36.

priestess perhaps represents an 'incarnation' of the prophecy of old-age, and in a twisting of the topical situation in which usually the old woman who is no longer wooed becomes *exclusa* (shut out), here it is she who is the main recipient of Hercules' pleas and has no problem keeping the door shut. However, yet another reason leads me not to underestimate the priestess of the *Bona Dea* by lowering her to the level of a *lena*, and that is the fact that her words hold one of the key allusions to the inspiration of this elegy: Hymn V of Callimachus 'The Bath of Pallas'[80] in which a similar thing happens to Tiresias when he comes (involuntarily, differently from Hercules) to a forbidden spring in which the goddess and her nymphs bathe. Propertius must have wished to cite his Alexandrian master directly and explicitly in this elegy in which he shows that he has assimilated many of the lessons of Hellenistic poetry; the adaptation of these topoi, from an erotic and urban genre such as the *paraklausithyron* to a bucolic and mythological situation, shows just how much he assimilated the lesson provided to him by Theocritus' *ΚΩΜΟΣ* and by the *Idyll* of Polyphemus and Galatea.

Alexandrian also is the coupling in the same elegy of two different episodes from Hercules' adventures united with a special attention to the landscape. This is a procedure similar to that used by the author of *Idyll* 25 of the *Corpus Theocriteum* when he tells of Herakles first speaking with a farmer, and then in the stables of Augeas, and finally traveling with the king's son, to whom he tells the story of the killing of the Nemean Lion.[81] The Alexandrian tradition regarding Herakles seems to have influenced Propertius' elegy through the *Aitia* of Callimachus as well[82] in which, as can be deduced from the remaining fragments, the hero was more than once at the center of aetiological tales that repeated the cliché of the meeting between a traveler

---

[80] Cf. Becker 1971: 452 and 465. V. 57 of Propertius translates Call. *Hymn.* 5.101f.: cf. Rothstein 1898 *ad loc.* It must not be by chance that Propertius was inspired by the only hymn written in elegiac distichs, on the tone of which Heinze 1919 (1960): 377 n. 120.

[81] Cf. the acute observations made by Gow 1950 (1965) II: 438–40. The words of Deubner 1921: 374 on *Idyll* 25 are fitting also to *Elegy* 4.9: '(Der Dichter) wollte Ausschnitte geben, die er aber trotzdem keineswegs ohne Verknüpfung gelassen hat' (the poet wanted to give excerpts, which he nevertheless by no means left without a narrative link). Cf. also Serrao 1971: 150.

[82] Cf. La Penna 1977: 88.

requesting hospitality and a local inhabitant;[83] in particular the fragments of the 'Sacrifice of Lindus' and of the 'Story of Thiodamas' tell two parallel stories in which Herakles, in a more comical than heroic light, is refused food by a farmer and reacts by killing and eating one of the man's oxen: the coincidence of the Callimachean cliché with the episode of Hercules in the *lucus* of the *Bona Dea* (and to a lesser extent with that of Hercules and Cacus) is clear.

In the course of this analysis we have seen the importance of Alexandrian poetry as an antecedent of Propertius' elegy both in terms of content (in the choice of an aetiological theme, in the humanization of a mythological character, and in the bucolic-elegiac 'reduction' of epic motifs), and in terms of form (in the allusions that place the topoi of the *paraklausithyron* in an unusual context, in the *variationes in imitando*). Elegy 4.9 appears definitely to be one of the most mature and successful products of Propertius' Callimachean works. It may not be by chance that only in this elegy did Propertius place a request for divine favor toward his book (v. 72 *velis libro dexter inesse meo!* May you deign to enter my book propitiously), feeling that this elegy might be the successful result of his attempt to give Rome a collection of *Aitia* worthy of its Callimachean model.[84]

---

[83] This topical situation can be related, in the end, to the meeting between Odysseus and Eumeus in *Od.* 14. George 1974: 26ff. points out the 'standard elements' of the Callimachean cliché (that he also finds in book VIII of the *Aeneid*). Cf. fr. 22–3 Pfeiffer (Sacrifice of Lindus), 24–5 Pf. (Story of Thiodamas), 55–9 Pf. (Story of Molorchus).

[84] Sullivan 1976 gathers many of the features of the Callimachean spirit and of the humor that are present in *Elegy* 4.9 (about which he speaks briefly at pp. 43 and 135f.), but he believes that their function is almost exclusively of ridicule toward Augustan ideology. Sullivan's general thesis in fact is synthesized thus at p. 138: 'I suggest that book 4, far from being a concession to Augustan pressures, is in fact Propertius' ultimate *recusatio*,' a thesis that sees a more or less openly parodic intent in all of Propertius' celebratory poetry. Sullivan, who studied the components that Ezra Pound got from Propertius in his *Homage to Sextus Propertius* (see Sullivan 1964), let himself be influenced by Pound, according to whom Propertius 'was tying a blue ribbon in the tails of Virgil and Horace' (cf. Sullivan 1964: 58 and 64). But in order to understand Propertius' aetiological-celebratory work it is better to take a more toned down attitude that takes into account the contrasting tendencies within the poet, his temperament as a man and as an artist (for Propertius the artist, the mixture of different elements and the contrast between these elements were principles to be used consciously by the poet). In this sense the essay of La Penna 1977 is useful. As a comparison one must remember, more than Sullivan does, the attitude that Ovid had toward official morals and ideology, regarding which see Scivoletto 1976, and Labate 1984.

# 6

## Propertius 1.4 and 1.5 and the 'Gallus' of the Monobiblos[1]

*Francis Cairns*

Since 1950, the arrangement by their authors of the distinct pieces making up republican and Augustan poetry books, and the associated question of linked pairs of poems within these books, have received increasing scholarly attention.[2] In the field of Roman elegy in particular, the monographs of Klaus Jäger[3] and John T. Davis[4] have forwarded the latter enquiry. Unfortunately, problems of poem division within the elegists have sometimes confused the issue;[5] but

---

[1] I am very grateful to Mr I.M. LeM. DuQuesnay, Dr Duncan F. Kennedy, Prof. Otto Skutsch and Prof. A.J. Woodman for their helpful and creative comments on the penultimate draft of this paper and for providing valuable additional material. It must however be emphasised that they are not necessarily in agreement with any views expressed in the paper and that I alone am responsible for any remaining errors or inadequacies. The present version grew out of a briefer paper given at the Colloquium of the Liverpool Latin Seminar *Carmina Gallo?* on 29 April 1983.

[2] Among numerous recent treatments the following may be noted as approaching such problems from different viewpoints: Skutsch 1963 (brief but fundamental); Courtney 1968; Wiseman 1969: 1–41; Van Sickle 1978; Hering 1979; Petersmann 1980.

[3] Jäger 1967 (1968).

[4] Davis 1977.

[5] The problem is less acute, but still noticeable, in Jäger 1967 (1968); more so in Davis 1977, some of whose 'dramatic pairings' are unfortunately disputed cases, particularly the notorious Prop. 1.8A and B. For arguments in favour of its unity based on generic considerations, cf. Cairns 1972: 148–52. These arguments, as he kindly informs me, have been accepted by Fedeli in his text of Propertius (i.e. Fedeli

an uncontroversial case, viz. Propertius 1.7 and 1.9,[6] where the presence of an interposed but unlinked poem between the pair prevents such confusion, guarantees the phenomenon for elegy; and there are other pairs, such as Tibullus 1.8 and 1.9, and 2.3 and 2.4, where both the linkage and the discreteness of the individual elegies are indubitable.[7] The phenomenon is not of course confined to elegy; and such lyric examples as Catullus 2 and 3, and 5 and 7,[8] and Horace *Odes* 1.34 and 1.35,[9] 2.2 and 2.3, 2.4 and 2.5, 2.6 and 2.7,[10] and 3.22 and 3.23,[11] are particularly helpful in their clarity.[12]

The inspiration for such linked pairs is not far to seek. The paired or grouped epigrams of Hellenistic anthologies are one obvious source.[13] Another (and this can be perceived more easily now that the old subjective/objective problem in the study of Roman elegy has been by-passed[14]) must lie in the linkages between different sections of longer hexameter or elegiac poems by Hellenistic Greek writers. The fragmentary character of these works in most cases prohibits perception of this feature; but a most illuminating understanding has now been reached of the layout of the most influential of them, Callimachus' *Aetia*, of which the latter two books seem to have consisted of detached but sometimes related elegies.[15] In this area

---

1984), although not previously in his commentary: Fedeli 1980: 207. See now Fedeli 1983: 1883–7.

[6] Cf. Quadlbauer 1970; Fedeli 1981: 228–31.

[7] On these poems cf. Cairns 1979c: 137–43, 147–53, 208–12; on Tibullus 1.8 and 1.9 McGann 1983: 1976–99 (delayed ten years in press) presents a view which is independent of, and was completed long before the publication of, Cairns 1979c, but for this reason is all the more valuable.

[8] On the latter pair cf. Cairns 1973; Ramminger 1937.

[9] Cf. Cairns 1978.

[10] On those of Horace *Odes* 2 cf. Nisbet and Hubbard 1978: 5f.

[11] Cf. Cairns 1977a, esp. 535–43; Cairns 1982.

[12] Linked pairs are not confined to contiguous or nearly contiguous pieces. On this point cf. Skutsch 1963, and for a pair in different books of the same collection cf. Cairns 1979b. It is of additional interest that both these poems themselves have been wrongly bisected by some editors and the two halves treated as linked poems. But for the correct interpretation see also Jäger 1967 (1968): 141–53. Another such pair is Prop. 1.3 and 2.29; cf. Cairns 1977c.

[13] Cf. e.g. Gow and Page 1968: I. xvii–xxi, on the Garland of Meleager.

[14] Cf. Cairns 1979c ch. 9, 'The Origins of Latin Love-Elegy'.

[15] Cf. esp. the most valuable paper of Parsons 1977: 46–50; and for some of the implications for Roman poetry, Thomas 1983.

too the *Metamorphoses*, where proximate and intercalated pairing of linked narratives is a prominent feature,[16] tells us about the practice both of Ovid's Hellenistic predecessors and of his Augustan contemporaries. For this, as for many other aspects of Augustan elegy, Pindar is of course a remote but important predecessor. Hellenistic commentators and modern scholars have seen linked pairs of poems in Pindar, e.g., *Olympian* 2 and 3, 4 and 5, and 10 and 11, *Pythian* 4 and 5, and *Nemean* 7 and *Paean* 6.[17]

Among Augustan elegiac books the Monobiblos of Propertius is a particularly fertile field for the study of linked pairs of poems;[18] and I shall begin by arguing that 1.4 and 1.5 are such a pair of separate poems closely associated in numerous ways. Scholars have of course discussed the possibility of a relationship between 1.4 and 1.5 before; and Otto Skutsch has come out clearly in favour of one.[19] But the views of other scholars have been mixed and on the whole sceptical. Although no one in recent times has denied all connection between the two poems, the commentary of Fedeli[20] and the monograph of Petersmann[21] both tend to stress the differences between 1.4 and 1.5 rather than what they have in common.

In this paper I shall examine first the overall analogies of subject matter and genre between Propertius 1.4 and 1.5 (§I. i) and second the general resemblances in their thematic structures (§I. ii). I shall then analyse the detailed verbal and conceptual coincidences between the two elegies (§I. iii). These sections in themselves aim at making a contribution to our understanding of Propertius' artistry and compositional technique; but they also suggest more wide-ranging

---

[16] Cf. most recently Crabbe 1981.
[17] Where evidence of ancient awareness of these links survives, it is usually in the *Scholia Vetera in Pindari Carmina*, Drachmann 1903–27; cf. I. 342 on *Ol.* XI, τόκος ἐπιγέγραπται, ἐπειδὴ ἐν προσθήκης μέρει τελευταῖον γέγραφε, καθάπερ καὶ ἐπὶ τῶν δανεισμάτων τὸ προστιθέμενον ἐκτὸς τοῦ ἀρχαίου, '[The word] *tokos* (interest) is written above the poem because he composed it last as an addition, in the same way as, in loans, the interest is separate from the principal.' The link between *Nem.* 7 and *Pae.* 6 is generally regarded by Pindaric scholars as fictitious. But for another view cf. Fogelmark 1972: Ch. 4, esp. 104–16. Such pairings may of course be more analogous to those between hymns (e.g., certain of the *Homeric Hymns*) and the epic narratives which they may have prefaced. Cf. N. J. Richardson 1974: 3f.
[18] Cf. Skutsch 1963.    [19] Skutsch 1963: 238.
[20] Fedeli 1980: 137, 152f.    [21] Petersmann 1980: 41–53.

and speculative conclusions about Bassus (§II. i), about the identity of Gallus in 1.5 (§II. ii), and about some of the historical (§II. iii) and literary (§II. iv) consequences of his identity. This paper, then, falls into two distinct portions. The first, studying the two poems as a linked pair, is independent of the second, which offers conclusions based on their linkage, so that the arguments of the first portion must be assessed on their own merits, irrespective of what follows.

I.I OVERALL SUBJECT-MATTER AND GENRE

The overall resemblances of subject-matter between Propertius 1.4 and 1.5 can be summarised briefly. In both elegies a third party is trying to create a rift between the lovers, Propertius and Cynthia: in 1.4 Bassus is ostensibly acting out of concern for Propertius in attempting to withdraw the poet from his love for Cynthia; in 1.5 Gallus is trying, so we are told, to steal Cynthia from Propertius. The differences between the treatment of Bassus in 1.4 and Gallus in 1.5 are perhaps meant to be less real than apparent. The hysterical and querulous tone adopted by Propertius suggests that his suspicions are running riot in both elegies, and that he is displaying two different behaviour patterns characteristic of jealousy: in 1.4 cunning reticence, and in 1.5 paranoiac verbosity. If this is so, it follows that, although Bassus' actions are not actually described in 1.4 as motivated by erotic interest in Cynthia, nevertheless this is what Propertius suspects; and the terms in which Bassus is threatened by the poet are intended to make the reader aware of these suspicions (although the reader might grasp them fully only in the light of 1.5). For among the dire activities on Cynthia's part which Propertius envisages as resulting from her anger at Bassus' interference in her love-affair with himself, the poet foresees that Cynthia will not only withdraw him from the company of Bassus but that she will avoid it herself (*nec te quaeret*, nor will she seek you out, 19f.).[22] In addition she will ensure that Bassus becomes *persona non grata* to all *puellae (heu nullo limine*

---

[22] Cf. Catullus 8,13f. with Kroll 1923 and Fordyce 1961 *ad loc.*

*carus eris*, alas, you will not be welcome at any threshold, 22). The prospect awaiting Bassus in 1.4 is thus similar to the one that awaits Gallus in 1.5: they will both become *exclusi amatores* (locked-out lovers, cf. 1.5.20), Bassus being excluded by all *puellae*, Gallus specifically by Cynthia (29). The view that Propertius suspects the motives of the apparently disinterested Bassus, who claims to be acting purely out of concern for Propertius' welfare, is confirmed by the chiastic distribution of the vocatives *Basse* (1.4.1) and *Galle* (1.5.31) in the two elegies, as well as by various other hints which will be noted below.

Another factor drawing the two elegies together is the emphasis in both on Cynthia's anger. In 1.4 it will be directed at Bassus; it will spring from Cynthia's actual or feared loss of Propertius as her lover; and it will result in that complete social ostracism of Bassus by the *puellae* which is Propertius' ultimate threat to him. Correspondingly, although with variations, Cynthia's anger in 1.5 will fall upon Gallus. He will be punished not for attempting to withdraw Propertius from Cynthia, but for attempting to withdraw Cynthia from Propertius. His punishment will be that total breakdown as an individual which is the inevitable fate of lovers of Cynthia; and this will be caused by Gallus' reduction to Propertius' own desperate status as an excluded lover of Cynthia.

The generic associations of Propertius 1.4 and 1.5 reinforce these resemblances in subject-matter. Both are erotodidactic, i.e. 1.4 offers Bassus, and 1.5 Gallus, a combination of instruction and apotreptic advice with regard to love. More specifically, both are examples of a specialised form of erotodidaxis which was first identified by Felix Jacoby,[23] and was shown by him to deal with some or all of the following topics:

(a) A lover displaying symptoms of love
(b) Another person asking questions or making surmises about the symptoms and about the identity of the beloved
(c) Comment on the beloved by this other person.[24]

---

[23] Jacoby 1914 (repr. in Jacoby 1961: 216–65).
[24] This formulation derives from Cairns 1972: 171–5; Cairns 1970; Cairns 1977b.

I have elsewhere carried further the work of Jacoby on this genre and have indicated new examples.[25] I have named it for convenience 'Symptoms of Love' and have stressed *inter alia* its symposiastic associations, its concentration on apotreptic, or, more rarely, protreptic assessment of the beloved, and its frequently interrogatory character. The group of Horatian examples of the genre treated in Cairns 1977b is particularly helpful for the interpretation of Propertius 1.4 and 1.5. The first, *Odes* 1.27, is fairly straightforward. But *Odes* 2.4 is acephalous: it omits the display of symptoms and the interrogation, concentrating instead solely on assessment, in this case the less usual positive alternative. *Odes* 1.8 is also suggestive of the variations to which the genre can be subject, since it is a very sophisticated example involving addressee-variation, subtle combination of topoi, and violent distortion in their order. Finally, *Odes* 3.12 is another example containing positive protreptic assessment of a beloved. Of the general associations of the 'Symptoms of Love,' its symposiastic links are not explicit in Propertius 1.4 and 1.5.[26] However, concentration on the assessment of a beloved is prominent in both 1.4 and 1.5; and the interrogative aspect of the genre is also, to some extent, visible in both (4.1–4; 5.3; 31f.).

Neither elegy however is a straightforward member of the genre: each is at least as complex as, e.g. Horace *Odes* 1.8, although in a different way. The principal complexity in both is 'inclusion':[27] in each the overall example of the genre 'Symptoms of Love,' in which Propertius is speaker, and in which he addresses Bassus and Gallus respectively in his capacities as lover and *magister amoris* (teacher of love), is preceded, and triggered off, by another, included example of the same genre. In this the roles of speaker and addressee are reversed: Bassus in 1.4 and Gallus in 1.5 are speakers and address

---

[25] Otherwise undocumented statements about the genre in this section are based on Jacoby 1914, and Cairns 1970; Cairns 1977b.
[26] It may be that the implied setting for the two elegies is a symposium, since, as well as the links between it and the genre, both elegy in general and the *komos* in particular, which is prominent in 1.4 and 1.5, have their own associations with the symposium. For those of elegy in general cf. Cairns 1971, esp. 205f.; and for those of the komos, Copley 1956, *passim*. But if present, the symposiastic setting is only an implicit background.
[27] Cf. Cairns 1972: Ch. 7.

Propertius. For an included genre to be the same as the overall genre is standard;[28] and it is paralleled for the 'Symptoms of Love' by, for example, Theocritus *Idyll* 14, in which the included example (2.12–42) is more easily identifiable than the overall one.

I begin with Propertius 1.5, which is somewhat closer than 1.4 to the simplest form of the genre. Its first and last couplets imply the following scenario: Gallus has approached Propertius and (32) has asked him *quid possit Cynthia* (what Cynthia is capable of, 31), i.e. Gallus has made the typical enquiry of the speaker in this genre about the beloved of the addressee, Propertius. The poet has responded in a heated and suspicious way: in the first line he stigmatises the speaker as *invide* (envious), which indicates that he thinks him hostile to and envious of his love-affair, and describes his questions as *voces molestas* (tiresome words). But then Propertius, instead of answering the speaker's questions about Cynthia in a straightforward fashion, reverses their roles: he does, in effect, tell Gallus what Cynthia is like as a beloved: but he does so by himself assuming the role of speaker in the overall example and by placing Gallus in that of addressee. Gallus is presumed to have laid himself open to this response by having revealed that he too, like Propertius, is in love with Cynthia.

Thus in the overall example the speaker, Propertius, is able to give his erotic advice as lover and as *magister amoris*, which are standard stances of speakers in this genre. The most explicit case of the lover-speaker is Callimachus *Epigram* 43 (Pfeiffer), where the speaker declares that he recognises his addressee's symptoms of love precisely because he himself is also a lover: φωρὸς δ' ἴχνια φὼρ ἔμαθον (a thief myself, I know the tracks of a thief, 1.6). There is of course an additional irony in Propertius 1.5—and also in 1.4, if my suggestion about Propertius' suspicion of Bassus' motivation is correct: Propertius not only casts both himself and his addressee as lovers, but the pair are in love with the same beloved, and so are rivals in love. But this type of irony may itself be traditional in the genre: in *Odes* 2.4, the speaker Horace, when giving a positive assessment of Phyllis, the beloved of Xanthias, takes some amusing pains to protest that he himself has no erotic interest in her (*fuge suspicari* [don't be at all

---

[28] Cf. Cairns 1972: 173–5.

suspicious], 22–4), a feature which suggests that the opposite might have been presumed. In addition, some of the Greek epigrammatic examples of the genre may imply the supposed situation of Propertius 1.5 (and 1.4), i.e. that speaker and addressee are in love with the same person: in Callimachus *Epigram* 30 (Pfeiffer) δαίμων οὑμὸς (my god, 3f.), the naming of the addressee's beloved (5) and the emphatic καὶ σύ in καὶ σὺ γὰρ ἐλθών (for you too, from the moment you came in, 5) all hint in this direction.[29] Less likely to be traditional in the genre is the possible implied sharing by Propertius and Gallus of the role of *magister amoris*. Propertius' stance as *magister amoris* is clear; but Gallus, by his confident questioning of Propertius in the included example, may also be claiming this status, despite Propertius' *invide* (1)—see also below (§II.ii).

Complications apart, Propertius and Gallus, *qua* speaker and addressee of the overall example, are not untypical of those who play these parts in the 'Symptoms of Love.' Their shared love for Cynthia could even be seen, to some extent, as that identification of interest which links speaker and addressee in many genres,[30] although it must be admitted that here it is ironically extreme, with the speaker sharing not only the addressee's beloved but also manifesting in the present the symptoms which the addressee will exhibit in the future! Standard 'Symptoms of Love' features of Propertius 1.5 are: copious amounts of apotreptic material (especially 1–6 and 31f.); revelation of the beloved's faults (esp. 7–12); and description of the actual symptoms of love (esp. 13–22). The advisory and consolatory role of the erotodidactic speaker is also emphasised, although in a roundabout way: his future effectiveness in this particular case is pointedly and strongly denied (27–30); but this is an additional argument to reinforce the value of his present precepts.

These topoi, then, appear in fairly standard form; but the relationship between them is quite abnormal: the symptoms are not being suffered in the present by the lover-addressee; and their effect is not, as is usual, to reveal that he is in love. Rather, if the speaker's warnings are ignored, the addressee will display these symptoms in

---

[29] It might also be argued, although less plausibly, that Call. *Ep.* 43 (Pfeiffer 1953) has a similar scenario.
[30] Cf. e.g. Cairns 1972: 211–16; 222–4.

the future.[31] The symptoms thus belong to the apotreptic advice and are not, as is more usual, the means whereby the lover is detected as requiring it. By a bold transference (which also reveals how Gallus, in the included example, detected Propertius' love for Cynthia) it is the speaker, Propertius, who is said to be exhibiting at present symptoms of love; and he, not untypically of the lover/*magister amoris* able to offer *erotodidaxis* in general (cf. Propertius 1.1.35-8: *hoc moneo vitate malum*..., I advise you, avoid this harm...), but, in our present state of knowledge, most untypically of the speaker in the specialised erotodidactic 'Symptoms of Love,' is thus able to warn his addressee to avoid his own present sufferings.

But again, and as if to balance these sophistications, most of the actual symptoms described in 1.5 are absolutely typical: madness, weeping, inability to speak, trembling, blotched countenance and pallor, and loss of all sense of place or identity.[32] But there is one novel, and at the same time poignantly comic touch, when in ll.29f. the speaker and the addressee are shown as a pair of rejected lovers of the same beloved weeping in each other's arms. This touch sums up the effect of the inclusion. I note, for completeness, that, as with many other cases of inclusion, there is a bridge passage which relates to both examples.[33] Lines 3–6, as part of the included example, contain the love-symptoms of the addressee, Propertius, while, in the overall example, they give a generalised warning to the addressee Gallus of his future miseries—to be particularised in ll.7–30.

The placing of 1.5, a more easily recognisable member of the genre, after 1.4, a less obvious example, is a compositional technique analogous to delayed generic identification.[34] In the Monobiblos two *propemptika* (1.6 and 1.8) display an illuminating parallelism: the more readily recognisable (1.8) is placed after the less so (1.6); and 1.6 includes, in its initial portion, a reported example of the more

---

[31] The madness which the addressee Aeschinas believes that he will suffer at Theocr. *Id.* 14.9 is a slightly different matter. It will be the end-result of his present symptoms (if no remedy is secured) rather than the sum of the symptoms of love, as it will be in Gallus' case.

[32] Cf. e.g. Enk 1946: II. 58–60; Fedeli 1980: 160–62; Hoelzer 1899: 32f.; Nisbet and Hubbard 1970: 169, 173f.

[33] Cf. Cairns 1972: 161; Cairns 1979c: 167, 171, 183.

[34] Cf. Cairns 1979c: 158.

recognisable form (ll.5–18).[35] In 1.6 and 1.8, as in 1.4 and 1.5, thematic similarities strengthen generic links: in 1.6 (as in 1.4) another man, in this case the *praetor* Tullus,[36] is trying to take Propertius away from Cynthia; in 1.8 (as in 1.5) another man, this time an unnamed *praetor*,[37] is trying to take Cynthia away from Propertius.

The placing of 1.5, the more obvious example, after 1.4, reinforces the belief that Propertius intended the pair to be read against each other as variations on a theme. A further argument for it is the presence in 1.4 of exactly the same technique of inclusion as is found in 1.5. In 1.4, the first ten lines are yet another 'Symptoms of Love,' in which Bassus is speaker and Propertius addressee. Bassus has approached Propertius and has offered him advice on his love-affair with Cynthia. What he actually did was to praise girls other than Cynthia, both virtuous (5ff.) and less reputable (11f.), thus acting to Cynthia's disadvantage. Presumably we are intended to imagine that Bassus had observed symptoms of love in Propertius. Bassus' explicit stance was clearly not that of a lover and/or *magister amoris* like Gallus, but rather was analogous to that of another moralising commentator on other people's love affairs, the Horace of *Odes* 1.8,[38] with perhaps a touch of the *irrisor amoris* 'derider of love' (see below).

In the overall example of 1.4, Propertius speaks, as in that of 1.5, as a lover/*magister amoris*. But Bassus, as addressee of the overall example, is not unambiguously a lover, as was Gallus. He retains from the included example overtones of that other standard speaker in the genre, the *irrisor amoris*, since he wants to end the love-affair between Propertius and Cynthia. But this aspect of Bassus should not be overstressed: first, as has been suggested, his motives and his feelings for Cynthia are suspected by Propertius—and the 'shared beloved' motif, if it was traditional in the genre (see above), would have ensured that Propertius' readers understood his suspicion; second, Bassus' implied association with *puellae* (21f.) shows that

---

[35] Cf. Cairns 1972: 3–16, 148–52.
[36] Cf. Cairns 1974a: 156–63.
[37] That he is a *praetor* does not emerge from 1.8 but is stated at 2.16.1, where he has returned to Rome and is once again involved with Cynthia.
[38] The fact that Bassus is an iambographer is of course relevant here—see §II.i.

in general he is not immune to love. As for the actual symptoms of love in 1.4, these are, unusually, associated with the beloved, Cynthia, and, as in 1.5, they are predicted for the future. Temporally, then, Cynthia's situation in 1.4 is similar to that of Gallus in 1.5. But 1.5 is more complicated in one respect in that the speaker, Propertius, is himself also experiencing these symptoms in the present, as befits his *persona* as elegiac lover-poet. Although Cynthia in 1.4 resembles the stock addressee of the genre by being a potential exhibitor of symptoms of love, her primary role is that of beloved and, as such, she is prominently, and characteristically for the genre, the object of an assessment. It focuses partly on her beauty and other positive traits, but also subsequently and strongly, as in 1.5, on her *ira* (wrath); and this makes it in essence, as such assessments usually are, negative. The speaker's warnings are directed, as is standard, at the addressee Bassus: it is he who will suffer the results of Cynthia's character and activities in 1.4, by being excluded, not only from Propertius' company, but from that of the *puellae*, including Cynthia. The poet does not go into further details about what this will mean to Bassus in terms of his sufferings: within 1.4 we are simply left to imagine that they will be those of any man who is rejected by *puellae*. But presumably we are also supposed, through the juxtaposition of 1.4 and 1.5, to envisage the detailed fate of Bassus in 1.4 as somewhat analogous to that of Gallus in 1.5.

1.4.5–10 is a generic bridge-passage of the kind discussed in connection with 1.5. In the overall example these lines form part of the assessment of the beloved, Cynthia. They make a favourable report about her beauty and so counterbalance some of the emphasis on her *ira* found elsewhere in 1.4. But, within the included example, they are Propertius' response, as addressee, to the speaker Bassus' implied criticisms of Cynthia. The passage has thus some of the functions of the description *cum* defence of Bombyca by her lover Bucaeus in Theocritus *Idyll* 10.24–37.[39]

---

[39] An alternative approach would see Prop. 1.4.5ff. and 1.5.2ff. as analogous to Theocr. *Id.* 10.24–37, which follow Milon's attack on Bombyca, the beloved of Bucaeus, and in which Bucaeus sings in praise of her. Thus the bulk of 1.4 would be taken as a 'reaction' (cf. Cairns 1972: Ch. 6) to Bassus' apotreptic and that of 1.5 to Gallus' interrogation. I doubt whether Propertius (or Theocritus) saw matters in this

*Propertius 1.4 and 1.5 and the 'Gallus' of the Monobiblos* 149

The bridge-passage of 1.4 naturally conforms with the main thrust of the elegy: Propertius turns the tables on Bassus in 1–10 not just by praising Cynthia's beauty, but by showing him that his relationship with Cynthia is an established one. Propertius will go on in ll.11ff. to develop these themes: he will not only reveal the depth of his own love for Cynthia, but will also show that Cynthia is not merely his beloved, as Bassus thinks, but is actively in love with him, so that she too may display symptoms of love. This in turn leads to the portrayal of Bassus himself as an actual or potential lover and victim of love.

The effect of all this is to deepen the impression, however unfounded it might be in reality, that Bassus is himself sexually interested in Cynthia. This notion is further strengthened by the series of role-changes undergone by the three actors of 1.4, which is partly paralleled by the similar switching of roles found in Theocritus *Idyll* 14. There the addressee in the overall example, Aeschinas, was the speaker in the included past example; and the beloved in the overall example, Kyniska, was the lover in the included example. Here in Propertius 1.4 the modifications in the roles are more subtle: again the speaker in the past included example (Bassus) is metamorphosed in the overall example into the generic addressee, the actual or potential lover who is the recipient of apotreptic advice. But Cynthia, who was the beloved under attack in the included example, remains the beloved in the overall example, although she is given characteristics which are more like those of a lover than a beloved, and her love affair, at least on the surface, is with the speaker, not the addressee. Propertius' own position is even more ambivalent: he is the lover-addressee in the included example, although we are not told anything specific about his symptoms of love there. In the overall example he is the speaker; but although himself a lover, he, uncharacteristically for the lover-speaker in this genre, gives apotreptic advice, albeit only in defence of his own love.

---

light. The main thrust of 1.4 and 1.5 is better explained in terms of 'inclusion'; and *Id.* 14 is a rare case where the generic pattern is repeated, in that Bucaeus' song adds to the information which he earlier gave about Bombyca and provokes further apotreptic criticism of her and of Bucaeus by Milon. Propertius' 'defence' of Cynthia is in any case different from Bucaeus' defence of Bombyca: it amounts in one sense to an admission that the implied criticism of Cynthia by Bassus was all too well-founded.

The way is thus prepared in 1.4 for 1.5: there too we find an included example, in which the roles of the speaker and addressee of the overall example are reversed; and there too, in the overall example, the speaker Propertius is a lover, and uses apotreptic, now quite explicitly, because the would-be beloved of his addressee is openly his own beloved.

## I.II THEMATIC STRUCTURES

The thematic structures[40] of 1.4 and 1.5 have approximately the same relationship one to the other as those of Tibullus 2.3 and 2.4, i.e. they share some themes and an overall similarity:

### 1.4

| | | | |
|---|---|---|---|
| $A_1$ | 1–4 | Bassus, why are you trying, by praising other girls, to persuade me to be a runaway from my *servitium* (slavery) to Cynthia? | |
| $B_1$ | 5–10 | Cynthia is more beautiful than the heroines and her contemporaries. | The positive side of Cynthia, and its effects on Propertius. |
| $C_1$ | 11–14 | Her beauty and her other good qualities together cause my *furor* (madness). | |
| D=A | 15–16 | You will not succeed in separating us because of our *fides* (loyalty). | |
| $C_2$ | 17–20 | Cynthia will go mad (*insana*), shun you and separate us. | The negative side of Cynthia, and its effects on Bassus |
| $B_2$ | 21–4 | She will defame you to other contemporary girls and to altars and sacred stones. | |
| $A_2$ | 25–8 | Cynthia is determined not to suffer the loss of me. | |

---

[40] On the concept and for extensive bibliography cf. Cairns 1979c: Ch. 8.

## 1.5

| | | |
|---|---|---|
| $A_1$ | 1–2 | Stop trying to disrupt, by your unpleasant words, our relationship as *pares* (a couple). |
| $B_1$ | 3–6 | You are mad (*insane*) and will suffer my own *furores* (frenzies). |
| $C_1$ | 7–12 | Cynthia is not like her contemporaries: she will bring on you cares and sleeplessness; she can deal with 'big men'. |
| $D_1$ | 13–18 | You will come running to my *limina* (threshold) in a state of total wretchedness and collapse. |
| E=A | 19–20 | Then you will understand the nature of my *servitium* to Cynthia and exclusion. |
| $D_2$ | 21–2 | and why I am pale and physically completely shattered. |
| $C_2$ | 23–6 | Your nobility and great name will not be able to help you. |
| $B_2$ | 27–30 | I will not be able to help you because I suffer my own *malum* (harm); we shall be unhappy lovers together. |
| $A_2$ | 31–2 | Stop trying to find out about my Cynthia, Gallus: she is a harsh mistress. |

Rows $B_1$–$D_1$ bracketed: Negative effects of Cynthia on Gallus

Rows $D_2$–$B_2$ bracketed: Negative effects of Cynthia on Gallus and Propertius

Like other pairs of linked Roman poems, Propertius 1.4 and 1.5 involve self-imitation with variation;[41] and, because they are adjacent, the reader is intended to perceive their links, including those of thematic structure, immediately. 1.5 is longer and more complex than 1.4, in that it contains one additional theme, the effects of Cynthia's *ira* on Gallus ($D_1$), and on Propertius ($D_2$), spelled out in detail. But both elegies consist, in essence, of a 'double sandwich,' in which the initial, middle and final portions, as indicated schematically above, deal with the interaction between, on the one hand, Bassus (1.4) or Gallus (1.5), and, on the other, Propertius and Cynthia, while the intervening portions, the 'fillings,' reveal the actual or potential effects of Cynthia upon Propertius, Bassus and Gallus, in isolation or in pairs. Thus, in the initial portion of 1.4, Bassus is

[41] Cf. Cairns 1979b.

warned to respect the relationship between Cynthia and Propertius, which is described there as *servitium*;[42] in the centre, the relationship is said to be one of *fides*, and Bassus is again warned off; and at the end, although it is a settled relationship, it seems again, by implication, to be *servitium*, since the loss of Propertius by Cynthia would be *damnum*, i.e. loss of property, viz. a slave. At the beginning of 1.5, Gallus is told not to interfere in the relationship between Propertius and Cynthia, at which point the metaphorical stress is on its parity;[43] but, in the middle of 1.5, the relationship is again *grave servitium* (burdensome slavery, 19); and the end, where Gallus is given his final warning, seems to imply that Propertius again sees himself as enslaved to a vengeful mistress.

The 'fillings' of the double sandwich of 1.4 consist, in the first instance, of a sketch of Cynthia's beauty and of its effect, namely Propertius' *furor* (11), and, in the second, of Cynthia's description as an *insana puella* (mad girl, 17), who will punish Bassus in various ways. To match the *furor* of Propertius in the first filling of 1.4, the first filling of 1.5 treats the *furores* of Propertius (3), which will be transferred to and shared by Gallus (*insane*, 3). The second filling of 1.5 stresses the irremediable nature of these future shared sufferings of Propertius and Gallus.

Thus 1.4 and 1.5, when read in sequence, reveal a conceptual progression similar to that found in Tibullus 2.3 and 2.4.[44] Propertius' concern throughout is with his own association with Cynthia, the various pressures which are placed on it, and the degree of confidence which he has in it. His confidence progressively ebbs away, and, by the middle of 1.5, he is forced by his fears to reveal that his relationship with Cynthia is not really one of settled contentment, as is suggested at 1.4.15ff. or even at the beginning of 1.5, but is rather *servitium*, involving not just total possession, as it

---

[42] The topos of erotic *servitium* derives of course from Greek literature, although it was heavily exploited by the Roman elegists, cf. Copley 1947. The odd attempt of Lyne 1979 to reduce the role of Greek literature in the development of the topos is implausible. See rather the excellent and thorough paper of Murgatroyd 1981 for a proper perspective on the problem.

[43] For the interpretation and parallels see Fedeli 1980 *ad loc*. The hypothesis of Moritz 1967, supported by Allen 1974: 113–15, that *pares* (1.5.2) refers to Propertius and Gallus is rightly rejected by Skutsch 1973: 317f., and by Fedeli 1980 *ad loc*.

[44] Cf. Cairns 1979c: 209–12.

already did at 1.4.1ff. and 25ff., but also extreme suffering. Parallel with this development in Propertius' own self-revelation is the unfolding of the character of Cynthia: she was lauded in 1.4.11ff. ($C_1$), although she was also revealed at 1.4.17ff. ($C_2$) as a girl possessing dangerous qualities when aroused, and as one likely (1.4.21ff., $B_2$) to impose upon Bassus an extreme form of social alienation, from Propertius, from other girls, and from the gods. But in 1.5 Cynthia emerges in even more horrendous colours: Bassus' threatened fate in 1.4 is left vague compared with what will befall Gallus in 1.5; at 1.5.7ff ($C_1$), it is Cynthia's *ira*, and not, as at 1.4.7ff., her beauty, which sets her apart from other girls; and the end result of Cynthia's *ira* in 1.5 will be that Gallus will come to occupy Propertius' own supremely wretched position (1.5.3ff. = $B_1$-$C_1$ and 1.5.23ff. = $C_2$-$B_2$).

By the close of 1.5 the theme of Cynthia and Propertius' mutual relationship, which occupies the beginning, middle and end of both poems, has, comparatively speaking, diminished in importance. It has been virtually replaced by the three-way tension between the parties involved in 1.5. To stress this, 1.5 ends with Propertius' simple warning to Gallus not to risk the terrible suffering which Cynthia will bring upon him. As noted above, the larger formal structure of 1.5 accommodates one extra theme, the detailed description of the effects of Cynthia on Propertius' rival, Gallus. Because Bassus was not cast explicitly as Propertius' rival in 1.4, the account of his future punishment there dwells more on his exclusion by other girls, although his real and heavy punishment, Cynthia's shunning of him, does receive mention (*post haec... nec te/quaeret*—after this... she will not seek you out, 1.4.19f.). But Gallus is Propertius' open rival in 1.5, and so great emphasis is placed on his exclusion by Cynthia and its results. The deterioration in the relationship between Propertius and Cynthia already seen in 1.4, and the greater openness of the threat posed to it by Gallus than by Bassus, are also signalled by the appearance earlier, and with less preamble, in 1.5 than in 1.4, of some concepts and details which the two elegies share (see §I.iii). In this way, since the two elegies present a similar tale, and since the atmosphere of jealousy, suspicion and fear is already well-established by the end of 1.4, 1.5 can be read *ab initio* as an intensification of it.

## I.III VERBAL AND CONCEPTUAL LINKS

There are numerous verbal and conceptual links between Propertius 1.4 and 1.5. Simply listing them might readily produce conviction about the pairing of the two elegies. But a more discursive treatment will be given here: each part of the thematic structure of 1.4 will be taken in turn and all correspondences between it and the remainder of the two elegies will be discussed. This will have the advantage of allowing internal echoes and those between the two elegies to be handled together, thus reinforcing the conclusions of §I.ii; and it will also permit the echoes to be partially interpreted as they are first noted.

But this procedure also has its disadvantages: first, and more serious, the abbreviated treatment required to handle so many echoes may suggest falsely that all the echoes noted are regarded as equally intentional or meaningful. The truth, as with all types of ancient *imitatio*, is of course that there is a sliding-scale from the fleeting to the substantial and from the merely verbal to the significantly conceptual;[45] and it is often unclear precisely what a single item may involve. In what follows, I have tried to stress those echoes which seem to me particularly striking or meaningful, while conceding that others may well be of less import. But it must be emphasised that the argument about pairing depends less on individual points than on their cumulative effect.

A second disadvantage of the procedure adopted here is that inevitably it will create the impression that the echoes between the first halves of the two elegies are much more numerous than those found later in the poems. Now this impression is not completely illusory: Propertius did indeed want to make his audience aware of the pairing as early as possible in 1.5; and so he tends to concentrate echoes there. But the concentration is not as great as it might at first seem. Two other, and fully real, trends in the asymmetric grouping of echoes will be discussed below. It should also be remembered that the structure of 1.5 contains one extra theme ($D_1/D_2$—the detailed sufferings of Propertius/Gallus). For this reason the equivalence of various themes in 1.4 and 1.5 will not always be immediately obvious

---

[45] Cf. Cairns 1979b: 121.

*Propertius 1.4 and 1.5 and the 'Gallus' of the Monobiblos* 155

from their coding. This drawback can be countered by frequent reference to the thematic structures of the pair as laid out above.

*1.4.1–4 (A₁)*

The first two couplets of 1.4 and 1.5 respectively exhibit complex mutual associations. These must, as suggested above, be intended as strong initial signals of the pairing of the two elegies:

*Quid mihi tam multas laudando, Basse, puellas*
  *mutatum domina cogis abire mea?*
*quid me non pateris vitae quodcumque sequetur*
  *hoc magis assueto ducere servitio?* 1.4.1–4, A₁

*Invide, tu tandem voces compesce molestas*
  *et sine nos cursu, quo sumus, ire pares!*
*quid tibi vis, insane? meos sentire furores?*
  *infelix, properas ultima nosse mala.* 1.5.1–4, A₁–B₁

Bassus, why by praising so many girls do you pressure me to change and leave my mistress? Why don't you allow me to lead whatever more of my life will follow in this my more familiar slavery?

You envious man, check at last your tiresome words and allow us to go on, as we are, as a couple. What do you want, you madman? To feel my frenzies? Unhappy man, you are rushing to experience the worst possible troubles.

1.4 begins with two indignant questions in asyndeton, each occupying a couplet (1f. and 2f.) and each introduced by *quid*. 1.5 starts with two indignant commands linked by a copula, which together make up a single couplet (1f.). But this couplet is followed by a third line introduced by *quid*, which contains two indignant questions in asyndeton. Complex grammatical and syntactical *imitatio cum variatione* is involved here. The vocatives *Basse* (1.4.1) and *invide* (1.5.1) answer each other, while *laudando* (1.4.1) and *voces molestas* (1.5.1) both refer to the addressee's utterances.[46] *Tandem* (1.4.1), i.e., *tam-dem*, occupies the same *sedes* as *tam multas* (1.5.1), and the adverbs in each case emphasise Propertius' strong feelings. Personal pronouns and adjectives reinforce the emotional impact of both elegy openings: *mihi*

---

[46] The antithesis praise/envy, which is standard in encomiastic poetry from the late sixth century BCE on, may add an extra touch; see also §II.i and Appendix.

(1.4.1), *mea* (2) and *me* (3) cf. *hoc* (4); *tu* (1.5.1), *nos* (2), *tibi* (3) and *meos* (3). *mutatum* (1.4.2) is opposed in sense by *cursu quo sumus* (1.5.2), while *abire* (1.4.2) corresponds with and overlaps in *sedes* with *ire* (1.5.2) and intensifies the contrast between the notion of compelling (*cogis*) to go away in 1.4.2 and that of allowing (*sine*) to go on in 1.5.2.

These initial multiple correspondences alert the reader to further links. So *Basse* (1.4.1), as well as being answered by *invide* (1.5.1), is also related to the vocative *Galle* in the first line of the final couplet of 5 (1.5.31. A$_2$), a relationship reinforced by *quid* (1.4.1; 3) and *quid* (1.5.31)! Similarly the idea of constancy/change found in *mutatum* (1.4.2) and *cursu* etc. (1.5.2) continues in 1.4.15f. (D = A): *quo magis et nostros contendis solvere amores,/hoc magis accepta fallit uterque fide* (and the more you try to pull our love apart, the more we both frustrate you with our pledged faith); in 1.4.27 (A$_2$), *maneat sic semper* (may she always remain of that mind) (which is the penultimate line of 1.4); and, with changed reference, in *pariter* (together, 1.5.29, B$_2$). *voces molestas* (1.5.1), as well as clashing with *laudando* (1.4.1), also picks up *non tacitis vocibus* (with unrestrained words) in 1.4.18 (C$_2$). Similarly Bassus' attempts at compulsion in 1.4.2 (*cogis abire*) are reflected ironically at 1.5.19f. (E = A), where it is Gallus who will be forced (*cogere*, 19) to learn what being enslaved to Cynthia is like and to go away (*abire*, 20) as an excluded lover. Again, the lovers' relationship is specifically said to be the *servitium* of Propertius to Cynthia in 1.4.4 (*assueto servitio*). But this notion is anticipated in 1.4.2: *mutatum domina cogis abire mea;* then *ingenuus color* (a well-bred complexion) at 1.4.13 (C$_1$) alludes to it by referring in contrast to Cynthia's freeborn appearance; and finally it is directly echoed in 1.5.19 (E = A), *tum grave servitium nostrae cogere puellae/ discere* (then you will be compelled to learn the harsh servitude that my mistress imposes), where the prospective *servitium* of Gallus to Cynthia, and by implication the present *servitium* of Propertius to Cynthia, is in question. The last echo conforms with the structure of 1.5 since it links A$_1$ and E = A. Lastly, although this may relate more to Propertius' style and mannerisms than his conceptual intentions, *tam multas*, at 1.4.1 (A$_1$) is followed by mention of Cynthia's *multis decus artibus* (many graceful accomplishments) at 1.4.13 (C$_1$), while 1.5.10 (C$_1$) speaks of the *curarum milia quanta* (how many thousand anxieties) which Cynthia will inflict on Gallus.

*Propertius 1.4 and 1.5 and the 'Gallus' of the Monobiblos* 157

## 1.4.5–10 (B1)

1.4.5 continues the excited personal pronouns (*tu, tu*) of the two elegy openings. Lines 5–8 refer to various heroines of the past who have inspired love: first two of them are named, Antiope and Hermione; then the whole class of such beautiful women is mentioned. B₁ of 1.5 (ll.3–6) also introduces paradeigmatic material, but in chiastic fashion: first (1.4), the whole class of *ultima mala* risked by Gallus is mentioned; then ll.5f. specify two particular metaphorical torments which he may experience, walking on fire and drinking Thessalian *toxica* (poisons). The *paradeigmata* in 1.4 and 1.5 are of course quite different in nature, but, almost as if partly in compensation for this, 1.4.6 and 1.5.6 are linked in another and more striking way. 1.4.6 begins with the adjective *Spartanae*, applied to the beautiful Hermione; 1.5.6 ends with the noun *Thessalia*, the source of the *toxica* which Gallus will be forced to drink. The link does not consist simply of the application of two geographical terms, one at the beginning and one at the end of the corresponding line in the two poems, a feature which of course wittily underlines the chiastic mode in which the exemplary material is presented. There is also a conceptual connection between these two names, since the two places referred to had long been associated in an expression, probably itself proverbial, first found at the beginning of Pindar *Pythian* 10: ὄλβια Λακεδαίμων, μάκαιρα Θεσσαλία (Happy is Lacedaimon, blessed is Thessaly). This combination of places appears to have had specifically erotic implications in the Hellenistic period, as is revealed by some lines of Theocritus *Idyll* 12 (on which see also Cairns 1972: 28f.), in which Laconian Amyclae and Thessaly are featured (12.12–16):

δίω δή τινε τώδε μετὰ προτέροισι γενέσθην
φῶθ', ὁ μὲν εἴσπνηλος, φαίη χ' Ὠμυκλαϊάζων,
τὸν δ' ἕτερον πάλιν ὥς κεν ὁ Θεσσαλὸς εἴποι ἀΐτην.
ἀλλήλους δ' ἐφίλησαν ἴσῳ ζυγῷ. ἦ ῥα τότ' ἦσαν
χρύσειοι πάλιν ἄνδρες, ὅτ' ἀντεφίλησ' ὁ φιληθείς.

Godlike were those two among men of the past; one the 'Inspirer', as a man speaking the dialect of Amyclae might say, the other, as a Thessalian would say, the 'Hearer'. They loved each other in perfect balance; they were revenants from the Golden Age, when the beloved loved in return.

In Theocritus the overtones are of lovers' bliss; if that significance was standard, then the Propertian juxtaposition in 1.4 and 1.5 would be ironic: it would serve partly to remind us of the concordant love of Propertius and Cynthia in 1.4 and in the first couplet of 1.5. but would also suggest *per contrariam* the miseries of that discordant love which Gallus will find if he persists in pursuing Cynthia, and which is now revealed as Propertius' fate also. Other correspondences between the early parts of 1.4 and 1.5 reinforce those already mentioned: the *levibus figuris* (minor beauties) of 1.4.9 ($B_1$) refer to the same individuals as the *vagis puellis* (flighty girls) of 1.5.7 ($C_1$); and in both phrases *collata* (compared) is placed, in the same *sedes*, between adjective and noun. Similarly *nomen* (name) (1.4.8, $B_1$) looks to *nosse* (know, 1.5.4, $B_1$) and *ignotos* (unknown, 1.5.5, $B_1$), as well as to the later *nomine* (1.5.26, $C_1$)—see also §II.ii.

*1.4.11–14 ($C_1$)*

*Mei furoris* (1.4.11, $C_1$) is echoed in *meos furores* (1.5.3, $B_1$), the nouns *furoris/furores* occupying the same *sedes*. It is also picked up at 1.4.17 ($C_2$), where Cynthia, on learning of Bassus' attempts to destroy her relationship with Propertius, will become *insana*. This notion in turn finds an echo in the same line of 1.5 which also echoes *furor*, i.e. 1.5.3 ($B_1$), where Gallus is addressed as *insane* in a line combining *insania* with *furores*: *quid tibi vis, insane? meos sentire furores?*[47] Thus in both elegies two persons are 'mad': in 1.4 these are Propertius and Cynthia, mutual lovers whose relationship should not be tampered with by Bassus; in 1.5 Propertius is at present mad and Gallus will join him in being mad, since they are both lovers of Cynthia, who will both suffer in future at her hands, as Propertius suffers now. But there is more: *ira* was commonly associated with *furor* in antiquity;[48] and in 1.5 Cynthia is above all *irata*. In this way she is, appropriately, implied to be the third mad person in 1.5. That the poet is aware of this implication is revealed by his coupling of *insana puella* at 1.4.17 ($C_2$) with *irata* at 1.4.21 ($B_2$) in a sustained description of Cynthia. Thus *molliter irasci*

---

[47] The overtones are legal. For the distinction in Roman law between *furor* and *insania* cf. Buckland and Stein 1975: 168.

[48] Cf. *TLL s.v. furor* II b; Ringeltaube 1913: 85.

*non solet illa tibi* (her anger with you is wont to be unrestrained, 1.5.8, C₁) can be read as a signal that Cynthia's madness is a factor in 1.5 as well as in 1.4.

### 1.4.15–16 (D = A)

In the centre of 1.4, at line 15, the key term *amores* appears at the end of a hexameter:

*quo magis et nostros contendis solvere amores*
and the more you try to pull our love apart

The term is echoed in a complex way throughout the two elegies: at 4.26 (A₂)

*quam sibi cum rapto cessat amore deus*
than when the god idles and a love is snatched from her

at 5.24 (C₂)

*nescit Amor priscis cedere imaginibus*
Love does not know how to defer to ancestral images

and at 5.29 (B₂)

*sed pariter miseri socio cogemur amore...*
but together in shared unhappy love we shall be forced...

The coincidence between *cessat amore deus* (4.26) and *nescit Amor cedere* (5.24), which involves not only the noun *amor* and the verb *cedere/cessare*, but also the element of personification, i.e. Amor the love god, supports the reading of O, viz *deus*, at 1.4.26 against the emendation *decus*.[49] Both the frequency with which *amores* is echoed and the contexts in which these echoes occur, which involve divine power, threats from third parties to end love and the shared nature of love, a topic ironically varied at 1.5.29, are a natural reflection of the role of love as the key theme of the two elegies.

### 1.4.17–20 (C₂)

Two as yet untreated correspondences can be observed in this section: *non impune feres* (you won't get away with it, 1.4.17, C₂) is echoed in *non*

---

[49] *deus* is rightly defended by Fedeli 1980 *ad loc.*

*impune illa rogata venit* (when invited, she comes with a high price, 1.5.32, $A_2$), and *quaeret* (1.4.20, $C_2$) in *quaerere* (seek, 1.5.32, $A_2$). Interesting variations in these echoes reinforce the similarities between Bassus and Gallus. The fact that *impune* can be either active or passive is exploited so that in 1.4 it is Bassus (the third party) who will not escape suffering, and Cynthia will cease to *quaerere* Bassus, whereas in 1.5 it is Cynthia who will impose suffering on the third party, Gallus, and Gallus is to cease to *quaerere* Cynthia. The most piquant aspect of the variation is, however, that in the two cases the end-result is the same: Cynthia will bring sorrow and punishment upon both Bassus and Gallus. In addition to these correspondences, those involving *insana* (1.4.17, $C_2$) have already been treated.

*1.4.21–24 ($B_2$)*

*Irata* (21) and its echoes have already been dealt with. Remaining correspondences are those between *limine* (1.4.22, $B_2$) and *limina* (1.5.13, $D_1$, cf. 1.5.20, $D_2$), and between *fletibus* (tears, 1.4.23, $B_2$), *fletibus* (1.5.15, $D_1$)—in the same *sedes*—and *flere* (to shed tears, 1.5.30, $B_2$). In addition these lines, in their repeated use of *illa* (that girl, 20, 22) and of parts of *nullus* (no-one/no, 22, 23, cf. 25), have a tone similar to portions of 1.5: cf. *illa* (1.5.7; 8; 11; 12, all $C_1$) and *nullus* (1.5.22, $D_2$), *nulla* (1.5.28, $B_2$). The repeated *illa* may be stressing the viciousness of Cynthia, and the parts of *nullus* the hopelessness of the states of Bassus and Gallus respectively.

*1.4.25–28 ($A_2$)*

Most of the correspondences in this section have been dealt with in earlier discussion: *non ullo* (25), *cessat amore* (26), *deus* (26), *maneat* (27) and *illa* (28). There remains only *querar* (I might complain, 1.4.28, $A_2$) and *querenti* (you complaining, 1.5.17, $D_1$), on which see also below.

The partly illusory concentration of echoes in the first halves of 1.4 and 1.5 has already been noted. Another, non-illusory feature of the distribution of echoes is that they are sometimes considerably out of phase as between the two elegies. This is seen first in the reproduction at an earlier stage in 1.5 of words and concepts which appeared at a later point in 1.4. This technique creates the impression of a progression of events between the two elegies; it also reinforces that sense of

## Propertius 1.4 and 1.5 and the 'Gallus' of the Monobiblos    161

deterioration in the relationship of Propertius and Cynthia already explored in §I.ii; and it produces a growing tension, as those minor irritations which Cynthia suffered in 1.4 are transferred *in toto*, first to Propertius, and then to Gallus, in 1.5, and as those undetailed sufferings with which Bassus is threatened in 1.4 are detailed fully, when the theme is applied to Propertius and Gallus in 1.5. So for example Cynthia's *fletus* (tears) at 1.4.23 (B$_2$) are, by implication, to be compared with Gallus' *fletus*, which appear in the same case and *sedes* at 1.5.15 (D$_1$). Again the *limen*, which Bassus will find is inaccessible to him at 1.4.22 (B$_2$), reappears in two different forms in 1.5. It turns up first in unexpected guise at 1.5.13 (D$_1$): Gallus will, paradoxically, run to Propertius' *limina*, complaining of his ill-treatment by Cynthia. The expected equivalent, namely Cynthia's *limen*, appears subsequently and obliquely (1.5.20, E = A), where Gallus is described as an *exclusus* (i.e. from Cynthia's *limen*). Finally the complaints (*querar*) which Propertius wishes never to have to make at 1.4.28 (A$_2$) are also picked up earlier in 1.5, at 17 (D$_1$), in the complaints (*querenti*) which Gallus will indeed have to make. These echoes employing *queri* may be linked with those using *quaerere* (1.4.20, C$_2$ and 1.5.32, A$_2$), i.e. at 1.4.28 (A$_2$), *quod querar inveniam*, 'finding' might suggest 'seeking,' and at 1.5.17 (D$_1$), *et quaecumque voles fugient tibi verba querenti* (and any words you might want to use in your complaints will fail you), *querenti* might in context allude to *quaerenti*, that is, he cannot find the words he is looking for. Another example is Propertius 1.7.5–8:

> *nos, ut consuemus, nostros agitamus amores,*
>     *atque aliquid duram quaerimus in dominam;*
> *nec tantum ingenio quantum servire dolori*
>     *cogor et aetatis tempora dura queri.*

> I, as is my wont, live out my love and seek some means to move my harsh mistress; I am compelled to serve my sorrow more than my genius, and to lament the hard times of my youth.

Here *quaerimus* (6) and *queri* (8) are coupled with *duram* and *dura* respectively to emphasise their connection. There is a possibility that the words might have been formally connected in ancient etymology, although the only evidence for this is that in Isidore *Etymologiae*

10.232f. *questus* and *querimoniae* are etymologised in sequence. Alternatively, the link might be a piece of creative etymologising on the part of Propertius.[50]

A second and compensatory pattern of out-of-phase echoes involves the picking up at a later point in 1.5 of items which appeared at an earlier point in 1.4. One example of this was the treatment of *non impune* and of *quaerere* (1.4.17.20, C$_2$ and 1.5.32, A$_2$). Another is the *ingenuus color* of Cynthia at 1.4.13 (C$_1$), that is her whiteness, which is ironically echoed in the pallor of 1.5.21 (D$_1$)—not so much a whiteness as an unhealthy pale yellowness—which is Propertius' badge as a lover, and which Gallus will soon share with him. This technique balances the converse pattern noted above and so contributes towards a sense of artistic symmetry, as well as giving the end of 1.5 the appearance of being the final summing-up of a situation.

All in all then, the numerous and detailed verbal and conceptual correspondences between Propertius 1.4 and 1.5 far exceed the number to be expected in any two elegies by the same poet, or explicable by the limited vocabulary and content of Roman, and Propertian, elegy. Furthermore, many of the correspondences are clearly significant. Thus the view that 1.4 and 1.5 have only limited connections must be abandoned, and the two elegies should be considered as a pair, composed as such by Propertius. The way is now open in §II for acceptance of the invitation offered by their intimate and omnipresent associations, namely to explore the implications of their being addressed to two real and named contemporaries of Propertius.

## II.I BASSUS

Bassus in 1.4 is universally identified as the iambographer Bassus, mentioned at only one other place, Ovid *Tristia* 4.10.47 (*Bassus quoque clarus iambis*, Bassus too, distinguished as an iambist) along with the epic poet Ponticus (addressee of Propertius 1.7 and 1.9), Tibullus, Horace, Virgil, Gallus, Aemilius Macer, and Propertius

---

[50] Cf. Cairns 1979c: Ch. 4.

himself, as one of a group of older writers contemporary with Ovid's own youth. Recently Thomas A. Suits has argued that Bassus' comments upon Propertius' love-life are linked in a sophisticated way with his own status as a writer of *iambi*.[51] Suits claims that there is something unexpected in the opening lines of Propertius 1.4: "For an iambist to be praising anyone would be surprising; for him to be praising women, especially so" (p.87). "The mere fact that such sentiments are somewhat out of character for Bassus' chosen genre gives an unexpected twist to the opening of the piece, which helps to set the stage for what follows" (p.88). Suits then shows that the 'requital motif' contained in *non impune feres* (1.4.17) is central to the iambic tradition, going back as it does to Archilochus. In making the threat "Propertius seems to be threatening, then, to play the iambist against Bassus" (p.88). Cynthia too, in her actions against Bassus, will implement her hostility "primarily through the iambist's own weapon: words (18)" (p.89). Her imprecations are also part of the same conceptual complex, because "calling upon the gods to effectuate one's curses, while not restricted to the iambic tradition, forms a natural part of it" (p.89). In being *insana* (mad, 17) and *irata* (angered, 21) Cynthia is again reminiscent of the iambist (p.89), *hostis* (enemy, 1.4.18) is the *mot propre* for the iambist (cf. Horace *Epode* 6.14, *acer hostis Bupalo*, a bitter enemy to Bupalus). Thus, according to Suits, Propertius "continues the pattern of reversal introduced at the outset (Bassus as eulogist instead of detractor) by whimsically portraying Cynthia in terms of the dread iambist and Bassus as her impotent victim. It can be seen that the way in which Bassus' poetic genre is turned against him is analogous to Propertius' depreciatory treatment of epic in the two elegies addressed to Ponticus" (p.90).

Suits' approach to Propertius 1.4 is, in my view, of fundamental importance; and its value is not affected by the minor modifications offered here. Two qualifications must be made to it: first, ancient iambographers are not a monolithic group in that Archilochus and Hipponax were differently regarded in antiquity, although the details

---

[51] Suits 1976. There are further useful comments (also modified in the present paper) at Fedeli 1981: 233f.

of this distinction are not yet clear;[52] and second, the overall image of the iambographer changed substantially between the archaic and the Hellenistic age.[53] C.W. Macleod had already noted that, in the latter period, iambographers could sometimes unexpectedly represent themselves as 'men of peace'.[54] So Callimachus in his first Iamb, while appearing as the new Hipponax, nevertheless abstains from Hipponax's quarrelsomeness and himself attempts to settle the quarrel of the *philologoi* (scholars) (p.306). In addition a certain sharing of characteristics between iambists and their victims had become conventional by Propertius' day. In collecting evidence for the juxtaposition in programmatic poetry of different literary types, including iamb, Macleod noted that it is "a feature of literary polemic to mimic sarcastically the other man's style" (p.307); and he had referred to certain contexts in which the iambographer is provoked by his adversaries and their insults into adopting the genre, after, in at least one case (Catullus 116), attempting a reconciliation. At one point (p.307 n.4) Macleod observed that in *Epode* 5.83–6 "it is another speaker [i.e. than the iambic poet] who finally breaks into curses." His thesis receives confirmation from Horace *Odes* 1.16, a palinode in which Horace and his female addressee both share the *ira* (anger) which led Horace to write iambs against the lady and which led to her fierce resentment of his action in so doing.[55] It is additionally reinforced by another valuable paper, by Matthew W. Dickie, discussing *invidia* in Roman iamb and satire.[56] Dickie has shown that the iambographer, who might traditionally be accused of φθόνος/ *invidia* (envy) in his dealings with the targets of his *iambi*, was frequently at pains, particularly in passages of literary polemic, to disprove this allegation and indeed to counter-accuse his addressee of this very fault. This is a particularly interesting shared characteristic

---

[52] The sharpest indications of this are the epodic self-identifications, with of course modifications, of Callimachus with Hipponax (cf. Fraser 1972: I. 733ff.) and of Horace with Archilochus (cf. Hor. *Epist.* 1.19.23ff.; Macleod 1977, esp. 372; Macleod 1973). Cf. also Degani 1973, revised version in Degani 1977: 106–26.

[53] Dickie 1981, esp. 199f., who explores the new Cynic image of the iambographer as a champion of virtue; see also Macleod 1973; Bühler 1964.

[54] Macleod 1973: 306f; Bühler 1964: 231–47.

[55] Cf. Cairns 1978: 549f.    [56] Dickie 1981.

in the present context, since Propertius shows, by beginning 1.5 with the vocative *invide*, that the notion of *invidia* was on his mind during the composition of the linked pair, 1.4 and 1.5 (see Appendix).

These considerations lead to a modified version of Suits' theory of a 'reversal' in Propertius' description of Bassus: for, if some iambographers can be conciliatory in their approaches, if iambic writers and their opponents in other cases can share characteristics, including *invidia* and *ira*, and if curses etc. are not restricted to the iambist, then an all-out reversal may not be in play in Propertius 1.4 but rather a more subtle interaction of literary types. Something in certain respects similar appears in Propertius 1.7 and 1.9, where Propertius elegantly blends the conventional characteristics of epic and elegy and the conventional *personae* of the epic and elegiac poets: the fates are to be (elegiacally) 'soft' to Ponticus' epic (1.7.4); Propertius complains about the (epic) 'hardness' of his elegiac lovelife (1.7.8); Ponticus will weep elegiac tears for his neglected epic subject (1.7.17f.); Propertius the elegist will be classed by Ponticus higher than Roman epic poets (*Romanis praeferar ingeniis*, 'I shall be ranked above the other poets of Rome,' 1.7.22);[57] and the epic poet Ponticus will himself become a lover and will try to write elegiac love poetry (1.7), as is actually seen to happen in 1.9.

The effect of this blending technique in the literary-polemical context of 1.7 and 1.9[58] is to make elegy the touchstone of literary excellence and so to exalt it over epic. In 1.4 however, the element of literary polemic is much less prominent; in contrast to 1.7 and 1.9, where Ponticus' epic poetry is openly discussed and the epic/elegy antithesis is clear throughout, it is nowhere made explicit in 1.4 that Bassus is an iambist or that epic and elegy are in tension. Indeed, if the line of Ovid's *Tristia* which reveals Bassus as an iambist had been lost, it is doubtful whether any modern scholar could have guessed this from Propertius 1.4. But nevertheless, it is indisputable that Propertius' first readers knew who Bassus was and that Propertius is, as Suits has shown, making considerable capital out of Bassus' literary identity. The only real question in this area is why the antithesis between the two forms in 1.4 is so low-key throughout.

[57] Cf. Fedeli 1981.   [58] Cf. Macleod 1973: 307.

The answer, I believe, is that, in Hellenistic and Roman literary thought, elegy and iamb were felt to have much more in common with each other in ideals and techniques, than, for example, either had with epic or drama.[59] The most striking indication of this is that Propertius' master, Callimachus, wrote both elegy and iamb. Such highly restrained literary by-play is also, if my suggestions (§II.ii below) about the addressee of 1.5 are correct, yet another feature shared by the pair.

Suits' interpretation, modified along these lines, remains therefore a valid perception of the literary dimension of 1.4. The elegist affects to be affronted by the iambist's interference in his love-life. He responds in a number of pointed ways: looking to a stock, and deliberately restricted, image of the iambographer, he insinuates that Bassus is behaving oddly by praising instead of blaming. Propertius follows this up with the threat that Bassus will meet his match in Cynthia, whose iambic qualities surpass his own.[60] On another level, the implication that Bassus himself is not immune to girls, or indeed to Cynthia, is a notion reminiscent of the handling of Ponticus in 1.7 and 1.9, where the ultimate polemical argument is that the opponent is going to be converted to the literary form he opposes. But in 1.4 Propertius' aim is the opposite: he does not wish to deter Bassus from iamb, or to claim that elegy is superior to iamb; rather he suggests that Bassus should mind his own business and thus, by implication, his own literary form, and leave Propertius and elegy in peace.

But, literary differences apart, since Bassus is a named and living contemporary of Propertius, and was probably also his friend and poetic associate, the *persona* of Bassus in 1.4 is, not surprisingly, carefully constructed so as to cast no discredit on him as an individual. To begin with, the characterisation of Bassus not as the spiteful type of iambographer who is motivated by malice and who concentrates on criticism of others, but as one who praises other women and

---

[59] Cf. Puelma Piwonka 1949, *passim*.
[60] The partial parallelism between Prop. 1.4 and Cat. 40 with respect to iambs may be noted here (cf. also Fedeli 1981: 233.) Because Ravidus made advances to Catullus' mistress, the poet threatens him with iambs. In 1.4, of course, Propertius is threatening Bassus with iambic behaviour on Cynthia's part.

thus denigrates Cynthia only by implication, absolves him from a number of the faults of the stock iambist. Again, the indications of erotic interests on Bassus' part soften the portrait further.

However, the most substantial element in the positive representation of Bassus is the implication that Bassus has adopted the iambist's favourite stance as the defender of public morality.[61] It is Propertius who offends against Roman social values by the *nequitia* (moral worthlessness) of his *amor*—a vice which, so it was thought, withdrew a man from the proper duties of a Roman citizen to state, family life and childrearing.[62] Bassus, by praising women other than Cynthia, and thus indirectly attacking her as the object of Propertius' *amor*, is attempting to lead Propertius back to the path of virtue. Bassus' actual strategy is again typical of Roman moral thinking: he praises two classes of women, first beautiful but chaste ancient heroines, analogues of marriageable Roman citizen girls, and secondly loose women, with whom Propertius might satisfy his lusts and so save himself from *amor*. Of these alternatives, marriage was of course the basis of conventional Roman morality—and marriage for Propertius would have meant the end of his life as a love-poet.[63] As for the *vulgivaga* (promiscuous) *Venus*, Bassus is following in the footsteps of the elder Cato, that *exempla*r of Roman morality, who approved of the young man whom he saw coming out of a brothel (Horace *Sat.* 1.2.31–5) and thus commended casual sex as the morally sound alternative to marriage (and of course to love). Bassus' high moral claims are of course undercut by the implication that he is in fact interested in Cynthia, and also by the kinds of punishment he is implied to fear. But Bassus, and the reader if he so wishes, are at liberty to dismiss these suggestions as unfounded fantasies on the part of Propertius.

---

[61] Cf. Dickie 1981: 199–203, on the self-image of Hellenistic and Roman iambographers. The self-image of Archilochus and Hipponax may well have been closer to this than we can realise, given the poor press which they had in the classical Greek period.
[62] Cf. Cairns 1979a.
[63] For a survey of Roman attitudes to sex etc., cf. Lyne 1980: Ch. 1.

## II.II GALLUS

The continuous linking at every level between Propertius 1.4 and 1.5, together with the interplay between iamb and elegy in 1.4 and the exploitation in it of Bassus' role as an iambographer, naturally prompts the hypothesis that the addressee of 1.5 is also a literary man. Indeed, only on this supposition could the pairing of the elegies be regarded as ultimately meaningful. Now any suggestion about the Gallus of 1.5 automatically involves us in the long-standing debate about the identity of the men called Gallus in the Monobiblos. It is clear that there are at least two such individuals and possibly more. The Gallus of Propertius 1.21.7, a kinsman of the poet, was already dead by 41 BCE and so cannot be the same man as the Gallus of the group 1.5, 1.10 and 1.13 or the Gallus of 1.20. The Gallus of 1.20 has long been identified by the majority of scholars as the elegiac poet C. Cornelius Gallus, an older contemporary of Propertius, a friend of Virgil and of Asinius Pollio, a successful general and 'the first to be put in charge of (Alexandria and) Egypt by Caesar (the son of the god) after the conquest of the kings (by Caesar)'.[64] Of late R. Syme[65] and Paolo Fedeli[66] have opposed this identification; but the majority view seems inescapable, particularly in view of the copious presence in Propertius 1.20 of those very characteristics recently established, mainly on other grounds, by Duncan F. Kennedy as diagnostic of Gallan influence in Augustan and post-Augustan poetry.[67] The identity of the Gallus of Propertius 1.5, 1.10 and 1.13 is however still

---

[64] On Gallus in general cf. Boucher 1966 and, for the Philae inscription, 38ff. I have conflated the Greek and Roman versions to give a fuller composite of the portion translated. The new Gallus fragments were first published by Anderson, Parsons and Nisbet 1979. The identification of the Gallus of 1.20 as the poet has been upheld, e.g. by Tränkle 1960: 23; Bramble 1974b, esp. 87; Monteleone 1979, esp. 38–53.

[65] Syme 1978: 99–103, who dismisses the identification as a 'fancy' (99 n.7), offers either a Caninius Gallus or an Aelius Gallus. Propertius was indeed probably related by marriage to the Aelii Galli (3.12.1), cf. Syme 1978: 102.

[66] Fedeli 1980: 153, on 1.5; Fedeli 1981: 235f. Another strong dissenter is Du-Quesnay 1978: 276f, in his review of Ross 1975a. But Fedeli and Syme rightly insist that the addressee of all four elegies is the same man.

[67] Kennedy 1982, esp. 379f. and n.54.

highly controversial: all that seems to be agreed is that the individual concerned, whoever he is, is the same in all three poems. The view that he too is the poet C. Cornelius Gallus was first propounded in 1901 by Franz Skutsch[68] and was revived in 1943 by Luigi Alfonsi.[69] But it was only in 1975 that the powerful advocacy of David O. Ross Jr brought the view back into prominence;[70] and only since then has it begun to win adherents, notably in recent times Richard F. Thomas[71] and Joy K. King.[72]

Each fresh convert to Franz Skutsch's view has brought new arguments to support it. These are too numerous and detailed to be summarised here,[73] although I shall later direct particular attention to one of them, an etymological complex in 1.5. The demonstration that 1.4 and 1.5 are a linked pair of poems generates yet another powerful argument in favour of C. Cornelius Gallus being the addressee of 1.5. If, as hypothesised above, the linking makes full sense only on the assumption that Gallus is, like Bassus, a literary man, then we can go one stage further: on the internal evidence of 1.5 it is highly probable that Gallus is a love-elegist; and this presumption is confirmed by 1.10 and 1.13; and if the Gallus of these elegies is indeed a love-elegist, then those wishing to deny that he is to be identified as C. Cornelius Gallus would have to adopt the unlikely position that there was a second, quite distinct, Augustan love-elegist also called 'Gallus.'

In all, the steady accumulation over the last eighty years of arguments in favour of identifying the Gallus of Propertius 1.5, 1.10, and 1.13 as the poet C. Cornelius Gallus is such that it would undoubtedly

---

[68] Skutsch 1901: 144f.   [69] Alfonsi 1943, publ. 1944: 54.
[70] Ross 1975a: 67, 83f., 95 n.3, 102.   [71] Thomas 1979: 203f.
[72] King 1980a: 212–14.
[73] One point which should however be noted is the effect of this view on the interpretation of Prop. 1.10. Skutsch first observed (1906: 144f.) that, if Gallus is the poet, then 1.10 may be an account of how Propertius read Gallus' love-elegies rather than of how he witnessed his love-making; cf. also Benjamin 1965. Although *AP* 5.255 (on which cf. Fedeli 1980: 251f., 311) does seem to argue on the other side, i.e. for a tradition of poetic voyeurism, the matter is not absolutely clear and Skutsch's approach has its attractions. On voyeurism in antiquity, cf. Krenkel 1977a; Krenkel 1977b.

have prevailed universally by now but for the seemingly insuperable obstacle presented by a single couplet (1.5.23f.):

> *nec tibi nobilitas poterit succurrere amanti:*
> *nescit Amor priscis cedere imaginibus.*
> Nor will 'nobility' be able to help you as a lover: Love does not know how to defer to ancestral images.

The hexameter (23) states that 'Gallus' is *nobilis* and the pentameter (24) appears to imply that he possesses *imagines*. The poet C. Cornelius Gallus was however a provincial *eques*.[74] As such, so the argument goes, he could not possess *nobilitas* or *imagines*; therefore the Gallus of 1.5 (and hence also of 1.10 and 1.13) cannot be the poet C. Cornelius Gallus.

It is, however, time to ask whether this objection should be allowed to prevail against the many arguments in favour of the identification. To begin with *imagines* in 24: there is no doubt that this term refers quite specifically to families with curule ancestors, a group to which C. Cornelius Gallus did not belong. If *imagines* in 24 were being attributed to the addressee, as *nobilitas* is indeed attributed to him in 23, then the two terms would be identical in meaning and that would be the end of the matter: Gallus could not be the poet. But the link between hexameter and pentameter is in fact much looser; although *nobilitas* is attributed to Gallus in 23, *imagines* in 24 are not; on a literal reading they are only implied to belong to Gallus. The observation, already made by other scholars who support the identification, that the pentameter (24) is probably either a quotation from or an adaptation of a line written by C. Cornelius Gallus,[75] loosens the link further. It makes it more plausible that the couplet contains a eulogistic hiatus between the *nobilitas* actually attributed to Gallus in the hexameter and the *imagines* which, on this reading, he would merely be implied to possess in the pentameter. Thus the couplet would mean: "Your *nobilitas* won't help you as a lover: [and, after all, it was you yourself who said] Love does not defer to distinguished pedigrees."

If the link between *nobilitas* and *imagines* is not a strict one, then *nobilitas* may have a non-technical sense. *Nobilis* and *nobilitas* are in origin broad terms, attributing to someone or something the quality

---

[74] Cf. Syme 1938.    [75] Cf. Tränkle 1960: 23; Ross 1975a: 83, 95 n.3.

of being outstanding, distinguished or excellent of his, her or its kind, i.e. *notabilitas*.[76] This quality could be predicated of virtually anyone or anything: so men, as members of the upper class, or in their particular occupations, or just as men, animals of all kinds, houses and other buildings and land could all be *nobilis*. The usages of these words which refer to Roman constitutional practice would not inevitably have been foremost in the minds of Latin speakers. If the *nobilitas* attributed to Gallus is non-technical, then it could simply be equivalent to the '*magnum nomen*' (great name) of Gallus at 1.5.26, *quam cito de tanto nomine rumor eris* (how quickly from being a 'great name' will you become tittle-tattle), and it could be seen as part of the etymological play on a number of words in Propertius 1.5, which has been noted by Joy K. King (1980a: 213f.) viz. *nosse* (4), *ignotos* (5), *notam* (16), *nosse* (18) and *nomine* (26), a feature which would then extend also to *nobilitas* i.e. *notabilitas* (23). It must be emphasized that etymologizing is not an oddity or an isolated phenomenon found by chance in this elegy. Rather, as has become increasingly clear in recent years, etymology and the related area of semantics together constitute one of the most constant and important intellectual sub-structures of Roman poetry.[77] The substantial complex of etymologies within Propertius 1.5 embracing the problematic lines 23f. may be intended by Propertius as a proof of the eulogistic contention that Gallus has *nobilitas*: the proof consists in the fact that he is *notus* (known), i.e. as a poet. It can hardly be a coincidence that the poet Gallus seems himself, in his elegiac *persona*, to have made claims to be *notus*. Hermann Tränkle has suggested that Propertius 1.18.8: *nunc in amore tuo cogor habere notam*, (now I am compelled to incur a black mark in your love) derives from Gallus, which would imply a claim on Gallus' part to notoriety as an elegiac lover.[78] Gallus' claim to fame through his mistress is also implied by Ovid *Amores* 1.15.29f.:[79]

---

[76] Unfortunately *TLL s.vv. nobilis; nobilitas* has not yet appeared. On the etymology and usage cf. Walde and Hofmann 1938/1954 *s.v. nosco*; Ernout and Meillet 1939 *s.v. nosco*; Merguet 1877–84; 1887–94; 1905–6, repr. 1964 all *s.vv. nosco; nobilitas*.
[77] Cf. Cairns 1979c: Ch.4.
[78] Boucher 1966: 24.
[79] Cf. Ross 1975a: 118. The suggestion which follows about Gallus' use of a part of *noscere* I owe to Dr D.F. Kennedy, who will treat the question in a future paper.

*Gallus et Hesperiis et Gallus **notus** Eois,*
*et sua cum Gallo **nota** Lycoris erit.*

Gallus is known in the West and in the East, and with Gallus will be known his Lycoris.

and also by *Ars Amatoria* 3.537: *Vesper et Eoae novere Lycorida terrae* (the West and the lands of the East know Lycoris). It is probable, then, that Gallus used some part of *noscere* to claim fame for himself, for his love-poetry, and for his mistress through his love-poetry.

But the very proximity of *imagines* (24) to *nobilitas* (23) suggests that there may be more to the couplet. The provincial family of Cornelius Gallus probably received the name Cornelius when it was enfranchised by some second- or first-century BCE Roman general of the name. But someone may have made the name Cornelius the basis for a dubious claim on behalf of Gallus to relationship with one of the families of noble Cornelii. Such fraudulent or semi-fraudulent claims to high descent were commonplace in the Augustan period.[80] Aristocratic genealogists like Messalla Corvinus might sneer at and expose such pretensions.[81] But the profusion of ancient and noble names which suddenly reappear in the Augustan *Fasti*, many of which vanish again just as suddenly, suggests that the regime sometimes found it convenient not to look too closely at the credentials of so-called *nobiles* presenting themselves for service. We need not suppose that C. Cornelius Gallus himself pressed such claims. The contemporary appearance of fantastic claims about the descent of the Tullii and the Octavii,[82] claims which do not seem to have enchanted Cicero and Augustus, shows that the imaginations of persons other than the principals were involved in this effort. On the other hand, it cannot have been easy for great men to reject well-meant concoctions out-of-hand. In the case of Gallus, we need only suppose that one of his eulogists had put about a story which Gallus had

---

[80] Syme 1978 admits this (100) but claims in connection with Propertius 1.5 that: "For a poet to attribute falsely a noble extraction to his friend, whether equestrian (as was Cornelius Gallus) or a minor senator, would expose them both to ridicule and contempt." Much however depends on the context and the sophistication of such claims, if indeed such a claim is involved here at all. For false claims to nobility cf. Brunt 1982; Syme 1939: 376f.; Wiseman 1971: 205f.

[81] Pliny *N.H.* 35.8.     [82] Brunt 1982: 3.

not absolutely denied; and on this supposition, the troublesome couplet (1.5.23f.) becomes more readily comprehensible.

It should also be remembered that Propertius is a poet, not a historian. The late republican and Augustan practice of eulogistic, and politically opportunistic, exaggeration in matters of genealogy was not uncongenial to poets.[83] Horace could address L. Aelius Lamia as: *Aeli vetusto nobilis ab Lamo* (Aelius, of noble descent from ancient Lamus), which is at least a hyperbole (*Odes* 3.17.1); and his dedicatory address to *Maecenas atavis edite regibus* (Maecenas, descended from royal ancestors, *Odes* 1.1.1) is even more fulsome. Loose uses of *nobilis* even in the politico-social sphere are in any case more common than has sometimes been realised. Some of them have been brought out recently in a valuable paper by P. A. Brunt, which also contains useful detailed evidence.[84] Brunt shows that a *nobilis* in Roman politics can range from a man with attested consular ancestors to one who is simply 'upper-class' or 'aristocratic.' Every intermediate state appears to have qualified a Roman to be called *nobilis* in specific circumstances: being a patrician, being a descendant of a curule magistrate, being related, although not necessarily in direct line of descent, to someone who had held appropriate office, even being a *gentilis* of a 'noble' *gens*. Not all individuals in all these categories would simultaneously have been described as *nobilis* by the same speaker; but there was clearly a great deal of room for manoeuvre.

When we move to a sphere which is larger but still politico-social, that is the public life of Italy and the Roman world in the first century BCE, the possibilities multiply. Indeed nobility could be predicated of men who were not even Roman citizens.[85] Within the citizen body it could be applied to provincial Italians who were *domi nobiles* (hometown nobles), e.g. *municipio suo nobilem* (noble in his own city, Cicero *Pro Cluentio* 109, cf.196). When thinking of men's standing in Italy and in the *res publica*, Cicero found no difficulty in declaring that an *eques* was *nobilis*, particularly if he was (as was Gallus) an important man who could have entered the Senate with ease, had he so wished. So,

---

[83] Cf. Thomas 1979: 204 n.84.   [84] Brunt 1982: 11f., 15f.
[85] Cf. e.g. Merguet 1905–6 *s. v. nobilis*.

for example, Cicero *Ad Familiares* 6.6.9 tells A. Caecina of Etruria that he is *hominem in parte Italiae minime contemnenda facile omnium nobilissimum* (easily the most noble man of all in a part of Italy least to be scorned); and at an earlier point in the same letter (6.6.3) Cicero had already said that Caecina's father was *nobilissimo atque optimo viro* (a very noble and excellent man).[86]

Propertius will have derived some learned humour from his quotation of Gallus' line in such misleading circumstances. He also achieved a teasing tension between this poem and 1.14, addressed to L. Volcacius Tullus, a man both rich and from a consular family. At 1.14.8 Tullus is told *nescit Amor magnis cedere divitiis* (Love doesn't know how to defer to great riches), a variant of the same original Gallan line which lies behind 1.5.24; while Gallus himself, certainly wealthy, but lacking *imagines*, except perhaps in his eulogists' fantasies, was told *nescit Amor priscis cedere imaginibus*. This parallelism is not an isolated feature in the Monobiblos: more of its background and significance will emerge in §II.iii, where a new relationship between Propertius, Tullus and Gallus will be hypothesised.

To sum up: it is one of the curiosities of Latin scholarship that, in the face of a steady accumulation of arguments in favour of identifying the addressee of Propertius 1.5, 1.10 and 1.13 as the poet C. Cornelius Gallus, an over-literal and unimaginative interpretation of a single couplet should still hold the day. It is perhaps too much to hope that the additional arguments presented in this paper will tilt the balance. But if, quite independently of any other considerations, the linking of 1.4 and 1.5 demands that we see in 1.5, 1.10 and 1.13 an elegiac love poet contemporary with Propertius and called Gallus, then to identify him as anyone other than C. Cornelius Gallus must surely be far-fetched.

## II.III HISTORICAL PROBLEMS AND IMPLICATIONS

The identification of the Gallus of the Monobiblos as C. Cornelius Gallus has historical consequences. These however do not affect and

---

[86] Cf. Rawson 1978: 137 and n.43.

are not affected by the well-known problems of dating and interpretation in the poetic and political careers of C. Cornelius Gallus. It makes no difference to the identification, for example, whether Gallus wrote his elegies, as most scholars believe, in the forties, or whether, as has recently been suggested, he was still writing in the thirties.[87] Propertius addresses Gallus as a living contemporary and imitates his work throughout the Monobiblos, but it does not follow that the work itself is contemporary.

Similarly the relationship between Propertius and Gallus which the identification implies (see below) has no consequences for the chronology or assessment of Gallus' political career from the mid-thirties on. Conversely, the identification is not open either to chronological objections based on the length of Gallus' stay in Egypt or to the argument that if Gallus were C. Cornelius Gallus, then Propertius would inevitably have made reference to his military successes in Egypt. To deal first with the chronology and the true nature of Gallus' activities in Egypt: on grounds quite unconnected with Propertius, it is now becoming clear that Gallus' status and tenure of office in Egypt, his military activities there, and his prominent commemoration of them on the pyramids were matters of less import than they have sometimes been represented, both in modern times and in antiquity. Gallus arrived in Egypt in 30 BCE and, after helping Octavian to demolish the rump of the Antonian forces and subsequently conducting a campaign to put down insurgents and secure the frontiers of Egypt, he probably returned to Rome in 29 BCE.[88] He was thus a temporary military commander appointed by Octavian; and his position cannot really be compared with that of the later prefects, who had wider functions and longer terms. His victories, won probably in a single campaign, and their place of inscription appear to have given his enemies grounds for blackening him at Rome.[89] But the Philae inscription is more modest than it at first seems; and this was a period when other commanders were

---

[87] So recently West 1983.
[88] Some of the judgments about Gallus in this section are influenced by and in part based on Daly and Reiter 1971, a profoundly original re-examination of some of the historical problems surrounding Gallus. The attempt to de-institutionalise Gallus' role in Egypt is however my own initiative.
[89] Cf. Dio 53.23.5f.

everywhere winning much more important successes. The *terminus ante quem* for Gallus' suicide is 26 BCE, but it may well have occurred earlier, in 27 BCE, since the clash with Agrippa, which began the process of Gallus' fall, took place in late 29 or 28.[90]

Thus there is time in the poetic career of Propertius for him to have been influenced by Gallus when he was present in Rome, both before and after his stay in Egypt. The date of the Monobiblos is not certain. Camps sums up the consensus in associating it with the year 30 but notes that the composition of poems could be spread over several years.[91] Since there are datable references to 28 and 27 BCE in Book 2, the years 30–28 are the closest we can come to a date for Book 1. But earlier dates for 1.5, 1.10, 1.13 and 1.20 are not ruled out; and it could be argued, although perhaps unnecessarily, that one reason why Gallus' Egyptian successes are not hinted at in these elegies is that they were written before Gallus went to Egypt.

Our historical judgments are however altered by the identification when it comes to the question of Propertius' patrons. Propertian scholars have always regarded L. Volcacius Tullus the younger, addressed in 1.1, 1.6, 1.14, and 1.22, as Propertius' first patron. This seems a reasonable view, particularly since Tullus receives the dedicatory first poem. But if C. Cornelius Gallus, not only himself an elegiac poet of distinction but, by the late thirties and early twenties, a wealthy and powerful man, is addressed by Propertius in four other elegies of the Monobiblos, then he was presumably also an important patron of Propertius. Indeed, given that the Monobiblos is full of echoes and influence from Gallus' elegies, he may even have been *de facto* a more important patron than Tullus, deferring to Tullus as dedicatee of the first elegy partly as *eques* to senator, but partly also because his own poetry was probably echoed prominently in that very elegy.[92] The view that Tullus and Gallus were joint patrons of Propertius would help to explain the symmetrical and interlaced arrangement of the poems addressed to them in the Monobiblos. Tullus has 1, then Gallus 5. Tullus immediately follows with 6. Next Gallus has 10, virtually the middle poem, and again 13, but here

---

[90] Cf. Daly and Reiter 1971: 297 and n. 27.
[91] Cf. Camps 1961: 6f.
[92] Cf. Ross 1975a: 59–70.

followed by Tullus with 14, thus reversing the situation of 1.5 and 1.6. Gallus has 20, a major piece perhaps balancing 1 in length, but Tullus has the actual epilogue, 22, a much briefer elegy, as he had the prologue.[93] Although one strand in these juxtapositions is the conceptual contrast between Gallus the lover, his military side suppressed in favour of the lover-*persona* of his own writings, and Tullus the anti-love *vir militaris*, military man (cf. esp. 1.5 and 1.6; 1.13 and 1.14), nevertheless the consistent balancing of poems addressed to Tullus and to Gallus throughout the Monobiblos strongly suggests their joint patronage of Propertius.

Two points arise from this new understanding of Propertius' patrons in the Monobiblos: first, instead of regarding the young Propertius from Assisi as simply the protégé of the Volcacii Tulli, a family of Caesarian magnates from neighbouring Perugia,[94] we should see him in his early career as moving in a larger and more elevated social circle, which included also C. Cornelius Gallus and perhaps older friends of Gallus like Asinius Pollio, Virgil, and possibly Varius. Second, if there were other connections between the younger Tullus and C. Cornelius Gallus, which in part led them to become joint patrons of Propertius, then the political career of Tullus can be clarified. Tullus seems to have been in high favour in 30–29 BCE, when, as Propertius 1.6 reveals, he was appointed to go as praetor to Asia with a special commission,[95] around the time when Gallus too was at the height of his power. But Tullus' career, for reasons which have never been explained, seems to have stuck at this point: he was not recalled from Asia until six to nine years later. Of course Tullus' consular uncle may have died in the meantime, thus diminishing the family's influence; and Tullus himself may have been less ambitious than 1.6 implies. But if the Volcacii Tulli were associates of Cornelius

---

[93] Such considerations are of course hampered by the problematic elegy 21, on which cf. Fedeli 1980: 485ff.

[94] The denial by Hubbard 1974: 25 that the Volcacii had links with Perugia was rightly set aside by Rawson 1978: 150. The convention operating in Prop. 1.21.1f., i.e. the fictional enquiry (for which cf. Cat. 7.1 with Kroll 1923 *ad loc.*; Hor. *Epod.* 14.5; Cairns 1972: 248 n. 31)—for Tullus certainly did not need to ask his protégé Propertius about his place of origin—is being continued in the equally fictional doubt of *si*, etc. (1.21.2).

[95] Cf. Cairns 1974a.

Gallus, then it is easier to see why, after Gallus' fall, the younger Tullus should have been neglected by Augustus and left to languish in Asia far from Rome.

The unexpected appearance of Maecenas in the first elegy of Book 2 is also now more readily explicable. Book 2 probably appeared in 26–25 BCE;[96] with Gallus dead and Tullus in Asia, Propertius would have needed a new patron; and he would perhaps have been all the more eager to show his loyalty to Augustus by entering Maecenas' circle if the loyalty of his former patrons was now suspect.[97] Again, if Tullus himself had been politically compromised by association with Gallus, this makes it easier to understand why Tullus relinquished his residual rights over Propertius to Maecenas. Propertius 3.22, which finally recalls Tullus to Rome in 24–21 BCE, could in these terms be seen both as a gracious gesture of repayment by Maecenas to Tullus for releasing Propertius to him, and as a public indication that Tullus was now forgiven, at least to the extent of being allowed to return to Italy.

## II.IV LITERARY PROBLEMS AND IMPLICATIONS

First, a minor point arising from the identification of the Gallus of 1.5, 1.10, and 1.13, as well as the Gallus of 1.20, with C. Cornelius Gallus. I argued above (§II. i) that the restraint in the literary by-play of 1.4 is due to the fact that iamb and elegy were kindred forms for Hellenistic and Roman writers; a *fortiori*, if in 1.5 Gallus, like Propertius, is a love-elegist, this explains why the literary by-play of 1.5 is even more restrained and why Propertius is, in effect, telling Gallus to stick to his own mistress. Propertius, recognising Gallus's superiority as an elegist to himself, is simply concerned with deterring Gallus from interesting himself in Cynthia, since he knows that he would lose her to Gallus if Gallus made any effort to win her. It must be remembered in this connection that Gallus' elegiac poetry was the

---

[96] Cf. Camps 1967: 1.
[97] His links with the Aelii Galli if, as is probable, they were already established at this time, may have been helpful in this connection. Maecenas was interestingly, like the Volcacii Tulli, Etruscan.

model for that of Propertius, so that Gallus is in a real sense Propertius' literary master.

On another level Propertius is exploiting the *personae* of his two patrons, Gallus and Tullus, along with his own *persona*, to create contrasts between the stock figures of the lover and the *vir militaris*. Propertius and Gallus both appear as lovers, but there is a marked difference between their success in love: Propertius is conspicuously lacking in it, while Gallus is portrayed as successful in love in all four poems of the Monobiblos in which he appears, with the possible exception of the last (1.20), which concerns his homosexual affair. Success is a factor differentiating Tullus and Propertius too, although in a more general way (cf. esp. 1.6 and 1.14); and these contrasts reflect their relationship as patron and poet. But the portrayal of Gallus as a successful lover, contrasting with both Tullus the *vir militaris* and Propertius the unsuccessful lover, poses problems requiring further comment. First, from Virgil *Eclogue* 10 and the first line of the new Gallus fragment in particular, it would seem that lack of success in love was a strong element in the self-portrayal of Gallus in his own work. Second, Gallus was an experienced military man and possibly, if the poems addressed to him do date from 30 BCE on, a recent victor in Egypt; but nowhere in the Monobiblos is there even a hint that he is a soldier, much less of achievements in Egypt. In contrast Tullus, who is really going off to the peaceful province of Asia, is writ large as a *vir militaris*.

The latter problem is perhaps easier to tackle first. It may well be that Gallus in his own work adopted exclusively a lover-*persona*, and that Propertius decided to retain this *persona*, particularly since the *eques* Gallus was to be praised so often in the proximity of the senator Tullus, whom he could so easily have overshadowed, if other aspects of his real character had been introduced. But if this concept answers the second problem, it only intensifies the first, namely Gallus' hypothesized lack of success in love in his own poetry and his great success as a lover in the poetry of Propertius. Here, it seems, Propertius must deliberately be reversing one aspect of Gallus' *persona*. Such a practice is not out of the question. Ancient poets do seem deliberately to have altered some aspects of the poetic *personae* of other poets when they wrote about them. So the Gallus of *Eclogue* 10 is generally regarded as being a bucolicised version of the real elegist;

and equally the Virgil of the *Eclogues* is transmuted into a love-elegist by the elegiac setting in which he appears in Propertius 2.34.67–76.

These examples however involve adaptations of *personae* to new contexts, not reversals of them. Much more striking, and for that reason deserving greater emphasis in the present context, are the two different and mutually inconsistent portaits of Tibullus offered by Horace:[98]

> *Albi, nostrorum sermonum candide iudex,*
> *quid nunc te dicam facere in regione Pedana?*
> *scribere quod Cassi Parmensis opuscula vincat,*
> *an tacitum silvas inter reptare salubris,*
> *curantem quidquid dignum sapiente bonoque est?*
> *non tu corpus eras sine pectore. di tibi formam,*
> *di tibi divitias dederunt artemque fruendi.*
> *quid voveat dulci nutricula maius alumno,*
> *qui sapere et fari possit quae sentiat, et cui*
> *gratia, fama, valetudo contingat abunde,*
> *et mundus victus non deficiente crumina?*
> *inter spem curamque, timores inter et iras,*
> *omnem crede diem tibi diluxisse supremam.*
> *grata superveniet quae non sperabitur hora.*
> *me pinguem et nitidum bene curata cute vises*
> *cum ridere voles Epicuri de grege porcum.*

Albius, impartial judge of my *Satires*, what shall I say you are up to now in the Pedum area? Writing something to surpass the trifles of Cassius of Parma? Or strolling silently amid the health-giving woods, intent on whatever is worthy of a 'wise good man'? You have never been a body lacking a mind. The gods have given you good looks, they have given you riches and knowledge of how to enjoy them. What greater blessing could a nurse wish for her dear charge than that he think aright and be able to express his thoughts, and possess in abundance influence, reputation, and good heath—along with a decent mode of life and resources that do not fail him? Amidst hope and care, amidst fears and rages, assume that every day that dawns is your last: the unhoped-for hour will come as an extra pleasure. You should come and see me when you want a laugh, a pig from the herd of Epicurus, fat and sleek and in good condition.
(*Epistles* 1.4)

---

[98] On these passages see, most recently, Dilke 1982.

*Albi, ne doleas plus nimio memor
immitis Glycerae neu miserabilis
decantes elegos, cur tibi iunior
   laesa praeniteat fide.*

Albus, don't grieve too much when you remember cruel Glycera, and don't sing pitiful elegies, because, your bond broken, a younger man outshines you. (*Odes* 1.33.1–4)

The more detailed *Epistles* 1.4 describes Tibullus as *nostrorum sermonum candide iudex* (1), says that his poetry is to surpass that of Cassius of Parma (3) and that he walks in the woods thinking about moral philosophy (5). Then Horace goes on to allege that Tibullus has all the internal and external goods, including a fine appearance, wealth, influence, fame and health (6–11). Horace recommends that he should enjoy each day as it comes (12–14). The portrait is so unlike the Tibullus of the elegies as to raise initial scepticism about the identity of *Albi* (1). But Albius is indeed Tibullus; and Horace is employing complex irony: most obviously the wealth attributed to Tibullus contradicts the *paupertas* (poverty) which he claimed, notably in his programmatic first elegy (esp. 1.1.1–4); his 'health' negates the morbid Tibullus 1.3, where the sick elegist contemplated imminent death. Horace has the same elegy in mind when he speaks of death to Tibullus (12–14), but only does so as an incentive to enjoyment. The *gratia* and *fama* of *Epistles* 1.4.10 combat the image of Tibullus, particularly in 1.10 and 2.1, as a humble and helpless dependant of Messalla; his walks in the woods while philosophising stand in opposition to his own descriptions of manual labour in the fields, both pleasant (1.1 and 1.5.21–34, the latter passage however a fantasy) and unpleasant (2.3), while occupied with thoughts of love. As for Tibullus being a *iudex* (1) of poetry, he is distinguished in his own work from Propertius precisely by his conspicuous rejection of the kinds of literary polemic which require the naming and assessment of other poets;[99] and as for

---

[99] Tibullus 2.6 would be an exception, if it were addressed to the epic poet Pompeius Macer, as is claimed by O'Neil 1967; it would be doubly exceptional if Macer's project of going off to war were indeed a metaphor for writing epic, as O'Neil further asserts.

Cassius of Parma, it is hard to believe that contemporaries really saw him as a significant predecessor for Tibullus.

How then are we to assess this portrait? It may well be more realistic in some particulars than the elegiac *persona* of Tibullus, although this can only be suspected. Some elements of it are clearly eulogistic, including those which do not seem to contradict the elegiac *persona*, viz. good looks and country living. There are also implied elements of literary polemic; and the philosophic concerns of Horace's *Epistles* have clearly been allowed to influence the sketch of Tibullus as a philosopher. But some remaining distortions may simply be humour on Horace's part. The second and briefer description of Tibullus in *Odes* 1.33.1–4 offers a different mix of truth and distortion. Here Tibullus is allowed to remain an elegiac lover; but the mistress named *inmitis Glycera* is absent from Tibullan elegy, unless this is an allusion to Nemesis; the lachrymose nature of Tibullus' elegy is exaggerated in a polemical flourish based on the etymology of *elegia*; and most striking of all, Tibullus is said to have lost his mistress to a younger rival, when the standard pattern in Tibullan elegy is for the rival to be richer than Tibullus. Thus some, but not all, of the same motives for distortion can be detected.

The representation of Gallus in the Monobiblos as successful in love and interested in Cynthia may therefore belong to the same type of misrepresentation of one poet by another; and again the motives are not fully clear. But the phenomenon leaves us in the same state with Gallus as with Bassus. Just as we can draw no conclusions about the nature or contents of Bassus' iambs from 1.4, partly because deliberate falsifications may be present there and partly because of the elegiac gloss given to Bassus by 1.4, so Gallus and his work may have been similarly affected in 1.5. For such reasons I would not wish to suggest that Propertius 1.5, 1.10, 1.13, and 1.20 necessarily allude to passages of Gallus' *Amores* in which Gallus interfered in other peoples' love affairs, attempted to steal other peoples' mistresses, played the excluded lover along with a friend, was a successful lover who sometimes abused the feelings of girls, and felt homosexual love for a boy called Hylas. Of course no one would be in the least surprised if new fragments of the *Amores* revealed all those themes. But to make any such deductions from the Monobiblos would be extremely perilous. Propertius may, after all, when he hints at any or all of these themes, be reversing polemically features of Gallus' *persona* in his *Amores*, as he seems to have altered certain features of Bassus' iambic *persona* in 1.4. At all events the portrait of Gallus in 1.5 contrasts piquantly with his representation in *Eclogue* 10 as the unsuccessful lover in that same lover/beloved/*miles* (soldier) triangle which also lies behind Propertius 1.8.

As well as polemical revisions, encomiastic alterations are a possibility: just as his other patron, the younger Tullus, is declared by Propertius to be anti-love (though we have no reason to think that he actually was) in order to make him seem morally superior to Propertius, so Gallus' success in love, revealed explicitly in 1.10 and 1.13, and implied by his capacity to interfere in Propertius' love-life in 1.5, may be a sheer invention by Propertius designed to show Gallus' superiority to himself as a lover. The encomium involved is subtle and is aimed at Gallus *qua* poet: the main (fictional) aim of a love-elegist is to be successful in his love, and specifically to achieve that success through his poetry; the representation of Gallus as a successful lover thus implicitly constitutes praise of his elegiac love-poetry, which is evidently superior to that of Propertius since Propertius is, as yet, unsuccessful in love. Another possibility, not necessarily inconsistent with the other suggestions made, is that concepts like that of Gallus' desire to interfere in Propertius' love-life, or that of Gallus ending up as a fellow excluded lover with Propertius, may simply be metaphors, expressing the closeness of their literary interests. All this does not rule out the possibility that Propertius 1.4 and 1.5 may be more heavily influenced by the style of Gallus than we are able at present to detect. In addition to 1.5.25 and the *nosco* complex, Gallan traits may be seen in *a* (13) and *medicina* (medicine, 28).[100] The fact that those stylistic features so far associated with Gallus on other evidence[101] are found more copiously in 1.20 than in 1.5, 1.10, and 1.13 could have a number of explanations.[102]

To compensate for this caution in the handling of specific themes which might be thought to be Gallan, a caution for which I make no

---

[100] Cf. Ross 1975a: 66f., 73.   [101] Cf. Kennedy 1982.

[102] One is suggested below; others might involve supposing pastiche of Gallus in 1.20 or/and deliberate avoidance of some features of Gallus' style in 1.5, 1.10, and 1.13.

apology, I end by stressing two more general, and perhaps safer, literary conclusions. First, Propertius 1.5, 1.10, and 1.13 do seem on the whole to confirm our present (1983) picture of a Gallus who wrote some 'subjective' erotic elegies as well as objective, mythological elegies.[103] Second, since the stylistic indications of Propertius 1.5, 1.10, and 1.13 are different from those of Propertius 1.20 and the other texts known to date to have been influenced by Gallus, there may have been greater stylistic variation within Gallus' work than we might have anticipated.

## APPENDIX: THE DELAYED IDENTIFICATION OF GALLUS IN 1.5

It was remarked above (p.156) that, whereas Bassus is named at the first line of 1.4, Gallus is identified only in the second to last line of 1.5, i.e. 31. The delayed identification of individuals, both real and mythical, goes back to early Greek lyric and is a common feature of ancient poetry.[104] It gave the audience the double pleasure of guessing the identity of the individual and then being proved right. In 1.5 something like this may have been involved: the readers were expected to conjecture the identity of Gallus from reminiscences of his work within 1.5, before having their conjecture confirmed at 1.5.31. Given that Gallan elegy was so well-known, this seems a likely view. The early identification of Bassus in 1.4 is not a counter argument: as far as we know, Bassus' iambs did not enjoy similar popularity and allusion to them would probably not have so easily been recognised.

But one feature of 1.5 raises further questions, the vocative *invide* at line 1. Since *invidia* was conventionally associated with 'anti-Callimachean' literary stances and with iambographers (see above, p.164) and given that only the latter association is meaningful in this

---

[103] This conclusion, which is of course an old one, was accepted in Cairns 1979c: 226f. (written without foreknowledge of the new Gallus fragments). The conclusion was of course confirmed by them when they appeared—cf. Anderson, Parsons, and Nisbet 1979.
[104] Cf. Cairns 1979c: 156.

context, we might well wonder if one of the species of 'deception' common in ancient poetry[105] is in play here: could Propertius be trying to deceive the reader into thinking that the addressee of 1.5 is an iambographer, who in this situation could only be Bassus? Or should we simply regard *invide* as another of the many verbal and conceptual links shared by 1.4 and 1.5? Since we do not know how individual poems making up a book were recited by the poet, or read by or to a reader, or what expectations an ancient audience had about the as yet unidentified addressee of a single poem within a book, no firm answers can be given. These questions should however be kept in mind, since, if any reader did have to wait until 1.5.31 to learn who was being addressed, he would have been both deceived, and yet untroubled, by 1.5.23f.

## POSTSCRIPT

This paper of 1984 appears to have played a part in accelerating the previously slow-paced acceptance of the role and presence of Cornelius Gallus in Propertius' *Monobiblos*. Intermediate bibliography which reveals this growing trend is noted at the beginning of Chapter 3 of my *Sextus Propertius: The Augustan Elegist* (Cambridge University Press 2006), reprinted in paperback 2009. Five of the twelve chapters of that monograph were devoted to following up in force the positions advanced in this paper. Chapters 3 and 4 sought to contextualize Cornelius Gallus within the historical framework of Propertius' career, and to provide criteria for detecting Gallan influence on Propertius' elegies in the form of numerous Gallan terms, motifs and themes (this material can also be referenced via the 'Index of Gallan words and concepts' at pp.483-7). Chapters 5 and 6 offered and worked through a new hypothesis about Gallan metrical features in the works of Propertius, while Chapter 7 analysed Elegy 1.20 as the product of the combined influence of Gallus himself and of one of his Greek sources, who is most likely to have been his mentor Parthenius.

---

[105] Cf. Cairns 1979c: Ch. 7.

7

# Propertius and the Unity of the Book[1]

## G. O. Hutchinson

How, in books of Roman poetry, are poems related to each other and to the book as a whole? The question is approached with divergent preconceptions. On the one hand, many assume that the design of a book will be symmetrical, and should be represented in a diagram.[2] In such a scheme, every connection must be plausible—which is never the case; and it must be supposed that ancient readers were given to making diagrams, through which alone such symmetry can be perceived. It is also remarkable how seldom such schemes illuminate the most salient questions about the books. Thus in Book I of Propertius it is the last three poems whose presence most needs to be explained. Skutsch detaches them from his scheme and refers to them as a 'coda or superstructure.'

On the other hand, it is often assumed that the individual poems in a book were written and finished before the poet considered how to order them: the arrangement was not a random process, but it was wholly distinct and secondary.[3] This idea is by no means self-evident; it seems to derive from the practice of modern poets, such as Housman.[4]

---

[1] Editors' note: The translations in this paper are all Hutchinson's own.
[2] So, in Propertius, O. Skutsch 1963: 238; Woolley 1967; Nethercut 1968; Juhnke 1971; Wille 1983, *et al.* But not even Homer has escaped.
[3] So e.g. G. Williams 1968: 177 and 1969: 23: 'Horace... collected the first six so-called "Roman Odes" at the beginning...'; Nisbet and Hubbard 1978: 6.
[4] See Housman, *Letters*, 197, 15 June 1922 (= Burnett 2007: 498). It is notable, however, that until he knows for certain which poems are to be included, he wishes all to be printed purely according to metre, and only later transposed into the quite different arrangement which he will then be able to devise.

Some poems plainly defy this conception. Propertius 1.9, for example (*Dicebam tibi venturos, irrisor, amores,* I said that love would come to you, you scoffer), cannot have been composed without a thought of 1.7, which it takes up explicitly. 3.5 must have been written to follow 3.4. Not only is there a pointed contrast between the opening words of each (*Arma deus Caesar*; *Pacis Amor deus est*, The god Caesar [is planning] war; Love is a god of peace), and between their final couplets; the reference at the end of poem 5 to the ensigns of Crassus (47f.) would seem intolerably abrupt if 3.4 had not been read first.[5] The assumption that the arrangement of the poems in a book was a distinct and secondary process, then, must certainly be abandoned sometimes. Hence, where it appears plausible that poems are connected otherwise than by subsequent collocation, the assumption can furnish no defence.

The question of plausibility is not a simple one. Even works which are moderate in their general approach make much of correspondences which I find strained.[6] Yet the matter is not wholly arbitrary. It is possible to emphasize the nature of reading in Rome, and to confine oneself to connections which could be apprehended readily, and yet to find in the Latin poets much satisfactory evidence for primary connections between poem and poem and between poem and book. The immediate object of this paper is to remove some of the obstacles which impede us from seeing two books of Propertius as real and significant unities. I hope, however, that the attempt will suggest the general importance of this area of study. Meaning—it will be insinuated—is not always confined within the individual poem: a part of the poet's meaning can be contained in the relations between the poems in a book. To miss this aspect will then be to miss the fullness of his sense.

---

[5] The contrasts prevent us from regarding the two as a single poem. On the other hand, it is most improbable that two originally unconnected poems were adapted to make a pair. Such a compromise is perhaps possible, though never preferable, elsewhere; it would not materially affect the case of this paper. My concern is not with biography but with intentions as manifested in the books: it matters less whether those intentions operated in the production of a first or of a final version of each poem. But, in this particular area, the importance of intentions of some kind is not to be denied.

[6] See, in particular, Burck 1966. He still gives more weight to numerical structures than I should care to; so too does Becker 1955, on the *Eclogues*.

Such a belief would be hard to reconcile with either of the approaches outlined above. One would be obliged to search for meaning either in a symmetrical pattern,[7] or in an assemblage of poems produced in isolation. Furthermore, adherents of the first view ought to regard as insignificant connections between poems which do not accord with their scheme. Adherents of the second view sometimes treat such matters with a scorn which the view itself does not necessarily demand.[8] If my own view is correct, this area of enquiry is not to be separated from the interpretation of the poetry.

For the student of the Golden Age of Latin poetry, the reading of books is a particularly important subject. It is commonly misrepresented, through romantic preconceptions about oral culture.[9] Even in the fifth century BCE books were read far more than is frequently assumed. 'Do you so despise the jury,' Plato makes Socrates ask, 'do you suppose them to be so $\mathring{a}\pi\epsilon\acute{\iota}\rho o\nu s$ $\gamma\rho a\mu\mu\acute{a}\tau\omega\nu$ (unfamiliar with letters) that they do not know that the books of Anaxagoras are full of such notions?' (*Ap.* 26d). However ironic this may be, the surface meaning must still bear considerable implications. Even dramas were read.[10] Nonetheless, poetic texts were largely collections of material designed primarily for performance. The Hellenistic poets, however, wrote to be read: the belief that Callimachus' *Hymns* were performed at festivals ought not to survive a perusal of the fifth or even the first. As a consequence, the *Aetia* and the *Argonautica* are designed in terms of the books into which they were physically divided; the brilliant structure of the latter remains largely neglected. Yet as a rule the poets represent themselves as singers, and their poems as songs. Thus Apollonius, in wishing for the immortality of his poem, prays that his 'songs' will grow ever sweeter for men 'to sing' (4.1773–5).

---

[7] A gallant attempt is made by Otis 1965.

[8] 'Minimal literary relevance,' G. Williams 1968: 23; 'trivialities,' Nisbet and Hubbard 1970: xxiii (in their second volume they are less forthright).

[9] See e.g. E. J. Kenney in the first paragraph of the *Cambridge History of Classical Literature* II (1982): 'In some respects... the literary life of Greece and Rome retained the characteristics of an oral culture... nearly all the books discussed in this history were written to be listened to.'

[10] In the second edition of the *Clouds*, for readers, Aristophanes exceeds the limits of the stage: thus at the end the school is burnt down, and there are five speakers (*contra* the edition of Dover, 1970: 266f.).

The Romans make it clear that they write for readers, and they often refer to their works as books. Catullus addresses any readers who may set their hands *nobis* (on me), that is, the scroll of his poems (14b). He begins his book of *nugae* (trifles) by contemplating the physical appearance of the *libellus* (book/little book). Propertius intends his books to be read by the neglected lover (1.7.13), to be read by the girl waiting alone for her man (3.3.20); his first book was read all over the Forum (2.24a.2). Readers were expected to start at the beginning and read through to the end, not to dip at random.[11] So in the *Eclogues* 4.1 *Sicelides Musae, paulo maiora canamus* (Sicilian Muses, let us sing of something a little grander) makes sense only in relation to the preceding poems; *Eclogue* 10 is marked out as the *extremum... laborem* (final effort); presumably the first paragraph of *Eclogue* 6 is displaced from the opening of the book as a deliberate surprise, and was intended to be read after *Eclogues* 1–5. Horace begins the tenth satire of his first book with a direct reference to the fourth: *Nempe... dixi* (I did indeed say);[12] this would puzzle the reader who dipped. The most striking passage of this kind in Propertius is 2.10.1f.: *Sed tempus lustrare aliis Helicona choreis,/et campum Haemonio iam dare tempus equo.* (But it is now time to circle round Helicon with dances of a different kind, and to allow the Thessalian horse the field.) The poet assumes that poems 1a–9 have just been read.[13] *Sed tempus*, and *iam* are used as they are at the end of *Georgics* 2.[14] It is now widely held, to be sure, that these words begin a new book. However, the words 'But now it is time to sing in another vein' demand imperiously that something should precede them.[15] Since the language of the authors indicates that a book would be read, and read consecutively, it need not be anachronistic or impractical to

---

[11] Contrast G. Williams 1968: 177.   [12] Fraenkel 1964.
[13] With Ribbeck 1885, I divide 2.1 into 1a and 1b (47–78).
[14] *Sed nos immensum spatiis confecimus aequor,/et iam tempus equum fumantia solvere colla* (But I have travelled over a plain immeasurable in expanse, and it is now time to release my horses' steaming necks.)
[15] Skutsch 1975: 230f. For this, the ἀλλά (but) at Tyrt. fr. 11.1 and fr. 10.15 would be a most doubtful parallel, even if fr.11 (transmitted by Stobaeus) were known to be a complete poem, and if fr.10 (despite Lycurgus) were known to be two. I suggest that fr.10.13f. are interpolated.

suppose that a Roman could notice relations between parts and the whole, or between different parts. On the contrary, the environment is propitious and encouraging.

In Book 4 we are forced to consider the relation of whole and parts by the book itself. In the first poem Propertius proposes to sing of Roman rituals and antiquities. He is then told by an astrologer that this plan runs contrary to the will of Apollo, and is reminded of Apollo's pronouncement that he should and would be a poet of love. The book itself contains four aetiological poems (2, 4, 9, 10), two poems on Cynthia (7, 8), poems on Actium (6), on the dead Cornelia Lepidi (11), and on a bawd (5), and a letter from a wife to her husband on campaign (3). The second half of poem 1 makes it surprising that any aetiological poems, and that only two poems on Cynthia, should appear in the rest of the book; the whole poem obliges us to expect more homogeneity in the book than we seem at first sight to find. To this last problem various solutions have been offered. The book is usually divided into aetiological poems and love-poems.[16] This attempt to deal with the non-aetiological poems is by no means convincing. In particular, the poem on Cornelia (11) cannot be accommodated satisfactorily into the scheme. While 3 is a letter from a loving wife, it is not a love-poem in the sense suggested by Apollo's speech (1.135ff.): it does not express the love of the poet.[17] It has also been suggested, on the other hand, that the book really is a collection of bits and pieces. It combines parts of an unfinished *Aetia*, some miscellaneous matter, and the topical poems on Actium and Cornelia which prompted the publication of the whole.[18] Thus the prologue to that *Aetia* has been retained as the first part of the prologue to Book 4, but has been followed by a section which contradicts it. This would be a very odd way to unite

---

[16] e.g. Dieterich 1911: 190f.; Grimal 1953: 46; Burck 1966: 408; Macleod 1976: 146.

[17] W. A. Camps classifies 3, 5, 7, and 8 more tentatively: 'a miscellany, but all in varying degrees related to the love theme which was the poet's earlier preoccupation' (p. 3 of his edition, 1965). This smooth formulation in part conceals, in part ignores, the problems that are raised by poem 1.

[18] M. Hubbard 1974: 116f.

the new collection, and the hypothesis does not bring us any closer to understanding the book that we possess.[19]

We may arrive at a more cohesive—and therefore a more satisfactory—conception of the book if we divide the poems between Rome in its beginnings and Rome in the poet's own day. Those poems in which Propertius is a character (5, 7, 8) of necessity belong to his own time. In each of them the poet carefully brings in Rome and the flavour of modern life, luxurious and cosmopolitan. So 5.11 *Collinas*, 52 *Foro*, 7.15 *Suburae*, 8.1 *Esquilias*, 29, *Aventinae*, 31 *Tarpeios*, 75f. *Pompeia . . . umbra* (the shade of Pompey's porticoes), *Forum*. In 5 we have much stress on modern luxuries, and we find the cult of Isis;[20] 7 is much concerned with Cynthia's household; in 8 we have a musician from Egypt and a dwarf, a theatre, and a *lectica* (litter with curtains). The poems on the battle of Actium and on the daughter of Scribonia (6, 11) require no comment. Of 3, the letter of Arethusa to her husband, H. Haffter has written, 'Fast zeitlos und wenig in römischer Situation beheimatet ist die Liebe dieses Paares.' (The love of this couple is almost timeless, and is not really embedded in a Roman setting.)[21] This is misleading. The contemporary and Roman setting is precisely marked. The mention of the *hasta pura* in line 68 shows the class of the young Lycotas.[22] It is in the winter that Arethusa expects to see him again (42): compare Suetonius, *DA* 24. The campaigns he is involved in are much like those that the poets imagine for Augustus. For our purpose it scarcely matters that some of the places mentioned are (to modern readers) implausibly

---

[19] It is doubtful whether *dies* (days) in 1.69 (*sacra diesque canam et cognomina prisca locorum*, I will sing of rites and days and the ancient names of places) gives evidence of an intention which would have been executed in the projected *Aetia*. *Dies* takes its sense from the context, and denotes *dies festi* (festival days): it is almost a synonym for *sacra*. The aetiological poems do not in fact explain directly any festivals of the state (although the festival of the Bona Dea is dwelt on in 9). But the phrase, in its context, gives an adequate notion of the type of poem in question. Programmatic statements need not be rigorously precise if this suits the dramatic or rhetorical purpose of the writer (cf. Russell 1981). Propertius wishes to stress his patriotism and his proximity to Callimachus.
[20] In the Rome of old *nulli cura fuit externos quaerere divos* (no one was concerned to seek out foreign gods, 4. 1.17).
[21] Haffter 1975: 163    [22] See Maxfield 1981: 85.

remote.[23] That the sentiment is un-Roman, no one would aver who bore in mind Cicero's letters to his wife from exile.[24]

The contrast between the two ages is the subject of the first 38 lines of poem 1.[25] The long chain of variations is closed with: *nil patrium nisi nomen habet Romanus alumnus;/sanguinis altricem non putet*[26] *esse lupam* (the offspring of Rome has nothing of his ancestry but the name; he would not think it was a she-wolf that nursed his blood). The aetiological poems themselves lay much weight on the antithesis, and in doing so often remind us of that opening section.[27] However, some of the elegies make unexpected links between the past and the present and between the two classes of poem. 8 begins with the modern Esquiline,[28] beautified by Maecenas (*novis... agris*, new... fields), filled with distributing stations for aqueducts (*aquosis*, watery), and inhabited by Propertius (3.23.24). The time is *hac nocte* (this night). We then proceed abruptly to an ancient rite, which is described for twelve lines before Cynthia suddenly appears. The rest of the poem is devoted to the happenings of the night. For his account of Tarpeia in poem 4, Propertius chooses or invents a version in which love, not avarice, drives her to betray the Capitol to Tatius.[29] This connects 4 with the 'modern' poems, in several of which love plays an important part. Probably the poem bears a particularly close relation to the poem which precedes it. Burck has already brought out the striking resemblances between them, not only in general situation but in detail.[30] Yet he does not emphasize

---

[23] See Syme 1978: 187f.
[24] *Fam.* XIV. 1–4 = 6–9 SB. Note especially the passion of XIV. 4.1 (cf. Prop. 4.3.6), 2.2; the tears of 3.1 (cf. Prop. 4.3.4), and elsewhere; Terentia's piety in 4.1 (cf. Prop. 4.3.57).
[25] These lines will be inspired by Tib. 2.5, as has long been recognized.
[26] *putat* recc. P's *pudet*, which Fedeli 1965 accepts, is clearly inappropriate. One might, however, have expected *quis* in place of *non*: might *non* have come from *nomen* above it?
[27] See especially 4.9.3f. (cf. 1.3f.), 5f., 19f.; 4.4.9–14, 73–8 (cf. 1.20f.—note also *Tarpeius pater* [father Jupiter of the Tarpeian rock] at 1.7): 4.10.18 (cf. 1.10), 25f., 27–30 (cf. 1.34f.?); 4.2.59f. (cf. 1.21, 5; in 2.60 one should perhaps read for *grata* [pleasing] the *parva* [small] suggested by a friend of Camps).
[28] See Platner-Ashby 1929: 203, 269.
[29] See Plut., *Rom.* 17, Lloyd-Jones and Parsons 1983, no. 724; *RE* IV A 2331ff., Hubbard 1974: 119f.
[30] Burck 1966: 422f.; the contrast had been noted by Celentano 1956: 55.

sufficiently the moral antithesis between the longing of the wife for her husband in 3 and the longing of the Vestal Virgin for the leader of the enemy in 4. The *fax* of Arethusa's passion for her husband is fanned by Venus herself (3.50). The *faces* of Tarpeia's monstrous desire are increased—with an alarming paradox—by the virgin Vesta (4.70). On her wedding-night Arethusa was becomingly modest (3.12). Tarpeia looks forward to that occasion with shocking (and amusing) sensuality (4.57–60). Both the ancient and the modern Roman love; but the love of the modern is proper and admirable, that of the ancient wicked to the last degree. The contrast pleasingly reverses expectation.

It has often been suggested that their position gives a particular emphasis to the central and the final poem (6 and 11).[31] Both these poems evince true and solid connections between the present and the past. In 6 Propertius stresses that the battle of Actium is a modern event and dwells on Augustus' temple to Apollo Actius (11, 67), which stands where once Evander's cattle lay (1.3f.). Yet Augustus is 'from' Alba Longa, and excels his Trojan ancestors (6.37f., cf. 1.35, 39ff.). The Egyptian fleet is condemned by the Trojan Quirinus (21f.); the augury of Romulus on the Palatine embraced this moment (43); the Roman standards are *signa Remi* (Remus' [Romulus'] standards, 80). By his race, and by his deliverance of the ancient city, Augustus stands in direct connection with the past. Both by her lineage and by the nobility of her nature, Cornelia, in poem 11, displays a profound continuity with the past of Rome. The whole of her central speech is devoted to this subject (29–62, with 63–72): note especially 43f., 47: *mi natura dedit leges a sanguine ductas* (to me nature gave laws that were drunk in from my blood). The theme is introduced early (11f.) and the poem closes with it (101f.).[32] The two elements which had mostly been contrasted, or paradoxically conjoined, are here brought to a satisfying unity.

We must now return to the problems raised by poem 1.[33] The interruption of Horos is a complete surprise: editors should not spoil

---

[31] Dieterich 1911: 191, etc.
[32] With Heinsius's *avis*, generally and rightly accepted. The *honoratis... aquis* of the MSS is incredible.
[33] The most important discussion of the poem is Macleod's, 1976.

it by inserting 'PROPERTIVS' and an inverted comma at the beginning of the poem.[34] Horos opposes explicitly the concerns of the first part, and his account of his successes (89–102) sets us abruptly in modern Rome. He thus conveys dramatically and forcefully the contrast between the two areas of the book. It is not the god Apollo who breaks in on the poet; it is a Babylonian astrologer, who professes to know his will. This surprise (again rather spoiled by the 'HOROS' of the editors) makes it more acceptable that the book should in fact contain αἴτια (aetiological accounts) after all.[35] Nonetheless, poem 2, on the Etruscan deity Vertumnus, is intended to startle. So, at first, is 3.4 '*Arma deus Caesar*' (The god Caesar [is planning] war): in the previous poem Propertius had been warned by the Muse and Apollo to sing of love, not Roman arms.

More puzzling, and deliberately more puzzling, is the speech made by Apollo at the beginning of the poet's career. Here the god commands the poet to write elegies, rather than martial epic (the usual genre to be renounced).[36] The poet's war will be love; one girl, Cynthia, will always have mastery over him. It is plainly implied— though not stated—that what Propertius must write is love-poetry. The reader will not be expecting what follows: five poems (2–6), only one of which (poem 5) could even possibly make reference to Cynthia. Poem 7 finally explains. Cynthia has died: her reign over his earthly life, and over his poetry, has ceased (93, 50). She commands him (77f.):

---

[34] We have long forgotten the *hospes* of the opening, who, as has often been realized, is simply a bold extension of the device used in epigrams on objects seen (cf. Alcaeus, *A. P.* IX 588 = *HE* 106ff., Theocr., *Ep.* 17 Gow). Catullus 4 exploits the same device. The first section of our poem does not read like a tour.

[35] Camps 1965 sees the reproof of Horos in 1.71f. as applying only to 87f., which he places with Marcilius after 68, and which he interprets as a proposal to write 'poetic prophecies' (p. 62 of his edition). It would seem that these prophecies are actually to be uttered by other people (so that '*dicere fata*' in 71 has an unexpected sense); and in any case the second line of the couplet cannot refer to them. I find it a very artificial notion that Horos can be understood to censure one part (one line) only of the programme, and to leave the rest intact. Besides, the tone of the couplet is quite out of place in the section 57–70—indeed, there is no niche for the lines anywhere in the poem.

[36] '*at tu finge elegos*' (135) shows that epic is in question. I do not agree with Macleod 1976 that 'the poem Propertius risked writing would have included, as lines 45–8 indicate, bellicose material'; and in fact poems 6 and 10 do treat of war.

> *et quoscumque meo fecisti nomine versus,*
> *ure mihi: laudes desine habere meas.*
>
> Whatever lines you have dedicated to me, kindly burn; cease to celebrate my praises.

The course marked out for the poet in his youth has been ended; he has been obliged to turn to other subjects.

This view of the book, it is hoped, springs naturally from what is emphasized in the book itself, accommodates without violence every poem, and makes sense of poem 1, which on any other view is a baffling production.[37] If it is correct, the book acquires the coherence which it leads the reader to expect, and each poem acquires a new force and point. The poet does not adopt, half-heartedly, the role of an ingenuous antiquarian and patriot. He remains piquant and unpredictable; but the poems on Augustus and Cornelia have especial weight, and form an integral part of the book, not merely in architecture but in theme.

There would be no difficulty in seeing Book 1 as a unity, were it not for the last three poems (20–2). The rest are strongly bound together, not only by various explicit or palpable connections, but by the theme of them all. Poems 1–19 all have the love of Propertius for Cynthia as a primary or secondary subject; where it is secondary, Propertius is treating the loves, actual or potential, of his friends. Poem 20 certainly begins with the love of his friend Gallus, for a boy, but the body of it narrates the myth of Hylas' abduction by nymphs. Poem 21 is an epigram put into the mouth of a Gallus who has died fleeing from Perusia (besieged by Octavian in 41 BCE). Poem 22 gives the origin of the poet: he comes from near Perusia, and his *propinquus* perished as a result of the fighting there. This sudden variety and heterogeneity should surprise. There is no reason to suppose that the poems in the first column of the Gallus papyrus[38] wanted connection with the other poems in the book, and so to make them a precedent for Propertius' filling out an otherwise unified book with

---

[37] Macleod 1976 sufficiently refutes the contention that 1.71–150 form a new poem (Sandbach 1962). If they did, the problems they raise would not be sensibly diminished.

[38] Anderson, Parsons, and Nisbet 1979.

extraneous matter. This is the feature of the book which requires explanation.

In the main part of the book, the love which engrosses our interest is given a well-defined setting. The world is that of the reader's own time and place. The incidents purport to be historical; but in themselves they have no significance to the reader outside the book, and the chief characters are given no name (the poet) or a false one (Cynthia). Poem 20, and poems 21–2, break out of this sphere in opposite directions. We may look first at 21–2. It is generally conceded that the two poems must be connected, that the kinsman of the poet who died by Perusia must be the speaker of poem 21.[39] I shall argue presently that that speaker, named Gallus, is a relative of the Gallus whom Propertius has addressed in four earlier poems; and that hitherto the Gallus addressed there, the poet's chief associate in love, had meant nothing to the reader outside the work. These two poems remove both characters from the world of love and connect them harshly with historical events not merely familiar to the reader but politically sensitive and disturbing. The poet does not fail to remind us that the siege was the work of Caesar (21.7); he parades his emotional involvement in the death of his kinsman (22.6); and he heightens the sense of audacity by withholding his own name.[40] The poems effect a sudden change of atmosphere from that of the rest of the book while maintaining contact with its characters. The poems also share with two poems closely preceding them the impressive theme of death. In 17 and 19 the lover had contemplated death with fantasies nostalgic or passionate. Here, appropriately, death becomes brutal fact. 17.11f. and 22.6–8 give a very different colour to the subject of unburied bones. We shall see further reason to accept this connection when we consider the sequence of poems from 17 to the end.

---

[39] See, for example, G. Williams 1968: 177f. He allows that the interrelation of the two poems must constitute an exception to what 'it is reasonable to assume' about most Roman poems.

[40] This reticence is startling in a *sphragis* which opens as this one does. It is notable also that the poet has not named himself hitherto. His name appears in the other books eight times, and Catullus, Tibullus, Sulpicia, and Ovid in his *Amores*, allow or compel their own names to enter. Rothstein (in his first edition, 1898) and Butler and Barber 1933 suppose that the disclosure of the name might be left to the title of the book; but the excuse is palpably unconvincing.

The change of feeling in 21 and 22 is heightened by the opposite change in the poem before. The poem is addressed to Gallus. *pro continuo... amore* (in accordance with my constant love for you [cf. Fronto p. 151. 9–10 Van den Hout]) in the first line refers us back to the earlier poems, and as in poem 10 the poet gives Gallus advice. But the advice given here removes us from reality: Gallus is to take care that the boy he loves is not snatched away by amorous nymphs.[41] The myth puts love itself in a fantastic setting and alters its atmosphere. The Boreadae sweep down to kiss the lovely Hylas (25–30);[42] fired with his beauty, the nymphs pull him into the water. The object of their passion is not an imperious and irascible mistress but a boy, who had rather pick flowers, *pueriliter* (like a child), than draw water, and who dallies with his own reflection (39–42).[43] This idyllic poem is modelled on Theocritus, the model of the *Eclogues*, and at several points the *Eclogues* themselves are imitated.[44] The poem before last had been based on the *Eclogues*. In both 18 and 20 the lover (Propertius or Gallus) is placed in the deserted countryside: compare especially 18.27 †*divini*† *montes (fontes codd.) et frigida rupes* (... hills [streams MSS] and a cold crag) and 20.13 *duros montes et frigida saxa* (hard hills and cold rocks). This locale is the more striking since in poems 1–16 Propertius has been in Rome; Cynthia has actually left Rome only to visit the decadence of Baiae (poem 11). The reader will surely connect the two poems, 18 and 20, and contrast their mood. In 18 Propertius puts himself into the pastoral world, as Virgil had put the poet Gallus in *Eclogue* 10; but he does not appear to find the countryside pleasing. He has come to the waste to complain out loud of the harshness of Cynthia. Here love is not transmuted into tranquil and airy fantasy.

Poems 17–22 may in some respects be regarded as a group. Poems 17 and 19 are both concerned with the imagined death of the lover, and the reaction of the beloved. *Non... nunc* (Not... now) in the

---

[41] A friend quoted by Camps thinks that the poet means by the nymphs ordinary Roman girls. Propertius gives us no reason to think this, and lines 7–10 (especially 7 and 10) are scarcely to be reconciled with this hypothesis.

[42] This picture is not found in Theocritus 13, Propertius' model. The Boreadae have a very different role in the story at A. R. 1.1300ff.

[43] Again, there is nothing of this in Theocritus or Apollonius.

[44] Compare 20.7–10 with *Ecl.* 8.6f., 20.36 with *Ecl.* 8.37, 20. 45 with *Ecl.* 5.59—and possibly 20.49f. with *Ecl.* 6.43f.

first line of 19 is most naturally seen as taking up poem 17. At any rate, the reader can hardly avoid connecting the two poems. It seems probable that the three poems at the end of the book continue the pattern of alternation. 20 is connected in theme with 18, 21–2 with 17 and 19. The connections give force and particularity to the divergence of 20–2 from the world of 1–19. In the case of 20, 18 to some degree prepares for the divergence by its quasi-pastoral character; but nonetheless 18, and 17 and 19, bring out the contrasts of tone. The characters of 20 and 21–2 link them not only to the rest of the book but to each other: 21–2, as I shall contend, throw light on the Gallus addressed in 20. Once again the link heightens the contrast, which is extreme, and which produces one of the most powerful effects in the book.[45] Gallus is suddenly abstracted from reality, and then as suddenly located in a reality more concrete than before. The surprises and deviations of the last three poems are not aimless or fortuitous but calculated. The ending of the book may be compared with the ending of Catullus 64. There, likewise, the reader is abruptly and surprisingly transported into a sombre present reality;[46] the preceding section (the song of the Parcae) makes this one seem the stranger. But the themes of this last section connect it with other parts of the poem, and the connections cause the surprise to seem forceful rather than odd. In both passages contemporary readers will have felt the poet's material to acquire a new and exciting immediacy. We may easily recapture this response.

I must now defend my view of the Galli. The Gallus of 21 is normally assumed to have nothing to do with the homonym who appears in four other poems, the last directly preceding this one. But surely the poet was not so negligent of his readers? Anyone who read the book continuously would naturally connect the two. Yet since Book 1 was not published before 30 BCE, and the second Gallus dies in 41 BCE, the reader cannot have supposed them to be the same. He

---

[45] Among the other effects in the book one may include the surprises of discovering that Cynthia will remain in Rome (8b), that Gallus is deeply in love (10), and that a poem in this book is being spoken by an ancient door (16).

[46] The sins described in 64. 399 ff. are all at home in Catullus' own day: compare with 399 Lucr. 3.72 (*sanguine civili* [by civil bloodshed] 70), contrast Hes., *Op.* 184; compare with 401f. the allegations at Cic., *Clu.* 27f. and Sall., *Cat.* 15, contrast Hes., *Op.* 182; compare with 403f. the allegation in Cat. 88, 89, and 90.

would assume that the Gallus of 21 was an elder relative of the Gallus of 5, 10, 13, and 20—presumably his father. This connection is welcome for another, though slighter, reason. Propertius gathered the bones of his own father, who must have perished at much the same time (4.1.127f.). If his object in poem 22 were simply to connect himself, through his family, with the victims of Octavian, it might have seemed more pointed in itself, and more natural as an answer to *unde genus, qui sint mihi... Penates* (where I come from in family, what is my home), if he had mentioned his father instead of a more distant relation. His proceeding is easier to understand if he positively wanted to touch on his associate Gallus.[47]

If the Gallus of poems 5, 10, 13, and 20 is related to Propertius, it becomes interesting to ponder on his identity; and to do so will prove germane to our wider concerns. We might be tempted to imagine that we had found support for a conjecture of Syme's: that this Gallus was a noble Aelius Gallus. The family had on other grounds been thought to be related to the poet's.[48] On reflection, however, one sees difficulties. This Aelius Gallus must be possessed of an eminence in society at least equal to that of Tullus, to whom several poems are also addressed (1, 6, 14, 22). Nothing is said of Tullus that does not do him honour. Even of the much obscurer Bassus and Ponticus,[49] addressed in poems 4, and 7, and 9, nothing is said that would cause embarrassment. To Gallus is addressed poem 13, which assumes that Gallus will enjoy the misfortunes of the poet, speaks of his notorious promiscuity, and describes with lavish fullness his physical union with his beloved. This description is malicious, as Lyne has argued persuasively of poem 10:[50] there too Propertius

---

[47] It would require a curious view of the poet to suppose that he had already written 21 before he contemplated collecting his poems, but could not bear to leave it out, and therefore wrote 22 to explain it for the general public (cf. G. Williams 1968: 177f.). On 22 the article of F. Leo in Fraenkel 1960: 169ff. is still worth consulting, for it brings out effectively the strangeness of the poem. But his conclusion is unwelcome: we have only the beginning of the poem.

[48] Syme 1978: 101f. On the Aelii Galli see also Nisbet and Hubbard 1978: 223f. The grounds for relating Propertius to the Aelii Galli are that the Postumus of 3.12, who is married to an Aelia Galla, may be the Propertius Postumus of *ILS* 914 (Rome). To the innocent outsider these grounds seem highly speculative.

[49] See Syme 1978: 98 (Ov., *Tr.* 4.10.47).

[50] Lyne 1980: 112ff.

exults in the sight he has obtained of his former rival's embraces (for their rivalry see poem 5). *Hoc pro continuo te, Galle, monemus amore* (I give you this warning, Gallus, in accordance with my constant love for you, 20.1) will sound less convincing than ironical. Would Propertius really write in this way of a distinguished *amicus* (friend)? It is not plausible to see all this as a hearty joke. I suspect that the poet has taken an obscure relation, unknown to the public, and has developed him as a foil without strict regard to veracity. The reference in 5.23f. to his *nobilitas* (noble origins) and to *priscis... imaginibus* (ancient ancestor masks) will appear in order to preclude confusion with Gallus the poet,[51] and to make a point about love. Even in prose dialogues Cicero can alter at will the philosophical allegiances of his brother (a figure not unknown to the public).[52] Gallus will stand as a historical being somewhere between Ponticus and (I imagine) Lygdamus. The poet can involve this half-fictional personage more freely in the world of love. He can thus play a major part in unifying the book.

Each of the books we have considered, then, should be seen as an artistic creation. Each forms a whole more organic and more interesting than a collection of wholly independent poems or a geometrical construction. The books themselves urge us to read them through in order, and not to restrict our view to the confines of each separate poem. On the other hand, we are not encouraged to search for devious and tangential connections. It now appears not unreasonable to suppose that relations within the book which are important to the poet will be natural, pointed, and striking. The assessment of particular cases will to some degree vary with the assessor; but a certain element of subjectivity does not mean that the whole matter is irredeemably arbitrary. It will seem to be so only if we permit the forced and the tenuous to obscure the significant.

This approach will, I believe, help to illuminate other books of Latin poetry. But even the two examples we have considered may serve to indicate that every book has its own kind of unity. Our conclusions about those two books invite us to look similarly at the

---

[51] Cf. Hutchinson 1981: 39.
[52] Compare Pease in his 1920 edition of the *De Divinatione* 1, 17, 20. On Quintus' career and writings, see D. R. Shackleton Bailey 1980: 3ff.

other two books of Propertius; if we do so, we shall find them to be no less individual. A picture of each may be hazarded. Book 2, which I hold to be one book,[53] is large and essentially homogeneous; it is bound together by continual and forceful variation of a number of themes. For example, the *Iliad* and its characters form a prominent concern which repays analysis. In Book 3, the subject-matter is expanded in a way which the prologue (poems 1–3) renders somewhat surprising; this leads to a renunciation of love as a way of life and as a serious theme for poetry. The book is not a disjointed miscellany of experiments. The poems which do not concern Cynthia are all linked with the prologue or with the connected pair of poems which opens the book proper (4 and 5, on the Parthian campaign); the last part of the book (poems 17–25) distorts the themes of the rest.

These suggestions about Books 2 and 3 would show further the variety of structure which a single poet may attain in a single medium. Different poets will diverge still further. This aspect of their art is no less personal than any other. The piquancy, the paradox, the dramatic surprises which we observed in the construction of Propertius' first and fourth books find ready parallels within his individual poems. The organization and design of a poet's books can form an integral part of his artistry and his meaning: that is why we should study them, and how.[54]

*Christ Church, Oxford*

---

[53] The contention that it is two, made popular again by O. Skutsch 1975, rests on shaky foundations. The mention of '*tres libelli*' (three books) in 2.13.25 may be met by the hypothesis—which could be supported on other grounds—that Books 2 and 3 were published together. The absence of Book 1 from the grammarians need have no significance in the light of the nature, and the paucity, of their citations from Propertius. The *De Natura Deorum* and the *Ad Herennium* are quoted a similar number of times by the grammarians, and their first books do not appear. For the nature of the quotations from Propertius, cf. Menes 1983: 136. It may also be noted that Book 2.1a–9 (supposedly the original Book 1) is quoted less often than Book 3 or the original Book 2: Skutsch illegitimately heaps together the figures for what on his hypothesis is two books.

[54] I am grateful to Mr. Jasper Griffin, Professor Hugh Lloyd-Jones, and Mr R. B. Rutherford for their encouragement, and to the Editorial Committee for their comments and advice.

## ADDENDUM

A less youthful account of poetry-books and of Propertius IV may be found in Hutchinson 2008 and Hutchinson 2006; on Propertius' Galli, note Hutchinson 2006: 77.

# 8

## Poetic Baldness and its Cure[1]

*James E. G. Zetzel*

This essay is an attempt to explore the life and death of some of the conventions of Roman elegy, concentrating on two related topics: the use of extended metaphors to describe poetry itself, and the relationship within some poems in Propertius' Monobiblos and the first book of Ovid's *Amores* between the elegist as a conscious participant in a poetic tradition and the elegist as lover within a—presumably fictitious—relationship. The starting point of my exploration is *Amores* 1.14, in which Ovid's mistress loses her hair as a result of the application of dye; that leads to a discussion of the first three poems of the Monobiblos, to an examination of Propertius' choice of metaphors for his own poetry in 1.5–10, and back, finally, to *Amores* 1.14. The larger issue addressed is the problem of poetic originality and self-definition within an extremely stylized poetic form—which is, I believe, the subject of *Amores* 1.14 itself.[2]

---

[1] Editors' note: all translations in this article are Zetzel's own.

[2] This article was begun long ago, in part as a reaction to D.O. Ross's *Backgrounds to Augustan Poetry* (1975a), for which see also my review (Zetzel 1977). A very brief summary of my interpretation of *Am.* 1.14 is also included in Zetzel 1992. Versions of this article or of parts of it have been presented as lectures at Mount Holyoke College, Princeton University, Harvard University, and Jesus College, Oxford. I am grateful to many of those present on those occasions for their suggestions; the anonymous referees for this journal have also made valuable comments. My greatest debt is to Susanna Zetzel for her many improvements of both the ideas and their presentation.

## AMORES 1.14

Although *Amores* 1.14 has received critical notice primarily because it appears to contain the latest datable allusion in the *Amores*,[3] it is a fine specimen of both Ovid's wit and his nastiness. Barsby perhaps goes too far in characterizing it as 'heartless,' but the speaker does not present himself—to put it mildly—as someone anyone would want for a lover.[4] The subject of the poem is hair—or rather its absence. Ovid's mistress (unnamed here, but I will call her Corinna for convenience) has been dyeing her hair despite the poet's admonitions; and as a result, her hair has fallen out. The poet expatiates on the beauty of his mistress's ex-tresses, their length, texture, color, and versatility; he compares her to a Bacchante sleeping after Maenadic frenzy; he reminds Corinna that he had warned against adorning her hair, or using combs and curling irons on it; he offers a lament on the death of the hair, which was worthy of the gods. Finally, he tells her to stop complaining: she has only herself to blame, and will have to wear a German wig until it grows back.

The poem is generally treated as a witty, rhetorical elaboration on the theme of beauty and its need for, or lack of need for, adornment, and as an inventive attack on female vanity.[5] To that extent, it is like many of the poems in the *Amores* or, indeed, large stretches of the *Ars amatoria*, and Ovid's interest in hair, particularly when disarrayed, is apparent to any reader of his poetry. As so often, Ovid is taking a theme of Propertian elegy (also a minor topic of Tibullus 1.8) and reducing it to the absurd, or nearly so. In this case, Propertius had written several poems against his mistress's adornment (1.2, 1.15,

---

[3] Cf. Cameron 1968: 331, who accepts the date of 16 BCE. Syme 1978: 3–5 suggests that the reference to the Sygambri as *triumphatae gentis* might better be taken as referring to the triumph of Tiberius in January of 7 BCE, but he also remarks (5, note 5): 'It is easier ... to take Ovid's reference as literary, rather than as an allusion to a historical event.' That might apply to the whole reference, not merely to the triumph: there were earlier triumphs over Germans, and the Sygambri appear as early as Caesar's campaigns in Gaul (cf. esp. *BG* 4.18f.). McKeown 1989 says nothing on the problem.

[4] Barsby 1973: 157. There is now a far more subtle reading of 1.14 as 'a dramatic mimesis of the lover's discourse' by Kennedy 1993: 71–7. The interpretation offered here takes a very different approach to the poem, but one not incompatible with Kennedy's.

[5] See, e.g. McKeown's 1989 introduction, 364–5.

2.18), with the implication—at times direct statement—that she would stick to simplicity if she were not still trying to attract other men. The first and best of these elegies is the second poem of the Monobiblos, and that is the poem that is being echoed by Ovid in 1.14.

The very first word of *Amores* 1.14, *dicebam*, presents a problem. 'I told you so' says the poet; but when? Ovid might simply be constructing a fictitious antecedent narrative—as with the self-quotation about curling irons at 27ff.—but there is no parallel for this opening in Augustan elegy. Editors refer to Propertius 1.9.1 '*dicebam tibi uenturos, irrisor, amores*' (I told you, you scoffer, that love would come to you), but that only raises further questions.[6] Propertius 1.9 begins that way precisely because it is the sequel to an earlier poem, 1.7. The first warns Ponticus of the dangers of love and the uselessness of writing epic; and in the second the predicted situation has come about: 'I told you so' is perfectly appropriate within the dramatic narrative of the Monobiblos. But no previous poem in *Amores* 1 warns against the use of hair dye, and there is not even a general admonition against adornment. Unless we wish to believe that the first edition of the *Amores* contained such a poem, which was then excised without the poet's realizing the difficulty left in 1.14.1—a hypothesis I do not take seriously—we must conclude that there was no such antecedent poem. At least, Ovid did not write one; but Propertius did. The second poem of the Monobiblos is an exhortation to the poet's mistress (and as in *Amores* 1.14 she is unnamed) not to use artificial adornment.[7] The poem begins with hair, proceeds to dress, and then goes on to cosmetics. The precept is illustrated with three couplets (9–14) giving arguments from nature and four (15–22) from myth. He concludes by saying that the gifts of the gods are enough, and that if she is pretty enough for Propertius without expensive accoutrements, then she should be satisfied with that.

The first lines of the two texts suggest their relationship immediately:

---

[6] E.g. Munari 1951; Barsby 1973; and McKeown 1989 *ad loc.*

[7] The specific subject of hair dye is the topic of Propertius 2.18B, which McKeown 1989 sees as the principal antecedent to *Amores* 1.14. But Ovid seems to borrow only a single word from 2.18B (*inepta*, 36), and the patterns of the poems are not at all alike. For *Amores* 1.14 as a sequel to Propertius 1.2, see also Kennedy 1993: 71–2. My analysis of Propertius 1.2 is indebted to Ross 1975a: 58–9; see further below, p. 219.

*Quid iuuat ornato procedere, uita, capillo* (Propertius 1.2.1)
*Dicebam 'medicare tuos desiste capillos'* (*Amores* 1.14.1)
What's the good, my life, of going about with your hair adorned
I kept saying 'stop dyeing your hair.'

The last words of the lines are the same, and the second is easily read as a reply to the first. And while *capillus* is scarcely a rare word in elegy, it is worth noting that Propertius, in the other poem (2.18B) to which Ovid might be alluding here, uses *coma* rather than *capillus*. There are other verbal similarities as well. In his first line, Ovid uses the verb *medicare*, here meaning 'to dye' (relatively uncommon in Ovid, other than once in *Am*. 1.12 and in the *Medicamina*). In line 7 of Propertius' poem we find:

*crede mihi, non ulla tuae est medicina figurae.*
Believe me, your beauty needs no help.

*Medicina* is a significant word for Propertius—as perhaps for Gallus before him—and it usually means 'cure,' but in this passage, it means not 'cure' but 'artificial improvement,' far closer to the meaning in Ovid's verse.[8] So too, at 1.14.5, Ovid uses *ornare*, as does Propertius in the first line of 1.2.

There are other possible reminiscences, although they are not quite so close. Propertius' subject in 1.2 is not only hair, but the entire range of feminine adornment: clothes, cosmetics, jewelry. Ovid limits his version to the topic of Propertius' first verse, and elaborates on that. Where Propertius 1.2.2 uses *tenuis* (slender) to refer to Cynthia's dress, Ovid in line 5 uses it to refer to the hair itself. In the same line, Propertius refers to *Coa ueste* as exotic and alluring foreign clothing; Ovid in line 6 compares the texture of Corinna's hair to '*uela colorati qualia Seres habent*' (like the fabrics of the tinted Chinese), and it is not unreasonable to see the two as parallel. The natural parallels adduced by Propertius (9–14) to attack feminine artifice correspond to the lines (7–12) devoted by Ovid to natural parallels for the texture and color of the hair, and both passages are marked by lyrical and

---

[8] On *medicina* in Propertius, cf. Tränkle 1960: 22–3, and Ross 1975a: 67–8 with Camps 1961 (1977) on this passage. *Medico* 'dye' is found in Horace, *C*. 3.5.8, Ovid, *Med*. 9, *Rem*. 707, *Am*. 1.12.11; for other uses of *medicina* as cosmetics, cf. *TLL* 8:540.22ff. s.v.

high-flown vocabulary.⁹ Both poets refer to the gods Apollo and Venus, although Propertius also has Calliope and Minerva, Ovid Bacchus. One further verbal parallel is possible: Propertius 1.2.13:

> litora natiuis persuadent picta lapillis
> Shores allure us by the paint of their natural pebbles

may, as McKeown suggests, influence the last line of Ovid's poem:

> postmodo natiua conspiciere coma.
> Later you will be admired with your natural hair.

*Natiuus* is not used elsewhere in the *Amores*. McKeown also makes a connection between Corinna's German wig and Propertius' objection in line 4 to *peregrinis muneribus* (foreign gifts) and points out the similar use of *sponte*.[10] Not all these parallels are equally convincing, but the combination of similar subject matter and verbal echoes is significant; Ovid probably had Propertius' poem in mind when writing his own and, among other things, he demonstrates how different an Ovidian sequel is from the one Propertius actually wrote in 1.15 and, indeed, from the poem Propertius wrote on hair-dye in 2.18.

There is more than the imitation of Propertius in *Amores* 1.14 that deserves attention. Corinna's hair is beautiful; and although it does not have a speaking part in the poem, Ovid describes it as learned and even didactic: *erudit admotas ipse capillus acus* ('the hair itself educates the pins applied to it,' 30). It is not impossible that we are supposed to think of another learned lock, that of Berenice, which lived a happier life and departed from its mistress's head in another direction.[11] And indeed, examination of the language used to describe the texture of the hair in lines 5–8 suggests that these locks are literary as well as literal. The first indication is the description of Corinna's hair as *tenuis* in line 5: while it would certainly seem an appropriate enough description, Ovid uses it of hair in only two of the 76 appearances of *tenuis* in his works.[12] On the other hand it is a very familiar element of the Roman critical

---

[9] For Propertius 1.2, cf. Tränkle 1960: 25–6; for Ovid, note especially the word order of lines 9, 11, 12, and the use of *cliuosus*. On words of that form, cf. Ross 1969: 53–60, Tränkle 1960: 59–60.
[10] McKeown 1989 on lines 56, 46, 28 respectively.
[11] The parallel is suggested by McKeown 1989: 365 and on 1.14.23–30.
[12] Here and *Am.* 3.10.3; McKeown 1989 cites also Tibullus 1.9.68.

vocabulary:[13] the opposition of *tenuis* and *grandis* runs through Augustan poetry, parallel to the conventional elegiac pairing of *mollis* and *durus* referring with equal relevance to beds, women, weapons, or poetry. Here, *tenuis* should be seen in conjunction with lines 7–8, a couplet that is a veritable anthology of major metaphors of Roman poetic theory:

> *uel pede quod gracili deducit aranea filum*
> *cum leue deserta sub trabe nectit opus.*
> or the thread the spider spins out with her graceful foot
> as she weaves her slight creation under a deserted beam.

Corinna's hair is compared to a delicate spider web under a deserted beam. *Deducere*, aside from being a technical term of spinning, is of course a metaphor for poetic skill; in *Ecl.* 6.5 *deductum* is the translation of Callimachus' λεπταλέην, and in *Epist.* 2.1.225 Horace refers to *tenui deducta poemata filo* (poems spun out on a slender thread); Ovid himself mocks the convention in the opening of the *Metamorphoses*, *ad mea perpetuum deducite tempora carmen* (spin down the unbroken song to my own times), a clear parody of Alexandrian poetic theory.[14]

But *deducere* is not the only word here that is drawn from the vocabulary of poetics. The spider web itself has similar connotations. That spiders' spinning was fine (*tenuis*) had appeared in poetry before Ovid's time,[15] but it took the genius of the poet of the *Culex* to carry it to its logical extreme.[16] He began his *paruum opus* as follows:

> *Lusimus, Octaui, gracili modulante Thalia*
> *atque ut araneoli tenuem formauimus orsum.*
> We have played, Octavius, with graceful Thalia supplying the tune,
> and like little spiders we have shaped our slight undertaking.

---

[13] On *tenuis* and its Greek equivalents see, among others, Reitzenstein 1931: 25–39; Puelma Piwonka 1949: 138–66; Clausen 1964: 194; Commager 1974: 45–7; Ross 1975a: 26–9.

[14] Cf. Kenney 1976: 51–2 with further references.

[15] Cf. Catullus 68.49–50 '*nec tenuem texens sublimis aranea telam/in deserto Alli nomine opus faciat*' (nor may the spider, weaving on high its slender web, construct its creation on Allius' deserted name), also in a context concerning poetry itself.

[16] Cf. Ross 1975a: 25–6 and 1975b: 252–3; on the language of the opening line see also Wimmel 1960: 307–8.

Since these verses include so many clichés of Augustan poetics—*ludo, gracilis* and *Thalia* from the Sixth *Eclogue*, not to mention the ever-present *tenuis*—it is reasonable to see the rest of his language as drawn from the same stock (and of course the spiders are completely appropriate in a poem about a gnat); the presence of *gracilis* in connection with the spider emphasizes the connection in *Amores* 1.14. On a less philological level, it is in any case evident that spiders and spinning are obvious metaphors for poetry; we need only read the story of Arachne in the *Metamorphoses* to see the similarity, in Callimachean terms, of all three activities. In the couplet of the *Amores*, moreover, one might suggest that the deserted beam is the equivalent of the Callimachean untrodden path, and that *pede gracili* refers to the metrical, as well as the arachnid foot.[17]

These are the major indications that connect Corinna's hair to poetry, but there are others. Her locks are *dociles* in line 13, which accords well with *erudit* in 30; her hair is fit for a hundred twists (13), a phrase remarkably applicable to Ovid's own poetry. The hair is such that Apollo or Bacchus would be proud of it (31f.), and they are the two presiding deities of Augustan poetry; and in the *Amores* Venus, who follows them, is a suitable companion. These descriptions are as appropriate to verse as to hair: learned as well as pliable, slight, and appealing to the gods of love, wine, and poetry itself.

Not every detail in a conceit like this is equally relevant to both sides of the metaphor. Combs and pins may not belong in a literary composition—although Cicero does refer to *calamistri* (curling irons) at *Orator* 78f. in speaking of literary ornament, and the whole concept of *fucatio*, dyeing, is important in the Roman rhetorical tradition.[18] But one other apparently irrelevant detail may be concerned with poetry. Corinna's hair color—before she used the ill-fated dye—was neither black nor golden, but something mixed and in between (9f.). There follows a remarkable simile:

qualem cliuosae madidis in uallibus Idae
    ardua derepto cortice cedrus habet.

---

[17] The Callimacheanism of the spider web is recognized by Kennedy 1993: 75–6.
[18] The elements of hair-styling (*ornatus, medicamenta*, and *calamistri*) have a long tradition as metaphors for style; cf. the parallels collected by Sandys 1885 on *Orator* 78–9 and Fantham 1972: 171–2. For *fucatio*, cf. Wiseman 1979: 3–8.

> like what the lofty cedar has in the damp valleys of steep Ida
> when its bark has been pulled off.

It is the color of a cedar tree after the bark has been stripped off. This is not an obvious comparison, and the elegance of the diction leads one to suspect something more. Cedar trees are not common in Latin literature; this is the earliest reference that I know.[19] The wood of the cedar is mentioned only three times before this: once in the *Georgics* (3.414), where it is used to fumigate a stable; and twice in *Aeneid* 7 (13, 178)—of which the first, I might note, is in connection with Circe's weaving and singing. But if the tree and its wood are rare, the oil is not, and it was important *to* poetry if not in it: it was used to preserve books.[20] Preservation of poetry by cedar oil indicates the worth of the poetry itself; that may be a partial explanation of Ovid's simile here.

But if the cedar itself is a sign of poetic worth, the fact that the bark is gone is not. When the bark is stripped from a tree, it dies. Less obvious, perhaps, is the importance of tree-bark as an image in Alexandrian and Augustan poetry. In the story of Acontius and Cydippe in Callimachus' *Aetia* (fr. 73 Pf.), Acontius in the woods carves *Kudippe kalê* on the bark of trees. A similar bark-graffito is found in Theocritus 18.47, and the scholiast on Aristophanes' *Acharnians* 144 (our source for the Callimachus fragment) says that it is the habit of lovers to write the names of their loved ones on walls, trees, or leaves. This unecological practice continued at Rome. To give only a few examples, Gallus in *Eclogue* 10.52ff. says that he will cut his *amores* on trees, and they will grow as the trees do. Propertius, playing Acontius-Gallus in 1.18.21f., does the same thing:[21]

> *a quotiens teneras resonant mea uerba sub umbras*
>    *scribitur et uestris Cynthia corticibus.*
> Ah, how often my words echo under your tender shade
>    and 'Cynthia' is written on your bark.

---

[19] The fact, discussed in a learned note by McKeown 1989, that such a tree in the Troad must be a juniper rather than a cedar, is not germane.

[20] Cf. Ovid, *Tristia* 1.1.7, 3.1.13; Horace, *Ars poetica* 332–3; Persius 1.42.

[21] This passage has been frequently discussed; Enk 1946 *ad loc.*, Pfeiffer 1949 (1965) on Callim. fr. 73; Ross 1975a: 71–3 with further references; and Cairns 1969: 131–4.

This tree carving would be irrelevant here if it were not for the Ovidian context. Ovid is talking about hair falling out, and it is the hair of poetry. If too much is carved on a tree, a similar effect is presumably produced. After you have carved all your lovers' names there, and so have all your amorously inclined friends, the bark comes off, and the tree dies. And some poetic figures carve rather more than a name: Mopsus in the Fifth *Eclogue* (13ff.) refers to poetry that he recently wrote on beech-bark; he then sings twenty-five lines. Later on, in Calpurnius Siculus 1.20, there are 52 verses on a *pagina* of beech bark. Either these rustic poets are lying, and used a giant sequoia instead of a beech, or the pastoral landscape was filled with dead trees.

It may appear—indeed, it probably is—frivolous to work out in detail the reality of situations described in the unreal worlds of pastoral and erotic poetry; but the image of carving on trees in Callimachean-neoteric verse is the act first of a lover, and then of a love poet; it may well stand as an emblem for poetic composition itself. If one accepts the occasionally arcane and precious symbolism proposed here, both the general subject of *Amores* 1.14—baldness resulting from the over-use of artificial aids—and the specific image of these lines can be interpreted as standing for the over-use of poetic convention.[22] If we read the poem as being concerned with poetry itself, it is virtually an epitaph for the conventions within which Ovid is writing. It has become too artificial, too unnatural; the subjects have become trite, all the fancy tricks of elegy have been done to death, and the vein has been worked out.[23]

## THE OPENING OF THE MONOBIBLOS

At this point, it is worth looking once more at the connection between *Amores* 1.14 and Propertius 1.2. There is further evidence

[22] Both anonymous readers for this journal were skeptical about this argument; I am myself more convinced about the importance of the bark-peeling than about that of the cedar tree, and the two parts of the argument are, I think, independent of one another.

[23] Roman poets did reflect explicitly on the repetitiveness of their own tradition; so, for instance, Vergil, *Georg.* 3.3–8 and, using a different but familiar poetic metaphor, Manilius 2.49–52.

for the link, with two aspects, one concerning imitations of other Propertian poems in Ovid's poem, the other involving the interpretation of Propertius 1.2 itself. In brief, Ovid looks at 1.2 as part of a linked group of texts, the first three poems of the Monobiblos; and 1.2 both independently and as part of this group needs to be read as a programmatic statement about the nature of Propertius' own poetic claims. One general observation: Roman elegy is a highly self-conscious and circumscribed form, working within a narrow set of conventions both defining the dramatic situations within the text and imposing a constant, and frequently ironic, identification on the one hand of poet and lover, on the other of poem as inscribed text and poem as either erotic scene or beloved person. In that context, to speak of a Roman elegy as being in some sense 'about poetry' is automatically redundant: the persona of the elegist is a poet/lover seeking a subject that is both text and mistress; there is no distance at all from bed to verse.[24] Ovid makes this relationship explicit in the opening poems of the *Amores*, but it is present as well in Propertius; in *Amores* 1.14 (as indeed elsewhere) Ovid echoes what I believe to be the double situation of the Propertian elegist in the opening of the Monobiblos, defining himself both as poet within his tradition and as lover within his erotic drama—in each case, seeking virgin territory.

To return to *Amores* 1.14. I have argued that it is based on Propertius 1.2, but it also contains distinct echoes of both 1.1 and 1.3. Thus Ovid says (39–42) that Corinna cannot blame magic or disease for her plight; in the opening poem of the Monobiblos, magic and medicine also appear in close proximity, as being of no use for curing lovers (19–28). There is also a precise verbal allusion, which has long been recognized:[25] Propertius (27f.) proclaims his willingness to undergo painful medical procedures in order to free himself from love:

---

[24] On the textual nature of the *puella*, cf. Commager 1974: 5–7 and more recently Wyke 1987b: 47–61. Wyke concentrates on Propertius 2.10–13, but what she says is equally applicable to the Monobiblos, even though Propertius' Callimachean allusiveness is less explicit and Cynthia is embedded in an apparently more 'realistic' narrative.

[25] Cf. Zingerle 1869: 91, and Ganzemüller 1911: 292; it is the only imitation in *Amores* 1.14 discussed by Morgan 1977: 41–2.

*fortiter et ferrum saeuos patiemur et ignes,*
   *sit modo libertas quae uelit ira loqui.*
We will courageously endure iron and savage fire
   so long as there is liberty to speak what anger wishes.

Ovid changes surgery and cautery to the application of curling irons (25f.):

*quam se praebuerant ferro patienter et igni*
   *ut fieret torto nexilis orbe sinus!*
With what endurance they submitted to iron and fire
   to create a woven curve in a twisted orb!

Less striking than this parody but equally valid, I hope, is the reminiscence in Ovid's poem of Propertius 1.3. Propertius included in his memorable opening triad of similes a comparison of Cynthia to a tired Bacchante (5f.):

*nec minus assiduis Edonis fessa choreis*
   *qualis in herboso concidit Apidano.*
and not unlike an an Edonian woman exhausted from constant dances
   as she collapses by the grassy Apidanus.

Ovid also described his mistress as a tired Bacchante (21f.):

*tum quoque erat neglecta decens, ut Thracia Bacche,*
   *cum temere in uiridi gramine lassa iacet.*
Then too she was comely in disarray, like a Thracian Bacchante,
   when she lies tired, spread out on the green grass.

The similarity of thought if not of diction is unmistakable, and one should have little doubt that Ovid, who knew this poem well and imitated it elsewhere, is referring to it here.[26]

Even though there are echoes of other poems on the theme of adornment in *Amores* 1.14 (Tibullus 1.8 and Propertius 2.18B are cited by McKeown), the group of allusions to the three opening poems of the Monobiblos is striking. Ovid was one of the best readers his predecessors have ever had, and—even if they are parodic—his

---

[26] The imitation is recognized by Rothstein 1898, Munari 1951, Schuster 1954 and Enk 1946 *ad locc.*; more hesitantly McKeown 1989. Ovid's principal imitation of 1.3 is *Amores* 1.10; cf. Morgan 1977: 70–2 and Curran 1964: 314–19.

allusions often serve as an oblique commentary on the texts from which they borrow. Using such commentary is, of course, risky: in particular, the links that are made by connected allusions themselves often constitute a tendentious reconstruction of literary history; but they are, in any case, worth pursuing.[27]

One of the clearest instances of allusion to multiple poems by the same author is particularly useful here, as it is also one of the poems that Ovid himself alludes to in 1.14: Propertius 1.3.[28] The dramatic situation of that poem is the poet's return from a drunken party to find Cynthia asleep. He puts fruit in her lap, without success, and she is awakened by the moonlight coming through the window; she reproaches Propertius for his absence, and accuses him of having been with another woman. The poem begins with a series of three mythological comparisons: Ariadne asleep after Theseus had deserted her; Andromeda after being rescued by Perseus; and a tired Bacchante. The first of these clearly establishes the tone of the poem and its allusive character (1.3.1f.):

> *Qualis Thesea iacuit cedente carina*
>   *languida desertis Cnosia litoribus.*
> As the maid of Cnossos lay limp on the deserted beach
>   As Theseus' ship sailed away.

The general scene reminds us of Catullus 64, and there is verbal reminiscence as well (64.249):

> *quae tum prospectans cedentem maesta carinam.*
> And she then looking off sadly at the ship sailing away.

But 1.3 also contains allusions to other Catullan poems; in particular, the verses (23–6) on the poet's attempt to place apples in Cynthia's lap:

---

[27] Morgan 1977 demonstrates clearly how important imitations in Ovid are for understanding his poetry, but she does not discuss the immense value of his imitations as explanations or interpretations of earlier poetry. I am at a loss to understand the statement of Tarrant 1979: 92–3: 'I know of no place in the *Amores* in which understanding a poem's essential character depends on identifying the source of an allusion.' Since so much of Ovid's poetry is parodic, it is hopeless to try to explain it without recognizing his victims.

[28] The interpretation of 1.3 offered here owes a great deal to Curran 1966: 189–207; see also Lyne 1970: 60–78. I am perplexed by the statement of Veyne 1988, that the mysteriousness of 1.3 'is due perhaps only to clumsiness.'

*et modo gaudebam lapsos formare capillos;*
 *nunc furtiua cauis poma dabam manibus;*
*omniaque ingrato largibar munera somno,*
 *munera de prono saepe uoluta sinu*
And now I took joy in shaping her loose hair;
 now I gave furtive apples with cupped hands;
I bestowed all these gifts to her ungrateful sleep,
 gifts that kept falling from her lap as she lay.

echo simultaneously Catullus 65.19–20:

*ut missum sponsi furtiuo munere malum*
 *procurrit casto uirginis e gremio*
Just as an apple sent by the secret gift of a lover
 runs down from the chaste lap of a girl

and 76.9:

*omnia quae ingratae perierunt credita menti.*
All these things have perished, entrusted to an ungrateful mind.

There are in 1.3 allusions not only to Catullus 64, but also to 76 and perhaps 65; moreover, as Ross has shown, this portion of the poem is filled with stylistic echoes of Catullus.[29] This complex of allusions has the same purpose that Ovid's set of allusions to Propertius 1.1–3 has: to demonstrate the connection that he has seen among the poems he has linked. As Ross says of Propertius here: 'Not only do elements of language and style from both the "learned" and the "personal" poems appear thoroughly mixed in this elegy, but also there is clearly no separating the world of poetic myth from the reality [which Ross rightly qualifies] of the personal experience.'

Where I part company with Ross, however, is in his insistence that Propertius' allusions are simply the result of his total assimilation of Catullan poetry and neoteric poetics, and thus that the linking of 'personal' and 'learned' is self-evident rather than programmatic, or even deliberate commentary on Catullus' collection. Even stranger is Ross's denial that the allusions to Catullus 64 contribute to the sense of Propertius 1.3. And since I want to argue that Ovid is justified in seeing a common theme in the first three poems of the Monobiblos,

---

[29] For all these echoes, cf. Ross 1975a: 54–5. The quotation below is from p.56.

and that that theme is poetry itself, a closer examination of the allusions to Catullus 64 and their purpose will be necessary.

The clearest echo of 64 in Propertius 1.3 is in the opening couplet, but as Curran has shown, Catullus' epyllion permeates Propertius' poem.[30] Not only does Cynthia's speech at the end remind the reader strongly of Ariadne's attack on the absent Theseus, but when Propertius describes his approach with the words (9)

> *ebria cum multo traherem uestigia Baccho,*
> when I dragged my footsteps drunk on a lot of Bacchic help

one is surely meant to think of the arrival of Dionysus to rescue Ariadne.

The simple presence of allusions to Catullus is, however, less striking than the way in which the central panel of Catullus 64 is used as a vehicle of expression by both the poet and his mistress. Propertius, perhaps because he is drunk, fondly sees himself as a rescuer; Cynthia clearly sees him as the deserting Theseus. In the same way, while Propertius would like to see Cynthia as a heroine of myth, he knows her true character all too well (18):

> *expertae metuens iurgia saeuitiae.*
> fearing the assaults of a rage I had experienced before

He sees himself as faithful and heroic; she pictures him as a drunken lecher—which his actions in fact show him to be. She sees herself as a Penelope or a Lucretia, while her words show that she justifies all too well Propertius' fears of her *saeuitia*.

One should not attempt to oversimplify a complex and beautiful poem. It seems evident, however, that the reminiscences of Catullus and the pattern of contradictory self-images and expectations are closely related and lie at the heart of the poem. Propertius is defining his love and his love poetry in relation to Catullus. By combining allusions to 64 and to more overtly autobiographical poems, he seems to suggest that Catullus saw himself in terms of the romantic myth of Theseus and Ariadne (or the reverse—the distinction does not matter here); similarly, by putting himself and Cynthia into

---

[30] Curran 1966: 207 with note 22 cites parallels between Catullus 64.200–1 and 1.3.39–40; 64.133 and 172 and 1.3.2. His other parallels are less compelling.

Catullus' myth, he shows how unrealistic such equations are. Propertius is, I think, deliberately oversimplifying Catullus 64 in order polemically to establish a greater distance between himself and Catullus: there is nothing in 1.3 that recognizes Catullus' ambivalence about the heroic age of poem 64,[31] nor does he seem to acknowledge the deliberate confusion of gender roles in the autobiographical aspects of Ariadne (as elsewhere in Catullus). Neither the elegist nor Cynthia is a good reader of Catullus—or maybe they are better than I think: within the poem, both Propertius and his mistress act out precisely the issues of misreading of myth and masculine/feminine that are central to Catullus in poem 64.

There is, I think, a very strong case for seeing 1.3 as a double comment on Catullus as a model for the elegiac poet in his capacities both as lover and as poet; and a similar case can be made for the first poem in Propertius' collection. The opening poem of the Monobiblos begins by declaring and defining the poet's love for Cynthia, in eight verses. It is a source of misery, the equivalent of both a wound and a disease. Cynthia is scornful, and forces the poet into *furor* and a life without *consilium*. These verses are balanced by another set of eight lines giving the tale of Milanion who, by dint of hard work and suffering, managed to win Atalanta (15f):[32]

> *ergo uelocem potuit domuisse puellam:*
> *   tantum in amore preces et bene facta ualent.*
> And so he was able to conquer the swift maiden:
>    such is the power in love of prayers and good deeds.

But the model of Milanion is shown by what follows to be invalid for the Propertian lover (17f.):[33]

---

[31] On Catullus 64, see particularly Curran 1969: 169–92 and Bramble 1970: 22–41.
[32] I do not believe, with Ross 1975a: 60 note 3 (following Housman) and others, that a couplet is missing after 1.11; see the various contrary arguments of Tränkle 1960: 15–16 and 1968: 255–6.
[33] Ross 1975a: 64 note 1 is surely wrong to read *non nullas* here, and his argument about the meaning of *in me* is obscure. The point of the couplet is to contrast the success of Milanion with the failure of Propertius: 'in my case (*in me*) love is slow (*tardus*, which contrasts with *uelocem* in the preceding couplet) and does not think of any tricks (i.e. methods of approach to Cynthia) nor does he remember his former paths.'

*in me tardus Amor non ullas cogitat artis,*
*nec meminit notas, ut prius, ire uias.*
In my case, Love is slow and thinks up no wiles,
nor does he remember to follow the familiar route, as he did before.

The poet then turns to other possible remedies for love, and denies, successively, the usefulness of magic (19–26), medicine (27–30)—the verses parodied in 1.14 by Ovid—and foreign travel (31–2). He concludes by bemoaning his lot once more, and he advises his friends to avoid his situation.

This is a bald summary of a difficult poem, and skirts many problems.[34] It is clear, however,—if only from its position in the book—that the poem is programmatic: it sets forth the conditions of Propertius' relationship to Cynthia and rejects a number of remedies. It provides the basic situations of the lover, which are then varied or elaborated in later poems. But one section of it, at least, is significant in terms of Propertius' relationship to previous poetry, and that is the Milanion *exemplum*. The language of these verses is consistently difficult; it combines archaism—*ibat* with the infinitive, *domuisse* for *domare* are examples—with Hellenistic obscurantism: Atalanta is unnamed, but is called first *Iasidos* and then *uelocem puellam*, which plays on the other, more familiar version of her story. The reason for this preciosity of style has been well explained by Ross, following Franz Skutsch and Hermann Tränkle: it is derived from Cornelius Gallus.[35]

In citing Gallus, however, Propertius need not be accepting him as model and precedent any more than he accepts Catullan poetics in 1.3. Milanion in Propertius is an odd creature, and the story as told by Propertius makes even less sense than the elliptical quality of learned poetry demands. Milanion is said to gain Atalanta by avoiding no labors (9), but the *labores* described are strange: he wanders in the mountains, looks at wild beasts, is beaten by a centaur, and moans from his wounds. *Therefore*, we are told, he was able to conquer her: so much do prayers and good deeds in love accomplish. We have heard nothing of prayers, and little of good deeds. This

---

[34] Other discussions which I have found useful are those of Commager 1974: 21–36 and Ahl 1974: 80–98.
[35] On these verses cf. Tränkle 1960: 12–5; Ross 1975a: 62–4; Zetzel 1977: 253–4; King 1980a: 221–2.

Milanion is not a brave and noble character; rather, as Shackleton Bailey suggested, he has taken on the coloring of the speaker of the poem, an attitude of helpless suffering.[36] And that this passage is a rejection, indeed, a parody of mythological elegy (as too, I think, is Vergil's version of Gallus in the Tenth *Eclogue*) is made explicit by the next lines: such deeds as Milanion's are no longer any use: Love has forgotten his old tricks and tracks.

The first poem, clearly, defines the attitude of the lover and the nature of love in positive terms (if one can call them that); but it also functions as a negative definition: Propertius is not the mythological lover of Gallus' poetry. The second half of the poem defines the attitude even further, by specifying the ways love cannot be cured. But what matters here is that Propertius begins by defining his love and his poetry in terms of his immediate predecessor, Gallus, and establishes his independence of Gallus in both areas. It is scarcely surprising that the two are taken together: as has already been said several times, the elegiac condition requires that love and love poetry be the same thing.

What, then, of the poem which Ovid is imitating most directly, 1.2? David Ross tentatively suggested that this poem might be read as being in some sense 'about' poetry.[37] The two sets of *exempla* would be examples of neoteric verse, and *uulgo conquirere amantis* (23) could be a reference to Callimachus' σικχαίνω πάντα τὰ δημόσια (Epigr. 28.4). In both texts, τὰ δημόσια/*uulgo* are probably an attack on the use of trite themes and forms by other poets. The reference to Apollo and Calliope as Cynthia's patrons (27f.) is appropriate in a text about poetry as well. But Ross did not find his own tentative reading of the poem entirely consistent. In particular, if the poem is

---

[36] Shackleton Bailey 1956: 2–4; cf. also Commager 1974: 25–7. The irony of *uidere* was pointed out by Rothstein 1898 *ad loc.*, and emendations (e.g. that of Courtney 1968: 257–8) are unnecessary. The most desperate attempt at emendation comes, as might be expected, from the most humorless of readers, Housman 1888: 22–5 = 1972: 1:44–6. I note particularly his comment on *preces* (16), on the oddity of which see Ahl 1974: 88–9: 'Prayers! Where has he said a word about prayers? . . . Those who defend the credit of a scribe will impute any imbecillity to a poet are, I suppose, capable of maintaining that Propertius here forgot what he had just said and imagined that he had said something else.' He accepted Fonteine's *fides*.

[37] Ross 1975a: 58–9. This interpretation was suggested to me independently by Professor Keith Nightenhelser.

metaphorical, then *Coa ueste* (2) ought to be a reference to Philitas, the poet of Cos and one of the poetic divinities of Propertius 3.1.1, and *tenuis* ought to have its usual implication of neoteric poetics; and as both of these are clearly rejected within the dramatic context of the poem, then it becomes difficult—to say the least—to read the entire text as a statement of adherence to the Alexandrian-neoteric tradition, as Ross would have it. As I have been suggesting in my readings of 1.3 and 1.1, however, that is not the way to look at 1.2: it is not a pledge of allegiance, any more than the Milanion *exemplum* is a statement of loyalty to Gallus or 1.3 to Catullus. In 1.2 Propertius is in fact condemning adornment, and rejecting made-up (in both senses) women and verse. He does so in two sets of *exempla* from nature and from myth, passages that are themselves ornate and elaborately neoteric in style. If the poem is to be read as a consistent metaphor, then these verses should not be examples of how to write poetry, but of how *not* to write it: Propertius may be indulging in parody. And if that is the case, and the poem is a call for simplicity, then the rejection of Philitas is perfectly consistent.[38] What is more, it is consistent with Ovid's parody: both poems are on one level attacks on female vanity and adornment, on another criticisms of the poetic tradition within which both poems are written. As is often the case, Ovid both adopts the Propertian conventions from which he starts, and simultaneously reveals by exaggeration his awareness of their artificiality and absurdity. Nor, of course, is Propertius unironic in the opening poems of the Monobiblos; if I am right in my interpretations, he too reveals his awareness of his debt to the tradition (Gallus, possibly Philitas, Catullus), exaggerates the tendencies of his models, and while apparently rejecting them, continues to remain well within the lines that they had laid out. It is a matter of eating

---

[38] There is an apparent inconsistency between the rejection of *Coa ueste* here and the acceptance of Cos, as fabric or style, at 2.1.5–6 (on which cf. Zetzel 1983: 90–3). But as the inconsistency remains true on any interpretation of these passages, literal or metaphorical, it does not affect the validity of the interpretation of 1.2 offered here. It should be noted here that the reading of the Monobiblos that I am proposing implies a significant break between it and books 2 and 3: the explicit Callimacheanism of 2.1 and later poems (particularly 2.10, 13; 3.1–3) can be seen as the work of a poet who has already (in the Monobiblos) come to terms with his own place in the tradition and hence adopts a less antagonistic stance.

one's cake and having it—but that is true of the entire tradition of Roman Alexandrianism, in which it is traditional to claim originality in words and phrases that are borrowed from other poets.

I have examined the first three poems of the Monobiblos purely in terms of Propertius' poetic relationship to his predecessors and his literary self-definition; and it could be argued that much of the first half of the book continues that pattern, in ways that are unfortunately no longer to be understood—and in any case, Ovid does not take them within his interpretation. It can hardly be coincidental that poem 4 is addressed to an iambic poet, Bassus, and poems 7 and 9 to an epic poet, Ponticus, while several poems are addressed to a Gallus who is probably not, but is homonymous with, the elegist.[39] But the first three poems (to return to them) are not simply metapoetic statements: they combine poetics with the internal development of the elegiac condition. If the first poem defines love from the poet's internal feelings and actions, the second defines his expectations of his mistress, what he hopes she will be. And if in 1.1 the *exemplum* acts out the situation of the poet, in the second poem the mistress is equated to the poem itself. The third poem moves beyond both previous ones: it concerns neither the poet nor his beloved in isolation, but develops the character of Cynthia and deals with the relationship between them; and it sets the relationship between texts on a par with the relationship between people.

## THE POET AS MAGICIAN

The self-definition of the elegist in the opening poems of the Monobiblos is almost necessarily negative: it establishes his position and his stance through a set of contrasts with various poetic possibilities, as represented by eminent predecessors. In fact, as I have suggested elsewhere, the true Callimachean can not remain passively imitative

---

[39] The interest in mathematical and structural patterns in the Monobiblos as in other Augustan books (cf. for Propertius Skutsch 1963: 238–9 and Otis 1965: 1–44) has tended to distract from the reading of the poems in order as an episodic narrative (as in Horace, *Satires* 1: cf. Zetzel 1980: 59–77).

of any model, no matter how great or how orthodox the predecessor may be: it is in the nature of the tradition to demand a sort of perpetual denial of the tradition in order to remain within it.[40] But along with the necessarily agonistic approach of the Callimachean, Propertius as elegist also develops in the first half of the Monobiblos a more positive self-definition, as both poet and lover. What is most interesting about it, I think, is that it stands entirely outside the normal range of Callimachean metaphors: not slender pipes or narrow paths or pure springs or insects, but magic.[41]

That magic is denounced as useless in 1.1 is clear. In lines 19–24, the poet starts from a description of the common power of magicians, and then ridicules them. *Deductae fallacia lunae* means, in all probability, not the true power to draw down the moon, but the ability to seem to do so. Propertius then claims that he will believe in the power of magicians to alter the course of nature only when they can make Cynthia (and there is clearly a play on the meaning of her name) suffer more than himself: in other words, he does not believe in this magic at all.[42] What is important, however, is that Cynthia's charms appear to be more powerful than common magic spells; that is to say, love is itself a magic more powerful than the familiar variety.

It is scarcely surprising to find traditional magic being mocked. No Roman poet of the period takes this sort of thing seriously, for all the frequency with which it is mentioned.[43] Thus, for instance, when Tibullus relates his visit to a witch in 1.2.41ff., her powers are described in detail. They are so great that she can permit Delia to deceive her husband—but not to deceive Tibullus himself. Such powers are much too convenient to be taken at face value. In the same way, the description of the *lena*'s power in Propertius 4.5 is irrelevant to the content of her speech, which is no more than the standard advice of bawd to *puella*. The purpose of the lengthy

---

[40] Cf. Zetzel 1977: 259.
[41] The image of the poet as magician is not limited to Rome; for an illuminating discussion of its role in Shakespeare, cf. Kernan 1979.
[42] Cf. Camps 1961 (1977) *ad loc.*, Shackleton Bailey 1949: 22–3, and Commager 1974: 32–4.
[43] The best discussion of magic in Roman poetry is that of Luck 1962, to which I owe much. The more recent study of Tupet 1976 offers little in the way of literary interpretation.

description of her magical powers is to establish her social position and to poke fun at her airs. The same lack of seriousness attends all major descriptions of this type of magic in elegy (e.g. Propertius 3.6, Ovid *Amores* 1.8, 3.7).

If this type of magic is not to be taken seriously, however, another variety is: the magic of love—or of love poetry. And because it does not involve the description of recipes and incantations, it is not so easy to recognize. The poem in which I think that magic makes its first significant appearance in Propertius is 1.5, which has several times been discussed in terms of religious imagery.[44] The two are clearly very close and the distinction may not be entirely valid; but there are some important differences.

1.5 is addressed to a Gallus—which one, is irrelevant—and it is a warning to stay away from Cynthia. She is described as dangerous, and somewhat evil: when she is mad at you it is unpleasant, and when she is not, it is even worse. This is, of course, merely an example of Propertius' normal masochistic stance: it is always more degrading to be in love than not to be, but love is still preferable to any other state. But the lover in 1.5 is described in much more specific ways: Cynthia is portrayed not just as a normal elegiac mistress, but as a magical spirit; and Gallus is both a lover and a magical suppliant. The inconsistencies between these roles add to the pains of love, but they also convey important implications, when read in the context of the Monobiblos, about the position of the poet himself.

The final couplet of the poem provides the clearest indication of the metaphor being employed (31f.):

> *quare, quid possit mea Cynthia, desine, Galle,*
> *quaerere: non impune illa rogata uenit.*
> Therefore, Gallus, stop asking about my Cynthia's powers:
> when summoned, her arrival is not without a penalty.

---

[44] Moritz 1967: 107, followed by Hubbard 1974: 26 and Lyne 1974: 263, recognizes the divine element in Cynthia in 1.5, but none of these scholars offers a complete analysis or sees any magical element in the poem. Luck's comment (1962: 39) comes closer to the truth: 'Die "aüssere" Magie operiert mit Kraütern..., die "innere" Magie eines Menschen wirkt allein durch Schönheit, Character, Geist. Cynthia besitzt diese innere Magie...' (The 'exterior' magic operates with magical herbs, the 'interior' magic of a person works alone through beauty, character, spirit. Cynthia possesses this inner magic.)

Most commentators seem to think that *rogare* and *uenire* are amatory terms: to proposition a woman, and to come to an assignation.[45] But they have other meanings as well, as Moritz, Hubbard, and Lyne have pointed out, as part of the language of prayer. *Rogare* along with its synonyms is frequently used of religious petitions;[46] *uenire* as a religious or magical term is the normal word for the approach of the divinity, whose presence is necessary for any request to be obtained. The use of the word (or its Greek equivalent) is attested in many prayers, from Sappho to Horace to Christian hymns.[47] There is another technical term in this couplet, which is also used in 1.10, to which I will return shortly: *possum*. It is not simply a statement of competence, but one of divine or unusual power. Aeneas tells the Sibyl *potes namque omnia* (*Aen.* 6.117: 'for you have all powers') and Horace addresses Canidia *et tu—potes nam— solue me dementia* (*Epod.* 17.45: 'you have the power: free me from madness'). This element, the *dunamis*, is a standard element of prayer.[48] In short, the final couplet of 1.5 is intended to warn Gallus not to seek the appearance of Cynthia, because her epiphany has terrible consequences.

It is scarcely surprising to find Cynthia having divine powers in this poem, as other women in Roman poetry are similarly described. Lesbia is a *candida diua* (68.70), and Cynthia's own pseudonym implies not only a connection with Callimachus, but also with Diana, the goddess of the moon and of magic. But the final couplet in 1.5 in particular, and the poem as a whole, suggest also a connection between Cynthia and forbidden knowledge, implying that she is not a creature to be treated frivolously. *Quaerere* in the last verse frequently refers to the search for illicit knowledge, including the use of astrologers.[49] And knowledge and experience run through the whole poem: Gallus is asked in the first line to stop talking—presumably the same action as is described by *quaerere* in the last line.

---

[45] So Enk 1946 and Camps 1961 (1977) *ad loc.*
[46] So Hubbard 1974 (1975): 26 note 1. *Rogare* is most clearly used in prayer at Horace, *C.* 2.16.1.
[47] See Hubbard 1974: 26 note 1, and Nisbet and Hubbard 1970 on Horace, *C.* 1.2.30.
[48] Cf. Norden 1903 (1981) on *Aen.* 6.117 and Norden 1913 (1956): 154.
[49] Cf. Nisbet and Hubbard 1970 on Horace, *C.* 1.11.1.

He is asked if he wants to experience (*sentire*, 3) Propertius' troubles; he will know (*nosse*, 4) evils; later on he will not know (*nosse* again, 18) where he is; he will learn (*discere*, 20) the sufferings of a lover.[50] Gallus, if he persists in his quest, will incur more than his share of pain by seeking knowledge of Cynthia, whose awesome attributes are best not discovered.

All this, of course, could be religious as well as magical, but other elements in the poem suggest a specifically magical context. In the first place, there is the reference to Thessalian poisons (6), beloved of witches. And one verse is a clear allusion to magical powers (12):[51]

*illa feros animis alligat una uiros.*
She binds together men fierce in their minds

The magical significance of *alligare*, binding, was explained by Norden, who cited a clear parallel to this verse from *Herc. Oet.* 453f:[52]

*artibus magicis fere*
*coniugia nuptae precibus admixtis ligant.*
Brides generally bind their marriages together
with magical arts and an admixture of prayers.

And, what is most germane, magical incantations from the papyri include the command to bind, κατάδησον, the person being sought.[53]

Closely connected to the powers of Cynthia as magical spirit are the symptoms of love in her victims. These include insomnia and blindness, loss of speech, pallor, and wasting away. All these are typical of the disease of love, but it is worth noting that they are also just the sort of thing that magical love charms in the papyri urge their familiar spirits to inflict on the woman loved. Thus, several

---

[50] On knowledge as a theme of 1.5, cf. King 1980a: 213–14.
[51] Lyne 1974: 263–4, rightly sees that *una* in this verse has a religious significance, but connects *alligat* with the *seruitium amoris*. With this interpretation, however, he is forced to admit that 'ideas have been merged in the line.' The reason for this difficulty is *feros*, which does not seem to belong in a religious context, and G. Luck 1979: 75 has suggested emending it to *ferox*. That is possible but also, I think, diminishes the magical or religious element in the verse. Rather, I suspect, the verse alludes obliquely to Circe's metamorphosis of men to beasts: note the similar juxtaposition of Circe and Medea in 2.1.53–4, and cf. also Tibullus 2.4.55.
[52] Norden 1903 (1927, 1981) on *Aen.* 6.439.
[53] E.g. *PGM* 4.349–50, 380.

want the woman to be unable to eat or sleep, or to enjoy sex, and one very thorough magician commands his familiar as follows:[54]

πέμπω σε ... πρὸς αὐτήν, ἵνα μοι ἄξῃς αὐτήν. εἰ κάθηται, μὴ καθήτω, εἰ λαλεῖ πρός τινα, μὴ λαλείτω, εἰ ἐμβλέπει τινί, μὴ ἐμβλεπέτω, εἰ προσέρχεταί τινι, μὴ προσερχέτω, εἰ περιπατεῖ, μὴ περιπατείτω, εἰ πίνει, μὴ πινέτω, εἰ ἐσθίει, μὴ ἐσθιέτω, εἰ καταφιλεῖ τινα, μὴ καταφιλείτω, εἰ τέρπεταί τινι ἡδονῇ, μὴ τερπέσθω, εἰ κοιμᾶται, μὴ κοιμάσθω, ἀλλ' ἐμὲ μόνον στεργέτω, τὰ ἐμὰ θελήματα πάντα ποιείτω.

I am sending you ... to her, for you to lead her to me. If she sits, let her not sit, if she speaks to someone, let her not speak, if she looks at someone, let her not look, if she approaches someone, let her not approach, if she is strolling around, let her not stroll, if she drinks, let her not drink, if she eats, let her not eat, if she is kissing someone, let her not kiss, if she is enjoying any pleasure, let her not enjoy it, if she sleeps, let her not sleep, but let her love me alone, let her do all my wishes.

There are generic features in such spells, and they coincide—rather less delicately—with Propertius' descriptions in 1.5. Not to be able to eat or drink, to see or sleep, to speak to, or kiss, or make love to, anyone else.[55] In Gallus' case, the manifestation seems supernatural: words will flee from his mouth (17).

For all these symptoms of love, Propertius in 1.5 has no cure (28):

*cum mihi nulla mei sit medicina mali.*
as there is no drug for my trouble.

But six poems later, in 1.10, the same Gallus has fallen hopelessly in love with another woman, and Propertius witnesses that love. But this time, he seems to be able to do something about it (15–18):

---

[54] PGM 4.1508f.; cf. 350ff. Even though the extant papyri to which reference is made here were written in late antiquity, it is very likely that they preserve earlier material. On this topic, cf. Nock 1972: 176–94, esp. 187–8. It should be pointed out that there was a revival of interest in magic and the more mystical forms of Platonism and Pythagoreanism in Rome in the first century BCE; see Nock 1972: 187 and Dodds 1952: 247–8 with note 70.

[55] One of the readers for this journal draws my attention to the description of similar magical effects in a contemporary text, Horace, *Epod.* 17.19–29.

*possum ego diuersos iterum coniungere amantis*
  *et dominae tardas possum aperire fores:*
*et possum alterius curas sanare recentis*
  *nec leuis in uerbis est medicina meis.*

I have the power to bring separated lovers back together
  and I have the power to open the reluctant doors of my mistress:
and I have the power to cure another's recent passions
  and the drug in my words is not mild.

The repetition of *possum* is emphatic, and must again mean the possession of special powers. The difference is that this time, it is Propertius who possesses them. One reason for the difference may be simply that it is no longer Cynthia whose powers he is attempting to overcome; but there is also a change in Propertius. He whose symptoms neither magic nor medicine could cure in 1.1 and 1.5 has acquired power, and that power lies in his words. It is, of course, the power of poetry that can join lovers.[56]

One interesting aspect of the power of song in this passage is that it can not only reconcile lovers, it can open doors as well. Hardly a magical function at first sight, but this simple skill is in some respects as magical as the ability to cause or cure disease. Even the paraclausithyron, the poem of the excluded lover to the door, is essentially an incantation, and this everyday action (not, of course, by turning the handle and walking in) was an important element of magical and religious ritual and pseudo-ritual. In one magical papyrus we find:[57]

σὺ δὲ πάλιν λέγε σιγή (λόγος), εἶτα ἄνοιξον τοὺς ὀφθαλμοὺς καὶ ὄψῃ ἀνεῳγυίας τὰς θύρας καὶ τὸν κόσμον τῶν θεῶν, ὅς ἔστιν ἐντὸς τῶν θυρῶν

And then you say 'silence' (speech), then open your eyes and you will see the gates open and the heaven of the gods which is within the gates.

---

[56] Luck 1959 on 1.10.15–8 comments (p. 138): 'His own experience has prepared him to give advice to the lovelorn; but his poetry is more than advice; it is magic, verbal incantation. Propertius speaks of his powers in terms which occur more frequently in descriptions of witchcraft.' See also Luck 1961: 222 note 17, 1962: 44. On the double meaning of *carmen* cf. also Commager 1974: 34. Poetry is explicitly described as a *pharmakon* for love by Theocritus 11.1ff.; on the relationship of magic, poetry, and rhetoric in Greece cf. de Romilly 1975: 3–22.

[57] *PGM* 4.623ff.; see also 12.323ff. and Norden 1903 (1981) on *Aen.* 6.81f.

And in another text, the papyrus includes among the powers of the *paredros* the ability to get women or gold, to free people from chains, and to open doors.[58] In fact, it was an important enough indication of supernatural powers that Hero of Alexandria (*Pneum.* 1.38f.) gave two methods for constructing a secret door-opener worked by the heat of the sacrificial fire. In 1.10, then, Propertius has acquired authentically supernatural powers.

The *medicina* that Propertius in 1.5 was lacking became his in 1.10 by virtue of his poetry. In the first poem of the book, he is a mere beginner; in 1.5 he is still struggling; but by 1.10 he has achieved some success in love and magic alike. Part of the motivation for this lies in the ambiguity of the word *carmen*: it is not only the word for the type of poetry Propertius writes, it is the normal word for a magical incantation, attested as early as the Twelve Tables.[59] It should be noted that in 1.1 he exploits the relationship between love and magic in another way: when he refers to witches as

*deductae quibus est fallacia lunae,*
who have the trick of drawing down the moon

*deducere* in context must mean the drawing down of the moon, but it is also a term of art for the Roman Callimacheans to describe the writing of elegant verse.[60] Magic and poetry are in one sense the same, just as in another magic and love are the same. And that love and poetry, in the elegiac convention, are the same is obvious.

It is no coincidence, I think, that between the helplessness of the poet in the face of magic in 1.5 and his powers in 1.10, there are several poems which are specifically concerned with the power of poetry, and express it in ways that are at least partly magical. 1.7 and 8A to Ponticus and Cynthia respectively express the helplessness of the lover, and they are answered in chiastic order by poetic solutions in 8B and 9. Ponticus in 7 is not in love; he is writing a *Thebaid*. Propertius contrasts his own situation, and warns that epic is useless to the lover (19f.):

*et frustra cupies mollem componere uersum*
   *nec tibi subiciet carmina serus Amor.*

---

[58] *PGM* 1.98ff.    [59] XII Tab. 8.1; cf. Horace, *Sat.* 2.1.82–3.
[60] See above note 14 and Ross 1975a: 65–6.

And you will yearn in vain to compose soft verse
and late Love will not supply you with poems.

In 8A, Propertius is in a situation similar to that which he imagines for Ponticus in 7: Cynthia is deserting him for her Illyrian lover. The poems balancing these both concern the power of love poetry: Ponticus when he falls in love is told to imitate Mimnermus instead of Homer, and in 8B Propertius exclaims (39–42):

> *hanc ego non auro, non Indis flectere conchis,*
>    *sed potui blandi carminis obsequio:*
> *sunt igitur Musae, neque amanti tardus Apollo,*
>    *quis ego fretus amo: Cynthia rara mea est.*
> It was not with gold or Indian shells that I had the power to bend her,
>    but with the service of enchanting song:
> so the Muses really exist, and Apollo is not slow for lovers.
>    In being a lover I rely on them: rare Cynthia is mine.

This is not merely a statement about poetry and its inspiration, although it is partly that; it is not just a substitution of Apollo for *tardus Amor* of poem 1. The idea that the *obsequium* of song is equivalent to the power of gold and jewels gives it more significance, and the description of his song as *blandum* is curious. *Blanditia* is a frequent attribute of medical, magical, and religious words and actions.[61] Even in this simple poem, the language used to describe divinely inspired poetry is equally relevant to magical incantation.

The reason for this use of the metaphor of magic for the power of song is not simply a function of the ambiguity of the word *carmen*: rather, it is related to the images of poetry presented by other Alexandrian or neoteric writers. One passage of 1.9 shows this very well (29–32):

> *qui non ante patet, donec manus attigit ossa:*
>    *quisquis es, assiduas a fuge blanditias!*
> *illis et silices et possint cedere quercus,*
>    *nedum tu possis, spiritus iste leuis.*

---

[61] For medicine cf. Celsus 5.28.2: *lenia medicamenta, quae quasi blandiantur* (gentle treatments, which almost blandish); for magic, cf. Ovid, *Am.* 3.1.46 *haec est blanditiis ianua laxa meis* (this door was opened by my blandishments); also *Met.* 2.815, Apuleius, *Metam.* 4.22.1. Note further *CGlL* 2.264.25–6: *blanditio* γοητεία ἐπὶ κολακίας, *blandior* γοητεύω ὅ ἐστι κολακεύω.

> He does not show himself until his hand touches your bones:
> whoever you are, run from his constant enticements!
> Flint and oak can yield to them;
> how will you resist, light spirit that you are?

*Blanditiae*, the word for Propertius' poetry in 8B and for the poem against the door in 1.16.16, here take on the power of moving rocks and trees. The power of moving trees belonged to one poet in particular, Orpheus, although it became a transferred characteristic of Hesiod and other poets admired by the neoterics.[62] But the implication is clear: love, or love poetry, is the equal of the magical power of Orpheus over nature. It is not too far-fetched, perhaps, to recall that one of the traditional accusations against a cruel man was that he was sprung from trees or rocks.[63] In such a situation, Orphic powers would indeed be useful.

My own suspicion is that, in using the language of magical song in the first half of the Monobiblos, Propertius is adapting and revising a convention of Vergil and, presumably, Gallus. In 2.13, Propertius specifically says that Amor had ordered him to write poetry not in order, like Orpheus, to lead trees and beasts, but so that Cynthia might marvel at his verse.[64] In the Monobiblos, Propertius is thus offering a new Orphism, a theory of poetry as magic, and of love poetry as the highest form of magic. The mechanism of Propertius' powers is clear. When he first falls in love, in poem 1, standard recipe magic is of no use, and in poem 5 he is still struggling and proclaiming his inability to overcome Cynthia's higher magic. But in 8B, 9, and 10 an antidote emerges, not without some irony. Cynthia's love has compelled him to write *carmina*, but those very songs turn out themselves to be a form of Orphic-magical incantation capable of overcoming Cynthia's own spells. The implication of the poet-lover as magician is, I think, consonant with the ironic rejection of Propertius' poetic predecessors in the opening poems of the book; indeed, the poet-sorcerer may itself be an ironic rejection of the poet-*uates*

---

[62] See Ross 1975a: 23–4.
[63] Cf. *Aen.* 4.366f. with Pease's exhaustive note (1935).
[64] Wyke 1987b: 57–60 rightly sees the transfer of spellbinding powers from the Gallus of *Eclogue* 6 to Propertius' own poetry as significant; but again, what is made explicit in Book 2 is already implicit in the Monobiblos.

beloved of some of Propertius' contemporaries. What it is, above all, is an exaltation of the effects of love on the poet, an assertion of the immediacy and poetic validity of his own elegiac experience. And yet, of course, that experience and even his assertion of poetic power are themselves conditioned by the work of his predecessors.

Let me return, finally and briefly, to my starting point, *Amores* 1.14. What Ovid sets out in vivid, even grotesque, terms is a fact that every Roman poet working in the Callimachean tradition knew—that what starts as a striking and novel image or technique quickly becomes a cliché: poetry, like poets and professors, becomes bald. There is a tendency, therefore, to claims of specious originality, or to novelty and variation for their own sake—practices which themselves rapidly become clichés. Ovid took a somewhat different tack: embracing the clichés, exaggerating them, drawing attention to the originality of his own unoriginality (or vice versa). That is what he does most clearly in 1.9, *militat omnis amans*, but also in 1.14 and other poems. In this case, indeed, he achieves a perverse kind of originality—he reverses expectations by writing about female baldness, and thus it might be suggested that he keeps his poetic hair by removing Corinna's. Ovid is aware of the risks of flaunting clichés as baldly as he does: his love poetry, despite moments of great beauty, is not love poetry, but parody of it. He has poured the hair-dye of elegiac convention all over his poetry, and if it is ultimately self-destructive, he knew that too. And he left nowhere for a love poet to go.

All this, however, is a rather sweeping interpretation of Augustan poetry, and it is possible that Ovid, in context, did not mean it that way. He does promise a cure: wear a German wig, he says, and sooner or later your own hair will grow back.[65] In fact, however, the cure has little relevance to the poetic part of the metaphor: poetic baldness has no cure. Perhaps Ovid was suggesting that he needed a rest from poetry; after all, there were two more books of *Amores* still to come. For Ovid, poetic hair grew in again; for Roman poetry, it never did. And the Sygambrian wig may have come back to haunt Ovid:

---

[65] One of the readers makes the appealing suggestion that *triumphatae...gentis* has a generic meaning as well, and indicates the possibility that worn-out elegy will be overtaken by epic.

perhaps he thought of it years later, as he sat in Tomi trying to write poetry in Gothic.

*Additional Note*, 2009

The text of Propertius cited here is Barber's OCT (ed. 2, 1960), which has recently been displaced by the unfortunate edition of Stephen Heyworth (2007a). In particular, I reject the following readings printed by Heyworth in passages discussed here (all from the Monobiblos; correct [Barber] text in parentheses): 1.11–12: *lacuna* (no *lacuna*); 1.12: *ferire* (*uidere*); 1.22: *umbras* (*amnis*); 1.33: *nam me* (*in me*); 2.9: *non fossa* (*formosa*); 2.13: *praelucent* (*persuadent* [wrongly obelized by Barber]); 2.24: *nimis . . . pudicitiae* (*satis . . . pudicitia*); 2.25: *ergo ego* (*non ego*); 3.16: *et arma* (rightly daggered by Barber; perhaps read *tarda*); 3.25: *omnia quae* (*omniaque*); 3.26: *malaque* (*munera*); 5.1–2: placed after 4.28 (placed as 5.1–2); 5.20: *domo* (*domum*); 9.31–32: deleted (in place); 10.16: *surdas* (*tardas*). On the other hand, I am more inclined now to accept, as does Heyworth, Luck's *ferox* for *feros* at 1.5.12 (see above, note 51).

# Part III

# Poetry and Politics

# 9

# A Farewell to Promethean Man[1]

*Hans Peter-Stahl*

I am aware of the possibility that, to some of my readers, Propertius' opposition to contemporary epic and his rejection of Augustan Zeitgeist is not as fundamental as I have outlined. They may claim that the outward submissiveness Propertius occasionally displays towards Vergil and Augustus is more sincere than I assume, and that, consequently, the signals of inner withdrawal and independence do not reflect anything vital, but stem from a rather marginal desire not to be bothered. In short, my reader may question whether the flame kindled by Octavian's Perusine massacre in general (1.22) and by the early loss of a close relative specifically (1.21) is still alive in our poet's breast and, rekindled by threatening new interference with his personal life (2.7) and poetry (2.1; 10), has led to a firm and permanent position. The answer to this question demands nothing less than an evaluation of Propertius' attitude towards Augustus' imperial ideology—an attitude which, if it amounts to a rejection (as I think it does), can hardly be expected to be open and comprehensive, but rather offered symbolically and in disguise. But an

---

[1] Editor's note: This paper is a chapter from Stahl's book *Propertius 'Love' and 'War'*. As such the original prose often refers to other parts of the book. The editors have chosen to retain Stahl's prose as closely as possible, but to omit phrases such as 'as was shown in chapter IV above' and to refer to those chapters simply with the date and page citations of the final publication. The Latin translations for the inset passages in this paper are the author's own except where noted; the editors have translated the embedded passages, and all the German, French, and Italian.

answer can be given. For this purpose I turn to some passages in Propertius' third book of elegies.

In parenthesis, it may be said that Books 2 and 3 are the two most closely related and most homogeneous, so that there is no difficulty in extending discussion of a topic from Book 2 into Book 3—provided, of course, that the context of the individual elegies discussed corroborates such continuity. The characterization I gave of Book 2 (as compared with the Monobiblos) in Stahl (1985: 139–171) is valid for Book 3 also: prominence of the long elegy; a theoretical and argumentative character; preoccupation with the Zeitgeist in order to set off an individual poetical message against it; increasing surrender to the political facts through lip service to the régime; loud self-advertisement of the elegist's greatness. Of new or newly prominent features, I mention the beginnings of objective elegy[2] and the growing emptiness of the personal love-theme, which finally leads to an outspoken farewell to Cynthia (the slow death of his love is, as I said in the Preface, an aspect of Propertius' poetry which this book will not treat in detail). Although a shift of emphasis doubtless takes place—a movement to and fro of certain themes between foreground and background—I do not see a change of basic attitudes, but rather a desire to express personal continuity in a changing environment.

To emphasize the continuity and, at the same time, to confirm my interpretation of Propertius' attitude towards Vergil (which, after all, is part of his attitude towards Augustus) I would like to draw my reader's attention to the proem of Book 3. It is certain that elegies 2.1 and 2.34 were purposefully conceived as a setting and guideline for the contents of that book, and we may accordingly be sure that elegy 3.1, as an introduction to Book 3, picks the reader up from the spot where elegy 2.34 left him.

In the opening lines (3.1.1–6),[3] Propertius, using almost religious language, introduces himself as the first poet to dress his Italian

---

[2] See Stahl 1985: 215–33.
[3] It is still worthwhile reading Luck's 1957: 175ff. circumspect explanation of the opening section. He attempts to find concrete answers (in 3.3) to the concrete questions of 3.1 by way of visualizing a consistent scenery from Propertius' hints. Luck's approach is not invalidated but rather modified by Baker's interpretation 1968b: 35ff. Comparing 3.9.43–6, Baker concludes that, as a love elegist, Propertius in 3.1.1f. expresses desire for the same worship (*sacra*) which his models receive. For

content in the forms employed by Callimachus and Philitas—the two Hellenistic writers of learned Small Poetry whom he had recommended to 'Lynceus' in the epilogue of Book 2 (line 31f.) as a prestage that would prepare him for the writing of personal love elegies (43ff.) in the Propertian manner (55ff.).

More interesting for us than the literary link Propertius sees between himself and Alexandrian form are the manifest implications and guidelines (hardly a matter of style alone) he finds for his own poetry in this pedigree:

> A valeat, Phoebum quicumque moratur in armis! (3.1.7)
> Ah, away with him, whoever wastes Apollo's time in arms!

The observant reader, I am afraid, cannot but individualize the innocent, general word 'whoever' (*quicumque*) when he recalls the 'pleasure' Vergil was alleged to find (2.34.61ff.) in being able to sing of Apollo's participation in the battle of Actium—Vergil

> qui nunc Aeneae Troiani suscitat arma. (63)
> who now rouses Trojan Aeneas' arms

If we still had some doubt about how to take the 'compliment' paid to the new Homer (*nescio quid maius nascitur Iliade*, 'something greater than the Iliad is being born,' 2.34.66), we may now claim that degree of certainty which irony allows without losing its fun.

Not very humbly, Propertius goes on to depict his own Fame as the master of the chiseled Small Form, even the triumph[4] of the poetry which he himself (!) has created (*a me/nata... Musa*, 9f.), followed

---

the whole complex of literary tradition alluded to in 3.1ff. (especially 3.3), see Kambylis 1965: 125–90.

[4] The most recent triumph in Rome was the Emperor's own in 29 BCE! The political scene of the day (and its implications for contemporary writers) seems not to exist for some scholars who distill almost every word of our text into just another '*stilkritische*' (stylistic-critical) allusion to Callimachus' Alexandrian literary criticism. See, for instance, Quadlbauer 1968: 97ff. Much more to the point is Galinsky (1969: 88): 'The usurpation of an epic and "official" custom for himself and his *exiguus sermo* (modest speech) reflects Propertius' self-confidence.' The poet's claim on a *triumphus* must be viewed in line with his habit of wresting established honors from his opponents and claiming them for himself (cf. 1.7.9ff.; [1.12.3ff.;] 1.6.30; 2.1.47; 2.7.13ff.; the last passage is evaluated by Galinsky 1969: 82f.). With regard to 'fame,' see Brouwers 1970.

by the 'crowd of the authors'—his rank-and-file army, we assume![5] There will be 'many' (*multi*, 15), to add Rome's new glories to history's annals (as once written by Ennius?), by singing of Bactra's incorporation into the *Imperium Romanum*, i.e. of the fulfillment of the old expansionists' dream that Parthia be added to the Roman domain—a dream just now revived under the slogan 'vengeance for the two Crassi'. But Propertius sets a new goal for Rome (it is Rome as a whole that he feels entitled to address!): peace poetry.

> *sed, quod pace legas, opus hoc de monte Sororum*
> *detulit intacta pagina nostra via.* (3.1.17–18)
> But offering a work which you (sc., Rome) may read in peace, our page brought this down from the Muses' mountain by an untrodden path.

The contrast between arms (7; cf. *laudes*, 15) and peace (17), *arma* and *pax*, comes into the open sharper than ever because it is now coupled with the contrast (*sed*, 17) of the 'many' (among whom we must count Vergil, too) who sing of Rome's military glory, and the one Propertius, who tries to introduce something which he feels is completely new (*intacta... via*, 18, as opposed to the *lata via*, 'wide path' of 14) to the Roman scene: love elegy as the poetry of peace—not so much peace which has been won through arms (peace as a postwar period, so to speak), but peace as the expression of a basic human attitude—love—which is conceived without the idea of war as its complement (cf. *pacis Amor deus est*, 3.5.1).[6] This of course

---

[5] Nothing but a preoccupation speaks for an interpretation which limits the *scriptorum turba* (crowd of authors) of line 12 to imitators in the field of elegy. In 2.34.65 the *scriptores* addressed are foremost epic poets. Quadlbauer (1968: 100) concedes: 'Aber auch andere sind nicht direkt ausgeschlossen' (But other sorts are not explicitly excluded). Of course we may also think of 'converted' epicists like Lynceus (2.34) and Ponticus (1.9).

[6] For the Augustan (Roman) idea of peace, cf. *Res Gestae* 13; *cum... esset parta victoriis pax* (when peace had been achieved through victories). etc. '*Pax* means "pacification" as much as "no fighting"', (Brunt and Moore 1973 *ad locum*). I cannot follow Quadlbauer 1968: 103 who finds in 3.1.17f. 'ein elegantes indirektes Kompliment für den Friedensbringer Augustus' (an elegant indirect compliment for Augustus bringer of peace). For Augustus' peace demands war poetry such as Vergil's, while Propertius' idea of peace is not recognized in Augustus' 'peacetime' Rome (although it ought to be, as our passage implies). Rightly, Galinsky asserts 1969: 89: 'The military preparations against the Parthians (15–16) which give rise to epic poetry, are contrasted with Propertius' poetry of *pax* (16ff.),' etc.

does not mean that Propertius' idea of peace cannot be enhanced or even given a sharper profile against the background of the threat of war—one need only think of its biographical origin as described in Stahl (1985: 99–132). It was, as we pointed out earlier, an unlucky circumstance for Propertius that the term *pax* had already been claimed by the victor of Perusia and Actium. This made it extremely difficult (and delicate) to outline a *Pax Propertiana* in the face of the *Pax Augusta*. Who would listen to a poet who could neither swim with the stream of his contemporaries nor spell out his message too openly? The sense of isolation that results from these conditions is voiced once again in 3.1: to ask for *mollia serta*, the garlands of the love elegist (19), because the *dura corona*, the wreath of the epic poet, does not fit one's head (20), is no way to earn acknowledgment from the 'many,' who approach the Muses on the 'broad road' (cf. *lata* via, 14) and who allegedly try in vain to compete with Propertius (*quid frustra . . . certatis . . . ?* 13). On the contrary, Propertius' exclusive poetry (honored by the Muses: vestro . . . *poetae*, 19), like Callimachus', even arouses envy among the 'crowd'—in this way he, showing no lack of self-confidence,[7] understands and interprets contemporary reaction to his work:

> *At mihi quod vivo detraxerit invida turba,*
> *post obitum duplici faenore reddet Honos.* (3.1.21–22)
> But what the envious crowd has detracted from me during my lifetime, the deity of Honor[8] will return to me with double interest after my death.

There is no shyness when he speaks about his own future fame. He even ventures to liken his situation to that of Homer (!), whose poetry grew more famous after its author's death (33f.), and then proceeds:

> *Meque inter seros laudabit Roma nepotes:*
> *illum post cineres auguror ipse diem.* (3.1.35–36)
> I, too, shall receive Rome's praise among later generations:
> I myself prophecy that day after my death.

---

[7] Self-confidence pervades the whole elegy. It is further expressed by the quotations from Callimachus (*Aitia*) and from Roman contemporaries. For a brief list, see Camps 1966 *ad* 3.1.

[8] 'Reputation,' Shackleton Bailey 1956: 295.

The situation is clear: Propertius has something to say to Rome, but Rome is not yet mature enough to listen. The *Pax Augusta* still prefers the glorious annals of war to the unglorious poetry of the *Pax Propertiana*. It is the daring generalization of his love's claim which lifts him above the heads of the forerunners mentioned in 2.34.85–92. They would never have dreamt of seriously recommending to Rome the lover's life as a human ideal which is difficult to attain. But of course they did not yet face a uniformed Rome, ruled by one strong hand. Now, the poet's lot truly is to be *unzeitgemäss* (out of sync with his times).

Propertius' refusal to join the *multi* (3.1.15) who will glorify Rome's victory over the Parthians leaves nothing to be desired in clarity. If further explanation is needed, Propertius gives it once more in 3.3, where Apollo himself is introduced, telling our poet in no uncertain terms (cf. *demens*, 3.15) not to think of writing a historic epic and becoming a successor to Ennius (cf. 6ff.), but directing him on a peculiar 'new path' (*nova... semita*, 26), which reminds us of the *intacta... via* ('intact path') of 3.1.18. That the new poetry envisaged by Propertius means Alexandrian Form, but personal (and appealing) contents, is the message we have understood continuously from elegy 1.7 through to 3.1 where we finally see the distinctive program of peace poetry announced (1.17; see also *cara legenti*, 'dear to the reader,' 3.2.15).

We are therefore surprised to find, in 3.4, our poet functioning as a priest and seer who prays in public for a successful outcome of Augustus' expedition against the Parthians. We are, however, in for a second surprise: the next elegy (3.5), taken by some as the last in a series of five coherent introductory poems,[9] denounces, if we can read on as well as between the lines, the spirit that leads to the Parthian expedition, in a voice shriller than ever—thus rendering the gap between the poet's public concessions to the régime and his personal standpoint wider than ever before. In the case of elegies

---

[9] Ites 1908: 51ff.; Solmsen 1948: 105, with n. 1; Nethercut 1961: 389ff. and 1970, 385ff.; Woolley 1967: 81; Courtney 1969: 70; Juhnke 1971: 113. This grouping should not, however, level the more substantial and much graver human concerns voiced in the pair 4 and 5 in comparison with 1–3 which move along lines of literary criticism. Cf. Jäger 1967: 74, who describes the new perspective of 4 and 5 as that of the poet facing the demands of his own time.

4 and 5, the contradiction between the views presented is so obvious that one may presuppose its existence without having to prove it,[10] and may proceed immediately to a detailed evaluation of its meaning in the context of Propertius' poetry. Both elegies can be read in themselves, especially 3.4. This poem is similar to 2.10 in starting on a high level—the speaker is a future epic poet there, a religious prophet here—and ending in an anticlimax: the end (or the other hand, as we said then) does not back up the beginning (the offer presented with one hand). The presence of two levels of meaning, the one promising, the other retracting, has been found in so many poems by now that we may rightly call it a Propertian technique. This time we shall find it enriched by a new twist: the retraction contained in the poem itself is outdone by an outright about-face in the following poem.

Elegy 3.4 displays a structure that can be easily described.[11]

A   1/2: Augustus' plan for an expedition to the east   1D
B   3–10: Propertius predicts great rewards to the soldiers and victory to Augustus: the ends of the world will yield triumphs, Parthia will become a Roman province.
  Poet and seer Propertius sends out the soldiers, sings of favorable omens: 'wash out the shame of the two Crassi's death (in 53 BC) and serve Roman history well!'   4D

[10] See for instance Camps' introductory remarks. A correspondence of their opening words (*Arma deus Caesar—Pacis Amor deus est*) has been observed by many interpreters. Jäger 1967: 76 has added that their concluding distichs (beside a reference of content in the latter to the earlier, seen by Ribbeck 1885: 483) correspond in form also: their hexameters are largely dedicated to the main person(s) of each poem, the pentameters to their counterparts.

[11] Interpreters have shown themselves confused by the shifting addresses in this poem; but the persons addressed offer the key to visualizing a consistent situation—as may be expected of Propertius' usual fondness for clarity and logic. The elegist here pretends to be a priest who sets out by addressing Augustus' soldiers in the presence of their warlord: 1/2 characterize and announce the campaign (Caesar = third person); 3–10 indoctrinate the soldiers (= second person throughout) with their mission (once in between the priest turns directly to the present Emperor: second person in *tua*, 4); in 11–22 the priest faces the altar and addresses the gods (= second persons in 11 and 19); during this time, he is turned away from the Emperor (= third person, 13 and 19; *hoc... caput* perhaps indicates a pointing gesture in the Emperor's direction); the soldiers, too, are out of sight during the prayer (= third person: *illis*, 21); only the priest himself and his personal concerns appear always in the first person because he is the one who speaks the prayer.

C  11–18: Prayer (*precor*) to Mars and Vesta that Propertius may live to see the day of Augustus' return and triumphal procession, of which (and of himself, reclining against his girl's bosom and watching) he gives a vivid picture in advance.  4D
D  19–20: Special prayer to Venus, to grant eternal life to Augustus, her latest descendant in the line originating from Aeneas.  1D
E  21–2: The poet leaves the expedition's booty to the warriors: for him it will be enough to be able to applaud the triumphal procession on the *Sacra Via*.  1D

It can be shown that elegy 3.4, like 2.10, implicitly contains the refusal of an epic praising the Emperor's deeds. The elegist will be present at the triumph, and he will applaud—but no more. The last section (E), like an epilogue, draws the line. This refusal, however, is in no way aggressive: it points to modesty and lack of ability (*posse*, 22), but not to lack of will. Even the disrespect we sense in the picture of Propertius watching the Emperor's triumph from the viewpoint which his girl's bosom allows him (*inque sinu carae nixus spectare puellae*, 'to watch entwined in the lap of my dear girl,' 15) is, in my eyes, not necessarily an insult if read by the Emperor, especially not in the face of the flattering prophecy preceding it: it may be taken to be the cheeky expression of devotion of a court clown who knows that a continuous panegyric tone is not expected from his lips. Once before already (2.1.1–16) we saw Propertius clownishly ridicule himself in the eyes of Maecenas and Augustus, without revealing his real attitude.

His lip service to the Emperor, on the other hand—most visible in unbalanced ('odd') section D which eternalizes Augustus—has here reached a degree of submissiveness which will be exceeded only by his elegy on the battle of Actium (4.6) where Julius Caesar will find his own deification confirmed by Augustus' victory over Cleopatra. In 3.4 Augustus himself is called *deus*—a fact that cannot be got around even by the most cunning interpretation, so striking is its singularity (even Horace and Vergil rarely went that far) and its insincerity (3.5 leaves no doubt that Propertius' *deus* is *not* the Emperor). The breakdown of the public resistance, or at least of open reserve, which made itself felt already in the change of tone from 1.22 to 2.10, is complete long before the unsuccessful poet of national themes announces himself in 4.1.

For elegy 3.4 certainly contains more than mere acknowledgment of the Emperor's power to use force (as did the unintimidated poem 2.7); even more than 2.10, it contains consent (*plaudere posse*, 'to be able to applaud,' 22) and, beyond consent, active participation by the 'seer-poet' who encourages the Emperor's troops to go to war (*magna, viri, merces... ite agite... date lintea... ducite... omina fausta cano... piate... ite... consulite!* 'the rewards are great, men ... go on... set sail... lead... I sing favorable omens... avenge... go... take counsel!' 3–10). This incitement to war is as flagrant an offense to the program of peace poetry (3.1.17f.) as is the poem's first word, *arma*, which, occupying the most emphatic position of all, makes the reader rightly expect something related in subject matter to the opening line of Vergil's *Aeneid* (alluded to but rejected as non-Propertian in spirit in 2.34.63, cf. 3.1.7). In the same way, the subject of punishment of the Parthians for killing father and son Crassus (3.4.9) in itself suggests a deviation from the range of subject matter set up in 3.1.15ff. (*multi..., qui finem imperii Bactra futura canent*, 'there are many who will sing that Bactra will be the boundary to your empire'). So does Propertius' interest in the promotion of *Romanae... historiae* (4.10), for which Camps rightly compares the spirit of Livy's *praefatio*.[12] Precisely this spirit had been superbly mocked in the opening poem of Book 2 (*maxima de nihilo nascitur historia*, 'the best history arises from nothing,' 1.16, Stahl 1985: 139–71). And—to mention one more matter—the prayer to Venus (3.4.19f.) displays, beside a surprising interest in Octavian's longevity (or even eternal existence), an unexpected endorsement of his official pedigree, the epic realization of which Propertius had termed *Caesaris in Phrygios condere nomen avos* a few years ago, 2.1.42 ('to plant the name of Caesar among Trojan ancestors').

There is no denying that elegy 3.4, if viewed against the general background of Propertius' poetry and independently from its pendant 3.5, is at odds with what we have learned to take as Propertius' personal attitude and outlook. In its approval of the Emperor's

---

[12] Livy *praef.*: *Iuvabit tamen rerum gestarum memoriae principis orbis terrarum populi et ipsum consuluisse* (It will be pleasing nevertheless for me to attend to the memory of the achievements of the foremost population on earth). Camps 1966 *ad loc.*: 'where Livy hopes to serve Rome's history by writing it.'

person and politics, it far exceeds even the sort of lip service an unsuspicious contemporary Augustan might have appreciated in poems like 2.10, 2.1, or 2.34; and its reserve, where pronounced, is soft, and does not appear to be a matter of principle. The principles are banished to and discussed in a separate elegy (this is the new[13] twist I mentioned above; the true rejection is uttered separately and fended off by some soft mock opposition). For my own interpretation, I must emphasize the increasing abyss between what has by now become public adulation and, on the other hand, the proud, but disguised denial of any common ground with the adulated. If we refuse to acknowledge the abyss (or ridicule it by calling it schizophrenia), and if we fail to see the pain and self-torture entailed by appearing in one's own book of peace-poetry as a priest blessing the arms of Octavian, we are bound to miss the vital interest which poems dealing with the Zeitgeist possessed for their author. It is hardly sufficient to ascribe the large part of his work that is concerned with its own function merely or even predominantly to his poetological interests. He must (to formulate a working hypothesis) have been under severe pressure to write something like 3.4 and to include it in the collection.

If one turns to the next elegy, one is surprised how soft the reserve voiced at the end of 4 seems in comparison with the new criticism contained in 5. For, once the character of 3.5 as a disguised recantation of 3.4 is recognized,[14] the meaning of 3.4 is reversed into the

---

[13] One may of course compare the manner in which 2.10 is preceded by 2.7. For an interpretation (not without followers) that locates Propertius' opposition inside 3.4 itself, see n. 27 below.

[14] It has proved difficult to weigh the two poems' individual intentions. Jäger 1967, for instance, first sees their author undecided ('in einem stark empfundenen Zwiespalt,' 'in a strong, keenly felt inner conflict,' p. 74); he also speaks of a 'Dialektik der Gegensätze Zustimmung—Ablehnung' ('the dialectic of the opposites, agreement–rejection,' p. 103). Later he declares the tensions between the opposites considerably lessened ('die Spannung... wesentlich herabgemindert') by a formal concord with the campaign program of Augustus ('eine formelle Zustimmung zum Feldzugplan des Augustus'), which makes the refusal 'only' personal ('welche die Ablehnung auf den persönlichen Bereich beschränkt,' 'which rejection was restricted to the personal realm,' p. 105). But is not the problem precisely the personal one, that Propertius fervently wishes to decline what he has been urged to support so fervently? Ites felt that 3.5 offers so strong a *recusatio*, '*ut ipsam el. 4 revocet*,' ('that it would revoke elegy 4 itself,' 1908: 53).

opposite of what it originally seemed, from blessing and praise to curse and condemnation.

I begin my interpretation by decoding the message of the first line, which, read for itself, appears rather harmless:

*Pacis Amor deus est, pacem veneramur amantes.* (3.5.1)
Of peace, Amor is the god, peace is what we lovers worship.

That love and peace go together is suggested also in the introductory poem of Book 3. Spice is added when we take into account the official imperial program of 'peace,' which means, rather, pacification. About ten years from now (13 BC), a symbol of this official 'peace,' the *Ara Pacis Augustae*, will be built when the Emperor will have returned from 'pacifying' Spain and Gallia—a situation well comparable to the present one in which the Parthian expedition of 3.4 (and 5) is expected to bring Parthia under Augustus' 'jurisdiction' (cf. *sub tua iura*, 3.4.4) and make it a *provincia* (4.5) of 'peacetime' Rome. The Zeitgeist, background for Propertius' formulation, once more finds its adequate expression, as in Augustus' *Res Gestae* (26ff.), so in the *Aeneid*, where *Augustus Caesar, divi genus, aurea condet/saecula, qui ... super et Garamantas et Indos proferet imperium; iacet extra sidera tellus*, etc. ('Augustus Caesar, born from a god, will found a golden age, which will bring the empire to the Garamantes and the Indus, his land will lie beyond the stars,' 6.792ff.), his worldwide (cf. *nec... tantum telluris*, 'not so much land,' 801) exterminator's activity being compared, among other things, to Heracles' 'pacifying' (*pacarit*, 803) act of killing the Erymanthian boar. By restoring the Golden Age (792f.) in this and similar ways, Augustus fulfills the Roman's mission in this world. It consists not so much in promoting the arts and sciences (847–850) as in 'ruling nations' and '*imposing* (the) order on (of) peace' (852). As we have seen Propertius to be conscious of the growing *Aeneid*'s spirit (2.1; 2.34; 3.1), it may be worthwhile to

---

In recent literature, only Wistrand 1977: 9ff. interprets 3.4 without any reference to 3.5. Consequently, he finds the poet 'wholeheartedly' accepting Roman imperialism and only 'personally' refusing 'to have anything to do with it' while showing 'the enthusiasm, loud and sincere but not so very deeply felt' of a national spectator 'attending an international sports competition' (pp. 18f.).

imagine in what way the famous lines about Rome's destiny must have impressed him:

> *tu regere imperio populos, Romane, memento*
> *(hae tibi erunt artes), paci(s)que imponere morem,*
> *parcere subiectis et debellare superbos. (Aen.* 6.851–853)
>
> You, Roman, take care to govern the people under your sway—these will be your arts—and impose upon them a custom of peace, spare the humbled and battle down the proud (editors' translation).

As we said earlier, Augustan peace may be defined (especially by those affected) as a postwar period in which the defeat (*debellare*) of independence (*superbos*) is followed by a grant of humiliating survival (*parcere subiectis*)—almost precisely what young Propertius and his family had experienced from Octavian the victor over Perusia (1.21; 22)—except for the fact that *parcere subiectis* had not at that time been an obligatory part of the peace program. Later, in 2.7, we heard Propertius assert that even powerful Caesar is unable to handle the loving individual the way he treats nations (*devictae gentes*, 'conquered peoples'), for (*nam*) the lover is willing to face execution rather than give in (2.7.5–7). This passage can help us understand why there is no difference in principle—but only in degree—between a pacified nation and Propertius himself in his precarious situation, and why the Parthian expedition—in my view, almost a matter of foreign policy—and the public enthusiasm surrounding it (which, moreover, Propertius himself felt obliged to join) are able to trigger a personal confession which may become dangerous once it is decoded and deprived of the disguise of popular philosophy.

The wording 'Of Peace, Amor is the god' (3.5.1) sounds as incomplete in Latin as it does in English, because, by its emphatic early position in the line, the notion 'of Peace' seems to point to an unmentioned but implied contrast, e.g. 'of War' or 'of Arms.' That war is in the air is proved by line 2, where we have to supply this meaning: 'hard enough, for my person, are the battles I fight with my lady (sc., in bed),' *Sat*[15] *mihi cum domina proelia dura mea.* The

---

[15] This is Livineius' conjecture for *stant* of the MSS (the latter is kept by Barber. Ingvarsson's interpretation 1955: 165ff. of *stant* = *sunt* does not give an adequate meaning to the context). See Shackleton Bailey 1947: 91f.

contrasting form has actually been supplied already and is still in the ear of the reader who recalls the foregoing poem's first line 'Arms God Caesar' ( ... intends to raise against the East ... ). The mutual logical complementation of the two head-lines (Arms—Love), in itself a reminder of a Propertian *leitmotif* ever since elegy 1.6, is underlined by an artful employment of positioning, sound, and word play:

> Arma *deus Caesar* (3.4.1)
> Pacis *Amor deus* (3.5.1)

While 'God Caesar' is tied up with arms, 'God Amor' is connected with the peace that Augustus would like to make his trademark. Something of Propertius' peculiar way of thinking, observed by us again and again, shines through here also: his inclination to state his own case in the terms in which his opponent is accustomed to think, even to wrest key terms away from the opponent in order to show that they belong to the elegist as well if he is to fulfill his task of interpreting essential aspects of man's destiny. In the present case, Propertius claims the term *pax* for his world of Love, while leaving to Augustus the sphere of War.

In a similar way—a parenthesis may strengthen my point—he can even wrest deification from 'God Caesar' and claim it for himself. When in 3.9 he refuses Maecenas an epic on Augustus, on the cheeky grounds of having chosen as his young life's model Maecenas himself (who always prefers to remain in the background: *in tenuis humilem te colligis umbras*, 'you humbly recede into the light shadows,' 29), he also adds, in his 'innocent' modesty, that the kind of appreciation that Callimachus and Philitas receive will be enough (*sat erit placuisse*, 43f.) for himself, and then proceeds to add that 'tiny' further touch of personal achievement which he has always claimed for his poetry:[16]

> *Haec urant pueros, haec urant scripta puellas,*
>    *meque deum clament et mibi sacra ferant!*(3.9.45–46.)
> Let these writings (of mine) kindle passion in boys, kindle passion in girls,
>    And *me* let them call a god, and to *me* offer sacrifices!

---

[16] Ever since 1.7.13f. and 23f.; see Stahl 1985: 48–71.

In the context of epic themes (35–42 and 47–56), which lead up to Augustus' success over the Parthians (54) and his defeated opponent Antonius' suicide (56), Propertius himself would hardly appear as a god, but would have to leave this honor to Augustus. He rather prefers, however, to receive it himself. The words *meque deum clament* can be appreciated fully only if seen before the background of Augustus' heroic deification in the epic which is requested by Maecenas but refused by Propertius.[17] And it is only logical in a poem such as 3.9 that we find repeated (cf. 1.6.29f., Stahl 1985: 72–98) that other claim of our poet, *viz.*, that peace is his, and war does not go with his 'nature':

> *Hic satus ad pacem, hic castrensibus utilis armis:*
> *naturae sequitur semina quisque suae.* (3.9.19–20)
> This one is born for *peace*, that one is useful for the *arms* of the camp: everyone follows the seeds of his nature.

By introducing the philosophical notion of *entelecheia*, he expresses here in one line what took him twenty-two in his other poem dedicated to Maecenas (2.1.57–78): every attempt to divert him from his destiny, which is the peace of love, is doomed to failure.[18]

---

[17] Even if Bennett 1968: 338ff. is right in thinking that in the rest of the poem (47–60) Propertius presents himself as asking his 'deified' patron to help him write an epic, such a request can hardly be serious after 45/46.

[18] The claim to be born for peace and not for war (3.9.19/20) is so central in Propertius' thinking that it must be considered a grave methodological error if Boyancé 1942: 65 declares the whole subsection 3.9.7–20 'une surcharge de redaction:' 'un petit poème dans le grand, une épigramme assez longue, dont le sujet n'est point sans rappeler une autre pièce adressée au même Mécène, l'ode I du livre premier d'Horace' ('an overload of editing... a small poem within the large one, a fairly long epigram, whose subject recalls another piece addressed to Maecenas, Horace *Odes* 1.1'). It is a common mistake of *Parallelstellenphilologie* to infer from verbal similarities an agreement in attitude or position, or even 'dependence' of one writer's attitude on the other's. Verbal similarities often result from use of the same material (situations, persons, paradigms, etc.) by two authors. Their purpose (which may include rivaling imitation, polemical reinterpretation, thematic—and independent—use of identical subject matter, exemplification of other, more difficult contexts, etc.) must always be established by and confirmed within the context in which the interpreter reads them.

With regard to the specific section 3.9.1–20, I refer my reader to Bennett's excellent investigation (1967) of the passage both within the poem and in the light of Propertius' use of gnomes. Bennett (p. 224) fails, however, to distinguish between the broader aspect of Propertius' inborn disinclination (*naturae... semina*, 'seeds of

I return to elegy 3.5. The categories of 3.9 provide a parallel example which helps explicate the overlapping notions of the beginning lines of elegies 3.4 and 5: *deus* Caesar faces competition from *deus* Amor; *pax* is the preserve of Amor and not so much of Augustus, who is characterized through *arma*. In fact, it looks as if Augustus gets his spelling wrong when claiming to be the lord of peace: for that purpose, one should spell *AMOR* (5.1), not *ARMA* (4.1). It is along these lines that we should look for the meaning implied in the paronomasia.

Once we realize that the opening of 3.5 wishes to refer the reader back to that of elegy 3.4, we cannot help keeping our eyes open for further allusions hidden behind the façade of moral philosophy displayed in 3.5.[19]

That Propertius claims the term *proelia* (2) for his loving embraces, and that he terms these battles hard, *dura* (2), like real battles, fits into the pattern of, e.g. 1.6 (36) and 2.1 (13f; 45.). But what is new is that, in the present poem, he goes on to denounce the attitude that leads to *proelia* in their original meaning (i.e. he castigates what he himself, in the rôle of an Augustan *vates*, has encouraged in the preceding poem!). For his own 'battles' are, in spite of the military metaphor, 'nevertheless' (*tamen*, 3) removed from the world of materialistic greed (3), senseless luxury (4), large estates (5), and, above all, profitable gains from other people's miseries (6). The series of four *necs* successfully drives one point home: the peace of love and lovers (1) is, in spite of its 'battles,' free from the guilt and crime of war—unlike all other *proelia* and the motives leading to war. Philosophically speaking, the τέλος, i.e. the wise man, of whom the

nature,' 20) against war and his momentary excuse (fear of public failure: *turpe*, 'shameful,' 5). By not making this distinction, Bennett 1968: 320ff. finds Propertius ready for compromise (3.9.47ff.) where he is not.

We must not believe (as Steidle 1962: 137 does) that the poet's emphasis on peace in Book 3 is 'geradezu eine neue Lebenswahl' ('really, a new lifestyle'). It is as a loving being (*amantes*, 'lovers,' 3.5.1), that he favors *pax* over *arma*.

[19] Although I go along with (and even further than) Solmsen 1948: 105, n. 1 and Nethercut 1961: 395f. in seeing the opening group of words in either poem in relation to the other poem's opening, I do not follow Nethercut's assumption of corresponding sections and of parallel key words in both poems. For these alleged parallels are not supported by parallel thought structure. Cf. Jäger 1967: 75ff.

*sapientes* of various popular schools try to talk more or less convincingly, is—the lover! He is the true opposite of the *miser* (6) castigated by every street preacher! Moral philosophy is another realm whose terms Propertius may claim for his own 'philosophy' of love, especially when he wishes to define what separates him from men of *arma*. The *pax Propertiana* turns out to be a philosophical position and a basic human condition rather than a political situation (1–6).

And that is exactly what he needs, because a definition of his position in philosophical terms grants him that degree of general and theoretical certainty (a *punctum Archimedis*, so to speak) which permits him to criticize man's given nature (7–12): in creating man, Prometheus showed neither a lucky hand nor the sense of foresight which his name implies (7/8). It seems to me that Propertius here purposely discredits Pro-metheus (cf. *parum caute* ('not careful enough,' the better MSS' reading in 8), who is seen elsewhere, in a hardly more optimistic interpretation of man's condition,[20] as the helper who finds amendments for the mistakes his brother Epimetheus committed. Propertius is like those pessimistic moral philosophers who see that man has made evil use of the tools of survival which Prometheus gave him: Prometheus cared for the body's 'straight way' (9/10), not for the mind's. The one example (*nunc*, 11) Propertius introduces of Promethean man's perverseness is that we go far over the sea,

> ... *et hostem*
> *quaerimus, atque armis nectimus arma nova.*    (3.5.11–12)
> ... and search after an enemy,
> and tie new wars (arms) to wars (arms).

I have no doubt at all that the poet here (as in lines 47f.) gives his condemnation of Augustus' plan for a Parthian expedition. The expedition is the natural point of reference, once we allow that 3.5 comments on 3.4. Augustus has literally to go overseas in search of an enemy (... *meditatur* ... *freta gemmiferi findere classe maris*, 'he plans to cleave the straits of the gem-bearing sea with his fleet,' 4.1f.), since at home everything is quiet; but prestige demands

---

[20] See, e.g. Protagoras in Plato (*Prot.* 322a ff.). For other versions, see Nisbet-Hubbard 1970 *ad* Horace, *C.* 1.16.3.

another victory, and so one has to dig up the defeat of the Crassi (by now, after all, thirty years ago) in order to find a cause for raising war, for 'tying new wars to wars.' If the poet cannot openly criticize the royal enterprise (which he even blessed in 3.4), the mask of philosophical preacher is probably the one most unlikely to be offensive (or even to be decoded) (7–12). He can be more open when he confines himself to his 'unserious' love subject matter—as in 3.12, where he blames Postumus, who left his wife Galla to follow Augustus (*Augusti fortia signa sequi*, 'follow the strong standards of Augustus,' 2) against the Parthians:

> *Si fas est, omnes pariter pereatis avari,*
> *et quisquis fido praetulit arma toro!* (3.12.5–6)
> If it is right to say, may all you greedy ones perish together
> and anyone (else), who ranked arms higher than a faithful wife!

Application to the concrete political situation is also in order for the following section—again three distichs (13–18)—in which, like a philosophical *diatribe*, the sermon finds its climax by addressing an imaginary listener: *stulte* ('fool,' 14). Concrete interpretation is supported by the fact that the addressee will subsequently have as his concrete counterpart the poet himself (*me*, 19 ... *me*, 21). Logically speaking, the new section (13–18) states the *reasons why* human behavior (as described in 7–12) must be considered wrong.

The first distich points to the fact that none of the riches acquired by Promethean man will accompany him to the underworld (13/14). This need not in itself be a reference to the Emperor's expedition, because the feature would apply just as well to, say, the nonpolitical businessman, who likewise, to Propertius' eyes, betrays man's true destiny. In a poem of similar fundamental importance (3.7), the money-chasing, worried life (*sollicitae ... vitae*, 7.1) of his friend Paetus is contrasted with his own condition of being *iners* (72), and Paetus' death at sea is to the poet a death caused by human guilt:

> *Ite, rates curvas et leti texite causas:*
> *ista per humanas mors venit acta manus.* (3.7.29–30)
> Go, build curved boats and thus create causes of destruction:
> this death is caused by human hands.

But in spite of his obsession with money (1ff.), and in spite of having neglected Propertius' advice (43–46), Paetus does not lose the poet's warm compassion, because the crime he committed against himself is, after all, not of the kind considered in 3.5. The *stultitia* ('foolishness') of the merchant is exceeded by that of the warlord.[21] It is therefore not before the second distich of our section (5.15f.), that the full impact of Propertius' judgment is expressed:

> Victor cum victis pariter miscebitur umbris:
> consule cum Mario, capte Iugurtha, sedes.(3.5.15–16)
> The victor's shade will be thrown together with the shades of the defeated: you, captive Iugurtha, sit together with consul Marius.

Who, exemplified by Consul Marius, can be the *future* (*miscebitur*) victor to share Iugurtha's fate as a shade? If we refrain from any speculative drawing of parallels and confine ourselves strictly to the situations outlined in elegies 3, 4 and 5, we cannot but compare the shade of Marius—who led defeated Iugurtha in his triumph and had him killed in the Tullianum at the end of the Sacra Via—to Augustus, whose triumph poem 4 predicts by vividly painting the procession on the Sacra Via, including the captive Parthian chieftains (*captos... duces*, 18) who, like Iugurtha, will be killed in the Tullianum, as soon as Augustus' triumphal procession has left the Sacra Via and the Forum Romanum, and before the Emperor climbs up the Capitoline Hill. Augustus is nothing but a shadow, like Marius, pursuing an empty and unworthy goal—this has been the poet's thought behind the splendid scene of 3.4![22] In retrospect, the vision of Augustus'

---

[21] We must not—because Paetus' avarice in 3.7 seems to lack individual features, and because 3.5, too, deals with the rôle of avarice (in the area of war)—conclude with Robertson 1969: 386 that 3.5 has no reference to the poet's personal concerns either. On the contrary, 3.5 may throw some light on the character of Propertius' involvement with the subject matter of 3.7.

[22] Solmsen 1948: 106 with n. 6 offers four passages from Horace's *Odes* to show that 'the equalizing function of death' was an idea conceived under Horatian influence. But I doubt that Propertius needed help from Horace in presenting Augustus' triumph as futile. A similar point can be made about the elegist's general use in 3.1–5 of Horace's self-eternalization in *Ode* 3.30 (see Solmsen 1948: 106ff., among others); it was not so much a revering poetic imitation as the outcry of the isolated elegist who was afraid he would not be heard among officially sanctioned and royally promoted colleagues that made Propertius prophecy his own future fame in shrill self-praise of Horatian colors.

triumph as seen in 3.4 now turns into a painting of his *stultitia* ('foolishness'), for in the same way as the consoling address to defeated Iugurtha (5.16) points to Augustus' Parthian victims (and, finally, perhaps—we recall 2.7 and 3.5.6—to Propertius himself), the address to the *stultus* (14), who pursues the riches of this world, comes to include the conquering Emperor,[23] once it is viewed in the whole context of lines 13–18. The poet's refusal of any part of the booty (3.4.21), then, did have a deeper reason.

It is a daring deed to mention Marius (whose victory over Iugurtha was supposed to have wiped out a national disgrace and whose victories in general could be, for 'official' use [2.1.24], summed up as *benefacta*) as a shade among shades in a poem that refers (47/48) negatively to Augustus' Parthian expedition (which likewise was supposed to wipe out a national disgrace). The historical example is probably as close to Augustus as Propertius could ever dare come when disclosing his true feelings. Thus we should not be surprised that the following distich (17/18), like the one preceding the crucial lines, is remote from Roman history: it denies that a difference exists between the fate of the rich king Croesus (almost a mythical figure) and that of the Homeric beggar Irus. Philosophically, of course, the distich makes the same point as its two predecessors, and it concludes by praising 'a natural death as opposed to drowning or death in battle.'[24]

So far, elegy 3.5 has proceeded on a well-balanced course: lines 1–6 declare the peace of love as free from all greedy motivations that are the causes of war; 7–12 blame Prometheus' creation for its emphasis on physical welfare instead of soundness of mind; 13–18 explain the *stultitia* involved in the pursuit of riches and military victory (and

---

[23] Nethercut 1961: 403 considers the identification *stulte* = Augustus possible, but decides in favor of a more general addressee (the *viri* of 4.3 or the *vos* of 5.47)—or just any 'individual' (cf. Nethercut 1961: 396 and 406). Closest to my own findings are the results of Jäger's approach because he systematically compares corresponding elements in both elegies. With regard to 5.15/16 he remarks: 'Deutlicher konnte im Hinblick auf einen vom Kaiser geplanten Feldzug Ruhm und Grösse nicht mehr abgewertet werden' ('More to the point, regarding a campaign planned by the emperor, one couldn't scorn fame and greatness,' 1967: 76). Before him, Ites 1908: 53f. gave a clear picture of the corresponding features in both elegies.

[24] Shackleton Bailey 1956 *ad loc.*

secretly condemn Augustus by way of correcting the false impression created by the foregoing elegy).

As often, the well-balanced structure of the beginning (3D; 3D; 3D) is purposefully interrupted by apparent disorder, stemming this time from the poet's introduction of his own person into the context. To express the contrast, he chooses the same formula he used to distinguish his own position from that of 'Lynceus' and Vergil (2.34.59; similar is 2.13.11): *me iuvat* (19) ... *me iuvat*[25] (21). It is *his* joy to have spent his early youth with poetry as it is *his* joy to have his head always (*semper*) crowned with the convivial wreath of roses (cf. 2.34, 59), and to '*chain* my mind with lots of *loosening* wine,' *multo mentem vincire Lyaeo* (21). The apparent paradox, that the wine-god, Dionysos 'Lyaeus,' who is usually believed to bring relaxation from worries, is said to 'chain' the poet's mind, must be taken together with Propertius' criticism of Pro-metheus' creation and interpreted along the same lines. It is not the happy relief from worries or any exuberant excesses of alcohol that Propertius appreciates in wine; rather, the paralyzing effect of wine is seen as a means of restraining the human mind from committing the outrages that are part of man's Promethean constitution.[26] The phrase <u>mentem vincire Lyaeo</u> (21) refers back to the defect of the mind (*mentem*) described earlier in lines 9/10, and shares the same basic pessimism about human nature. The emphatic *me... me* shows that 3.5.1–18 is not an irrelevant catalogue of opinions held by popular philosophy, but that, so far, notions of popular philosophy have helped to express the poet's own position and led up to the personal statement of lines 19–22. That enervation or diversion by alcohol means prevention of crime, and thus, under the circumstances of man's condition, comes close to being a moral achievement, is, as we shall see (2.15, see Stahl 1985: 215–33), a serious thought of the poet's which is most easily understood if we recall the political conditions that formed and threatened him in his younger years—years which he consciously dedicated to the Muses (*me iuvat in prima coluisse Helicona iuventa*, 'I am happy to have tended Helicon in my tender years,' etc., 19f.).

---

[25] Or *me iuvet... me iuvet*.
[26] By no means should we follow Bury 1939: 7 and 'amend' the transmitted text ("to bind with the Loosener' sounds strange,' *loc. cit.*).

What we read in 3.5 is, taking into account the conditions of 'free' speech at Rome in the late twenties BC, still the same rejection of the Active Life that forbade him to join his friend Tullus on his official mission to purge Asia Minor of any remnants of Antonian rule (1.6), and made the poet defend his own *militia*, which denounced *arma* and *laus* in favor of *extrema nequitia* ('utmost disgrace,' 1.6.25–30, see Stahl 1985: 72–98).

But such open and unrestrained claims would, when Book 3 was being written (ca. 24–21 BC), sound almost revolutionary. They cannot be maintained, therefore, except in the disguised and indirectly alluding form of 3.5, which mentions Marius and means Augustus. We may even, as in the case of 2.7 and 2.10, conjecture that 3.4 was destined for the Emperor and the court to read, whereas 3.5 was not. The lengths to which Propertius could go in complying with official wishes and in disowning his true position will be seen from elegy 3.22, an invitation to his friend Tullus to come home from the East. A short description of this poem at the end of this chapter will help us to appreciate the relative openness of 3.5.

After three sections of 3D each, the reader may well expect that the fourth section, which deals with the poet's own views and attitude, may also be limited to 3D. We are surprised, however, that the third distich (23/24) introduces a lengthy description (11D) of the philosophical subjects which the poet may choose to concern himself with at a later date. After speaking of his youth (19f.), and the unchanging (*semper*) present (21f.), he is going to speak of his future life (23f.), when love will have yielded to grey hair:

> *Tum mihi naturae libeat perdiscere mores...*  (3.5.25)
> Then may it please me to learn thoroughly the ways of nature,

The list of possible subjects of investigation comprises a surprisingly wide variety of philosophical problems, ranging from natural philosophy to men's fears about an afterlife. The large number of topics presented in these eleven distichs has eluded all attempts to find a convincing pattern of balanced subgroups. This has not prevented inventive philologists from seeing here an announced program (never realized, alas) for future philosophical writings—as if *perdiscere* means 'to write.' (In a similar way 2.34 has been made into a catalogue of Varius' writings.)

No one, as far as I can see, has taken this pile of philosophical problems for what it is: an unordered mass of difficult questions that present themselves to a thinking mind, engaging it in such a way that a thorough and detailed investigation (*per-discere*) will certainly take up more than one lifetime. What the poet means to say by this impressively long list is this: 'For the rest of my life (if I shall live longer than I love), I am already booked up completely for philosophical studies: may no one try to bother me with the occupations of Pro-methean man!' This interpretation (a) allows the list of questions to be long because the poet *wants* it to be long—just as in 2.1 he lengthily demonstrates to Maecenas (lines 57–70) that absolutely nothing can distract him from his love; and (b) preserves a logical connection between the three distichs that precede (19–22) and introduce (23/24) the list and the one distich (the last in the poem, 47f.) following it:[27]

---

[27] The words *exitus hic vitae superest mihi* ('this is what remains for the rest of my life,' 47) pick up 23/24 (*atque ubi iam Venerem gravis interceperit aetas*, 'and when heavy old age has cut short my Love,' etc.) and identify the same period of time as *tum* (25) denotes (hardly apposite: *exitus... vitae* = 'way of leaving life', Shackleton Bailey 1956: Appendix). The biographical timetable leaves no gap at all. I should like to give credit to Nethercut 1970: 397. Although not concerning himself with Propertius' condemnation of human nature, but rather taking 3.5 to be the usual *recusatio* (and the catalogue of philosophical problems a substitute for the customary promise of an Augustan epic; cf. Wilkinson 1960: 1102), Nethercut has felt that the sheer length of the 'inflated' passage 25–46 hangs together with the poet's antipathy against the Emperor's campaign. In this he probably comes closer to the poet's intention than Courtney (1969: 70ff.), who, deriving the *excursus* from a Vergilian source (*Georg.* 2.458–506), thinks that Vergil serves as a 'warrant' ('what better authority could be found?') when the poet proceeds from 'dissociation' from the Parthian campaign (= end of 3.4) to 'distaste' (= 3.5). Wilkinson 1960, in his prudent discussion of the elegist's continued resistance against Augustus, has correctly diagnosed the implications from the last couplet in 3.5 for elegy 4: 'He could hardly have contrived more effectively to negative any enthusiasm a superficial reading of the previous poem might have conveyed' (1960: 1102). The immanent argument of 3.5 apparently escaped Paratore's search (1936: 186ff.) for anti-Augustan features; although seeing the implications the last distich (47/48) has both for 3.5 itself ('un enorme valore di aperta ribellione agli intendimenti fondamentali della politica del monarca,' 'a tremendous courage for outright rebellion to the fundamental intentions of the politics of the monarch') and for 3.4, he nevertheless assigns to the philosophical *excursus* the function of parodying Horace's and Vergil's philosophical aspirations rather than interpreting it in the context in which it occurs. As in 3.4 (Paratore 1936: 152ff.)— and elsewhere—he weakens the case he tries to build, looking for far-fetched allusions rather than verifying the actual consequences of a poem's argument. *Merces*, 3.4.3, for

> *Exitus hic vitae superest mihi: vos, quibus arma*
> *grata magis, Crassi signa referte domum!* (3.5.47–48)
> This is what remains for the rest of my life. But you to whom war (arms)
> is more pleasing, bring home Crassus' standards!

If he is ever forced to retire from the innocence of love, it will be in the direction of the pure contemplation of philosophy but there is no room in his life for the crimes of arms. They will not even be his δεύτεραι φροντίδες (on the back burner)! He wants to have nothing in common with the man whose drum he felt urged to beat in the foregoing poem (*Arma deus Caesar...*). and when he now utters another of those imperatives (cf. *ite... ducite... piate... ite et Romanae consulite historiae!* 'go... lead... avenge... go take care of Roman history,' 4.7–10), the meaning is no longer *omina fausta cano* ('I sing favorable omens,' 4.9), but rather like *omnes pariter pereatis avari* ('may all you greedy men perish alike,' 12.5), i.e. 'have done with you' (who leave their love for Augustus' Parthian expedition, 12.1–4). I interpret *Crassi signa referte domum* ('bring home the standards of Crassus,' 5.48) in exactly the same way as I interpreted the imperatives addressed to Tullus in 1.6.19/20 (cf. Stahl 1985: 72–98).

> *tu patrui meritas conare anteire securis*
> *et vetera oblitis iura refer sociis!* (1.6.19–20)
> Try to supersede the well-earned trophies of your uncle,
> and restore the old rights to forgotten allies!

Propertius is sending the other away on a road on which he would never be willing to follow: 'You go!' can mean (if two parties only are

---

instance, according to Paratore, reveals the 'spirito di preda' ('zeal for spoils') of Augustus' Parthian campaign—whereas in truth the poem itself, in the same line, explains the *metaphorical* use made here of the word: the soldiers' reward should be seen not in the usual booty but in their contribution to the greatness of Rome and her empire. It appears odd to me to read a second metaphor (*viz.*, the whole campaign is predatory) into the context. In a similar way, I find it difficult to believe with Nethercut 1970: 395 that in line 21 of 3.4 Propertius turns against Vergil's idea of *labor*, giving a 'definition of *labor* as brigandage and robbery.' The line expresses a point in its own context. For further considerations concerning Paratore's method, see our remarks on 3.22 in this chapter and also Chapter X below ('Aggressive Self-preservation: From Cynthia to Cleopatra: 3.11,' Stahl 1985: 234–47); *praeda* at 3.4.21 receives no negative connotation either from its immediate context (but see Stahl 1985: 200).

involved), as we said, 'Your way is not my way'. And the reason given in 1.6 was already the same—and expressed by the same paronomasia *arma—amor*—as years later in 3.5:

> *nam tua non aetas umquam cessavit <u>amori</u>,*
> *    semper at <u>armatae</u> cura fuit patriae.* (1.6.21–22)
> Your youth has never yielded to love,
>     And your care was always for the country at arms.

It is this kind of continuity I had in mind when, in the prefatory note to Part Two of this book (Stahl 1985: 133–6), I expressed concern about rashly established hypotheses of 'development' which are introduced to reconcile surface contradictions in an author's works, but which fail to account for the possibility of personal and inner consistency in the face of a changing environment and mounting outward pressure. We fail to understand a major part (by sheer number of lines, perhaps the major part) of Propertius' poetry if we do not recognize the precautionary facades he erected, which allowed his true attitude to hide behind them and peep out only occasionally. We are now entitled to say that he never intended to write epic court poetry in the event his love poetry gave out (but he did give that false impression in 2.10. Lines 7/8 of 2.10 are refuted by 3.5.23ff.);[28] that he probably never had any detailed plan of studying certain philosophical problems in his later years (although, it must be said, his nature is not unphilosophical); that he never appreciated Augustus' Parthian expedition (though, as seer-poet, he pretended to bless the arms of the departing soldiers in 3.4). We would fail to see one tragic aspect of his life if we took the tribute paid to Caesar Augustus at its face value, and not as mere lip service rendered with greatest reluctance and performed under the severest emotional pain. An interpreter is obliged to observe the small bores of dissent hidden in the facades of praise and submission. We may not like the insincerity involved; but before passing a negative judgment and diagnosing a character flaw, we should recall three points in favor of the defendant: he is a victim of the régime and doubtless feels strong

---

[28] Because of this reference, Courtney sees the main purpose of 3.5 as a retraction of the promise given in 2.10: 'He is now taking back what he then said' (1969: 71). In this way 3.4 becomes 'a very necessary preliminary.'

pressure upon himself;[29] there are not many poems of adulation that fail to give the attentive reader a key to the author's true attitude, either by their own structure and content or by some sort of pendant; addresses of submission are not written for their own sake (or to support the official political program), but are used as a protective cover that allows the channels to remain open through which the poet's personal message may reach the public.

I do not deny the possibility that, with his love's hopes slowly dying, he may have been in danger of shifting his position. While the return from insane love to *Mens Bona* (3.24.19) does not necessarily mean more than recovery from sickness to health, the wish to end his torture by leaving Rome and Cynthia for Greece and philosophy (3.21) might in some way be seen to reflect the philistine faultfinder's line of thinking in 1.12 (see Stahl 1985: 3–21); and the acceptance into his own vocabulary of society's judgment on his 'dishonorable' or 'ignominious' love (*turpi fractus amore*, 'broken by shameful love,' 3.21.33, see Stahl 1985: 234–47 on 2.16.36 and 39) can be seen as a partial surrender—as can his hope that the day of his death will be *honesta* (3.21.34).[30] At least we know that he suffers from the contempt he meets. But we also know from the fourth book (4.1) that even the announced end of his relationship with Cynthia (end of Book 3) could not fundamentally change, at least not for long, the direction of his life and poetry, but could only modify it—although he himself had apparently believed the change might happen. And we

---

[29] Though not proved, our working hypothesis about the poet being urged to write pro-Augustan poetry has so far consistently explained his contrasting utterances. Why else would he (unless he was a schizophrenic—a less likely hypothesis) repeatedly contradict himself in writing? We shall return to the problem in due course.

[30] Nothing in the poems concerned with his ending love (3.17; 21; 24; 25) points to the new poetical beginning that will open Book 4 (not even 17, which promises Bacchus Dionysiac poetry in case the god helps Propertius; and 3.21 points to noncreative studies in Greece, *tacito... sinu* ['in my silent breast,' 32]: should he not die and open his mouth at all, it would be to lament for his lost love). We underestimate the fatal seriousness of his crisis, if we, with E. Burck (1959 'Abschied von der *Liebes*dichtung;' italics mine, 'Farewell to love poetry'), see Propertius in 3.24 and 25 already defined by 'Hoffnung auf neue dichterische Aufgaben und Leistungen' ('hope for a new poetic role and achievement,' p. 211). 'Abschied von der *Dichtung*' ('Farewell to poetry') would have been a title more appropriate to the poet's desperate situation.

shall find his old outlook cautiously restated (4.4, see Stahl 1985: 265–306). But before that the increasing discrepancy we have observed between public lip service and personal reserve reaches a final peak that, in my eyes, even surpasses the one between elegies 3.4 and 5, because it must sound like a palinode inside his own personal domain of poetry. This is, as I indicated before, his attempt to call friend Tullus home from the East.

Elegy 3.22 is composed in the well-balanced manner that is found already in poems of the first book. Its structure almost surpasses the smoothness of its counterpart 1.6 (see Stahl 1985: 72–98), which dismissed Tullus on his political mission. A short outline of the contents may lead us to the poem's core:[31]

| | | | |
|---|---|---|---|
| A | 1–4: Tullus, you have preferred to stay at cool Cyzicus for many years. | | 2D |
| B | 5–16: Though you may travel in any part of the world (in the West, East, South, etc.) <let me tell you>: | | 6D |
| C | 17–26: 17/18: Rome's advantages will prove unsurpassed: | 1D | |
|   | (1) 19–22: its history, | 2D | 5D |
|   | (2) 23–6: its natural attractions. | 2D | |
| D | 27–38: Crimes (of Greek myth) that are unknown in Rome. | | 6D |
| E | 39–42: Tullus, you should come home where you belong and found a family! | | 6D |

The elegy almost reverses the situation of the two friends at the time of Tullus' departure: Propertius, then dedicated to *extremae... nequitiae* ('utmost disgrace,' 1.6.26), refused to join the friend on his uncle's political, pro-Octavian mission. Since then, several years have passed, and Tullus, whom we knew as the privileged young career man of high family and high prospects, has chosen not to return home (to continue his career) but to stay at pleasantly (*placuit*) cool (*frigida*)[32] Cyzicus on the Propontis. Now Propertius of all persons

---

[31] I do not share Barber's belief that a distich is missing after line 36 of the transmitted text. See Rothstein *ad loc.* By no means can lines 37f. be forced from their abhorrent context and squeezed into the section on tourist attractions (between 10 and 11, Otto and Hanslik). This transposition destroys the poem's clear balance.

[32] Cf. Hor. *Carm.* 3.4.21ff.:

> ... seu mihi frigidum
> Praeneste, seu Tibur supinum,

calls him home, not so much for the sake of their friendship (the personal ties, although enhanced by the address *Tulle*, are mentioned in one line [6] only, and then in the negative: *si... nec desiderio, Tulle, movere meo,* 'if, Tullus, you are not moved by love for me'), but rather by on his part outlining to the friend those patriotic values and motives by which the poet once characterized nephew and uncle in 1.6.

I see two possible lines of interpretation:

(1) Propertius is longing for his friend Tullus and tries to sweeten the idea of homecoming by describing Rome and Italy in the patriotic terms which Tullus himself will appreciate—at least the Tullus whom we know from elegy 1.6.

Two points make me reject this line of interpretation:

(a) At the time when Propertius asks him to come home, Tullus has been away at least six (at most nine) years, i.e. he overstayed the return of his uncle's cohort for so many years that no real interest in a further political career on Tullus' part can any longer be assumed; on the contrary, an appeal to patriotic motives might even contribute to making him stay at Cyzicus.
(b) In the foregoing elegy (3.21), Propertius himself takes leave of Rome for Greece; if he really desires to see Tullus again, it would be better to ask him to expect the poet's arrival in Greece than to come to Rome. This consideration does not hypothesize a greater consistency than there actually is between the situations of poems 3.21 and 22. For 21, besides taking into account other passages of the Monobiblos,[33] also contains a revocation of Propertius' refusal in 1.6.13–18 to leave Cynthia for Tullus and Athens; and it also refers literally to the fear of the sea which had been earlier alleged as the reason for Propertius' refusal to accompany Tullus (*Non ego nunc Hadriae vereor mare noscere tecum,* 'I am not afraid to become acquainted with the Adriatic Sea with you,' etc., 1.6. 1ff.). The echo cannot be missed: 'So it is now that I will go by boat

---

*seu liquidae placuere Baiae.*
...whether I like cool Praeneste, or sloping Tibur, or watery Baiae.

[33] For example, 3.21.11–16 refer to Propertius' request of 1.1.29ff. that his friends take him away from Rome. For more details, see now also Burck 1981.

as a guest of the rough Adriatic Sea' (*ergo ego nunc rudis Hadriaci vehar aequoris hospes* ... 3.21.17).

It is thus doubly improbable that Propertius in 3.22 is formulating a serious personal call to a friend he has been missing for a long time.[34] From all we know about Propertius, he must have been delighted rather than disappointed to see his friend give up thinking in patriotic terms of a public career; perhaps (it has been assumed) it is even love which keeps Tullus in the East and has destroyed his taste for politics. After all, he would in this way only fulfill Propertius' earlier diagnosis:

> *Nam tua non aetas umquam cessavit amori,*
> *semper at armatae cura fuit patriae.* (1.6.21–22)
>
> Your youth has never yielded to love,
> And your care was always for the country at arms (editors' translation).

[34] When analyzing the structure of Book 3, Courtney 1970: 51f., viewing the surface only of 3.22, states a contrast between the anti-Hellenism in 3.22 and the philhellenic journey of 3.21. Another investigation of book structure (Woolley 1967: 81), likewise taking seriously 'the claim expressed in poem 22 of the superiority of Italy over Greece', puts 3.22 in corresponding contrast to the Spartan girls of easy access in 3.14, finding in 14 'praise of Sparta,' 'a superiority in one respect to Rome.' The journey to Greece (3.21), on the other hand, is (mis)-matched to the Lycinna poem 3.15 in another 'contrast' (p. 81). No indication whatsoever is given in Woolley's geometrical graph and its 'panels' (1967: 80) of the deeper common ground 3.21 and 22 share with each other and with Book 1. Like the unsuccessful schematic explanations interpreters have given of the Monobiblos, Woolley's of Book 3 is shipwrecked by its inherent disregard for the task of securing an interpretation of the single elegy, a book's construction element, in the first place. A more flexible approach to his own schematizing method is perhaps displayed in Juhnke's 1971 essay on the structure of Books 2 and 3. But it, too, offers unverified assumptions about single elegies; 3.21 and 22 are seen equally to point to 'erfüllte Lebensmöglichkeiten jenseits der brüchigen elegischen Welt' ('a fulfilled life beyond the crumbling elegiac world,' p. 116); 3.22 itself, offering 'römisches Land und Leben als Überhöhung der elegischen Welt' ('Roman land and life as extreme exaltation of the elegiac world'), is matched to 3.4 (the power of the Roman Empire), while 3.21 is seen as a counter-piece to 3.5 ('Flucht in die Geistigkeit,' 'flight into the intellect,' p. 121). The implications of Juhnke's assumptions are far-reaching: he is paving a one-way road, on which the Propertius of Book 3, dissatisfied with his 'broken elegiac world,' is unfalteringly progressing towards Augustus' Rome. One may compare also the interpretations which E. Burck has given of 3.24 and 25 (Burck 1959) and, subsequently, of the structure of Book 4 (Burck 1966). (See also the final section of this chapter and n. 29 above). Since 3.21 is doubtless serious (it shares the tendency of 3.17; 24; 25: the poet seeking liberation from the disease of his love), its contrast to the anti-Hellenic elegy 3.22 suggests that the latter is another façade poem, the surface of which may cover up its author's true attitude. Daut's 1975 insistence on a military tone in 3.21 appears to be not in focus.

Surely, love would, in Propertius' eyes, be a valid motive for staying away from Rome—even at a time when the poet himself thinks of freeing himself from his own *turpis amor* ('shameful love,' cf. 3.21.33). We are not informed, however, about Tullus' motive for staying, and I therefore exclude this speculation from my train of thought.[35]

(2) The other and more convincing hypothesis is that Tullus' family (see Stahl 1985: 72–98, that his uncle had been a consul together with Octavian, and had, as proconsul of Asia Minor, served Octavian's interests) would like to see the young man back in Rome and active in politics (possibly the Emperor himself has indicated a gracious interest in Tullus?). Why not exercise a soft pressure on Tullus' old friend (and former client?) Propertius to use his poetical talents and personal ties for the good purpose of reminding Tullus of his Roman obligations? My hypothesis would sufficiently explain the strange reversal in Propertius' attitude towards what Tullus is doing: the poetic letter to Cyzicus is in the first place written to accommodate certain circles in Rome—while the addressee may be sure of the correspondent's deep-seated understanding for his extended stay in Cyzicus. Thus viewed, the letter becomes another document of the disguises (or self-denials) Propertius was forced into, in his effort to survive as a poet of personal goals.

The words of elegy 3.22 speak for themselves,[36] as does the structure which I outlined before: in the center (17–26 = 5D) we find the praise of Rome, surrounded by two shells. The outer shell (1–4, 39–42, 2D each) addresses Tullus in his actual and in his proper environment; the inner shell in its earlier half (5–16, 6D) describes the rest of the

---

[35] Brakman 1926: 77f. takes the *ampla nepotum spes* of 3.22.41f. as an ironical allusion (made to tease Tullus) to Priam's many bedrooms and *spes ampla nepotum* in Vergil (*Aen.* 2.503), and from the stress on *aptus amor* (3.22.42) he understands *Tullum a muliere Graeca immemorem esse reditus patriae* (because of a Greek woman Tullus is heedless of a return to the fatherland). Understood along these lines, the 'esaltazione del matrimonio fecondo' (praise of fruitful marriage) in lines 41f. is far from being a step in 'un processo catartico, che si sviluppa da una turbinosa passione verso più santi ideali di vita' ('a process of catharsis, which evolves from a stormy passion toward more blessed ideals of life'), as Fontana 1950: 76 would like to see it. Defining the degree of Propertius' irony or of his personal involvement is still an urgent methodological problem.

[36] On the whole, Schuster and Dornseiff's 1954 text is more convincing here than Barber's 1953 (1960), (and Hanslik's 1979).

world as contrasted with Rome, and in its latter half (27–38, 6D) contrasts some horrors of Greek mythology with Rome's more benign character.

The center itself, in an introductory distich (17/18), makes Rome's miracles surpass everything else in the world. Its second main part (23–6) praises Rome for its healthy (and cool) waters (so Rome can rival 'cool Cyzicus', 1—an advantage the contemporary reader cannot adequately appreciate). The first of the two main parts (19–22) brings a positive evaluation of Roman history:

> *Armis apta magis tellus quam commoda noxae:*
>     *famam, Roma, tuae non pudet historiae!*
> *Nam quantum ferro tantum pietate potentes*
>     *stamus: victrices temperat ira manus.*     (3.22.19–22)
> Land more apt for arms than fit for crime:
>     *Fama*, oh Rome, is not ashamed of your history!
> For as through our sword, so through our piety powerful
>     we stand: our anger restrains its hand in victory.

Here, finally, we see Propertius publicly signing the *pax Augusta*. He clearly joins the pattern we find in the *Aeneid*, especially the programmatic lines cited earlier in this paper (6.851–3): reinterpretation of Rome's bloody history in terms of an ultrareligious, all-pervading piety (we may compare *pius Aeneas*), self-moderation after victory as a Roman characteristic, a distinction drawn between arms and crime. This is the language of 3.4 raised to the level of principle, with no pendant like 3.5 to show the reader the reverse side of the coin where we would find Iugurtha instead of Marius, the defeated nations instead of the Roman soldiers, Propertius instead of Augustus.[37] More than anything hitherto (but like some later

---

[37] According to Putnam (1979: 243), *ira* here (and in *Aeneid* 12, when Aeneas kills Turnus) carries a moral blemish. But this idea is perhaps (if not Stoic) more Christian than Roman. On 'just wrath' and 'just fury' in the *Aeneid*, see Stahl 1981: 166.

Vergilian language (and that means, of course, contents also) or spirit has been found independently from my own investigation in the two façade poems 3.22 (cp. Rothstein 1898 *passim*; La Penna 1951b: 50; 1977: 81f.) and 3.4 (Hanslik 1967: 187ff.), and, in addition, Horace has been adduced to confirm the Augustan attitude of 3.4 (Haffter 1970: 61). These findings are of methodological importance for judgments on Propertius' *Dichtersprache*: when intending to please the representatives of the Zeitgeist by depicting official ideology, he may be found to borrow freely from the

poems), these lines mean Propertius' political surrender—whatever his feelings may have been. Perhaps he hoped that he himself would experience Augustus' moderation in victory and be allowed to continue in his vocation. But—for other reasons—that was hardly possible, for—if we may draw a conclusion from the position of elegy 3.22 in the neighborhood of poems that say farewell to Cynthia[38]—the time of final surrender to political pressure seems to have coincided with a period when he felt that his love must cease to be his

thought and linguistic achievements in Vergil's poetry. But such stylistically elevated passages should not go unchecked as if indicating a priori 'Propertius at his very own'. The result would be a misunderstanding like Hanslik's, who seems to take seriously Propertius' manner of appearance in 3.4: 'Zwischen dem *deus Caesar* (1) und dem kleinen Menschen Properz (22) steht der Dichter als erhabener *vates* (9). Damit ist schon etwas für die grosse Struktur des Gedichtes gewonnen' ('Between 'god Caesar' [1] and 'little man Propertius' [22] the poet stands as sublime *vates* [9]. Thereby something is already achieved for the overall configuration of the poem.'), 1967: 183. Cf. Woolley 1967: 81, in whose eyes the concluding distich reveals 'humility—a sentiment which also finds expression in Horace'). Similarly, it is inadequate to regard poem 3.4 as difficult because of an allegedly mutilated textual tradition. The truth, as confirmed by 3.22, is vice versa: the elegist's mannered court language (his 'Vergilian' style) led to misunderstanding (and possibly changing) of the original text.

We are now in a position to say a few words also about 'official' court propaganda: Rothstein 1898 concludes that in 3.1.15f. (as in 2.10 and, of course, 3.4) Propertius expresses current martial expectations about the Emperor which Augustus himself never intended to fulfill. A historian, H. D. Meyer 1961, pointing to what are to him apparent misrepresentations of official foreign policy, calls the poet 'naïve' (the word appears at least five times in about ten pages), since he 'im Sinne des Kaisers zu sprechen glaubt' ('since he believes he is speaking on Caesar's behalf,' 1961: 76; Meyer apparently takes 3.4 seriously and has no idea that the poet's true opinion is revealed only in the subsequent elegy). But it seems odd (and even uncritical) to assume that, in a poem written to please the court and to show the author's cooperation, His Highness would not be represented in the light and glory he himself desires to be seen in (including a few exaggerations). The naïveté would be rather with the historian who expects of and assigns to a public address the same function as to a memo circulating in the Department of Foreign Affairs. Even more inadequate than the historian's approach is that of philologists who deplore that the rhetoric of Propertius' panegyric lacks Horace's deep religious feeling toward the Emperor (see, e.g. Doblhofer 1961: 114ff.). Such blame appears inappropriate because it leaves no room for the tragic conflict and pain under which the elegist performed his adulatory duties. The problem of whether or not the Augustan poets rightly depicted Augustus as a great conqueror is an old one (see already Ferrero 1908–9 *passim*) and has been answered differently. Most revealing perhaps is the wishful self-portrait the Emperor himself sketches in his *Res Gestae* (26–33).

[38] Elegy 3.17; 21; 24; 25.

life's center if he was to survive. The crisis sets in on both flanks of his endangered personality at about the same time.

The crisis even invades the poet's own world of similes and imagination. The following section (22, 27–38) reminds Tullus that the horrors of Greece, especially of Greek myth, do not exist in Rome. Examples are: a daughter in chains, suffering for the hubris of her mother (for the benefit of a monster); a father being served his two sons for dinner; a mother killing her son by magic; a man chased and torn to pieces by his mother and her associates; a father sacrificing his daughter (to satisfy his political ambition); a goddess changing her human rival into a cow; etc. It was often, and especially in times of heightened national consciousness, fashionable in Rome to characterize the Greeks as inhuman, unreliable, treacherous. And it was part of Augustan ideology that Rome's domination of Greece (accompanied perhaps by feelings of guilt in some educated minds) was justified because it only paid back to contemporary Greeks what their ancestors had done to Rome's—i.e. the Iulians'—alleged Trojan ancestors by capturing Troy (the *Aeneid* relies heavily on this scheme).[39] How crudely this line of thinking could be pursued at times, we may see from the table of horrors that Propertius feels free to offer his Augustan readers. But the question which the more educated among his readers must raise is this: 'How could he thus betray the world in which not only his much-praised forerunners Philitas and Callimachus but also his own mind and thoughts were so much at home that he seriously considered the study of Greek art (together with Greek philosophy and literature, 3, 21, 25–30) as an alternative to his life of a love-poet now ending?' Had he not from the very beginning—we need only recall Milanion and Atalante as symbols for Propertius and Cynthia in 1.1—used Greek myth to help him express what he wished his readers to understand? The alternative interpretation—Propertius was suddenly and truly converted to seeing Greek myth as a collection of nightmarish excesses—will

---

[39] A good example of Vergil's suggestive manner can be seen in Aeneas' words (*Aen.* 2.65f.): *accipe nunc Danaum insidias et crimine ab uno/disce omnes* ('Hear now the treachery of the Greeks; learn about them all from this one crime'). We should never forget that Augustan ideology requires a reversal of Greek national values. Since the Iulians are the divinely guided descendants of innocent Trojan Aeneas, the Greeks must be the godless aggressors of Troy. See Stahl 1981 *passim*.

not hold, especially in the face of the foregoing poem 3.21, and must be excluded. Therefore, I can only ascribe this cheap and almost rhetorical declamation to the pressure and taste of the circles who ordered the poem. Perhaps Propertius felt he could count on the addressee and the educated among his contemporary readers to understand his reasons for including yet another patriotic piece in his book.

The pledge of loyalty to Roman values is still incomplete. The peak of self-denial is reserved for the last four lines:

> *Haec tibi, Tulle, parens, haec est pulcherrima sedes,*
>    *hic tibi pro digna gente petendus honos,*
> *hic tibi ad eloquium cives, hic ampla nepotum*
>    *spes et venturae coniugis aptus amor.* (3.22.39–42)
> This country has given you birth, Tullus, this is the most beautiful of countries,
>    here you must strive for honor and office worthy of your noble family,
> here are the citizens to listen to your oratory, here you have rich hope
>    for offspring, here you find the proper love of a future wife.

This passage mentions the family (which, according to my hypothesis, urged the poet to write this elegy) and its ambitious hopes for Tullus' career. Moreover, by speaking of marriage and begetting children, it also lays a bait for Tullus which Propertius himself has, so far, never found alluring; on the contrary: *Unde mihi patriis natos praebere triumphis?* ('Whence should I provide soldiers for patriotic triumphs?,' 2.7.13). But the bait is definitely in line with the Emperor's reforms. The discrepancy cannot be denied: there is no bridge leading over the abyss between the poet's true feelings and the public statements he has felt obliged to make. The argument of this paper—which shall not be repeated here at length—has been that we must acknowledge the discrepancy if we are to understand the poet's personal difficulties and to see the extent to which his creative powers were involved in dealing with the Zeitgeist.[40] That some of this

---

[40] In the special case of elegy 3.22, one may wonder whether, although no bridge crosses the abyss, a footpath leads around it. Much depends on the reasons that kept Tullus far from home. We know that he had become forgetful of his career. No more is indicated by Propertius (who must know more) nor perhaps could be indicated without embarrassing the noble family at Rome. But if—provided the reader would

involuntary investment came back, with interest, was shown in Stahl 1985: 213–306. But here, a few remarks on scholarship are in place. The failure of Augustan interpretation to recognize a discrepancy between Augustan surface and personal attitude has resulted in a tragic misunderstanding which takes the façade poems as indicators of a true and smooth development towards Augustanism, 'passaggio dalla poesia erotica ad un' altra quasi epica o meglio civile', as Alfonsi's chapter on Book 3 puts it ('transition from erotic poetry to a poetry almost epic, or better, civic,' 1945: 65). Because of the implications for correctly understanding Book 4, I ask my reader to compare my above results with two statements on 3.4 and 22. First, La Penna (1951b: 50) with regard to 3.22: 'L'invito all' amico è la cornice, le lodi dell' Italia sono l'essenziale. È evidente che Properzio ha davanti à se e cerca di rifare, variando, Virgilio, *Georg.* 2, 136sgg.' . . . '3,22 è già un avviamento abbastanza netto verso la poesia etiologica nazionale dell' ultimo libro, dove Virgilio è spesso presente' (The invitation to the friend is the cornerstone, the praise of Italy is essential. It is clear that Propertius has in the background and seeks to refashion, with variation, Vergil's *Georgics* 2.136ff... 3.22 is already a sufficiently refined exercise toward the national aetiological poetry of the final book, where Vergil is always present).

Next, Haffter (1970: 61f.): 'Die Elegie 22, was gibt sie anderes als *laudes Italiae* und zugleich *laudes Romae*? Natürlich ist dieser Lobpreis nicht für sich allein vorgebracht, sondern irgendwie [*sic*!] mit der Nennung einer Person verbunden, mit Tullus, dem das erste Buch gewidmet ist.' (Elegy 22, which presents itself other than as a *laudes Italiae* and equally *laudes Romae*? Naturally this glorification is not put forth only for its own sake, but rather is somehow (*sic*!) connected to the naming of the person—Tullus—to whom the first book is dedicated). Then follow remarks on Propertius' being in agreement with Vergil's *laudes Italiae* in the *Georgics* and with the *Aeneid's parcere subjectis et debellare superbos*. The poem's final call to Tullus for fulfillment of his civic duties and for marriage at Rome elicits the following comment: 'Dieser unmittelbare Gedichtschluss,

---

wish to continue Brakman's speculation (n. 35 above)—the reason for his stay was that he loved a *puella*, then the prospect of a career, dutiful marriage, and propagation of a family could be a deterrent on the efficacy of which the author of the Letter to Cyzicus could safely rely.

wie sehr weist er auch für sich allein wieder voraus auf das vierte Buch! ('This abrupt ending of the poem, all by itself, signposts once again the fourth book!'). Generally, Haffter says, in Books 2 and 3 'wird das Römische mehr und mehr ausführlich beschrieben und es verliert mehr und mehr seinen negativ-distanzierten Ton. Betrachten wir gleich im dritten Buch die kurze Elegie 4...den Soldaten ruft Properz zu, sie sollten...für die römische Geschichte sorgen. Dieser römische Tenor füllt bis auf zwei oder drei Verse das ganze Gedicht,' etc. ('The Roman world is written with ever more detail and loses ever more and more its distant, critical tone. Let us regard in the third book the brief 4th elegy...Propertius addresses the soldiers who should be concerned with Roman history This Roman stance fills the entire poem save two or three verses,' p. 60f.).

We see once again that it was not only contemporary opinion which the poet successfully eluded by his game of political hide and seek. Even Paratore (1936: 157ff.; cf. 1942), usually anxious to avoid a patriotic interpretation, goes into the trap. Dismissing any search for a logical argument in 3.22, he explains the poem on the basis of opposition to Vergil's *laudes Italiae*, but finds in the last distich (but only there) 'una nota di più umana romanità' ('the mark of a more personal *Romanitas*,' p. 169). Paratore goes out of his way to prove that Propertius writes *laudes Romae* (or *Latii*), but not, as Vergil does, *Italiae*. The reason for this, he says, is that egoistic Propertius is interested only in the joys of the capital, where his mistress resides ('dove era trascorsa la sua vita di avido gaudente', 'where he passed his life of pleasure-seeking,' 1936: 166)...I prefer to stay with the poem's argument which implies that it was Tullus' noble family who wanted to see him back in Rome (and not only in Italy). This keeps another road open for interpreting Book 4.

Philologically speaking, the most instructive misunderstanding of 3.22 is again provided by G. Williams (1968: 417ff.; and cf. Stahl 1985: 99–132). Eager to explain the poem in terms of a poor copy depending on a superb model (i.e. Vergil, *Georg.* 2.136–74), he finds it 'weak and trivial,' its logic 'not powerful,' etc. Once more he is blind to the fact that the main deficiencies he finds are caused by his own method, which does not verify the alleged copy's immanent and independent train of thought. Let us hear him on 3.22.23–6: '...the lakes appear in what is mainly a review of Italian water resources which has little point and no logic' (p. 422). But already by the emphatic first word in the poem's first line (*Frigida*) Propertius voices concern that friend Tullus is not returning to Rome because of Cyzicus' attractively (*placuit*) cool climate[41] which results from its being surrounded by water (cf. *isthmos, aqua, fluit*, line 2)! How can it be a 'mistake' if, in inviting Tullus to come home, Propertius undertakes 'a review of Italian water resources', to point out that Rome is able to rival Cyzicus' sea climate? '...essentially the same mistake as he made when he adopted the theme of Italian lakes from Virgil, but ignored the way in which Virgil had set them' (p. 425). Williams' faultfinding words turn against himself, because not Propertius but he is the one who 'ignored the way in which' the elegist 'set them'. Unable to understand a passage within the logical context designed by its author, the scholar is quick to see in it a mere stylistic reference to a passage in another, earlier author; then proceeds to declare the alleged copy poetically and logically inferior to its alleged source.

The other alleged 'mistake' our censorious literary critic finds is that (in 3.22.27ff.) for Vergil's 'monsters he substitutes a series of monstrous acts from Greek mythology' (Williams 1968: p. 424). Again the critic misses Propertius' point, which is not a mere stylistic substitution but the argument that Tullus should leave the alien Greek world, which is here represented as being dominated by a crime-ridden religion, and return to where he belongs, i.e. to Rome's innocent religiosity (cf. *armis—noxae* 'arms (not) crime,' 19; *pietate potentes*, 'powerful in our piety,' 21—terms unintelligible in their context to our mistaken critic, p. 424). There is no way the poet could possibly have integrated Vergilian monsters into his argument—except to justify Professor Williams' theories. Obsessed

---

[41] Cf. Hor. *Carm.* 3.4.21ff. (note 32) and Rothstein 1898 *ad loc.* Wrongly Tränkle 1960: 51; cf. 101ff. assumes that Propertius is negative and ironical concerning Cyzicus in 3.22.1–2. Lines 3/4 are perhaps on a different level because they may already indicate the negative features of Greek myth that play an important rôle in persuading Tullus to leave Greece (27ff.).

In similar fashion, Tränkle (1960: 102) should not tie together the words *salubris Pollucis equo* in line 26. Apart from being grammatically wrong (the dative *equo* goes with *pota*, not with *salubris*), his understanding narrows the poet's emphasis on the *general* healthiness of the *Iuturna* down to a single case and thus spoils the point of *salubris* within the train of thought.

with searching for models and copies, Williams blurs the difference between stylistic devices (some of which do indeed, in this official poem, imitate Vergil praising fertile Italy and her presumably greatest fruit: *te, maxime Caesar*, 'you, greatest Caesar,' *Georg.* 2.170), on the one hand, and discursive thinking (which here demonstrates to Tullus the superiority of Roman healthy climate and Roman piety over Greek pleasant climate and Greek crime), on the other.

Once more it turns out that stylistic investigation, when practiced without proper regard for logic, cannot even explain the surface level of the artifact (not to mention its true meaning). If the critic nevertheless feels entitled to develop his mistaken understanding into a theory of 'Tradition and Originality', and, by means of his theory, condemns the innocent poem as lacking, one might rightly despair of philological interpretation. This is especially true because a political, pro-Augustan attitude, an 'emotion for patriotism' (Williams 1968: 425) on the poet's part, is taken for granted by Williams all along (and not by Williams only). A poet's dissent is a priori limited to matters of style and, if discovered, blamed lavishly: 'The result is feeble and silly. The reader who knows the passage of Virgil is astonished at the tasteless ineptitude of style and content in Propertius' (p. 425). It is interesting to see how swiftly the word 'content' (i.e. the not understood argument of 3.22) is slipped into the sentence just quoted along with the judgment of style.

From another viewpoint, it may be remarked that the approach which my interpretations try to keep open is one which theoretical literary criticism often considers naïve and uncritical (cf. Allen 1962, *passim*). The poetical 'ego' speaking in the elegies, we are told, must not be confused or identified with the poet's own. This is, as far as this paper is concerned, true for instance insofar as Propertius never did as a *vates* bless the arms of Augustus' soldiers. Kraus (1965) has in this manner checked through all the poems in the first book of Tibullus and concluded about its bitter core that it 'eben nicht wörtlich als ein einzelnes, individuelles Erlebnis genommen werden soll' ('should not be taken literally as the experience of a single individual,' p. 163). This may be true about Tibullus 1, and, to a degree (as we saw), even about Propertius 1, but set absolute, the demand to exclude the poet's ego from his poetry would a priori prevent the interpreter from even considering as real the dilemma of façade and personal poetry to which this paper is dedicated—in short: the literary theory would wipe out the essential conflict reflected in the work of art.

Let the preceding pages be enough of a necessary exercise in dealing with existing scholarship. Today's reader of Propertius faces difficulties that arise not only from his author's text (and personal situation) but also from the fixations of scholarship, which can perhaps be roughly outlined in two opposing opinions. On the one hand, 'Propertius, the lesser Augustan, comes to imitate his greater contemporaries Horace and Vergil because he has recognized their superiority.' On the other hand (a position less widely discussed so far), 'Propertius, though somewhat individualistic, has not as obligingly presented the lonely individual as has Vergil in the hero of his *Aeneid*.' May the elegist's interpreter be forgiven if, in this situation, he has taken a detailed route to show, in Stahl (1985: 137–212), how the old dilemma of 'love' versus 'war' is alive and continuing. The new forms of public disguise and personal consistency (or opposition), once analyzed, will help us in approaching the poet's later work (Stahl 1985: 213–306). Also of help will be the knowledge acquired of the elegist's growing artistic and personal loneliness. The situation in Book 3 does not even allow for an opening address to a Tullus or a Maecenas any longer.

# 10

## Propertius 2.7: *Militia Amoris* and the Ironies of Elegy[1]

*Monica Gale*

Criticism of Propertius 2.7 has usually centered around the elegy's role as evidence for the poet's attitude towards Augustus. Treated as such, it has been used to support a surprising variety of conclusions. For Stahl and Lyne, the poem represents a courageous defence of individualism under a repressive and intolerant regime. At the other end of the spectrum, Cairns has tried to show that the poet's deliberate presentation of himself as 'a morally tainted individual' undercuts his argument to such an extent that the poem is effectively an endorsement of the legislation which it purports to attack.[2] Between these two extremes, Baker detects 'a cautious blend of levity and gravity' and suggests that, while emphasizing the value of *amor*, the elegy hints at a tension between Propertius' personal inclinations and the demands of others or his own sense of duty; Boucher, who believes that Propertius is generally pro-Augustan, reads 2.7 as an open and straightforward critique of the *princeps*' attempts at moral reform, which, by its very openness, militates against the reading of subtle irony into apparently patriotic elegies such as 3.11 and 4.6; and Camps speaks of 'a certain extravagance, even shrillness, in the manner in which Propertius expresses his defiance of ordinary

---

[1] All translations in this paper are the author's own.
[2] Stahl 1985: 140–55; Lyne 1980: 77–8; Cairns 1979a: 185–204.

Roman values' which 'may reflect tensions within the poet himself.'[3] More recently, Cloud[4] has argued that Propertius has simply used the marriage law[5] as a peg on which to hang his working out of a collection of Hellenistic erotic topoi, and that the poem cannot be read as a serious statement of opposition to the *princeps*.

It is remarkable that such a short and apparently straightforward poem should have elicited such a variety of readings. One way of explaining the diversity of opinion is to point to the different agendas (open or hidden) of the critics, most of whom set out to 'prove' that Propertius is either pro- or anti-Augustan, and find in the text what they expect to find. Almost all approach the poem with the expectation that it can and should be interpreted as more or less univocal, and they therefore suppress or explain away details which appear to conflict with such a reading. The terms of the debate have, in fact, often been over-simplified: as a number of more recent critics have pointed out, 'pro-Augustan' and 'anti-Augustan' are not in themselves unproblematic concepts.[6] At the very least, the commentator should beware of suggesting that 'Augustanism' was the single-handed creation of an individual: the historical Augustus could more accurately be described as the representative—or even the creation—of a pre-existing set of values. Secondly, it is clear that political readings of elegy (and of Augustan poetry in general) are always conditioned to a greater or lesser extent by the ideology of the interpreter: if we set out to find a defiant and rebellious Propertius, we will no doubt succeed; equally, the reader who is sufficiently determined to prove that the poet gave the new regime his full support will not be short of supporting 'evidence.'

My aim in what follows is to transcend the misleading categories of earlier critics and, rather than asking whether the poem (still less the poet) is pro- or anti-Augustan, to trace the ways in which the text opens up the possibility of either reading. The notion suggested by

---

[3] Baker 1968a; Boucher 1965: 135–6; Camps 1967: 97.
[4] Cloud 1993.
[5] Whatever its nature may have been; most recently, it has been argued that it was not in fact a piece of Augustan legislation, but an earlier law *repealed* by Octavian (along with other Triumviral measures of dubious legality) in 28 BC. See Badian 1985; Badian's theory is dealt with in more detail below.
[6] See esp. Kennedy 1992; cf. also Sharrock 1994b.

Baker and Camps, that the elegy reflects a tension of some kind in Propertius' writing, offers a useful point of departure. If, as my introductory doxography suggests, the poem can be read in a number of different ways, that may be because conflicting and self-contradictory elements are inherent in the text itself. I will suggest that what earlier readings of the poem have missed is a pervasive and sophisticated irony (which seems to me characteristic of Propertius and of elegy as a genre): the poem sets up a series of oppositions—between poetry and war, between love and respectability, between the 'elegiac lifestyle' and Augustan ideology—which it then proceeds to undermine and collapse in various ways. In the end, the individual reader may choose to interpret the poem as pro-Augustan or as anti-Augustan; but in either case, the possibility of an ironic sub-text still persists.

With this end in view, I shall begin by focussing on the opposition between love and war, which is central to Propertius 2.7 and to the elegiac genre as a whole. The characteristic doubleness of elegiac discourse is clearly exemplified by the conceit of *militia amoris*, the 'warfare of love,' which tends both to privilege and to devalue the life of love in comparison with the acceptable public career of the soldier or statesman. My discussion of *militia amoris* will then serve as the basis for a detailed reading of 2.7 in Section II of this paper.

I

The idea that love is a kind of warfare is an old one.[7] There are isolated references in Greek lyric and tragedy to the weapons of Eros;[8] the image of the lover struggling against his divine assailant, and the familiar iconography of the winged archer, were subsequently more fully developed by the Hellenistic poets.[9] It is in

---

[7] For more detailed discussion, see Spies 1930 (repr. 1978), Thomas 1964; Murgatroyd 1975; Lyne 1980: 71–8.

[8] e.g. Anacreon, frs. 27 and 46 (and cf. Sappho, fr. 1.28 and Theognis, fr. 1285–6 for the metaphor of erotic pursuit as warfare), Aesch., *P.V.* 649–51, Soph., *Ant.* 781, *Trach.* 497–8, Eur., *Hipp.* 392–3, 530–2 and 727.

[9] e.g. A.P. 5.176–8; 12.23, 37, 45, 50, 76 and 144.

Roman poetry, however, that the ramifications of the comparison are most fully worked out. In Plautus and Terence, the metaphor becomes much more common, and is extended to include lovers' quarrels, the mistress' financial 'plundering' of her lover and 'fights' against rivals, as well as the 'war' with unconquerable Eros.[10] Lyne suggests that the popularity of this kind of imagery in comedy results from its potential to be either 'wittily discordant or unexpectedly and amusingly appropriate—love is both violent and supremely non-violent.'[11] This analysis is worth bearing in mind when we come to consider Propertius' use of military imagery, which, I would suggest, relies on precisely this ambiguity: love is both like and unlike *militia*. In Propertius' case, however, though wit and humour are certainly present (and more prominent than traditional accounts of the 'anguished' Propertius would lead us to believe), the doubleness of the conceit also reflects elegy's essential ambivalence towards the traditional ideology of military *gloria* and public life.

Horace occasionally uses military metaphors in an erotic context,[12] but it is in elegy that the *militia amoris* topos really comes into its own. There are some half dozen examples in the poems of Tibullus. These range from passing allusions (such as *adsidue proelia miscet amor*, 'love engages continually in warfare,' 1.3.64, or *contra quis ferat arma deos?*, 'who would bear arms against the gods?,' 1.6.30) to more extensive programmatic passages. In 1.1 and 1.10, Tibullus rejects wealth and military service in favour of a life of love and pastoral *otium* ('leisure'), which is represented as a kind of alternative *militia*, incompatible with a respectable public career:

*hic ego dux milesque bonus; vos, signa tubaeque,*
  *ite procul; cupidis vulnera ferte viris,*

---

[10] e.g. Ter., *Eun.* 59–61 (lovers' quarrels), Pl., *Trin.* 239 and Ter., *Hec.* 65 (the mistress plunders her lover), Pl., *Cist.* 300 (the war against love), Pl., *Pers.* 231–2, *Truc.* 230 (love as *militia*). In Greek new comedy, by contrast, the metaphor is strikingly rare: Alexis, fr. 234K is an isolated example. The language of warfare or conquest should also be distinguished from gymnastic metaphors (e.g 'wrestling' as a euphemism for sex); a particularly striking example is Apuleius, *Met.* 2.17, as compared with [Lucian], *Onos* 9 (the lover in Apuleius' version is clearly figured as a soldier doing battle rather than as an athlete).

[11] Lyne 1980: 72.

[12] e.g. *Carm.* 1.6.17, 3.26, 4.1.1–2. and 16. Cf. also Cat. 37.3 and 66.13–14.

*ferte et opes: ego composito securus acervo*
*dites despiciam, despiciamque famem.*
(1.1.75–8)

Here I am a good general, a good soldier; away with you, standards and trumpets; bring wounds and riches to men who desire them: as for me, secure in my garnered harvest, I will scorn both wealth and want.

Similarly, in 1.2.65ff., war is rejected in favour of life with Delia; in 1.10 it is implicitly contrasted with the relatively harmless *Veneris bella* ('wars of Venus') of l. 53; in 2.3.37–50 the poet inveighs against *praeda* ('booty' or 'loot'), which is the weapon of the poet's rival, 'campaigning' in Tibullus' own *domus* ('household'); and in 2.4.20, we find an example of the characteristically Propertian and Ovidian rejection of epic on the grounds that elegy is more 'useful' to the lover. For the first time,[13] *militia amoris* becomes the defining feature of a poetic programme and a way of life: by speaking of love in terms of *militia*, Tibullus both contrasts it with literal warfare and simultaneously asserts that love and love-poetry have equal validity with a more conventionally respectable career. Again, Tibullus' use of the topos relies on the fact that love is both like war (and therefore the elegist is as good as the soldier/politician and the epic poet) and unlike war (which is rejected in favour of the life of peace, love and *otium*). This simultaneous acceptance and rejection of *militia* leads to a certain tension: the problem is that the elegist needs to subscribe to conventional social values for the first part of the comparison (the claim to respectability) to work, even as he rejects them in favour of his alternative system of values. This irony comes to the surface in 2.6, in which Tibullus considers deserting from Cupid's army to join Macer on a real campaign, but proves unable to escape his painful fate. Here, the military metaphor has the opposite effect from its use in 1.1. Rather than rejecting war in favour of love, Tibullus now depicts both kinds of *militia* as harsh and unpleasant. He is unable to escape Cupid, because one cannot bear arms against a god; here,

---

[13] There is some evidence that the conceit was employed by Gallus, however: see Virgil, *Ecl.* 10.44–5 and 69, with Coleman's 1977 commentary, *ad loc.*

though, he is no longer *dux milesque bonus* ('a good general, a good soldier'), but rather an unwilling conscript to love's army.[14]

In Tibullus, then, *militia amoris* is expressive of a characteristic equivocation between acceptance and rejection of the prevailing ideology of upper-class Roman society. Traditionally, military and political success are seen as appropriate goals in life, while love is dismissed either as non-serious or as harmful and demeaning (if indulged in to an excessive degree).[15] Similarly, love poetry is light and insubstantial, by contrast with the weighty seriousness of epic. Tibullus challenges these conventional values in their own terms: rather than rejecting the view that the lover is a degenerate idler, and the poetry of love lacking in weight, he responds by privileging 'idleness' over the corruption of public life, and 'light' poetry over the dead weight of epic. But by accepting the conventional labels, Tibullus exposes the inadequacy of the 'elegiac lifestyle' as an ideal: love is desired, but also painful and humiliating; war and public life are devalued, but also likened to the lover's own experience.

In Propertius, both the contrasts and the similarities between war and *otium*, between real warfare and the *militia amoris*, become an extremely prominent theme, particularly in Books Two and Three. This may reflect Tibullan influence, but Propertius develops the topos much more thoroughly than his contemporary, to the extent that *militia amoris* can be seen as one of the major themes of Book Two. In fact, about half the elegies in the book contain some reference to the relationship between love and *militia*. Propertius applies the comparison and explores its implications in a variety of different ways and different contexts; the Tibullan phrase *adsidue proelia miscet amor* ('love engages continually in warfare') could be used as a kind of epigraph for the book, in which Propertius works out the metaphor in all its possible ramifications.

---

[14] Both Spies 1930 (1978): 72–3 and Murgatroyd 1975: 77 are aware of the double-edged nature of the topos; but neither fully brings out the ironies which result from the tension between acceptance and rejection.

[15] These attitudes are most clearly exemplified by Cicero's treatment of Caelius' relationship with Clodia in the *Pro Caelio*: Caelius' behaviour is defended on the grounds that he was never deeply involved, and that in due course he gave up the affair in order to devote himself fully to a public career.

## Propertius 2.7: Militia Amoris and the Ironies of Elegy 279

The most straightforward use of the metaphor is as a euphemism for sex: in 2.1, the poet speaks of 'wrestling' with his naked mistress, and irreverently describes such encounters as *longae Iliades* ('lengthy *Iliads*'); and in 2.14 a new conquest (or perhaps a reconciliation with Cynthia) is compared to the sack of Troy and to victory over the Parthians. Alternatively, the war may be against the lover's rivals: as the poet bitterly remarks in 2.8.7–10, *vinceris aut vincis, haec in amore rota est* ('you are conquered or you conquer: such are the vicissitudes of love'). Or, as in the Hellenistic epigrams, the enemy may be Amor himself, who breaks a treaty (2.2), triumphs over the poet (2.8.39–40), and is asked, in imitation of an epigram of Asclepiades (*A.P.* 12.166), to keep shooting at the wretched lover until he is dead and out of his misery (2.9.37–40). There are also several passing references to the weapons of Amor.[16] A less direct analogy between love and war is set up by the numerous comparisons in Book Two between Propertius' situation and scenes or characters from the *Iliad*, to which there are no fewer than ten references in different poems.[17] Yet another group of poems contrasts the lover's life and the soldier's, or elegiac and martial poetry: these include the programmatic elegies 2.1, 2.10 and 2.34, and passages (e.g. 2.7, 2.14.23–4 and 2.15.41–6) which reject war in favour of a life of idleness and love.

In Book Two, then, Propertius displays some ingenuity in his exploration of various different ways in which the comparison between love and war can be applied.[18] But this complex manipulation of the topos is not simply a literary exercise: it also serves to develop

---

[16] See 2.13.1–2, 2.30.31, and the more developed working out of the image in 2.12.9–24.
[17] 2.1.14 and 49–50, 2.3.32–40, 2.6.16, 2.8.29–40, 2.9.16, 2.13.37–8, 2.14.1–2, 2.15.13–14, 2.20.1–2, 2.22.29–34.
[18] Indeed, it might be argued that Ovid's more explicit elaboration in *Am.* 1.9 functions as a kind of commentary on Propertius 2. Like Propertius, Ovid self-consciously applies the comparison in a number of different ways: in ll. 4–8, the mistress plays the role of general, with the lover as her soldier; in 9–16 and 19–20, the mistress is the object of the lover's *militia*; in 17–18 and 21–8, the lover is at war with his rivals, or the mistress's husband or *custodes* ('guards'); and in 33–8, Ovid introduces figures from the Trojan War as *exempla*. Cf. also Otis 1965, which raises the possibility of reading Book One as a 'working out' of the theme of *servitium amoris* through a series of contrasts and symmetries between poems. My analysis of Book Two is rather similar.

an analogously complex and ambiguous picture of Propertius' attitude towards the establishment and towards conventional morality.

Before looking in more detail at the way *militia amoris* operates in Book Two, it is worth turning back briefly to 1.6, in which Propertius first refers to his own lifestyle as *militia*. Tullus has asked the poet to accompany him to Asia on the staff of his uncle, the proconsul of the province. Propertius turns down the offer on the grounds that Cynthia has begged him to stay, and continues:

> *me sine, quem semper voluit fortuna iacere,*
> *    hanc animam extremae reddere nequitiae.*
> *multi longinquo periere in amore libenter,*
> *    in quorum numero me quoque terra tegat.*
> *non ego sum laudi, non natus idoneus armis:*
> *    hanc me militiam fata subire volunt.*
>
> (1.6.25–30)

Since fortune has always wanted me to lie low, allow me to give up my life to utter worthlessness. Many have perished gladly in lasting love, in whose company may the earth cover me, too. I was not fitted by my birth to praise or feats of arms: this is the soldiering which my fate wills me to undertake.

Here, the poet sets out what we might call the elegiac dilemma. On the one hand, love is *nequitia* ('worthlessness'); it involves the lover in suffering, loss of reputation and all the other evils associated with erotic passion by moralists as different as Cicero and Lucretius. On the other, it is not only desirable—a death one would gladly die—but even, in some sense, as valid a 'career' as the more conventional path pursued by Tullus. It is hard—perhaps, finally, impossible—to decide who is the butt of the irony which pervades these lines. There is, at some level, a rejection (or defiance) of conventional social values here; but the tone of helpless regret, and the poet's overt acceptance of terms like *nequitia* ('worthlessness') and *non laudi idoneus* ('not fitted for praise'), can also be seen as deflating.[19] Line 30 can be read either way: either it expresses pride in the *militia amoris*, as some-

---

[19] This kind of self-mockery also occurs in Roman comedy (e.g. Plaut., *Most.* 85–156), where the 'reprobate' lover laments his own downfall. The humour here is derived from the young man's application *to himself* of the kind of language conventionally directed against the follies of love by the moralists.

thing ultimately as valuable as literal *militia*; or it carries the ironic implication that, by rejecting one kind of *militia*, Propertius has simply bound himself to another kind, which is both more gruelling and—in conventional terms—less rewarding. Or we can accept both possibilities, and say that the line sums up the paradoxical and mocking stance which is characteristic of Propertius' poetry, in which love is viewed simultaneously through the eyes of the obsessed lover and of an ideology which condemns such obsession as diametrically opposed to the duties and rewards of public life. In sum, Propertius' mockery is directed both at conventional morality and at the pretentions of his own elegiac *persona*.

In several passages in Book Two, the regretful tone of 1.6 is replaced by a more defiant note. The theme of the poet's unfitness for any other kind of life is picked up in 2.1, Propertius' *recusatio* to Maecenas. Here he excuses himself from writing epic on the grounds that, like Callimachus, he is not up to 'thundering;' yet the tone of the poem is far from modest.[20] The phrase *longae Iliades* ('lengthy *Iliads*'), the suggestion in lines 43–6 that 'battles in a narrow bed' are just as respectable a profession as farming, sailing or soldiering, and the bold claim *laus in amore mori* ('it's glorious to die of love') are all deliberately provocative, simultaneously claiming for elegy a status equal with that of epic and mocking the traditional morality which would term his relationship with Cynthia *extrema nequitia* ('utter worthlessness'). On the other hand, the high ideal of a faithful lifelong relationship (47–8) is somewhat undercut by Propertius' lack of certainty that he will be the only one to enjoy Cynthia's love, and her supposed condemnation of the *Iliad* on the grounds of Helen's immorality (50) is highly ironic in view of the fact that she is herself compared to Helen (explicitly or implicitly) in several other elegies.[21]

In 2.1, Propertius challenges the conventional view that elegy and the so-called 'elegiac lifestyle' are morally inferior to epic and a public career; yet the humorous extravagance of his claims tends to soften their impact, and to open up the possibility of a reading in which

---

[20] On the paradoxical interplay between weakness and strength characteristic of the Callimachean *recusatio*, and its relationship to the self-abasement of the elegiac lover, cf. Sharrock 1995.

[21] See esp. 2.3.32, 2.6.16, 3.8.32.

Propertius' *persona* is viewed as absurdly and comically exaggerated.[22]

Two elegies seem to go much further. In 2.15.41–8, the poet claims that if everyone lived a life of 'wine, women and song,' there would have been no Actium and no Civil Wars; and in 2.14, he celebrates his 'conquest' (or reconciliation, if we assume that the girl is Cynthia) as *devictis potior Parthis* ('preferable to the defeat of the Parthians'). Both statements are certainly irreverent and mocking, and have been read by critics like Stahl as overt defiance of the Augustan regime. But is the issue really that straightforward? The context is important. In both poems, Propertius expresses the exultant feelings of the successful lover through a series of extravagantly hyperbolical protestations. His joy exceeds that of Agamemnon, Ulysses, Electra or Ariadne (2.14.1–4); he will become immortal if such bliss continues (2.14.10, 2.15.39–40); his conquest is better than *spolia*, *reges* and *currus* ('spoils,' 'kings' and '[triumphal] chariots,' 2.14.23–4); the girl holds the power of life and death over her lover (2.14.31–2), and he will be faithful to her in death as in life (2.15.31–6). The references to the Parthians and to Actium stand in each poem as the climactic assertion of the validity of the poet's way of life. The conquest of the Parthians is introduced as the *summum bonum* of the conventional military and political career which Propertius rejects for himself (he does not, after all, say that such a campaign would be worthless, but that he himself prefers a different kind of conquest). In 2.15, he seems to come closer to saying 'make love not war,' but there is something

---

[22] cf. Veyne 1988 (trans. Pellauer): esp. 97–100. Veyne, however, sees elegiac discourse as entirely humorous: 'the Roman elegists smile about what they are talking about—love, heroines, Ego—but they are absolutely serious about the rules of the genre' (99). This is, I think, an over-simplification. Although, as I have argued, Propertius' self-irony makes it difficult to take his anti-conformist stance at face value, neither can we take him to mean exactly the opposite of what he seems to be saying. If the elegiac ideal of love, fidelity, *otium* ('leisure') and freedom from the demands of society is shown to be unattainable and in some ways absurd, that does not alter the fact that the elegists are, on one level, putting it forward as an ideal. The fact that Propertius constantly undercuts his 'rebellious' stance does not prevent his poetry from being provocative. The complexity of elegiac irony makes it possible either to take the poems straight, or to read them as a joke; but both approaches are, in my view, equally partial. For a critique of Veyne, see Conte 1994a (trans. Most): 158–60, n. 19; cf. also the reviews by Wyke 1989b: 166–70 and Fowler 1990: 104–6.

slightly ridiculous in the implication that drunkenness is a preferable alternative to the ambitions which lead to war. Line 44 recalls the Golden Age imagery used (for instance) by Tibullus at the beginning of 1.10; but the fact that it is *pocula* ('wine-cups')[23] rather than rustic simplicity or old-world piety that is opposed to warfare tends to subvert the commonplace antithesis between pastoral innocence and military–political strife. The eight lines devoted to Actium here also form a kind of diptych with eight lines (35–42) on the same subject in the next poem, 2.16. Here, Propertius is in a gloomier mood, lamenting Cynthia's financial greed, and love is now seen as something humiliating rather than elevating. The poet's assessment of Actium is also strikingly different: Antony is now described as subject to *infamis amor* ('disreputable love'), which causes him to turn tail at the crucial moment, and his cowardice contrasts with Caesar's *virtus* and *gloria* ('courage' and 'glory'). The poet's equivocation in his handling of the battle thus corresponds very clearly to his equivocal presentation of love and the elegiac lifestyle itself. Both passages are in one sense subversive: the first exploits the conventional association between civil war and moral guilt to justify Propertius' 'immoral' lifestyle; in the second, he 'excuses' his weakness on the grounds that much greater men have fallen prey to love. But by characterizing himself as a drunken degenerate, by appearing to accept society's evaluation of his way of life, even as he rejects what society conventionally regards as success, he has again left open the possibility of two (or more) readings.[24] We can take him either to be mocking the conventions of Augustan panegyric, or to be satirizing the pretentions of his own *persona*—the rebellious youth, who thinks the world well lost for love.

There is also a latent uncertainty in both 2.14 and 2.15 that the ideal of 'love till death' can actually be carried through. While sure of his own loyalty, the poet can do no more than hope for the loyalty of his mistress (2.14.29–32, 2.15.25–8), and the opening *exempla* in 2.14

---

[23] This interpretation assumes that the MS reading *pocula* is accepted; most recent editors prefer Fontein's conjecture *proelia* ('battles').

[24] Much the same could be said of the reference to Antony which some critics (e.g. Griffin 1985: 35) have seen in 2.15. If the allusion in one sense aligns the poet with Augustus' rival, it also undermines itself by accepting the anti-Antonian propaganda which portrayed him as a drunkard.

do not bode well. The victories of Agamemnon and Ariadne were both followed by sticky ends, and the rejoicing of Electra and Ulysses was, to say the least, premature. The juxtaposition of these two poems with two (2.16 and 17) in which the poet laments his separation from his fickle mistress tends to confirm these hints.

So far, then, we have seen that Propertius exploits the topos of *militia amoris* as a way of dissociating himself from conventional morality and social values and of asserting the validity of the elegiac lifestyle and elegiac poetry as an alternative to an official career and to 'official' poetry. *Militia* in its literal sense stands for the kind of activity which a young man in Propertius' position might be expected to pursue: by referring to his affair with Cynthia in the same terms, he excuses his lack of ambition and rejection of *negotium* ('business' or 'occupation') on the grounds that to live and die a lover is just as worthy a goal in life. At the same time, the language he uses points to a degree of irony in these claims. While he mocks both overtly and implicitly the values of the Augustan establishment, he also exposes his own *persona* to mockery as the fatuous devotee of unworthy ideals. From this point of view, the role of the addressee may be seen as particularly significant: unlike Catullus, who addresses himself primarily either to Lesbia herself, or to members of his circle who can be expected to share his views on life and love, Propertius' reader is generally characterized as a more conventional figure. Despite his claims to write for an audience of young lovers,[25] his addressees (Tullus in 1.1 and 1.6, Bassus in 1.4, Maecenas in 2.1, or the anonymous friend of 2.8) are often represented as attempting to dissuade him from his devotion to Cynthia. Thus, the audience is characterized, by and large, as hostile to (or at least, not automatically in agreement with) the ideals the poet proclaims. This again tends to open up scope for irony, as we are distanced from the speaker and alerted to the possibility that he, rather than the *senes duri* ('stern old men'), may in the end be the butt of his own mockery.

Some of the other ways in which the topos is used in Book Two point to an even more ambivalent and ironical attitude. One of these

---

[25] See 1.7.11–24, 2.13.11–12.

is the frequent comparison with the *Iliad*. On the one hand, the way Propertius uses this comparison is supremely self-confident: his 'battles' with his mistress have the status of *longae Iliades* ('lengthy *Iliads*,' 2.1.14), his tomb will be as famous as Achilles' (2.13B.37–8), Cynthia is another Helen (2.3.32ff.), and so on. Moreover, he persists in reading the *Iliad* as a work of love-poetry: it is about a *levis puella* ('fickle girl,' 2.1.50), and the relationship between Achilles and Briseis is several times treated as an *exemplum*, particularly at the end of 2.8, where all the effects of Achilles' wrath are ascribed to his frustrated love for *formosa Briseis* ('lovely Briseis').[26] This somewhat perverse reading of the epic may constitute another justification for writing love-poetry—usually seen as the antithesis of epic. On the other hand, the comparison which Propertius draws between himself and the Homeric heroes is often so wildly incongruous that it amounts to a deliberate undermining of the poet's overt claims. The most extreme example of this occurs in 2.22A, where Propertius compares his 'staying power' to the ability of Achilles and Hector to fight after a night of love. But in other contexts, too, the contrast with the heroic exploits of the *Iliad* tends to qualify the idea that love really is the most important thing in life. The last couplet of 2.8, for example, draws attention to this disparity, and to the perversity of reading the *Iliad* simply as a love story exemplifying the triumph of Amor:

> *inferior multo cum sim vel matre vel armis,*
> *mirum, si de me iure triumphat amor?*
>
> Since I am far inferior both in birth and in arms, is it any wonder that love justly triumphs over me?

Here, the references to Achilles' *mater* and *arma* ('birth' and 'arms') remind us of the other issues involved: Homer's Achilles was not in fact motivated solely by Briseis' beauty, but by concern for his social

---

[26] cf. 2.9.9–16, 2.10.1, 2.22.29–30. Penelope's exemplary loyalty is similarly invoked in 2.9.4–8 and 3.13.24. Galinsky's term *reductio ad amorem* (coined to describe Ovid's allusions to the *Aeneid*) could equally well be applied to Propertius, who can often be shown to have anticipated traits which are usually thought of as peculiarly Ovidian.

status and for recognition of his military superiority[27]—precisely the kind of concern which Propertius claims to repudiate. Moreover, the mingling in this couplet of literal and figurative senses of *militia* (Achilles' arms are literal, but the triumph of *Amor* is figurative) exposes the factitious basis of the comparison. These ironies are carried further by the reference to Briseis in the following poem, where Briseis' loyalty is contrasted with Cynthia's unfaithfulness.[28]

The idea that love is a battle against Amor, which also occurs quite frequently,[29] is another version of *militia amoris* which tends to

---

[27] cf. *Il.* 1.280: εἰ δὲ σὺ καρτερός ἐσσι θεὰ δέ σε γείνατο μήτηρ, 'even if you are strong, and a goddess bore you.'

[28] The Iliadic theme in taken up again briefly in Book Three (see especially 3.1.25–6 and 3.8.29–32). The Homeric poems again act as a kind of foil in Book Four, where the two Cynthia poems, 4.7 and 4.8, can be read as parodic versions of episodes from the closing sequences of the *Iliad* and *Odyssey* respectively (cf. Hubbard 1974: 149–55). Cynthia's ghost in Poem 7 has strong affinities with the ghost of Patroclus as it appears to Achilles in *Il.* 23 (cf. esp. ἦ ῥά τίς ἐστι καὶ εἰν Ἀίδαο δόμοισι/ψυχὴ καὶ εἴδωλον, ἀτὰρ φρένες οὐκ ἔνι πάμπαν· παννυχίη γάρ μοι Πατροκλῆος δειλοῖο/ψυχὴ ἐφεστήκει ('so, then, some kind of spirit or image exists even in the house of Hades... for all night long the spirit of ill-fated Patroclus stood over me,' *Il.* 23.103–6) with *sunt aliquid Manes... Cynthia namque meo visa est incumbere fulcro* ('ghosts do exist... for Cynthia seemed to lean over my bed,' Prop. 4.7.1–3); more generally, 4.7.5–6 ~ *Il.* 23.62–4; 7–8 ~ *Il.* 23.66–7; 13–14 ~ *Il.* 23.69–70; both ghosts issue instructions relating to their burial; 93–4 ~ *Il.* 23.91–2; and 96 ~ *Il.* 23.99–101). In Poem 8, the 'rout' of Phyllis and Teia, the punishment of the disloyal slave Lygdamus, the purification of the house, and the conclusion *toto solvimus arma toro* ('we made our peace all over the bed') recall the sequence of events in *Odyssey* 22–3 (rout of the suitors, punishment of disloyal slaves, purification, and reunion between Odysseus and Penelope). As in Book Two, the implicit comparison between the heroic and elegiac milieux contains a great deal of irony and humour (especially in 4.8). In neither poem do the protagonists live up to the characters of their Homeric models: in 7, the spite and vindictiveness of Cynthia's ghost contrast with Patroclus' pathetic pleas, and Propertius' apparent disloyalty to her memory with Achilles' devotion. The gruesome details of 7–12 and the evocation of contemporary 'low-life' in Cynthia's speech also mark the distance between this almost sordid world and the glamorous life and death of the Homeric heroes. There may also be a further example of creative 'misreading' of Homer, in Propertius' use of the relationship between Patroclus and Achilles as a model for his own erotic connection with Cynthia. In 4.8, neither character has the fidelity of Homer's Penelope (though there may be an ironic echo of her resistance to the suitors in Propertius' assertion that Phyllis and Teia proved unable to arouse him because his mind was on the absent Cynthia); and there is further irony in the fact that Propertius casts himself in the feminine role, while Cynthia plays the avenging Odysseus.

[29] e.g. 2.2.1–2, 2.9.37–40, 2.12, 2.13.1–2.

devalue the status of the life of love. To describe Love as a being with whom the lover is in conflict presupposes the old idea that love is a plague, a madness, something to be avoided—a view in fact diametrically opposed to the elegiac ideal of love as a lifelong *foedus* ('pact'). This is the view expressed in 1.1, where love is seen as a *furor* ('frenzy'), an incurable illness, from which the poet would like to escape. Admittedly, Propertius tends to use the impossibility of conquering the god, like his own unfitness for physical *militia*, as an 'excuse' for continuing in his present way of life, as in 2.30.31–2, where he complains that he alone is taken to task for what is really a *communis culpa* ('common failing'); but the idea that love is ideally something to be avoided runs through Book Two, counteracting the notion that the *vita iners* ('life of idleness') is wholly to be desired.

In Book Two, and throughout the collection, then, *militia amoris* is used as a way of exploring and developing the generally anti-establishment and anti-conformist stance of elegy as a genre. Propertius parades his rejection of conventional values and standards of behaviour:

> haec ubi contigerint, populi confusa valeto
>     fabula.                                              (2.13.13–14)

When these things have fallen to my lot, let the babbling gossip of the people go hang.

> ista senes licet accusent convivia duri:
>     nos modo propositum, vita, teramus iter.
>                                                          (2.30B.13–14)[30]

Stern old men may complain about those parties of ours: but let us, my life, follow the road we have embarked upon.

This is, of course, also a poetic creed, and the rejection of a respectable career in favour of the *vita iners* is intimately connected with the rejection of epic in favour of elegy. Both oppositions are encapsulated in the contrast between love and *militia*. But because love is also like *militia*, the opposition constantly tends to collapse. Love is not

---

[30] There is an obvious echo of Catullus 5 here, but the difference in tone is instructive. In Propertius' version, defiance of conventional morality is played off against the idea that Amor is a tyrannical conqueror who will not let his victims escape (31–2, and cf. Poem 30A—although most editors regard this as a separate poem, the juxtaposition is still significant).

consistently held up as an ideal: like real warfare, it is also connected with hardship, uncertainty and death. The lover is not always the proud warrior under the standards of Amor; he is also the unwilling slave of his mistress or of love itself. He is both an Achillean hero and a feeble degenerate.[31] On the poetic level, the claim that elegy is as good as epic entails acceptance of the conventional evaluation of epic as the highest genre, and Propertius undermines his self-assertion by the extravagance of his misreading of the *Iliad* as a love poem. On the political level, the poet both accepts and refuses to celebrate the status quo. Augustus is automatically regarded as 'one of them,' as the supreme representative of the *senes duri* ('stern old men') who would have Propertius abandon his scandalous lifestyle, and of those who engage in real *militia*. As such, he is treated with a mixture of humility and defiance, just as Tullus is in 1.6. Where Propertius takes the line that his affairs are just as important as war or epic, the tone is almost insolent: in 2.1, he virtually puts his own 'battles' on a par with Caesar's, and (perhaps) cites some of the less glorious episodes of the recent civil wars as examples of what he would write about had his fate allowed him to compose an epic.[32] In the second *recusatio* in Book Two, Poem 10, he takes the opposite line: he is prepared to sing of Augustus' exploits, but has not yet attained the heights of Helicon, and so must regretfully postpone the enterprise.

These equivocations seem to me one of the most characteristic features of the elegiac genre. While the elegiac poets proclaim the ideals of lifelong fidelity and the rejection of conventional values, they are constantly showing us that these ideals are unattainable. The final renunciation of the beloved is an integral part of the story, as are her infidelity, greed and cruelty. The lover is both godlike and enslaved. He poses as an anti-establishment figure, but is only able to express himself in the language of the society he claims to distance himself from.[33] The extravagance of his gestures and the stereotypical nature of his *persona* constantly draw attention to

---

[31] cf. La Penna 1977: 135–6 and 170 on the *incoerenza* ('incoherence') of Propertius' ideology. Cf. also Boucher 1965: 24–35 and Sharrock 1995.

[32] cf. Camps 1967 *ad loc.*; Sullivan 1976: 57–8; Stahl 1985: 164–7.

[33] Note especially the paradoxical condemnation of contemporary immorality and *luxuria* in passages like 2.6.35–6, 2.9.3–18, 2.16.15–22 and 3.13, which recall the Augustan moralizing of Horace or Virgil.

*Propertius 2.7:* Militia Amoris *and the Ironies of Elegy*   289

themselves, leaving us uncertain whether he is finally challenging convention, or reaffirming it by exposing the absurdity and implausibility of the ideals he proclaims. These ironies are fully apparent in 2.7, where the ambiguous figure of *militia amoris* again has an important role to play.

II

*Gavisa es certe sublatam, Cynthia, legem*
 *qua quondam edicta flemus uterque diu,*
*ni nos divideret: quamvis diducere amantis*
 *non queat invitos Iuppiter ipse duos.*
*"At magnus Caesar." sed magnus Caesar in armis:*   5
 *devictae gentes nil in amore valent.*
*nam citius paterer caput hoc discedere collo*
 *quam possem ⟨e⟩ nuptae perdere more faces,*
*aut ego transirem tua limina clausa maritus,*
 *respiciens udis prodita luminibus.*   10
*a mea tum qualis caneret tibi tibia somnos,*
 *tibia, funesta tristior illa tuba!*
*unde mihi patriis natos praebere triumphis?*
 *nullus de nostro sanguine miles erit.*
*quod si vera meae comitarem castra puellae,*   15
 *non mihi sat magnus Castoris iret equus.*
*hinc etenim tantum meruit mea gloria nomen*
 *gloria ad hibernos lata Borysthenidas.*
*tu mihi sola places: placeam tibi, Cynthia, solus:*
 *hic erit et patrio sanguine pluris amor.*[34]   20

You rejoiced, to be sure, Cynthia, when the edict was withdrawn— the edict which once cost us both so many tears, lest it should divide us; though Jupiter himself could not divide two lovers who did not wish it. 'But Caesar is mighty.' Yes, Caesar is mighty in arms: but conquered tribes have no power in matters of love. For I would

---

[34] The text is taken from Camps, except for the reading '⟨e⟩ more' in l. 8, on which see n. 48 below.

sooner allow this head to be severed from my neck, than waste torches and live like a bride, or pass your closed door, once wed, looking back with wet eyes on the scene of my betrayal. Ah, what a lullaby my flute would play for you then, that flute more mournful than the funeral trumpet! How am I to get sons to serve my country's triumphs? No one of my blood will be a soldier. But if I could really follow my girl's camp, Castor's horse would not be big enough for me. Indeed, it is from this that my name has won such fame—fame that has travelled as far as the wintry Borysthenides. I love you alone: may you, Cynthia, love me alone: this love will be worth even more to me than the blood of my ancestors.

In this short poem, the opposing images of the lover as a degenerate idler and as a heroic figure with his own loyalties and his own kind of *gloria* are played off against each other in complex ways, which tend to undermine neat oppositions, and make it difficult to come up with a definitive reading of the poem as either 'pro-Augustan' or 'anti-Augustan.'

To illustrate my point, it is worth glancing briefly at two of the more extreme interpretations advanced by representatives of the 'pro-Augustan Propertius' and 'anti-Augustan Propertius' schools of thought. Cairns and Stahl approach the poem from opposite directions. Cairns contends that it is impossible to take the poem at face value, as an attack on Augustan marriage legislation, because Augustus would simply not have countenanced such an attack from one of Maecenas' protégés. His main argument rests on an analysis of the poet's *persona*, which has affinities with the wastrel youth of Roman comedy and characterizes the speaker as 'a morally tainted individual.' His attack on the law is deliberately inadequate,[35] and would not have impressed the contemporary reader; and his eulogy of Augustus in ll. 1–6 would be all the more flattering, coming as it

---

[35] For reasons of space, I have omitted detailed consideration of Cairns' generic argument: the poem is based, he suggests, on the rhetorical *progymnasma* devoted to the criticism of legislation, but Propertius has drawn attention to the inadequacy of his own critique by using only one of the four standard headings under which the law should be discussed. Again, this argument relies on a particular view of the audience's expectations; and it is not clear to me that even a contemporary audience would have expected a full working-out of the rhetorical model in a short, personal poem.

does from 'the last man on earth to appreciate or value military success.'

Stahl, by contrast, assesses the tone of the poem as 'defiant,' taking the first six lines to be ironic, and the protestations of ll. 7–10 to be sincere. He admits that the language is hyperbolical, but assumes that the exaggeration and the 'jocular' tone of the closing lines are 'designed to take the potential political sting out of the poem.' Propertius, he argues, is characterized as a kind of anti-type of Virgil's hero in *Aeneid* 4, rejecting duty for love.

It should be clear from these summaries to what an extent the 'meaning' of the poem is conditioned by the values and assumptions the reader brings to the text.[36] Cairns shows that it is possible (with some ingenuity) to read the poem as pro-Augustan if (and only if) one begins by assuming that 'the commonplace guise of the lover-poet' is both morally objectionable and not to be taken seriously. Stahl shows that it is possible to take it the other way, though only by glossing over elements in the poem which conflict with his reading. Line 13, for example, is taken to mean 'why should I bear sons?,' in the face of more convincing parallels for the alternative translation 'how could I ... ?,'[37] on the grounds that such a note of 'obliging despondency' would be out of keeping with the defiant tone of the rest of the poem. Similarly, the opposition with *Aeneid* 4 is less clear-cut if we remember Virgil's sympathetic treatment of Dido, which Stahl ignores.[38]

It is notable that both Cairns and Stahl see irony as a crucial element in the poem, but differ as to which parts of the poem are to be seen as 'sincere' and which as ironic. It seems to me that Propertius does not in fact give the reader enough authorial guidance

---

[36] I am not, of course, claiming to approach the poem without any preconceptions of my own; I hope, however, that, by emphasizing the openness of the poem to differing interpretations, I have produced a reading which is more satisfying than the univocal interpretations I have discussed.

[37] See Shackleton-Bailey 1956: *ad loc.*

[38] Stahl's reading of the *Aeneid* as fully in sympathy with the ideals of the new regime is worked out in more detail elsewhere (Stahl 1981 and 1991). In both articles, Stahl sets himself firmly against readings based on the 'two voices' theory of the so-called Harvard school. His view of Propertius as a 'truly independent' poet is an obvious corollary to his interpretation of 'Augustan Virgil' as unambiguously imperialist.

to force the issue one way or the other. The relationship between poet (or implied author) and *persona* is not clear-cut enough to enable us to decide whether, as it were, to side with the speaker, in his *persona* of suffering, rebellious lover, or with the more conventional system of values represented, in this poem, by Augustus and his *lex*. The reader who approaches the poem expecting to find a straightforward attack on or eulogy of Augustus will find it, because in a sense both are there in the text. Cairns' observation that 2.7 has affinities with the *recusatio* is, I think, an important one, since the refusal-poem is characterized by a similarly double-edged quality. Though the writer does, in general, end up praising his patron while claiming not to, he may also have serious things to say about the conventional generic hierarchy and the relative status of poet and statesman.

Propertius begins by telling us that Cynthia rejoiced when a law, which might have separated the lovers, was finally withdrawn. Propertius, on the other hand, argues that the legislation could not have parted them anyway, since not even Jupiter has the power to divide *amantis invitos* ('lovers who did not wish it'). This assertion prompts a series of reflections in which the poet contrasts political and military might with the power of love, and the claims of society with the claims of his relationship with Cynthia. But even before we launch into the antithesis between love and war in ll. 5–6, some ironies and ambiguities have begun to appear beneath the surface of the poem. The reference to Jupiter in l. 4 is a neat variation on the commonplace that even the king of the gods succumbed to love;[39] but there is also an implied comparison between Jupiter and Augustus, the tone of which is hard to assess. Is this simply flattery (as Cairns would have us believe), or should we see some irony in the juxtaposition *Iuppiter ipse... magnus Caesar* ('Jupiter himself... mighty Caesar')? Certainly the latter phrase sounds somewhat lame after the ringing hyperbole of the previous line. But, if so, self-irony is also apparent, particularly in the word *invitos* ('unwilling'). Propertius has already told us that he is unwilling to be separated from Cynthia: the previous poem concludes *nos uxor numquam, numquam diducet amica: | semper amica mihi, semper et uxor eris*

---

[39] E.g. Meleager, *A.P.* 12.101 (also the model for the opening of Prop. 1.1).

('neither wife nor mistress will ever separate us: you will forever be both mistress and wife to me'), and 2.7 picks up and develops this idea—no wife will separate them, despite the demands of Augustus and society at large. But there may nevertheless be an obstacle to this idyllic relationship: Cynthia herself. Propertius' uncertainty that her devotion is as strong as his is implied in the tentative subjunctive *placeam* ('may you love') in l. 19, and we should also remember the context of Poem 7, which forms part of a sequence leading up to 2.11, a kind of 'failed' *renuntiatio amoris*. This cycle is foreshadowed in 2.3.33–40, where Cynthia is compared to Helen, the bone of contention between the rival lovers Paris and Menelaus. The theme of erotic rivalry is developed over the next six poems. In 2.4, Propertius reflects on the inconstancy of women (compared with boys); in 2.5, he tries to persuade himself to give Cynthia up, after hearing rumours of infidelity; in 2.6, he reflects on the irrationality of his jealousy, and concludes with the declaration of eternal fidelity quoted above; but in 2.8 and 9, he has lost her to a rival, suggesting that his jealousy was not absolutely without foundation. In 2.10 and 2.11, he teases the reader with the possibility that he will finally abandon Cynthia and elegy, before reaffirming his devotion, and the impossibility of escaping Amor, in 2.12 and 13.[40]

Throughout this group of poems, then, Propertius' declared ideal of lifelong fidelity is undermined by Cynthia's inconstancy, and the protestations of 2.7 should be read in the light of this tension. Even while he proclaims the power of love, Propertius hints that the possibility of a lasting romantic relationship may be open to

[40] I am obviously assuming here that the poems should be read in the order transmitted by the manuscripts; contrast, for example, Heyworth 1986 (unpublished). Heyworth argues that our Book Two originally consisted of two separate books (cf. also Hubbard 1974: 41–4), and that serious dislocation has also taken place in the ordering of the poems. 2.10 was the last poem of the original 'Book Two,' while 2.13 opened a new book (2.11 and 2.12 belong elsewhere). My analysis of the cycle stretching from 2.3 to 2.13 provides an alternative explanation for what I would see as 'false' closural features in 2.10, and for the new beginning in 2.13; and I have already suggested that the whole book as we have it is unified by the recurrence of references to *militia amoris* and to the *Iliad*. It is true that the book is exceptionally long; but the total number of lines (1,362) is still surpassed by Lucretius 5 (1,457 lines), and the books of other Augustan poets vary considerably in length. On *tres libelli* ('three books') in 2.13.25, see Camps 1967 *ad loc.*

question. In fact, though not even Jupiter can separate two lovers, they *will* be separated, temporarily in Book Two, and finally at the end of Book Three, by rival lovers and Cynthia's own infidelity. A flaw in the 'alternative' morality which the poet puts forward in 2.7 is revealed through the way that Cynthia is characterized, both in Book Two and throughout the collection, so that it is never possible to be sure that the poet is not laughing at himself, drawing attention to the extravagance of the impossible ideal of the Catullan *foedus amicitiae* ('pact of friendship').

In ll. 5–6, Propertius introduces the familiar opposition between *amor* and *arma* ('love' and 'arms'). Caesar's greatness is limited to the latter field; he has no power in the former, since Propertius would rather die than be parted from Cynthia. This assertion picks up two recurrent elegiac topoi: the contrast between love and war, and the motif of 'love till death.'[41] Both look forward ironically to the next poem, in which Propertius will be 'defeated' by his rival, despite the assertion that this is worse than having his throat cut (2.8.3–4). The hyperbolical language[42] of l. 7 is also undercut by the much more uncertain tone of the closing lines, as already noted, and it should perhaps also be remarked that the 'love till death' motif is elsewhere used to indicate the harshness, not of society, but of Cynthia herself, who will 'be the death of him.'[43] As in the case of *militia amoris*, the different ways that Propertius applies this topos point to ambiguities in his presentation of *amor*, which is both supremely desirable, and supremely painful.

The idea that physical death is preferable to the death of love is further developed in the extraordinarily complex imagery of lines 8–11, where Propertius pictures his marriage procession passing his mistress' closed door. This is at once a marriage and a funeral procession, and also a kind of failed *komos*. The torches of l. 8 are

---

[41] Cf., for example, 2.15.29–36.

[42] Both Cairns and Stahl are aware of the exaggeration here. We do not, of course, know the terms of the *lex* but, judging from the legislation of 18 BC and AD 9, the worst that could have happened to Propertius would have been to lose out on certain public privileges (such as special seats in the theatre), and the right to inherit property from relatives not within the sixth degree, or from unrelated benefactors.

[43] E.g. 2.1.74–7.

both marriage and funeral torches,[44] and the flute would sound more dreary than the funeral trumpet (l. 12). The *faces* ('torches') perhaps also suggest the flame of passion, which Propertius would be destroying (*perdere*) in parting from Cynthia. This imagery continues the sentiment of l. 7: separation from Cynthia would be worse than death. But the picture of the lover passing the closed door (ll. 9–10) also suggests the *exclusus amator* or 'locked-out lover,'[45] and thus once again we are given an ironic reminder that Cynthia herself has been in the past, and will be in the future, the cause of the lovers' separation. Propertius would rather die than pass her closed door as a husband; but there is little he can do when Cynthia herself shuts him out, as she will in the very next poem.

But the lines also imply that the marriage would not have the desired effect. Far from becoming a useful member of society, Propertius is portrayed as a feeble, womanish figure in these lines. The marriage-torches would be wasted,[46] because this feeble character would be unable to produce warlike sons, as he tells us in l. 13. Instead of acting as a proper *maritus* ('bridegroom'), he seems rather to play the bride's role. The tearful departure from Cynthia's threshold recalls the bride's traditional reluctance to leave her mother's embrace[47] and her childhood pursuits, and the puzzling phrase *nuptae ... more* ('like a bride') can also be explained in similar terms: Propertius would take the wifely role of humble obedience, rather than the husband's part.[48]

---

[44] Cairns 1979a: 195, n. 27, aptly compares 4.3.13f. and 4.11.46.

[45] Cf. Tib. 1.5.67–74. Note also the references to *limina/ianuae* ('threshold,' 'doors') in Prop. 2.6.37, 2.16.6 and 3.25.9–10. The tears of the departing lover in the *renuntiatio amoris*, 3.25, also recall the *uda lumina* ('wet eyes') of 2.7.10.

[46] The 'wasted' marriage torches perhaps also recall the very common idea that the lover 'wastes' his patrimony on his mistress: cf. *OLD* s.v. *perdere* § 6.

[47] Cf., for example, Cat. 61.79–82 and 62.20–4.

[48] On *nuptae more* see Williams 1958: 27–8. Williams argues for the reading '‹e› nuptae ... more,' which he interprets as 'a very condensed form of *ut qui ex more nuptae viverem* (or more archaically *ut qui nuptae morigerus essem*), meaning "in living a wife's life"' (28). Propertius, he suggests, assumes 'that married life would consist in his being *morigerus* to his wife and not the reverse.' This is certainly more convincing than the alternatives: Butler and Barber and Camps retain the manuscript reading, translating 'at the whim/behest of a bride' (but the parallels cited by Camps are unconvincing, and *nuptae more* would surely have to mean 'in the manner of a bride'); Enk prefers *amore* (but, as Shackleton-Bailey points out, there is surely no

The defiance of l. 7 thus begins to evaporate in these lines, leading up to the 'obliging despondency' of l. 13. The poet equivocates between the proud claim that he would rather die than leave Cynthia, and the more apologetic stance of the central lines, which recalls the *non ego sum laudi, non natus idoneus armis* ('I was not fitted by my birth to praise or feats of arms') of 1.6. This reading again supports Shackleton-Bailey's translation of *unde* in l. 13 as 'how?' rather than 'why?.' But with *quod si* ('but if') in the following line, the tone changes again. Propertius has protested his feebleness, which would prevent him from fulfilling the role of a useful and productive member of society. Now, paradoxically, he tells us that as a lover, and a poet of love, far from being feeble, he will be able to match the military prowess of Caesar himself. If Cynthia's camp were 'real' (*vera*[49]), the poet would be transformed into a hero of the stature of Castor. He has his own kind of glory, which has spread as far as the distant Dneiper, conquering the limits of the known world as Augustus is often represented as doing elsewhere.[50] Again, this claim is provocative, but it is also undercut by the whimsical conceit of ll. 15–16 and the extravagance of the boast in l. 18 (as Cloud notes, Propertius can hardly be claiming seriously to have literary admirers in the Ukraine). There may, too, be some sexual innuendo in the reference to Castor's horse, since riding is a common metaphor for intercourse in Latin poetry.[51] Propertius' sexual potency, like his

question of Propertius *loving* his hypothetical bride); Shackleton-Bailey suggests *in ore*, which makes very little sense after *perdere faces*. Propertius depicts himself in a similarly feminine role in 1.11.23–4, where he paraphrases Andromache's famous speech in *Iliad* 6: his dependence on Cynthia has reduced him to playing the woman's part. Cf. also 4.8 (discussed in n. 28 above); and 2.1.48 and 2.13.36, which (as Hubbard points out, 1974: 101) entail a similar role reversal, recalling the ideal of *univiratus*, which was frequently celebrated in the epitaphs on women's tombs.

[49] The meaning of *vera* is also disputed: Camps and Shackleton-Bailey take it to mean 'the right kind' or 'the only true soldiering,' while Butler and Barber and Enk translate 'if it were real warfare.' The latter interpretation is defended by Stahl 1985: 150, n. 26.

[50] Cloud 1993 compares Hor., *Carm.* 3.5.2–4, Virg., *Aen.* 6.794–5 and Prop. 2.10. On the topos of 'world-wide fame,' see further Nisbet and Hubbard on Hor., *Carm.* 2.20.14. A similar parallelism between the 'conquests' of poet and *princeps* can be seen in the proem to *Georgics* 3: cf. Buchheit 1972: 92–159.

[51] See Adams 1982: 165–6. The metaphor is usually used as a euphemism for the 'female superior' position, but for a more general sense, cf. Lucr. 4.1195–6, Ovid, *Ars.*

poetry, is inspired solely by Cynthia; separate him from her, and he would become the feeble wimp of ll. 8–14, rather than the macho hero of l. 16. Again, the outrageousness of this claim undermines the defiance of the opening lines.

Finally, as already noted, the last couplet sheds doubt on the idea that Cynthia's fidelity is as strong as the poet's. His decision to sacrifice respectability and his *patrius sanguis* ('the blood of [his] ancestors') for her love becomes rather pathetic in the light of this uncertainty, and, although the confident assertion of the final line picks up the apparent assurance of l. 4, we have already seen that Propertius undermines that confidence in various ways.

The poem as a whole, then, sets up a series of oppositions: between the realms of *amor* and *arma*; between poetry and war; between the public sphere and the private sphere; between the power of the state (or of respectable society) and the power of love. But this neat structure is also undermined by a series of ironies: the paradoxical notion that respectability itself would make Propertius useless; the contrast between 'reality' (the feeble poet-lover) and fantasy (the heroic conqueror of ll. 15–18); the implicit reminders of his subservience to Cynthia, which contrast with his defiance of Augustus; and, finally, Caesar's (acknowledged) greatness as against the uncertainty of Cynthia's fidelity. In the last instance, in particular, it is not clear which way the irony cuts. Do we take the poet's flattery of Augustus[52] as ironic and Propertius' protestations at face value? or vice versa? I have argued that to try to decide the question one way or the other is to over-simplify the poem.

I have so far avoided discussing the precise nature of the *lex* which is the starting-point of the poem. Two facts are fairly clear. Firstly, the legislation has either been withdrawn or cancelled, so that Propertius is not actually attacking a policy which is *currently* being pursued by the *princeps*. Secondly, the language of l. 3 is evidently exaggerated:

---

2.726 and *R.A.* 429–30, and esp. Mart. 7.57 (where the reference to Castor and Polydeuces probably has a sexual reference: see Adams 1982: 166, n. 3). Castor's horse Cyllarus is mentioned by several classical poets: see especially Sen., *Phaedr.* 811, where Cyllarus is specifically associated with heroic prowess.

[52] The speaker of the first part of l. 5 is either an anonymous objector (of the kind common in oratory and diatribe) or Cynthia herself; but Propertius does not deny Caesar's claim to greatness in the military sphere.

there is no way that any law could actually have forced Propertius to marry, unless its provisions were significantly harsher than those of the later *Leges Iuliae* and *Lex Papia Poppaea*, which seems highly unlikely. Hence, it is a mistake to see the poem as a head-on attack on Augustus; the withdrawal of the legislation is rather used as the starting point for a series of reflections on the conflicting demands of love and society. This reading would be strengthened if we were to accept the conclusions reached in the recent analysis of the issue by Badian,[53] who argues that there is no solid evidence for the promulgation of any marriage legislation at the period when the elegy is likely to have been written.[54] On this view, either the historians are improbably silent about Propertius' *lex*, or the poet must be referring to legislation which dated from some time *before* 28 BC. Badian (following Ferrero Raditsa[55]) suggests that the reference is in fact to a Triumviral measure, and that (unlike Augustus' later marriage laws) it was introduced for the purposes of raising funds, rather than maintaining moral standards. Propertius would then be referring to a general abolition of irregular Triumviral ordinances in 28 BC. If Badian is right, it becomes still more difficult to see Propertius as launching an all-out attack on Augustus' attempts at moral reform. The poem would still seem provocative: Propertius' stance is directly opposed to Augustan ideals, as he makes clear by the reference to Caesar in l. 4 (Augustus would evidently like to separate the lovers if he could, on Propertius' view); but Augustus would now figure not so much as the proponent of moral reform as the representative of the *senes duri* ('stern old men') who condemn the poet's relationship with Cynthia as immoral. Thus, the elegy need not be seen as directly challenging the power of the *princeps*, but rather as ironically manipulating elements of Augustan ideology.

---

[53] Badian 1985. Something of a critical consensus against Badian's theory seems to be forming, however: see, for example, Treggiari 1991: 59–60 and n. 91.
[54] Badian argues that the ancient sources which are usually cited as mentioning the law are in fact referring either to later legislation or to legislation unconnected with the issue of marriage.
[55] Raditsa 1980: 295–6.

## III

Propertius' use of the *militia amoris* topos in 2.7, as elsewhere in Book Two, is both witty and ironic. Both the superficial flattery of ll. 4–5 and the superficial defiance of ll. 6–20 are undermined, and it is, in the end, not possible to be certain which aspect we should privilege. The readings of Cairns and Stahl are unsatisfying because they both involve over-simplifying, and jettisoning either the poet's self-irony, or the irony which he directs at the establishment.

This complex use of irony is characteristic of elegy as a genre—perhaps in part because of the way the elegiac poet represents himself. The defining features of elegy are all negative: it is anti-conformist, anti-establishment, not-epic; its values and ideology are the antithesis of those held in respectable society. The elegist is thus an outsider, someone who has explicitly put himself beyond the pale. The very prominent use of conventional language and stereotyped situations also serve as constant reminders to the reader of the distinction between poet and *persona* (or Propertius and Ego, to use Veyne's terminology). But this does not mean that the poet entirely repudiates his *persona*; rather, the reader is invited to become aware of the inadequacies and inconsistencies both in the conventional morality from which elegy distances itself and in the ideals which it sets up on its own account. We might usefully compare the multiple levels of irony which Horace constructs in Book Two of the *Satires*, where he often delegates the moralizing voice to other characters, so that we receive the 'message' of the poems at second or third hand. The narrator thus distances himself from the surface meaning of the text, and it becomes unclear how seriously we are to take it, particularly where Horace himself becomes the butt of the joke.[56]

---

[56] See especially *Sat.* 2.7, where Davus' moralizing turns out to be derived at second-hand from a second-rate philosopher's door-keeper. At the same time, Horace 'proves' Davus' point, not only by his own past behaviour, but also by losing his temper at the end of the poem. On Horace's *persona*, see also Freudenburg 1993: 3–51. Freudenburg argues that the *persona* of the 'diatribe satires,' 1.1–4, is based on the *doctor ineptus* of comedy, and is thus not to be taken seriously. His underlying assumption that humour and parody are incompatible with serious moral reflection needs some qualification, however: cf. Fowler 1994.

In sum, the literary and political (or ideological) levels of meaning are not separable, and we should not simply dismiss Propertius' use of the *militia amoris*, and his anti-establishment stance more generally, as literary conventions. On the other hand, the very overt 'literariness' of elegy opens up levels of irony which make it impossible (or at least inadequate) to regard the poet as offering us a straightforward ideological programme or political message.

## POSTSCRIPT (2010)

Since the original publication of this article in 1997, much important work has been done on the relation between gender and genre in Roman elegy: it is now widely recognised that Propertius' self-representation as effeminate and unwarlike, along with his use of the *militia amoris* trope, is part of a complex and deeply ambiguous engagement both with epic poetry (as the 'establishment' genre *par excellence*) and with normative Roman values in general. For discussions of *militia amoris* in this connection, see e.g. Greene 1998: 41–3, De Brohun 2002: 73–85, and Miller 2004: 146–57. For two very different—but equally stimulating—analyses of the characteristic 'doubleness' of (Propertian) elegy discussed at the end of section I and in section III above, see Gibson 2007: 43–69, and Miller 2004: 130–59 (esp. 143–6, on 2.7). On Propertius and imperialism, see also Keith 2008: 139–65, who seeks to reformulate discussion of the politics of elegy by focussing on *otium* and luxury as products of empire, rather than as symptoms of elegiac *mollitia*.

The text of Book 2 has received considerable attention in recent years, particularly with the publication of P. Fedeli's monumental commentary (Cambridge, 2005) and the new Oxford Classical Text of S. J. Heyworth (2007a), with its companion volume, *Cynthia: A Companion to the Text of Propertius* (Oxford, 2007b): the textual problem at 2.7.8 is examined by Fedeli at 229–30 and by Heyworth at *Cynthia*, 140–1. Fedeli's introductory remarks on the poem (221–5) include extensive discussion of the nature of Propertius' *lex*, with a useful *historia quaestionis*, and offer further support for the hypothesis of Badian. In contrast, M. Beck (2000) seeks to cut the Gordian knot by classifying the poem, on stylistic as well as historical grounds, as spurious. The issue of book division raised in n. 40 above is addressed at length by the late R.O.A.M. Lyne (1998b), and by C. E. Murgia (2000), both of whom endorse (versions of) the position espoused by Heyworth; *contra*, see the brief remarks of J. Butrica 2006: 27–30 and (more cautiously) R. Tarrant 2006: 55–7.

# 11

## Images of the City: Propertius' New-Old Rome[1]

*Elaine Fantham*

If ever Rome was full of unfinished buildings, it must have been in the years after, or even before, Actium, when the new monuments were rising on the Palatine, and the Campus Martius was taken over by temples and theaters and porticoes and the towering Augustan Mausoleum. It is not as though major elements of the city had been destroyed, as they were in the Sullan assault of 83, and would be again in Nero's great fire and five years later in the battle between the supporters of Vitellius and those of Vespasian. The stimulus for this fever of construction came instead from an ambitious vision of the city, a desire shared by Caesar and his heir, to emulate Alexandria and other Hellenistic imperial capitals. Augustan poets hailed the gilded roofs and luxurious statuary, but as Rome's residents watched the heart of their city transformed, they must have passed years living in an extended construction site, with the old disfigured and the new still incomplete or raw.

I have chosen Propertius as my witness to this process, although he is not, like Virgil, the originator of the classic contrast of Then and Now, because the genre of elegy permits him a realistic evocation of both city scenes and activities, and the chronology of his four books is well enough defined to allow a sense of his evolving vision. Let me

---

[1] Editors' note: except where noted, all translations in this paper are Fantham's own.

see how much it is possible to deduce his attitude to the changes taking place around him from his representation of the old city as well as his allusions to the new.

Inevitably any interpretation of the poet's response must be to some extent conditional. In the first place we have to take into account the influence upon Propertius of his poetic predecessors: indeed it would be totally misleading to reconstruct his representation of Rome without mapping on to it the landmarks offered by the poetic models available to him. Luckily elements of imitation in the relationship of Propertius' account of the early city to the *Ur-Rom* of Virgil and Tibullus have been traced, and expertly traced, by La Penna, Solmsen, and others,[2] while Buchheit has examined in detail the dependence of Propertius' fullest contrast of *Einst und Jetzt* in elegy 4.1a on Tibullus' virtuoso elegy 2.5, and on book 8 of the *Aeneid*.[3]

Virgil's way had been to evoke Rome in her first miraculous beginnings with the few scattered cottages of Evander's idyllic settlement in the eighth book of the *Aeneid*. With Evander's retrospective narrative these passages from book 8 provided inspiration for the pastoral vignettes of *Ur-Rom* in Tibullus' elegy for young Messalinus. Indeed it seems to me highly likely that besides *Aeneid* 2, 4 and 6—known to have been recited to Augustus in 23 BCE—Virgil would have chosen to compose and recite these passages with their immense appeal to local patriotism as early as possible in his epic undertaking.[4] Certainly much of the *Aeneid* and probably of Tibullus' second book was known to court circles of Rome before 19, when both poets died, and it is easy to show that one important elegy of Propertius' third book (if not also his salute to Virgil in 2.34)[5] is familiar with the parts of the *Aeneid* that introduce early Rome.

---

[2] See La Penna 1977, esp. part II ch. 4, 'Scoperta poetica della città e d'intorni': 176–82, 187–91, and, on formal echoes, La Penna 1950/1951, Solmsen 1961, Weeber 1978.
[3] Buchheit 1965.
[4] We need not go all the way with Grimal 1952 to accept his conviction that Virgil himself composed the Roman scenes of book 8 as an early homage to Augustus.
[5] Pillinger 1969:195 argues that 2.34 shows Propertius' 'familiarity with the Actium motif in the *Aeneid* then in progress,' noting also that beside 4.6 'several passages elsewhere in book 4 point to his special interest in the eighth book of Virgil's epic.'I would go beyond his argument to suggest that 2.34 is Propertius' response to the books opening the second half of the *Aeneid*. It defines the *Aeneid* in four lines before hailing it with an accolade that could also be read as a lictor's proclamation to clear

Balancing the great *Recusatio* to Maecenas in book 3, the Cleopatra elegy 3.11 foreshadows much in book 4, and I shall make it my point of departure for understanding how Propertius came to write his poems for Rome (*Roma fave: tibi surgit opus*, 'give me your favor, Rome, this work arises on your honor', 4.1.67), and evoke his 'ancient names of places', *cognomina prisca locorum* (4.1.69).

When I come to consider book 4 itself, I want to argue that not only the opening guided tour, 4.1a and the etiological elegies (4.1; 4.2; 4.4; 4.9 and 4.10) but the whole book was designed to reflect the shape and life of the city. In particular I believe that Propertius' image of Rome was shaped by Varro's conception of Romulus' archetypal city, which would also be known to him through its transformation in the opening chapters (1–12) of Livy's first book, composed between 29 and 25 BCE.

With one conspicuous exception Propertius makes few references to the new city of gold and marble: instead he invites us to deduce his response to the *new* city from his imaginative devotion to the *old*.

the way for a triumphal procession. *Nescioquid maius nascitur Iliade* ('Something even greater than the *Iliad* is coming to birth') suggests, not Virgil's first proem, but his second, from the seventh book, just as the references to the Actian shore of guardian Phoebus and gallant ships of Caesar (2.34.61) mark his acknowledgement of the great image on the shield of Aeneas in book 8. Here the poet is saluting the *Aeneid* in terms of the *Iliad*, that is, the warfare of its second half: he even borrows the comparative from Virgil's proem to book 7: *maior rerum mihi nascitur ordo*|*maius opus moveo*, 'a greater series of events is coming to birth: I attempt a greater task.' But while Virgil is only asserting the greater grandeur of his war narrative over his Odyssean wanderings, Propertius has changed the context of the comparative to make Virgil a more extravagant compliment. Propertius will develop the nexus between the arms given to Aeneas by Venus and the ships that bring Caesar victory without any fundamental change of direction in 4.1. 39–40 and 45–8. His description of Virgil's present task in 2.34.63, echoing the metrical form but not the syntax of *Aen.* 2.618, has adapted the phrase *arma suscitare* 'raising up arms' to suggest the warfare of *Aeneid* 7–12 rather than the voyages of 1–5. By its wording it also points to Aeneas' literal *arma*, the shield on which is depicted the panoramic battle scene of Actium. As a result he has put the cart (or triumphal chariot) of Augustus' Actian victory before the horse of Aeneas' warfare and role as founder. Rome's walls are the natural symbol of the foundation and undoubtedly 'the arms of Trojan Aeneas and city-walls raised on Lavinian shores' (2.34.63–4) echoes 'arms and the man who first...came to Italy and the shores of Lavinia' (*Aen.* 1.1–3). But Propertius has telescoped into a single phrase places and times that Virgil set apart: the shores of Lavinium and the walls, not of Lavinium but of Rome herself (*atque altae moenia Romae*, *Aen.* 1.1–7). It is these walls that will symbolize the city throughout its appearances in Propertius' text.

# Images of the City: Propertius' New-Old Rome

Indeed, in the proud evocation that opens book 4, contrasting Rome's greatness with the earliest settlement shared precariously between man and nature, his symbol for the mature city is itself old: 'Wolf of Mars, best of nurses for our community, what walls grew up from your milk!' (4.1.55–6).

Rome's greatness is symbolized by the walls she had in Propertius' time long outgrown, so that the city he is celebrating is not the new metropolis; instead he presents himself as the poet planner founding or marking out the old city: 'for I would attempt to lay out the walls in loyal verse', *moenia namque pio coner disponere versu* (4.1.57). Propertius sees himself as another Amphion, the poet architect first mentioned in the second Ponticus elegy (1.9.10) then cited with Orpheus as a model for Propertius' creative power in 3.2.5–6: 'men say Cithaeron's rocks were driven to Thebes by his art, and of their own accord were fused into its walls.'

Thus the poetic city Propertius creates is a nostalgic counterpart of Augustus' physical creation of the new monuments.

But the first occasion on which Propertius presents the city of Rome as a symbol of patriotism[6] is elegy 3.11, which is also his first certain allusion to the eighth book of the *Aeneid*. The opening theme of the poem is his own submission to the tyranny of his lover: this leads to the denunciation of female tyranny whose worst and last example, Cleopatra, is evoked in lines 41–6:

> She who dared to pit the barking Anubis against our Jupiter, and force the Tiber to endure the threats of the Nile, to drive back the Roman bugle with the rattling sistrum and chase the Liburnian prows with Egyptian puntpoles, and cast vile mosquito nets towards the Tarpeian rock and lay down the law between the statues and trophies of Marius.

Besides the obvious echoes of Horace's famous Actium epode (*Ep.* 9) and the Cleopatra ode (*C.* 1.37),[7] these lines draw specifically

---

[6] Propertius has portrayed the social amenities offered by Rome to the lover in 2.32, and evoked the primeval Rome of Romulus in 3.9.

[7] Compare *foeda...conopia* ('foul tents,' 45) with *turpe conopium* ('shameful tent'), *Epode* 9.15–16, and the threats to Jupiter Capitolinus, *Iovi nostro* ('our Jupiter,' 41), *Tarpeio...saxo* ('Tarpeian rock,' 45), and demand for the city, *coniugis obsceni pretium Romana poposcit | moenia* ('she sought Rome's walls as the prize of her tainted husband,' 31–2), with *dum Capitolio | regina dementes ruinas...parabat* ('while the queen was planning senseless ruin for the Capitol'), *Odes* 1.37.6–8.

on *Aen.* 8.696 and 698 for Anubis and the *sistrum*. Propertius draws again on the shield ecphrasis for the image of the protective Nile offering refuge in 3.11.51: 'yet you fled to the wandering streams of the fearful Nile', *fugisti tamen in timidi vaga flumina Nili* (cf. *Aen.* 8.711–3). There can be no doubt that this elegy reflects Virgil's representation of Actium and his association of Augustus' victory with the triumph of Italy and Rome herself. But in contrast with Virgil's Actium vignette, Propertius' poem foregrounds the physical city of Rome. Here too his inspiration may be Virgilian. Virgil's craftsman god depicted the early city in the shield ecphrasis at 635 and 647 (*urbem*) and made the Capitoline the visual focus of the climactic scene of Gallic assault at 652–4, alongside Romulus' Palatine hut at 655. Again, in the culminating triumph vignette Vulcan shows Augustus Caesar first entering the city walls in triple triumph, *triplici invectus Romana triumpho | moenia* ('carried within Roman walls in triple triumph,' 714–15), against a backdrop of three hundred shrines, then finally at his destination on the snow-white threshold of gleaming Phoebus (720).

In 3.11, the city itself becomes ever more important for Propertius as the elegy advances. Thus initially Propertius damns women by representing them as threatening to control the male world of the community. He prepares the way for Cleopatra with Semiramis' foundation of Babylon (21, 25) and her commands to Bactria to submit to her *imperium* (26). Cleopatra herself is designated but needs no naming. The symbol of her arrogance is her demand for Rome's walls and the subjection of her Senate:

... *Romana poposcit*
*moenia, et addictos in sua iura patres* (31–32)
She demanded Rome's walls and a senate bound to her laws (editors' transl.)

The *sedes* of *Romana...moenia* echoes that of *Aen.* 8.714–15: the enslaved senate recalls Caesar in *Aen.* 8.679 advancing 'with Senate and people', *cum patribus populoque*. For Propertius the walls of Rome, celebrated by Virgil in *Georgics* and *Aeneid* alike,[8] signify the prize of

---

[8] Cf. *Georg.*2.535 'and set around her seven hills with a wall,' *septemque una sibi muro circumdedit arces* = *Aen.* 6.783; and the walls that symbolize Rome's power in *Aen.*1.7 and 276.

contention and frame his meditation on the naval victory. After the walls the Tiber (42) and the Capitoline (*Tarpeio... saxo*, 45) are evoked to symbolize the city and its defences, followed by its natural defences 'high on her seven hills' (57).[9] Propertius also names other sites of defensive resistance, the cistern in the Forum recalling Curtius' death, and the path commemorating Horatius' demolition of the bridge, before he brings his poem back emphatically to the walls, founded by the gods and still to be preserved by them:

> *haec di condiderant, haec di quoque moenia servant:*
>    *vix timeat salvo Caesare Roma Iovem. (65–6)*
> These walls the gods had established; these they also keep safe. Rome would scarce fear Jove himself while Caesar thrives.

The next and last site to be mentioned is the temple of Leucadian Apollo (69).[10] The Augustan temple on the Palatine wins pride of place as climax and conclusion to Propertius' evocation of the city. After the walls, the river, the citadel and seven hills that together defended Rome, comes finally the votive temple of victory commemorating the end of its need for defences: *tantum operis belli sustulit una dies*, 'one day abolished such a struggle of warfare' (3.11.70).

There is a further signal that already in this book Propertius was preparing to make the city his theme. The elegant *recusatio* of 3.9 includes among Propertius' promises, always contingent on Maecenas setting him an example, the promise that he would write a national foundation epic of his city:

> *eductosque pares silvestri ex ubere reges* (51)
>    *ordiar et caeso moenia firma Remo* (50)
> *celsaque Romanis decerpta Palatia tauris* (49)[11]
> I shall tell of equal kings reared by a woodland udder and walls made safe by Remus' slaughter, the lofty Palatine grazed by Roman cattle ...

---

[9] On Rome's natural defences, note Cicero's account in *Rep.* 1.5 stressing the advantages of the Tiber and the *nativa praesidia* of steep hills enhanced by the Romulean walls. Tiber, hills, and walls will constitute the city for Propertius.

[10] Propertius is cited from Fedeli's 1984 text, in which only 67–8 are transposed to precede 59.

[11] Here I go against Fedeli 1984, retaining Peiper's transposition of 51 and 49.

The proposed, but postponed, celebration of Rome will begin with Romulus and Remus and honor the walls and the safe heights of the Palatine. In 3.9 the Palatine is singled out as the original walled community of Romulus (matching that of Livy 1.7) and associated by etymology with the original pastoral economy of Rome: but when the temple of Leucadian Apollo culminates the evocation of Rome in 3.11, there is no need to name its Palatine site, for the temple and its porticoes must have been the best known and most celebrated of Octavian's new monuments even before he entered Propertius' poetry as *tuus... Caesar* in the dedicatory poem of book 2 (2.1.25).

Let us give a moment to Propertius' ecphrastic encomium of this temple and its porticoes, the pointedly short and symmetrical 2.31.

> You ask why I am late for you? The golden portico of Apollo has just been opened by Caesar. It was so great a sight, articulated by Punic columns, the female brood of old Danaus set between them. Here indeed I thought the marble likeness of Apollo more handsome than the god himself, mouthing its song to the silent lyre: and round the altar stood Myron's herd, four crafty oxen, lifelike images. Then at its center rose the temple in brilliant marble, dearer to Apollo than his natal Delos: as its features there was the sun-chariot above the roof-ridge, and the doors, the famous work of Libyan tusk; one panel showed the Gauls cast down from the peak of Parnassus, the other mourned the death of Tantalus' daughter. Then finally the god himself, between his mother and his sister, clad in the long robe sounds out, as Pythian, his songs.

Scholars have been grateful to this elegy for its documentation of the appropriated Greek cult statues and iconographic scheme of the ensemble. We in turn know from our historians the occasion in October 28 BCE recorded by Propertius.[12] But this poem is filled with representations of gods and divine acts, not with the monument itself or its setting. Since the temple itself had already been consecrated at Caesar's triumph in 29, one would expect Propertius to focus on the newly finished porticoes, and he certainly devotes ingenuity to evoking the range of Numidian *giallo antico* columns with Danaus' daughters (their daggers half-concealed beneath their robes) filling the intercolumnar

---

[12] Dio 53.1.3: 'Moreover he completed and dedicated the temple of Apollo on the Palatine, the precinct surrounding it, and the Libraries.'

spaces.[13] In lines 5–6 the poet concentrates on the statue of Apollo, set apparently before the altar in front of the temple around which were set the famous lifelike heifers of Myron.[14] The hyperbolic compliment 'almost more beautiful than the god himself' has naturally led scholars to assimilate this statue, not otherwise identified, to the image set by Octavian in the library complex, reported by a scholiast on Horace *Epistles* 1.3.17 to have had Octavian's face and deportment.

So far each artistic element has had its couplet. In the second half of the poem the temple briefly looms in the foreground, dazzling in its marble, and exalted as the god's new favorite place of worship. With the distich describing the cult statue of Apollo Citharoedus by Scopas (15–16), this distich frames four lines devoted to the frontal ornamentation, one to the sun-chariot on the roof-ridge (or possibly to a pedimental relief),[15] the other three to the ivory-panelled doors celebrating two acts of vengeance by the leader's patron god.

Does such an enumeration of respected works of the best Greek classical period make a good poem? Does it even offer a natural sequence of visual experiences as they would affect the onlooker? To me this seems a frigid and unelegiac elegy, without flow or climax, and troubled by extraordinary ellipses, such as the yoking of the mourning for the children of Niobe with the presumably unmourned Gauls, or the odd zeugma *in quo* of 11, combining the statuary group aloft with the doors as part of the temple itself. Finally, as commentators have noted, the superlative praise of the first statue outshines the simple description of the cult statue that should have formed the climax of the poem. It would be easy to transpose lines 5–6, harder to justify the transposition, or to explain the ensuing leap from the Danaids to the

[13] Cf. Ovid *Ars* 1.71–6; *Tr.*3.1.60–2: 'I am led to the shining white temple of the unshorn god, where stand the foreign statues between the columns, the daughters of Belus and the father with drawn sword.' Also see Kellum 1986.

[14] Cf. Pliny *NH* 34.57. Both the Apollo and the cattle are praised in terms of their naturalism, which was a famous aspect of Myron's art recorded in many epigrams.

[15] La Penna 1977 and others have referred this to the (otherwise unknown) subject of the pediment, but archaeologists Coarelli (1980: 257) and Zanker (1988: 85) refer Propertius' language to the rooftop chariot sculpted by Lysias, in which both Apollo and Diana ride. Propertius himself is the primary source for many details, but the classical sculptors of most of the statuary are identified in Pliny's chapters on the history of sculpture, *NH* 36. 24 (on the shrine) and sections 13, 32 and 34–5. See now Richardson 1992: 14 and figure 64.

insufficiently located altar. The poem gives the modern reader little pleasure: what aesthetic appeal, beyond that of a Baedeker, would it have for Propertius' Hellenized readers? Did Propertius regret it? Is that why he does not attempt any similar architectural ecphrasis again?

Was he trying to conform to the new ideology? Inevitably allusions to the Palatine suggest to the modern reader the ideological conflict between the Augustan Palatine and Republican Capitoline hills—a contest that would be played out in other Augustan public acts, such as the ritual of the Secular Games in 17. The Secular hymn with its stress on the new Palatine triad would be sung in more than one place, but certainly in front of this same temple, within the residential precinct of Augustus himself. Most readers of Propertius seek to interpret in these political terms the poet's choice of sites for celebration, scrutinizing his poetry for a hint of polarisation or even favoritism between the two focal hills.

Keeping in mind these oppositions of old and new, architecture and nature, Imperial and Republican symbols, we come at last to the image of the city offered by the Romano-centric fourth book. Although the opening line of 4.1: *Hoc quodcumque vides... qua maxima Roma est*, 'all that you see here, where mighty Rome extends' introduces the most expansive representation of the city, past and present, I suggest that we begin by following Propertius' urban topography through the sequence of poems 4.2 to 4.10 that form the body of the book.[16]

First a word about those walls, so prominent in 2.34 and 3.9 and 11. Remnants of the Servian walls still survive and were surely more fully preserved in the Augustan era, but by Propertius' life-time the old Romulean walls must already have been purely conceptual, defined only by the surviving gates of the Palatine itself, since even the ritual Pomerium had been expanded by Sulla and Caesar. Yet in 4.1, as in 2.34 and 3.11, the walls of Rome serve repeatedly to symbolize the city.

*optima nutricum nostris lupa Martia rebus*
　*qualia creverunt moenia lacte tuo*
*moenia namque pio coner disponere versu*

---

[16] Scivoletto 1981 offers little assistance.

Wolf of Mars, best of nurses for our history, what walls grew up
sustained by your milk! For I would try to lay out the city walls in
loyal verse. (4.1. 55–57)

Reformulating his promise to celebrate the city, Propertius makes its
walls a symbol of his own ordering and constructive powers (*disponere
versu*) and expresses his rise to metropolitan fame by contrasting Rome's
fortifications with the walled hilltops of his native Assisi (65–6, cf.
125–6).[17] In contrast, the story of Tarpeia in 4.4, Propertius' counterpart
of Virgil's vignette of the Gallic capture on Aeneas' shield, marks the
importance of Rome's walls by stressing their absence and the Romulean
city's reliance on its natural defences: *murus erant montes*, 'the hills
served as its wall' (4.13); compare their pointed omission and substitution in Tarpeia's mock farewell in 4.35–6: *Romani montes et montibus
addita Roma|et valeat... Vesta*, 'farewell you Roman hills and Rome
attached to its hills, and Vesta ...'.[18] Only the slope of the 'Tarpeian
rock' (remember 3.11.45) defends Rome, and Propertius' elegy purports
to honor Tarpeia's tomb and tell how she gave the cliff her name.[19]

Varro's *De Lingua latina* is neither a *descriptio urbis* nor a periegesis
but a word list, in which the ordering of the place-names and their
origins is still likely to reflect his perception of their spatial and
historic sequence, and more systematic accounts given in other
works now lost. After introducing the *septimontium* (not our seven
hills but the multiple crests of Palatine and Capitoline with the Velia)
Varro starts his list with the Capitoline and explains its name from

---

[17] Propertius' *creverunt moenia* seems to have no parallel in Latin, but for the
emotive connotation of walls cf. *Aen.* 1.365–6 and 4370, *fortunati quorum iam moenia
surgunt*: 'Happy are those whose walls are now | already arising!' Outside Virgil
*crescere* and *surgere* are found with *moenia* only in Ovid's imitations at *Heroides*
7.11 and *Met.* 15.452.

[18] Goold 1990 has recently been inspired by the precedent of *Murus erat montes* to
revive the conjecture *et Tiberis nostris advena murus erat* in 4.1.8 (Goold's translation:
'the Tiber, though foreign, was our forebears' wall').

[19] Wiseman 1978 has shown that the *rupes Tarpeia* refers specifically to the southeast face of the summit by the arx overlooking the Forum. Since there was not yet
any temple of Jupiter on the other crest, Prop. 4.4.2 *antiqui limina capta Iovis*
('the threshold of old Jove was taken') must be an anachronism. The naming of the
summit after Tarpeia may be pointed by the text of 4.4.29 if we adopt Palmer's
transposition '*et Tarpeia sua... ab arce*', stressing the etymology of the place name,
rather than the paradosis *sua Tarpeia* which construes *Tarpeia* (abl.) with *arce*.

the mythical omen of the head discovered by the Tarquins laying the foundations of the temple of Jupiter. He adds that it was previously called Mons Tarpeia from the crime and death of the Vestal Tarpeia, and even now the cliff is called *Tarpeium saxum* (5.41): before that again it was *Mons Saturnius*, just as Latium had been called *Saturnia*. Virgil elaborated this last etymology in *Aen.* 8.347–58; Propertius turned to its successor.

From the Capitoline Varro proceeds *not* to the Palatine but to the Aventine and Velabrum (5.43–44). The ritual of the Argei leads him to the first listing of the four names of the urban, district-based, tribes *Suburana, Esquilina, Collina* and *Palatina*, then to his account of the Mons Caelius and Vicus Tuscus 'in which stands the Statue of Vertumnus' (5.46), and of the Carinae (47, cf. *Aen.* 8.361). It is then he treats the Palatine with its various etymologies, and its two crests, Cermalus and Velia. For Varro, writing in 47 BCE, the Palatine was simply the wealthy residential area occupied by such as Cicero and Hortensius: only its role as a district naming one of the tribes (the list is reprised at 56 with *Palatina* in second place) seems to earn it any special attention.

In contrast, Livy's chronological narrative starts with the Palatine as Evander's original settlement, first walled by Romulus, who extended the 'city,' but set up his asylum or reception center for fugitives between the two crests of the unenclosed Capitoline (1.7). In fact Livy's next few chapters are focused on the Capitoline: 1.10 reports Romulus' dedication of his *spolia opima* to the sacred oak of Jupiter Feretrius and demarcation of a site for the future temple, 1.11.6–9 describes how Tarpeia as daughter of the garrison commander on the Arx betrayed the cliff access to the Sabines, and 1.12 sets the Sabines on the citadel, from which they descend to fight the Romans in the open valley of the future Forum between the two hills, *in media convalle duarum montium* (1.12.10).

Propertius follows Livy's configuration of early Rome for the betrayal, defeat and victory of the Sabine war in the valley between the two hills evoked in his Tarpeia elegy: but Propertius' fantasy, like Dionysius of Halicarnassus' archaizing history,[20] reforests the terrain:

---

[20] Compare Dionysius Halicarnassus 2.15, 'He consecrated the place between the Capitol and the citadel... "the place between the two groves," a term that was really descriptive at that time of the actual conditions, as the place was shaded by thick

it starts from a Grove of Tarpeia (*Tarpeium nemus*)[21] and generates a clearing by the Tiber inlet where Tatius can camp and exercise in view of the citadel, and Tarpeia goes to fetch water for the service of Vesta. Livy has other topographical features—the old gate of the Palatine, the marsh that bogs down Mettus Curtius—but essentially it is his Romulean city that Propertius portrays in 4.4, as also in 4.1.

Yet it is a mistake for modern readers of Propertius to look for Propertius' Rome only in the overtly etymological elegies. Consider the locations named in successive elegies from 4.2 to 4.10. Pride of place in 4.2 is given to the Forum—*Romanum satis est posse videre forum* ('it is enough to be able to look upon the Roman forum,' 4.2.6)—and the old river inlet of the Tiber, associating his name with the river bend (*Vert-amnis*) and Velabrum (7–10). But the poem lingers in the crowded Vicus Tuscus, linking the site with the legendary force of Caelius Vibenna as in Varro. The third elegy, like Arethusa, is confined to her home until she makes her votive journey to the Porta Capena between Caelian and Aventine to meet her returning husband. After the Capitoline emphasis of 4.4, the fifth elegy takes us through the red-light district and outside the city to the burial grounds of the poor; no place is named except for a swift allusion to the waste ground beyond the Colline gate as source of *Collinae herbae* (4.5.10–11). The adjective should not be passed over, since it names one of the four districts of the urban tribes. Subura and Esquiline, the eponyms of two more tribes, are named in the great Cynthia elegies 4.7 and 8.[22] Between them comes the commemoration of Actium, Propertius' most elaborate variation on the great Virgilian theme with its focus on the temple of Palatine Apollo (11).

---

woods on both sides where it joined the hills' and 2.49 'after cutting down the wood that grew on the plain at the foot of the Capitoline and filling up the greatest part of the lake... they converted this plain into a forum.' (Tr. Cary, Loeb Classical Library, 1950.)

[21] There is no reason to adopt Kraffert's (1883: 147) conjecture *Tarpeium scelus* as do Camps 1965 and Goold 1990; even without the transposition Propertius is clearly referring to three places, two of which relate to the Varronian aetiological tale: Tarpeia's grove, her tomb and the ancient shrine of Jupiter (?Feretrius). See below for Propertius' stress on the wooded aspects of unpopulated early Rome.

[22] Cf. *vigilacis furta Suburae* ('secrets of the sleepless Subura,' 4.7.15), and *Esquilias... aquosas* ('watery Esquiline,' 4.8.1).

This is indeed the only time that Propertius will call Apollo *Palatinus*,[23] and he may have chosen to do so precisely to evoke the fourth of the urban tribal districts, offering the sequence Collinus, Palatinus, Subura(nus), Esquili(nus) in 4.5 through 8. The poem itself, like Virgil's shield, transports the reader to Actium and thence to the Nile before returning to the god's *monumenta* in Rome.

Now to 4.9 and 4.10.[24] The former perversely displaces the traditional Aventine associations of Cacus with a conspicuous early allusion to the Palatine (4.9.3, 'the sheep-rich Palatine, unconquered hills') before the expected reference to the Velabrum and river shallows (9.5–6), the Forum Boarium (9.19–20), and Ara Maxima (67). Hercules' promise in 19–20 is ambiguous, for as he invites the oxen to sanctify the *arva Bovaria* with a mighty moo (*longo... mugitu*), he promises that their pasture will become the *nobile... Romae... Forum*: not, then, the region of the Forum Boarium but the future republican forum. These displacements seem designed to edge the scene of Hercules' thirst towards the far end of the Palatine: the whole episode, including his final curse excluding women from the Ara Maxima, is again moved away, set not at the celebrated altar, but in this imaginary secluded spot where the birds sing in the abundant shade as the long-branched poplar marks the ruined shrine. This pastoral setting, worthy of a Third style wallpainting, replaces the topography of Roman legend, excluding from the text both traditional heroic events, the battle with Cacus and the founding of the altar, and both their traditional sites.

Propertius' final aetion is almost equally coy about the site of Romulus' dedication to Jupiter Feretrius. His readers knew, as Livy did, that the altar and temple stood on the Capitoline, but the poet speaks only of the city's gates (7), her territories (10), her towers (13), and Romulus' humble home (*parvo... Lare*, 18). From this first Palatine settlement he radiates outwards to Veii and the villages of Cora and Nomentum, before moving away from the Tiber to the

---

[23] Compare 4.1.3 *Navali stant sacra Palatia Phoebo* 'where stand the Palatine buildings sacred to Phoebus of the ships,' and contrast 2.31 (*Phoebus* 3 times, *Pythius* once) 3.11.69 (*Leucadius*) 4.6.67 (*Actius*).

[24] On 4.9 see Anderson 1964, Pillinger 1969:182–9, and Cairns 1992, with response by Anderson 1992.

Rhine (39) and Marcellus' victory over Brennus' descendant, Virdomarus.[25] Unsatisfactory as the brusque narrative may seem to the modern reader, the elegy depends for its effect as much on spatial as on temporal advance, from the first defence of the original city to the victory that ensured the safety of Italy itself from the barbarian.

There remains the resumptive opening poem with all its problems. Guey (1952) imaginatively converted the first part of the elegy (up to line 50) into a walk around the summit of the Palatine, but of the four alleged viewpoints only the first and second, at the foot of the Cermalus and on its crest near Augustus' Palatine precinct, seem to be needed. If we read the first fifty lines without transpositions or reinterpretation, they offer a view of Rome that pans in from an opening focus on the grassy hills of the entire city ('all that you see,' 4.1.1) to the Palatine temple and, facing it, the once bare Tarpeian rock, now bearing the gilded gables of the temple of Jupiter Optimus Maximus. Below it lies the Tiber, opposite again *domus ista Remi* ('that house of Remus,' 4.1.10: despite the reference to 'rising on steps' not the temple of Romulus on the Quirinal, but the *casa Romuli* rebuilt on the Cermalus in the 30s). Beneath in the Forum area is the new Senate house where the old senators once met in the open, and the Comitium of the Quirites; beyond, the new theaters of Marcellus and Pompey with their awnings lead towards the Campus Martius, now being adorned by Augustus with monuments to himself and his family.

With this poem Propertius is doing more than reconstruct his image of the old city: he is renewing the foundation of Rome. His final invocation 'be favorable to me, Rome; this work arises for you' and appeal to his fellow citizens for fair omens and good auspices (*candida... omina... dextera cantet avis*, 68) surely recalls Romulus' celebrated auspices and rounds off his earlier claim 'I would attempt to lay out your walls in verse.'[26] Here then is a new and living portrait of the Rome of old.

---

[25] That Propertius has Virgil's vignette of the Gallic capture in mind is clear from his adaptation of the Gaul's striped breeches *virgatis... bracis* of 4.9.43, from the striped cloaks *virgatis... sagulis* of *Aen.* 8.660.

[26] Cf. Ovid *Fasti.* 4.827–36, in which Romulus' prayer is followed by good omens, the citizens lay the foundations and in a brief space of time the new wall came into being, *et novus exiguo tempore murus erat.*

La Penna has argued that Propertius must have felt even more acutely than most of his generation the contradictions between the old models based on the standards of an agrarian society, and the convenience, pleasures and attractions of the Hellenized urban community he now lived in.[27] Most recently Martindale, speaking of Virgil's *Ur-Rome* in *Aeneid* 8, sees Virgil's 'blurring of epic with pastoral' in Evander's Rome as a necessary 'contradiction within the spiritual idea of Rome, which is simultaneously the *caput rerum*, the metropolis which Augustus found brick and left marble, and an idyll of primitivism and rural simplicity.' But he transforms this fair description of conflicting sentiment into an imputation of disingenuity, of 'an (attempted) erasure of conflict, in the interests of Roman identity and Augustan ideology.'[28]

If this opposition of images and values of Rome then and now does not require us to read disingenuity into Virgil, why should we give a different reading to Propertius, treating him as either hypocrite or dissident? Do his images of the old city discredit the new monuments that express Augustan pride in renewal? Given his double inheritance of pastoral nostalgia from both Virgil and Tibullus, even the cattle, hides and straw littered around 4.1[29] may be as traditional as the earthenware gods of 4.1.5. Ovid would develop these rustic textures further in the *Fasti*, suppressing the elegant contempt that he had expressed for such primitive rusticity in *Ars Amatoria*.[30]

The nostalgia that rejects modern landscaping as part of luxury and corruption is very real in Juvenal's third satire, where Umbricius seems to incriminate the marble of Egeria's cistern for the degrading of her grove:

> we went down to the valley of Egeria and her grottoes so unlike the real caves. Her divinity would have been so much more vividly present,

---

[27] La Penna 1977: 182.
[28] Martindale 1993: 51. The contrast between early pastoralism and Virgil's *Romano...foro et lautis...Carinis* ('The Roman forum and the elegant Carinae,' *Aen.* 8.361) or Propertius' *aurea templa* ('golden temples,' 4.1.5) is proper to the different stages in Rome's organic growth and is cause for neither conflict nor embarrassment.
[29] Cattle, 4.1.4 and 22; straw 4.1.19; hides, 4.1.12 and 25.
[30] *Ars* 3.113–22. Ovid's deprecation of ancient primitive conditions (*simplicitas rudis*) was inherited in part from Propertius' recognition of the past as irrecoverable, cf. 2.32 'he who looks for the Tatii and Sabines of old, has only recently set foot in our city.' (cited by La Penna 1977: 182).

if grass fringed the waters with a green border and no marble violated the native tufa stone![31] (*Sat.* 3.17–20)

However, as Eleanor Leach shows in her paper 'Horace and the Material Culture of Augustan Rome,' we cannot assume a simple monolithic attitude to urban change on the part of our poets, or of Augustus himself.[32] Horace reflects in *Odes* 2.15 the appeal of the very pleasure gardens he is deprecating, and his enjoyment of material luxury colors many other poems. Augustus too cultivated his reputation for simple living[33] and certainly condemned the ostentation of private luxury in building: the demolition of Vedius Pollio's palace was as much a reaction against the man's luxury as against his notorious cruelty.[34] But however modest Augustus' private living space, his precinct, once enhanced by the Apolline temple and its libraries, and later the shrine of Vesta, took on the glory of a public monument, and the *princeps*, with a personal wealth from inheritance and spoils equal to or greater than that of the state treasury, would add further monuments from his own pocket.[35]

I think we forget that what Augustus was replacing may have once been woodland and hills, but surely was no longer green by the time he purchased the ground needed for the new Rome. Most probably the contemporary Republican city was nothing for a sentimentalist to regret. Hence Propertius may well have had no cause to feel or conceal resentment of the fine new public buildings, but at the same time his poetic imagination turns away from the city around him in nostalgic

---

[31] The preceding allusion (3.16) to the Camenae being evicted from their grove and the wood reduced to beggary also maintains the note of regret for the numinous world of woodland.

[32] Leach 1997: 116–18.

[33] Cf. Suet. *Aug.* 73: 'he later lived on the Palatine but in the modest house of Hortensius, conspicuous neither for its expanse nor its adornment, having only short porticos with Alban columns and inner rooms without any marble or notable mosaic pavement.' The 'house of Augustus' certainly has a simpler decor than the later Julio-Claudian and Flavian palaces, but Hortensius was in his day a by-word for luxury.

[34] On Vedius' palace, and his *luxuria*, cf. Ovid *Fasti* 6.640–4, *quia luxuria visa nocere sua*, 'because it seemed corrupting by its luxury', and Tac. *Ann.* 1.10.5.

[35] Much of his wealth came from his father. As Lucan would comment on Julius Caesar in 49 BCE, 'now for the first time Rome was poorer than (a) Caesar' (*BC* 3.163). For money paid out from Augustus' private purse, cf. *Res Gestae* 16–18, and add 19–21 for public monuments restored or built 'from the proceeds of booty.'

distaste. His imaginative preference for the distant past emerges from details, such as the epithets in 4.1a: alluding to primitive materials and textures (earthenware, artless, skin-clad [twice!], rustic, bristly, lean, cheap and rough) and to modest scale and simplicity (*nuda, parva*)[36] all associated with emotive words like *prisci, patrio, annua*.

The elegist is clearly not unhappy with the unofficial city of Vertumnus, the Subura and his well-watered Esquiline; and he is careful to give praise to Augustus' new Palatine precinct in 2.31 and 4.1. But Propertius' recurring evocations of natural untilled land, in particular the *loci amoeni* of 4.4. and 4.9 24–30, are reinforced by his encomiastic use of *Natura* (cf. 2.18.25, 3.22.18) and the adjective *nativus* for the natural beauty of seashells (1.2.13), the lush natural couch of grass (*nativus torus* 3.13.36), and the natural springs (*nativae... aquae* 4.4.4) of Tarpeia's grove. Propertius' old Rome is full of trees, undergrowth and brooklets, exploiting to the full the traditional picture of wooded hills that we find in Dionysius of Halicarnassus (2.15.4 on the grove of the asylum) and *Aeneid* 8 (of the copses and brambles of the Capitoline): Virgil's brambles and thickets (*dumi*, *Aen*. 8. 348, repeated 657; *vepres*, 8.645) are recalled by Propertius' hairy brambles *hirsuti... rubi* (4.4.27); his Capitoline is moist with dew and rivulets (4.4.48, 50), his Palatine and Capitoline alike blossom with epithets of natural abundance, rich in ivy, foliage, cattle, and shade (*hederoso, ramosa, pecorosa, umbroso*: 4.4.3; 4.4.5; 4.9.3; 4.9.24), a pastoral world also recalled in more overtly idyllic settings like the passage on the happiness of former young country people in 3.13.25 (*felix agrestum quondam pacta iuventus*) mentioned above. The best evidence for Propertian regret of the present built-up city and its marble monuments is this sensual delight in the unsettled wilderness surrounding Rome's first citizens.

Propertius is not, after all, aiming to write bucolic poetry;[37] neither his Tarpeia nor his Hercules is represented as enjoying the

---

[36] La Penna 1977: 90 is more justified in speaking of Propertius' love of rustic purity and poverty than in attributing to this fourth book the association of contemporary splendor with excess and corruption. Poems in Propertius' earlier books denounce the present *mores* chiefly in connection with sexual licence and infidelity. The only criticism of current behavior that I find is the implied condemnation of foreign cults in 4.117.

[37] But La Penna 1977: 86 rightly stresses the bucolic setting of Tarpeia's passionate love.

spring and shade of the pre-civic landscape. Yet without any generic pressure to enhance the wilderness the poet has let his image of Rome be dominated by groves and grottoes and waters that outbid the glitter and luxury of the new Augustan city: against the ostensible glorification of the gilded and marble temples and their precincts, the lost—and irretrievable—natural innocence of the unpopulated pre-urban community emerges as the world privileged by both the former dissident and the ostensibly reconciled composer of patriotic elegy.

#  Part IV

# Gender

# 12

# Mistress and Metaphor in Augustan Elegy[1]

*Maria Wyke*

## WRITTEN AND LIVING WOMEN[2]

A pressing and persistent problem confronts work on the women of ancient Rome: a need to determine the relation between the realities of women's lives and their representation in Latin literature. Several of the volumes on women in antiquity which appeared in the course of the 1980s exposed the methodological problems associated with any study of women in Greek and Roman literary texts.[3] Twenty years later, moreover, the historian Susanne Dixon opens *Reading Roman Women: Sources, Genres and Real Life* (2001) with the admission that she finds herself more sceptical than ever about the possibilities of extracting substantive information about Roman women from the ancient sources.[4] In any study of the relations between Rome's written

---

[1] Editors' note: This paper appears as a chapter in Wyke's 2002 book, *The Roman Mistress. Ancient and Modern Representations*. Where Wyke in this paper refers to other places in that book, the editors have simply amended to traditional name-date citation.

[2] Quotations from Propertius, Tibullus, and Ovid have followed the Oxford Classical Texts of E.A. Barber 1953 (1960), J.P. Postgate 1915 (1963), and E.J. Kenney 1961 (1994), respectively. Translations of both ancient and modern works are my own unless otherwise indicated.

[3] See, for example, the comments of Foley in her preface to *Reflections of Women in Antiquity* (1981), the survey by Fantham 1986, and the articles of Skinner and Culham in *Helios* 2 (1986).

[4] I am extremely grateful to Susanne Dixon for providing me with access to the manuscript of her book before it was published.

and living women, the heroines of Augustan elegy deserve particular scrutiny because the literary discourse in which they appear purports to be an author's personal confession of love.[5] The texts of Latin love poetry are frequently constructed as first-person, authorial narratives of desire for women who are individuated by name, physique, and temperament. This poetic technique tempts us to suppose that, in some measure, elegy's female subjects reflect the lives of specific Augustan women.

Moreover, Augustan elegy has set an especially seductive trap for historians of women's lives in antiquity. For, written in an autobiographical mode, it appears to confide to its readers a poet's personal confession of love for a woman who is not his wife. Read uncritically, such love poetry has been employed to confirm the existence in Augustan Rome of a whole movement of sophisticated and sexually liberated ladies, as in J.P.V.D. Balsdon's study *Roman Women: Their History and Habits* (1962) and Sarah Pomeroy's *Goddesses, Whores, Wives and Slaves* (1975).[6] Propertius' Cynthia, Tibullus' Delia and Nemesis, at times even Ovid's Corinna, have been extracted from their poetic world to become representative of a cultured society *où l'émancipation féminine se traduit avant tout par la recherche d'une liberté dans l'amour* (where female emancipation expresses itself above all in the search for erotic freedom).[7] Working from a somewhat different perspective, Ronald Syme suggested a more cautious assessment of the elegiac heroine's place in history. Although proposing that Ovid's poetry has much to offer the historian, Syme did not himself employ the *Amores* as source material for the construction of an Augustan demimonde. Yet he still set out the general social conditions in which he saw the mistresses of elegy operating: a post-civil war period that would have witnessed a number of women reduced to a marginal existence through either calamity or a love of pleasure.[8]

---

[5] In the preface to her book on Roman women, Dixon 2001 calls elegy (along with the genres of satire and the novel) an essential if troubling historical source, and devotes a chapter to the analysis of its deceptive strategies of representation.
[6] Balsdon 1962: 191–2, 226; Pomeroy 1975: 172.
[7] Fau 1978: 103, and cf. Grimal 1963.   [8] Syme 1978: 200–3.

In presenting a first-person narrator who is indifferent to marriage and subject to a mistress, Augustan elegy also poses an intriguing question of important literary and social dimensions: if it focuses on a female subject who apparently operates outside the traditional constraints of marriage and motherhood, could it constitute the advocacy of a better place for women in the ancient world? Could Augustan elegy be offering its readers realistic representations of women bound up with a feminist message?[9] This question has generated considerable controversy, as revealed by the initiatory debate between Judith Hallett and Aya Betensky that took place in a special issue of the journal *Arethusa* (1973) dedicated to the study of women in antiquity. The special issue itself formed part of the initiatory debates on women in antiquity instituted by feminist scholarship of the 1970s.[10]

In particular, the corpus of Propertian poems seems to hold out the hope that we may read through its written woman, Cynthia, to a living mistress. Poem 1.3, for example, conjures up before its readers a vision of an autobiographical event. The first-person narrator recalls the night he arrived late and drunk by his mistress's bed. The remembered occasion unfolds through time, from the moment of the lover's arrival to his beloved's awakening. The details of the beloved's sleeping posture, her past cruelty, and her present words of reproach all seem further to authenticate the tale. The portrait of a Cynthia possessed of a beautiful body, a bad temper, and direct speech inclines us to believe that she once lived beyond the poetic world as the flesh and blood mistress of an Augustan poet.[11]

Even the existence of Cynthia within a literary work appears to be explained away. Poem 1.8 creates the illusion that it constitutes a fragment of a real conversation. The persistent employment of the second-person pronoun, the punctuation of the text by questions and wishes that centre on 'you,' turns the poem itself into an event. As we read, Cynthia is being implored to remain at Rome with her

---

[9] As Hallett 1993: 65, reformulating her earlier views on Propertius' poetry in particular.

[10] On which, see Hallett 1993: 62–5, Miller and Platter 1999a: 405, and the discussion in Wyke 2002 chapter 5.

[11] For a deconstruction of the apparent realism of poem 1.3, see Wyke 1984 and Greene 1998: 51–9.

poet. Subsequently, we are told that this poetic act of persuasion has been successful:

> hanc ego non auro, non Indis flectere conchis,
> sed potui blandi carminis obsequio.
> sunt igitur Musae, neque amanti tardus Apollo,
> quis ego fretus amo: Cynthia rara mea est! (1.8.39-42)[12]
> Her I, not with gold, not with Indian pearls, could
> turn, but with a caressing song's compliance.
> There are Muses then, and, for a lover, Apollo is not slow:
> relying on these I love: rare Cynthia is mine!

Writing poetry, on this account, is only the instrument of an act of courtship. The text itself encourages us to overlook its status as an Augustan poetry-book and to search beyond it for the living mistress it seems to woo.[13]

There are, however, some recognised dangers in responding to Propertian poetry in this way, for other prominent features of Augustan elegy conflict with its apparently autobiographical narrative structure. Not only is elegy's personal confession of passion articulated in a manner which is highly stylised and conventional, but Hellenistic and Roman traditions for erotic writing also contribute clearly to the formation of the world in which the elegiac lover and his mistress move. Once recognised, such discrepancies undermine any attempt to construct a simple relation between elegiac verse and the world in which it was composed.[14] Augustan elegy has therefore been identified as poetic fiction, and the extreme biographical methodology of the nineteenth and early twentieth centuries—the search for close correspondences between the individual characters and events of the text and those of its author and his milieu—has long since been abandoned. Yet neither has the opposite view (that the mistresses of elegy are entirely artificial constructs) proved satisfactory; for, like the Platonic assessment of literary processes, the theory that Latin erotic discourse is modelled on Hellenistic literature, which is itself modelled on Hellenistic life, leaves Augustan poetry and its female subjects at several

---

[12] The text is Barber 1953 (1960).
[13] For the theme of poetry as courtship, see Wyke 2002 chapter 2.
[14] See e.g. Du Quesnay 1973: 1–2; Veyne 1983: 11–12; Griffin 1985: ix.

removes from reality. Most commonly, critics have recognised the presence of considerable artifice in the elegiac texts, yet continued to treat their female figures as belonging to a special category of discourse; a window onto the reality of female lives at Rome. The reader is allowed to move along an unobstructed pathway from woman of fiction to woman of flesh.

An early example of the critical strategies employed to isolate the elegiac mistress from poetic artifice, and to safeguard her status as a living individual, can be found in Jean-Paul Boucher's *Études sur Properce: problèmes d'inspiration et d'art* (1965). There, despite his considerable interest in the impact of Hellenistic literary practices on the Propertian corpus, the author concluded his studies by trying to construct a plausible portrait of a Roman woman out of Cynthia's poetic characteristics. A chapter entitled 'Poésie et vérité' conveniently provided a bridge between formalistic accounts of Propertian poetic techniques and romantic readings of the narrative's heroine. The textual characteristics of a fictive female are disengaged from their context in a poetry-book and reshaped into the detailed portrait of a girlfriend by whom the text was inspired.[15] So constructed, Cynthia is then positioned in the social formation of the Augustan epoch; the female beloved is read as referring out of the poetic sphere to a specific 'emancipated' woman of the late first century BC. Out of the elegiac text is born the historical reality of a liberated lady.

In the latter part of the twentieth century, other critics explicitly presented models of the relation between elegiac representations and the realities of women's lives in Rome that they thought capable of accommodating the literariness of elegiac writing while keeping elegy's written women placed firmly on the map of the Augustan world. Poets deal in 'verbal artefacts,' according to R.O.A.M. Lyne in *The Latin Love Poets: From Catullus to Horace* (1980, reprinted 1996 and 2000), yet their poetry 'adumbrates,' 'embodies,' or 'emblazons' life.[16] Love elegy, Jasper Griffin argues in *Latin Poets and Roman Life* (1985), is neither an open window affording glimpses of individual Roman lives, nor a mirror offering their clear reflection, but a *picture* of Roman realities over which has been painted a

---

[15] See esp. Boucher 1965: 468–9.  [16] Lyne 1980: viii and *passim*.

dignifying, idealising veneer of poetic devices. Poetic artifice can now be readily accommodated to autobiographical narratives, for it simply raises the realities of Roman life to the level of idealised art: Cynthia is a profit-making courtesan over whom the heroines of myth cast a glittering sheen; stylised depictions of female nakedness constitute reflections transposed into poetry of encounters with professionals in Rome.[17] Thus Augustan love poetry has continued to be beset by the romantic theory that it was produced to express its authors' own amatory experiences.

Idioms such as 'adumbrations' or 'transposed reflections' form the ingredients of a critical discourse that no longer treats elegiac poems as accurate, chronological documents of an author's affairs, yet still describes their stylised heroines as somehow concealing specific Augustan girlfriends.[18] Hans-Peter Stahl's contribution to the literature on the Propertian corpus, *Propertius: 'Love' and 'War,' Individual and State under Augustus* (1985), for example, reveals the critical laxity that is often at work. Stahl recognises that Cynthia possesses 'literary qualities,' admits nevertheless that his own work is constructed from a naive standpoint, and leaves it to his readers to draw the line they deem appropriate between Augustan reality and elegiac literariness. Yet the structure of his book does not otherwise assist such an enterprise, for neither recognition nor admission appears until the last footnote of Stahl's fifth chapter, while throughout the main text frequent reference is made to two formative experiences of love and war in Propertius' life—a torturing love for Cynthia and the massacre of Perusia. Readers of Stahl's book are actively directed to look out of the Propertian corpus to the inspiring realities of a woman's love life in Augustan Rome.[19]

Thus the realism of the elegiac texts continues to tempt us. While reading of women who possess some realistic features, we may think that—once we make some allowances for the distortions that a male lover's perspective and a poet's self-conscious literary concerns may impose—we still have an opportunity to reconstruct the lives of some real Augustan mistresses. Controversy arises, however, when

[17] See esp. Griffin 1985: 105, 139 and 110. On Griffin, see Kennedy 1993: 2–5.
[18] See e.g. Williams 1968: 542.
[19] On Stahl, see further Wyke 1989b and Kennedy 1993: 35–7.

we ask exactly what allowances should be made. Is the process of relating women in poetic texts to women in society simply a matter of removing a veneer of poetic devices to disclose the true picture of living women concealed beneath?

It is precisely because readers of Cynthia have encountered such difficulties as these that I propose to explore aspects of the problematic relation between women in texts and women in society by focusing on the Propertian corpus of elegiac poems. My purpose is, first, to survey approaches to the issue of elegiac realism and by placing renewed emphasis on Cynthia as a *written* woman to argue that she should be related not to the love life of her poet but to the 'grammar' of his poetry; second, to demonstrate that the poetic discourse of which she forms a part is firmly engaged with and shaped by the political, moral, and literary discourses of the Augustan period, and therefore that to deny Cynthia an existence outside poetry is not to deny her a relation to society; and, third, to suggest that a study of elegiac metaphors and their application to elegiac mistresses may provide a fruitful means of reassessing whether Augustan elegy carries the attraction of a feminist message.

## AUGUSTAN GIRLFRIENDS/ELEGIAC WOMEN

The first-person narratives of the elegiac texts and their partial realism entice us. They lead us to suppose that these texts form poetic paintings of reality and their female subjects poetic portraits of real women.[20] Yet realism itself is a quality of a text, not a direct manifestation of a real world. Analysis of textual realism discloses that it is not natural but conventional. To create the aesthetic effect of an open window onto a reality lying just beyond, literary works employ a number of formal strategies that change through time and between discourses.[21]

---

[20] See Kennedy 1993: 1–23 on the centrality to scholarship on elegy of a concern with the relationship between representation and reality, and his analysis of some of the methodological problems attached to explications of that relationship (including my own).

[21] A classic exposition of the disjunction between textual realism and reality, and a detailed exploration of the strategies of nineteenth-century French realist writing, can

As early as the 1950s, Archibald Allen drew attention to this disjunction between realism and reality in the production of Augustan elegy. He noted that the realism of the Propertian corpus is partial since, for example, it does not extend to the provision of a convincing chronology for a supposedly extratextual affair. And, focusing on the issue of 'sincerity,' Allen argued that the ancient world was capable of drawing a distinction that we should continue to observe, between a poet's art and his life. From Catullus to Apuleius, ancient writers could claim that poetry was distinct from its poet and ancient readers could construe 'sincere' expressions of personal passion as a function of poetic style.[22]

In *L'Élégie érotique romaine: l'amour, la poésie et l'occident* (1983), Paul Veyne pursued the idea that the *I* of ancient poets belongs to a different order than do later '*Is*' and suggested that *ego* confers a naturalness on elegy that ancient readers would have recognised as spurious. Exploring the quality of *ego* in elegy's narrative, Veyne further argued that the ancient stylistic rules for 'sincerity' observed in the Catullan corpus were scarcely obeyed in Augustan love elegy. Full of traditional poetic conceits, literary games, mannerisms, and inconsistencies, the texts themselves raise doubts about their potential as autobiography.[23]

Both these readings of elegiac first-person narratives warn us to be cautious in equating a stylistic realism with Augustan reality. But what of the particular realist devices used to depict women? Some modern critics have thought, for example, that the elegiac texts do offer sufficient materials from which to sketch the characteristics and habits of their authors' girlfriends or, at the very least, contain scattered details that together make up plausible portraits. From couplets of the Propertian corpus, John Sullivan assembles a physique for Cynthia: 'She had a milk-and-roses complexion. Her long blonde hair was either over-elaborately groomed or else, in less

---

be found in Barthes' *S/Z* 1970 (1975). For the importance of this work, see Hawkes 1977: 106–22.

[22] Allen 1950a and b.
[23] Veyne 1983. On Veyne see Wyke 1989b, and Kennedy 1993: 91–100; Miller and Platter 1999a: 404; Janan 2001: 7. Cf. Sharrock 2000 on how Propertian elegy entices its readers to take its elegiac world as real while simultaneously inviting them to see how the perspective of its narrator is undermined.

guarded moments, it strayed over her forehead in disarray... Those attractive eyes were black. She was tall, with long slim fingers.'[24] Oliver Lyne adds credible psychological characteristics:

> We find a woman of fine artistic accomplishments who is also fond of the lower sympotic pleasures; superstitious, imperious, wilful, fearsome in temper—but plaintive if she chooses, or feels threatened; pleasurably passionate—again if she chooses. I could go on: Propertius provides a lot of detail, direct and circumstantial. But the point I simply want to make is that the figure who emerges is rounded and credible: a compelling 'courtesan' amateur or professional.[25]

An ancient tradition seems to provide some justification for this process of extracting plausible portraits of Augustan girlfriends out of the features of elegiac poetry-books. Some two centuries after the production of elegy's written women, in *Apologia* 10, Apuleius listed the 'real' names that he claimed lay behind the elegiac labels *Cynthia* and *Delia*. Propertius, we are informed, hid his mistress Hostia behind *Cynthia*, and Tibullus had Plania in mind when he put *Delia* in verse. If we accept these identifications then, however stylised, idealised, or mythicised the elegiac women Cynthia and Delia may be, their titles are to be read as pseudonyms and their textual characteristics as reflections of the features of two extratextual mistresses.[26]

From the outset, however, the difficulty involved in assimilating all the written women of elegy to living, liberated ladies has been clear. Beginning with the ancient tradition that does not offer 'real' names to substitute for *Nemesis* or *Corinna*, the procedure is not uniformly applied. The inappropriateness of attempting to assimilate Ovid's Corinna to a living woman is generally acknowledged, because the text in which she appears easily reads as a playful travesty of earlier love elegy. Many commentators have agreed with the view that Corinna does not have *un carattere precisamente individuabile ed è priva di autenticità, perché in realtà non esiste* (does not have a precisely recognisable character and is without authenticity, because

---

[24] Sullivan 1976: 80.   [25] Lyne 1980: 62.
[26] For *Cynthia* and *Delia* as pseudonyms, see e.g. Williams 1968: 526–42 and Newman 1997: 301–4.

in reality she does not exist). She constitutes, rather, a generalised figure of the mistress.[27]

The Tibullan corpus has been classified as manifestly more 'sincere' than the Ovidian, yet the second Tibullan heroine has likewise aroused suspicion. David Bright offers detailed support for an earlier reading of Nemesis 'as a shadowy background for conventional motifs.'[28] Nor, for Bright, is this fictive mistress Nemesis preceded in the Tibullan corpus by at least one poeticised girlfriend. The first Tibullan heroine, Delia, also seems to be entangled in elegy's literary concerns, as the characteristics of Nemesis in Tibullus's second poetry-book are counterbalanced by the characteristics of Delia in the first to produce a poetic polarity. Delia is goddess of Day, Nemesis daughter of Night.[29] Bright states, 'the flexibility of fundamental characteristics and the meaning of the two names, indicates that Delia and Nemesis should be regarded as essentially literary creations.'[30]

In *The Latin Love Poets* (1980), Oliver Lyne questioned the need for even these concessions to poetic artifice. He found no compelling reason to doubt that Nemesis and Delia were pseudonyms of particular women, and even attempted tentatively to reappropriate Corinna for realism by drawing attention to a physique which John Sullivan had earlier assembled: 'physically she was *candida* with rosy cheeks, tall and dignified... with small feet and an abundance of fine closely-curled hair.'[31] The fabric of a poetic text is again turned into a mistress's flesh. Thus despite accounts which foreground the artifice of elegiac poetry and its mistresses, many critics have persisted in

---

[27] Bertini 1983: xvi. Cf. for instance Grimal 1963: 156; Bright 1978: 104; Barsby 1973 (1979): 15–16. The question of whether Corinna had an identity independently of the elegiac text is insoluble for Du Quesnay 1973: 2–3, and of no literary interest for Sullivan 1961: 522–8. On the fictiveness of Corinna, see also Wyke 2002 chapter 4 and Boyd 1997: 132–64.

[28] Williams 1968: 537.

[29] Bright 1978: 99–123. See Fineberg 1993 on the female personifications of Age, Punishment, Death, and Night who form part of the narrative transition from bright Delia to dark Nemesis.

[30] Bright 1978: 123.

[31] Lyne 1980: 239–40 argues that 'a reasonable picture does emerge from the poems' of Corinna, and draws attention to, but does not quote, the physique assembled by Sullivan 1961: 524 n.5. For a living Corinna, cf. Fau 1978: 112 and Green 1982: 22–5. See also the more cautious arguments of McKeown 1987.

reading out from the female subjects of its discourse to specific liberated ladies. Faced with such romantic readings of Augustan love poetry, we may want to ask whether Propertian realism is anchored any more securely to reality than that of Ovid and Tibullus.

Realist portraits of a mistress do not seem to have so bold an outline, or so persistent a presence, in Propertian poetry as to guarantee for Cynthia a life beyond the elegiac world, because realism is not consistently employed in the corpus and sometimes is challenged or undermined by other narrative devices. Even in Propertius's first poetry-book the apparent confession of an author's love is not everywhere sustained. Poem 1.16, for example, interrupts the realistic use of a first-person narrative. At this point the narrative *I* ceases to be plausible because it is not identifiable with an author and is voiced by a door. Poem 1.20 substitutes for expressions of personal passion the mythic tale of Hercules' tragic love for the boy Hylas. The poetry-book closes with the narrator establishing his identity (*qualis*) in terms not of a mistress but of the site of civil war.[32]

The formal strategies that produce for us the sense of an Augustan reality and an extratextual affair are even less prominent or coherent in Propertius's second poetry-book. The *ego* often speaks without such apparently authenticating details as a location, an occasion, or a named addressee. The object of desire is not always specified and sometimes clearly excludes identification with Cynthia. The margins of the poetry-book and its core are peopled by patrons and poets or take for their landscape the Greek mountains and brooks of poetic inspiration. At these points, the text's evident concern is not to delineate a mistress but to define its author's poetic practice.[33]

By the third and fourth poetry-books a realistically depicted, individuated mistress has ceased to be a narrative focus of Propertian elegy. The third poetry-book claims as its inspiration not a girlfriend but another poet. Callimachus has replaced Cynthia as the motivating

---

[32] See Greene 1998: 37–66 and Sharrock 2000 on the strategies deployed even in the Monobiblos that challenge or undercut its apparent realism. Cf. Janan 2001: 33–52 on the 'Gallus' poems in particular and their extreme, and disorienting, disjunction.

[33] On the second book's distinctive style, see Veyne 1983: 67, 71; Papanghelis 1987: 93–7; Wyke 2002 chapter two. Cf. McNamee 1993 who argues that book 2 begins to make explicit the Callimachean poetic concerns expressed implicitly in book 1.

force for poetic production. The title *Cynthia* appears only as the text looks back at the initial poems of the corpus and draws Cynthia-centred erotic discourse to an apparent close. Far more frequently the first-person authorial narrator speaks of love without specifying a beloved, and poetic eroticism takes on a less personal mode.

In the fourth book there is not even a consistent lover's perspective. Several poems are concerned with new themes, such as the aetiology of *Roma*, rather than the motivations for *amor*. And the narrative *I* fluctuates between a reassuring authorial viewpoint and the implausible voices of a statue, a soldier's wife, and a dead *matrona*. When the more familiar mistress appears, the sequence of poems does not follow a realistic chronology but moves from the stratagems of a dead Cynthia who haunts the underworld (4.7) to those of a living Cynthia who raids a dinner party (4.8).[34]

These inconsistencies and developments in the Propertian mode of incorporating a mistress into elegiac discourse cannot be imputed merely to an author's unhappy experiences in love (to Propertius's progressive disillusionment with a Hostia) for each of the poetry-books and their Cynthias seem to be responding to changes in the public world of writing. The general shift from personal confessions of love toward more impersonal histories of Rome may be determined partially by changes in the material processes of patronage in the Augustan era, from the gradual establishment of Maecenas's circle through to the unmediated patronage of the *princeps*,[35] and the particular character of individual poetry-books by the progressive publication of other poetic discourses such as Tibullan elegy, Horatian lyric, and Virgilian epic.[36] But are the individual, realistically depicted Cynthias of the Propertian corpus then immune from such influences?

Literary concerns permeate even the activities and habits of the Cynthias who appear in the first two books. Poem 1.8, for example, implores its Cynthia not to depart for foreign climes and asks: *tu pedibus teneris positas fulcire pruinas, | tu potes insolitas, Cynthia, ferre nives?* (Can you on delicate feet support settled frost? Can you, Cynthia,

---

[34] For the narrative techniques of book 4 in particular, see Wyke 2002 chapter 3 and Janan 2001.
[35] See e.g. Stahl 1985, and Miller in this volume.
[36] See e.g. Hubbard 1974.

strange snows endure? 1.8.7–8) The Gallan character of this Cynthia, and the trip from which she is dissuaded, is well known. In Virgil's tenth *Eclogue* attention already had been focused on the laments of the earlier elegiac poet over the absence of another snow-bound elegiac mistress. Propertius caps the Virgilian Gallus, in the field of erotic writing, by contrasting his ultimately loyal Cynthia with the faithless Lycoris. Cynthia's delicate feet both recall and surpass the *teneras plantas* of the wandering Lycoris (*Ecl.* 10.49). Simultaneously, they give her a realisable shape and mark a new place in the Roman tradition for written mistresses.[37]

Similarly, it has been observed that the disturbing narrative techniques of the second book (its discursiveness, parentheses, and abrupt transitions) constitute a response to the publication of Tibullus's first elegiac book.[38] And the process of transforming Propertian elegy in response to another erotic discourse again extends to realist depictions of the elegiac beloved. Poem 2.19 presents a Tibullanised Cynthia, closer in kind to the images of Delia in the countryside than to the first formulation of Cynthia in the Monobiblos:

> *etsi me inuito discedis, Cynthia, Roma,*
>    *laetor quod sine me devia rura coles...*
> *sola eris et solos spectabis, Cynthia, montis*
>    *et pecus et finis pauperis agricolae.* (2.19.1-2, 7-8)
>
> Even though against my will you leave, Cynthia, Rome,
>    I'm glad that without me you'll cultivate wayward fields...
> Alone you'll be and the lonely mountains, Cynthia, you'll watch
>    and the sheep and the borders of the poor farmer.

Tibullus began his fanciful sketch of a countrified mistress—the guardian (*custos*) of a country estate—with the words *rura colam* (1.5.21). So here *rura coles* begins Cynthia's departure from the generally urban terrain of Propertian discourse. The apparently realistic reference to Cynthia's country visit contains within its terms a challenge to the textual characteristics of a rustic Delia.

---

[37] For a convenient summary of views on this literary relationship, see Fedeli 1980: 203–5 and 211. Cf. Newman 1997: 17–53 and Janan 2001: 33–52. For a detailed analysis of how literary concerns are expressed through the Cynthias of books 1 and 2, see Wyke 1984, and McNamee 1993.

[38] E.g. Hubbard 1974: 57–8 and Lyne 1980: 132.

The Cynthias of the third and fourth books also disclose the influence of recently published literary works. The third Propertian poetry-book initiates an occasionally playful accommodation of Horatian lyric within erotic elegy. This literary challenge is articulated not only through the enlargement of poetic themes to include social commentary and the elevation of the poet to the rank of priest,[39] but also through the alteration of the elegiac mistress's physique.

The book opens with an erotic twist to the Horatian claim that poetry is an everlasting monument to the poet. For, at 3.2.17–24, Propertian poetry is said to immortalise female beauty (*forma*).[40] The book closes appropriately with the dissolution of that monument to beauty and the threatened construction of one to ugliness:

> *exclusa inque uicem fastus patiare superbos,*
> *et quae fecisti facta queraris anus!*
> *has tibi fatalis cecinit mea pagina diras*:
> *euentum formae disce timere tuae!* (3.25.15-18)

> Shut out in turn—may you suffer arrogant contempt,
> and of deeds that you've done may you complain—an old hag!
> These curses deadly for you my page has sung:
> learn to fear the outcome of your beauty!

The threatened transformation of Cynthia on the page from beauty to hag (the dissolution of the familiar elegiac edifice) mirrors similar predictions made about the Horatian Lydia in *Odes* 1.25.9–10.[41]

The two Cynthias of the fourth book take on Homeric rather than Horatian shapes. Although multiple literary influences on the features of these Cynthias may be noted (such as comedy, aetiology, tragedy, epigram, and mime) their pairing takes up the literary challenge recently issued by Virgil. Just as the Virgilian epic narrative conflates an Odyssean and an Iliadic hero in the character of Aeneas, so the Propertian elegiac narrative constructs a Cynthia who becomes first an Iliadic Patroclus returning from the grave (4.7) and then a vengeful Odysseus returning from the war (4.8).

---

[39] See e.g. Nethercut 1970: 385–407.
[40] For the comparison with *Odes* 3.30.1–7, see Nethercut 1970: 387 and Fedeli 1985: 90.
[41] Fedeli 1985: 674, 692–3.

In the last book of the Propertian corpus, the precarious status of realism is put on display. Whole incidents in the lives of a poet and his mistress now reproduce the plots of the Homeric poems, while their details echo passages of the *Aeneid*. In poem 4.7, the first-person authorial narrator recalls the occasion on which he had a vision of his dead mistress. Her reproaches are replete with apparently authenticating incidentals such as a busy red light district of Rome, worn-down windows, warming cloaks, branded slaves, ex-prostitutes, and wool work. Yet the ghost's arrival and departure, her appearance, and her reproofs sustain persistent links with the heroic world of *Iliad* 23 and the general conventions of epic discourse on visions of the dead. Similarly, in poem 4.8, the first-person narrator recalls the night when Cynthia caught him in the company of other women. The narrative of that night is also littered with apparently authenticating details such as the setting on the Esquiline, local girls, a dwarf, dice, a slave cowering behind a couch, and orders not to stroll in Pompey's portico. Yet Cynthia's sudden return finds her playing the role of an Odysseus to her poet's aberrant Penelope. Echoes of *Odyssey* 22 dissolve the poetic edifice of a real Roman event.[42]

When critics attempt to provide a plausible portrait of Cynthia, they must undertake an active process of building a rounded and consistent character out of physical and psychological characteristics that are scattered throughout the corpus and are often fragmentary, sometimes contradictory, and usually entangled in mythological and highly literary lore. Yet the discovery of Gallan, Tibullan, Horatian, and Virgilian Cynthias in the Propertian corpus argues against the helpfulness of this process. The strategies employed in the construction of a realistic mistress appear to change according to the requirements of a poetic project that commences in rivalry with the elegists Gallus and Tibullus and ends in appropriation of the terms of Horatian lyric and Virgilian epic.

It is misleading, therefore, to disengage the textual features of an elegiac mistress from their context in a poetry-book so as to reshape them into the plausible portrait of an Augustan girlfriend, for even the physical features, psychological characteristics, direct speeches,

---

[42] For references to the extensive literature on these two poems, see Papanghelis 1987: 145–98 and Wyke 2002 chapters 3 and 5. See also Janan 2001: 100–27.

and erotic activities with which Cynthia is provided often seem subject to literary concerns. Thus the realist devices of the Propertian corpus map out only a precarious pathway to the realities of women's lives in Augustan society and often direct us instead toward the features and habits of characters in other Augustan texts.

Yet the repetition of the title *Cynthia* through the course of the Propertian poetry-books may still create the impression of a series of poems about one consistent female figure.[43] Does support remain, then, for a direct link between Cynthia and a Roman woman in the ancient tradition, namely that *Cynthia* operates in elegy as a pseudonym for a living mistress Hostia?

On entry into the Propertian corpus, the epithet *Cynthia* brings with it a history as the marker of a poetic programme. The Hellenistic poet Callimachus had linked Mount Cynthus on Delos with Apollo as the mouthpiece of a poetic creed. That association was reproduced in Virgil's sixth *Eclogue* where the god directing Virgilian discourse away from epic material was given the cult title *Cynthius*.[44] The Propertian text itself draws attention to that history at, for example, the close of the second poetry-book where Callimachus, Virgil, Cynthius, and Cynthia are all associated with writing-styles. First Callimachean elegy is suggested as a suitable model for poetic production (2.34.31–2) then, in a direct address to Virgil, *Cynthius* is employed as the epithet of a god with whose artistry the works of Virgil are explicitly compared: *tale facis carmen docta testudine quale | Cynthius impositis temperat articulis* (Such song you make, on the learned lyre, as | Cynthius with applied fingers controls, 2.34.79–80). Finally, a reference to *Cynthia* closes the poem and its catalogue of the male authors and female subjects of earlier Latin love poetry: *Cynthia quin etiam uersu laudata Properti—|hos inter si me ponere Fama uolet* (Cynthia also praised in verse of Propertius—| if among these men Fame shall wish to place me, 2.34.93–4).

The alignment within a single poem of Callimachus, Virgil, Cynthius, and Cynthia constructs for Propertian elegy and its elegiac mistress a literary ancestry. The title *Cynthia* may be read as a term in the statement of a poetics, as a proper name for the erotic embodiment of a particular poetic creed. In a corpus of poems that

---

[43] Cf. Veyne 1983 on *Delia*.
[44] See Clausen 1976: 245–7 and Boyance 1956: 172–5.

frequently voices a preference for elegiac over epic styles of writing, that uses a critical discourse inherited from Callimachus and developed in Virgil's *Eclogues*, the title *Cynthia* contributes significantly to the expression of literary concerns.[45]

The name of the elegiac mistress does not offer us a route out of a literary world to the realities of women's lives at Rome. Yet, as with her other apparently plausible features, her name is inextricably entangled in issues of poetic practice. Any attempt to read through the name *Cynthia* to a living mistress, therefore, overlooks its place in the 'grammar' of elegiac poetry where *Propertius* and *Cynthia* do not perform the same semantic operations. In the language of elegy, a poet generates a different range and level of connotation than his mistress.

The issue of the elegiac mistress's social status further elucidates the peculiar role women play in the poetic language of Augustan love poetry; for, when attempts have been made to reconstruct a real girl-friend out of Cynthia's features, no clear clues have been found in the poems to the social status of a living mistress, and conclusions have ranged from adulterous Roman wife to foreign prostitute, or the evident textual ambiguities have been read as reflections of the fluidity of social status to be expected within an Augustan demimonde.[46]

In Propertius 2.7, for example, the narrator describes his mistress as having rejoiced at the removal of a law that would have separated the lovers. He declares that he prefers death to marriage:

> *nam citius paterer caput hoc discedere collo*
> *quam possem nuptae perdere more faces,*
> *aut ego transirem tua limina clausa maritus,*
> *respiciens udis prodita luminibus.* (2.7.7-10)

> For faster would I suffer this head and neck to part
>   than be able at a bride's humour to squander torches,
> or myself a husband pass your shut doors,
>   looking back at their betrayal with moist eyes.[47]

---

[45] See Wimmel 1960. For the intimate association of Cynthia and Callimachus in the Propertian corpus, see also Wyke 1984, Wyke 2002 chapter 2, and McNamee 1993.

[46] Respectively, Williams 1968: 529–35; Cairns 1972: 156–7; Griffin 1985: 27–8.

[47] The interpretation of verse 8 is open to much dispute. See Gale in this volume on 2.7, who reads the poem as highly ambiguous or ironic, and cf. Miller in this volume.

And he rejects his civic duty to produce children who would then participate in Augustus Caesar's wars: *unde mihi Parthis natos praebere triumphis? | nullus de nostro sanguine miles erit* (From what cause for Parthian triumphs to offer my sons? | None from my blood will be a soldier, 2.7.13–14). Here, if nowhere else in Augustan elegy, we might expect to find a clearly defined social status allocated to the elegiac mistress, because, at this point in the elegiac corpus, the text seems to be directly challenging legal constraints on sexual behaviour.

Nevertheless, even when the elegiac narrative takes as its central focus a legislative issue, no clear social position is allocated to Cynthia. We learn instead that men and women play different semantic roles in this poetic discourse. The female is employed in the text only as a means to defining the male. Her social status is not clearly defined because the dominating perspective is that of the male narrator. What matters is his social and political position as an elite male citizen who, in having a mistress (however indifferent she may be), refuses to be a *maritus* or the father of *milites*.[48]

What this analysis of elegiac realism seems to reveal is that the notion of *concealment* (the idea that the stylised heroines of elegy somehow conceal the identities of specific Augustan girlfriends) is not a helpful term in critical discourse on elegiac women. Perhaps Apuleius's identification of Cynthia with a Hostia is suspect, since it forms part of a theatrical self-defence and should be read in the light of a long-standing interest in biographical speculation. (We do not now accept, for example, Apuleius's identification of Corydon with Virgil or of Alexis with a slave boy of Pollio.)[49] But the point is that, whether or not a Hostia existed who was associated with Propertius, the Cynthia of our text is part of no simple act of concealment.[50]

---

[48] See esp. Veyne 1983, who argues that it is sufficient for elegy's purposes to locate its *ego chez les marginales* and cf. Conte 1989: 445. See Konstan 1994: 150–9, who notes that in the elegiac tradition the beloved is neither a *virgo* awaiting a legitimate marriage nor a *matrona* running the marital household, and 'is thus located outside the patrilineal structure that constitutes the status and the horizons of a proper Roman girl' (p. 157). Cf. Myers 1996: 4–6 who adds that the beloved is neither *virgo*, nor *matrona*, nor easily purchasable *meretrix*.

[49] See e.g. Fairweather 1974: 232–6.

[50] See Kennedy 1993: 83–100 for a detailed discussion of scholarship's concern with the problem of identifying names in the elegiac texts with real people.

While the combination of realist techniques and parodic strategies in the Ovidian corpus is generally thought to deny Corinna any reality, the realist strategies of the Propertian corpus have been isolated from other narrative techniques and left largely unexplored in order to secure for Cynthia an existence outside the text in which we meet her. I have argued, however, that even the realist devices of Propertian elegy can disclose the unreality of elegiac mistresses. Cynthia too is a poetic fiction: a woman in a text, whose physique, temperament, name, and status are all subject to the idiom of that text. So, as part of a poetic language of love, Cynthia should not be related to the love life of her poet but to the 'grammar' of his poetry.[51]

The Propertian elegiac narrative does not, then, celebrate a Hostia, but creates a fictive female whose minimally defined status as mistress, physical characteristics, and name are all determined by the grammar of the erotic discourse in which she appears. The employment of terms like 'pseudonym' in modern critical discourse overlooks the positive act of creation involved in the depiction of elegy's mistresses.[52] Therefore, when reading Augustan elegy, it seems most appropriate to talk not of pseudonyms and poeticised girlfriends but of poetic or elegiac women.

## METAPHORS

So the bond between elegiac women and particular Augustan girlfriends has proved to be very fragile. The realistic features of elegy's heroines seem to owe a greater debt to poetic programmes than to the realities of female forms. But if we deny to Cynthia an existence outside poetry, are we also denying her any relation to society? If elegiac narratives are concerned with fictive females, how do women enter their discourse? What relation might still hold between women in Augustan society and women in its poetic texts? And what function could a realistically depicted yet fictive mistress serve in elegy's aesthetics?

---

[51] See further Gold 1993a: 87–8 and 1993b: 291–2; McNamee 1993; Kennedy 1993; Flaschenriem 1997.
[52] Bright 1978: 103–4.

One possible approach to some of these questions has already been suggested, as I have argued that the characteristics of elegiac women are determined by the general idioms of the elegiac discourse of which they form a part, and that Cynthia should be read as firmly shaped by the Propertian poetic project. Yet elegiac discourses and poetic projects are, in turn, firmly engaged with and shaped by the political, moral, and aesthetic discourses of the Augustan period. And so it is through the relation of elegiac narratives to all the other cultural discourses of the specific period in which they were produced that we can at last see a more secure fit between women in elegiac texts and women in Augustan society.

The general idioms peculiar to elegiac writing have been as intriguing to the reader as the specific attributes provided for women at various points in the elegiac corpus, for they seem to be offering a challenging new role for the female, a poetic break away from the traditional duties of marriage and motherhood.

First of all, features of the elegiac vocabulary seem to overturn the traditional Roman discourses of sexuality. In the poetic texts the elegiac hero is frequently portrayed as sexually loyal while his mistress is not.[53] The Propertian lover protests: *tu mihi sola places: placeam tibi, Cynthia, solus* (You alone please me: may I alone please you, Cynthia, 2.7.19). He desires as the wording on his epitaph: *unius hic quondam seruus amoris erat* (Of a single love this man once was the slave, 2.13.36). Now this elegiac expectation of eternal male faithfulness, according to one analysis, 'spurns the double standard characterizing Roman male-female relationships' because, traditionally, extramarital sex was tolerated for husbands while their wives were legally required to uphold the principle of *fides marita* (marital fidelity).[54] It was the ideal of a woman's faithfulness to one man that was most frequently expressed on Roman epitaphs and, furthermore, it was expressed in the same terms as the elegiac ideal: *solo contenta*

---

[53] For male faithfulness in the elegiac corpus, see Lilja 1965: 172–86 and Lyne 1980: 65–7.
[54] Hallett 1973: 111. On the double sexual standard for Roman husbands and wives, see Dixon 1992: 88; Edwards 1993: 49–53; Williams 1999: 47–56.

*marito, uno contenta marito* (content with her husband alone; content with but one husband).[55]

Another feature commonly cited as a central structuring principle of elegiac desire, and as crucial evidence for an elegiac transformation of traditional sexual roles, is the application of the *seruitium amoris* metaphor to a heterosexual liaison.[56] A parallel for the topos of the lover-as-enslaver can be found in Hellenistic erotic writing, but Augustan elegy's casting of the female in the dominant sexual role seems to work against the operations of other Roman sexual discourses. The Propertian narrator asks: *quid mirare, meam si uersat femina uitam | et trahit addictum sub sua iura uirum?* (Why are you astonished if a woman drives my life | and drags, bound beneath her own laws, a man? 3.11.1–2).[57]

The male narrator is portrayed as enslaved, the female narrative subject as his enslaver. The Tibullan lover, for example, says farewell to his freedom: *hic mihi seruitium uideo dominamque paratam: | iam mihi, libertas illa paterna, uale* (Here for me I see slavery and a mistress at the ready: | now from me, that fathers' freedom, adieu, 2.4.1–2). Thus the control of household slaves, a woman's version of the economic status of a *dominus*, has been transformed figuratively into the erotic condition of control over sexual slaves. The sexual domain of the elegiac *domina* contrasts with that traditionally prescribed for Roman *matronae*, namely keeping house and working wool.[58]

A third significant feature of this poetic discourse is the declaration that the pursuit of love and poetry is a worthy alternative to more traditional equestrian careers. This elegiac declaration is best known in its formulation as the *militia amoris* metaphor.[59] The elegiac hero

---

[55] *Carm. Epigr.* 455 and 643.5, for which see Williams 1958: 23–5. See also Treggiari 1991: 229–319 and Dixon 1992: 88–90.

[56] For erotic *seruitium* in the elegiac corpus, see Lilja 1965: 76–89; Copley 1947: 285–300; Lyne 1979: 117–30; Conte 1989: 443–4. See also McCarthy 1998; Fitzgerald 2000: 72–7.

[57] For further discussion of Prop. 3.11, see Wyke 2002 chapter 6.

[58] Hallett 1973: 103 contrasts the epitaph of Claudia (*ILS* 8403): *domum seruauit, lanam fecit* (she kept her house; she made wool). See Gold 1993b: 288–9, who notes that the term *domina* (unlike *dominus*) effectively constrains the powers of the elegiac mistress to the domestic and the sexual.

[59] For erotic *militia* in the elegiac corpus, see Lilja 1965: 64–6; Lyne 1980: 67–78; Conte 1989: 444–5. See also Gale 1997, reprinted in this volume; Davis 1999: 438–42.

is portrayed as already enlisted in a kind of military service, battling with love or his beloved. The Propertian narrator receives the following instructions:

> at tu finge elegos, fallax opus: haec tua castra! –
> scribat ut exemplo cetera turba tuo.
> militiam Veneris blandis patiere sub armis,
> et Veneris pueris utilis hostis eris.
> nam tibi uictrices quascumque labore parasti,
> eludit palmas una puella tuas. (4.1.135-40)

> But you, devise elegies, a tricky task: this is your camp! –
> That they, the remaining crowd, write at your example.
> The warfare of Venus you'll endure under alluring weapons
> and to Venus's boys a profitable enemy you'll be.
> Because for you whatever Victorias your effort's procured,
> one girl escapes your awards.

Similarly an Ovidian poem entirely dedicated to the exploration of the metaphor of *militia* begins *militat omnis amans, et habet sua castra Cupido* (Every lover soldiers, and Cupid has his own barracks, *Am.* 1.9.1).

Augustan elegy represents its hero as faithful to his usually disloyal mistress, and as engaged metaphorically in either sexual servitude or erotic battles. Yet the unconventional sexual role bestowed, through poetic metaphor, on the elegiac male seems to implicate the elegiac female in equally unconventional behaviour: he slights the responsibilities of being citizen and soldier, while she operates outside the conventional roles of wife and mother. So, if specific features of the elegiac mistresses do not seem to reflect the realities of particular women's lives, might not the general idioms employed about them nevertheless reflect general conditions for the female in Augustan society? Is the elegiac woman unconventional because there are now some unconventional women in the world?

Once again, the elegiac texts tempt us: if, as Georg Luck has argued, 'the woman's role in the Roman society of the first century BC explains to a large extent the unique character of the love poetry of that period,'[60] then elegy would be invested with a social dimension of substantial interest to the student of women in antiquity. The

---

[60] Luck 1974: 15.

mistresses stylised in elegy might then constitute poetic representatives of a whole movement of sexually liberated ladies and may be read as 'symbolic of the new freedom for women in Rome's social life in the first century BC.'[61] To establish such a connection between elegiac mistresses and Augustan women it is first necessary to find parallel portraits of the female outside the poetic sphere. If external evidence can be found for the gradual emergence of a breed of 'emancipated' women, then it might be possible to argue that such women *provoked* elegiac production.

Sallust's description of an unconventional Sempronia provides the most frequently cited historical parallel for the elegiac heroines:

*litteris Graecis et Latinis docta, psallere, saltare elegantius quam necesse est probae, multa alia, quae instrumenta luxuriae sunt. Sed ei cariora semper omnia quam decus atque pudicitia fuit... lubido sic accensa ut saepius peteret uiros quam peteretur.* (Cat. 25.2-4)

Well educated in Greek and Latin literature, she had greater skill in lyre-playing and dancing than there is any need for a respectable woman to acquire, besides many other accomplishments such as minister to dissipation. There was nothing that she set a smaller value on than seemliness and chastity... Her passions were so ardent that she more often made advances to men than they did to her.[62]

Similarly, the Clodia Metelli who appears in Cicero's forensic speech *pro Caelio* is often adduced as an example of the kind of emancipated woman with whom Roman poets fell in love in the first century BC and about whom (thus inspired) they composed erotic verse. The early identification of Clodia Metelli with Catullus's *Lesbia* seems to strengthen such a link between living and written women and to bind the habits of a late republican noble woman (as evidenced by Cicero's *pro Caelio*) to poetic depictions of a mistress in the Catullan corpus.[63]

---

[61] King 1976: 70. On the social dimensions of elegy, see further Wyke 2002 chapter 5.
[62] The translation is that of Lefkowitz and Fant 1982: 205. For Sempronia's use as part of the social backdrop for elegiac production, see Lyne 1980: 14 and King 1976: 70 and n.7. See also Newman 1997: 280–1.
[63] See e.g. Lyne 1980: 8–18 and Griffin 1985: 15–28. Wiseman 1985: 15–53 uses Clodia extensively as an example of women of high society in Catullus' time while, more cautiously, identifying Lesbia only with a member of Clodia Metelli's family—probably a sister (pp. 136–7).

However, the process of matching love poetry's heroines with a new breed of 'emancipated' women raises methodological problems. Sallust's Sempronia and Cicero's Clodia have often been employed as evidence for the phenomenon of the New Woman (as elegy's historical twin is sometimes called).[64] Yet it is important to observe that, even outside the poetic sphere, our principal evidence for the lives of ancient women is still on the level of representations, not realities. We encounter not real women, but representations shaped by the conventions of wall paintings, tombstones, and, most frequently, literary texts. Any comparison between elegiac women and emancipated ladies tends, therefore, to be a comparison between two forms of discourse about the female.[65]

Sempronia and Clodia are both to be found in literary texts. And as written women, they are (like their elegiac sisters) no accurate reflection of particular female lives. Sallust's Sempronia is written into a particular form of literary discourse, for, in the context of his historical monograph, she is structured as a female counterpart to Catiline. Her features also belong to a larger historiographic tradition in which the decline of Roman *uirtus* and the rise of *luxuria* are commonly associated with aberrant female sexuality. Sempronia's qualities contradict the norms for a *matrona*. She is whorish because a whore embodies moral degeneracy and thus discredits the Catilinarian conspiracy.[66] Clodia is also written into a text. The villainous features of this prosecution witness are put together from the stock characteristics of the comic *meretrix* and the tragic Medea. Cicero's Clodia is a *proterua meretrix procaxque* (bold and insistent prostitute, *pro Cael.* 49) because sexual promiscuity was a long-standing topos in the invective tradition against women. As part of a forensic discourse, the sexually active woman is designed to sway a jury. The

---

[64] Balsdon 1962: 45.

[65] See Edwards 1993: esp. 34–62, where she argues that the adulteresses to be found in Roman moralising discourses should be read as resonant metaphors for social and political disorder, but not necessarily as matching the behaviours of specific people. Cf. Dixon 2001: esp. chs. 2 and 5.

[66] Paul 1966: 92; Boyd 1987; and Dixon 2001: chs. 2 and 9. For this use of the aberrant female in Roman discourses of moral and political disorder, see Edwards 1993: esp. 43 and Dixon 2001: chs. 2, 5, and 9. Cf. Wyke 2002 chapters 6 and 9 on Roman representations of Cleopatra and Messalina respectively.

rapaciousness of this supposedly injured party turns the young, male defendant into a victim and her sexual guilt thus underscores his innocence.[67]

When attempting to reconstruct the lives of ancient women from textual materials, some critics have drawn upon a kind of hierarchy of discourses graded according to their usefulness as evidence. Marilyn Skinner, for example, argues that Cicero's letters offer a less tendentious version of Clodia Metelli than does his oratory. And the Clodia she recuperates from that source is one concerned not with sexual debauchery, but with the political activities of her brother and husband and with property management.[68] Perhaps this picture of a wealthy, public woman is a better guide to the new opportunities of the first century BC, but it is not the picture of female behaviour that Augustan elegy paints. The term *domina* could identify a woman of property, an owner of household slaves. Within the discourse of Augustan elegy, however, it takes on an erotic (not an economic) significance. The female subject that the poetic narrative constructs is not an independent woman of property but one dependent on men for gifts: *Cynthia non sequitur fascis nec curat honores,* | *semper amatorum ponderat una sinus* (Cynthia doesn't pursue power or care for glory, | always her lovers' pockets only she weighs, 2.16.11–12). Augustan elegy, then, does not seem to be a response to the lives of particular emancipated women, but another manifestation of a particular patterning of female sexuality to be found in the cultural discourses of Rome.

Rome was essentially a patriarchal society sustained by a familial ideology. The basic Roman social unit was the *familia* whose head was the father (*pater*): 'a woman, even if legally independent, socially and politically had no function in Roman society in the way that a man, as actual or potential head of a *familia*, did.'[69] Using the Ciceronian Clodia as her starting-point, Mary Lefkowitz has documented the prevalence of this way of structuring femininity in antiquity. Praise or

---

[67] Lefkowitz 1981: 32–40 and Skinner 1983: 275–6. Wiseman 1985: 15 recognises the need for caution in reading Cicero's portrait of Clodia Metelli, but still sees no reason to doubt its accuracy (p. 30). See also Edwards 1993: 46; Fitzgerald 1995: 21–2; Dixon 2001: chs. 3 and 9.
[68] Skinner 1983.
[69] Gardner 1986: 77; see too Dixon 1988: 13–40; Dixon 1992.

blame of women, Lefkowitz argues, is customarily articulated with reference to their biological role, assigned according to their conformity with male norms for female behaviour. The good woman is lauded for her chastity, her fertility, her loyalty to her husband, and her selfless concern for others. The bad woman is constantly vilified for her faithlessness, her inattentiveness to household duties, and her selfish disregard for others.[70] In the conceptual framework of Roman society, female sexuality takes on positive value only when ordered in terms that will be socially effective for patriarchy, that is in the satisfactory performance of marital and reproductive duties. Sexually unrestrained women are marginalised. Displaced from a central position in cultural categories, they are associated with social and political disruption.[71] A notable example of this politically charged polarisation of women into the chaste and the depraved occurs at the beginning of the principate: 'In the propaganda which represented Octavian's war with Antony as a crusade, it was convenient to depict [Octavia] as a deeply wronged woman, the chaste Roman foil of the voluptuous foreigner Cleopatra.'[72]

This patterning of discourses about the female can be grounded in history. A figure like Sempronia was not articulated in Roman texts before the middle of the second century BC, after Rome's rise to empire (and its consequent wealth and Hellenisation) had brought with it significant social and cultural change.[73] From this period there began a proliferation of moral discourses associating female sexual misconduct with social and political disorder. And by the first century BC marriage, adultery, procreation, and childlessness were appearing regularly as subjects for concern in the texts of writers such as Cicero, Sallust, Horace, and Livy interlocked with anxieties about the collapse of traditional Roman society and the outbreak of civil war.[74]

[70] Lefkowitz 1981: 32–40. Cf. Dixon 2001: chs. 5 and 9.
[71] Richlin 1983; Dixon 1988. See also Edwards 1993: esp. 35–6; Skinner 1997: 9–11; McGinn 1998: esp. 17; Hemelrijk 1998 (1999): 7–21; Williams 1999: 113–15; Dixon 2001: chs. 3, 5, and 9; Wyke 2002 chapter 6 (on Cleopatra) and 9 (on Messalina).
[72] Balsdon 1962: 69, and see further Wyke 2002 chapter 6.
[73] I am indebted to Elizabeth Rawson for this observation.
[74] See e.g. Richlin 1981: 379–404; Dixon 1988: 92–7. Cf. Treggiari 1991: 211–15; Dixon 1992: 119–23 and 2001: chs. 3 and 5; Edwards 1993: 42–7 and 93–7; McGinn 1998: 78–9.

So persuasive have these discourses on the female been that they have often been taken for truth. Many of the histories on which elegy's commentators once relied for reconstructions of Rome's New Woman invested their accounts of changes in women's social position with elements of moral turpitude transferred wholesale from the writings of the Roman moralists. For example, the first edition of *The Cambridge Ancient History* claimed that 'by the last century of the Republic, females had in practice obtained their independence, and nothing but social convention and a sense of responsibility barred the way to a dangerous exploitation of their privilege.'[75] Similarly, Balsdon's *Roman Women* stated emphatically: 'Women emancipated themselves. They acquired liberty, then with the late Republic and the Empire they enjoyed unrestrained licence.'[76] Thus in the ready association of liberty with licence, the strictures of Roman moralists were turned into the realities of republican lives.[77]

One particular form of discourse about female sexuality had considerable and significant currency during the period in which elegiac eroticism was produced. From 18 BC on, legislation began to appear that criminalised adultery and offered inducements to marry and reproduce.[78] However, the production of elegy's female figures cannot be read as a direct poetic protest against this social legislation, although it appears to be the subject of one Propertian poem:

> *gauisa est certe sublatam Cynthia legem,*
>   *qua quondam edicta flemus uterque diu,*
> *ni nos diuideret.* (2.7.1-3)
>
> She was delighted for sure at the law's removal—Cynthia—
>   over whose publication once we both cried long,
> in case it should part us.

Since the tradition of erotic writing to which the Propertian Cynthia belongs stretched back at least as far as the Gallan corpus, the earliest

---

[75] Last 1934: 440.  [76] Balsdon 1962: 14–15.
[77] Cf. Gardner 1986: 261. See also Edwards 1993: 35–6; Dixon 2001: chs. 1, 5, and 9.
[78] For the details of the Augustan legislation, see Last 1934: 441–56; Brunt 1971: 558–66; Dixon 1988: 84–6. See also Treggiari 1991: 60–80, 277–98; Dixon 1992: 78–81; McGinn 1998: 70–104, 140–215.

examples of the elegiac mistress considerably predate the legislation.[79] Yet the appearance of the Augustan domestic legislation from 18 BC does demonstrate that the discourses about female sexuality with which elegy was already engaged were now being institutionalised: female sexual practice was now enshrined in law as a problematic issue with which the whole state should be concerned.[80]

Augustan elegy and its mistresses constitute, therefore, a response to, and a part of, a multiplication of discourses about the female that occurred in the late republic and early empire. Similarly, in his first volume on the history of sexuality, Michel Foucault demonstrates that, when 'population' emerged as an economic and political problem in the eighteenth century, 'between the state and the individual, sex became an issue, and a public issue no less: a whole web of discourses, special knowledges, analyses, and injunctions settled upon it.'[81] In the first century BC, at a time when female sexuality was seen as a highly problematic and public concern, the poetic depiction of the elegiac hero's subjection to a mistress would have carried a wide range of social and political connotations. And the elegiac mistress, in particular, would have brought to her poetic discourse a considerable potential as metaphor for danger and social disruption.

A brief outline of the operations of realism and of metaphor in Augustan elegy discloses that elegy's mistresses do not enter literary language reflecting the realities of women's lives at Rome. An examination of their characteristics reveals that they are fictive females engaged with at least two broad (but not necessarily distinct) categories of discourse. Shaped by developments in the production of literary texts and in the social construction of female sexuality, they possess potential as metaphors for both poetic projects and political order.

---

[79] Badian 1985: 82–98 doubts that even by the time Propertius's second book was published any attempt had yet been made to introduce the legislation concerning marriage. Cf. Gale 1997: 89–90 (= Gale in this volume) and Miller in this volume. For the relation between Augustan elegy and the moral legislation, see also Wallace-Hadrill 1985: 180–4. Cf. Sharrock 1994: esp. 113 and Davis 1999: 435, 444–9.

[80] See Edwards 1993: 34–62 and Galinsky 1996: 128–40. Contrast Habinek 1997 who argues that Ovid's *Amores* and *Ars Amatoria* record the invention of sexuality as a discrete topic of discussion, now disembedded from other socio-political relations.

[81] Foucault 1981: 26.

# Mistress and Metaphor in Augustan Elegy 351

The second of these two categories will be further explored in the remainder of this chapter; for it is the range of connotations that the elegiac mistress gains as a result of her association with the erotic metaphors of *seruitium* and *militia* (rather than those arising from her identification with the Muse and the practice of writing elegy) that may most intrigue the student of women in antiquity.[82] Amy Richlin argues that on entry into a variety of Rome's poetic and prose genres (such as invective and satire) the ordering of female sexuality is determined by the central narrative viewpoint which is that of a sexually active, adult male.[83] So, in depicting their hero as subject to and in the service of a sexually unrestrained mistress, do the elegiac texts offer any challenging new role for the female, or for the male alone?

Some critics have made much of the boldness of appropriating the term *laus* for the erotic sphere and *fides* for male sexual behaviour, but their descriptions of such strategies are seriously misleading. The Propertian narrator declares: *laus in amore mori: laus altera, si datur uno | posse frui: fruar o solus amore meo!* (Glorious in love to die: glorious again, if granted one love | to enjoy: o may I enjoy alone my love! 2.1.47–8). Both Judith Hallett and Margaret Hubbard, for example, frequently refer to such material as involving a bold reversal or inversion of sex roles—the elegiac hero sheds male public virtues and takes on the female domestic virtue of sexual loyalty.[84] Such terminology suggests, erroneously, that in elegiac poetry the female subject gains a position of social responsibility at the same time as it is removed from the male.

It is not the concern of elegiac poetry to upgrade the position of women, only to portray the male narrator as alienated from positions of power and to differentiate him from other, socially responsible male types. For example, in the same poem of Propertius's second book, the narrator's erotic battles are contrasted with the activities of the *nauita*, the *arator*, the *miles*, and the *pastor*, without any reference to a female partner:

---

[82] For the elegiac mistress as a metaphor for her author's poetics, see further Veyne 1983 and Wyke 2002 chapters 2–5.
[83] Richlin 1983.   [84] Hallett 1973 and Hubbard 1974.

> *nauita de uentis, de tauris narrat arator,*
>   *enumerat miles uulnera, pastor ouis;*
> *nos contra angusto uersantes proelia lecto:*
>   *qua pote quisque, in ea conterat arte diem.* (2.1.43-6)
>
> The sailor tells of winds, of bulls the farmer,
>   the soldier numbers wounds the shepherd sheep;
> we instead turning battles on a narrow bed:
>   in what each can, in that art let him wear down the day.

Similarly, in the first poetry-book the Propertian lover expresses, in the abstract terms of an erotic militancy, his difference from the soldier Tullus (1.6.19–36).

Furthermore, the elegiac texts take little interest in elaborating their metaphors in terms of female power but explore, rather, the concept of male dependency. The elegiac mistress may possess a camp in which her lover parades (Prop. 2.7.15–16) or choose her lovers as a general chooses his soldiers (*Am.* 1.9.5–6), but generally elegiac metaphors are concerned with male servitude not female mastery, and with male military service not female generalship. In *Amores* 1.2 it is Cupid who leads a triumphal procession of captive lovers, not the Ovidian mistress, and in *Amores* 1.9 it is the equation *miles/amans* (soldier/lover) not *domina/dux* (mistress/commander) that receives the fullest treatment.[85]

The metaphors of *servitium* and *militia amoris* thus disclose the ideological repercussions for a man of association with a realistically depicted mistress. In a society that depended on a slave mode of production, and in which citizenship carried the obligation of military service, these two metaphors define the elegiac male as socially irresponsible. As a slave to love, he is precluded from participating in the customary occupations of male citizens. As a soldier of love, he is not available to fight military campaigns.

The heterodoxy of the elegiac portrayal of love, therefore, lies in the absence of a political or social role for the male narrator, not in

---

[85] See Greene 1998 against Hallett's reading of elegy as empowering women. Greene argues instead that the use of the *militia* metaphor connects conquest in war with the male lover's violent desire to overcome his hard mistress, while the *seruitium* metaphor operates both as an erotic ruse (designed to sway the beloved) and as an aesthetic pose (designed to gain a poetic reputation). See further Wyke 2002 chapter 5.

any attempt to provide or demand a new social role for the female subject. The temporary alignment with a sexually unrestrained mistress that Augustan elegy depicts does not bestow on the female a new, challenging role but alienates the male from his traditional responsibilities. The elegiac poets exploit the traditional methods of ordering female sexuality (that locate the sexually unrestrained and therefore socially ineffective female at the margins of society) in order to portray their first-person heroes as displaced from a central position in the social categories of Augustan Rome. And, moreover, they evaluate that displacement in conventional terms. At the beginning of the second book of the *Amores*, the poet is introduced as *ille ego nequitiae Naso poeta meae* (I, Naso, that poet of my own depravity, 2.1.2) and in the Propertian corpus the lover and poet of Cynthia is also associated with the scandal of *nequitia* ('vice' or 'depravity,' 1.6.26 and 2.24.6). Thus, the poetic depiction of subjection to a mistress is aligned, in a conventional moral framework, with depravity.

Finally, despite claims of eternal devotion, none of the elegiac poets maintain this pose consistently or indefinitely. At the end of the third poetry-book, the Propertian lover repudiates his heroine and describes himself as restored to Good Sense (*Mens Bona*). At the end of his first poetry-book, the Tibullan hero finds himself dragged off to war. And, toward the end of the *Amores*, the appearance of a *coniunx* on the elegiac scene disrupts the dramatic pretence that the narrator is a romantic lover involved in an obsessive and exclusive relationship.[86]

The purpose of this chapter has been to suggest that, when looking at the relations between women in Augustan elegy and women in Augustan society, we should not describe the literary image of a mistress as a kind of poetic painting whose surface we can remove to reveal a real Roman woman hidden underneath. Instead, an exploration of the idioms of realism and metaphor has demonstrated that elegiac mistresses are inextricably entangled in, and shaped by, a whole range of discourses that bestow on them a potential as metaphors for the poetic projects and political interests of their authors.

This analysis is designed only as the starting-point for a critical study of elegy's heroines and their constructive power as metaphors

---

[86] Cf. Butrica 1982: 87.

for poetic and political concerns. Yet already one aspect of this analysis may seem unsatisfactory or unsatisfying, for it seems to offer no adequate place for living Augustan women in the production of elegiac poetry. Further questions immediately confront us. How did women read or even write such male-oriented verse? Would a female reader in Augustan Rome be drawn into the male narrative perspective? And how did a female writer, such as Sulpicia, construct her *ego* and its male beloved? In such a context, would the erotic metaphors of *seruitium* and *militia* be appropriate or have the same range of connotative power?

# 13

## The Natural and Unnatural Silence of Women in the Elegies of Propertius[1]

*Barbara K. Gold*

I begin with a quote from W. R. Johnson on Propertius 4.11: 'When we have finally gotten to Cornelia, whose central message is that the game of *recusatio* has ended, overwhelmed by her chilly sublimities and conquered by the powers of her Roman Truths and Virtues— when the performance ends and the silence begins, we may be shocked to hear Cynthia laughing loudly at the lachrymose deity and the metonymic skid that has now enfolded him.'[2]

So Ralph Johnson describes the final poem of Propertius Book 4, the long, rambling speech of Cornelia, paragon of Roman aristocratic maternal virtue. She is one of several women to take the podium in Book 4: she is accompanied by Arethusa, the Roman wife left behind by her soldier/husband Lycotas (4.3); Tarpeia, the love-struck girl who betrayed Rome to the Sabine king, Titus Tatius (4.4); Acanthis, the grasping and vile *lena*, who gives the poet's mistress advice on how to get as rich as possible (4.5); and Cynthia herself, featured in two poems (once dead in 4.7 and once alive in 4.8). The range of women presented in Book 4 of Propertius is characteristic of the many ways that female characters are depicted throughout his four

---

[1] Translations in this paper are the author's own. In the very few citations in which the author refers to Maria Wyke's two articles ('*Scripta Puella...*' and 'Mistress and Metaphor') both in their original publication venue and in their reprise in her 2002 book *The Roman Mistress*, the editors have omitted the latter.

[2] Johnson 1997: 180.

books of elegies: some are purely mythical (e.g. Thetis in 2.9, 3.7), some figured as more fictional (Cynthia throughout), and others as historical (e.g. Cornelia in 4.11). All, however, are figured as fictional in the end.

What does it mean to have so many women speaking out of Propertius' pages, to end with Cornelia's spirited posthumous defense of her life? And why does Johnson hear, in the silence after 4.11, a laughing Cynthia, making fun of a poem that many critics have accepted as Propertius' final conversion to an Augustan vision and Augustan ideals of marriage and womanhood?[3] To laugh is to have a presence, to make a judgment, to declare an identity separate from the text. If we allow Cynthia to laugh in our imaginations, we are granting to her a position as the creator and judge of poetry, a signmaker, rather than simply consigning her to the role of the 'Written Woman.'[4]

But this is Johnson's fantasy (it might be important that he is a man: can women hear Cynthia laughing?). I am interested in the methods used to silence women and in how Propertius figures this silence through his garrulous women.

I propose to investigate the silent women of Propertian elegy by examining first, the meanings of silence, particularly when it is used to suppress alienated groups; second, the ways silence can be put into play by those who wield the instruments of depiction (the pen, stylus, computer, or paintbrush); third, the women of Propertius' elegies

---

[3] Janan 2001: Chapter 9, for a summary of the different interpretations of 4.11. The two main critical assessments are: that 4.11 is either genuine praise of Roman virtues and Augustan ideals with the figure of Cornelia at the center and a renunciation of Propertius' earlier poems, or that the figure of Cornelia represents the bleakness, emptiness, and meaninglessness of a matron's life in Rome.

[4] Wyke 1987b = Wyke 2002: 46–77. If we grant to Cynthia such powers, we acknowledge that Propertius himself is, through Cynthia, questioning many of the very values he has seemed to espouse throughout Book 4. See on this Janan 2001; she says that 'the poet, out of his mistress' mouth, subtly lays bare the degree to which his own medium is implicated in perpetuating an unsustainable 'truth' about women' (112). See also McCoskey 1999: 16–39. She argues, in frustration with much current scholarship that disallows Cynthia any real identity and 'makes her subordinate . . . to other questions, such as Propertius' literary self-identification or his so-called feminism' (32), that we should try to reclaim Cynthia—'to give her shape precisely when Propertius seeks so adamantly to deny both the visibility and indeed the significance of that shape'—and to read 'Cynthia *qua* Cynthia' (33).

who are silenced even through their speaking; and fourth, particular women in Book Four of Propertius' elegies, especially Cornelia and Cynthia, who speak from beyond the grave and thus exemplify another kind of silent speaking.

## I THE MEANINGS OF SILENCE

It is generally true that, in most societies, the dominant group has control over the means and methods of representation while the Other, those marginalized and excluded from sources of power, are silent or silenced. Silence is, of course, as multivalent as other forms of communication. It is usually, but not always or inevitably, the mark of powerlessness. The words 'silent' and 'silenced' reveal very different sides of this posture. To be *silent* can be an active choice: we can speak of a strong, silent type, or silent disapproval, or silent protest. Silence, if figured as nothingness or space, is essential to any conceptual way of thinking, be it in mathematics, where the zero is essential now to mathematical systems; astronomy, where space is the place in which our planet revolves; art, where figures can only be inscribed in space, and form must be balanced against emptiness; music, where silence is as necessary as the notes that punctuate it; or religion, where silence often allows the most important forms of communication to happen.[5] Silence need not be 'the absence of sound' but can be the presence of something else. It can mean 'focusing on what matters most.'[6] As Adrienne Rich describes it in her 'Cartographies of Silence,' 'silence can be a plan rigorously executed//the blueprint to a life//It is a presence/It has a history—a form//Do not confuse it with any kind of absence.'[7]

Silence is powerful in many situations; it can lead to action and to dominance over those who speak out. As we will see, in Propertius'

---

[5] See McCrone 1988: 7.   [6] Ericsson 1988: 8.
[7] Rich 1978: 16. See also Montiglio 2000, who discusses both the active nature of silence ('silence is a more complex condition than an absence of words: originally it is a state, a way of behaving, an "adverb,"' 289) and the gendering of silence (290–2 and *passim*).

poetry the silent are sometimes those who are in control, who have chosen that mode as their way to gain and hold position, and who are *listened to*.[8] Conversely, those who speak, the garrulous, do not necessarily gain their ends by using this approach. Words can be valueless (see Prop. 2.22b.2). When we use terms like 'chatterbox,' 'wordy,' or 'logorrhea,' we denigrate the power of speech.

The word *silenced* bespeaks a very different side of this speech phenomenon. One never chooses to be silenced. It is imposed on the unwilling, the powerless, the alienated. Silencing deprives them of having a means to communicate, makes them speechless, and imprisons them in another kind of oppression. The silenced are not those who have chosen speechlessness as a way of defiance or communication. They have been relegated to this position by those who wish to speak for them. Some have their words snatched away by others who interrupt or shout over them; some by being imprisoned so that their words, even if uttered, cannot be heard, and some by having the organ of speech cut out of their mouths (e.g. Philomela, raped by her despicable brother-in-law Tereus, who then cuts out her tongue to prevent her from telling the tale. Ovid has his own comments on this barbarous act of surgery; Philomela finds other means of speaking—weaving her story into a tapestry—and her tongue gains new life in Ovid [*Met.* 6.424–674; see 557–601 for the tongue as a serpent tail] when it crawls like a serpent along the ground, separated from the voice box that activated it and gave it words).

This, then, is the kind of silence that is used to oppress and marginalize. This is the silence that the writer Tilly Olsen calls 'unnatural silences: the unnatural thwarting of what struggles to come into being, but cannot.'[9] A natural silence would allow a 'necessary time for renewal, lying fallow, gestation, in the natural cycle of gestation.' But this unnatural silence is not productive, active, or creative; rather it signals an 'absence of creativity . . . that suicide of

---

[8] See Foucault 1978: 3–13, 77–131 and *passim*. Foucault challenges the conventional idea that sexuality has been repressed and silenced in modern societies and that it is through critical discourse that we unlock that repression. Rather, he claims that, by putting sexuality into discourse (of any sort), we bring it under the control of normalizing structures and forms of power.

[9] Olsen 1978: 6.

the creative process.'[10] And it is a silence that only humans, not the natural world, can produce or receive.

This kind of silence requires two elements: a perpetrator and a victim. The perpetrator is someone whose discursive practices are governed by 'conventions of the linguistic community,'[11] whereas the victim is excluded from these practices and from the community. Such discursive practices are often gendered; the central narrative viewpoint of most genres, elegy among them, is that of a sexually-defined, aggressive male who orders female sexuality and female forms of expression.[12] Fictive women in such texts are the victims of a silence of oppression (even those who are granted the power of speaking within the narrative). Many techniques are used in such a silencing process: among them are negative stereotyping, namelessness, denial, erasure, non-naming, partial naming, encoding, omission, veiling, fragmentation, lying.[13] Through such tactics, silenced groups (such as elegiac women) are deprived of any official means of expression,[14] excluded from male constructions of meaning and experience, and are made to serve as signs or vehicles of the discourse in which they are inscribed.[15]

## II WRITING INTO SILENCE

How then can silence be used to advantage by those who wield the instruments of representation and depiction? How does a poet like Propertius organize his medium in order to let his female characters speak out at some length, often drowning out the poet's own voice

---

[10] Olsen 1978: 7.   [11] Herrnstein Smith 1978: 135.
[12] See Richlin 1983 (1992): 41.   [13] C. Kramarae cited by A. Jaworski 1993: 119.
[14] Jaworski 1993: 128.
[15] For another interesting example of a woman silenced in Augustan poetry, cf. Lara in Ovid *Fasti* 2.571–616 (Lara, the mother of the Lares Compitales, like Philomela, had her tongue torn out; she became identified as the *dea Muta*. Her story is told by an old woman who performs a ritual in honor of Tacita); see Newlands 1995: 160–1, who argues that we can see, in the restricted speech of this episode, Augustus' 'authority over freedom of speech' (160). See also Keith 1992: esp. 135–6 for a consideration of how Ovid's interest in language and speech might reflect the political conditions under the principate and the 'imperial controls encroaching upon all modes of discourse' (7).

within the framework of the poem, and yet use the silences to control his characters? Where are the silences in the poems? The work of Pierre Macherey might help here. Macherey, in *A Theory of Literary Production*, provides insight into how we can learn from silence: 'It can be shown that it is the juxtaposition and conflict of several meanings which produces the radical otherness which shapes [a] work: this conflict is not resolved or absorbed, but simply *displayed*. Thus the work cannot speak of the more or less complex opposition which structures it, though it is its expression and embodiment. In its every particle, the work *manifests*, uncovers what it cannot say. This silence gives it life.'[16]

As I have argued elsewhere,[17] Propertius and some other classical authors create a space in the fabric of the text where there is an uneasiness in the representation of gender for both the author and reader, where the language seems to have more potentiality to be interpreted from many different perspectives, where the marginalized characters seem to be trying to 'speak,' and where there are voices speaking against the text.[18] There are, for example, Sappho's explicit rereadings of Homer, Sulpicia's of elegy, and characters such as women in Aristophanes' *Lysistrata*, *Thesmophoriazusae*, *Ecclesiazusae* and Euripides' plays, freed slaves in Petronius' *Satyricon*, Statius' Hypsipyle, and, of course, Propertius' elegiac women. I proposed that we look in these texts for what is hidden, deemphasized, left out, or denied articulation, and try to expose and bring to light the spaces produced in these texts over which the writer has less control and in which 'woman' can be found. This kind of reading of texts against themselves in order to uncover new levels of meaning for women has already been done for Catullus, Horace, Ovid, Propertius, Comedy, Satire, and Latin literature more generally.[19] Propertius, calling into

---

[16] Macherey 1978 (1985): 84. See also Iser 1974: 31.
[17] Gold 1993a.
[18] Gold 1993a: 84.
[19] I list here only a representative sampling of the many treatments of women in Latin texts in this ever-burgeoning field. **Catullus**: Greene 1998; Richlin 1983 (1992); Skinner 1983: 273–87; **Horace**: Ancona 1994; **Ovid**: Gamel 1989: 183–206; James 1997: 60–76; Nugent 1990: 160–85; Richlin 1983 (1992); Sharrock 1991b: 169–82; **Propertius**: Gold 1993a; Janan 2001; McCoskey 1999; Miller 2004: 130–59 (= Miller in this volume); Welch 2005a; Wyke 1987b (= Wyke 2002: 46–77); Wyke 1989a: 25–47

question just who and what Cynthia represents, creates new possibilities for gender reversals and gender confusions. He destabilizes the traditional roles and qualities assigned to women by casting both Cynthia and himself in many different and conflicting roles and by problematizing his representation of her.[20]

Thus, I have argued that, although Propertius never really relinquishes control over his material, he opens up spaces in his text in which we can feel and see the presence of 'woman' and in which he interacts with her.[21] He thus shows us new ways of organizing and reading sexual difference and forces us to rethink our known categories of what 'woman' or 'the female' might mean in Roman elegy.

I would like now to progress from my previous discussion of Propertius' opening up of silent spaces in the text—which provide us with new ways of thinking about sidelined characters—to consider both the good and bad effects of silences and silencing for such characters. I need to be clear here once again about the differences between silence and silencing (one perhaps chosen and one not) and about the several effects of silence. Silence is a technique not inimical to women writers and stylists: indeed it has frequently been put into play by female authors from Sappho to Virginia Woolf as a nontraditional means of making their voices heard.[22] Female and feminist writers often have resorted to creating their own styles of expression, both 'exploring the communicative and symbolic values of silence' and breaking silence to 'speak with new voices.' This might

---

(= 2002: 11–45); Wyke 1995: 110–28; **Vergil**: duBois 1976: 14–22; McManus 1997; Perkell 1981: 355–77; Rose 1993: 211–37; **Comedy**: Gold 1998a: 17–29; Packman 1993: 42–55; Smith 1994: 21–38; **Satire**: Braund 1995: 207–19; Braund and Gold 1998: 247–56; Gold 1998b: 369–86; Richlin 1984: 67–80; Richlin 1983 (1992); **Latin literature in general**: Hallett 1984: 241–62 (originally printed in *Arethusa* 6 1973: 103–24); Hallett 1989a: 209–27; Hallett 1989b: 59–78. See also the bibliography in these books and articles for other treatments of women in Latin poetry.

[20] The argument could also be made that he is not really interested in asserting a new gender structure but rather in reverting to a traditional form of masculine behavior and roles encoded in earlier, Greek literature and thus reasserting traditional male dominance. See Gutzwiller and Michelini 1991: 66–84; Gold 1993a; Miller 2004: especially p. 173.

[21] See G. Williams 1991: 19 on finding the shape of the woman described by her absence.

[22] For the uses of silence in Virginia Woolf's work, see Walker Mendez 1980: 94–112.

include associative thinking, intuitive reasoning, use of neologisms, renaming, and altered diction and syntax.[23] As I have argued above, male writers can use silence in similar fashion to create spaces for different ways of thinking in their texts. But silence (or silencing) can also be used to negative effect, to shut out and subdue voices, to marginalize and exclude. And, in a male-produced text, silence can take on very different value depending upon whether it is lodged in the male writer or character or in a female character. The final issue really is: who controls the silence?

For now we need to consider in more detail some of the particular techniques of silencing listed earlier. Propertius has a whole potential arsenal of these at hand. One is negative stereotyping. Women in antiquity were frequently polarized into the chaste and the depraved, and female sexual misconduct was associated with political and social breakdown.[24] Discourses about women in most ancient texts are grounded in this structuring of the female.[25] One need only think of Cleopatra, Sempronia, or Messalina, or Cynthia, who is, Propertius says, both depraved and the cause of his *nequitia* (see Propertius 1.6.26, 2.24.6, 3.11, 3.19). Another silencing technique is namelessness. Propertius names two lovers in his elegies: Cynthia and (briefly) Lycinna (3.15). Cynthia receives prominent mention in the Monobiblos, headlining the marquis of poem 1.1 (which begins *Cynthia prima*) and appearing in 13 out of the 22 poems often as both addressee and subject. In subsequent books, Propertius uses her name less and less (12 of 34 poems in Book 2, only 3 of 25 in Book 3, and 2 of 11 in Book 4). This is not to say that Propertius does not continue to write his love poetry; only that his women become less and less articulated, more and more unidentified, shadowy figures who lack name and substance. Richardson assumes that 'all the poems addressed to unnamed women who have a hold on the poet are to Cynthia, unless they clearly cannot be,'[26] but I think that we need not make this assumption or fixate on retaining a stable identity and role for Cynthia. I would maintain that this not naming is a

---

[23] Jaworski 1993: 121–2.
[24] See on this Gold 1998b; Edwards 1993; Carson 1990: 135–69; Wyke 2002: 37–42 and *passim*.
[25] Wyke 1989a: 40–3.    [26] Richardson 1977: 4.

deliberate technique of Propertius, a harbinger of Ovid, who felt no real need for even a fictively-identified woman. Propertius used this technique to control the features and very existence of his women. In 3.2, where Propertius celebrates the power of song, he addresses a nameless *fortunata* (happy woman), 'whoever you may be, who are praised in my book of poems' (*meo si qua es celebrata libello*, 17); he continues: 'my poems will be monuments to your beauty' (*carmina erunt formae tot monumenta tuae*). The woman is beautiful, the woman might or might not be Cynthia (it is tantalizing to identify her as such but it could be anyone), but the woman is nameless and her main role here is to be the subject matter for Propertius' verse.[27]

This leads us to another means of silencing, well described by Maria Wyke. This is the 'written woman' technique.[28] Wyke maintains that we cannot hope to discover a specific Augustan woman in Propertius' poetry but must view Propertius' women as written women, "related not to the love life of her poet but to the 'grammar' of his poetry, as 'metaphoric mistresses.'"[29] As Paul Veyne says (about Propertius), 'This poetry devoted to a woman is really quite egocentric. The poet speaks almost exclusively of the actions, passions, sorrows and words of Ego, who talks only about himself... what we learn of Cynthia comes down to two things: on the one hand, she has every possible attraction... and seems made to fulfill every wish; on the other, she makes her poet suffer.'[30]

Elegiac mistresses are 'inextricably entangled in and shaped by a whole range of discourses, which bestow on them a potential as metaphors for the poetic projects and political interests of their authors.'[31] For example, in 1.8, Propertius begs Cynthia to stay in

---

[27] Cf. Ovid *Am.*1.1.2 (*materia*), 19–20; 1.3.19–26.

[28] See Wyke 1987a and b and 1989a (these three articles together are Wyke 2002: 11–114), and 1995. Wyke frequently uses the term 'written woman' or 'elegiac woman' to refer to the poeticized women addressed and described in elegy who should be seen less as flesh and blood lovers of the poet than grammatical elements of his poetry.

[29] Wyke 1989a: 27–41; see also Wyke 1987b (together these are Wyke 2002: 11–77).

[30] Veyne 1988: 136. Elegy is not the only genre that is egocentric and more about the author than about his female subject. See Hunink 1998: 275–91 on Pudentilla: 'The *Apology* is not about Pudentilla, it is about Apuleius' (290).

[31] Wyke 1989a: 43.

Rome and not to go off with a wealthy rival to foreign lands. Cynthia becomes 'Gallanized,' that is, Propertius embeds Cynthia in the language and situation of Gallus' characters, Cynthia is compared to Gallus' mistress Lycoris, and Cynthia's delicate feet recall the *teneras plantas* of Lycoris in *Eclogue* 10. Elsewhere, Cynthia becomes 'Tibullanized,' resembling the rural Delia.[32] Thus Propertius can project any image onto the pliable figure of the mistress; he also pushes her one step farther away from reality by borrowing characteristics for her from previous fictive characters.

Performance is another technique by which the poet could subsume and ventriloquize the role of the women in his poetry. Although it has been argued that 'performing the other' can call into question normative male/female values and give women a more prominent role,[33] it is just as possible to argue that when the poet played both his role and the role of female characters, this deep and active involvement with the female roles enabled him to dominate and control these characters and that this is another, active form of silencing.[34]

These are just a few of the many ways available to the male poet to gain total control over the women in his poetry, making these women 'subservient to the narrator's poetics'[35] and ultimately making them silent characters.

### III *TACITUS VIR, GARRULA PUELLA*

The most important aspect of silence is the control of it. We have already said that, in and of itself, silence is a neutral state, able to nurture or destroy, to highlight or to erase, to preserve a way of life and express defiance, or to lose a voice and an existence. One of Propertius' most interesting uses of the verb *taceo* is in a rather

---

[32] Wyke 1989a: 30–1.
[33] See, on 'playing the other' (in Greek drama), Zeitlin 1996: 341–74.
[34] See, on performing elegy as a way of opening up female roles, Gamel 1998: 79–95.
[35] Wyke 1995: 112. See also the quote from Barthes on this page (cited by Kennedy 1993: 70).

insignificant four-line poetic fragment (appropriately fragmentary) that appears to contain advice to the male lover from an anonymous source. So this speaker advises:

*assiduae multis odium peperere querelae:*
  *frangitur in tacito femina saepe viro.*
*si quid vidisti, semper vidisse negato!*
  *aut si quid doluit forte, dolere nega!* (2.18a)

... constant complaining has brought ill favor on many: often has a woman been broken by a man's silence. If you have seen anything, always say that you have not! Or, if anything perchance has hurt you, deny that you are hurt.[36]

Women, who are often the source of *querelae* elsewhere in Propertius,[37] are more likely, Propertius says here, to be favorably influenced by silence. The word *frangitur* in line 2 is a key word here and is, I believe, mistaken by the Loeb translator (Goold), who softens the harsh meaning of it when he renders it as 'won.' Rather, I would say that the woman here is described metaphorically as an animal who is 'broken' by the man's silence.[38] The man in question, using silence as a horserider would use a bit or a whip, forces her into submission with his silence, not his words, pretending to deny both his visual capacity and his negative emotions. The power of silence in this scenario rests on deception (that is, the male lover only pretends not to see or feel hurt); the so-called speaker can accomplish much more by using an open-ended silence than he could if he were limited

---

[36] The translation here is partly mine and partly based on Goold's. See Richardson 1977 for a possible reconstruction of 2.18, which he puts together with 2.17 and 2.22b (275–8).

[37] See Prop. 1.6.8,11; 2.20.4; 4.3.31; 4.8.79.

[38] *Frangere* can mean 'to influence,' 'to prevail upon,' 'to win over,' but it is generally used in this cluster of meanings with an ablative of means (OLD, *frango*, #10, p. 731). It is under this meaning that the OLD puts Propertius 2.18.2 (wrongly, I believe). *Frangere* can also mean 'to check,' 'to curb,' 'to break in,' 'to reduce to obedience' (OLD, *frango*, #11). Cf. TLL vol. VI 1,1250, 12–13, where *frangere* in Propertius 2.18 and elsewhere (2.28.34, 2.33.25) is taken metaphorically to mean 'wear down,' 'relent.' The phrase *in tacito viro* is troubling and odd syntactically. *In* here appears to mean 'on the occasion of,' 'in the circumstance of,' 'on account of;' cf. Prop. 2.8.36, *in erepto... amore*, for a similar use of *in* and Richardson 1977: 235 *ad* 2.8.36 for other similar uses of *in* + abl. In nearly every case, the *in* + abl. phrase is used with a verb or adjective expressing extreme emotion or dire circumstance.

by speech.[39] And the speech here in lines 3–4 is only negative (*negato... nega*). The manipulated and deceived woman is thus figured as a broken animal, and the male lover's silencing becomes an active form of oppression.

In other elegies, Propertius gives similar advice to himself in his attempts to win over his unreliable lover. He admonishes himself to 'keep his bliss locked up in his *silent* breast' (2.25.30) since a man's boastful words (*maxima verba*) can do harm to a love affair. Elsewhere, he embarks on a trip to Athens to escape from a love affair gone wrong (*gravi amore*, 3.21.2) and hopes thereby to ease the wounds locked in his *silent* breast (*tacito sinu*, 3.21.32). To keep something (speech, erotic feelings) hidden is to contain it and to have power over it; to let it turn into speech is far riskier.[40] Through his silence the male lover accomplishes his goals.

This power of the poet/male lover to gain his objectives through silence takes a dramatic turn in 3.23 where the poet has lost his writing tablets, the centerpiece of his amatory campaign. So powerful a vehicle are they for his persuasions that they can proceed without the author's presence: *illae iam sine me norant placare puellas,/et quaedam sine me verba diserta loqui* ('They had learned now to please girls without my help and without my help to utter some persuasive phrases,' 3.23.5–6). His words have abandoned the author and taken on a life of their own, eloquent and persuasive and able to achieve *effectus bonos* ('good results,' 10). The poet thus figures himself as disconnected from the very words that help him to achieve his goals, both literary and amatory, a silent overseer of a band of wayward words that somehow nevertheless retain the characteristics of their maker.

And what of women's silence in Propertius? Do women achieve their goals more easily through speech or silence? In the same poem discussed above, the lost tablet poem (3.23), Propertius envisions his tablets in the possession of another, a *puella garrula* (17–18), who has commandeered these tablets and inscribed her own story on them. He imagines that, on the tablets, she berates him for staying away with another woman, recapitulating the complaint already issued directly to Propertius in 1.3, or she invites him to spend the night

---

[39] Another artist, Apollo, sings tales with his 'silent lyre' (*tacita carmen hiare lyra*) in 2.31.6.
[40] Cf. Foucault 1978, who makes this claim about myth.

*The Natural and Unnatural Silence of Women* 367

with her (a less likely possibility for the Cynthia we have come to know). The words here are attributed to her by the owner of the tablets and the poem, who calls her *garrula*, a woman who talks a little too much and whose words therefore carry little importance (cf. 2.22b.44). Perhaps the invitation inscribed on the tablets here will carry no more weight than the woman's promises in 2.22b, where Propertius talks about words that have no value *(nullo pondere verba,* 2.22b.44).[41]

Elsewhere, in the Monobiblos, Propertius rebukes his friend and fellow poet, Bassus, who tries to break up Propertius and Cynthia by praising the beauty of other women. Cynthia will be enraged, Propertius says, and 'will be hostile to you with no words left unspoken' (*et tibi non tacitis vocibus hostis erit*, 18). Like the *puella garrula* in 3.23, this scorned woman in 1.4 is hardly silent. The litotes here in *non tacitis vocibus* delivers a strong image of the garrulous woman whose words are more threatening than silence and are out of control. Propertius' women are not allowed to consider their words nor do they have any power over them.[42] These women talk whether dead or alive; the only time they are silent is when they are silenced.

## IV THE SCREAM OF AN ILLEGITIMATE VOICE[43]

So Propertius' women stand in conflicted relationship to silence. In many of his poems, especially in Book 4, women become the main speakers, ostensibly controlling the action and taking over the position of chief narrator. Let us look in on Cornelia in the final poem of Book 4, poem 11. Here the self-confessed paragon of Roman maternal and patriotic virtue delivers a sober, 102-line defense of herself to her husband, L. Aemilius Paullus Lepidus, from beyond the grave, narrating her own funeral elegy. Gone seems to be the elegiac woman whose identity was a mere function of the elegiac poetry in which she

---

[41] *Pondere* in 2.22b.44 is an emendation by Beroaldus for *ponere*, the reading adopted by the OCT text of Barber.
[42] Cf. the talkative Cynthia in 2.8.17–28.
[43] I take this epitaph from Rich 1978: 18.

is inscribed.[44] This is a woman who speaks her mind and seems to reveal herself as the perfect Roman wife, mother and daughter.[45]

But Cornelia makes a very telling statement in line 84. She asks her husband Paullus to wait to show his grief until late at night when her image appears to him in his dreams. And, she says:

> *utque ubi secreto nostra ad simulacra loqueris*
>     *ut responsurae singula verba iace* (83–4)
> And when in private you speak to my image, speak every word to me as though I will reply

This break in the logic of the poem cuts through the illusion that Cornelia is standing before us, a dream given substance and features, suddenly become an anti-elegiac woman. How strange, we think as we arrive at this juncture, suddenly to be given, as Propertius' final word, a strong, aristocratic *matrona*, the resounding answer to the *meretrix* who has dominated the work, a spokesperson for Roman patriarchal imperialism. Is this a conversion? A *petitio benevolentiae* to Augustus? How could we have had Propertius so wrong?

But, as Cornelia tells Paullus in line 84, she isn't really talking. Paullus can pretend, just as the reader has been doing, that she can answer, but he will need to understand that this is a fiction and speak to her *ut responsurae*, 'to me as though I will reply.' She cannot, of course: she is dead (within the frame of the poem) and she is a fictive character, a part of Propertius' literary landscape.

After the briefest of reality checks, Cornelia retakes the floor to finish off her admonitions with a rousing peroration. Cornelia may be dead, but she has a powerful voice, one that makes us listen and believe.

Cornelia's presentation in 4.11 seems to contradict Cynthia, who is the main character in the Monobiblos and has been recently revived in poems 4.7 and 4.8. Cornelia here at the end appears to have gained the upper hand and to have driven Cynthia out of this book. She is,

---

[44] Cornelia can be seen as the 'anti-elegiac woman' since she, unlike other women in Propertius' verse (most notably Cynthia), embodies the traditional Roman virtues and acts as a guarantor of Roman integrity with her insistence on chastity as a primary virtue. See Janan 2001: 146–64; Wyke 1987a: 171–2; Wyke 2002: 108–14.

[45] On Cornelia, see further Gold 2007: 170–2, 178–80; she makes the case that Cornelia is not as perfect as she seems to be.

by all appearances, the exact opposite of Cynthia: the solid and virtuous matron, very different from the frenetic, naughty, and dangerous *meretrix* and *dominatrix*. Cynthia in 4.7 also returns as a ghost (*manes*, 1), intruding on the *frigida regna* (6) of Propertius' bed. Again, as with Cornelia, little bits of reality break through the illusion of her spectral visit. Although charred by the funeral pyre (as we would imagine her to be), her look is still the same (7–8) and her spirit and voice (*spirantis... animos et vocem*, 11) undiminished.

Cornelia and Cynthia share many other things in common. Both come to give advice and admonishment to a lover or husband, both give the two longest speeches by women in Propertius' corpus, both claim to be loyal to one man, and both implicitly take their places among the memorable women before them. Cynthia, like Cornelia, is given the opportunity to represent herself, a rare opportunity indeed for an elegiac woman.[46] And she takes matters entirely into her own hands, even opposing Propertius' earlier fantasies about her (e.g. 1.3, 2.29a/b) in which she assumed the roles of Bacchant or Naiad. She lets Propertius know that it is he who is the faithless partner while she kept the faith (4.7.51–3).

Cornelia and Cynthia share two other bonds. Each is brought into the world of the Other by an amalgamation of their characters and the spaces they inhabit. The Roman *matrona* is always perched precariously between the two worlds of the public/official/political and the private/domestic/experiential. Cornelia defines herself in relation to the military and political careers of her male relatives but does so in the comfort of her world, that of the private, elegiac woman.[47] Likewise, Cynthia moves out of her private elegiac sphere when she writes her own epitaph that speaks of her glory (*laus*) and lends her an epic touch (4.7.85–6). In addition, each of these women is defined by her relationship to a man. The ideology of the good woman rests on the close identification of woman and man; she gains her defining characteristics from a husband, son or father.

Both Cornelia and Cynthia, then, are powerful narrating voices. They speak in magisterial imperatives, ask sharp questions, and

---

[46] See Janan 2001: 100–13.
[47] See Wyke 1987a: 172–3; Wyke 2002: 108–14.

demand answers.[48] But why is it that the most powerful and dominating voices belong to the dead women, while the living (e.g. Arethusa in 4.3 and Tarpeia in 4.4) are characterized as softer and less dominating figures? Death for such women as Cornelia and Cynthia means not silence, as we would anticipate, but an even more powerful voice. Death for these women gives them a verbal power that they did not have while they were alive.[49]

Propertius suggests, in granting power only to the dead, a fear of living female words, which could destabilize and exert a dangerous control. But women who are conjured up from beyond the grave or are given putative words by the poet (e.g. 3.23) belong to an imaginary that cannot threaten or violate the images created by the poet beyond the discursive boundaries he puts in place. They are characterized by different kinds of silences, speaking like a Cassandra without being understood, or having the poet 'speak for them,' or being erased and eclipsed by the poet. They have no real authorial power over the words they speak; the poet has discursive mastery over his elegiac women.[50]

---

[48] Other, softer women, like Arethusa in 4.3 and Tarpeia in 4.4, speak in a more suasive, gentle, conditional mode and are creatures of the men they serve.

[49] For another interpretation of Cornelia's silence, see Janan 2001: 161, who translates Prop. 4.11.84 as 'speak your words at intervals (*singula*)' and says that Cornelia exists 'only as the pauses between his words—precisely as *nothing*, silence, non-meaning.'

[50] See Wyke 1995: 123. There are critics who take a very different view of the authorial figure of women in Propertius and maintain that there is a 'feminine voice' detectable in Propertius' elegies. See, e.g. Flaschenriem 1998: 49–64, who analyzes the figure of Cynthia in Propertius 1.15, 2.5, and 4.7 and says that we can find there Cynthia 'depicted as an authorial figure in her own right, and as a maker of "texts" that emphasize her autonomy from the poet-lover' (49). She reads Cynthia as 'a metaphor for a feminine perspective' who 'signifies the existence of an autonomous, though largely unrepresented, female point of view' (63). In a different vein, see Miller 2004, who, using Lacanian and post-Lacanian analysis, discusses Propertius' feminized subject position and discourse; Propertius' many contradictions and complexities are interestingly explained through this filter. Another way to frame this complex poetic problem is to look at Propertius' poetry as an artifact reflecting his own social identity. Although this is more usually claimed for poets like Horace and Persius (so Freudenburg 2001: 173–83 and n. 98; Cucchiarelli 2005: 62–80, esp. 68–9, 71–5), one might equally see Propertius' foregrounded gaps in logic as descriptive of his own self-identity.

Likewise the implication of dominance in the term *domina* is heavily problematized by Propertius. The word is used 32 times in the four books of elegies, often of Cynthia, while the word *dominus* appears only four times in all.[51] The word *domina* is a word with multiple registers. On one level, it means a master/mistress of a household and slaves.[52] And Propertius underscores this role for his elegiac woman by having himself take the position of *servus amator*, a slave/lover. Thus the poetic logic is that Cynthia rules over Propertius and his whole household. But in fact, each such woman would have herself been a slave on two levels: economic and poetic. The lives of these women must have been fraught with economic uncertainty; Micaela Janan calls them part of 'an entire underclass world disadvantaged in a struggle for accurate visibility.'[53] The poet's stress on their greed must imply something about the harsh economic realities they faced. Similarly, they were slaves of a signifying system, a part of the grammar of a literary system.[54]

So, the overuse of the word *domina* to denote the elegiac women of Propertius' world and the underuse of the word *dominus* for the male characters is illusory and misleading.[55] Propertius is playing with his language, his characters, and his readers. Such verbal legerdemain cannot disguise the inferior position of the women represented in the elegies and indeed only serves to call our attention to it just as the

---

[51] Johnson 1995: 14.
[52] Gold 1993b: 288–9; Hallett 1984: 249–52 and note 43; Miller 2004: 137.
[53] Janan 2001: 107.
[54] See Wyke 1987a and b (= Wyke 2002: 46–114).
[55] Other such terms denoting social status are used by the Roman poets in a similarly misleading and opaque manner. Cf., e.g. *amicus*, a term applied equally to both partners in a patronage relationship. The relative positions of the two people in question were, however, quite clear to everyone and the purposefully misleading use of terminology only serves to underline their inequality. So with *domina* and *dominus*: the relative social and familial positions would have been clear to everyone. See Gold 1987: 8, 75, 206. On the use of the term *dominus* in a largely non-amatory context (but with some interesting observations that might shed light on the amatory usages), see Noreña 2007: 248–9; Dickey: 2002: Chapter 2. Dickey distinguishes between the vocative and referential uses of *dominus* (the vocative being the 'more innocuous' of the two, 95); Noreña points out that *dominus* (which began as an amatory address, as Dickey says) can be a negative, neutral or cordial form of address. I would maintain that this ambiguity is there already in elegiac poetry.

clashes in the text and reality checks discussed above signal a problem in the surface meanings of 4.11.[56]

But before we decide that Propertius is simply a gamesman, wickedly using his considerable literary talents to confuse his readers, let us go back to the meanings of silence and the possibilities in the rifts in the text. There are reasons to believe that Propertius' elegiac women are more than simply creatures of the poet, prisoners of his grammar, or slaves to his sign system. The breaks in logic we have encountered—and these could be endlessly multiplied—signal Propertius' willingness to give up some control and his possible dual position as creator of a sign system and underminer of that system.[57] Another signal of this yielding of control is the power behind the voices of the women in Book 4, whether dead or alive. It is here, in a place of disruption and rifts, where we hear the women of elegy speak through their silences and sense the dangers that such speaking women might have posed.[58]

---

[56] For other layers of reading of 4.11, see Johnson 1997.

[57] Janan 2001: 109 where she says that Propertius 4.7 'interrogates . . . the world its own elegiac genre has imagined.'

[58] For claims on both sides of the question, see Wyke 1987a; 1989a and 1995; 1987b for the argument that the elegiac woman is a function of the poet's grammar and text; Miller 2004 (= Miller in this volume), Janan 2001; Gold 1993a; all these argue for a particular sensitivity and awareness in Propertius that could be described as 'speaking in the feminine, a discourse that eludes the conventional binary oppositions of official and subversive, pro and con, conscious and unconscious' (Miller 2004: 146). Wyke 1995: 120–1 also argues that Propertius' subject position cannot be precisely located within conventional Roman (masculine) ideological space. In this way, Propertius calls into question norms of gender, discourse, power and desire in a more radical way than 'the concept of opposition can convey' (Miller 2004: 146).

# 14

## Gender and Genre in Propertius 2.8 and 2.9[1]

*Ellen Greene*

I argued in a previous paper that despite the Propertian lover's avowed identification with feminine powerlessness and vulnerability and his concomitant classification of elegy as a distinctly 'feminine' genre, the *amator* in the Monobiblos often subverts his own rhetoric of subservience by linking himself in his *exempla* with powerful masculine mythological heroes.[2] This linkage, I argue, serves to associate the effeminized male lover with figures in myth notorious for their domination and violence toward women. In the second book, however, the *amator*'s imagined heroic persona becomes much more blatant. We begin to see the *amator* vacillate more openly between epic and elegiac discourses and between conflicting images of himself as both lover and poet, master and mastered. Moreover, the increased association of the elegiac mistress with literary production in Book 2 heightens the indeterminate nature of both the speaker's gender identity and his poetic discourse.[3]

Elegy 2.1, Propertius' opening programmatic poem, shows that his project in Book 2 is predicated on both an acceptance of elegiac discourse and a resistance to it. Although the *amator* in 2.1 exploits

---

[1] All translations in this paper are the author's own.
[2] See Greene 1995; also Greene 1998: chapter 3.
[3] In Wyke 1987b see discussion of how Book 2 is characterized, in part, by increasing references to Cynthia as matter for poetic composition.

elegy's conventional rhetoric of subservience toward both his mistress and his patron, he nonetheless allies the elegiac enterprise with the heroic values of epic, thus undermining the hierarchical relationships implicit in his position as abject lover and poet. In particular, by linking *amor* to images of death and glory in his *recusatio* and identifying himself with renowned mythical heroes, the Propertian speaker subverts his own claim that epic lies beyond his grasp and sphere of interest. The Propertian *amator* in Book 2 not only undermines the feminine persona he establishes for himself in the Monobiblos, but also reveals a discourse that constantly defies classification.[4]

I will argue in this paper that in his second book Propertius constitutes elegy as a generic category precisely through the way it discloses its own contradictions and paradoxes at every turn.[5] Moreover, as the *recusationes* of elegy make clear, elegy—as a genre—is not only discursively aligned with the feminine, but is explicitly defined through its opposition to other kinds of verse traditionally marked as male such as epic or encomium. At the same time, the elegist appears to defy conventional gender roles by declaring himself the *mollis* poet of elegy and occupying the 'feminine' position in the amatory relationship. However, as I will argue, Propertius' male lover constantly undermines not only his own elegiac discourse but also the position of subservience he appears to embrace. Unlike the Catullan lover, whose identity is often defined by the fragmentation arising from conflicting values and sensibilities, the Propertian *amator*'s fluid gender identity allows him to recast the feminine role to his own advantage and elevate the elegiac lover to heroic status.

As Maria Wyke has argued, Propertius' second book of elegies is characterized by an increasing emphasis on the mistress as matter for literary discourse and a curtailment of the more realistic mechanisms for depicting the amatory relationship.[6] Indeed, Book 1 opens with a

---

[4] See Gold 1993a. Gold argues that Propertius destabilizes traditional Roman categories of gender by putting the male narrator 'into play as the feminine.'

[5] One may argue that genres in general are constituted through a dialectical relationship to other genres. In Poem 2.1 Propertius identifies elegy as a generic category precisely through its opposition to epic, thus suggesting that elegy derives its meaning through a constant reference to what is *other*. On genre, see especially Derrida 1991 and 1992.

[6] On the image of Cynthia as a literary construction in Book 2, see Wyke 1987b and 1989; see also Keith 1994, and Fredrick 1997.

dramatic reference to Cynthia's eyes, while Propertius' second book of elegies begins by invoking the process of poetic composition. I agree that Cynthia's dramatic function in Book 2 diminishes significantly. But I will show that the increased association of the elegiac mistress with poetic production is linked inextricably with the *amator*'s more explicit identification with the discourses and values of epic poetry. Despite the narrator's declarations in Poem 2.1 that he rejects the lofty occupation of epic poet, he nonetheless describes his slender verse in epic terms and characterizes himself as an epic hero whose own *fama* will guarantee the posterity of both *puella* and patron.[7] Thus, Propertius frames his second book of elegies not only by identifying the elegiac mistress more explicitly with the raw material of his verse, but also by imagining the male lover achieving the glory worthy of a great epic hero. My study here will focus on Poems 2.8 and 2.9, texts that offer striking illustrations of the ways in which the male lover in Book 2 presents an image of himself as the *mollis* poet of elegy and, at the same time, often identifies himself with the ideals and discourses of epic.

I E. 2.8

In Poem 2.8, despite his presentation of himself as *miser*, the *amator* implicates himself in the world of male public culture by identifying himself with the tragic deaths of epic heroes. The speaker begins by emphasizing his abject status; the passive *eripitur* in line 1 evokes the familiar image of the elegiac lover as *servus amoris*.[8]

*Eripitur nobis iam pridem cara puella:*
  *et tu me lacrimas fundere, amice, vetas?*
*nullae sunt inimicitiae nisi amoris acerbae:*
  *ipsum me iugula, lenior hostis ero.*

---

[7] See a more expanded argument on this point in Greene 2000. See also Miller 1998b for a discussion of the Propertian lover's vacillations between epic and elegiac discourses.

[8] For discussions of the *servitium amoris* topos in Roman elegy, see especially Copley 1947; Day 1938; Kennedy 1993; Lyne 1979; McCarthy 1998; Veyne 1988.

*possum ego in alterius positam spectare lacerto?* 5
    *nec mea dicetur, quae modo dicta mea est?*
*omnia vertuntur: certe vertuntur amores:*
    *vinceris aut vincis, haec in amore rota est.*
*magni saepe duces, magni cecidere tyranni,*
    *et Thebae steterunt altaque Troia fuit.* 10
*munera quanta dedi vel qualia carmina feci!*
    *illa tamen numquam ferrea dixit 'Amo.'*
The girl I have loved so long is snatched away,
    and you, my friend, forbid me to shed tears?
No enmities are bitter except those in love.
    Slay me and I'll be a milder foe.
Can I watch her couched in another man's arms?
    Has she been, and will not be, called mine?
All things change: assuredly love changes.
    You are conquered or conquer, so turns the wheel of love.
Often great leaders, great tyrants fall,
    And Thebes once stood, and lofty Troy once was.
How many gifts I have given, what poems I composed!
    Yet she, iron, never said 'I love.'

The speaker has been robbed of his *cara puella* and the reference to the longevity (*pridem*) of his love for her recalls the painful vicissitudes we have come to associate with this love. In line 2, the speaker addresses an unnamed *amicus* who appears to forbid the *amator's* shedding of tears. The speaker's apostrophe to a male friend, who is clearly in favor of a more stoical approach to amatory affairs, not only evokes the network of relations between men in Roman society but also implicitly inserts the value of *amicitia* in the context of conventional elegiac complaint. The word *amicus* can refer to a patron; given that Book 2 opens with the lover's apostrophe to Maecenas, it is reasonable to believe that the *amicus* in Poem 2.8 may also be Maecenas.[9] Moreover, in Poem 2.1, as is typical in an elegiac *recusatio*, the speaker begins the poem by defending his choice to write elegy. Here the speaker also suggests that his addressee, the *amicus*, voices disapproval toward the lover's unmanly expression of emotion and its attendant amatory rhetoric. As Ellen Oliensis argues, the hierarchical structure of the

---

[9] See Greene 2000 for a discussion of Maecenas in Propertius 2.1. In Oliensis 1997 see an illuminating analysis of the role of the patron in elegiac verse.

client-patron relationship mirrors the fiction of gender reversal in the bond between the male lover and his mistress. Within the dominant ideology of Rome, Oliensis writes, 'the client is a respectable, the lover a disreputable figure.'[10] Roman males were expected to grow up, get over their youthful dalliances, and ultimately devote themselves to participation in public culture.[11] Indeed, the *amicus*' opposition to the lover's tears suggests an impatience with the speaker's concern for his private emotions. But rather than defend his position as a lover and writer of elegies, the narrator launches into a description of *amor* in precisely the terms demanded by aristocratic male culture—terms that valorize rather than oppose epic ideals.

The invocation of the unnamed *amicus* (as friend or reader), with its implications of male public culture, immediately gives rise to the *amator*'s characterization of himself as a *hostis*. In Poem 2.1 the speaker made clear that amatory violence is what inspires poetic composition: *seu nuda erepto mecum luctatur amictu,/tum vero longas condimus Iliadas* ('or if she wrestles with me nude, her clothes torn away, then we really do make some long *Iliads*,' 13–14). Here the *amator* also uses military metaphors to describe the amatory relationship.[12] But the speaker's abrupt shift from the image of the *puella* as *cara* to the images of a savage *amor* invoked in line 3 suggests the reconfiguration of the elegist's soft verse as *durus*—an attribute chiefly associated with both the elegiac mistress and masculine epic. In Poem 2.1 the speaker claimed that the *durus versus* of epic is beyond the capability of the 'soft' poet. But here the implied military metaphors to describe the hostilities of *amor* identify the *amator* with the *durus* style of epic— with the violent imagery and ethic of personal vengeance associated with the literary genre the elegist claims to reject. The *amator*'s assertion that 'no enmities are bitter except those in love' implies that *amor* is actually more savage than war. The speaker thus overturns the characteristically passive position of the male lover by envisioning

---

[10] Oliensis 1997.
[11] See Edwards 1996: 52–63 on how the genre of elegy is associated with a resistance to public concerns.
[12] See Cahoon 1985 for a discussion of the use of military metaphors in Ovid's *Amores*. Cahoon's analysis may be usefully applied to Roman elegy in general.

himself as a *hostis* whose rage can only be mollified by death itself (*ipsum me iugula, lenior hostis ero*).

In lines 5–6, the speaker's rhetorical questions to his *amicus* seem to reinforce his reasons for shedding tears in the first place. These questions also resonate with the image of the speaker as abject lover; he appears powerless to change circumstances beyond his control. However, the speaker's rational approach to his dilemma, expressed in lines 7–8, undermines the characteristic portrayal of the elegiac lover as *miser*, as hopelessly bound to his hard-hearted mistress. Despite the implication that the *amator* cannot endure the *puella*'s rejection of him, his calm philosophical response to his own impassioned questions reveals a far greater degree of emotional control and mastery than is typically associated with the elegiac lover. The speaker implicitly answers his own questions about whether he is able to tolerate his mistress 'couched in another man's arms' and 'no longer being called his.' The specificity of the speaker's love for his mistress and its attendant emotionality become assimilated to the speaker's sudden intellectual awareness that *omnia vertuntur: certe vertuntur amores*. The speaker abruptly frames his *amor* within the larger context of the flux of life in general, showing that he *can* bear his mistress' rejection of him. The speaker thus proves to his *amicus* that he does have the fortitude and discernment demanded of a *doctus vir*—a man worthy not only of *dignitas* but of the homosocial bonds at the core of aristocratic culture. In addition, the *amator* applies military terms to the vicissitudes of *amor* by claiming that in the realm of love, as in war, one can only either conquer or be conquered: *vinceris a victis, haec in amore rota est* (l. 8). *Amor* is thus cast in the terms of masculine epic; the vicissitudes of conquest and defeat in war normally serve to valorize male heroic endeavor. By reconstituting the *amator*'s passivity in the context of masculine heroic achievement, the speaker implicitly grants heroic status to the traditionally disempowered male lover.

That heroic status is heightened in lines 9–10 when the speaker compares his defeat in love not only to the defeats of great leaders and despots but also to the fall of great legendary Greek cities. These mythological references suggest that the male lover, although vanquished for the moment, will nonetheless receive the *fama* accorded to great mythical heroes and places. Not only does the *amator* describe his amatory troubles in epic proportions, but he also implicitly elevates elegy as a genre to epic status. In lines 11–12, the speaker suddenly evokes the characteristically abject condition of the lover by exclaiming about the futility of his amatory gifts and the poetic compositions that accompanied those gifts. The speaker appears to be speaking in the feminine once again, depicting the male lover lamenting his fruitless efforts to win his mistress' love. Yet the speaker's efforts are presented within the context of his allusions to epic. Poems and presents are presented as analogous to the achievements of great epic heroes on the battlefield. Moreover, the speaker's characterization of his mistress as *ferrea* ('iron') again metamorphosizes the *puella* into the epic *hostis*. She is just the adversary hardhearted enough to be worthy of a great epic hero. The image of the *puella* as *ferrea* here also evokes the *amator*'s more typical description of his mistress as *dura*. In Poem 2.1 the speaker claims that the *durus versus* of epic is beyond his abilities. Yet by characterizing the subject of his verse, Cynthia, as also *dura*, he identifies elegy with epic and suggests that elegy is as rigorous a form of poetic composition as epic itself. Describing the *puella* as *ferrea* in Poem 2.8 expands upon the image of her as *dura* and serves to link her more definitively with masculine epic. Indeed the quality of *ferreus* is less abstract than *durus* and is associated more specifically with weaponry and war. This association further implicates elegy in the world of male public culture and, at the same time, implicitly transforms the *cara puella* into a mute, unyielding object—a tool in the heroic exploits of men. The word *ferreus* is also sometimes used to describe the rigidity associated with death itself.[13] On the one hand, the speaker's characterization of his mistress as *ferrea* here reinscribes the mistress' dominant status in the amatory relationship. On the other hand, the speaker inverts the normative gender roles associated with elegy by conferring a kind of death on the elegiac mistress and describing her in a way that dehumanizes her.

In lines 13–16 the speaker makes explicit his implied invective against Cynthia by depicting her not only as morally base but as someone who misuses language. After attributing non-human traits

---

[13] See *Aeneid* 10, 745 where Virgil characterizes death as an 'iron sleep' (*ferreus somnus*).

to Cynthia, the *amator* suddenly brings her back to life by apostrophizing her directly for the first time in the poem.

> *ergo ego tam multos nimium temerarius annos,*
> *improba, qui tulerim teque tuamque domum?*
> *ecquandone tibi liber sum visus? an usque*
> *in nostrum iacies verba superba caput?*
> So all these years I have been rash, have I, wicked woman,
> I who have borne you and your household?
> Did I ever seem free to you? Will you continually
> throw insolent words at my head?

These lines seem to reinforce the traditional association of the male lover with passivity and subservience. Yet here it is the *amator* who hurls insults at his mistress—accusing her of both moral depravity and the abuse of language. The latter abuse is especially striking in light of the speaker's earlier references to his own poetic offerings to his mistress. The speaker wields language here as a weapon, and shows in the following stanzas that words can kill.

> *sic igitur prima moriere aetate, Properti?*
> *sed morere; interitu gaudeat illa tuo!*
> *exagitet nostros Manes, sectetur et umbras,*
> *insultetque rogis, calcet et ossa mea!*      20
> *quid? Non Antigonae tumulo Boeotius Haemon*
> *corruit ipse suo saucius ense latus,*
> *et sua cum miserae permiscuit ossa puellae,*
> *qua sine Thebanam noluit ire domum?*
> So are you to die in the prime of your life, Propertius?
> Then die. Let her take pleasure in your destruction!
> Let her harass my ghost, and pursue my shade.
> Let her insult my pyre, and trample on my bones!
> What? Didn't Boeotian Haemon fall at Antigone's tomb,
> stabbed in the side with his own sword,
> and did he not mingle his bones with those of the unhappy girl,
> without whom he did not wish to enter his Theban home?

These lines recall the speaker's earlier comparisons between his destruction at the hands of his *ferrea puella* and the fall of great men and mythical cities. Here the *amator* circumvents the putative opposition between epic and elegiac poetry by imagining himself fulfilling the dictum he expressed in Poem 2.1, that 'to die in love is glory' (*laus in amore mori*). In Poem 2.1 the speaker makes it clear that the epic ideal of glory in death achieves greater *kleos* (renown) for the male lover than the *laus altera* ('other praise') of possessing the elegiac mistress.

Although the *amator* perpetuates the image of Cynthia as cruel and hard-hearted in the way he portrays her reaction to his imagined death, he also envisions her committing moral transgressions worthy of an *improbae puellae* ('immoral girl'). The five-fold repetition of the hortatory subjunctives in lines 19–20 ('Let her enjoy, harass, pursue, insult, trample') suggests that the speaker relishes imagining his mistress gloating over his demise and violating his corpse. The *puella*'s imagined persecution of the speaker's poor shade allows the *amator* to envision for himself a noble death. In lines 21–24 the speaker implicitly compares himself to Haemon who takes his own life because he cannot bear to be departed from his beloved Antigone. Just as the elegiac mistress provides the *materia* for the *amator*'s poetic compositions, Antigone's death produces the occasion that allows Haemon to achieve his own glory. Throughout Propertius' first book of elegies the figure of Cynthia is inextricably linked to her role as narrative *materia* in the poet's writing, and the speaker often makes clear that the poet's place in posterity is dependent on the mistress' own *fama*—in particular a *fama* that will result from the mistress continuing to be the subject of his verse.[14] Here the speaker's image of Haemon nobly mingling his bones with those of Antigone offers a sharp contrast to the image of Cynthia trampling on the bones of 'Propertius.' On the one hand, the identification of the speaker with Haemon reinforces the abject position of the male lover. But, on the other hand, the speaker's description of Antigone as *miser* in line 23 invokes the characteristically wretched emotional condition of the elegiac lover. This confusion in the attribution of gender identities in the speaker's *exemplum* underscores the ambivalent nature of the gender roles the speaker imagines for both himself and his mistress. Moreover, in implicitly associating Cynthia with *miser* Antigone the speaker not only transforms his *ferrea puella* into a victim of male

---

[14] Propertius 1.11 provides a particularly striking illustration of the way in which Cynthia becomes equated with the elegiac book.

authority, but also transfers the traditional attribute of the male lover to the female beloved. At the same time, Antigone is a figure who transgresses male norms for female behavior in much the same way as Cynthia is often pictured as acting outside of Roman social mores. By invoking Antigone's death in this way, the speaker imagines the elegiac beloved as a lifeless text he can imbue with whatever noble or ignoble, male or female, characteristics he chooses.[15]

The glorious death the speaker imagines for both himself and his mistress comes to fruition in the following couplets where the *amator* magisterially announces that Cynthia will not escape the death he envisions for her.

> *Sed non effugies: mecum moriaris oportet;*                   25
>    *Hoc eodem ferro stillet uterque cruor.*
> *Quamvis ista mihi mors est inhonesta futura:*
>    *Mors inhonesta quidem, tu moriere tamen.*
> Still you will not escape: you must die with me;
>    Let the blood of both drip from the same sword.
> Although that death will be dishonorable for me,
>    Indeed a dishonorable death, but even so you shall die.

Here the speaker imagines the male lover and his mistress as adversaries engaged in mutual slaughter. However, the speaker's use of the future tense to predict what will in fact happen to the mistress emphasizes the male lover's agency in subduing the *ferrea puella* and subjecting her to the speaker's rhetorical control. As iron, as *ferrea*, the mistress provides the *materia* that may afford both of them a glorious epic death in the poet's imagination. Yet twice the speaker characterizes this death as *inhonesta*. It is not clear from the syntax of Propertius' lines whether *inhonesta* refers to both their deaths, to his, or only to hers. Richardson suggests that this passage recalls Aeneas' desire to kill Helen in *Aen.* 2 (759–867), since Aeneas realizes that killing a woman will bring him no glory.[16] However, in light of

---

[15] Although the Haemon/Antigone exemplum is drawn from tragedy and not epic, the speaker emphasizes its association with Thebes. Troy and Thebes are the mythical places immediately linked to violent and glorious death. As Richardson 1977: 233 points out, the choice of Thebes and Troy as the two exempla in the poem 'is a natural one, since these were the great cities of ancient epic.'

[16] Richardson 1977: 234.

the *exemplum* in the previous lines, it seems unlikely that the speaker is referring to their mutual death as dishonorable. Both Haemon and Antigone achieve glory through their tragic deaths, and the aims of both (certainly in Sophocles' version) are presented as honorable. In Propertius' poem it seems that *inhonesta* ('cheating') recalls the speaker's earlier reference to Cynthia as *improba*. The possible allusion to Helen here would thus serve to reinforce the speaker's characterization of his mistress as morally bankrupt, while emphasizing the male lover's manly fortitude and moral rectitude through his implicit identification with Aeneas. Since the speaker's sword is a rhetorical one, the image of the elegiac woman as a figure who transgresses acceptable moral standards serves as a reminder of the poet's power to assign moral blame to the female beloved. Further, the speaker's bold promise to Cynthia that she will not escape his vengeance (*sed non effugies*) contradicts the speaker's characteristically powerless stance and, at the same time, asserts the confidence of the poet to link inextricably the fates of the male lover and the elegiac mistress in his poetic texts. The blood of both drips from the same sword, the same *ferrea materia* ('iron matter') the poet uses for his art.

The speaker's tone of wrathfulness toward his mistress (*tu moriere*, 'you will die') is reinforced in the final couplets of the poem when the *amator* implicitly compares his sorrow at losing Cynthia to Achilles' grief over the loss of Briseis. However, the comparison between the male lover and Achilles serves again to link *amor* to images of death and glory and to emphasize the speaker's reconfiguration of himself as a heroic figure.

> *ille etiam abrepta desertus coniuge Achilles*
>    *cessare in Teucris pertulit arma sua.*                                 30
> *viderat ille fuga stratos in litore Achivos,*
>    *fervere et Hectorea Dorica castra face;*
> *viderat informem multa Patroclon harena*
>    *porrectum et sparsas caede iacere comas,*
> *omnia formosam propter Briseida passus:*                             35
>    *tantus in erepto saevit amore dolor.*
> *at postquam sera captiva est reddita poena,*
>    *fortem illum Haemoniis Hectora traxit equis.*
> Even Achilles, abandoned, his wife snatched away,
>    allowed his arms to lie idle in the face of the Trojans.

> He had seen the Achaeans in flight scattered on the shore,
> and the Greek camp ablaze with Hector's torch;
> he had seen the shapeless corpse of Patroklos lying stretched out
> on a heap of sand and his hair strewn with blood,
> suffering all for the sake of lovely Briseis:
> such grief rages for a love snatched away.
> But when with late retribution his captive was restored,
> he dragged the brave Hector behind his Thessalian horses.

Monica Gale argues that Poem 2.8 shows that Propertius 'persists in reading the *Iliad* as a work of love-poetry ... and the relationship between Achilles and Briseis is several times treated as an *exemplum*, particularly at the end of 2.8, where all the effects of Achilles' wrath are ascribed to his frustrated love for "*formosa* Briseis."'[17] In misreading Homer, Gale argues, Propertius undermines his assertion that elegy is as good a genre as epic. It is certainly true that the speaker in 2.8 begins his *exemplum* by emphasizing how Achilles' withdrawal from battle and his alienation from warrior culture in general occur as a result of losing Briseis. But as in Homer's poem where Achilles' grief ultimately turns into action—into a passionate desire for revenge that will lead to his death and ensure his *kleos*—in Propertius' poem Achilles' sorrow turns to rage: *tantus in erepto saevit amore dolor*. The speaker describes Achilles' *dolor* as itself ruthless and raging, just as the male lover's sorrow at losing Cynthia quickly turns to invective and fantasies of revenge. Moreover, the images of Briseis as the 'wife' and 'love' of Achilles correspondingly change in line 37 to a description of her as Achilles' captive. The action of revenge, which finds fulfillment in Achilles dragging Hector's body through the dust, affirms Achilles' re-identification with his warrior identity. The description of Briseis as Achilles' captive resonates with the Propertian lover's implicit comparison between Cynthia and the captive Antigone (in her cave tomb). In addition, the association of Achilles' wrath with the portrayal of Briseis as a slave suggests that the speaker's own expressions of rage at his mistress are also linked to an image of Cynthia as someone the poet hopes to subdue with his rhetorical sword.

---

[17] Gale 1997: 83.

Indeed, the last two lines of the speaker's *exemplum* not only serve to underscore the image of the male lover as a hero who embraces his death and the glory attendant on it, but also to emphasize the close association between the activation of male heroism and the restoration of the female beloved to her rightfully subordinate position. Moreover, the speaker's mention of Patroklos calls to mind the bond between the male hero and his *amicus*—whose demise (in the case of Patroklos) spurs the 'lover' Achilles to return to the male arena and win his *kleos*. Alison Sharrock makes the intriguing point that the reference to Achilles' other beloved, Patroklos, emphasizes the centrality of the image of the male friend in constructing a heroic identity for the male speaker. 'The *amicus*,' Sharrock writes, 'at some subliminal, symbolic level, could "be" Patroklos.'[18] Although clearly the speaker's male friend has not been 'snatched away' from him, one may well argue that the male lover's potential defeat by *amor* imperils his standing in the masculine sphere of heroic achievement.

The last two lines of the poem, however, seem to return us to the poem's opening, to the image of a bereft *amator* lamenting the loss of his *dura puella*. The speaker appears to disavow the comparison between the heroic exploits of Achilles and his own amatory adventures.

*inferior multo cum sim vel matre vel armis,*
    *mirum, si de me iure triumphat Amor?*        40
Since I am inferior in mother and in arms,
    why wonder if Love justly triumphs over me?

The references to Achilles' *mater* and *arma* here reinforce the speaker's emphasis on the *kleos* achieved by the warrior in battle. In particular, the speaker reminds us of the hero's semi-divine status by recalling Achilles' divine mother and the arms procured by her from Hephaistos. Although the Propertian speaker asserts that he cannot claim for himself a similar divinity, his earlier references to his own imagined epic death and, in particular, to the sword that will be the tool of that demise, suggest that the poet does possess the means to win the glory attendant on the death he imagines for himself and his mistress. Indeed, he has shown that words are his weapons, and they can kill

---

[18] Sharrock 2000: 279.

his enemies or at least render them extinct as far as posterity is concerned.

The speaker seems to ask a merely rhetorical question at the end when he asks, 'why wonder if Love justly triumphs over me?' It is by no means certain that *Amor* has vanquished the speaker. First, the *amator*'s defeat is predicated on the condition that he is inferior to Achilles, particularly with respect to the immortality Achilles receives as a result of his prowess on the battlefield. But the speaker has shown his own skill in defeating his adversaries with the *ferrea materia* of his art. In Poem 2.1 the male lover demonstrates that the *amor* which constitutes the *amator*'s *insania* ('lover's irrationality') defines his place in posterity and guarantees for him a *iusta gloria* ('proper glory').[19] Second, the suggestion at the end that the *amator* has been defeated by Love is undermined by the speaker's earlier assertions about the changeability of *amor*. The images of *amor* as a wheel that turns and of the lover as both conqueror and conquered suggest that *Amor*'s defeat of the speaker is transient at best. In Propertius' *exemplum*, Achilles too suffers defeat temporarily but is able to reclaim his heroic stature once he gains mastery over the beloved and is thus able to re-enter the male arena. Moreover, earlier in the poem the speaker imagined himself killing both himself and Cynthia. Given that the speaker made *amor* the cause of Achilles' rage, it stands to reason that the speaker, avowedly more susceptible to the effects of love than Achilles, would outdo Achilles himself in wreaking vengeance on his enemies.[20]

The speaker again addresses his friend, after demonstrating to him that the elegiac lover can master the effects of *amor* not only by according love its proper place in the scheme of things, but also by confronting his enemy—the *ferrea puella*—with the ruthless rage worthy of a great epic hero. The speaker's question at the end recalls the *amator*'s earlier queries to his friend about his own ability to endure the vicissitudes of love. It seems that the elegist has proven to his friend just how *dura* his poetic *materia* is and how adept he is at

---

[19] At the end of Poem 2.1, the speaker refers to his addressee and patron Maecenas as his *iusta gloria* in life and death. Earlier in the poem, however, the speaker makes it clear that the patron's posterity, like the *puella*'s, depends on the poet to endow him with the attributes worthy of inclusion in commemorative verse.

[20] See Sharrock 2000: 279–80 for a perceptive analysis of this point.

using it as a weapon to subdue his *ferrea puella*. The *kleos* the male lover imagines for himself arises out of the dishonorable death of the elegiac mistress; the moral turpitude he associates with Cynthia makes his imagined slaughter of her seem noble. The speaker's rhetorical question at the end has a generalizing force that seems directed at anyone who will listen; who *can* wonder about the capability of the soft poet to wield his poetic *arma* with as much *virtus* as Achilles himself?

## II 2.9

In his commentary on Propertius' *Elegies*, Richardson asserts that Poems 2.8 and 2.9 are a pair. He points out a number of themes in 2.8 that reappear in 2.9, including the images of the wheel of fortune, Achilles and Briseis, the poet dying for love, and the use of *exempla* from the Theban epic cycle.[21] My own analysis of 2.9 will focus on how the poem reinforces the heroic persona of the elegiac lover we saw in 2.8, and more explicitly links the construction of his heroic identity with the homosocial relations that circumscribe the lover's relationship to his mistress. My interpretation of 2.9 is predicated on including the last two distichs of the poem in the body of the text.[22] Scholars have long been perplexed by the final four lines of the poem.

---

[21] Richardson 1977: 232–41. See also Bobrowski 1994; Lyne 1998b groups together Poems 2.8, 2.9(a), 2.10/11, arguing that these poems constitute the end of the original Book 2. Most recently, Sharrock 2000 argues for important links between 2.8 and 2.9, primarily on the basis of their shared mythological material and links between the *amicus* of 2.8 and the rival (the other man) in 2.9.

[22] Goold 1990, in the Loeb edition, prints lines 49–52 as fragment 9b. Similarly, Camps 1967 presents these lines as a separate poem (9a) but avows that they refer to the same incident as 9a. Butler and Barber 1933 assert that the tone of the final quatrain clashes with that of the whole elegy, while Papanghelis 1987 reads the quatrain as central but doesn't take a position on whether it ought to be included with the rest of the poem. Richardson 1977: 240, on the other hand, argues that lines 49–52 present a 'natural development' of the previous lines and that attempts to remove these lines to a separate poem are 'clearly mistaken.' Although she does not examine 2.9 in detail, Sharrock's arguments 2000 in favor of taking '9a' and '9b' as one poem are most germane to my own reading of 2.9. She points out some very important mythological parallels between 2.8 and 2.9 that take into account the

But I believe, along with Sharrock and others, that the pattern of mythological allusions in both 2.8 and 2.9, and more importantly the emphasis on the lover's rival at the beginning of 2.9, offer persuasive evidence that lines 49–52 ought to be read as a logical development of the preceding lines.

As Sharrock astutely observes, in 2.8 the speaker's identification with Achilles links the *amator* not only to the experience of erotic abandonment (in Achilles' loss of Briseis) but also to the enactment of epic vengeance against one's rivals or enemies. While in 2.8 the speaker imagines himself violently defeating his adversaries (Cynthia and *Amor*), one may also argue that he hints at the defeat of his rival as well. The parallel between the speaker and Achilles, who wins his *kleos* by violently slaughtering his rival Hector, not only may suggest an implicit concern in 2.8 with 'the other man,' but also serves to link 2.8 directly to the opening of 2.9, to the explicit identification of the man (*iste*) who, at least for the moment, claims the beloved's attentions.[23]

Like Poem 2.8, 2.9 seemingly begins by invoking the powerless position of the elegiac lover who apparently has been supplanted by another man.

*iste quod est, ego saepe fui: sed fors et in hora*
    *hoc ipso eiecto carior alter erit.* 2
What that man is, I have often been: but perhaps even
    in an hour, he will be cast out and another will be dearer.

However, unlike 2.8, here the speaker implicitly expresses from the start the awareness that *omnia vertuntur: certe vertuntur amores* ('all things change; for sure love changes'). The speaker quickly dispenses with the earlier images of himself as passive and subservient and instead constructs an image of himself as a man with enough distance and perspective to see himself as part of the 'wheel of love.' In addition, the speaker's immediate and explicit concern with his rival suggests that the bond between the lover and his mistress is subordinated to

---

reference to Theban princes in the final quatrain. Sharrock also emphasizes the central role of the rival in the construction of "Propertius'" character in the poem.

[23] See Sharrock 2000: 279–80, for an excellent discussion of how Hector stands metaphorically for the implicit 'rival' in Poem 2.8, with 'military rivalry merging into erotic rivalry, as we know erotic discourse is inclined to do at Rome.'

relations between the two male rivals in the poem. Indeed, in structural terms the poem (taking '9a' and '9b' as one) is framed by the speaker's references to his rival, by his overriding concern for 'who is up and who is down' not only in the cycles of erotic success and failure but in the assertion of dominance within the context of male public culture. The emphatic position of *iste* in the first line of the poem may recall the use of *ille* in Catullus 51. To be sure, Catullus' use of the demonstrative pronoun to refer to 'the other man' serves to point up the differences between 'Catullus' and his rival, while the speaker in Propertius' poem emphasizes the interchangeability of their positions. However, in both poems a male rival is the figure of separation between the lover and his mistress. By giving so much prominence to the presence of 'that man,' both poems foreground a situation of erotic triangulation. As René Girard and Eve Sedgwick have argued, in the context of male-dominated societies the bond between two male rivals in an erotic triangle is often stronger than that between the lover and his mistress.[24] Erotic triangles involving two males and a woman place men in primary relation to one another while the woman is merely the conduit for that relationship. Propertius' Poem 2.9 seems in my view to underscore this point. The image of the unnamed rival, much like the *amicus* in 2.8, animates the lover's imagined epic persona and provides a framework within which the elegiac lover may construct various heroic roles for himself.

In lines 3–18 the speaker in 2.9 turns his attention away from the other man, and presents the *exempla* of faithful women ostensibly in order to highlight Cynthia's unfaithfulness.

*Penelope poterat bis denos salva per annos*
　　*vivere, tam multis femina digna procis;*
*coniugium falsa poterat differe Minerva,* 　　　　　　　　　　5
　　*nocturno solvens texta diurna dolo;*
*visura et quamvis numquam speraret Ulixem,*
　　*illum exspectando facta remansit anus.*

---

[24] Girard 1965 has an illuminating discussion of a system of power structured around the rivalry between two active members of an erotic triangle. See also Sedgwick 1985 for a perceptive analysis of erotic triangulation (males competing for a female) in the context of male homosocial desire.

*nec non exanimem amplectens Briseis Achillem*
*candida vesana verberat ora manu;*   10
*et dominum lavit maerens captiva cruentum,*
*propositum flavis in Simoente vadis,*
*foedavitque comas, et tanti corpus Achille*
*maximaque in parva sustulit ossa manu;*
*cum tibi nec Peleus aderat nec caerula mater,*   15
*Scyria nec viduo Deidamia toro.*
*tunc igitur veris gaudebat Graecia nuptis,*
*tunc etiam felix inter et arma pudor.*

Penelope was able to live sound for twice ten years,
    a woman worthy of so many suitors;
her false weaving enabled her to defer marriage,
    undoing the day's weaving in nightly deceit;
and although she never expected to see Ulysses again,
    she stayed true, grown old in waiting for him.
And Briseis too embracing the lifeless Achilles
    beat her white cheeks with her raging hand;
and the mourning captive washed her bloody master,
    laid out by the golden waters of Simois;
she soiled her hair and in her small hands took up
    the body of the huge Achilles and his mighty bones.
Since neither Peleus nor your sea-born mother were with you,
    nor Scyrian Deidamia, whose bed was widowed.
Thus, in those days, Greece rejoiced in true brides,
    and in those days decency flourished even amid warfare.

What is intriguing about these lines is not only their more blatant identification of the elegiac lover with epic heroes but also the way in which they envision a complex picture of gender identities for both the *amator* and his mistress. Although the *exemplum* of Penelope seems simply to invoke an ideal of chastity, the image of Penelope 'worthy of so many suitors' recalls the wayward Cynthia whose attractiveness to other men at times produces a measure of voyeuristic titillation that fuels the lover's literary and erotic imaginations.[25] Indeed, the speaker's reference to Penelope's many suitors

---

[25] Poem 1.11 is a good example of how the Propertian lover seems aroused by fantasizing about Cynthia's possible transgressions. For further discussion of this point, see Greene 1995.

leads directly to images of female trickery and deceit.[26] These images not only echo the speaker's chronic invectives toward Cynthia, but also his more general recurring characterization of women as inherently deceitful creatures—a characterization he articulates to Cynthia later on in the poem. The speaker presents Penelope not only as an *exemplum* of female devotion but also as another version of the *dura puella*. When the *amator* again emphasizes Penelope's fidelity in lines 7–8, he presents her as an old woman whose sexuality no longer poses a threat. The speaker's dual images of Penelope here recall in Poem 1.11 the lover's ambivalent images of Cynthia as both seductress and nurturing mother. In 2.9 Penelope's facility in practicing deceit is implicitly linked to her sexual attractiveness, while the image of her as an old woman (a mother perhaps) is explicitly associated with her fidelity. The *exemplum* of Penelope shows the way in which a woman's autonomy is closely linked to a sexuality that potentially endangers the social order and ultimately threatens male hegemony. The speaker's version of the Penelope/Odysseus myth suggests that Odysseus' *kleos* is predicated on control over the beloved's sexuality. This is analogous to the linkage in 2.8 between the activation of Achilles' heroism and the characterization of the female beloved as the hero's captive.

Briseis, the second *exemplum* of female devotion invoked by the speaker, is explicitly described as a *captiva*. As in Poem 2.8, the description of Briseis as Achilles' captive here is closely linked to the re-affirmation of the hero's warrior identity. The image of the bloody Achilles (*cruentum*) constitutes fulfillment of the male lover's imagined death in 2.8. In 2.9 the ideal of a glorious epic death seems inextricable from the image of the captive female beloved whose diminutive hands stand in sharp contrast to the male hero's huge body and mighty bones. Not only does the image of Briseis taking up Achilles' bones contrast with Cynthia treading on the bones of 'Propertius' in 2.8, but it also recalls the image of Haemon mixing his bones with those of Antigone. Propertius seems to use the figure of Briseis here to underscore an ambivalence in the roles of lover and

---

[26] Sharrock 2000: 281 agrees that the mention of Penelope's trickery points up the similarities rather than differences between her and Cynthia. Sharrock argues, however, that these similarities offer the possibility of a heroic role for Cynthia just as 'various heroic roles are offered as a possibility for Propertius.'

beloved. In her expressions of grief and loss over Achilles Briseis is cast in the role of lover, much like the figure of Haemon in 2.8. However, in 2.8, Briseis is the beloved whose loss Achilles mourns. And the speaker's characterization of Briseis as *vesana* (insane) in turn links her with an emotional state often associated with the male lover.[27] Moreover, the images of Briseis, frenzied in her grief, hair befouled, recall the extravagant laments of Achilles for Patroklos in the *Iliad*. These topsy-turvy attributions of gender roles mirror the speaker's own vacillations between his identities as the *mollis* poet of elegy (often lamenting the loss of his beloved) and the epic hero whose death and mastery of the beloved ensure his *kleos*. In addition, the reversible roles of Achilles and Briseis not only evoke the speaker's images in 2.8 of *amor* as a turning wheel and of the lover as both conqueror and conquered, but also in 2.9 the speaker's matter-of-fact reference to love's vicissitudes.

The speaker's fluid identification of himself as both abject/feminine and heroic/masculine is reinforced in the image of the widowed Deidamia whose name evokes the transgendered Achilles on Scyros temporarily evading his masculine duties. Interestingly, here the speaker's identification with Achilles seems to be the most intense. He interrupts the impersonal third-person narrative and addresses the dead hero directly, perhaps suggesting that it is when Achilles is in his feminine guise that he is most sympathetic to the male lover. There may even be a hint here of homoeroticism in the speaker's seemingly more personal appeal to the feminized Achilles. The speaker's ambiguous gender identity and poetic discourse culminate in line 18 when he announces that *tunc etiam felix inter et arma pudor* ('and in those days modesty flourished even among warfare'). The happy (*felix*) marriage of *arma* and *pudor* in the speaker's invocation of an idealized past suggests that the intermingling of typical masculine and feminine virtues and spheres of activity constitutes an ideal for the male lover that encompasses the epic and elegiac personas so characteristic of him throughout the first two books of the *Elegies*.

In line 19 the speaker abruptly interrupts his images of a heroic past and addresses the *puella*, implicitly contrasting the noble Achilles to the impious Cynthia.

---

[27] See Catullus 7.10, where the speaker refers to 'Catullus' as *vesanus*.

*at tu non una potuisti nocte vacare,*
  *impia, non unum sola manere diem!*  20
*quin etiam multo duxistis pocula risu:*
  *forsitan et de me verba fuere mala.*
*hic etiam petitur, qui te prius ipse reliquit:*
  *di faciant, isto capta fruare viro!*
*haec mihi vota tuam propter suscepta salutem,*  25
  *cum capite hoc Stygiae iam poterentur aquae,*
*et lectum flentes circum staremus amici?*
  *hic ubi tum, pro di, perfida, quie fuit?*

But you were not able to be unoccupied even for one night,
  impious one, nor to remain alone for one day!
Moreover, you prolonged your drinking with much laughter:
  and perhaps there were nasty words about me.
This man is even being pursued, this man who before left you:
  May the gods grant that you, a captive, enjoy that man!
Were these the vows I took up for your safety,
  when the waters of Styx all but covered your head.
and crying we your friends stood around your bed?
  Where was this man then, before the gods, faithless one,
  and what was he then?

The speaker begins by berating his mistress for never being without male company. But the use of *vacare* to describe the condition in which the male lover prefers his mistress echoes in Poem 2.1 the speaker's implied characterization of the elegiac beloved as the 'nothing' (*nihil*) that inspires his verse.[28] *Vacare* also resonates more generally with the speaker's identification of the elegiac mistress as narrative *materia* for his writing. In Poem 2.9 the speaker implies that he prefers his mistress to be 'empty' or 'unfilled'—to continue to be the *tabula rasa* that he may use to satisfy both his sexual desires and his literary ambitions.[29]

---

[28] In Poem 2.1 the *amator* declares that the *puella*'s words and deeds inspire him to write verse but admits finally that a *maxima de nihilo nascitur historia* ('a great story is born out of nothing'). In Greene 2000: 246, I argue that the logic of the speaker's argument in 2.1 necessitates equating the 'nothing' (*nihil*) that generates the speaker's verse with the mistress herself. As *poeta*, the speaker constructs a *maxima historia* ('greatest account') out of a woman, or *de nihilo*.

[29] *Vacare* can also mean 'to be unoccupied by a syllable.' This reinforces the close association of the elegiac mistress with poetic production.

If another man 'occupies' her then the elegiac lover is not free either to perpetuate his poetic practice or to control her sexuality.

Although the *amator* launches into his characteristic invective toward Cynthia and the vilification of women in general, his primary focus continues to be the presence of the 'other man.' Cynthia's absence, her inaccessibility, gives rise to the *amator*'s fantasies of his mistress enjoying herself with another man. It seems that the speaker evokes the amatory scene not primarily to castigate his beloved but to envision himself as an integral part of that scene. Although the speaker imagines Cynthia and the other man 'laughing in their cups,' he also pictures them exchanging 'nasty words' about him. Now the speaker becomes the 'other man'—the one whose presence not only disrupts the apparent merriment of the two lovers but also brings to the forefront the relationship between the two male rivals in the poem. Moreover, the speaker's presence in the erotic scene evokes the speaker's opening comments about the reversible roles of *iste* and *ego*. In the first line of the poem the words *iste* and *ego* are presented in opposition to one another; the speaker then undercuts that opposition with the words *sed fors*—words that introduce the speaker's assertion that the positions of the two men can change 'even in an hour.' In line 22 the words *forsitan et* echo *sed fors*, and at least implicitly call to mind how quickly the male lover (who is *eiectus*, 'cast out,' for the moment) may reclaim his beloved's attentions.[30]

The interchangeability of the speaker and his male rival intensifies in line 23. Although the emphatic *hic* refers back to the *iste* of line 1, the speaker's statement has a generalizing force that recalls the speaker's earlier comments about the vicissitudes of the rivals' respective positions. Considering how the 'wheel of love' works the speaker could quickly become *hic*, the man who is sought, the beloved instead of the lover. Indeed, the *amator* imagines his own ideal scenario in which the beloved woman, the *domina*, becomes the lover. The

---

[30] Although the speaker imagines his mistress and his rival making nasty remarks about him, the speaker does nonetheless picture himself occupying Cynthia's consciousness. In fact, it is a topos in Roman amatory poetry for the *amator* to admit that he really knows his mistress loves him if she insults him—especially in the presence of others. Catullus 83 is a prime example of this. In the poem the speaker asserts that he knows that Lesbia still desires him because she says *mala plurima* ('many bad things') about him to her husband.

speaker characterizes his ideal mistress as *capta*, evoking the image of the captive Briseis lamenting her dead hero. The speaker's earlier identification with Achilles thus implicitly casts the *amator* in the role of 'that man' (*iste vir*), the *dominum* to a helpless, subservient mistress.

In lines 25–28 the speaker seemingly plays the lover again, reminding Cynthia of *his* fidelity and devotion despite her perfidiousness. Although he describes himself crying by her bed, his depiction of male camaraderie and his intense focus on his rival in line 28 closely link *amicitia* and *amor*. The speaker refers to his amatory vows in the context of describing himself as part of a circle of male companions. Not only does the speaker's reference to his *amici* bring into focus the world of male public culture, but it also suggests a contrast between the faithless vows made by women and the manly pledges among *amici*. The picture of men standing together in solidarity circumscribes the male lover's bond with his mistress within a network of male social relations. In addition, the reference to the speaker's *amici* here recalls the *amicus* of Poem 2.8—whose stoical perspective offers a corrective to the lover's tears. In 2.9 male solidarity (even in tears) seems to provoke the speaker to turn from tears to rage—much like Achilles in 2.8 whose grief changes to wrath and whose focus on the female beloved becomes subordinated to his concern for both his *amicus* (Patroklos) and his rival (Hector).[31] Although the speaker in 2.9 angrily addresses Cynthia as *perfida*, his main object of rage is the 'other man.' Like his heroic *exempla*r Achilles, the speaker 'kills' his rival—only with words as his weapons. By asking Cynthia 'where this man is?,' and 'what or who was he?' the speaker practically calls into question the rival's very existence.

There is also a suggestion of voyeurism here in the image of the male lover looking at his beloved with his male friends. Sharrock has pointed out that the Propertian lover often invites his male addressees to join him in looking at Cynthia and experiencing both the pleasure and pain of loving her.[32] Here too in Poem 2.9 the shared

---

[31] In Sharrock 2000: 270, she points out that in Poem 1.5 Gallus and the speaker (friends and potential rivals over Cynthia) end up crying together, 'comrades in suffering.'
[32] Sharrock 2000: 270.

sorrow of the speaker and his *amici* serves to underscore the primacy of male friendship and its potential for reinforcing traditional heroic values. Indeed, after virtually erasing his rival's existence the *amator* implicitly identifies with both Achilles and Odysseus, imagining himself as both warrior and wanderer.

> *quid si longinquos retinerer miles ad Indos,*
> *aut mea si staret navis in Oceano?* 30
> What if, a soldier, I should be detained in far-off India,
> or my ship were anchored in the sea?

Here the speaker pictures himself as a *durus vir* engaging in the traditional exploits of an epic hero, and in turn invokes the conventional portrait of women as deceitful liars.[33]

> *sed vobis facile est verba et componere fraudes:*
> *hoc unum didicit femina semper opus.*
> *non sic incerto mutantur flamine Syrtes,*
> *nec folia hiberno tam tremefacta Noto,*
> *quam cito feminea non constat foedus in ira,* 35
> *sive ea causa gravis sive ea causa levis.*
> But it is easy for you (women) to contrive falsehoods and deceits:
> this one achievement women have always learned.
> The Syrtes are not so changed by a shifting breeze,
> nor do leaves flutter so in the wintry south wind,
> as quickly as a woman's bond does not stand fast when she is angry,
> whether the cause is serious or slight.

The speaker's invective reiterates a familiar topos in elegy and appears to reinforce the male lover's position of subservience toward his mistress—by implicitly portraying himself as the victim of female treachery. However, this passage describes the mistress' attributes and activities in a way that closely associates the elegiac beloved with the narrator's own poetics. The speaker uses the verb *componere* to characterize what women do most easily, a verb associated earlier in

---

[33] Throughout Propertian elegy, Cynthia is often characterized as *perfida* ('untrustworthy'). In Catullus 70.3–4, the male lover explicitly describes women as deceitful: *sed mulier cupido quod dicit amanti/in vento et rapida scribere oportet aqua* ('what a woman says to her craving lover ought to be written on wind and water').

the *Elegies* with the elegist's particular form of poetic discourse.[34] The close link between woman and *opus* in line 32 more explicitly equates the mistress with the elegiac book. On the one hand, the portrayal of the woman here reiterates the standard image of the mistress as *dura puella*. On the other hand, the association of woman with the poetic *corpus* of the narrator suggests that the speaker asserts mastery over the beloved by subjecting her to his rhetorical control. In addition, the speaker's assertion that women break their bonds whether the cause is 'serious' or 'slight' not only emphasizes women's inherent irrationality but also suggests that the speaker's verse can be identified with both epic and elegy. *Gravis* and *levis* characterize two kinds of poetic discourse and are linked by the speaker to the subject of his verse—the elegiac mistress. In Poem 2.1 the speaker describes his poetic inventions as *causas*.[35] In 2.9 he uses the same word (*causa*) to characterize the motivating force behind the mistress' mobility of temper, thus implying that his own poetics and persona, like the mistress' moods, may be either *gravis* or *levis*, *durus* or *mollis*. In addition, the speaker's association of female deceit with both the *gravis* and *levis* forms of verse suggests that women are the same in both genres, as either elegiac beloveds or epic heroines. Even Penelope—the epitome of female devotion—practices deceit and breaks promises (if only to the suitors). The speaker's vilification of women thus serves to affirm the value of *amicitia*. The image of the mistress violating the bonds of public and private trust (*foedus*) stands in sharp contrast to the ideal of male friendship invoked by the speaker.

Despite the vilification of women in his invective, the speaker's characterization of the elegiac mistress as especially subject to *ira* (*in feminea ira*) also links her with Achilles—whose anger is not only his most defining trait but is also the emotion that motivates him to seek vengeance on his enemies. As in Poem 2.8 (and also in 2.1), here the speaker also transforms the *puella* into the *hostis* of epic by attributing to her the very same emotion most associated with the

---

[34] See Poem 1.7 in particular, where the *amator* suggests to his addressee, Ponticus, that the ability to compose (*componere*) *mollem versum* ('soft verse') may constitute an antidote to the lover's pain.

[35] See a more extensive discussion of Propertius' identification of the elegist's verse as *causa* in Greene 2000: 246.

epic hero with whom the *amator* identifies himself. Moreover, in line 37 the speaker implicitly refers to the mistress' *ira* as a *sententia*, an attribution that accords to the elegiac beloved a purposefulness characteristic of an epic hero. *Sententia* can also refer to a sentence or clause or more generally to the theme of an author's work, which again links the *puella* with the elegiac book and suggests that the mistress' anger is part of an identity the poet/lover has constructed for her so that he himself can play the hero who faces her in 'combat.' The speaker's offer to 'yield' to the *puella* may thus be construed not so much as a reversion to his elegiac identity but as an expression of his recognition that a worthy adversary has, for the moment, vanquished him.

> *nunc, quoniam ista tibi placuit sententia, cedam:*
> > *tela, precor, pueri, promite acuta magis,*
> *figite certantes atque hanc mihi solvite vitam!*
> > *sanguis erit vobis maxima palma meus.*        40
> *sidera sunt testes et matutina pruina*
> > *et furtim misero ianua aperta mihi,*
> *te nihil in vita nobis acceptius umquam:*
> > *nunc quoque erit, quamvis sis inimica, nihil.*
>
> Now, since that decision pleases you, I will yield:
> > Cupids, I beg you, let loose sharper arrows,
> Compete to pierce me and free me from this life!
> > My blood will be the greatest victory for you.
> The stars will be my witnesses and the morning frost
> > and the door opened in secret to wretched me,
> nothing has ever been more pleasing to me in life than you:
> > now nothing will be, although you are an enemy.

In spite of the speaker's seeming willingness to admit defeat and his characteristeric portrayal of himself as *miser* in line 42, his acknowledgement that he yields because the *puella*'s anger 'pleases' her suggests that the *amator*'s position of subservience is simply part of the elegiac game.[36] In Poem 2.1, the speaker asserts that the mistress' resistance and the amatory 'violence' resulting from it give rise to his poetic compositions. Here there is also the suggestion that the mistress' anger

---

[36] For the humorous, theatrical, and artificial aspects of Roman elegy, see Veyne 1988: especially chapter 3.

Gender and Genre in Propertius 2.8 and 2.9  399

may be a source of pleasure for both of them. If the *amator* yields, then the *puella* can once again be cast in the conventional role of *domina* in the poet's verse. And indeed in lines 38–9, the speaker re-casts himself in the conventional role of lover, beseeching the Cupids to increase his emotional pain and end his life. In line 40 the images of blood and the palm tree of victory, however, recall the bloody corpse of Achilles and his glorious victory over Hector. To be sure, the speaker envisions himself here not as the conqueror but as the conquered. Yet he pictures himself dying a bloody death for love—the same death he imagines in 2.8 and describes in 2.1 as a death worthy of an epic hero.

Although the speaker asserts in line 43 that nothing in his life is more pleasing to him than Cynthia, the apposition of *te* and *nihil* (as well as their adjacent positions to one another) recalls the implication in Poem 2.1 that the speaker constructs a *maxima historia de nihilo*, or out of woman.[37] In 2.9 the speaker thus suggests that what really pleases him are the possibilities for poetic composition offered by the elegiac beloved. Indeed, the identification of *te* with the neuter *nihil* reinforces the image of the mistress as a dehumanized object, an image that resonates with the speaker's characterization of her as *ferrea* in Poem 2.8. Also, the fact that the speaker depicts Cynthia as both pleasing and an enemy (*inimica*) implies not only that her resistance to him animates the lover's desire but that the mistress' status as *dura puella* fuels the poet's literary imagination as well. As in 2.8, here the speaker's characterization of the beloved as *inimica* implicitly identifies the male lover as a *hostis* and also associates his poetic discourse with the *durus* style of epic. But unlike in 2.8, in Poem 2.9 the poet/lover constitutes himself as a *hostis* primarily in relation to his male rival. The mistress is the medium of exchange between men, offering the possibility of heroic action for the lovers seemingly competing for Cynthia's attentions. In lines 47–8, despite adopting the characteristically abject pose of the lover, the speaker prays that his rival will turn to stone in the act of love.

---

[37] Earlier in 2.1 the speaker declares the *puella* as the source of his verse and then admits that a *maxima de nihilo nascitur historia* (a momentous history is being born from nothing). In Greene 2000: 246, I argue that the logic of the poem necessitates equating the 'nothing' (*nihil*) that generates the speaker's verse with the mistress herself.

> nec domina ulla meo ponet vestigia lecto: 45
> solus ero, quoniam non licet esse tuum.
> atque utinam, si forte pios eduximus annos,
> ille vir in medio fiat amore lapis!
> No other mistress will step into my bed:
> I will be alone, since I cannot be yours.
> And yet I wish that, if I have spent pious years,
> that man should turn to stone in the midst of love!

Although the speaker's focus on revenge against his rival may seem sudden, his invocation of *ille vir* recalls the figure of the other man (*iste*) at the beginning of the poem. The fact that the speaker imagines his rival as *lapis* serves to elevate his prayer to the status of a curse, since *lapis* is a stone thought to have divine or magical properties.[38] The implication here is that the speaker pictures the other man not only being unable to satisfy the *puella*, but also turning into a lifeless statue. One of the most intriguing features of this image is the fact that in elegy it is women who are usually depicted as statues.[39] Propertius suggests that the *amator*'s revenge on his rival not only involves feminizing the other man, but also turning him into an art-object. The image of *ille vir* as passive matter links him with the elegiac mistress who is associated throughout the *Elegies* with the narrative *materia* for the poet's verse. The speaker thus imagines himself perpetrating revenge on his rival by turning him into an inanimate object over which the *amator*, as artist, may exercise supreme control. Picturing the other man as *lapis* also allows the speaker to imagine 'killing off' his rival; the association of lapis with tombstones reinforces the sense that the speaker imagines his rival dead as well as impotent.

In the last four lines of the poem the speaker evokes a bloody scene that again links *amor* to images of death and glory.

> Non ob regna magis diris cecidere sub armis
> Thebani media non sine matre duces, 50

---

[38] See *Oxford Latin Dictionary* 1001, under *lapis* (1b and 4d).

[39] See especially Propertius 1.3, in which Cynthia is portrayed as a statue-like figure while the male lover is the artist arranging her as the 'real' Cynthia sleeps. See also Ovid *Amores* 1.7, where the narrator explicitly compares the elegiac mistress to blocks of white Parian marble. For discussions of the elegiac woman as art-object, see Sharrock 1991a; also Greene 1995: 308.

*quam, mihi si media liceat pugnare puella,*
    *mortem ego non fugiam morte subire tua.*
No more did the Theban princes fall under dreadful arms
    for the sake of the throne, their mother in between,
than I, if I could fight with my mistress between us,
    would willingly die in killing you.

Here the *amator* imagines himself fighting his rival to the death and again uses a mythological *exemplum* not only to align himself with the heroic values of epic but also to dramatize quite forcefully the way in which the mediating *puella* facilitates male reciprocity. While earlier in the poem the *puella*'s nearly fatal illness allowed friends to exchange tears, here 'with the mistress in the middle' the speaker imagines himself exchanging deaths with his rival. The implicit comparison between the two rivals and the brothers Eteocles and Polynices (*Thebani duces*, 'Theban leaders') heightens the closeness of the connection between the speaker and the other man. The two men (*iste* and the *ego* of the poem) are in fact closer than Achilles and Patroklos or than the speaker and his *amici*.[40] This closeness between the two male rivals reinforces the speaker's assertion at the beginning of the poem about the interchangeability of their positions. Although the Theban princes are fighting for a throne and not for a woman, the parallel between the princes and the two male lovers suggests that the acquisition of political power and the possession of the beloved are analogous endeavors. Propertius implies that what counts most for the lover is not union with his mistress but the demonstration of his superiority in the male arena. Indeed Achilles, the speaker's heroic *exemplar* here and in 2.8, does want to win back Briseis, but that is not what activates his heroism. Rather, it is his desire to wreak vengeance on his rival that satisfies his demand for justice and wins him his *kleos*. The speaker's declaration in line 52 that he would not flee death parallels Achilles' conscious decision to pursue a path of glory. Unlike Achilles, however, the speaker does not conquer his opponent. Rather, the *amator* envisions himself and his rival engaged in a reciprocity that is nearly always absent in the imagined relationship between the

---

[40] See Sharrock 2000: 280–1, for an interesting discussion of the last four lines of Poem 2.9.

lover and his mistress. The exchange of one death for another in the last line of 2.9 reinforces the way in which the elegiac lover defines himself through symmetrical homosocial relations.

The parallel between the *puella* and Jocasta at the end emphasizes the way in which the dual roles of the elegiac mistress— as both 'wife' and 'mother'—serve both to catalyze and to thwart male heroic endeavor.[41] It is not entirely clear whether Jocasta's role in the scene is merely as a spectator or as a mediator between her two sons. Both Camps and Richardson argue that it has to be the former for the parallel between Jocasta and the *puella* to be consistent. Camps, however, does acknowledge that there may also be a reminiscence here of the version of the story in which Jocasta attempts to separate the two brothers and then kills herself when she is unsuccessful.[42] In any case, Propertius was probably familiar with the two versions of the story and may very well be invoking both of them here. This would be entirely consistent with his portrayal of Cynthia throughout the first two books of the *Elegies*. On the one hand, the wayward Cynthia distracts the male lover from his masculine duties. On the other hand, the image of the *puella* as the 'mother' of the *amator* can suggest the importance of the woman's role in the continuation of the speaker's poetic practice. In addition, as Sharrock points out, the reference to Theban kings may also allude to Oedipus and Laius—who become unwitting rivals for the same woman.[43] In that case, the parallel between Cynthia and Jocasta becomes less ambiguous. Just as Jocasta is both wife and mother to Oedipus, Cynthia has also been depicted as both 'wife' and 'mother' to the *amator*. Whether the *puella* is pictured as a passive spectator or as a 'meddling mother,' she is nonetheless presented as subordinate to an overarching structure that privileges *amicitia* over *amor*. The whole poem is framed by an image of the interlocking identities of the two male rivals. From the very first line,

---

[41] In Propertius 1.11 the speaker compares Cynthia to his own mother. In Greene 1995: 314, I argue that the shift in Poem 1.11 from the image of Cynthia as seductress to an image of her as a nurturing mother points up the bi-polar representation of women in the poem as either good or bad, virtuous or depraved.

[42] See Richardson 1977: 240; and Camps 1967: 108.

[43] See Sharrock 2000: 280–1, for a discussion of how the *Thebani duces* may also refer to Oedipus and Laius.

with its syntactic link between *ego* and *iste,* the poem dramatizes the extent to which the bond between the two men is stronger than that between the male lover and his mistress. The final image of the two men dying together as equals, with the woman 'in the middle,' casts the *puella* as the third person in the triangle, as either a peripheral presence or an obstructive force in the fulfillment of masculine, heroic identity.

# 15

# 'Beyond Good and Evil': Tarpeia and Philosophy in the Feminine (4.4)[1]

*Micaela Janan*

> Past and past the waters glide,
> And I bathe my hands and hair,
> Lo, my hands stain not the stream.
> Did I not say this was a dream?
> Face nor hands are hard and red,
> And soft leaves drop all round my head,
> And soft weeds round my dipping feet
> Stir and change and gleam.
> I rest! My rest is very sweet.
>
> Swinburne[2]

Propertius 4.4 retells as a love story how the Vestal Virgin Tarpeia betrayed Rome to the Sabines. As in other versions of the tale, she bargains with Rome's enemy and leads them into the Capitoline citadel by an unsuspected path; the Sabine king, Tatius, rewards her by having his soldiers crush her to death beneath their shields. But Propertius uniquely attributes her treason to passionate love for Tatius: she bargained to be his queen, not for gold, as more cynical

---

[1] All translations in this paper are the author's own except where noted. Where the author has left French untranslated we have done the same. This paper is a chapter of Janan's 2001 book *The Politics of Desire*. Where Janan refers to other chapters the editors have simply changed that to name-date citation.

[2] 'The Dream by the River' (Swinburne 1925 vol I: 99).

authors have it.[3] How to interpret this elegy's revision of a founding Roman myth has puzzled numerous commentators, who commonly throw all questions onto the axis of Augustan politics. Some see the poem as evidence of the poet's tardy sympathy with Augustus' program: Propertius allegedly repudiates pure love-elegy as inimical to Augustus' moral and political reforms and condemns Tarpeia to prove he has rejected his old elegiac sympathies.[4] Others detect irony beneath his patriotism, proclaiming his 'Augustan' moral severity but a thin veneer, donned for protection from an increasingly intolerant regime: Propertius reveals his still-warm elegiac loyalty, they say, when he converts a tale of Tarpeia's greed into a chronicle of her star-crossed love for the Sabine king.[5]

Yet this poem's ambiguities, which lend themselves to such divergent interpretations, exceed the frame of Augustan politics alone. This chapter argues that elegy 4.4 interrogates the very binary logic implied in framing its loyalties as either 'pro-Augustan' or 'anti-Augustan.'[6] One of Lacan's most inspired and unorthodox disciples, Luce Irigaray, can help us here by extending the trajectory of Lacan's

[3] Zofia Gansiniec offers a useful conspectus both of the ancient evidence for, and previous scholarship on, the legend of Tarpeia—though, rather surprisingly, she dismisses Propertius' version from consideration in a contemptuous footnote (1949: 22.53).

[4] E.g. Alfonsi 1945: 78 (with some caution: he attributes to all of Propertius' work, including Book 4, the same reservations about the Augustan program that the *Aeneid* reveals to have haunted Vergil); Grimal 1951b; Grimal 1952: 315–18; Boucher 1965: 148 (who in fact sees the whole of Book 4 as the flowering of a patriotism that he argues was always present, though more muted, in Propertius' verse); Weeber 1977: 101–2.

[5] E.g. Paratore 1936: 130; Baker 1968a: 342–4; Hallett 1971: 115–21 (with some reservations: Hallett argues that Propertius despises Tarpeia's actual betrayal of Rome and her 'materialistic beliefs' that lead her to try to win Tatius with the gift of the city rather than herself); Sullivan 1976: 136–7; La Penna 1977: 87; Sullivan 1984: 31; Stahl 1985: 279–305.

[6] Duncan Kennedy's work makes the very assumptions behind the conceptual division 'pro-' vs. 'anti-Augustan' seem appallingly naïve. Assessing whether a given text supports, opposes, or is neutral towards Augustus involves us in logical contradiction: 'a situation deemed historically determined is studied in accordance with terms and criteria thought not to be so determined' (Kennedy 1992: 26). Take, for example, his analysis of Ovid's flippant agnosticism: *expedit esse deos et, ut expedit, esse putemus* ('it is useful that the gods exist, and since it's useful, let's think they do,' *Ars* 1.637, editors' translation) is usually taken as ironic and 'anti-Augustan' insofar as it interprets moral crusades as a cynical form of social control.

thought on the feminine far beyond where it stood at the time of his death in 1981.[7] Her work confronts contemporary thought with the problematic elements of a consistently unacknowledged symbolization system that does *not* cleanly divide into binary oppositions—a system she calls 'feminine' insofar as culture has (as we have already noted often in this book) traditionally assigned the messier ambiguities of thought to Woman as a force of disruption and disorder.[8] Guided principally by Irigaray's critique of conventional epistemology, I shall show that the Tarpeia poem abounds in details that cannot be captured in 'either/or' logic—details linked (non-coincidentally) to feminine desire.

Take, for example, the fatal body of water that initially brings together Tarpeia and Tatius. The paths of Sabine king and Vestal

---

However, Ovid's statement, although rhetorically resisting its own implication in this logic of explanation, cannot be exempted from its effects, for Ovid's ironic and flippant appropriation is part of what gives this logic its social meaning and force, and so helps to render legitimate the moral and religious programme of Augustus. This is the discursive context which both enables the *Ars Amatoria* as witty and sophisticated text *and* constitutes it at the same time as what-must-be-repressed. This is the logic that helps to generate the 'necessity' of an 'Augustus,' and thus plays an integral part in creating and sustaining the position of Augustus (Kennedy 1992: 45).

Kennedy does not claim to be able to avoid the dilemma he has so well elucidated; language functions pragmatically on the basis of binary oppositions, an inescapable impasse. He does, however, put the key dyads that have long governed the analysis of 'Augustan' poetry into question as a tactical maneuver designed to defamiliarize seemingly 'well-known' territory. I, too, aware that the shifty properties of binaries cannot be evaded, nonetheless hope to raise questions in this paper either never posed, or posed with insufficient force, about Propertius' text.

[7] I do not wish to pass over lightly the split between Irigaray and Lacan that resulted in her expulsion from the *École freudienne* in 1974. However, the only difference between them that is relevant to the present discussion is that she elaborated the possible conceptual content of the feminine as a category of thought, while his last seminars largely abandoned the project in favor of articulating the exact relationship between the registers of the Real, the Symbolic and the Imaginary. Her meditations are an original extension of Lacan's thought on the feminine, compatible with its principles, and at the same time a brilliant innovation on its fundamental assumptions. Margaret Whitford incorporates, in her discussion of Irigaray's thought, an evenhanded assessment of its debt to Lacan (Whitford 1991).

[8] For a discussion of the ancient manifestation of conceptual chaos associated with Woman, see Lovibond 1994 on the Pythagorean table of opposites. I also discuss the Pythagorean table's implications for gender conceptualization at greater length below.

Virgin cross at a shepherd's spring that Tatius palisades for his military camp; Tarpeia sees him when she draws water from the spring, and falls passionately in love. But how she *can* draw water despite Tatius' barricade has baffled commentators. Emendations and line transpositions have been freely offered to try to bring these puzzling verses into sensible coordination. Some scholars make two springs from one,[9] or banish one of the irreconcilable allusions to it;[10] others poke holes in the barrier;[11] still others try a combination of approaches.[12] Yet each suggested change to the text garners trenchant objections and small assent.

The spring's inconvenience to smooth explanation is striking: both carefully guarded and easily available to an unarmed enemy girl, it cuts across the very conceptual categories that seek to define it. The spring deconstructs such oppositions as enemy territory/native territory; inside/outside; martial/pastoral; closed/open. Tarpeia's act of daily devotion to Vesta marks this mysterious fount as intractable to conventional logic; we can neither locate it entirely within, nor entirely without, Tatius' barricade.

Moreover, as the work of Harry Rutledge, John Warden, and F.E. Brenk makes clear, water is throughout the poem's central point of reference.[13] Stunned by Tatius' good looks, Tarpeia drops her ritual water-jar when she first sees him (21–2); she invents ritual excuses to visit the sacred spring, so that she can spy on her beloved (22–3); she worries that her tears of amorous frustration may have quenched the perpetual flame on Vesta's altar (45–6). The elegy's liquid imagery measures Tarpeia's desire for Tatius as a passion that exceeds all 'proper' bounds. But *why* water—why does *that* element in particular

---

[9] Baehrens 1880, Postgate 1894 (as indicated by their texts and *apparati critici*; both rearrange the relevant lines, while Postgate prints *exili* for *ex illo* in 4.4.14); Rothstein 1898 (1966) *ad* 4.4.15; Richardson 1977 *ad* 4.4.15; Marr 1970: 167–9; Walsh 1983: 75.

[10] So Enk 1911: 311–12 (*montem* for *fontem* in 7, after Heinsius); Richmond 1928 (*furtim* rather than *fontem* in 15); Camps 1965 (*contra* for *fontem* in 7).

[11] For example, Wellesley 1969: 97–8 (following Karsten 1915) makes the barricade three-sided, leaving one approach open; similarly, Hanslik 1962: 237–9, declares that *praecingit* (7) means 'bordered,' so that Tatius does not fully enclose the *fons*.

[12] E.g. Butler-Barber 1933 (1964): 344–5.

[13] Rutledge 1964: 70–1; Warden 1978: 177–8; Brenk 1979.

govern this poem (rather than, say, the commoner erotic metaphors of fire or heat)?[14]

## THE MECHANICS OF FLUIDS

Luce Irigaray's essay 'The Mechanics of Fluids' can illuminate the water imagery that organizes this poem's resistant ambiguities; her thought also sheds light on why the heart of the elegy takes shape in Tarpeia's own words, a long soliloquy that mimes desire articulated from a 'feminine' vantage point. Irigaray assesses conventional epistemology as (mis)informed by an exclusionary model of understanding—a model that grapples with the welter of phenomena by calling upon binary opposition to establish distinctive classes. Such a model takes 'black' to be the opposite and exclusion of 'white,' for example, as 'male' of 'female,' 'rational' of 'irrational,' 'good' of 'bad.' Each term is logically impenetrable to the other, as if founded upon a metaphorical 'mechanics of solids.' Moreover, the meaning produced by such binarisms is never neutral: one term is always posited as inferior and supplementary to the other, as 'female' commonly is to 'male.' Various types of post-structuralism have demonstrated the falsity of this construction, by showing the putative 'superior' term to operate according to principles embodied in the 'inferior, supplementary' term, which is thus transformed.

Yet Irigaray goes beyond demonstrating 'bad faith' to show the putative knowledge produced by these binarisms to be implicitly gendered male. Her assumption should be familiar territory to classicists; Genevieve Lloyd has shown that the Pythagoreans offered an early example of it. Their famous table of opposites construes the 'bounded'—that is, that which can be grasped by the rational subject as precise and clearly determined—as male and good. The female and bad aligns with the 'unbounded'—the unlimited, irregular and

---

[14] On fire or heat as metaphors for love, see Nisbet-Hubbard 1970 *ad* Horace *Odes* 1.19.5, 1.33.6, Onians 1951: 151–2.

disorderly.[15] In contrast to this tradition, Irigaray seeks out a 'feminine' logic that escapes the conceptual tyranny of stable forms, and that offers a new metaphorical basis for thinking—a logic analogous to the 'mechanics of fluids.' Fluids 'resist' in that they refuse to be reduced to mathematical formulae, like the more biddable nature of solids. Fluids challenge the idea that dividing the world into clean oppositions ('either $x$ or not-$x$') adequately expresses some underlying truth.[16]

The metaphoric logic behind Irigaray's quest would have been familiar not only to the Pythagoreans, but to Romans near Propertius' own time. Sandra Joshel and Catharine Edwards have recently documented the extent to which Rome characterized the rejected, inferior, and untrue as liquid and feminine, while ascribing hardness, dryness, fixity and masculinity to 'the good.' Sallust, Horace, Seneca and others speak of vice in images of insidious flood that wash away both personal virtue and the social order, softening and effeminizing Roman moral rigor.[17] Joshel and Edwards concern themselves chiefly with ethical discourse but, set in the wider context of Roman moral philosophy, the trajectory of their thought intersects epistemology itself. Cicero, for example, treats 'the good' as virtually synonymous with 'the real,' with 'being' as opposed to 'seeming,' as in the Platonic and Stoic traditions he inherits. The truth the vicious person fails to

---

[15] Lloyd 1984: 3. For more on the Pythagorean table of opposites, see Janan 2001 chapter 1.

[16] Here and in the previous paragraph, I have summarized the ideas of Irigaray 1977 (1985): 106–18, but Irigaray 1991 takes up these thoughts again and expands on them. The best guide to Irigaray's thought on these and other matters remains Whitford 1991.

[17] Joshel 1992a: 117–21; Edwards 1993: 173–5. Support for the idea that greater liquidity, weakness, deviance, and propensity for irrationality characterized the feminine was also available to Romans from a 'scientific' quarter, i.e. from medicine. Heinrich von Staden and Monica Green have both demonstrated, for example, that Celsus (writing in the first quarter of the first century CE, under Tiberius) inherits the prevalent Greek conceptualization of women, attested throughout the Hippocratic corpus' gynecological writings: women are wetter than men, and their health (including their mental health) depends upon the proper management of their bodily fluids (von Staden 1991; Green 1985). The overabundance or improper situation of women's bodily fluids—particularly menstrual blood—may result in delirium. Though Celsus was no slave to Greek medical ideas, he does bring into Roman discourse a muted version of the Greek view of female physiology as damp chaos. For an overview of Greek gynecological beliefs, see King 1983, Hanson 1990 and 1992.

see resembles the Platonic Forms—solid, stable, measurable.[18] Cicero also plays upon the etymological connection between *virtus* and *vir*, depicting moral truth as something solid and masculine in the midst of feminine flux; his philosophy can justly be described as a masculinist 'mechanics of solids.'[19]

These associative links among untruth-as-vice, the feminine and liquidity—as opposed to truth-as-virtue, the masculine and solidity—clarify some of the recalcitrant details of the Tarpeia elegy. Yet the poem does not simply reproduce Roman conceptions of 'masculine' vs. 'feminine' properties. Rather, Propertius questions Rome's cultural prejudices by revealing the hasty sutures in logic that support them. When he unfolds Tarpeia's story and grants her a voice, he sketches an epistemology much closer to the beliefs of Heraclitus, for example, or the Skeptic philosopher Carneades (whose visit to Rome so deeply impressed its citizens in the century before Propertius' own).[20] Both these thinkers deny that philosophy elucidates a truth conceived as the fixed substrate beneath phenomena in flux. Both challenge the idea that the universe naturally divides into fixed and stable binarisms; for neither is philosophy the grasping of stable forms.[21] Taken to its logical

---

[18] On truth as solid and stable, see, e.g. *Tusc.* 2.21.48 (the part of the soul devoid of reason is *mollis*), 4 *passim*, esp. 4.5.10–6.11 (*placida quietaque constantia* [calm and quiet consistency] characterizes the rational soul), 4.10.23 (by contrast, corrupt beliefs are like bad blood or an overflow of phlegm or bile); 4.13.31 (the essence of virtue is consistency of beliefs and judgments, firmness and stability [*firmitas, stabilitas*]). On truth as measurable, see, e.g. *Off.* 1.59 (ethical duty can be calculated, like a problem in accounting), 3 *passim*, (which focuses entirely on comparing two goods in order to distinguish the true from the apparent good—e.g. 3.3.11: measuring one good against another is like comparing weights in a balance scale).

[19] *Tusc.* 2.18.43.

[20] Carneades visited Rome in 155 BCE, about a century before Propertius' birth; however, Cicero features a précis of Carneades' addresses to the city in *De Republica*, finished in 51 BCE, which indicates that the philosopher's ideas were still matters of lively debate in Propertius' youth.

[21] For Heraclitus' views on change, see the fragments collected and discussed by Kirk-Raven 1957 (esp. pages 196–202). Though assessing Heraclitus' cosmology on the basis of our scanty fragments is a matter of controversy, the ancients certainly believe that his views denied a stable substrate to phenomena: see Plato, *Cra.* 401d, *Tht.* 160d, 179e–180b; Aristotle, *de An.* 405a25, *Metaph.* 987a33, 1005b25. Indeed, Heraclitus' conviction that binary opposition is an illusion drives Aristotle to distraction: he returns repeatedly to this doctrine, trying to refute it (see *Top.* 159b30, *Ph.* 185b20, *Metaph.* 1010a13, 1012a24, 1012a34, 1062a32, 1063b25). See also Cherniss 1935, esp. 380–2; Kirk 1954 (who offers a bolder and—to my mind—more

conclusion, this alternate frame of reference not only undermines the hierarchy that raises Man over Woman, but denies that such dichotomies order existence in any meaningful way.

## IN A STRANGE LAND

With this philosophical background in mind, let us turn to the poem's opening and consider the uneasy montage of disjunctive images that shuffles before the reader's eyes:

*Tarpeium nemus et Tarpeiae turpe sepulcrum*
  *fabor et antiqui limina capta Iovis.*
*lucus erat felix hederoso conditus antro,*
  *multaque nativis obstrepit arbor aquis,*
*Silvani ramosa domus, quo dulcis ab aestu*
  *fistula poturas ire iubebat ovis.*
*hunc Tatius fontem vallo praecingit acerno,*
  *fidaque suggesta castra coronat humo.* (1–8)

I shall speak of the Tarpeian grove and the sordid tomb of Tarpeia and the captured threshold of ancient Jove. There was a fertile grove enclosed in an ivy-covered dell, and many a tree murmurs in reply to nature's waters—the branchy home of Silvanus, to which the sweet shepherd's pipe bade the sheep withdraw from the heat and drink. This spring Tatius bounds with a maple palisade, and encircles his loyal camp with piled-up earth.

We are offered the queer juxtaposition of a grove, a tomb, and a hostage god's threshold—a completely imaginary triad, to boot. Tarquin destroyed Tarpeia's burial place when he built the temple

---

satisfying interpretation of the fragments than that found in Kirk-Raven 1957); Guthrie 1962: 435–69 (whose notes usefully summarize previous bibliography); Kahn 1979 is also a useful companion to the fragments (though I believe him mistaken in interpreting the crucial fr. D90 as a record of Heraclitus' belief in periodic cosmic conflagration). As for Carneades' views: Cicero, in *De Republica*, has 'Philus' painstakingly summarize a speech Carneades is said to have made defending ethical relativism (*Rep.* 3.8–31). Although 'Laelius' refutes the argument, it must have seemed a formidable threat to merit the considerable trouble Cicero takes both to redact and refute it.

of *Iuppiter Capitolinus*;[22] the two monuments never shared the hill.[23] As for the 'Tarpeian grove' (*Tarpeium nemus*): many reasonably find this element disturbing, insofar as Propertius introduces and drops it with equally little ceremony, even though his aetiological program should compel him to trace its history; moreover, no other source attests its existence. Accordingly, some adopt Kraffert's emendation to *scelus* ('curse; crime') while others assimilate the *nemus* to the *lucus* in line 3—though that helps little, given that neither does the *lucus* inspire an aetion, it just colorfully shades the background.[24] The question of what these and the other prominently placed elements of the ekphrasis have to do with one another—how we might reconcile the elements of a peaceful pastoral scene (grove, spring, sheep, shepherd's pipe) with a tomb, or, more strangely still, with the martial elements picked out by 'Jove's captured threshold,' Tatius palisading the spring and arraying his army around it—Propertius leaves unanswered.[25] But the obscurity of the opening ekphrasis dramatizes the role interpretation plays in what passes for perception. Ancient as well as modern analyses of perception recognize the way that convention inscribes and naturalizes interpretation in the visual artifact, so as to make a legible whole out of disparate objects.[26] Stripped of such subtle framing, the opening lines, in their obstinate opacity, baffle any claim to the 'pure' perception of truth,

---

[22] Plut. *Rom.* 18.1.

[23] Richardson construes the *limina* as indicating the temple of *Iuppiter Feretrius* (Richardson 1977 *ad* 4.4.1–2). But Propertius himself thinks of 'Tarpeian' Jupiter as having no temple on the Capitoline at this time (*Tarpeiusque pater nuda de rupe tonabat*, 'Tarpeian Jupiter used to thunder from a bare rock,' 4.1.7, editors' translation); he must, therefore, be thinking of *Iuppiter Capitolinus*.

[24] W.A. Camps amends *nemus* to *lucus* outright (Camps 1965: 21 and *ad* 4.4.1); Shackleton-Bailey preserves the vulgate reading, but calls Kraffert's conjecture 'tempting' (Shackleton-Bailey 1956: 234). Among those who take *nemus* in 4.1 to be identical with the *lucus* of 4.3: Butler-Barber 1933: 344; Wellesley 1969: 96; Marr 1970: 170–1; King 1990: 226.

[25] Stahl remarks upon the conflict between martial and pastoral imagery (Stahl 1985: 281).

[26] Among Propertius' near-contemporaries, Lucretius emphasizes this necessary intentionality when he intricately imbricates the physiology of perception and erotic love (*DRN* IV). Some objects impinge upon the sight willy-nilly, but perception of others requires active projection of the subject's will (4.805–17): desire and perception influence one another (4.1061–67, 1153–70). For an illuminating discussion of relations between perception and desire in Lucretius, see Nussbaum 1989; for a

truth unmediated by representation: their apparent heterogeny demands a new way of seeing the (previously) unimaginable. The rest of the poem elaborates upon that need for a different vantage.

In the next moment after this serenely pastoral opening strangely stained with martial and morbid elements, Tarpeia sees Tatius for the first time and the water-jar slips from her nerveless fingers.[27] Graeco-Roman art and legend lend her gesture sinister significance. Giulia Sissa has discussed the ways in which the ancients associated vessels, especially water vessels, with female sexuality.[28] A woman's sexuality is a container for the precious resource of fertility, a container properly unbreached. That metaphorical thinking shapes Roman folk-legend when, for example, Tuccia the Vestal disproves the rumors of her unchastity by miraculously carrying water in a sieve.[29] Being chaste, she can magically seal a container that should leak—but the Vestal Tarpeia, whose love has made her ritual chastity impossible to her, makes even an unperforated container spill its contents. Moreover, as Tarpeia drew this water to clean Vesta's temple, the poet remarks that the jar 'hurt her head' (*at illi/urgebat medium fictilis urna caput*, 4.4.15–16). That phrase eerily echoes another Propertian heroine (whose story I scrutinize further in Janan 2001 chapter 9): when his idealized Roman matron Cornelia swears to her own chastity under threat of the Danaids' suffering, she says 'if I lie, may that fruitless water jar, the punishment of the sisters, hurt my shoulders' (*si fallo, poena sororum/infelix umeros urgeat urna meos*, 4.11.27–28). Sissa has shown that the Danaids' unfillable sieves represent their flawed sexuality, failed as maidens and failed as brides.[30] Propertius' elaborate cross-referencing between his two elegies casts the shadow of those sieves upon Tarpeia's oozy, burdensome water-jar.

---

sophisticated application of ancient theories of the imbrication of vision and desire to Propertius 2.31/32, see Hubbard 1984.

[27] On the jarring effect of this passage's mixing of pastoral with military imagery, that brings their assumed mutual exclusion into question, see the subtle analysis of Miller-Platter 1999b.

[28] Sissa 1990: esp. 127–77.

[29] Sissa 1990: 127–9, discusses Tuccia's miracle as recorded in V. Max. 8.1.5 and Dion. Hal. 2.69.

[30] Sissa 1990: 127–34, 162–3, 171–2.

Yet the symbol of these murderous brides does not unambiguously condemn Tarpeia: Propertius writes her story as both the same and significantly different. True that Tarpeia expects to wed Tatius. She says, for example, 'Rome betrayed comes to you as no insignificant dowry' (*dos tibi non humilis prodita Roma venit*, 4.4.56). Tatius' last words to her echo this expectation when he says '*Marry*, and ascend the bed of my kingdom!' ('*nube*' ait '*et regni scande cubile mei!*,' 4.4.90). But in contrast to the Danaid myth, this bridegroom kills the bride: the Capitoline that Tatius mockingly calls his 'marriage bed' sees *his* murderous duplicity, not Tarpeia's. And though scrupulous to punish her, Tatius happily keeps the fruit of her treachery, Rome. Tatius lies and deceives—the very acts supposed to define women, especially in sexual affairs.[31] The poem proffers this, *à l'air naïf*, as the benchmark of his honor: he dupes Tarpeia and thus 'not even as an enemy gave honor to crime' (*neque enim sceleri dedit hostis honorem*, 4.4.89). Yet this articulation ironically makes the 'superior' term depend upon principles defined by the rejected, subordinate term: 'masculine honor' becomes a subset of 'feminine wiles.'

## A BEND IN THE WALL

Even without the hypocrite Tatius as her foil, Tarpeia-as-flawed-vessel embodies a principle strangely necessary to Rome's welfare, if little acknowledged: the breach she opens in Rome's walls gives them a necessary elasticity. David Konstan has elucidated the way Roman historiography grapples with the contradictory effects of boundaries: boundaries define the city-state, but they also limit its growth and expansion.[32] Sandra Joshel and Patricia Joplin have, in turn, demonstrated the metaphorical alignment between physical and conceptual boundaries of the state, and female sexuality; sexual unions, whether

---

[31] Instances of this calumny are too numerous in classical literature to list here, but as representative examples consider: Catullus 70; Horace *Odes* 2.8 and Nisbet-Hubbard 1970's introductory note citing parallel examples of women forsworn in love; Propertius 2.16.47–8; Ovid *Amores* 3.3.

[32] Konstan 1986: 198–201.

'Beyond Good and Evil': Tarpeia and Philosophy    415

rapes, marriages, or seductions, regularly 'breach' the polity's defining limits so that it may move on to a new phase. Livy, for example, dramatically connects the ultimately fatal sexual assaults upon Lucretia and Verginia to the downfall of the Roman monarchy and of the *decemviri*'s tyranny respectively.[33] Similarly, Tarpeia makes possible Rome as Propertius and his contemporaries know it. Pierre Grimal notes that the Caesars proudly traced their ancestry all the way back to the Sabine king, Tatius; the Sabines in general figure importantly in Roman history. Their stealthy entry into Rome sets the stage for eventually reconciling the two warring factions and, gradually, for Rome to absorb her former enemies completely.[34] Tarpeia's action is both abhorred and utterly necessary—the type of *felix culpa* that Roman legend regularly stages and that just as regularly demands the sacrifice of a woman.[35]

Tarpeia thus bears the unhappy burden of history: the resolution she proposes to Rome's conflict with the Sabines foreshadows the principles of their eventual reconciliation.[36] Tarpeia says that her marriage will 'dissolve' (*solvere*, 59) the two established battle lines and 'soften' (*molliet*, 62) their arms (her metaphors of liquescence and plasticity are telling). Marriage does do so, but not hers to Tatius; rather, the Sabine women's to Roman men.[37] Yet her ironically

---

[33] Joplin 1990, Joshel 1992a, discussing *Ab Urbe Condita* 1.57–60, 3.44–8 (the story of Appius and Verginia receives further attention in Janan 2001 chapter 15 of this book, because of its importance to understanding Prop. 4.11, the Cornelia elegy). Joplin 1991 analyzes the Tereus-Procne-Philomela story from Ovid's *Metamorphoses*, further illuminating the way Roman literature allegorically links women's body boundaries to the limits of the state.

[34] Grimal 1951b, 1952: 315–18.

[35] Joseph Rykwert notes that a quasi-apotheosized Tarpeia, albeit a traitor of legendary stature, received state sacrifice at the opening of the Parentalia, the Roman feast of All Souls. Such dubious heroines regularly figure in foundation stories; Tarpeia is to be identified, Rykwert declares, as 'the virgin at the sacred hearth [by whose] guilty or substitute intercourse with god or hero, as well as its punishment, a new city, a new alliance, a new nation, a new state are founded' (Rykwert 1976: 160). Miles 1992 deftly uses Rykwert's observations to explicate Tarpeia's significance for the Roman conceptualization of marriage (183–4).

[36] Lucia Beltrami and Pierre Grimal both see the similarity between the aim of Tarpeia's project and the Sabines', though neither expands upon the observation (Grimal 1952: 316 n3; Beltrami 1989: 270–1).

[37] The principal late Republican and Imperial accounts of the Sabine women's abduction all report legitimate marriage to Roman men as the outcome; cf. Cicero,

prophetic scheme again shows the 'dominant' term to depend upon principles established by the 'subordinate, contingent' term: Rome's integrity as a polity—what it means to *be* Rome—depends on the city's infiltration by foreigners because of women. By this process, the poem not only transforms the subordinate term, so that Tarpeia's betrayal becomes a blessing, but questions the very logic that sees 'integrity' and 'infiltration' as antitheses.

Water images plot the progression of Tarpeia's passion: she invents ritual needs to wash her hair in the river so that she can gaze upon Tatius more often (4.4.23–24); she laments Vesta's extinguished sacred flame, 'spattered by my tears' (4.4.45–46); her plan to betray the city revolves equally around guiding the Sabines along a hidden Capitoline path slippery with invisible springs (47–50), and taking advantage of Rome's holiday drunkenness, its watches 'dissolved' at Romulus' command (*Romulus excubias decrevit in otia solvi/atque intermissa castra silere tuba*—'Romulus decreed that the watches be dissolved for the holiday, and also that the camps fall silent, with the martial trumpets temporarily discontinued,' 79–80). Mere plot exigencies cannot explain this strange concatenation of liquidity: for example, though three whole lines are devoted to describing the oozy path to the Capitoline, no one slips under Tarpeia's guidance, and the expansive detail seems otiose.[38] Yet all these passages feature liquid creeping out of its 'proper' place to create minor or major instances of upheaval, a chaos chiefly defined by law or ritual. Tarpeia's hair-washing, while not culpable per se, falsifies ritual, in that she invents bad omens as her pretext. Her tears extinguish Vesta's flame, the religious sign that corroborates Rome's own integrity and continuity as a state. The hidden waters on the Capitoline threaten not only those who tread the path, but the Romans, too, by giving them a false sense of security (they do not bother to guard this slippery 'back door' to the city); and the city's drunkenness relaxes discipline under siege, very nearly to its inhabitants' destruction.

---

*Rep.* 2.7; D.H. 2.30–1; Livy, 1.9.14–16, 13.1–5; Ovid *Fasti* 3.202–28. For an insightful analysis of the rape of the Sabines as represented in these and other ancient texts, see Miles 1992.

[38] Noticed by King 1990: 239.

## BACCHANT OR AMAZON?

Most of these images are intriguing but minor stitches in a complex tapestry—save one: as Tarpeia rushes to find Tatius and offer him Rome, Propertius compares her to a woman running alongside a river. The Vestal 'rushes headlong, just as a woman from Strymon, her breast bared by the torn fold of her dress, alongside the swift Thermodon' (*illa ruit, qualis celerem prope Thermodonta/Strymonis abscisso pectus aperta sinu,* 4.4.71–2). The cunning oddity of this image sketches a woman 'out of place,' for whom no clear context can be found. John Warden elucidates the picture's duplicity: mentioning the Thermodon suggests an Amazon and the woman's nude breast corroborates this, given Graeco-Roman sculpture's tradition of Amazons with one breast bared.[39] But, as Warden points out, Amazons belted back their garments to expose the breast, rather than tearing them. Torn garment and headlong haste imply a Bacchant, especially since erotic passion drives Tarpeia; Latin literature often represents women's love as inspiring maenad-like behavior.[40]

Warden principally elucidates the parallels between Propertius' Tarpeia and Vergil's Dido, reading the Vestal as a response to the Sidonian queen. His fine exposition renders his point inescapable, yet some observations he prematurely subordinates to Dido's image, and these deserve consideration in a fuller context.

For example, although Warden initially finds tension in the juxtaposition of Bacchant, so often a convenient figure for a woman passionately in love, and a traditionally 'manhating' Amazon, he later observes: 'As one gazes more steadily at the two figures, one begins to suspect that they are not as diametrically opposed as might appear at first sight. The pack of wild women who tore apart Orpheus and Pentheus might seem, at least to the threatened male, all too reminiscent of the women warriors of the Thermodon.'[41] He

---

[39] A tradition upon which Propertius himself regularly draws: cf. 3.14.13–14, 4.3.43–44 (Warden 1978: 179).

[40] Warden 1978: 177–80; he points to Vergil (*Aen.* 4.300–301) and Propertius himself (3.8.14) as examples of Latin writers who compare women in erotic distress to Bacchants (Miller 1995: 227, aptly cites *Aen.* 7.385–405 as another instance).

[41] Warden 1978: 182.

marshalls this duplicity to support reading Dido, the chaste warrior-queen turned impassioned lover, behind Tarpeia; yet, when seen in the context of Propertius' other references to Maenads and Amazons, the implications of 4.4's composite *sauvagesse* open out onto the intertwined problems of the feminine within and without the state, and the inadequacy of thought to frame her.

Propertius' own sketches of Bacchants are few, but richly suggestive: in 3.22, Bacchants figure as fierce manhunters, who define Greek 'barbarity' as opposed to Roman decorum (however ironic the comparison may be). Italy may congratulate itself, he says, that here 'savage Bacchants do not hunt Pentheus in the woods' (*Penthea non saevae venantur in arbore Bacchae*, 3.22.23). In 1.3, Propertius compares his lover, insensibly slumbering and thus unresponsive to his attentions, to an exhausted maenad wrapped in a sleep indifferent to man after communion with her god (*nec minus assiduis Edonis fessa choreis/qualis in herboso concidit Apidano*, 1.3.5–8). Cynthia is the sleeping maenad of Greek vase paintings, and Propertius the satyr who spies upon her—but as on those vases, always in vain, the object of the maenad's sleeping inattention or waking rejection.[42] Propertius represents Amazons with like ambiguity: Warden notes that the poet's women-warriors disquietingly juxtapose the eroticism of female nudity with weapons and belligerence.[43]

When brought to bear upon the Tarpeia poem, these vignettes attest aspects of Woman's desire that escape Man's calculation: beside blind hatred or blind love for his sex arises a mystifying passion for war or for god, passion that places Man nearer margin than center of any epistemology—*if* he figures at all. In the light of these images, as well as of their wider cultural context, the Bacchant and Amazon evoked by Tarpeia in flight together sketch the extremes of Woman's figuration, but extremes that keep eerily collapsing into one another. Bacchant and Amazon share a passion for the divine, whether Ares,

---

[42] See McNally 1978: 121–4; Lissarague 1990: esp. 62–4. Literary sources also echo this theme of the Bacchant as inviolate, even—or especially—when most vulnerable in sleep: see Plutarch *Moralia* ('*Mulierum Virtutes*') 249e–f.

[43] Warden 1978: 179.

Artemis or Dionysos;[44] they share a penchant for violence and a capacity to exceed the place marked out for Woman within the polity.[45] They can be construed as opposites, given their reversed—though oddly symmetrical—relations to Man and the state. Love-mad women behave like maenads, and so inscribe the Bacchant as 'manlover,' while the Amazon is 'manhater' par excellence;[46] the Bacchant originates within the city-state and is drawn outside its confines, while the Amazon dwells at civilization's borders, but is drawn into war with those at its heart.[47] Yet Propertius' juxtaposition emphasizes all the elements that overlap in their respective mythologies. This disturbing tendency of one figuration of Woman to collapse into another suggests some fundamental miscalculation: if 'manhater' and 'manlover' are fundamentally so indistinguishable, if feminine margin and center of the state exchange places so readily, are 'Man' and 'state' meaningful reference points? Something incalculable by these yardsticks flashes in Woman's desire, something that collapses categories previously seen as mutually exclusive and stable.

That 'something' erupts at the very heart of the city, in the figure of its stability and continuity—the goddess Vesta. The virgin goddess paradoxically fans the flame of Tarpeia's love as she sleeps:

> dixit, et incerto permisit bracchia somno,
>     nescia se furiis accubuisse novis.
> nam Vesta, Iliacae felix tutela favillae
>     culpam alit et plures condit in ossa faces. (4.4.67–70).

---

[44] On the Amazons' worship of Ares and Artemis, see Bennett 1967: 30–72; duBois 1982, 34; Tyrrell 1984: 16, 55, 77, 86–7. The myth of the Amazons' divine attachments offers yet another curious parallel to the maenads: some accounts have it that the Amazons, too, followed the maenads' god as Dionysus' martial allies when he conquered the East (cf. D.S. 3.71.4); others that Dionysus was their enemy initially, but pardoned them when they became his suppliants (cf. Paus. 7.2.7–8, Tac. *Ann.* 3.61 and W. R. Halliday's discussion of Plut. *Quaest. Gr.* 56 (Halliday 1928: 210–11).

[45] Tyrrell 1984: esp. 40–63.

[46] Various strands of the Amazons' myth indicate their hostility to men: they mutilate male children for slaves, or send them away to their fathers; they will have sex with men, but they steadfastly reject marriage; sometimes they are reported to refuse even cohabitation, choosing to live in a single-sex society. See duBois 1982: 34; Tyrrell 1984: 53–5.

[47] For the Amazons' homelands as always at civilization's borders, see Tyrrell 1984: 56–8; for their propensity to be drawn into war with 'civilized' peoples (such as the Greeks), see duBois 1982: 32–6.

[Tarpeia] spoke, and stretched out her arms/surrendered her embrace[48] to uncertain sleep, not knowing that she slept with fresh furies. For Vesta, happy guardian of the flame of Troy, nurtured her [Tarpeia's] guilt and buried more torches in her bones.

This witchlike Vesta answers to the twin images of Bacchant and Amazon she inspires Tarpeia to emulate, in their broadly overlapping contradictions. Vesta here feeds passion, though herself ritually its enemy; she overturns Rome, her own city, from its very heart, stretching its extremes to include the Sabines; she modulates erotic passion into war and violence.[49] Her flame itself embodies irresolvable contradiction. The flame came from the ruins of Troy; as evidence of Rome's continuity and stability, it nonetheless bears the trace of transience and destruction, especially since that flame now incites Tarpeia's betrayal of Rome.[50] Vesta's weird image points to aspects of the very heart and origins of Rome—aspects characterized as feminine—whose conceptual intractability Rome dissimulates.[51] The poem marks feminine desire as a different economy of thought, wherein traditional categories of thought are exceeded and binary opposition, as the foundation of meaning, collapses under the weight of its own conceptual inadequacy.

Vesta also inspires images that elaborate the spatial contradictions she embodies, as the foreign transient at Rome's heart who nonetheless 'protects' its boundaries (after her fashion). Let us return for a moment to the Bacchant-Amazon whom Tarpeia imitates under Vesta's goading: this woman in mad career cannot easily be located in anything like recognizable space. If she is a woman from Strymon, why does she run alongside the Thermodon a thousand miles from her home?[52] Like the mysterious spring that opened this poem, we

---

[48] Regarding the ambiguity of *permisit bracchia*, see Richardson 1977 *ad loc.*
[49] On Vesta as tutelary deity of the community, see Latte 1960: 108. To enable a breach in the walls that protect that community—in this case, Rome—abrogates her peculiar function.
[50] On Vesta's flame as Trojan in origin, see Ovid *F.* 3.417–18, 6.365, 455–6. Aeneas, according to legend, was charged with conveying the goddess' fire from Troy to Rome (*Aeneid* 2.296–7).
[51] On Vesta's ambiguity, see Miller-Platter 1999b, Miller 1995: 226.
[52] Warden notes the peculiarity, but sees it only as a reference to the woman's Amazon associations: the Strymon bordered Thrace, a legendary haunt of the Amazons (Warden 1978: 177).

are offered yet another surreal geography of water; it, too, suggests eerie mobility in apparently stable categories (such as Cappadocia vs. Thrace), and it marks that mobility as feminine. Always, before thought can overtake it in this poem, the feminine is already elsewhere.

## WANTING IT ALL

Not surprisingly, just this aspect of Woman's desire—its mobility and collapsing of conceptual categories—marks Tarpeia's passion. As we have seen, this poem's imagery hospitably embraces categories Roman culture generally construes as polar opposites, antitheses upon which 'reason' and 'truth' putatively rest. The poem disturbs, displaces, and recombines classification in dizzyingly fluid formations that undermine the easy familiarity of the original categories themselves. Consider how the following passages describe Tarpeia's bewitched fascination with Tatius.

*vidit harenosis Tatium proludere campis*
    *pictaque per flavas arma levare iubas:*
*obstipuit regis facie et regalibus armis,*
    *interque oblitas excidit urna manus.* (4.4.19–22)

She saw Tatius practicing on the sandy fields and raising his ornamented weapons above his tawny crest;[53] she was struck dumb by his face and his kingly weapons, and the urn fell from her oblivious hands.

'*Ignes castrorum et Tatiae praetoria turmae*
    *et formosa oculis arma Sabina meis,*
*o utinam ad vestros sedeam captiva Penatis,*
    *dum captiva mei conspicer ora Tati!*' (4.4.31–32)

'O fires of the camps and headquarters of Tatius' bodyguard and Sabine arms, beautiful to my eyes!' [I shall discuss the translation of the second distich below]

---

[53] I follow Richardson's suggestion in my translation (who takes *per* to stand for *super*), but the puzzling phrase *per flavas... iubas*' has provoked a wide range of interpretations. Butler and Barber offer a fair summary of the possible readings (Butler-Barber 1933 *ad loc.*); I have not concerned myself to argue the case here, as the phrase's exact meaning does not impinge on my interpretation of the poem.

'ille equus, ille meos in castra reponet amores,
  cui Tatius dextras collocat ipse iubas!
quid mirum in patrios Scyllam saevisse capillos,
  candidaque in saevos inguina versa canis?
prodita quid mirum fraterni cornua monstri,
  cum patuit lecto stamine torta via?' (4.4.37–42)

'That horse, that's the one who will take my love back into camp, whose mane Tatius himself will arrange to fall to the right! What wonder that Scylla attacked her father's hair, and that her fair limbs were turned to savage dogs? What wonder that the horns of the monstrous brother were betrayed, when the twisted way lay open as [Ariadne's guiding] thread was reeled in?'

'te toga picta decet, non quem sine matris honore
  nutrit inhumanae dura papilla lupae.' (4.4.53–54)
'You the toga with its insignia suits, not he whom the hard pap of a she-wolf nursed, without the honor of a mother!'

Tarpeia's admiration for Tatius' appearance curiously revolves as much or more around what is *not* Tatius as what is: his horse, his weapons, the weapons of his soldiers, his imagined beauty in an ornamented toga. True, erotic poetry sometimes praises the beloved's dress alongside the elegance of her or his features (though more often in describing women than men), but such descriptions usually subordinate dress to person. By contrast, 4.4 sets Tatius' arms (*regalibus armis*) paratactically side by side with his face (*regis facie*) as if both excited Tarpeia's wonder equally. Moreover, nothing affords a precedent to the way her desire spreads so as to encompass his horse (37–38) and even his entire army and their arms (31).[54] Stahl rightly perceives the embarrassment of these lines, and strives to explain it away: 'Although her affection now seems to widen from Tatius (19, 21) and his arms (*arma*, 20, *armis*, 21) to Tatius' soldiers and their arms (31/32), this plural is rather to be seen psychologically as a multiplication of beloved

---

[54] Her admiration for the shields curiously echoes another version of the Tarpeia legend in which she remains, despite appearances, loyal to Rome. She acted (so the story runs) as Rome's double agent, sending a message to Romulus that she would lead them into the city, and then demanding the Sabines' shields as her reward once she has them inside the city. However, the messenger betrays her to Tatius, and the Sabines crush her with their shields (L. Calpurnius Piso in his *Annales*, as recorded by Dion. Hal. 2.38–40).

Tatius himself... .[55] Yet saying that she 'multiplies Tatius himself' hardly lessens the oddity: she thus makes of Tatius Hobbes' Leviathan in military dress. As for her queer fixation on her beloved's horse (37–38), it moves Stahl, like Rothstein before him, to rationalize it as her envy of the attention horse receives from rider.

> She identifies the horse as the one she now sees every day from her rock and which enjoys the privilege of Tatius' personal care (how much she herself would like to receive his attention!)[56]
> 
> *Statt des einfachen, das Roß, das Tatius reitet, hebt Tarpeia das beneidenswerte Glück des Rosses hervor, das von Tatius selbst gepflegt wird; eine Art des Empfindens, die der antike wie der modernen Erotik geläufig ist.*[57]

Yet Stahl cites no textual support for thus translating Tarpeia's thoughts, and Rothstein's attempts to find parallels in Greek poetry are inexact at best: his citations all *explicitly* articulate the wish to be some object that offers proximity to the beloved, an element crucially missing here. The poem offers no gloss on Tarpeia's fascination with the steed; rather, like the passions of Bacchant and Amazon, Tarpeia's love for Tatius encompasses also the beasts of the field and the implements of war, while—again like these wild women—her ardor displaces Man and state as central, unified points of reference, gliding indifferently between singular and plural, animate and inanimate, beast and human and monster.

Tarpeia's gaze, that restlessly creates new 'wholes' for its delight out of a list-like collection of objects (arms, man, horse, toga), takes to its logical extremes an operation inherent in the cultural construction of desire. Culture writes conventional readings of what is desirable (or not), organically united (or not), onto the object, offering interpretation as 'perception;' Tarpeia's novel fetishism throws this bad faith into relief.[58] Her eclecticism steps just far enough outside the bounds

---

[55] Stahl 1985: 286.   [56] Stahl 1985: 287.

[57] 'Instead of the simple, "the horse that Tatius rides," Tarpeia throws into sharp relief the enviable luck of the steed, which is tended by Tatius himself; a type of feeling that is familiar to ancient eroticism, as it is to modern' (Rothstein 1898 *ad* 4.4.37).

[58] A bad faith familiar to antiquity: Lucretius, after Epicurus, expounds eloquently on desire's ability to create an object for itself (see above, note 26) and his conviction finds a distinct echo in Prop. 3.24, for example, when Propertius tells Cynthia that his poetry granted her the appearance it purported to record:

of quotidian expectation to undermine the notion that the content of passion defines natural complementarities or natural objects. Her gaze thus repeats and reverses an effect of the poem's montage-like opening, where we were baffled of constructing a sensible whole out of the disparate symbolic resonances grove, spring, sheep, shepherd's pipe, tomb and army brought to the picture. Divested of any obvious guidelines, her visions of the beloved render uncanny and unreadable the homely furniture of human desire.

Fittingly, Tarpeia expatiates on her ardor by likening it to mythical passions that wrought monsters.

> '*quid mirum in patrios Scyllam saevisse capillos,*
>   *candidaque in saevos inguina vera canis?*
> *prodita quid mirum fraterni cornua monstri,*
>   *cum patuit lecto stamine torta via?*' (4.4.39–42)

> 'What wonder that Scylla attacked her father's hair, and that her fair limbs were turned to savage dogs? What wonder that the horns of the monstrous brother were betrayed, when the twisted way lay open as [Ariadne's guiding] thread was reeled in?'

It does not puzzle her that, for love, Scylla would suffer herself to be metamorphosed into half-maiden, half-monster; no longer wonderful to her are the histories of the house of Minos, whose wife Pasiphaë loved a bull and disguised herself as a cow to enjoy him. Tarpeia lays claim to annals of passion that make nonsense out of any notion of what is 'natural;' love's assumed objects, its expected effects, turn topsy-turvy. She claims instead a history of desire, marked as feminine, that exceeds any notion of Man and Woman as natural complementaries, or the state as the lodestone of human loyalties. The

> *mixtam te varia laudavi saepe figura,*
>   *ut, quod non esses, esse putaret amor;*
> *et color est totiens roseo collatus Eoo*
>   *cum tibi quaesitus candor in ore foret* (3.24.5–8)

> Often have I praised you as a composite of different kinds of beauty, so that love would think you what you were not; and so often your complexion was compared to the rosy dawn when an artificial pallor was on your cheeks.

> Note that in this passage, he does not contrast his verse's praise of her beauty with any real ugliness—'candor' is only another type of beauty; rather, he contrasts the projection of his desire onto her (seeing her with a rosy complexion, and with whatever other permutations '*varia figura*' implies) with her shaping of her appearance (she makes herself up to be pale, but he simply dismisses *her* cosmetic standards as if unworthy of aesthetic evaluation, saying simply: 'what you were not, love thought you were'). I discuss this passage further in Janan 2001 chapter 5.

icons of Tarpeia's love stand perforce outside human sexual relations: Scylla's genitals become dogs; Minos' daughter, Ariadne, eventually becomes a god's (Dionysus') consort rather than Theseus'. Such longing shapes grotesques of indifference, confusing the realms of beast and god, erasing assumed touchstones of human identity, unraveling existing social order without regret.

## FEMININE SYNTAX

Tarpeia's strange amalgamations that sketch the shifting amorous subject and object parallel her mobile position in articulating her love. Tarpeia assumes, Amazonlike, the role of autonomous subject of desire and diplomacy in making her own marriage pact and treaty (*hoc Tarpeia suum tempus rata convenit hostem/pacta ligat, pactis ipsa futura comes*—'Tarpeia, having decided that this was her time, met with her enemy; she concludes a pact, with herself as companion according to the terms of the pact [or, 'with herself as companion to those with whom she had concluded the pact'], 4.4.81–82).[59] Even were she not a Roman woman and a Vestal consecrated to chastity, these prerogatives would be her father's and Romulus' respectively rather than hers; her independent marriage brokering and her treason are set paratactically side by side as virtually equivalent acts (*prodiderat portaeque fidem patriamque iacentem/nubendique petit, quem velit, ipsa diem*—'she had betrayed both the entrusted responsibility of the gate and her fatherland lying helpless, and she herself seeks what she wants, the day of her marriage,' 4.4.87–88). Yet, even as she fantasizes offering herself to Tatius, her terms play curiously and paradoxically between subject and object, active and passive positions:

---

[59] On the Amazons as reversing the bride's traditional passivity in their liaisons—demanding, for example, that their husbands be the ones to bring a dowry, move where the Amazons feel most comfortable, and attend to all household tasks—see Tyrrell 1984: 41–3, 53–5, 66, 71, 77. On the ambiguity of *pactis*, and the way that it implies Tarpeia's marriage pact with Tatius, see Richardson 1977 *ad* 4.4.82.

'o utinam ad vestros sedeam captiva Penatis,
   dum captiva mei conspicer ora Tati!' (4.4.33–34)
[I shall discuss the translation of these lines below]
'o utinam magicae nossem cantamina Musae!
   haec quoque formoso lingua tulisset opem.
te toga picta decet, non quem sine matris honore
   nutrit inhumanae dura papilla lupae.
hic, hospes, patria metuar regina sub aula?
   dos tibi non humilis prodita Roma venit.
si minus, at raptae ne sint impune Sabinae,
   me rape et alterna lege repende vices!' (4.4.51–58)

'O would that I knew the songs of the sorceress-Muse! Even this tongue would help my handsome man! You the toga with its insignia suits, not he whom the hard pap of a she-wolf nursed, without the honor of a mother! Shall I thus, my foe, be feared as queen in my father's hall?[60] Rome comes to you as no humble dowry! Or at least, lest the Sabines' ravishment go unpunished, rape me and pay back in turn with the law of "an eye for an eye".'

Take, for example, the difficulties of 4.33–34: is Barber correct in printing Gronovius' suggestion *ora* or should the major manuscripts' *esse* be preferred—a reading that dictates *conspicer* be read as truly passive rather than deponent? And what about the ambiguity of the second *captiva* in 34: does it modify the implied subject of *conspicer* or the emendation *ora*? Between the emended and unemended versions of these lines, we have as possible translations 'would that I, a captive, might see the face of my Tatius;' 'would that I might be seen to be the captive of my Tatius;' 'would that I might see the captive face of my Tatius'—the last imagining a reciprocal love-match in which each would be the captive of the other. But, as Paul Allen Miller and Charles Platter have pointed out, 'there is no way to decide between these competing readings on grammatical bases alone.... Each of these readings is defensible and the attempt to promote one over the other reveals more about the reader than the

---

[60] Another famous crux: Butler-Barber and Shackleton-Bailey between them fairly summarize the problems, and the solutions proffered to date (Butler-Barber 1933 *ad* 4.4.55; Shackleton-Bailey 1956 *ad* 4.4.53). I follow Butler's text and (in the main) his and Barber's interpretation; but the precise translation of this distich does not affect my argument.

poem. Rather the very inability to assign absolute agency to either party is consonant with the structure of the poem as a whole.'[61] The rest of Tarpeia's soliloquy elaborates upon just that indeterminacy: she imagines herself actively offering herself, as passive object, to Tatius, sees herself as war-captive, strangely pliant witch, bride, rape-victim. The oddity of saying 'she offers herself as rape victim'—how can she be raped when she longs for the embrace of her addressee?— underlines, by its very logical contradiction, the slippery duplicity of fantasy, the way in which it deconstructs the notion of unified subjects and objects that underwrite normative conceptions of desire. Tarpeia's soliloquy anticipates the logical moves in Freud's key essay on fantasy, wherein he analyzes the phenomenon as a series of syntactical permutations on the sentence 'a child is being beaten' that shift the fantasizer back and forth between observer and participant, active and passive, subject and object, even female and male.[62] Irigaray lays claim to psychoanalysis' instructive elucidation of that language-based instability in conceptual divisions when she imagines 'feminine' syntax:

> What a feminine syntax might be is not simple or easy to state, because in that 'syntax' there would no longer be either subject or object, 'oneness' would no longer be privileged, there would no longer be proper meanings, proper names, 'proper' attributes... Instead, that 'syntax' would involve nearness, proximity, but in such an extreme form that it would preclude any distinction of identities, any establishment of ownership, thus any form of appropriation.[63]

The form and content of Tarpeia's fantasies trace that syntax exactly: 'I wish that I were your captive/your sorceress/your bride/your rape victim' scatters Tarpeia among vagaries of will, consent, and power. On the one hand, if Tatius captures or rapes her, her consent to the action ceases to be at issue and (as Livy argued for Lucretia) she

---

[61] Miller-Platter 1999b.　　[62] Freud 1953–74 vol. 17:179–204.
[63] '*Ce que serait une syntaxe de féminin, ce n'est pas simple, ni aisé à dire, parce que dan cette «syntaxe» il n'y aurait plus ni sujet ni objet, le «un» n'y serait plus privilégié, il n'y aurait plus de sens propre, de nom propre, d'attributs «propres»... Cette «syntaxe» mettrait plutôt en jeu le proche, mais un si proche qu'il rendrait impossible toute discrimination d'identité, toute constitution d'appartenance, donc tout forme d'appropriation*' (Irigaray 1977 (1985): 134/132; ellipsis in original).

cannot be held responsible.[64] The infractions against Vesta and Rome she so wants would then be freed of moral consequences—in theory. Yet Tarpeia complicates her will when she herself constructs herself as passive victim within the fantasy: her daydream oxymoronically reads as 'I desire not to desire the thing I desire: I wish to have it forced upon me.'

But in addition to object of rape or capture, Tarpeia also wishes herself Tatius' bride, or powerful witch. I have already noted the oddity of Tarpeia's arranging her own marriage with Tatius: while the formalities of Roman marriage pact and ceremony construct a bride as passive party, the object of exchange between two men, Tarpeia imagines herself as marriage broker.[65] But she does not thus unambiguously usurp power: she becomes both subject and object in this exchange, giving herself away. Similarly, while the witch she wants to be represents a feared pinnacle of female power, Tarpeia's wish to be only Tatius' instrument also complicates this image: her incantations would forward her *lover*'s agenda, not her own (*haec quoque formoso lingua tulisset opem*, 52).

Within this complex picture of Woman's desire, we cannot settle upon a simple answer to the question 'what does Tarpeia want?,' and therefore to 'what is she—traitor, victim or benefactor? what is her degree of culpability?' Rather, we revolve dizzyingly among imponderables, among fractions of subjects organized around epicenters of will, power, and desire. The entire congeries of volition and submission grows even more complex because Vesta renders inevitable what Tarpeia had only debated.[66] Who, then, is culpable for Tarpeia's

---

[64] On consent as the logical fulcrum that divides rape from adultery, see Livy 1.58.9.

[65] Despite the influence Roman women could, and undoubtedly did, exert over the marriages of their children, they had no legal right to do so. Moreover, as Emile Benveniste has shown, the very language of the marriage ceremony constructs men as its agents, women as its object: a father gives his daughter in marriage (*filiam dare in matrimoniam*), a man leads someone's daughter in marriage (*alicuius filiam ducere in matrimonium*), but a woman enters into marriage (*ire in matrimonium*), as into a place constructed for her by someone else (Benveniste 1969: 1:239–44).

[66] Nor can we seek comfort in an allegorical reading of a goddess fixing Tarpeia's determination, as we might if she were Venus rather than Vesta: Vesta does not traditionally personify passion.

'Beyond Good and Evil': Tarpeia and Philosophy    429

actions? I have argued against reading Tarpeia solely as a response to Vergil's Dido, but here she does conjure up the same unresolvable problem of agency hinged upon a woman's fatal and fated 'offense' (*culpa*) that *Aeneid* 4 broaches.[67] Yet Propertius has replayed the enigma such that the characterization of Tarpeia's desire shifts into the field of its conceptualization, and stages the impossibility of its being conceived. Tarpeia dramatizes an impasse in 'reason' that, without making the questions of guilt and innocence, betrayal and benefit, offender and victim any less importunate, renders them not only unanswerable, but unaskable in the terms laid down by received thought.

Given the uneasy conceptual fluidity Tarpeia embodies within Roman myth, Tatius' response reads as a particularly brutal concrete metaphor: crushing her beneath Sabine shields 'puts the lid on' the vertiginous questions her brief history poses.[68] Or almost so: the poem closes with the lines 'the name of the mountain was got from Tarpeia as leader; watcher, you have the reward of an unjust lot!' (*a duce Tarpeia mons est cognomen adeptus/o vigil, iniustae praemia sortis habes*, 4.4.93–94). The Capitoline is hers, finally, as *mons Tarpeius*—but whose is the injustice? The perfectly ambiguous *vigil*, 'watcher,' glances both toward Tarpeia and Jupiter, the Capitoline's god: Propertius has told us that she watched to open up Rome and the god watched to punish her for it.[69] Was it unjust to kill her, or to make the god's invaded home her monument? The poem ends in a studied refusal to sort out who is offender and who offended. The final distich's irreducible ambiguity insists that any choice would be based on the same false conceptual distinctions the elegy as a whole has exploded; the Tarpeia poem refuses that choice as its ultimate ethical gesture.

---

[67] Dido's affair with Aeneas is consistently referred to as a *culpa* in *Aeneid* 4 (cf. *Aen.* 4.19. 4, 4.172), not only as a breach of faith with her former husband Sychaeus, but also implicitly as the beginning of all the trouble she brings upon herself and her city. Nonetheless, the affair was inspired in (forced upon?) Dido by two powerful gods, Venus and Cupid (*Aen.* 1.657–722).

[68] Miller 1995 insightfully analyzes the Roman conceptualization of women as a potentially destructive, but necessary, force to be contained both literally (within the domestic space) and metaphorically (within the boundaries of decorum).

[69] Butler-Barber 1933 *ad* 93–4 gives a fair summary of the possible interpretations of the vulgate reading of these lines, as well as some suggested emendations.

# 16

## Why Propertius is a Woman[1]

*Paul Allen Miller*

... la vraie question n'est pas celle de leur inconduite, mais celle de leur incohérence. (Maleuvre 1998: 2)[2]

---

[1] Author's note: This chapter began as the 2000 Walsh Lecture given at the Classics Department of the University of Chicago. It was published in *Classical Philology* before being revised for my 2004 book, *Subjecting Verses: Latin Love Elegy and the Emergence of the Real*. There it forms part of a larger theoretical argument. It will be helpful in this new context to introduce and briefly define three terms originating from Lacanian psychoanalysis that are used throughout it. They are Imaginary, Symbolic, and Real. These terms are conventionally capitalized in English usage to indicate that they are being used in a specialized sense, although Lacan himself never followed this practice. The Imaginary is a term derived from the Freudian concept of the Imago. While there are many subtleties to Lacan's theorization of it, on the most basic level it refers to the image of ourselves that we project upon the world. The Symbolic in contrast is the world of rules and codes. It includes language and all other shared semiotic systems. It is based on the concept of *langue* in Saussurean linguistics and represents the shared communal grid of intelligibility that defines a community. We are recognized as subjects by others only through assuming a position in the Symbolic. That position may correspond either more or less well to the vision we have formed of ourselves in the Imaginary. The Real is that which falls outside of either of the two preceding categories. It is not 'reality' because it is precisely what escapes linguistic expression and Imaginary appropriation. Thus the Real cannot be the object of conscious experience. It is important to note that the Imaginary, the Symbolic, and the Real do not denote mutually exclusive realms, but interpenetrating registers of existence. Our Imaginary projections are bathed in the codes and norms of the Symbolic and the Symbolic offers rules, codes, and forms for processing the work of the Imaginary. The Real represents not so much a world outside these two as their necessary limitations.

[2] 'The real question is not of their misconduct but of their incoherence.' Editors' note: All translations are Miller's own, except where specified. Miller chose to

> In the genre of Propertian love elegy... the narrating ego is
> constituted as an effeminate voice. (Wyke 1995: 120)

Propertius Book 2 moves from the initial establishment of the poet's style in the Monobiblos to its institutionalization and consequent engagement with the recuperative force of Roman ideological norms, embodied in the Symbolic. It is no accident that this book commences with a *recusatio* or that the figures of Maecenas and Augustus loom large over it. Propertius has begun to move in the imperial circle. This, however, does not mean that his poetry becomes less oppositional. Rather to the extent that poetry referring to, or refusing to refer to, the emperor, Maecenas, and their coterie, is more prominent in this collection (Gold 1985: 158), then the recuperative pressures of the Roman Symbolic stand in proportionately sharper opposition to the erotic Imaginary's desire for asocial union (as exemplified in words like *nequitia, inertia*, etc.)[3] that stands at the heart of elegiac discourse.

In this chapter, I shall examine four related areas. First, I shall look at the ways in which Propertius in Book 2 fashions an anomalous subject position by identifying himself simultaneously with Augustan and anti-Augustan positions, paying special attention to poems 2.15's and 2.16's depictions of the battle of Actium. Second, I shall argue that the Propertian subject position thus created closely approximates that of Woman as defined by post-Lacanian feminists such as Clément, Cixous, Kristeva, and Irigaray. Third, I shall contend that this identification not only helps explain the frequent deployment of the trope of gender inversion in elegiac discourse, but also that it provides a useful explanatory framework for examining the formal rhetoric of elegy in Book 2, as exemplified in two important political poems 2.1 and 2.7, in which the poet displays both a newfound closeness with the imperial regime and a refusal of its embrace. Finally, I shall examine the ways in which these same essential contradictions are also embodied in Book 3, with special emphasis on poems 3.4 and 3.5,

---

translate some French texts and to leave others in French; we have followed his lead and left the French alone.

[3] See for example Propertius 1.6.25–26; Tibullus 1.1.57–58; Gaisser 1983: 65; Wimmel 1976: 37–8; Veyne 1988: 106; Copley 1956: 100; Sullivan 1976: 62; and Tracy 1979: 343, '*Nequitia* in the Roman elegists has been defined as the freeing of self from community consciousness, the retreating into one's own "I".'

even as the field of their articulation is narrowed and their intensity strengthened.

## I WHEN OPPOSITES ATTRACT

When I say that the recuperative pressures of the Roman Symbolic stand in sharper opposition to the Imaginary's desire for asocial union, I do not mean that Propertius' poetry reflects an oppositional stance in a naive, thematic sense. It is not a question of the poet's 'attitude' toward the regime. What I am addressing is an objective structure of the poetry, and its clearest evidence is the unending debates on whether Propertius should be seen as: a) Augustus' political critic (Hallett 1973: 109; Stahl 1985: 147); b) his ally (Alfonsi 1945 [1979]: 37; Cairns 1979a: 201–02; Newman 1997: 6); or c) an apolitical Callimachean ironist who just happens to be the beneficiary of imperial patronage (Veyne 1988: 3, 30, 108). None of these options does sufficient justice to the complex and contradictory nature of Propertius' later poetry (Santirocco 1995: 226–28), which, as we shall see, is simultaneously more and less political than that in the Monobiblos. It is more political because aspects of the imperial regime are envisioned as possible themes, as in 2.15 and 2.16 where the poet treats the *princeps*' recent victory at Actium. It is less political because those same themes are almost always deferred, as in 2.10, where the composition of an epic celebrating Octavian's conquests is promised but put off to the Greek calends (Stahl 1985: 157–60). The complexity of the gesture embodied in such a *recusatio*, as Cameron (1995: 472–73) and Commager (1974: 56–58) note, is heightened by the fact that its structure is dependent upon accepting the superiority of the very genre of eulogistic epic that it is rejecting. Such a poem thus demands a double reading[4] that can take account both of the possibility of

---

[4] See Enk 1962: 2.151 citing Fleischmann, '*Nihil certi promittere voluit Propertius hoc carmine Augusto; "itaque fit, ut quae altero versu elatiore quodam animo et singulari quadam alacritate se aggressurum promittat ea iam altero versu refringat et quodam modo retrahat"*' ('Propertius didn't want to promise anything certain to Augustus with this poem; "and so it happens that, what he promises he will undertake

infinite deferral and of what many commentators have seen as a sincere promise to provide Maecenas and Augustus the epic they desired (Lachmann 1816 [1973]: xxi–xxiii; Lemaire 1832: 192; Paley 1853: 88–90; Butler and Barber 1933 (1969): 208; Camps 1967: 108–09). Similarly, when these Augustan themes are addressed, they are dealt with in an ambiguous and problematic fashion. Thus in 2.15.41–46 the poet claims that if only everyone else pursued a life of drunken carousing, then the Actian sea would not now be churning Roman bones nor Rome exhausted from triumphing over its own citizens (Commager 1974: 48–49; Sullivan 1976: 58; Stahl 1985: 226–27; Gurval 1995: 181). On the surface, this sounds like opposition to the Augustan regime's program of moral reform and martial virtue. It is not a celebration of the victory at Actium. At the same time, however, it can hardly be thought to outline a serious political program. In fact, Rothstein reads the passage as implicit praise for Augustus as opposed to the explicit depiction of a decadence that can only recall Antony's portrayal in Augustan propaganda (1898 [1979]) 1.313–14).[5] Is this, then, political opposition, implicit praise, or self-subverting irony? If opposition, then to what and, more importantly, from what standpoint? Where would it be located on the map of Roman ideology? If the poem is either implicitly Augustan or merely ironic, then how do we explain the disturbing image of Roman bones denied final rest in the churning waters off Actium (Gurval 1995: 181), or the force of the uncanny feat of poetic alchemy whereby those same bones are transformed into dry leaves floating in a wine bowl at the end of the evening's revels (2.15.51–52)? Decadence and death, it seems, await us no matter the path we choose.

Poem 2.15's evocation of Actium, however, cannot be read in isolation from its companion piece, poem 2.16. There, in lines 35–40, the poet compares his own *turpis amor* with that of Antony for Cleopatra, a gesture he will repeat in poem 3.11. This is a position that simultaneously puts him in direct opposition to Augustus (Propertius = Antony) and

---

in one verse with some sort of higher enthusiasm and particular speed, he cuts short in the next verse, and somewhat retracts [his promise],'" editors' translation).

[5] Butler and Barber 1933 (1969): 217 agree but assert 'there is no real inappropriateness.' Giardina 1977: 157 is similarly ambivalent: '*Minime ad Antonium refertur sermo eiusque amores*' ('This is concerned to the smallest degree with Antony and his love affairs,' editors' translation). Tränkle 1983: 157 argues that 2.16's condemnation of Antony shows that 2.15 should be read in a negative light as well.

condemns that opposition (Propertius = *turpis*), while attributing *gloria* and *virtus* to Caesar (Rothstein 1898 [1979]: 1.314; Stahl 1985: 229). Propertius is thus simultaneously pro- and anti-Augustan. But even this contradictory formulation oversimplifies his position. For, on the one hand, while Propertius grants Augustus *virtus*, he defines it as almost the opposite of what it normally means in Roman ideology, *Caesaris haec virtus et gloria Caesaris haec est:/illa, qua vicit, condidit arma manu* ('This is the manly courage of Caesar, this is Caesar's fame: with the very hand by which he conquered, he put away his arms,' 2.16.41–42). As Gurval has recently observed:

> ... the poet's concluding compliment to Octavian (lines 41–42) is a most unusual manner in which to praise a Roman victor in battle. The *virtus* and *gloria* come not from his courage in fighting or military success over the enemy but from the pardon that the victor bestowed on the vanquished. (1995: 184–85)

For Propertius, Augustus can be said to embody *virtus*, but only so long as it does not mean *virtus*.

On the other hand, it would be a mistake to accept Propertius' identification with Antony at face value, in the manner of Jasper Griffin (1977). Indeed Gurval wants to separate Propertius completely from this implied 'self-comparison' on the grounds that the poet condemns Antony's *amor* as *infamis* and labels it a cause for shame while blaming it for the destruction of his fleet (1995: 184): *cerne ducem, modo qui fremitu complevit inani/Actia damnatis aequora militibus* ('behold the commander who just now filled the waters of Actium with the empty cry of his doomed soldiers').[6] Clearly, there are limits to how far the identification between the poet and Antony can be taken. Propertius' love for Cynthia cannot be posited as the efficient cause of the debacle at Actium, whereas Antony's for Cleopatra was and is so construed.

Gurval's denial of any relationship at all, however, goes too far.[7] There are at least two objections that can be raised to this position. First, Propertius uses *turpis* and *infamis* elsewhere to characterize his

---

[6] All texts are cited from Barber's 1953 OCT unless otherwise noted.

[7] As Walter 1999: 94 shrewdly observes, Propertius is less concerned with his personal likeness with Antony than with the opposition between Antony and Augustus and the homologous one between the excessive Dionysian lover and the restrained Apollonian image of Augustus.

own affair and the poetry that pretends to chronicle it (1.16.7, 2.3.4, 2.24.1–10; Wyke 1995: 119). Indeed, as Stahl notes, Propertius consistently adopts the language of those who would condemn him (1985: 92–93). If both Antony's and Propertius' love can be considered under the same rubric, at least from the standpoint of the emergent imperial ideology, then how different are they? If Propertius were in the same position as Antony in relation to Cleopatra, would he not have done the same thing? Second, if Antony is presented in 2.16 as responsible for the debacle at Actium, and if Propertius in 2.15 portrays his own 'Antonian' lifestyle as a potential antidote to Rome's recent civil slaughter, then, where is the real opposition between Caesar's virtue and Antony's (or Propertius') vice? Each in turn can be cast as both the cause of war and the agent of peace. From the perspective of the dead at Actium, the pro- and anti-Augustan (or pro- and anti-Antonian) positions would be essentially interchangeable. As Propertius in 3.5 wryly observes, *victor cum victis pariter miscebitur umbris* ('the conqueror and the conquered will be equally mixed in the land of the shades,' 3.5.15). Each side may define itself as opposed to the other, but each produces the same effect as the other.

What we have in these poems is a very intricate language game in which the poet, by occupying both sides of the opposition but never being wholly present on either side, inscribes the possibility of a third position that can only be expressed in terms of the simultaneous contradiction between and equivalence of both sides. The poet's contradictory self-positionings within this ideological matrix are, therefore, more an indication of the impossibility of a normative Propertian subject within the terms of the late republican and early imperial Symbolic than of the need to assign priority to one of these positions as 'truly Propertian' and denigrate the other as either a misreading or a mystification designed to deceive the uninitiated.

Indeed, the search for the true Propertius is a fool's game that can be played *ad infinitum*, as each side of the argument always seeks to trump the other rather than acknowledge that the text always already includes the Other.[8] What we see in Book 2 is neither a rebel in Augustus' camp, nor a collaborator, nor an abstracted aesthete, but

---

[8] This is precisely the problem with Stahl's brilliant and provocative reading of the poet. He posits a double structure to later Propertian poetry, but feels consistently

the vision of an erotic subject who is placed under more and more tension as he is brought into closer and closer contact with the discourse of the Augustan regime. This tension both makes this subject position possible and, at the same time, threatens to implode it. The task of the critic is not to privilege one reading over the other, nor to deconstruct the opposition in the name of irony, but to accept the contradiction itself as the fullest instantiation of the Propertian subject.

In the end, the poetic consciousness of Book 2 is not only dialogically constituted out of its own intratextual relations (Miller 1994: chps. 3–4), as in the example of 2.15 and 2.16, but is also projected onto a space that is both manifestly constructed from the terms of contemporary Roman ideology and not able to be precisely located anywhere within it. It is both inside and outside, adopting and inverting traditional Roman values,[9] while projecting images of utopian beauty that are forever tinged with death:

*ac veluti folia arentis liquere corollas,*
  *quae passim calathis strata natare vides,*
*sic nobis, qui nunc magnum spiramus amantes,*
  *forsitan includet crastina fata dies. (2.15.51–4)*
and just as the leaves fallen from withered garlands,
  which you see swimming here and there,
  piled one on top of another in the wine bowl

---

compelled to demonstrate that such duplicity can be resolved back into a monological whole once the 'truth' is recognized. 'The discrepancy cannot be denied: there is no bridge leading over the abyss between the poet's true feelings and the public statements he has felt obliged to make' (1985: 209 = Stahl in this volume). The question of what gives him the epistemological and ontological privilege to distinguish the true from the false, especially if as he says they share no point of contact, is never answered. What is at stake, as Duncan Kennedy observes, is a desperate effort to save the unified liberal, male subject of the Western 'ideology of the individual' (1993: 35–8). The search for the one true meaning lurking behind the necessarily deceptive appearances ultimately produces a paranoid style of reading in which all ambiguities and ambivalences must be ruthlessly shorn away. The best recent example of this paranoid style is Maleuvre, whose recent book on elegy acutely diagnoses the incoherence of the elegiac subject position, and then proceeds magisterially to resolve it by demonstrating how the entire elegiac canon can be shown to be an elaborately encoded allegory of Augustus' seduction of Maecenas' wife Terentia (1998).

[9] On Propertius as both inside and outside traditional Roman ideology, see Platter 1995. On elegy performing 'the ambiguities of equestrian status,' see Fitzgerald 1995: 9.

at the end of evening's revels,
so perhaps tomorrow holds the fatal day for us,
who now breathe the full inspiration of love.

This passage presents a moving image of sensuality and decay that is the counterpart and pendent of the churning bones of Actium. The layering of dead leaves in the wine bowl and the evocation of the *carpe diem* motif combine to produce a call for absolute commitment to the present moment and for an erotic transcendence that has no place in traditional Roman categories of manhood or *virtus* (Sharrock 1995: 166). Here, in this moment of poetic *jouissance*, with 'its strange yoking of ecstasy, pain, and death [that] menaces the Symbolic as the symptom of what cannot enter into the logic of signification' (Janan 1994: 30), the Propertian subject finds its own irreducible kernel of enjoyment, the hard core of its being that is beyond the pleasure and reality principles and beyond the Symbolic categories that make them possible (Kristeva 1979: 13; Zizek 1989: 135; 1991: 169; 1993: 90; Irigaray 1977a: 95).[10]

## II '*WAS WILL DAS WEIB?*' ('WHAT DOES THE BODY WANT?')

Je plaiderai... en faveur d'une théorie analytique des systèmes et des pratiques signifiantes qui chercheraient dans le phénomène signifiant la crise ou le procès du sens et du sujet plutôt que la cohérence ou l'identité d'une ou d'une multiplicité de structures.

(Kristeva 1977: 150)[11]

The interstitial space of *jouissance*[12] just described for the Propertian subject is in fact analogous to what Cathérine Clément identifies as

---

[10] Zizek admirably sums up the psychoanalytic theory behind this reading when he writes, 'what lies beyond [the pleasure principle] is not the symbolic order but a real kernel, a traumatic core. To designate it, Lacan uses the Freudian term: *das Ding*, the Thing as an incarnation of the impossible *jouissance*...' (1989: 132).

[11] 'I will plead... in favor of an analytic theory of signifying systems and practices that would search within the signifying phenomenon for the crisis point or the trial of sense and the subject rather than the coherence or the identity of one or of a multiplicity of structures.'

[12] On *jouissance* as essentially feminine, see Lacan 1975: 13, 76–7.

woman's eccentric position in relation to communal Symbolic norms. Woman, she claims, occupies a position that is both radically critical and deeply conservative, both inside and outside the system (1975: 13–14). Julia Kristeva (Eagleton 1983: 164–65; Moi 1985: 133–34, 163, 166; Kristeva 1979: 8, 15) echoes this view. What I want to argue is that this psychoanalytically based and politically charged definition of the feminine not only has the potential to shed light on the elegiac practice of assuming traits conventionally assigned by Roman ideology to women or effeminate men—passivity, *mollitia*, and *servitium* (Edwards 1993: 93; Kennedy 1993: 33–34)—but can also be used to demonstrate a determined and necessary link between the practice of gender inversion and the elegists' rhetoric of ambivalence, oxymoron, and paradox. The rhetoric of undecidability and the practice of gender inversion are two sides of the same coin, which together reveal the Propertian text to be symptomatic of a profound dissociation between Symbolic norms and the possibilities of self-representation that lie at the heart of the elegiac enterprise.

Clément's and Kristeva's definitions of 'Woman' are of course founded on the psychoanalytic work of Jacques Lacan. Indeed, French feminism from the 1970s to the present constitutes itself both in reaction to and in the tradition of Lacanian psychoanalysis.[13] *Exemplary* in this regard is the case of Luce Irigaray. A member of Lacan's *Ecole Freudienne* at Paris until her expulsion in 1974 after the publication of *Speculum de l'autre femme,* Irigaray's work is both grounded in the Lacanian theory of the subject's sexualization in language and deeply critical of it. Of the many places in which this ambivalent and all but oedipal relation between teacher and student is played out, it is perhaps best seen in her essay 'Cosi fan tutti.' In this tour de force, she revisits Lacan's *Séminaire XX, Encore*, on feminine sexuality, and through a strategy of extensive quotation, commentary, and parody presents the discourse of the master in the guise of a Mozartian comedy of seduction, only with the genders reversed. By changing

---

[13] See *inter alia*, Moi 1985: 99: 'Cixous, Irigaray, and Kristeva are all heavily indebted to Lacan's (post-) structuralist reading of Freud ...' and Weed 1994: 87.

Mozart's title 'Cosi fan tutte' to 'Cosi fan tutti,' Irigaray makes us see the subje.ct presumed to know travestied by the Other.

Parody, as Bakhtin tells us, is always double-voiced.[14] In parodic texts, by definition the voice being parodied cannot be absolutely distinguished from the voice of the parodist, if the effect is not to be lost and the discourse degenerate into a monologic attack that seeks to annihilate rather than subvert the other. Two systems of accentuation are present in parodic texts, each in its most extreme manifestations clearly distinguishable from the other, but also each overlapping with and mutually determining the other at precisely those moments of contact that make parody possible. Parodic discourse is, thus, always already internally dialogized. Consequently, it must presume the authoritative status of the speech it seeks to inhabit.[15] Parody like the *recusatio*, therefore, always begins with a concession to the ground of the other, but continues with a simultaneous refusal to grant that territory absolute status and an imperative that the monologic dreams of the other be relativized and opened to the speech of the interlocutor. Such indeed would seem to be the case in 'Cosi fan tutti.' For, as Elizabeth Weed has argued, 'Virtually every element of the essay... comes from the twentieth *Séminaire*' (1994: 90). Consequently, the point where Lacan's discourse leaves off and Irigaray's begins is impossible to determine with absolute precision, yet the result is not the annulling of either Lacan's or Irigaray's discursive claims, but rather the opening of the former to the interrogation of the latter. 'Cosi fan tutti,' then, is one of the purest manifestations of the dialogic possibilities inherent in Irigaray's concept of a feminist mimetic discourse.[16] It also provides a very precise model for the complex relationship maintained between Propertian erotic poetry and the normative Symbolic of the emergent imperial regime.

---

[14] Bakhtin 1984: 127, '... parody was inseparably linked to a carnival sense of the world. Parodying is the creation of a decrowning double; it is that same "world turned inside out." For this reason parody is ambivalent.' On the distinction between negative, monological satire and the ambivalence of carnival laughter, see Miller 1998a.

[15] Bakhtin 1981: 68–9, 75–6; Morson 1989: 63, 65, 73.

[16] Irigaray 1977a: 183, '*elles sont «objets» pour et entre hommes et ne peuvent, par ailleurs, que mimer un «langage» qu'elles n'ont pas produit*;' Irigaray 1977b: 76–7; Herndl 1991: 11; Schwab 1991: 57–9; Weed 1994: 82.

This inherently complex relationship between Irigaray and Lacan's texts is further complicated by several factors. In a real sense, Lacan's discourse is self-parodic. When Lacan says of women, '*elles ne savent pas ce qu'elles disent, c'est toute la différence entre elles et moi*' (1975: 68), it must be remembered that for Lacan knowledge, *le savoir*, is itself constituted within the phallic order of the Symbolic, that realm of ordered rationality and non-contradiction that psychoanalysis, both in spite of and because of its own scientific pretensions, must always see as a mystified realm of rationalization and one whose protocols Lacan's own discursive practice violates at every turn.[17] Women don't 'know' what they are saying because the feminine position within the phallic economy is located outside the Symbolic, but it is only within the Symbolic that 'knowledge,' defined as information processed in accord with the formal dictates of reason (i.e. the laws of Symbolic substitution recognized by a given community), can occur. Lacan, Irigaray, Clément, Kristeva, and Cixous agree that woman is not representable within the phallic order of the Symbolic.[18] It is for this reason that Lacan argues that '*La femme*' does not exist, since the article '*la*' implies a universal and the concept of universality is the logical category that constitutes the very heart of the Symbolic order.[19] Woman thus represents a hole in the Symbolic, not because she is

---

[17] Weed 1994: 89, 'Lacan... sees the knowledge (*savoir*) involved in symbolic processes as indissociable from the knowledge (*connaissance*) produced in the early imaginary demarcations of "psyche" and "body," a *connaissance* that is, in turn, activated differently in the symbolic depending on whether the subject is sexed through language as male or female. If anything, Lacan sees women as knowing they don't know what they're saying—by virtue of their position in the symbolic order—while men are dupes of Truth.' On the Symbolic as realm of ordered rationality, see Janan 1994: 35, 79; Butler 1990: 82–3.

[18] Janan 1994: 28, 'for Lacan, Woman is a position outside clear meaning and grammatical language—she is *hors-sens*, outside meaning/sense. As such, Woman signifies the antithesis of masculine certitude, based on identification with rules, order, Law. Thus the feminine is for Lacan an attitude toward knowledge and procedure, rather than a category defined strictly by gender;' and Goux 1990: 223. On woman as unrepresentable within the symbolic, see Lacan 1975: 74; Herndl 1991: 16; Moi 1985: 117, 133–4, 163, 166; Irigaray 1977a: 184, '*Les femmes... vont assurer la possibilité de l'usage et de circulation du symbolique sans y être pour autant partie prenante. C'est le non-accès, pour elles, qui établit l'ordre social*;' Irigaray 1977c: 25; Butler 1990: 9–10, 27–8, 154 n. 27; Goux 1990: 147; Weed 1994: 81, 88–90.

[19] Lacan 1975: 53, 54, 57, 64, and 68, '*Il n'y a pas La femme, article défini pour désigner l'universel.*' See Kristeva 1979: 15 for her reading of this passage.

lacking (although that is the only way the patriarchal Symbolic can represent her) but because she is exorbitant in relation to its totalizing claims. The shudder of her *jouissance* takes place beyond words and thus beyond the Symbolic's power to categorize, anatomize, and atomize. It partakes of that Real from which the primary repression of our entry into the Symbolic has forever severed us.[20] She gives the lie to the Symbolic's claim to representing universality, *tout*. She says no to that. She is thus the *pas-toute*.[21] She is, as Irigaray argues, the ground on which the phallic figure of totality and totalitarianism is erected, the space that makes its calculation possible.[22] Thus her excess, which the Symbolic figures as lack, is man's necessity. It is precisely this space of intrinsic eccentricity that Propertius occupies in Book 2.

### III 'WHEN DOES NO MEAN NO?'

The elegists, in fact, represent a travesty of Roman conventions of masculinity that both questions those conventions and implicitly accepts them as the ground of their questioning (Hallett 1974: 212). This travesty of the masculine and its Symbolic norms, in turn, accounts for the anomalous position of the elegiac beloved or *domina*, who is simultaneously the cruel mistress of the *servus amoris* and the victim of the poet's, and Roman masculinity in general's, complex games of power and manipulation. Thus Propertius, as has been widely recognized, frequently assumes the feminine discursive position and promotes Cynthia to a pseudo-masculinity without ever forfeiting his phallic privileges (Luck 1960: 121–22; Stahl 1985: 263; Gold 1993a: 89; Wyke 1995: 118).[23] As Gutzwiller and Michelini

---

[20] Lacan 1975: 13, 57, 69, 76–7; Janan 1994: 30; Julien 1990: 173, 176, 208; Irigaray 1977b: 87–8, 95, 109; Butler 1990: 56; Eagleton 1983: 168.

[21] Lacan 1975: 69, "*Ce n'est pas parce qu'elle est pas toute dans la fonction phallique qu'elle y est pas du tout. Elle y est pas pas du tout. Elle y est à plein. Mais il y a quelque chose en plus.*" See also 13 and 75.

[22] Irigaray 1977d: 106–7, '*Donc le «tout»—de x, mais aussi du système—aura déjà préscrit le «pas-toute» de chaque mise en relation particulière, et ce «tout» ne l'est que par une définition de l'extension qui ne peut se passer de projection sur un espace-plan «donné», dont l'entre, les entre(s), seront évalués grâce à des repères de type ponctuel.*"

[23] For a brief synopsis of passages in which Propertius plays the woman, see Wyke 1995: 116.

note, while the elegists followed the lead of the Hellenistic poets in their reversal of normative gender values, 'Roman love poets found ways of reasserting traditional male dominance in matters of sex' (1991: 76; see also Gold 1993a: 91; Hallett 1993: 64). The rhetoric of undecidability and inversion is not in itself therefore a tool of liberation, as Hallett in more optimistic times had asserted (1973). Rather it is symptomatic of a disruption in those social structures that produce the gendered subject (Gold 1993a: 83). It is precisely this moment of disruption, as manifested in poems 2.1 and 2.7 as well as 3.4 and 3.5, that I will be examining in the remainder of this chapter. Each text exhibits, as we shall see, an analogously double-voiced strategy that at once deconstructs the laws of gender and genre.

Poem 2.1 is both the opening programmatic poem of Propertius' second book and another example of the *recusatio*, already seen in 2.10, a form whose ambivalent rhetoric simultaneously refuses a closer engagement with an alien kind of discourse (epic, encomium, etc.) and grants that engagement through this negation. It is a form that must assume the rhetorical plausibility of Maecenas' suggesting to the poet that he produce an epic on Augustus (Rothstein 1898 (1979): 1.209; Hubbard 1974: 99–100). And some have read 2.1 as a response to stronger pressures still (Stahl 1985: 164; Gold 1985: 127). It is a poem that at minimum stages the possibility of poetry's engagement with political and social power. Throughout this poem, Propertius founds his project in Book 2 on both his refusal of the embrace of normative Augustan discourse and his acceptance of it. As such, the specific difference that constitutes elegiac discourse—exemplified in the poet's inability to perform his traditional encomiastic function, his rhetorical impotence—is problematized in the very gesture that marks that discourse's programmatic institutionalization.

More specifically, in 2.1 the poet begins by offering his reader a *mollis* or 'effeminate' *liber* (2.1.2) that is inspired not by Apollo or the Muses but by the poet's *puella* or 'girl' (2.1.3–4) (Wyke 1995: 117).[24]

---

[24] Bramble 1974a: 44, 'Sexual overtones load the vocabulary of the critics: *tener, mollis, fractus, effeminatus enervis*, and their opposite epithets like *fortis* or *virilis*. This patently moralistic terminology often acted as substitute for rational criticism, as at Quint. 12. 10.12, where we hear that in his own day, Cicero was taxed with being *in compositione fractum, exultantem, ac paene, quod procul absit, viro molliorem*' (editors'

There then follows a list of possible topics concerning his beloved upon which the poet proposes to write *longae Iliades* (2.1.14). This allusion to epic, so seemingly out of place in the programmatically *mollis* genre of elegy,[25] is anticipated by a specific reference to amorous violence in the preceding line (*nuda erepto mecum luctatur amictu*, 'Naked she fought with me, her wrap ripped away,' 2.1.13) that at once naturalizes the identification of elegy with epic and underlines the paradox. The overt inversion of genres in this passage is paralleled by an implicit inversion of genders as the epic *hostis* metamorphoses into the *puella* of the poet's *militia amoris* (Kennedy 1993: 31–32). The conflation of genders and genres becomes complete, and the oxymoronic character of the verse explicit, when later in the same poem the possibility of Propertius producing an encomiastic epic on Augustus is rejected. Such *durus versus* (2.1.41) would be beyond the compass of the soft poet. At the same time, Cynthia, the subject of the poet's own *mollis liber*, is also characterized as *dura* (2.1.78), so that the elegiac beloved is attributed the same traits as epic itself (Wiggers 1977: 341; Kennedy 1993: 32–33; Fredrick 1997: 180).

How then are we to understand the poet's claim that the crown of epic lies beyond his grasp? The production of an annalistic epic on the *res gestae* of Augustus and his trusty companion Maecenas—the very topic Propertius says he would treat had he the ability (2.1.25–38)—seems simple compared to the act of sheer rhetorical prestidigitation the poet claims to accomplish: the creation of a *maxima de nihilo . . . historia* ('a great history out of nothing,' 2.1.16). This phrase moreover follows immediately upon the formulation of the poet's own amorous adventures as *longae Iliades* and directly precedes his apostrophe to Maecenas on his inability to write heroic verse, *quod mihi si tantum, Maecenas, fata dedissent,/ut possem heroas ducere in arma manus* (2.1.17–18) (But if only the fates, Maecenas, had granted to me to be able to lead heroic bands into arms.). The effect of this juxtaposition is at once to underline the difference between Propertius' amorous epic and the more traditional tales he professes to be unable to recount and to reduce the distance between these poles to the most

---

transl.: 'affected, showy, and—far be it from the truth—almost effeminate in his composition').

[25] Lemaire 1832: 145; Rothstein 1898 (1979): 1.210; Enk 1962: 13–14; Giardina 1977: 90; Richardson 1977: 211.

negligible possible by casting the one in terms of the other (Gold 1985: 159). The masculine genres of history and epic are here subordinated to and surpassed by elegy.[26]

At the same time, there is in these lines a deliberate confusion of form and content, since what Propertius literally says is, 'if only the fates granted me this much, Maecenas, so that I might be able to lead bands of heroes in arms.' The normal gloss on the pentameter, 'i.e. write an epic describing such events' (Camps 1967 *ad loc.*), erases the line's polysemic character. The basic sentiment does indeed seem to be the same as that expressed later in lines 43–44, *navita de ventis, de tauris narrat arator,/enumerat miles vulnera, pastor ovis* ('the sailor tells about the winds, the ploughman about his bulls,/the soldier recounts his wounds, the shepherd his sheep'), that is, if I were a general I would write epic. However, the literal reading must be maintained as well, if the line is not to lose much of its point, for Maecenas too was not born to lead men into battle. Indeed, he had made a conscious decision to lead a life of equestrian *otium* (Nicolet 1966: 704; Veyne 1988: 104–05) pursuing a career neither in the military nor in electoral politics, a fact that Propertius deliberately exploits in 3.9 to justify his own life of elegiac *mollitia* (Gold 1982).[27] The point becomes all the sharper when we recall that Maecenas himself, unlike Tibullus' patron Messalla, was accused of effeminacy (Juvenal 1.66; 12.39; Seneca, *Epistles* 114). Hence, the conflation of genres implicit in the poet's proposal to write *longae Iliades* on his beloved is doubled by a conflation of genders shared by the elegist and his patron in their mutual *mollitia*. Indeed, this whole unstable constellation of values is nowhere better exemplified than in the poem's final couplets:

> *si te forte meo ducet via proxima busto,*
> *esseda caelatis siste Britanna iugis,*
> *taliaque illacrimans mutae iace verba favillae:*
> *'Huic misero fatum dura puella fuit.'* (2.1.75–8)
> If perchance your way should bring you past my grave,

---

[26] As Wiggers 1977: 339 points, out the later comparison of Cynthia's fidelity to Helen's adultery (2.1.49–50) implicitly, if perversely, argues for elegy's superiority to epic on the grounds of moral seriousness.

[27] On the pursuit of *otium* as linked to *mollitia* or effeminacy, see Edwards 1993: 85.

stop your British gig with its carved yokes
and weeping utter such words to my mute ashes:
'a hard girl was the fate of this wretch.'

The oxymoron of the *dura puella* has already been discussed, but it is here paralleled by another inversion of gender traits connoted by Maecenas' use of the British war chariot or *essedum*. This was not a vehicle of machismo. Ovid in *Amores* 2.16.49–50 tells us it is the kind of chariot driven by a woman, a sentiment echoed in Propertius 2.32.5. Cicero treats the *essedum* as a sign of effeminate luxury and notes that it is all the more disgusting when driven by Antony while serving in the traditionally virile office of tribune of the *plebs* (*Epistulae ad Atticum* 6.1.25; *Orationes Phlippicae* 2.24).[28] The transformation from epic battle-car to elegiac chick-chariot, which the *essedum* undergoes as the price of entry into the Roman Symbolic, in many ways sums up the entire thrust of this poem, as elegy and epic change places in a dance that Roman culture can only conceive as feminine.

In fact, there is consistent practice of *contaminatio* throughout the poem, as one generic and gendered frame is invaded by another and what appears to be the outside is revealed to be always already inside. This violation of the law of genre—whereby the *mollis* and the *durus*, the masculine and the feminine, epic, history, and elegy are deliberately confused—is, as Sheri Benstock argues in *Textualizing the Feminine*, one of the most consistent features of discourse traditionally marked feminine, even when produced by male writers (1991).[29] The law of genre is, of course, the textual manifestation of the Oedipal law of the father whose primary social function is to institute the Symbolic and draw clear and distinct boundaries between recognized bodies and maintain category distinctions. Its most striking manifestation is in the incest taboo, but it is at work wherever the 'universal' strives to draw clear and distinct boundaries between discrete classes of persons and things so as to regulate their intercourse (Goux 1990: 222–23, 242; Rabinowitz 1993: 15; Althusser 1996: 27). It is precisely this phallic concept of the boundaries of

---

[28] See Lemaire 1832 *ad loc.*; Rothstein 1898 (1979) *ad loc.*; Enk 1962 *ad loc.*; Hubbard 1974: 102n1; Giardina 1977 *ad loc.*

[29] Benstock looks not only at H. D. Stein, and Woolf, but also at Joyce and Derrida.

discourse that Propertius violates at every turn. The clearest example in the present poem of this confusion of inside and outside, and hence of the problematization of the boundaries, is the old controversy over whether 2.1 is one, two, or even three poems,[30] but it is felt at all levels of diction throughout its troubled text.

Thus, the first three couplets present what is on the one hand a straightforward declaration of poetic intent, and on another a sustained meditation on the relation between form and content, signifier and signified, inside and outside:

> Quaeritis, unde mihi totiens scribantur amores,
>   unde meus veniat mollis in ora liber.
> non haec Calliope, non haec mihi cantat Apollo.
>   ingenium nobis ipsa puella facit.
> sive illam Cois fulgentem incedere †cogis†[31],
>   hac totum e Coa veste volumen erit. (2.1.1-6).
> You ask, why my loves so frequently become literature,
>   why my soft book should be on the lips.
> Neither Calliope nor Apollo sings these things for me.
>   my own genius the girl herself creates.
> If you would have her go forth shining in Coan silks,
>   a whole book will be made from this Coan dress.

We have already noted that *mollis* in line 2 is generally read as programmatic, referring to the subject matter contained in the *liber* (i.e. elegy), rather than the texture of the book itself. Yet the distinctions become much cloudier when we move on to the question, 'To whom is the poet referring in the phrase *in ora*, himself or his readers, and what does this mean?' While the majority of readers including

---

[30] For a good review of the early literature on this point Enk 1962: 8–9. The contemporary consensus is for the unity of the text, see Boucher 1965 (1980): 381.

[31] Either the ms. tradition is corrupt and *cogis* needs to be emended (Lachmann 1816 (1973); Lemaire 1832; Paley 1853; Butler and Barber 1933 (1969) propose *coccis*; Enk 1962; Camps 1967; and Goold 1990 follow the *codices deteriores* with *vidi*) or *cogis* here has the attenuated sense of *adducere*, which is all but unexampled (Rothstein 1898 (1979); Butler 1926; Shackleton Bailey 1956 [1967]: 61). Many simply mark the text with daggers in despair (Barber 1953—though he proposes *iuvit* in the *apparatus criticus*; Giardina 1977; Richardson 1977; Fedeli 1984). I have chosen to translate the consensus reading of the best mss. in what seems a reasonable fashion, following Butler 1926, while leaving the OCT's daggers to denote the perilous nature of any such reading.

Enk (1962 *ad loc.*), Camps (1967 *ad loc.*), Richardson (1977 *ad loc.*), Giardina (1977 *ad loc.*), and Butler and Barber (1933 [1969] *ad loc.*) read the phrase as monologically and unproblematically referring to the fame the poet achieves through his verse—he is on the lips of everyone—Goold (1990 *ad loc.*) interprets it as a question of poetics, 'how is it that my book sounds so soft upon the lips?'[32] Yet if we look at the immediately preceding hexameter and the following couplet, it becomes clear that what is most at issue is the question of origins: 'whence does my soft book come softly on the lips?' This reading does not invalidate either the majority position nor that of Goold, for none of these readings are mutually exclusive, from a logical point of view, and all are grammatically possible owing to the extreme concision of the line. Rather it reveals their interdependence. For the question of the origin of the poetry (whence it came), its nature (soft upon the lips), and its ultimate destination (as a topic of conversation for its audience) are all three at issue in this poem. But if we cannot make a firm distinction between subject matter (*res*), style (*verba*), and reception (*res publica*), then the difference between inter-, intra-, and extratextual relations becomes impossible to maintain.[33]

Nor is this an isolated instance of the transgression of fundamental boundaries. The violation of the law of genre/gender is pervasive throughout both this passage and the poem as a whole (Greene 2000: 244). Indeed, there is an ambiguity in the very first line: does *amores* refer to the poet's love affair or the poetry that purports to chronicle it (Giardina 1977 *ad loc.*; Gold 1985: 158–59)? This very confusion, however, forces us to pose the even more fundamental question of whether any such distinction can be made. On one level, the poet seems to tell us that his experience dictates the song he sings, *ingenium nobis ipsa puella facit*. Nevertheless, even this seemingly straightforward line is problematic when read in context, for the poet has just told us that his poetry is not the product of Apollo and the Muses. The next words beneath the reader's eyes are *ingenium nobis*.

---

[32] Butler (1926) prints the reading of the Neapolitanus, *in ore*, and translates in the same way. Rothstein 1898 (1979) reads *in ora*, but takes it to mean not 'in the mouth' but before the eyes.

[33] On Propertius' deliberate undermining of the classical distinction between *res* and *verba*, see Benediktson 1989: 30–1.

This poetry is not the product of the gods but of the poet's own genius![34] *Ipsa* does nothing to change our mind, since it could as easily be neuter plural as feminine singular. It is only once we reach *puella* that the process of interpretive revision has to take place. The sequence runs as follows: I need no external source of inspiration; my own innate talents are my girl's creation. But if the *amores* themselves, as Giardina points out, serve as a title for Book 2, and hence have no necessary referent beyond the book we hold in our hands, then in what sense can the *puella* herself be extratextual?

This ambivalence should come as no surprise. It is now a truism of Propertian criticism that Cynthia stands for Propertius' poetry as much as or more than for a consistent character in a novelistic romance, let alone a person of flesh and blood (Veyne 1988: 3, 7, 89; Wyke 1989a: 28, 32–34; Gold 1993a: 88; Kennedy 1993: 50–51).[35] Thus when the poet tells us that, if she should wear Coan silks, a fabric known for its see-through qualities, he will make an entire book from the fabric, he means not only a volume of erotic titillation, but also a deluxe edition fashioned from the fabric itself, whose style, like that of Catullus' *libellum . . . pumice expolitum* ('slender volume polished with pumice,' 1.1–2), will be as smooth as the material from which it is made (Rothstein 1898 (1979) *ad loc.*). It will be silken inside and out. That would indeed be a *mollis in ora liber!*[36] Thus from the very opening of 2.1, what falls within and without the realm of elegy, let alone the book-roll itself, is deliberately and intensely problematized. Within such a context, the line to be drawn between *mollis* and *durus*, masculine and feminine, epic and elegy becomes problematic indeed.

It is of course part and parcel of the *recusatio* both to grant and refuse the requested verse form, and Propertius not only delivers on

---

[34] Thus Rothstein notes that these lines far from reflecting modesty actually equate the poet's *ingenium* with divine inspiration, if they do not claim its outright superiority (1898 [1979] *ad loc.*).

[35] See 2.23.1–2, *Tu loqueris, cum sis iam noto fabula libro/et tua sit toto Cynthia lecta foro?* ('Do you speak, when you are now a story in a well-known book/and your Cynthia is read in all the forum?'). These lines in addition to treating the name Cynthia as the title of the poet's book also play on the joke that characters in books cannot speak.

[36] On this whole passage, see Fredrick 1997: 180, with whom I am in substantial agreement.

this promise by casting elegy in terms of epic, but also by providing an example of the kind of encomiastic verse he claims to be unable to write. Indeed, immediately following the poet's profession of epic incompetence, he provides a brief history of the genre's themes from the gigantomachy through Herodotus' *maxima historia* of the Persian wars to the deeds of Marius. His account of topics that cannot be treated culminates in a fourteen-line excursus on the feats of Augustus himself. Yet the ambivalence expressed with regard to the poet's ability to write encomiastic epic is paralleled in the subjects he proposes to treat if he were to praise Caesar: the graves at Philippi (l. 27) and the desecrated hearths from the Perusine war (l. 29) (Wiggers 1977: 336). The slaughter of civilians and prisoners at the end of the siege of Perusia was, of course, a topic with which he had already dealt in poems 1.21 and 1.22. It was a page from the history of the civil wars that the *princeps* would have far rather had forgotten than memorialized. In fact, Propertius is the only Augustan poet so tactless as to mention it. Yet he not only includes it in his list of possible topics of epic celebration, he highlights it: for, while all the others appear in strict chronological order, the battle of Perusia (41 BCE) is found between Naulochus (36 BCE) and Augustus' triple triumph (29 BCE). Moreover the list of possible topics itself is the longest of any *recusatio* in Augustan poetry. Propertius clearly does not want either his readers or his patrons to miss the point (Nethercut 1963: 11, 46–48; Nethercut 1983: 1840). Poem 2.1 thus presents effeminized elegy in the terms of masculine epic, while simultaneously both confessing the poet's inability to produce epic verse and giving an example of that same form that would make the poet's patron thankful for the latter's declining of his invitation. At the same time, the very existence of 2.1 stands as a testimonial to Maecenas' discretion and Augustus' *clementia* and respect for the traditional virtue of *libertas* (Cairns 1979a: 186, 201–02).

## IV 'MAKING UP IS HARD TO DO'

Poem 2.7, likewise, appears on first reading to be a refusal of the existing order. It is generally read as a celebration of the repeal of one of Augustus' moral reform laws and a declaration of pure opposition to the Augustan regime's efforts to rewrite the Roman Symbolic. Instead of celebrating the return of the *mos maiorum*, the poet's vision of himself in a strictly dyadic relation with Cynthia, one which would exclude all forms of third-party interaction, is promoted to the status of a norm (*tu mihi sola places: placeam tibi, Cynthia, solus:/hic erit et patrio sanguine*[37] *pluris amor,* 'you alone please me, may I alone please you, Cynthia, and this love will be worth more than a father's blood,' ll.19–20). Yet this reading of the poem is highly problematic, since, as Badian has shown (1985), and others have agreed (Konstan 1994: 152; and Edwards 1993: 41n.26), none of the laws promoted by Augustus had been passed at this time, let alone repealed. Badian's elegant solution to this historical conundrum is to argue that the poems' actual reference is to the repeal by Augustus of a tax imposed on unmarried men by the second triumvirate in order to raise money for the civil wars. The repeal, then, would represent part of the normalization process undertaken by Augustus, commonly referred to as 'the restoration of the republic.' Implicit in Badian's reading is the idea that 2.7 rather than being an attack on Augustus' moral reform legislation is actually a celebration of his fiscal restraint.

Yet, while Badian's solution to the problem of the legal reference in 2.7 is compelling, it hardly eliminates the interpretive difficulties that beset the poem. What Propertius and Cynthia celebrate is not their ability 'to keep what they earn,' but their refusal to enter into a recognized marital relationship and to provide citizens for the imperial armies of Rome (*unde mihi Parthis natos praebere triumphis?/nullus de nostro sanguine miles erit,* 'why should I offer sons for a Parthian triumph?/There will be no soldier from our blood,' 2.7.13–14), neither of which can be seen as supporting what Galinsky calls the moral basis of the restoration of the republic (1996: 8). Hence, Propertius' support of Augustus' repeal of the repressive triumviral legislation continues to be a statement of opposition to an Augustan ideology whose articulation had begun well in advance of any actually recorded legislation (Besnier 1979: 202; Wallace-Hadrill 1985: 180–84).

---

[37] There is no good reason not to follow the manuscripts here and read *sanguine* instead of Postgate's 1881 (1884) *nomine*.

Indeed, it is in order to account for the anomaly of the poet's critical stance vis-à-vis the moral tenor of the Augustan regime, even as he remained the acknowledged recipient of its patronage, that Francis Cairns produced the brilliant, if reductive, expedient of interpreting 2.7 as a covert endorsement of the policy it seems to oppose. Cairns notes that Propertius' casting of himself as the decadent, effeminate poet in opposition to Augustus' policy of moral regeneration merely underlines the evils the *princeps* sought to combat (1979a: 187, 190). The poet's lack of moral credibility in traditional Roman terms provides the best possible endorsement for the proposed reforms. Poem 2.7, thus, offers a double-voiced form of discourse analogous to that of 2.1's *recusatio*. As Cairns observes, 'In writing what is ostensibly a rejection of his patrons' proposals, but actually giving a favorable impression of them to the reader, Propertius is doing something paralleled in his own work and that of his contemporaries. The best-known Augustan parallels are *recusationes*' (1979a: 200). Poem 2.7, then, presents precisely the same kind of doubleness as that observed in 2.1.

Yet, even this double-voiced reading of 2.7 is an oversimplification. It merely inverts what Galinsky refers to as the 'inane dichotomies' of '"pro-" and "anti-Augustan"' (1996: 5) but does not posit that which eludes such binary oppositions, and hence what makes them possible: a subject position that is both inside and outside the norms of Symbolic discourse, that situates itself in the interstices of the dominant order, and that consequently assumes that feminine position which Propertius elsewhere more explicitly claimed as his own (Clément 1975: 17–18; Gold 1993a: 91; Hallett 1993: 63; Wyke 1995: 119–20). Cairns' position then cannot really account for both readings of 2.7, but merely demonstrates the possibility of replacing one with the other. Yet, as we saw in 2.1, Propertius' deployment of the *recusatio* form not only grants what it refuses, but it then also calls into question what it has granted by concentrating on Augustus' actions during the civil war. In particular, we noted the reference to the cruelties of the Perusine war in which Propertius lost a kinsman as he tells us in 1.22. It would be surprising indeed if at the beginning of the next book all this had been forgotten and

Propertius been converted into a subtle but unrepentant apologist for the Augustan regime.[38]

Clearly, a more complex and nuanced interpretation is required if we are to account for all the data. Poem 2.7, as we have seen, is capable of being read as a defense of the *princeps'* policy of fiscal restraint, an implicit attack on his soon to be launched moral reform program, and a covert endorsement of that same policy. All of these readings are not only textually but also historically possible and plausible. They bespeak an unresolvable ambiguity in the poet's relation to the realm of Augustan public discourse, and hence to the Symbolic norms of his time, analogous to that already seen in the case of poems 2.15 and 2.16.

This symptomatic undecidablity is evident even on the level of 2.7's poetic diction. Thus in lines 1–6 the poet writes:

*Gavisa est certe sublatam Cynthia legem,*
　　*qua quondam edicta flemus uterque diu,*
*ni nos divideret: quamvis diducere amantis*
　　*non queat invitos Iuppiter ipse duos.*
*'At magnus Caesar.' sed magnus Caesar in armis:*
　　*devictae gentes nil in amore valent.*
Cynthia certainly rejoiced when the law was revoked,
　　at whose proclamation we both long wept
lest it should divide us, although Jupiter himself
　　cannot split apart two lovers if they are not willing.
'But Caesar is great.' But Caesar is great in arms:
　　conquered peoples are worth nothing in love.

The reference to Jupiter can be read as a covert allusion to Augustus thematically preparing his explicit mention in the next couplet. As Cairns notes, the association of Jupiter and Augustus is a common encomiastic strategy in Augustan poetry, allowing the poet implicitly to deify the emperor without risking impiety or a political *faux pas* (1979a: 187–88).[39] The metonymic identification of Jupiter and Augustus, however, is not always benign. The same trope appears in Ovid's *Tristia*, first as an ironic insinuation of despotism (*Tristia* 2)

---

[38] On 2.1's deliberate echoes of 1.22, see Gold 1985: 158.
[39] See, *inter alia, Odes* 3.1.

and then as an explicit recognition of the poet's abjection in the face of imperial power. It is because of the inherent ambiguity of the identification with the father of the gods that what is for Cairns an implicit encomium becomes for Nancy Wiggers a subtle condemnation of imperial brutality (1977: 337).

The text is more elusive still. It neither quakes before the power of Jupiter, nor indicts his brutality, but proclaims the god's inability to separate lovers against their will. Moreover, the juxtaposition of Jupiter and Caesar underlines not only these figures' metonymic identification, but also their substantive difference. Indeed, Caesar is introduced as a potentially more powerful adversary than Jupiter himself, *At magnus Caesar* (Postgate 1881 (1884) *ad loc.*; Richardson 1977 *ad loc.*). This first adversative construction is not, however, allowed to stand alone, but is answered by a second, *sed magnus Caesar in armis*. It notes that while Caesar is great in arms, and hence a potentially more formidable opponent than the distant Jupiter, his greatness is circumscribed to a realm that has no relevance to lovers. 'Conquered peoples are worth nothing in love.' Thus, Caesar like Jupiter is impotent before the power of love. The claim of a complete lack of relation between love and war, however, is belied by the poet's own use of the trope of *militia amoris* in both 2.1 and 2.7 (King 1980b: 73). What this string of adversatives and negations points to then is a position that eludes the sterile dichotomies of pro- and anti-Augustan: for, what Richardson reads as a 'defiant defense of liberty' (1977 *ad loc.*), Cairns sees as 'open praise of Augustus' military glory' (1979a: 187); and what Wallace-Hadrill reads as an attempt to define and limit 'Augustus' proper sphere of action,' the battlefield but not the heart (1985: 184), Badian interprets as the celebration of a return to fiscal normalcy (1985) and Postgate as 'gross flattery' (1881 [1884] *ad loc.*).[40]

To this extent, then, both 2.7 and 2.1, like 2.15 and 2.16, present Propertius as speaking in the feminine, a discourse that eludes the conventional binary oppositions of official and subversive, pro and con, conscious and unconscious. Propertius is a woman because his subject position cannot be precisely located in any one spot within

---

[40] Tränkle argues for interpreting the poem as an 'elegy of praise full of respect and distance' (1983: 155, author's translation).

conventional Roman ideological space (Wyke 1995: 120–21). In this context, his inversion of normative gender roles in assuming the pose of *servus amoris* can be seen as part of a wider ideological and rhetorical strategy in which the norms of gender, discourse, power, and desire are called into question in a more radical fashion than the concept of mere opposition can convey. To that degree, the Propertian text can be read as symptomatic of a more profound dissension at the heart of the Symbolic itself, one that figures the norms of discourse as radically incommensurate with the poet's Imaginary reflections of the self's experience. The gap that is thereby revealed is a truer gauge of this poetry's engagement with History and the Real than any reduction of the text to a state of permanent ontological inferiority, to the status of a mere reflection of a pre-existing reality, political or otherwise. Unlike other women, however, Propertius, at least theoretically, retains the option of being a man. His appropriation of the feminine position does not imply a new symmetry in sexual power relations so much as a destabilization of the category of the masculine. In the final analysis, it remains an appropriation that was not equally open to all. And that is real power too.[41]

## V 'LOVING YOUR ENEMY'

The clue may be supplied by one of the ideal demands, as we have called them, of civilized society. It runs: 'Thou shalt love thy neighbour as thyself.' ... Why should we do it? What good will it do us? ... Indeed, if this grandiose commandment had run 'Love thy neighbour as thy neighbour loves thee,' I should not take exception to it. And there is a second commandment, which seems to me even more incomprehensible and arouses still stronger opposition in me. It is 'Love thine enemies.' If I think it over, however, I see that I am wrong in treating it as a greater imposition. At bottom it is the same thing.
(Freud 1961a: 56-57)

---

[41] The fact that racial, gendered, class, and sexual subject positions may be in large part social constructions does not mean that they are all equally available to everybody. See Steele 1997: 202.

Augustus takes on an increasingly prominent role in the poetry of Book 3, although few of the references to him could be construed as complimentary. Poem 3.5, which directly contradicts 3.4.1 in its first line (cf. *Arma deus Caesar meditatur* with *Pacis Amor deus est*), again confuses questions of ethics with poetic style.

(Gold 1985: 163-64)

Book 3 exhibits the same confusions and conflations of basic categories that we have identified in Book 2 (Stahl 1985: 189–90 = Stahl in this volume).[42] It does not, however, merely repeat Book 2's problematic: for in it, the circle that defines the gap between Imaginary self-definition and Symbolic law has been reduced. The distinctions between elegy and epic, public and private, masculine and feminine have been more sharply defined in relation to one another and the distance between them reduced. Book 3 opens with reflections on the contradictions between martial themes and the poet's erotic and Callimachean aims (3.1–3)[43] and closes with the dismissal of Cynthia and amatory poetry (3.24–25; Gold 1985: 163; Wyke 1987a: 154; 1989: 30). It juxtaposes the poet's proposed journey to Athens, as a means of escaping unhappy love, with an exhortation to Tullus to return to Rome and enjoy the fruits of the Augustan peace (3.21–22; Stahl 1985: 207–08 = Stahl in this volume page 326).[44] It stages the poet's own refusal of epic verse as parallel to Maecenas' unwillingness to accede to the ranks of the senate (3.9; Gold 1985: 166–67; Boucher 1965 [1980]: 304), and it, like Book 2 (2.15–16), justifies the poet's subjugation to a woman by citing Antony's subjection to Cleopatra (3.11; Gurval 1995: 206–07).

Poem 3.11 is particularly symptomatic of the kind of ideological conundra presented by Book 3's conflation of even the most basic categories, including those of friend and foe. It closes by celebrating Augustus' power as equal, if not superior, to Jupiter's own: *haec di condiderant, haec di quoque moenia servant:/vix timeat salvo Caesare Roma Iovem* ('the gods founded these walls, the gods still watch

---

[42] On 3.1 continuing the themes and style of 2.1 and 2.34, see Stahl 1985: 190 (= Stahl in this volume).

[43] On 3.1–5 as a response to Horace's 'Roman Odes,' see Sullivan 1976: 14; Cremona 1987. On the apparently Callimachean pose adopted by the poet actually being profoundly imbued with Roman models, see Cameron 1995: 473–4.

[44] Gold (1985: 155–6) notes that 3.21 and 3.22 represent a rejection of the position taken by the poet in 1.6, where the poet stays home and Tullus goes abroad.

over them/Rome should hardly fear Jupiter while Caesar is safe,' 3.11.65–66). The statement is problematic. On one level, it is certainly laudatory of Augustus (Fantham 1996: 124–25). On another, it borders on sacrilege by exalting the *princeps* above the father of the gods, a position that sorts ill with his preferred image as the restorer of traditional piety. Propertius goes well beyond the more nuanced position staked out by Horace:

> *Caelo tonantem credidimus Iovem*
> *regnare; praesens divus habebitur*
> > *Augustus adiectis Britannis*
> > > *imperio gravibusque Persis* (*Odes* 3.5.1-4)
>
> We trust that thundering Jupiter reigns in heaven; Augustus will be considered godlike in the here and now by the conquered Britons and through his power over the dread Persians

In this closing poem of the Roman Odes, Augustus is a god only to those barbarians at the far edges of the known world who are about to be subjected to Roman *imperium*.[45] In Rome, he is merely the first citizen. His reign may be the earthly instantiation of Jupiter's rule (*Odes* 3.1.5–8), but he is not a god himself, let alone Jupiter's superior. His subsequent deification is alluded to by Horace, but his status in this world is clearly that of a man (White 1993: 169–82).

The extremity of the Propertian position cannot help but raise eyebrows. It is deliberately provocative. Is this a compliment or an insult? The question becomes more difficult to answer the closer we look at the poem itself. Jupiter may be compared to Augustus at the end of 3.11, but earlier in the poem he is portrayed as one who, like Propertius, disgraces himself and his household through submission to a woman (3.11.27–28). Jupiter like Propertius, then, functions as an analogue to Antony in his submission to Cleopatra: no wonder Augustus is portrayed as the god's potential superior! Yet Augustus' own line is not exempt from this taint: for the poem's mention of Pompey's death on the shores of Egypt not only calls to mind the origins of the civil wars but also reminds the reader of the deified Julius' own erotic submission to the *noxia Alexandria* (3.11.33–38;

---

[45] Of course the Horatian subtext is made clearest in elegy 3.11's relation to *Odes* 1.37. See Sullivan 1976: 23–4.

Stahl 1985: 237, 242–47; Gurval 1995: 198). This last association is especially important because the deification of Augustus' uncle and adoptive father is what established the warrant for the *princeps'* own impending divine status, though only once he has left behind the realm of the here and now (cf. *Odes* 1.2.45).

As we can see then, in poems like 3.11, rather than sticking to safe topics, as Hubbard alleges (1974: 95), Propertius in Book 3 has moved into an even closer engagement with the Augustan regime. Such proximity, however, not only more firmly plants Propertius' star in the imperial firmament, it also necessarily exacerbates the contradictory relations that characterize the rapport of elegy with the imperial Symbolic. The ratcheting up of the tensions inherent in this rapprochement is at the heart of the Propertian project in Book 3, and it is nowhere better exemplified than in the relation between poems 3.4 and 3.5, a pair whose opening lines both recall and directly contradict each other: *Arma deus Caesar dites meditatur ad Indos* ('Caesar the god is planning to take up arms against India,' 3.4.1); *Pacis Amor deus est, pacem veneramur amantes* ('Love is the god of peace, we lovers worship peace,' 3.5.1) (Boucher 1965 (1980): 69; Stahl 1985: 196–97 = Stahl in this volume; Camps 1966 *ad loc.*). The remainder of this chapter shall be concerned with the complex and multivalent relations between these last two poems of the programmatic sequence that introduces the third book (Camps 1966 *ad loc.*; Nethercut 1983: 1839). As we shall see, these poems intermingle political, erotic, poetic, and generic frames in such a fashion as both to preserve elegy's irrecuperable remainder and to make its posited externality to the emerging imperial Symbolic ever harder to maintain. Propertius is still a woman, but now more than ever he is woman as the formal expression of a simultaneous excess and lack (Benstock 1991: 119)

Poems 3.4 and 3.5, in the manner of all of Propertius' later work, are not simple texts. The difficulties in interpreting 3.4 begin with the very first line. *Arma deus Caesar* echoes the opening of the *Aeneid*, extracts of which were already circulating at the time Propertius was finishing Book 2 circa 25 BCE[46] and are explicitly alluded to in

---

[46] The exact dating of Propertius' books is open to question, depending on whether one accepts Lachmann's thesis that Book 2 was originally two separate

2.34.61–66. This initial reference to the poem has been the cause of critical debate as to whether it is laudatory (Newman 1997: 220), critical of Vergil's lapsing from the orthodox Callimachean line of eschewing epic (Benediktson 1989: 45), or engaged in a subtle polemic about the proper progression of a poet's career (Stahl 1985: 182–85). Nonetheless, it has been difficult to read the final couplet referring to Vergil's forthcoming epic, *cedite Romani scriptores, cedite Grai!/nescio quid maius nascitur Iliade* (Make way Roman writers! make way Greeks! Something greater than the *Iliad* is being born.), as less than ironic since Pound's brilliant mistranslation:

> Make way, ye Roman authors,
>                      clear the street, O ye Greeks,
> For a much larger Iliad is in the course of construction
>                      (and to Imperial order)
> Clear the streets, O ye Greeks! (Sullivan 1964: 169)

Thus when Propertius begins a poem *arma deus Caesar*—immediately after being told by Calliope in 3.3 to eschew epic and arms, *Contentus niveis semper vectabere cycnis,/nec te fortis equi ducet ad arma sonus* ('you will always be content to be carried by snowy swans/nor will the sound of a brave horse lead you to arms,' 3.3.39.40)—it is hard not to see it as a critical echo of *arma virumque cano*. Indeed, the only puzzling thing is that no previous commentary has observed this

---

books. There is strong evidence of manuscript corruption in Book 2, as evidenced by the widespread disagreement over how many poems the volume contains, ranging from 34 to 46 depending on the editor (Hubbard 1974: 44–5), and many have found the notion of dividing the second book attractive, especially in light of 2.13.25–26's reference to there being three books, i.e. the Monobiblos plus two others (Lachmann 1816 (1973): xxi–xxii; Paley 1853 *ad loc.*; Hubbard 1974: 41–2; Sullivan 1976: 6–7; Lyne 1980: 120; King 1980b: 61–84; Günther 1997: 6–10). This notion has not won universal assent, but the alternative explanations that 'three' either represents an indefinite number (Richardson 1977 *ad loc.*; Camps 1967 *ad loc.*) or a selection of representative books from Propertius' library (Rothstein 1898 (1979) *ad loc.*) are not convincing. King's argument that poems 2.1 to 2.12 form a coherent unity in terms of both thematic and numerical correspondences has much to recommend it (1980: 66, 70, 80), while Fredrick observes the dominance of the Iliadic theme in poems 2.1 to 2.15 (1997: 182). If one accepts Lachmann's thesis then Hubbard's and Sullivan's datings of the books seem reasonable: Monobiblos 29–8, Book 2a 28–7, Book 2b 26–5, Book 3 22–1, Book 4 after 16 (Hubbard 1974: 44; Sullivan 1976: 3, 7–8). In any case, 2.34's reference to the *Aeneid* only makes sense if the poem's basic outline was already known; it is therefore not unreasonable to assume that by 22 BCE the circle of poets gathered around Maecenas had heard some version of the poem's opening lines.

allusion, even as Ovid's *arma gravi numero* ('weapons in a serious meter,' *Amores* 1.1.1) is universally conceded to be an echo of *Aeneid* 1.1 (Green 1981: 268; McKeown 1987 *ad loc.*; Mack 1988: 54–55; Buchan 1995: 54n.5).

The Propertian allusion, in fact, is more precise than its Ovidian recollection. The substitution of *deus* for *vir* keeps the basic structure of the opening hemistich of *Aeneid* 1.1, in which the agent wielding the *arma* is the second word of the hexameter. At the same time, Propertius' reformulation also makes explicit that the *vir*, Aeneas, was but a stand-in for the *deus*, Caesar, all along, even as it implicitly recalls that both Aeneas and Augustus were really only *viri*. Thus, the use of *deus* for Augustus here, as in 3.11, can be read as both genuinely encomiastic[47] and a covert slap.[48] Likewise, the echo of the *Aeneid* presents the same essential ambiguity on the poetic level—is it complimentary or critical? In addition, the nature of that intertextual relation is in no way made less problematic by the *Aeneid's* own notoriously complex relation to the *princeps*. Finally, the alliteration between *cano* and *Caesar* drives the parallels between the two passages home.

Such complexities are not limited to the first line. In fact, the whole of poem 3.4 is compounded from a similarly unstable mixture of contradictory elements. Thus, on the one hand, the poem labels the motive for war and the subsequent celebration of triumphs as greed (cf. 3.4.2 *gemmiferi... maris*, 'the gem rich ocean'; and 3.4.3, *magna, viri, merces*, 'great wages, men!'). On the other, the image of Caesar giving laws to the Tigris and Euphrates and recovering the lost standards of Crassus was almost necessarily genuinely encomiastic. These were themes with such broad appeal that they cannot be immediately discounted as simple kowtowing to the party line or as imperial propaganda, nor can they, in themselves, be reduced to mere pretexts for greed (3.4.4–10; Boucher 1965 [1980]: 117; White 1993: 159–68; *pace* Stahl 1985: 195 = Stahl in this volume). It was certainly possible to loot without establishing a constitutional order or giving laws, and there were far easier targets of potential pillage than the feared Parthians.

---

[47] Richardson 1977 *ad loc.*; Camps 1966 *ad loc.*; Butler and Barber 1933 (1969) *ad loc.*; Newman 1997: 250.

[48] Rothstein 1898 (1979) *ad loc.*, citing Philo *leg. ad Gaium* 23; Hubbard 1974: 104; Stahl 1985: 194 = Stahl in this volume.

By the same token, however, Propertius' claim that he will watch Caesar's triumph while propped on his girlfriend's lap is, as Richardson notes, 'a flagrant breech of decorum' (1977 *ad loc.*). Such statements are hardly designed to rally the troops for a program of imperial expansion. Still, the sting of the barb is substantially reduced by the final couplet, which on its own would demand to be read as a simple restatement of traditional Roman values:

> *praeda sit haec illis, quorum meruere labores:*
> *me sat erit Sacra plaudere posse Via. (3.4.21–2)*
> Let this booty be for those whose labors have earned it:
> It will be enough for me to be able to applaud from the Sacred Way.

The sentiment is, 'Let the prizes goes to those who earn them; for the rest of us there is nothing to do but express our admiration.' This is a mere affirmation of an ideological truism: those who possess wealth and power are those who deserve it. It does not challenge the traditional social order and the system of rewards reserved for *otium* and *negotium* but reaffirms them (Conte 1994b: 256). But why then say it? The one question the normative position cannot answer is why someone would choose not to play the game. Yet, that person is precisely the elegist. The very statement of the norm implies the existence of a position that cannot be articulated within its bounds. This is the position of Propertius, of Woman.

The tensions inherent in such a position cannot be reduced without sacrificing much of the poem's interest. Indeed, it is precisely with regard to this sort of *aporia* that a symptomatic reading of elegy proves its mettle: for it is in the symptom itself that the force of History is made manifest. As Boucher eloquently observes, 'Les contradictions du développement élégiaque sont l'écho des contradictions du poète… l'écho des contradictions d'une époque qui sort durement des guerres civiles et d'une révolution' (1980: 386–87).[49] Such contradictions are not to be resolved by critical fiat into a univalent picture of pro- or anti-Augustan sentiment. Rather they are, like woman herself, a symptom,

---

[49] 'The contradictions of the development of elegy are the contradictions of the poet… the echo of the contradictions of an epoch that with difficulty has just come through the civil wars and a revolution.'

a trace of the Symbolic's own foundational moment of exclusion, its attempt to wrest a self-consistent, and hence monological, system of signification from language's web of infinite difference (Lacan 1975: 68; 1982: 168; Janan 1994: 31). It is less Propertius' attitude toward Augustan ideology that is on display in such undecidable moments than the elegist as the unassimilable remainder, as that which cannot be processed by the categories of Augustan ideology without either falsifying elegy or itself (Boucher 1965 [1980]: 136–37).

The symptomatic visibility of that remainder is best seen in 3.4's penultimate couplet where the poet achieves a momentary fusion of the amorous and the imperial, in an image that simultaneously gives elegy's blessing to epic and confirms our earlier reading of 3.4.1 as a parody of *Aeneid* 1.1:

> *ipsa tuam serva prolem, Venus: hoc sit in aevum,*
> *cernis ab Aenea quod superesse caput.* (3.4.19-20)
> You yourself keep watch over your child, Venus: may he live forever,
> whom you see to be the descendant of Aeneas

Venus is the appropriate guardian of Augustus since she is the mother of Aeneas, the founder of the Julian line. She is of course also the goddess of love and mother of Amor, Aeneas' brother, as Ovid reminds us (*Amores* 1.2.51–52). But whereas in Ovid this reference, coming at the end of Amor's triumph over the poet, is a moment of pure irony containing neither a specifiable political content nor a credible encomiastic purpose (Barsby 1973 [1979] *ad loc.*; Mack 1988: 64; Buchan 1995: 64), in Propertius the reference to an Augustan triumph at the end of the long-planned Parthian campaign, and in a context evoking the *Aeneid*, must leave open the possibility of a genuinely eulogistic intent (Stahl 1985: 193–94 = Stahl in this volume). It is precisely in the gap between the equally plausible positive and negative readings of this couplet that the Propertian subject is situated. Venus is the suture between the realms of Propertius and Augustus, the point of articulation that allows the effeminate world of elegy to be momentarily joined with the masculine, warlike world of Augustus and epic, without being assimilated to it.

At the same time, Venus is the poetic hinge point that allows the poet to prepare the reader for the opposition between 3.4 and 3.5 announced by *pacis Amor deus est* ('Love is the god of peace'), in which *pax* is substituted for 3.4.1's *arma* and *Amor* for *Caesar*. Propertius does not, however, strictly refuse battle but rather in the following line modulates directly into the *militia amoris* motif, claiming that his *dura proelia* will be with his mistress rather than the Parthians. In contrast to the battles outlined in 3.4, though, his amorous tussles will not be fought for the acquisition of *praeda*. Indeed, where 3.4.2 looked expectantly to the *freta gemmiferi... maris* ['the straits of the *gem-bearing* seas'], 3.5.4 directly denies that *bibit e gemma divite nostra sitis* ['our thirst drinks from a *bejeweled* cup']. Moreover, in 3.5.3–18, greed, imperial expansion, and the sack of Corinth are attributed to a congenital perversity of the human spirit that forces us ever to seek new satisfactions for new desires (Liberman 1995: 319), and hence to establish new boundaries to cross and new enemies to crush, as we become embroiled in a continual dialectic between the search for limits and the necessity of their transgression (Barton 1993: 57–58). Each new set of categorical distinctions is annihilated, each new boundary is erased, as the foundation of our desire in an original lack, a marking of the limits of the self, can only be ultimately expunged in the absolute negation that is death (Bataille 1957: 155). Propertius limns this narrative for us in the first half of 3.5:

>   nec tamen inviso pectus mihi carpitur auro,
>     nec bibit e gemma divite nostra sitis,
>   nec mihi mille iugis Campania pinguis aratur,
>     nec miser aera paro clade, Corinthe, tua.
>   o prima infelix fingenti terra Prometheo!
>     ille parum cauti pectoris egit opus.
>   corpora disponens mentem non vidit in arte:
>     recta animi primum debuit esse via.
>   nunc maris in tantum vento iactamur, et hostem
>     quaerimus, atque armis nectimus arma nova.
>   haud ullas portabis opes Acherontis ad undas:
>     nudus ad infernas, stulte, vehere rates.[50]

---

[50] This line is much disputed. I have chosen to follow Lachmann 1816 (1973), Lemaire 1832, Paley 1853, Rothstein 1898 (1979), Butler 1926, Paganelli 1964, Richardson 1977, and the reading of the better codices rather than that offered by Barber's 1953 OCT or pick one of the numerous other emendations that have been advocated by Enk 1911 (1978), Butler and Barber 1933 (1969), Shackleton Bailey 1956 (1967), Camps 1966, Goold 1990, and Fedeli 1984, and have yielded no better sense nor garnered much assent.

> *victor cum victis pariter miscebitur umbris:*
>     *consule cum Mario, capte Iugurtha, sedes.*
> *Lydus Dulchio non distat Croesus ab Iro:*
>     *optima mors Parcae*[51] *quae venit acta die.* (3.5.3–18)

Neither nonetheless is my heart seized by unseen gold,
    nor does our thirst drink from a bejeweled cup,
nor are a thousand rich acres ploughed in Campania for me
    nor do I, like a wretch, procure your bronzes, Corinth, with my sword.
Oh unhappy first earth to yield to Prometheus' craft!
    That one wrought the work of a too little cautious soul.
Putting the bodies in order he did not oversee the mind with skill.
    First the way of the spirit ought to be straight.
Now we are tossed about on the sea by so much wind, and we seek
    an enemy, and we lash new arms to arms.
You will not take any riches to the waves of Acheron:
    Fool, you will be carried naked to the infernal rafts.
The victor will be equally mixed with the conquered shades:
    you, captured Jugurtha, will sit with the consul Marius.
Lydian Croesus does not stand apart from Ithacan Irus:
    Best is the death that comes on the day appointed by Fate.

On one level, this is a stinging indictment of the transgressive desire that powers the dreams of eastern conquest in 3.4 and sets up a clear opposition between the lover who worships peace and Caesar who plans war. There is never enough (Stahl 1985: 195–200 = Stahl in this volume). New enemies must always be found, new boundaries established between us and the other, an other who must always then be annihilated and incorporated into ourselves, into the dominant order, until we reach the point at which all boundaries, all distinctions between self and other collapse (Black 1991: 108).[52] The logical conclusion of this aggressive desire, which Propertius attributes to us as original sin owed to the fault of Prometheus, is death, the *telos* to which the passage leads (Freud 1961a: 65–66, 69; Freud 1961b: 30–33). This is

---

[51] I have adopted the reading of Lachmann et al. A discussion of this crux can be found below.

[52] See Butler 1999: 6, 'desire, according to Hegel, is the incessant human effort to overcome external differences, a project to become a self-sufficient subject for whom all things apparently different emerge as immanent features of the subject itself.'

the only possible complete fulfillment, the erasure of the distinction between self and other, of the boundaries that constitute the hierarchies wherein our identity is founded and our subjectivity positioned: Marius versus Jugurtha, Croesus versus Irus, victor versus vanquished, Roman versus barbarian, rich versus poor, inside versus outside, same versus other.[53] The logic of desire, however, is fundamentally deconstructive. It both requires these kinds of binary oppositions and undoes them, including that between lover and soldier. Thus on another level, this same logic is what aligns Propertius and Augustus within the dialectic of transgression and desire,[54] so that each becomes the ironic mirror image of the other.

This homology is made apparent on a number of levels, the most obvious of which is the poet's deployment of the motif of *militia amoris* (3.5.2). Yet, this trope is sufficiently common that, despite its use immediately after 3.4's vision of future triumphs over eastern foes, it might be thought to be purely conventional. More convincing, however, is a pair of textual anomalies that have never been adequately explained, each of which demonstrates the homology of the Propertian and Augustan positions with respect to desire. The first is found in the last line of the passage just cited, *optima mors Parcae quae venit acta die* ('best is the death that comes on the day appointed by fate'). This line has caused much vexation. The main problem is the word *Parcae*. Barber's 1953 OCT prints the reading of the best mss., *parca*, in daggers. Lachmann 1816 notes that *parca dies* as first explained by Scaliger—'the fated day'—is nonsense in Latin. *Parcae dies*, however, gives excellent sense, is easily explained, and is paralleled in *Aeneid* 12.149.[55] The issue that has impeded its universal acceptance is one of interpretation rather than grammar, paleography, or usage: for, are not all deaths those that come on the day of fate? But if that is the case then what is the point of the distinction Propertius seems to be drawing between the life

---

[53] Bataille 1957: 26–7; Lacan 1986: 341; Black 1991: 110, 205; Guyomard 1992: 53–4; Butler 1999: 9.

[54] On the fundamental structure of eroticism as the violation of boundaries and the dissolution of the closed structure of being, see Bataille 1957: 22.

[55] Thus Lemaire 1832 *ad loc.*; Rothstein 1898 (1979) *ad loc.*; Camps 1966 *ad loc.*; Shackleton Bailey 1956 (1967): 145–6; Fedeli 1984 *ad loc.*

(and death) of the lover and the soldier? We all die on our appointed days. Enk admirably sums up the logic of this counterargument:[56]

> apparet eam correctionem sensum dare huic loco non aptum. Nam si quis ob stultiam in mari aut in acie perit, ea quoque mors acta venit die Parcarum. Sensus, quem flagitat contextus arsque logica, hic est: optimum est mori, cum confectus annis vitam relinquis. Hunc sensum restituit emendatio Baeherensii: carpta[57] qua recepta etiam lectio apta[58] in textu ponenda est.

[It appears that this correction gives an inappropriate sense to this passage. For if anyone, on account of foolishness, dies either at sea or in battle, that death also comes on the day appointed by the fates. The sense that the context and logical consistency demands is this: the best death is that which comes when you leave life weighed down with years. The emendation of Baehrens restores this sense: *carpta*, whereby the received reading *apta* is also to be placed in the text.]

The problem, of course, is that Enk assumes that Propertius' goal is logical consistency and that the purpose of the passage is to present a straightforward rhetorical distinction between two opposed styles of life, which we can for our purposes refer to as the Augustan and the elegiac.[59] But as numerous commentators have noted the essence of Propertian style is just the opposite: it does not present the reader with unproblematic rhetorical demonstrations, but sharp juxtapositions, unstated transitions, and ironic reversals (Luck 1960: 114; Elder 1962: 71–72; Boucher 1965 [1980]: 316–17; 370; Benediktson 1989: 29). Moreover, this tidying up of the rhetorical distinctions between the Augustan and the elegiac modes of life is in direct contradiction with thrust of the passage itself, which states that all such categories are invalid in the realm of the dead, *victor cum victis pariter miscebitur umbris* ('ghosts of victor and victim will mingle,' editor's transl.). The fact that no matter when or how one dies one

---

[56] Enk 1978 (1911): 220.
[57] Butler 1912 (1924) and Goold 1990 also follow Baehrens.
[58] The oldest of the mss., N, has the reading *acta*; this is accepted by Lachmann 1816 (1973) and those who agree with him. It is also the reading of Butler 1912 (1924), Barber's OCT 1960, and Richardson 1977 Some of the later mss. read *apta*, as do Paley 1853, and Butler and Barber 1933 (1969).
[59] See also Rothstein's 1898 (1979) comments on l. 3.

always dies on the day appointed by fate does not render the passage meaningless, but rather proves its point. Thus, on the one hand, the poet's message is certainly that the pursuit of wealth is to be shunned since 'you can't take it with you.' However, on the other, since there are no distinctions in the underworld, then the lover and the soldier, the poor man and the rich man are both counted the same.[60] We all share equally in Prometheus' mistake. From this perspective, the poet's deployment of the *militia amoris* motif at the poem's beginning is more than the invocation of a well-worn topos. It is a statement of ultimate equality.

Thus, the first of our two textual anomalies clearly reveals as much the aporetical nature of the poet's relation with Augustus as it does the corrupt nature of the text. Most proposed emendations of Propertius have been efforts to smooth out these contradictions and produce a monological text (Boucher 1965 [1980]: 117 n.1), rather than to read such cruxes symptomatically from the perspective of the emergence of the Real. The homology of the Augustan and elegiac subject positions is, in fact, most interesting in its simultaneous assertion of formal difference (the lover versus the soldier) and substantive identity (the originary or Promethean lack that is desire). It is the contradiction between these two opposed asseverations that constitutes the final irrecuperable remainder, the moment of the Real that can only be attributed to that which must be excluded from a self-consistent Symbolic economy, to that which must be abjected: that is to woman as the excluded ground that makes the

---

[60] Paley 1853 *ad loc.* and Richardson 1977 *ad loc.* each defend the original reading of the mss., taking *parca* as an adjective meaning 'poor' or 'mean.' Neither offers any parallel passages for the phrase *parca dies* meaning 'day of poverty.' Both interpret the passage to mean that the best death comes when one is poor. The reasoning here is unclear, nor does it address the passage's fundamental point that death treats rich and poor alike. Paganelli 1964 too accepts *parca*, but treats it as a proper name without explanation. This is a position that cannot be defended. The most important thing, however, is not which reading of the text to accept, but rather to see the confusion itself as symptomatic of the instability of the fundamental Symbolic categories out of which, and in opposition to which, Propertius constructs the elegist's subject position (see Miller and Platter 1999b). It thus becomes increasingly difficult to define a position outside of Augustan norms, as the very gestures of opposition themselves become assimilated to the structures of the emerging imperial ideology.

masculinist synthesis possible (Kristeva 1977: 165; Moi 1985: 166; Butler 1990: 93).[61]

The same homological structure that unites the opposed positions of the Augustan and elegist can be seen in our second anomaly as well. The last twenty-two lines of the poem consist of a list of topics the poet will study when love has ceased to hold him in thrall (Rothstein 1898 [1979]: 2.33). This repetitive catalog, which occupies almost half the poem, is by far the longest in the Propertian corpus. It is an aesthetic blemish. Its very length serves to undermine the otherwise symmetrical structures linking 3.4 and 3.5 (Richardson 1977: 333). How do we explain such a gaffe? Was the poet simply carried away? Is he so infatuated with Alexandrian learning that he cannot resist detailing all the possible topics in natural science, philosophy, and metaphysics that his later studies might cover? Or might this list, in its very repetitive insistence, relate to the theme of the poem itself, that is, to the fundamental inability of desire to be satisfied (except by death)?

It is helpful at this juncture to recall that desire, from a rhetorical perspective, is metonymic in structure. It is an endless series of displacements and inadequate substitutions; its verbal embodiment is the list (Lacan 1986: 143, 340; 1991: 201–02; Zizek 1991: 7; Guyomard 1992: 50). Propertius in the last half of 3.5 asks us to envision him as moving from one realm of intellectual conquest to the next in the same way that his soldierly counterpart must move from one enemy to the next in the first half of the poem and in 3.4. There is a structural symmetry to their respective enterprises. Similarly, just as the first half of the poem ends in the underworld so does the second. Thus, the poet will finish his career by investigating whether:

*sub terris sint iura deum et tormenta gigantum,*
    *Tisiphones atro si furit angue caput,*
*aut Alcamaeoniae furiae aut ieiunia Phinei,*
    *num rota, num scopuli, num sitis inter aquas,*

---

[61] The abject is precisely that which links us most firmly with the Real, the reminder/remainder of our pre-Symbolic origins. It is literally non-sense. On the ideological equivalence of cadavers, feces, menstrual blood, and sexual fluids, see Bataille 1957: 64.

> *num tribus infernum custodit faucibus antrum*
>     *Cerberus, et Tityo iugera pauca novem,*
> *an ficta in miseras descendit fabula gentis*
>     *et timor haud ultra quam rogus esse potest. (3.5.39–46)*
> if the laws of the gods and the torments of the giants exist beneath the earth
>     if the head of Tisiphone rages with a black snake,
> or the furies of Alcmaeon or the hungers of Phineus,
>     are there wheels, cliffs, and thirsts in the middle of water,
> does Cerberus with three throats guard the mouth of the cave,
>     and are there nine little acres for Tityus,
> or does a fictive story descend among the wretched peoples,
>     and is there able to be no fear beyond the pyre?

The question of whether the underworld exists might be thought to contradict the earlier claim that all social distinctions will be erased in the underworld, but as in our first instance we are dealing with a formal assertion of difference that masks an underlying substantial identity: for how can there be social distinctions beyond the grave if there is no beyond? In either case—'the best death comes on its appointed day' or 'there are no rich men in the underworld unless it doesn't exist'—we are all equal before death and desire. What remains in both cases then is an assertion of difference that can neither articulate its own underlying assumptions nor be reduced to the terms of mere opposition to an ideological norm. The moment of difference that it enunciates is precisely that which cannot be assimilated to either Augustan imperial ideology or its opposite. Instead, that difference articulates itself as a kind of circularity embodied in the final couplet of the poem, which both functions as an envoi and returns us to the beginning of 3.4, *exitus hic vitae superest mihi: vos, quibus arma/grata magis, Crassi signa referte domum* ('this is what the end of life has in store for me: you to whom arms/give more pleasure, bring the standards of Crassus home,' 3.5.47–48).

## VI REMAINDERS

> ... the feminine separates and sutures, it is an effect of 'the vigilance and failure of censorship.' (Benstock 1991: 118)

That which will not be pinned down by truth is, in truth, <u>feminine</u>.
(Derrida, *Spurs*, cited by Benstock 1991: 119)

Peter White has taught us that it is a vast oversimplification to view the relationship of poets to the Augustan regime as either one of simple conformity to the dictates of an all-powerful patron or of heroic resistance to the forces of tyranny. Neither did Maecenas act as a kind of minister of propaganda nor did Augustus dictate the specific kinds of poems that should be written. Nonetheless, as White also points out, it would be a mistake to see the various kind of encomiastic verse produced by not only Horace and Vergil, but also by Propertius and even Ovid, as unprompted and spontaneous outpourings of genuine emotion. There was a culture of patronage existing at all levels of Roman society that located the individual within a vast web of mutual obligations to his or her social superiors and inferiors. These were often of an informal nature, but had direct political consequences and could have legal force. Such relations were the foundation of traditional republican politics. They were also the social fabric into which the poetry of the period was woven. With the collapse of the republic and the coming of the principate, there naturally occurred a centralization of patronage relations as the cultural and political life of the city increasingly came to revolve around the imperial household and those closest to it (1993: 28, 119–22, 138, 145, 150–52, 163–67, 208).[62] In any such environment, in which the legitimacy of a given form of discourse is founded upon relations that either no longer obtain or have been fundamentally altered, the choice for the speaker between conformity and resistance is a false one, predicated more on a bourgeois view of the subject as a unified source of meaning than on the semantic conditions of possibility for a given discursive formation (Habinek 1998: 8). Thus what we see in this period is not the institution of, and the resistance to, a planned program of poetic propaganda, but the gradual restructuring of the field of social, discursive, and power relations that made poetic discourse possible within imperial society. Elegy is a symptom of that restructuration.

---

[62] See also the valuable discussions of Gold 1985; Cairns 1979a: 202; Boucher 1965 (1980): 37; Santirocco 1986: 154; de Ste. Croix 1981: 342; Wyke 1989a: 30; and Conte 1994b: 251.

Whereas earlier in the century the collapse of the republic and of the normative ideology of Roman aristocratic *virtus* had opened up new discursive spaces and created slippages in the semiotic system that constituted the Roman Symbolic, as exemplified in the poetry of Catullus, Gallus, and to a lesser extent the Monobiblos, the subsequent consolidation of the principate recentered discursive norms in a way that altered the nature of what it meant to be a speaking subject (Cairns 1979c: 32; Maltby 1980: 4). Who spoke to whom and for what purposes all underwent fundamental changes in this period. With the collapse of the traditionally decentered (or better, multipolar) web of associations that regulated discursive power in republican Rome, the privileged interlocutor naturally became the *princeps* and his associates. This, as White points out, was not a deviation from the conditions under which poetry was produced under the republic but its natural outgrowth (1993: 139–40, 207). Poets wanted maximum visibility and thus sought the support of the most prominent and influential patrons. With the rise of the *princeps*, a single center of discursive gravity naturally formed. Augustus did not so much change the rules of the game as the grounds on which the game was played.[63] He became the patron of all patrons so that, rather than interpersonal relations between the elite being conceptualized on the model of mutual aristocratic obligation in the pursuit of *negotium*, the norm became one of dependant clientage in the pursuit of a cultivated and thus, from a traditional perspective, effeminized *otium*.[64] Therefore not only did the poets become women but so did their former patrons as well (Joshel 1992b: 151; Edwards 1993: 85; Barton 1993: 29n.63; Oliensis 1997: 154).[65]

This change itself, however, took place within the existing set of social institutions and was consistently presented as a return to the status quo ante, a restoration of the republic. As such, the change itself could only be articulated, within the terms available, as a contradiction.

---

[63] As Habinek 1998: 121 makes clear, the normative function of Roman literature was to contribute 'to the amalgamation of Roman identity to subject status and help reconstitute the potentially free reader of the widely circulated literary text as a subject of an imperial regime.'

[64] On the case of Messalla, see note 24.

[65] On the collapse of the republic and the collapse of the traditional discourse of aristocratic manhood or *virtus*, see Edwards 1993: 57; Fredrick 1997: 179.

This history becomes most manifest to us precisely in the moments of poetic *aporia* that result from the speaking subject being placed in an impossible position: one which allows it neither to accede to a traditional web of aristocratic mutual obligations nor to reject the values inherent in that web; one that neither allows traditional republican *libertas* nor denies it; one that no longer allows the practice of *virtus* as traditionally understood and yet launches a deliberate legislative, religious, and artistic program to encourage its restoration (Last 1934: 456, 459; Littlewood 1983: 2138; Wallace-Hadrill 1985: 183; Edwards 1993: 41–42; Edwards 1996: 49–50, 57).

Propertius, then, is a woman because her excess is the only authentic place from which he can speak, because she simultaneously marks the gap between the Imaginary and the Symbolic and sutures them together. Propertius is a woman because he articulates the rules of the game of power from a position that both accepts that game and finds itself outside the Symbolic system that prescribes it. Propertius is a woman because under the empire, in spite of the variability of individual responses, even a senator can no longer be a man, at least, as the republic understood *dignitas*, manhood and *virtus*. Propertius is a woman because Propertius too is a symptom.

# Works Cited

Adams, J. N. 1982. *The Latin sexual vocabulary*. Johns Hopkins Press, Baltimore, MD.
Ahl, F. 1974. 'Propertius 1.1.' *WS* 27: 80–98.
Alfonsi, L. 1943, publ. 1944. 'L'elegia di Gallo.' *Rivista di Filologia* 21: 46–56.
―― 1945 (1979). *L'elegia di Properzio*. Vita e pensiero, Milan (repr. New York).
―― 1971. 'Sul mito di Ercole e Caco in Properzio.' In *Fons perennis. Studi in onore di V. d'Agostino. Rivista di Studi Classici.* Amministrazione della Rivista di studi classici, Torino: 1–6.
Allen, A. 1962. "Sunt qui Propertium malint." In J. P. Sullivan, ed. *Critical Essays on Roman literature: Elegy and Lyric*: 107–48. Harvard University Press, Cambridge. Mass.
Allen, A.W. 1950a. '"Sincerity" and the Roman elegists.' *CP* 45: 145–60.
―― 1950b. 'Elegy and the classical attitude toward love: Propertius 1.1.' *YCS* 11: 253–77.
―― 1974. 'Propertiana' *CP* 69: 113–16.
Althusser, L. 1996. *Writings on Psychoanalysis: Freud and Lacan*. Eds. Olivier Corpet and François Matheron. Trans. Jeffrey Mehlman. Columbia University Press, New York.
Álvarez-Hernández, A. 1997. *La Poética Propercio. Autobiografía artística del 'Calimaco Romano.'* Accademia properziana del Subasio, Assisi.
Ancona, R. 1994. *Time and the Erotic in Horace's Odes*. Duke University Press, Durham.
Anderson, R. D., P. J. Parsons, and R. G. M. Nisbet. 1979. 'Elegiacs by Gallus from Qasr Ibrim.' *JRS* 69: 125–55.
Anderson, W. S. 1964. 'Hercules *Exclusus*. Propertius IV.9.' *AJP* 85: 1–12.
―― 1992. 'The Limits of Genre.' In G. K. Galinsky, ed., *The Interpretation of Roman Poetry: Empiricism or Hermeneutics*. Studien sue classischen Philologie 67, 96–103. Peter Lang, Frankfurt.
Axelson, B. 1945. *Unpoetische Wörter. Ein Beitrag zur Kenntnis der Lateinischen Dichtersprache*. Gleerup, Lund.
Badian, E. 1985. 'A Phantom Marriage Law.' *Philologus* 129: 82–98.
Baehrens, E. 1880. *Sex. Propertii elegiarum libri IV*. Teubner, Leipzig.
Baehrens, W. 1913. 'Propertiana.' *Philologus* 72: 263–77.

Baker, R. J. 1968a. '*Miles Annosus*: the Military Motif in Propertius.' *Latomus* 27: 322–49.
——1968b. 'Propertius 3.1.1-6 Again. Intimations of Immortality?' *Mnemosyne* 21: 35–9.
Bakhtin, M. M. 1981. 'From the Prehistory of Novelistic Discourse.' In M. Holquist, ed. *The Dialogic Imagination*. Trans. C. Emerson and M. Holquist, 41–83. University of Texas Press, Austin.
——1984. *Problems of Dostoevsky's Poetics*. Ed. and trans. C. Emerson. University of Minnesota Press, Minneapolis.
Balsdon, J. P. V. D. 1962. *Roman Women: Their History and Habits*. The Bodley Head, London.
——1979. *Romans and Aliens*. Duckworth, London.
Barber, E. A. 1953 (1960). *Sexti Properti Carmina*. Clarendon Press, Oxford.
Barsby, J. A. 1973 (1979). *Ovid: Amores Book I*. Oxford University Press, Oxford, reprinted Bristol.
Barth, F. G. 1777. *Sex. Aurel. Propertius*. Schwickert, Leipzig.
Barthes, R. 1970 (1975). *S/Z*. Trans. R. Miller. Jonathan Cape, London.
Barton, C. 1993. *Sorrows of the Ancient Romans*. Princeton University Press, Princeton.
Bataille, G. 1957. *L'érotisme*. Éditions de Minuit, Paris.
Batstone, W. 1992. '*Amor improbus, felix qui,* and *tardus Apollo*: The *Monobiblos* and the *Georgics*.' *CP* 87: 287–302.
Beck, M. 2000. 'Properzens Elegie 2, 7 und die augusteische Ehegesetzgebung.' *Philologus* 144: 303–24.
Becker, C. 1955. 'Virgils Eklogenbuch.' *Hermes* 83: 314–49.
——1971. 'Die späten Elegien des Properz.' *Hermes* 99: 449–80.
Bellen, H. 1963. '*Adventus dei*. Der Gegenwartsbezug in Vergils Darstellung der Geschichte von Cacus und Hercules.' *RM* 106: 23–30.
Beltrami, L. 1989. 'Properzio 4, 4: La colpa della Vestale.' In Giuseppe Catanzaro and Francesco Santucci, eds., *Tredici secoli di elegia latina: Atti del convegno internazionale, Assisi, 22–24 aprile 1988*, 262–72. Accademia properziana del Subasio, Assisi.
Benediktson, D. 1989. *Propertius: Modernist Poet of Antiquity*. Southern Illinois University, Carbondale and Edwardsville.
Benjamin, Anna S. 1965. 'A Note on Propertius 1. 10; *O iucunda quies*.' *CP* 60: 178.
Bennett, A. W. 1967. 'Sententia and Catalogue in Propertius (III 9, 1–20).' *Hermes* 95: 222–43.
——1968. 'The Patron and Poetical Inspiration. Propertius III 9.' *Hermes* 96: 318–40.
Bennett, F. M. 1967. *Religious Cults Associated with the Amazons*. AMS Press, New York.

Benstock, S. 1991. *Textualizing the Feminine: On the Limits of Genre.* University of Oklahoma Press, Norman.
Benveniste, E. 1969. *Le vocabulaire des institutions indo-européennes.* 2 vols. Éditions de Minuit, Paris.
Bertini, F. 1983. *Ovidio: Amori.* Garzanti, Milan.
Besnier, R. 1979. 'Properce (Elégies II, VII et VIIa) et le premier échec de la législation démographique d'Auguste.' *Revue historique droit français et étranger* 57: 191–203.
Betensky, A. 1973. 'Forum.' *Arethusa* 6: 267–9.
Binder, G. 1971. *Aeneas und Augustus.* A. Hain, Meisenheim am Glan.
Black, J. 1991. *The Aesthetics of Murder.* Johns Hopkins University Press, Baltimore.
Bobrowski, A. 1994. 'Propertius 2.8 and 2.9 as Counterparts.' *SO* 69: 108–20.
Booth, J. 2001. 'Moonshine: Intertextual Illumination in Propertius 1.3.31–3 and Philodemus, *Anth. Pal.* 5.123.' *CQ* 51: 537–44.
Boucher, J. P. 1965 (1980). *Etudes sur Properce: problèmes d'inspiration et d'art.* E. de Boccard, Paris.
——1966. *Caius Cornelius Gallus.* In *Bibliothèque de la faculté des lettres de Lyon* 11. Les Belles Lettres, Paris.
Bowra, C. M. 1958. 'A Love Duet.' *AJP* 79: 376–91.
Boyancé, P. 1942. 'Surcharges de redaction chez Properce.' *REL* 20: 54–69.
——1956. *L'influence grecque sur la poésie latine de Catulle à Ovide.* Fondation Hardt pour l'Étude de l'Antiquité Classique, Geneva.
Boyd, B. W. 1987. '*Virtus effeminata* and Sallust's Sempronia.' *TAPA* 117: 183–201.
——1997. *Ovid's Literary Loves: Influence and Innovation in the* Amores. University of Michigan Press, Ann Arbor.
Brakman, C. 1926. 'Propertiana.' *Mnemosyne* 54: 77–80.
Bramble, J. C. 1970. 'Structure and Ambiguity in Catullus XLIV.' *PCPS* 16: 22–41.
——1974a. *Persius and the Programmatic Satire: A Study in Form and Imagery.* Cambridge University Press, Cambridge.
——1974b. '*Cui non dictus Hylas puer?* Propertius 1.20.' In A. Woodman and D. West, eds. *Quality and Pleasure in Latin Poetry,* 81–93. Cambridge University Press, Cambridge.
Braund, S. M. 1995. 'A Woman's Voice?—Laronia's Role in Juvenal *Satire* 2.' In B. Levick and R. Hawley, eds. *Women in Antiquity,* 207–19. Routledge, New York.
——and B. K. Gold. 1998. 'Introduction.' *Vile Bodies: Roman Satire and Corporeal Discourse.* Special Issue of *Arethusa* 31: 247–56.

Brenk, F. E. 1979. 'Tarpeia among the Celts: Watery Romance, from Simylos to Propertius.' *Studies in Latin Literature and Roman History* 1: 166–74.

Bright, D. F. 1978. *Haec mihi fingebam: Tibullus in his World.* Brill, Leiden.

Broekhuizen, J. 1727. *Sex. Prop. Elegiarum Libri IV.* Wetstenios, Amsterdam.

Brouwers, J. H. 1970. 'Properce et la gloire.' *Mnemosyne* 23: 42–61.

Brunt, P. A. 1971. *Italian Manpower.* Oxford University Press, Oxford.

——1982. '*Nobilitas* and *Novitas*.' JRS 72: 1–17.

——and J. M. Moore. 1973 (1967). *Res Gestae Divi Augusti. The Achievements of the Divine Augustus.* Oxford University Press, Oxford.

Buchan, M. 1995. '*Ovidius Imperamator*.' *Arethusa* 28: 53–85.

Buchheit, V. 1965. 'Tibull 2.5.' *Philologus* 109: 184–200.

——1972. *Der Anspruch des Dichters in Vergils Georgika: Dichtertum u. Heilsweg/Vinzenz Buchheit.* Wissen Schaftliche Buchgesell shaft, Darmstadt.

Buckland, W. W. and Peter Stein. 1975. *A Text-Book of Roman Law from Augustus to Justinian*, 3rd ed., Cambridge University Press, Cambridge.

Bühler, W. 1964. 'Archilochos und Kallimachos.' *Entretiens Hardt* 10: 225–47.

Buonocore, M. 1995. *Properzio nei codici della Biblioteca Apostolica Vaticana.* Accademia properziana del Subasio, Assisi.

Burck, E. 1959. 'Abschied von der Liebesdichtung (Properz III 24 und 25).' *Hermes* 87: 191–211.

——1966. 'Zur Komposition des vierten Buches des Properz.' *WS* 79: 405–27.

——1981. 'Liebesbindung und Liebesbefreiung. Die Lebenswahl des Properz in den Elegien 1,6 und 3,21.' In E. Lefèvre, ed. *Vom Menschenbild in der Römischen Literatur.* Vol. 2, 349–72. C. Winter, Heidelberg.

Burnett, A., ed. 2007. *The Letters of A.E. Housman.* Oxford University Press, Oxford.

Bury, R. G. 1939. 'Notes on Propertius.' *PCPS* 172–4: 6–7.

Butler, H. E. 1905. *Sex. Propertii opera omnia.* A. Constable and Co., London.

——1926. *Propertius.* Harvard University Press, Cambridge, MA.

——and E. A. Barber. 1933 (1964, 1969). *The Elegies of Propertius.* Clarendon Press, Oxford (Reprinted Hildesheim, G. Olms).

Butler, J. 1990. *Gender Trouble: Feminism and the Subversion of Identities.* Routledge, New York.

——1999. *Subjects of Desire: Hegelian Reflections in Twentieth-Century France.* 2nd ed. Columbia University Press, New York.

Butrica, J. 1982. 'Review article: the Latin love poets.' *EMC* 1: 82–95.

——1983. 'Propertius 3.3.7–12 and Ennius.' *CQ* 33: 464–8.

——1984. *The Manuscript Tradition of Propertius. Phoenix* Supplementary Volume 17. University of Toronto Press, Toronto.

Butrica, J. 2006. 'The transmission of the text of Propertius.' In H. C. Gunther, ed. *Brill's Companion to Propertius*. Brill, Leiden: 25–43.

Cahoon, L. 1985. 'The Bed as Battlefield: Erotic Conquest and Military Metaphor in Ovid's *Amores*.' *TAPA* 118: 293–307.

Cairns, F. 1969. 'Propertius 1.18 and Callimachus, *Akontius and Kydippe*.' *CR* 19: 31–4.

——1970. 'Theocritus *Idyll* 10.' *Hermes* 98: 38–44.

——1971. 'Propertius, 2,30 A & B.' *CQ* 21: 204–13.

——1972. *Generic Composition in Greek and Latin Poetry*. Edinburgh University Press, Edinburgh.

——1973. 'Catullus' Basia poems (5, 7, 48).' *Mnemosyne* 26: 15–22.

——1974a. 'Some Problems in Propertius 1.6.' *AJP* 95: 150–63.

——1974b. 'Some Observations on Propertius 1. 1.' *CQ*: 24: 94–110.

——1977a. 'Horace, Odes, III, 13 and III.23.' *Ant. Class.* 46: 523–43.

——1977b. 'Horace on Other People's Love Affairs (*Odes* I 27; II 4; I 8; III 12).' *QUCC* 24: 121–47.

——1977c. 'Two Unidentified Komoi of Propertius. I 3 and II 29.' *Emerita* 45: 325–53.

——1978. 'The genre Palinode and three Horatian examples: Epode 17; Odes, I, 16; Odes, I, 34.' *Ant. Class.* 47: 546–52.

——1979a. 'Propertius on Augustus' Marriage Law (II.7).' *Grazer Beiträge* 8: 185–204.

——1979b. 'Self-Imitation within a Generic Framework: Ovid *Amores* 2.9 and 3.11 and the *renuntiatio amoris*.' In A. Woodman and D. West, eds. *Creative Imitation and Latin Literature,*121–41. Cambridge University Press, Cambridge.

——1979c. *Tibullus: a Hellenistic poet at Rome*. Cambridge University Press, Cambridge.

——1982. 'Horace Odes 3, 22: Genre and Sources.' *Philologus* 126: 227–46.

——1984. 'Propertius and the Battle of Actium.' In A. Woodman and D. West, eds. *Poetry and Politics in the Age of Augustus*, 129–68. Cambridge University Press, Cambridge.

——1987. '*AP* 9.588 (Alcaeus of Messene) and *nam modo* in Prop. 1.1.11.' In *Filologia e forme letterarie. Studi offerte a Francesco della Corte*. Edizione Quattro Venti, Urbino: I.377–83.

——1992. 'Propertius 4.9. *Hercules Exclusus* and the Dimensions of Genre' In G. K. Galinsky, ed. *The Interpretation of Roman Poetry: Empiricism or Hermeneutics*, Studien zue classischen Philologie 67, 65–95. Peter Lang, Frankfurt.

——2006. *Sextus Propertius: The Augustan Elegist*. Cambridge University Press, Cambridge.

Cameron, A. 1968. 'The First Edition of Ovid's *Amores*.' *CQ* 18: 320–33.
——1995. *Callimachus and His Critics*. Princeton University Press, Princeton.
Camps, W. A. 1961. *Propertius Elegies Book I*. Cambridge University Press, Cambridge. Reprinted 1977.
——1965. *Propertius Elegies Book IV*. Cambridge University Press, Cambridge.
——1966. *Propertius Elegies Book III*. Cambridge University Press, Cambridge.
——1967. *Propertius Elegies Book II*. Cambridge University Press, Cambridge.
Canter, H. V. 1920. 'The Paraklausithyron as a Literary Theme.' *AJP* 41: 355–68.
Carson, A. 1990. 'Putting Her in Her Place: Woman, Dirt, and Desire.' In *Before Sexuality: The Construction of Erotic Experience in the Ancient Greek World*, edited by D. M. Halperin, J. Winkler, and F. Zeitlin, 135–69. Princeton University Press, Princeton.
Celentano, L. 1956. 'Significato e Valore de IV Libro di Properzio.' *Annali della Facoltà di letteratura e filosofia* 6: 33–68.
Cherniss, H. 1935. *Aristotle's Criticism of Presocratic Philosophy*. Johns Hopkins University Press, Baltimore.
Clausen, W. V. 1964. 'Callimachus and Latin poetry.' *GRBS* 5: 181–96.
——1976. 'Cynthius.' *AJP* 97: 245–7.
Clément, C. B. 1975. 'La Coupable.' *La jeune née*, 8–113. Union générale d' Éditions, Paris.
Cloud, D. 1993. 'Roman Poetry and Anti–Militarism.' In J. Rich and G. Shipley (eds.), *War and Society in the Roman World*. Leicester-Nottingham studies in ancient society, v. 5. London.
Coarelli, F. 1980. *Guida archeologica di Roma*. Arnoldo Mondadori Editore, Bari.
Coleman, R. 1977. *Vergil Eclogues*. Cambridge University Press, Cambridge.
Coli, E. 1978. 'Properzio IV.9 e il culto della Bona Dea.' *GIF* 9: 298–305.
Commager, S. 1974. *A Prolegomenon to Propertius*. University of Cincinnati, Cincinnati.
Conington, J. and Nettleship, H. 1883 (1963). *The Works of Vergil with a Commentary*. Vol. III (*Aeneid* VII–XII). Whittaker, London.
Conte, G. B. 1974. *Memoria dei poeti e sistema letterario*. G. Einaudi, Turin.
——1989. 'Love without elegy: the *remedia amoris* and the logic of a genre.' *Poetics Today* 10: 441–69. Reprinted 1994 in *Genres and Readers: Lucretius, Love Elegy, Pliny's Encyclopedia*. Trans. by G. W. Most. Baltimore.

Conte, G. B. 1994a. *Genres and readers: Lucretius, love elegy, Pliny's Encyclopedia.* Johns Hopkins University Press, Baltimore.
——1994b. *Latin Literature: A History.* Trans. Joseph B. Solodow. Revised by D Fowler and G W. Most. Johns Hopkins University Press, Baltimore.
Copley, F. O. 1947. '*Servitium amoris* in the Roman elegists.' *TAPA* 78: 285–300.
——1956. *Exclusus Amator. A Study in Latin Love Poetry.* American Philological Association, Madison.
Courtney, E. 1968. 'The Structure of Propertius Book I and some Textual Consequences.' *Phoenix* 22: 250–8.
——1969. 'Three Poems of Propertius.' *BICS* 16: 70–87.
——1970. 'The Structure of Propertius Book III.' *BICS* 16: 70–87.
Crabbe, A. 1981. 'Structure and Content in Ovid's *Metamorphoses*.' *ANRW* 2.31.4: 2274–327.
Cremona, V. 1987. 'Emulazione e polemica: Properzio III, 1–5: Orazio III, 1–6.' *Euphrosyne* 15: 247–56.
Cucchiarelli, A. 2005. 'Speaking from Silence: the Stoic Paradoxes of Persius.' In K. Freudenburg, ed. *The Cambridge Companion to Roman Satire*, 62–80. Cambridge University Press, Cambridge.
Culham, P. 1986. 'Ten years after Pomeroy: studies of the image and reality of women in antiquity.' *Helios* 13.2: 9–30.
Cupaiuolo, F. 1963. *Un capitolo sull' esametro latino.* Libreria Scientifica Editrice, Naples.
Curran, L. 1964. 'Ovid *Amores* 1.10.' *Phoenix* 18: 314–18.
——1966. 'Vision and Reality in Propertius I.3.' *YCS* 19: 189–207.
——1969. 'Catullus 64 and the Heroic Age.' *YCS* 21: 169–92.
Daly, L. J. and W. L. Reiter. 1971. 'The Gallus Affair and Augustus' *lex Iulia maiestatis*: a Study in Historical Chronology and Causality.' *Coll. Latomus* 164. In *Studies in Latin Literature and Roman History.* C. Deroux (ed.) Latomus, Brussels.
Daut, R. 1975. 'Zu Properz 3, 21.' In P. T. Brannan, ed. *Classica et Iberica. A Festschrift in honor of Joseph M. F. Marique*, 293–302. Institute for Early Christian Iberian Studies, Worcester, MA.
Davis, J. T. 1977. *Dramatic Pairings in the Elegies of Propertius and Ovid. Noctes Romanae* 15. Paul Haupt, Bern-Stuttgart.
Davis, P. J. 1999. 'Ovid's *Amores*: a political reading.' *CP* 94: 431–49.
Day, A. A. 1938. *The Origins of Latin Love Elegy.* Blackwell, Oxford.
De Brohun, J. B. 2002. *Roman Propertius and the Reinvention of Elegy.* University of Michigan Press, Ann Arbor.

De Romilly, J. 1975. *Magic and Rhetoric in Ancient Greece*. Harvard University Press, Cambridge.

de Ste Croix, G. E. M. 1981. *The Class Struggle in the Ancient Greek World: From the Archaic Age to the Arab Conquests*. Cornell University Press, Ithaca.

Degani, E. 1973. 'Note sulla fortuna di Archiloco e di Ipponatte in epoca ellenistica.' *QUCC* 16: 79–104.

——(ed.) 1977. *Poeti greci giambici ed elegiaci*. Ugo Mursia Editore, Milan.

Derrida, J. 1991. 'Living On: Border Lines.' In P. Kamuf, ed., *A Derrida Reader: Between the Blinds*: 254–68. Columbia University Press, New York.

——1992. 'The Law of Genre.' In *Acts of Literature*: 221–52. Routledge, New York.

de Sanctis, A. 1973. *Saggio d'interpretazione psicologia*. Bibliotheca Bibliographica 9.

Deubner, L. 1921. 'Ein Stilprinzip hellenistischer Dichtkunst.' *NJA* 47: 361–78.

Dickey, E. 2002. *Latin Forms of Address: From Plautus to Apuleius*. Oxford University Press, Oxford.

Dickie, M. W. 1981. 'The Disavowal of Invidia in Roman Iamb and Satire.' *PLLS* 3: 183–208.

Dieterich, A. 1911. 'Die Widmungselegie des letzten Buches des Propertius.' In *Kleine Schriften*, 164–92. Teubner, Leipzig.

Diggle, J. and F. R. D. Goodyear, eds. 1972. *The Classical Papers of A. E. Housman*. Cambridge University Press, Cambridge.

Dilke, O. A. W. 1982. 'De Horatio et Tibullo.' In *De Tibullo eiusque aetate*. *Academia Latinitati Fovendae Commentarii* 6: 7–14. 1st Nazionale di Studi Romani, Rome.

Dimundo, R. 2000. *Tears in Propertius, Ovid and Greek Epistolographers*. De Gruyter, Berlin.

Dixon, S. 1988. *The Roman Mother*. Croom Helm, London.

——1992. *The Roman Family*. Johns Hopkins University Press, Baltimore.

——2001. *Reading Roman Women: Sources, Genres and Real Life*. Duckworth, London.

Doblhofer, E. 1961. *Die Augustuspanegyrik des Horaz in formalhistorischer Sicht*. Winter, Heidelberg.

Dodds, E. R. 1952. *The Greeks and the Irrational*. University of California Press, Berkeley and Los Angeles.

Dover, K. J. 1970. *Aristophanes' Clouds with Introduction and Commentary*. Oxford University Press, Oxford.

Drachmann, A. B., ed. 1903–27. *Scholia Vetera in Pindari Carmina*. Teubner, Leipzig.

duBois, P. 1976. 'The *Pharmakos* of Virgil: Dido as Scapegoat.' *Vergilius* 22: 14–22.

——1982. *Centaurs and Amazons: Women and the Pre-history of the Great Chain of Being*. Ann Arbor.

DuQuesnay, I. M. LeM. 1973. 'The *Amore*.' In J. W. Binns (ed.), *Greek and Latin Studies, Classical Literature and Its Influence: Ovid*, 1–48. Routledge, London.

——1978. 'Review: Backgrounds to Augustan Poetry: Gallus, Elegy and Rome.' *CR* 28: 276–7.

Eagleton, T. 1983. *Literary Theory: An Introduction*. University of Minnesota Press, Minneapolis.

Edwards, C. 1993. *The Politics of Immorality in Ancient Rome*. Cambridge University Press, Cambridge.

——1996. *Writing Rome: Textual Approaches to the City*. Cambridge University Press, Cambridge.

Eisenhut, W. 1975. *Wege zu Properz.* = *Wege der Forschung* 237. Wissenschaftliche Buchgesellschaft, Darmstadt.

Elder, J. P. 1962. 'Tibullus: *Tersus atque elegans*.' in J. P. Sullivan, ed. *Critical Essays on Roman Literature: Elegy and Lyric*, 65–105. Routledge, London.

Enk, P. J. 1911 (1978). *Ad Propertii Carmina Commentarius Criticus*. Brill, Zutphen, reprinted New York.

——1946. *Sex. Propertii Elegiarum Liber I*. 2 vols. Leiden: Brill.

——1962. *Sex. Propertii Elegiarum Liber Secundus*. Leiden: Sÿthoff.

Ericsson, D. 1988. 'Silence.' *Friends Journal* 44: 8.

Ernout, A and A. Meillet. 1939. *Dictionnaire étymologique de la langue latine*, 2nd edn. C. Klincksieck, Paris.

Fairweather, J. 1974. 'Fiction in the biographies of ancient writers.' *Ancient Society* 5: 231–75.

Fantham, E. 1972. *Comparative Studies in Republican Latin Imagery*. University of Toronto Press, Toronto.

——1986. 'Women in antiquity: a selective (and subjective) survey 1979–84.' *EMC* 5.1: 1–24.

——1996. *Roman Literary Culture: From Cicero to Apuleius*. Johns Hopkins University Press, Baltimore.

Farrell, J. 2009. 'The Impermanent Text in Catullus and Other Poets.' In W. A. Johnson and H. Parker, eds. *Ancient literacies: The Culture of Reading in Greece and Rome*, 164–85. Oxford University Press, Oxford.

Fau, G. 1978. *L'Emancipation féminine à Rome*. Les Belles Lettres, Paris.

Fedeli, P. 1965. *Properzio Elegie Libro IV*. (Studi e commenti, 3), Adriatica Editrice, Bari.

——1969. 'Osservazioni sullo stile di Properzio.' *SIFC* 41: 81–94.

——1980. *Sesto Properzio Il primo libro delle elegie, introduzione, testo critico e commento a cura di Paolo Fedeli*. *Accademia Toscana di Scienze e Lettere 'La Colombaria,' Studi* 53. Olschki, Florence.
——1981. 'Elegy and Literary Polemic in Propertius' Monobiblos.' *PLLS* 3: 227–42.
——1983. 'Propertii monobiblos: Struttura e motivi.' *ANRW* 2.30.3: 1858–1922.
——1984. *Sexti Properti Elegiarum Libri IV*. Teubner, Stuttgart.
——1985. *Properzio: Il libro terzo delle elegie*. (Studi e commenti, 3), Adriatica Editrice Bari.
——1986. *Il libro terzo delle elegie. Introduzione testo e commento. RFIC* 114.
——1987. 'Properzio, fra culto del testo tradito e caccia alla corruttela.' In *Bulletin dela Faculté des Lettres de Mulhouse* 15: 107–12.
——2005. *Properzio: Elegie, Libro II. Introduzione, testo e commento. ARCA Classical Texts, Papers and Monographs* 45. Francis Cairns, Cambridge.
Ferrero, G. 1908–1909. *The Greatness and Decline of Rome*. Vols. 4 and 5. G. P. Putnam & Sons, New York.
Fineberg, B. H. 1993. 'From a sure foot to faltering meters: the dark ladies of Tibullan elegy.' In M. DeForest, ed. *Woman's Power, Man's Game: Essays in Honor of Joy King*, 249–56. Bolchazy-Carducci, Wauconda, IL.
Fitzgerald, W. 1995. *Catullan Provocations*. University of California Press, Berkeley.
——2000. *Slavery and the Roman Literary Imagination*. Cambridge University Press, Cambridge.
Flaschenriem, B. L. 1997. 'Loss, desire, and writing in Propertius 1.19 and 2.15.' *CA* 16.2: 259–77.
——1998. 'Speaking of Women: 'Female Voice' in Propertius.' *Helios* 25.1: 49–64.
Fogelmark, S. 1972. *Studies in Pindar with particular reference to Paean VI and Nemean VII*. Gleerup, Lund.
Foley, H. P., ed. 1981. *Reflections of Women in Antiquity*. Gordon and Breach, New York.
Fontana, M. 1950. 'Properzio e il matrimonio.' *GIF* 3: 73–6.
Fordyce, C. J. 1961. *Catullus. A Commentary*. Oxford University Press, Oxford.
Foucault, M. 1976 (1981). *The History of Sexuality. Volume 1: An Introduction*. Penguin, Middlesex.
——1978. *The History of Sexuality*, trans. by R. Hurley. Vol. 1. Pantheon Books, New York.

Fowler, D. 1990. 'Roman Literature. (review article).' *GR* 37: 104–11.
—— 1994. 'Postmodernism, Romantic Irony and Classical Closure.' In I. De Jong and J. P. Sullivan (eds) *Modern Critical Theory and Classical Literature*, 231–56. E. J. Brill, Leiden.
—— 1996. 'Even Better than the Real Thing: A Tale of Two Cities.' In J. Elsner, ed. *Art and Text in Roman Culture*, 57–74. Cambridge University Press, Cambridge.
Fraenkel, E. 1960. *Friedrich Leo Ausgewählte Kl. Schriften*, Vol I–II. Edizioni di Storia e Letteratura, Rome.
—— 1964. '*Lucili quam sit mendosus.*' *Kleine Beiträge zur klassischen Philologie* II: 199–208.
Fraser, P. M. 1972. *Ptolemaic Alexandria*. Clarendon Press, Oxford.
Frassinetti, P. 1949. 'Scuola di poesia e poesia di scuola nelle lettere latine.' *GIF* 2.4: 352–60.
Frazer, J. G. 1929. *The Fasti of Ovid. Text and Commentary*. Macmillan, London.
Fredrick, D. 1997. 'Reading Broken Skin: Violence in Roman Elegy.' In J. Hallett and M. Skinner, eds., *Roman Sexualities*: 172–96. Princeton University Press, Princeton.
Freud, S. 1953–74. *The Standard Edition of the Complete Works of Signumd Freud*. 24 Vols. Ed. James Strachey, *et al.* Hogarth Press, London.
—— 1961a. *Civilization and Its Discontents*. Trans. James Strachey. The Standard Edition. New York.
—— 1961b. *Beyond the Pleasure Principle*. Trans. James Strachey. The Standard Edition. New York.
Freudenburg, K. 1993. *The Walking Muse: Horace on the theory of satire*. Princeton University Press, Princeton.
—— 2001. *Satires of Rome: Threatening Poses from Lucilius to Juvenal*. Cambridge University Press, Cambridge.
Führer, R. 1975. 'Eufonia e critica testuale (a proposito del primo libro di Properzio).' *Maia*. 27: 217–20.
Gadda, C. E. 1982. *Il tempo e le opere*. Adelphi, Milan.
Gaisser, J. 1983. '*Amor, Rura,* and *Militia* in Three Elegies of Tibullus.' *Latomus* 42: 58–72.
Gale, M. 1997. 'Propertius 2.7: *Militia amoris* and the ironies of elegy.' *JRS* 87: 77–91.
Galinsky, G. K. 1966. 'The Hercules-Cacus Episode in *Aen.* VIII.' *AJP* 87: 18–51.
—— 1969. 'The Triumph Theme in Augustan Elegy.' *WS* 82: 75–107.
—— 1972. *The Herakles Theme. The Adaptations of the Hero in Literature from Homer to the Twentieth Century*. Rowman & Littlefield, Oxford.

——1975. *Ovid's Metamorphoses. An Introduction to Basic Aspects.* University of California Press, Berkeley.

——1996. *Augustan Culture: An Intrepretive Introduction.* Princeton University Press, Princeton.

Gamel, M. 1989. '*Non sine caede*: Abortion Politics in Ovid's *Amores*.' *Helios* 16: 183–206.

——1998. 'Reading as a Man: Performance and Gender in Roman Elegy.' *Helios* 25.1: 79–95.

Gansiniec, Z. 1949. *Tarpeia: The Making of a Myth.* In K. Majewski, ed. *Acta Societatis Archaeologicae Polonorum* 1. Societas Archaeologica Polonorum, Wroclow.

Ganzemüller, C. 1911. 'Aus Ovids Werkstatt,' *Philol.* 70: 274–311, 397–437.

Gardner, J. F. 1986. *Women in Roman Law and Society.* Croom Helm, London.

George, E. V. 1974. *Aeneid VIII and the Aetia of Callimachus. Mnemosyne* Supplement 27. Brill, Leiden.

Giangrande, G. 1980. 'An Alleged Fragment of Gallus.' *QUCC* 34: 141–53.

——1986. 'Review of Fedeli *Elegiarum Libri IV* (Teubner, 1984)'. *RFIC* 114: 210–18.

Giardina, G. 1977. *Propertius: Elegiarum Liber II.* Corpus Scriptorum Latinorum Paravianum, Torino.

——2003. *Contributi di critica testuale: Da Catullo alla Historia Augusta.* Herder, Rome.

——2005. *Properzio. Elegie. Edizione critica e traduzione.* Edizioni dell'Ateneo, Rome.

Gibson, R. K. 2007. *Excess and Restraint: Propertius, Horace and Ovid's Ars Amatoria. BICS* Suppl. 89. BICS, London.

Girard, R. 1965. *Deceit, Desire, and the Novel: Self and Other in Literary Structure.* Johns Hopkins University Press, Baltimore.

Gold, B. K. 1982. 'Propertius 3.9: Maecenas as *Eques, Dux, Fautor.*' *Literary and Artistic Patronage in Ancient Rome.* Ed. Barbara K. Gold, 103–17. University of Texas Press, Austin.

——1987. *Literary Patronage in Greece and Rome.* University of North Carolina Press, Chapel Hill.

——1993a. '"But Ariadne Was Never There in the First Place:" Finding the Female in Roman Poetry.' In N. S. Rabinowitz and A. Richlin, eds. *Feminist Theory and the Classics,* 75–101. Routledge, New York.

——1993b. '"The Master Mistress of my Passion:" The Lady as Patron in Ancient and Renaissance Literature.' In M. DeForest, ed. *Woman's Power,*

*Man's Game: Essays on Classical Antiquity in Honor of Joy King*, 279–304. Bolchazy-Carducci, Wauconda, IL.

Gold, B. K. 1998a. '"Vested Interests" in Plautus' *Casina*: Cross-Dressing in Roman Comedy.' *Helios* 25: 17–29.

——1998b. '"The House I Live in is Not My Own:" Women's Bodies in Juvenal's *Satires*.' *Arethusa* 31.3: 369–86.

——2007. 'How Women (Re)Act in Roman Love Poetry: Inhuman She-Wolves and Unhelpful Mothers in Propertius's *Elegies*.' *Helios* 33.2: 165–87.

Goold, G. P. 1966. '*Noctes Propertianae*.' *HSCP* 71: 59–106.

——1987. 'On Editing Propertius.' *Papers in Honour of Otto Skutsch*. *BICS* Supplement 5: 27–38.

——1989. 'Problems in Editing Propertius.' In J. Grant, ed. *Editing Greek and Latin Texts*, 97–119. AMS Press, New York.

——1990. *Propertius: Elegies*. Harvard University Press, Cambridge, MA.

——1992. '*Paralipomena Propertiana*.' *HSCP* 94: 287–320.

Goux, J. J. 1990. *Symbolic Economies After Marx and Freud*. Trans. Jennifer Curtiss Gage. Cornell University Press, Ithaca.

Gow, A. S. F. 1950 (1965). *Theocritus. Edited with translation and commentary*. Vol. I–II. Cambridge University Press, Cambridge.

——and D. L. Page. 1968. *The Greek Anthology: The Garland of Philip and some contemporary Epigrams*. Cambridge.

Graf, F. 1982. 'Die Gallus-Verse von Qasr Ibrim.' *Gymnasium* 89: 21–36.

Green, M. 1985. *The Transmission of Ancient Theories of Female Physiology and Disease through the Early Middle Ages*. Diss. Princeton University.

Green, P. 1981. *Ovid: The Erotic Poems*. Penguin, London.

——1982. *Ovid. The Erotic Poems*. Penguin, London.

Greene, E. 1995. 'Elegiac Woman: Fantasy, *Materia*, and Male Desire in Propertius 1.3 and 1.11.' *AJP* 116: 303–18.

——1998. *The Erotics of Domination: Male Desire and the Mistress in Latin Love Poetry*. Johns Hopkins University Press, Baltimore.

——2000. 'Gender Identity and the Hero: Propertius 2.1.' *Arethusa* 33: 241–61.

Griffin, J. 1977. 'Propertius and Antony.' *JRS* 67: 17–26.

——1985 (1986, 1994). *Latin Poets and Roman Life*. University of North Carolina Press, London (Reprinted Chapel Hill, Bristol).

Grimal, P. 1951a. 'Enée à Rome et le triomphe d'Octave.' *REA* 53: 51–61.

——1951b. 'Etudes sur Properce, II: César et la legende de Tarpeia.' *REL* 29: 201–14.

——1952. *Les intentions de Properce et la composition du livre IV des Élégies.* Latomus 11: 183–97, 315–25, 437–50.
——1953. *Les intentions de Properce et la composition du livre IV des Élégies.* Collection Latomus 12. Latomus, Brussels.
——1963. *L'Amour à Rome.* Les Belles Lettres, Paris.
Grumach, E. 1949. *Goethe und die Antike: eine Sammlung.* Vols. I–II. W. de Gruyter, Berlin.
Guey, J. 1952. 'Avec Properce au Palatin: legendes et promenades.' *REL* 30: 186–202.
Günther, H. C. 1997. *Quaestiones Propertianae.* Brill, Leiden.
——1998. 'Römische Liebeselegie und hellenistische Dichtung.' *Hellenika* 48: 7–27.
——2006. *Brill's Companion to Propertius.* Brill, Leiden.
Gurval, R. A. 1995. *Actium and Augustus: The Politics and Emotions of Civil War.* University of Michigan Press, Ann Arbor.
Guthrie, W. K. S. 1962. *A History of Greek Philosophy. Vol I: The Earlier Presocratics and the Pythagoreans.* Cambridge University Press, Cambridge.
Gutzwiller, K. J. and Michelini, A. N. 1991. 'Women and Other Strangers: Feminist Perspectives in Classical Literature.' In J. E. Hartman and E. Messer-Davidow, eds. *(En)Gendering Knowledge: Feminists in Academe,* 66–84, University of Tennessee Press, Knoxville.
Guyet, F., Guyomard, P. 1992. *La jouissance tragique: Antigone, Lacan et le désir de l'analyste.* Aubier, Paris.
Habinek, T. 1997. 'The invention of sexuality in the world-city of Rome.' In T. Habinek and A. Schiesaro, eds. *The Roman Cultural Revolution.* Cambridge University Press, Cambridge: 23–43.
——1998. *The Politics of Latin Literature: Writing, Identity, and Empire in Ancient Rome.* Princeton University Press, Princeton.
Haffter, H. 1970. 'Das Gedichtbuch als dichterische Aussage. Überlegungen zu den Elegien des Properz.' In D. Ableitinger and H. Gugel, eds. *Festschrift Karl Vretska,* 53–67. C. Winter, Heidelberg.
——1975. 'Das Gedichtbuch als dichterische Aussage—Überlegungen zu den Elegien des Properz.' In W. Eisenhut, ed. *Wege zu Properz. Wege der Forschung* 237: 160–73.
Hallett, J. P. 1971. *Book IV. Propertius' Recusatio to Augustus and Augustan Ideals.* Diss. Harvard University, Harvard.
——1973. 'The Role of Women in Roman Elegy: Counter-Cultural Feminism.' *Arethusa* 6: 103–23. Reprinted as Hallett 1984, below.

Hallett, J. P. 1974. 'Women in Roman Elegy: A Reply.' *Arethusa* 7: 211–17.
——1984. 'The Role of Women in Roman Elegy.' In J. Peradotto and J. P. Sullivan, eds. *Women in the Ancient World: The Arethusa Papers*, 241–62. State University of New York Press, Albany.
——1989a. 'Female Homoeroticism and the Denial of Roman Reality in Latin Literature.' *Yale Journal of Criticism* 3: 209–27.
——1989b. 'Women as *Same* and *Other* in the Classical Roman Elite.' *Helios* 16: 59–78.
——1993. 'Feminist Theory, Historical Periods, Literary Canons, and the Study of Greco-Roman Antiquity.' In N. S. Rabinowitz and A. Richlin, eds. *Feminist Theory and the Classics*, 44–72. Routledge, New York.
Halliday, W. R. 1928. *The Greek Questions of Plutarch*. Clarendon Press, Oxford.
Hanslik, R. 1962. 'Textkritisches in Properz Buch IV.' *RhM* 105: 236–52.
——1967. 'Properz III 4.' *WS* 80: 183–9.
——1979. *Sex. Propertii Elegiarum Libri IV*. Teubner, Leipzig.
Hanson, A. 1992. 'Conception, Gestation, and the Origin of Female Nature in the *Corpus Hippocraticum*.' *Helios* 19: 31–71.
Hanson, A. E. 1990. 'The Medical Writer's Woman.' In D. M. Halperin, J. J. Winkler, and F. I. Zeitlin, eds. *Before Sexuality: The Construction of Erotic Experience in the Ancient Greek World*, 309–37. Princeton University Press, Princeton.
Hawkes, T. 1977. *Structuralism and Semiotics*. Methuen, London.
Heinze, R. 1915 (= 3rd ed., 1965). *Vergils epische Technik*. Teubner, Leipzig, repr. Stuttgart.
——1919 (1960). *Ovids elegische Erzählung*. Teubner, Leipzig, repr. Stuffgart.
——1921 (1967). *Q. Horatius Flaccus Satiren*. Dublin.
Hemelrijk, E. A. 1998 (1999). Matrona Docta: *Educated Women in the Roman Élite from Cornelia to Julia Domna*. Diss. Katholieke Universiteit Nijmegen. Published in 1999 by Routledge, London.
Hering, W. 1979. *Die Dialektik von Inhalt und Form bei Horaz. Schriften zur Geschichte und Kultur der Antike* 20.
Herndl, D. P. 1991. 'The Dilemmas of a Feminine Dialogic.' In D. M. Bauer and S. J. McKinstry, eds. *Feminism, Bakhtin, and the Dialogic*, 7–24. State University of New York Press, Albany.
Herrnstein Smith, B. 1978. *On the Margins of Discourse. The Relation of Literature to Language*. University of Chicago Press, Chicago.
Hertzberg, G. A. B. 1843. *Sexti Aurelii Propertii elegiarum libri IV*. Lippert und Schmidt, Halle.

Heyworth, S. J. 1986. *The Manuscripts of Propertius: Toward a Critical Edition.* Diss. Cambridge.
——1995. 'Propertius: Division, Transmission, and the Editor's Task.' *PLLS* 8: 165–85.
——2007a. *Sexti Properti Elegi.* Oxford University Press, Oxford.
——2007b. *Cynthia. A Companion to the Text of Propertius.* Oxford University Press, Oxford.
——2007c. "Propertius, Patronage, and Politics." *BICS* 50: 93–128.
Highet, G. 1972. *The Speeches in Vergil's Aeneid.* Princeton University Press, Princeton.
Hinds, S. 1998. *Allusion and Intertextuality.* Cambridge University Press, Cambridge.
Hoelzer, V. 1899. *De Poesi amatoria a comicis atticis exculta, ab elegiacis imitatione expressa, pars prior.* Philipps-Universität Marburg, Marburg.
Hofmann, J. B., A. Szantyr, M. Leumann, F. Stolz, and J. H. Schmalz. 1965. *Lateinische Syntax und Stilistik.* C.H. Beck, Munich.
Holleman, A. W. J. 1977. 'Propertius IV 9: An Augustan View of Roman Religion.' *RBPh* 55: 79–92.
Hollis, A. 1996. 'Heroic honours for Philetas?' *ZPE* 110: 56–62.
——2006. 'Propertius and Hellenistic Poetry.' In H. C. Günther, ed. *Brill's Companion to Propertius*, 97–125. Brill, Leiden.
Housman, A. E. 1888. '*Emendationes Propertianae.*' *JPh* 16: 1–35. (= 1972 *Classical Papers* I: 29–54).
——1893. 'The Manuscripts of Propertius I.' *JPhil.* 21: 161–97 (= 1972 *Classical Papers* I: 277–304).
——1905. 'Butler's Propertius. *Sexti Properti opera omnia.*' *CR* 19: 317–20 (= 1972 *Classical Papers* II: 630–6).
——1972. *The Classical Papers of A. E. Housman*, Vols I–III. Ed. J. Diggle and F. R. D. Goodyear. Cambridge University Press, Cambridge.
Hubbard, M. 1968. '*Propertiana.*' *CQ* 18: 315–19.
——1974 (1975). *Propertius.* Scribner, London, reprinted New York.
Hubbard, T. 1984. 'Art and Vision in Propertius 2. 31/32.' *TAPA* 114: 281–97.
Hunink, V. 1998. 'The Enigmatic Lady Pudentilla.' *AJP* 119: 275–91.
Hutchinson, G. O. 1981. 'Notes on the New Gallus.' *ZPE* 41: 37–42.
——2002. 'The New Posidippus and Latin Poetry.' *ZPE* 138: 1–10.
——2006. *Propertius, Elegies Book IV.* Cambridge University Press, Cambridge.
——2008. *Talking Books: Readings in Hellenistic and Roman Books of Poetry.* Oxford University Press, Oxford.
Iglesias Monteil, R. M. 1975. 'Nacionalismo en Propercio.' *CFC* 9: 79–131.

Ingvarsson, E. 1955. 'Zu Properz III 5.2.' *Eranos* 53: 165–71.
Irigaray, L. 1977a. 'Des marchandises entre elles.' *Ce sexe qui n'en est pas un*, 189–93. Éditions de Minuit, Paris.
―― 1977b. 'Cosi fan tutti.' *Ce sexe qui n'en est pas un*, 85–101. Éditions de Minuit, Paris.
―― 1977c. 'Ce sexe qui n'en est pas un.' *Ce sexe qui n'en est pas un*, 23–32. Éditions de Minuit, Paris.
―― 1977d. 'La «méchanique» des fluides.' *Ce sexe qui n'en est pas un*, 103–15. Éditions de Minuit, Paris.
―― 1977e (1985). *This Sex Which Is Not One*. Trans. by Catherine Porter. Cornell University Press, Ithaca.
―― 1991. *The Marine Lover of Friedrich Nietzsche*. Éditions de Minuit, Paris.
Iser, W. 1974. *The Implied Reader: Patterns of Communication in Prose Fiction from Bunyan to Beckett*. Johns Hopkins University Press, Baltimore.
Ites, M. 1908. *De Propertii elegiis inter se conexis*. Diss. Georg-August-Universität, Gottingen. Bielefeld.
Jacoby, F. 1914. 'Drei Gedichte des Properz.' *RhM* 69: 393–413, 427–63.
―― 1961. *Kleine Philologische Schriften*. H. J. Mette, ed. *Deutsche Akademie der Wissenschaften zu Berlin, Schriften der Sektion für Altertumswissenschaft* 21: 216–65.
Jäger, K. 1967 (1968). *Zweigliedrige Gedichte und Gedichtpaare bei Properz und in Ovids Amores*. Diss. Eberhard-Karls-Universität, Tübingen, later published Tübingen.
James, S. 1997. 'Slave-Rape and Female Silence in Ovid's Love Poetry.' *Helios* 24: 60–76.
―― 2003. *Learned Girls and Male Persuasion: Gender and Reading in Roman Love Poetry*. University of California Press, Berkeley.
Janan, M. 1994. *'When the Lamp is Shattered:' Desire and Narrative in Catullus*. Southern Illinois University Press, Carbondale.
―― 1999. "Beyond Good and Evil: Tarpeia and Philosophy in the feminine." *CW* 92: 429–44.
―― 2001. *The Politics of Desire: Propertius IV*. University of California Press, Berkeley.
Jaworski, A. 1993. *The Power of Silence: Social and Pragmatic Perspectives*. Sage Publications, Newbury Park, California.
Johnson, W. R. 1973. 'The Emotions of Patriotism. Propertius 4.6.' *CSCA* 6: 151–80.
―― 1995. 'Foreword.' In *Charm: Sextus Propertius*, trans. by Vincent Katz, 9–15. Sun and Moon Press, Los Angeles.
―― 1997. 'Final Exit: Propertius 4.11.' In D. H. Roberts, F. Dunn and D. Fowler, eds. *Classical Closure: Reading the End in Greek and Latin Literature*, 163–80. Princeton University Press, Princeton.

——2009. *Propertius A Latin Lover in Ancient Rome*. Ohio State University Press, Columbus.

Joplin, P. K. 1990. 'Ritual Work on Human Flesh: Livy's Lucretia and the Rape of the Body Politic.' *Helios* 17: 51–70.

——1991. 'The Voice of the Shuttle is Ours.' In L. A. Higgins and B. R. Silver, eds. *Rape and Representation*, 35–64. Columbia University Press, New York.

Joshel, S. R 1992a. 'The Body Female and the Body Politic: Livy's Lucretia and Verginia.' In A. Richlin, ed. *Pornography and Representation in Greece and Rome*, 112–30. Oxford University Press, Oxford.

——1992b. *Work, Identity and Legal Status at Rome: A Study of the Occupational Inscriptions*. University of Oklahoma Press, Norman.

Juhnke, H. 1971. 'Zum Aufbau des zweiten und dritten Buches des Properz.' *Hermes* 99: 91–125.

Julien, P. 1990. *Pour lire Jacques Lacan*. 2nd edn. Seuil, Paris.

Kahn, C. H. 1979. *The Art and Thought of Heraclitus*. Cambridge Univesity Press, Cambridge.

Kambylis, A. 1965. *Die Dichterweihe und ihre Symbolik. Untersuchungen zu Hesiodos, Kallimachos, Properz und Ennius*. Kiel. Bibl. d. Klass. Altertumswiss. N.F. 2. Reihe. C. Winter, Heidelberg.

Karsten, H. T. 1915. 'Propertii Elegia IV 4.' *Mnemosyne* 45: 357–64.

Keith, A. M. 1992. *The Play of Fictions: Studies in Ovid's Metamorphoses Book 2*. University of Michigan Press, Ann Arbor.

——1994. '*Corpus Eroticum*: Elegiac Poetics and Elegiac *Puellae* in Ovid's *Amores*.' *CW* 88: 27–40.

——2008. *Propertius. Poet of Love and Leisure*. Duckworth, London.

Kellum, B. A. 1986. 'Sculptural Programs and Propaganda in Augustan Rome: The Temple of Apollo on the Palatine.' In R. Winkes, ed. *The Age of Augustus: Interdisciplinary Conference Heldat Brown University, April 30th–May 2nd, 1982*, 169–76. Louvain-la-Neuve, Institut supérieur d'archéologie et d'histoire de l'art, Collège Erasme Belgium.

Kennedy, D. 1982. 'Gallus and the Culex.' *CQ* 32: 371–89.

——1992. '"Augustan" and "Anti-Augustan:" Reflections on Terms of Reference.' In A. Powell, ed., *Roman Poetry and Propaganda in the Age of Augustus*, 26–58. Bristol Classical Press, London.

——1993. *The Arts of Love: Five Studies in the Discourse of Roman Love Elegy*. Cambridge University Press, Cambridge.

Kenney, E. J. 1961 (1994). *Ovid Amores, Medicamina faciei femineae, Ars amatoria, Remedia amoris*. Oxford University Press, Oxford.

——1976. 'Ovidius Prooemians.' *PCPS* 22: 46–53.

Kernan, A. B. 1979. *The Playwright as Magician*. Yale University Press, New Haven.

King, H. 1983. 'Bound to Bleed: Artemis and Greek Women.' In A. Cameron and A. Kuhrt, eds. *Images of Women in Antiquity*, 109–27. Wayne State University Press, Detroit.

King, J. K. 1976. 'Sophistication vs. chastity in Propertius' Latin love elegy.' *Helios* 4: 67–76.

——1980a. 'The Two Galluses of Propertius' *Monobiblos*.' *Philologus* 124: 212–30.

——1980b. 'Propertius 2.1–12: His Callimachean Second Libellus.' *Würzburger Jahrbücher für die Altertumswissenschaft* N. F. 6: 61–84.

King, R. 1990. 'Creative Landscaping: Inspiration and Artifice in Propertius 4.4.' *CJ* 85: 225–46.

Kirk, G. S. 1954. *Heraclitus: The Cosmic Fragments*. Cambridge University Press, Cambridge.

——and J. E. Raven. 1957. *The Presocratic Philosophers*. Cambridge University Press, Cambridge.

Koechly, H. 1857. *Nonni Panopolitani Dionysiacorum Libri XLVIII*. Teubner, Leipzig.

Konstan, D. 1986. 'Narrative and Ideology in Livy: Book 1.' *CA* 5: 198–215.

——1994. *Sexual Symmetry: Love in the Ancient Novel and Related Genres*. Princeton University Press, Princeton.

Kraffert, H. 1883. *Beitrage zur Kritik und Erklarung lateinischer Autoren*. Tapper, Aurich.

Kraus, W. 1965 "Zur Idealität des 'Ich' und der Situation in der römischen Elegie: Tibull, Erstes Buch, Zweite Elegie." F. Schalk, ed. *Ideen und Formen. Festschr. H. Friedrich*: 153–63. Klostermann, Frankfurt.

Krenkel, W. 1977a. 'Exhibitionismus in der Antike.' *Wissenschaftliche Zeitschrift der Wilhelm-Pieck-Universität Rostock Jahrgang* 26: 613–18.

——1977b. 'Skopophilie in der Antike.' *Wissenschaftliche Zeitschrift der Wilhelm-Pieck-Universität Rostock Jahrgang* 26: 619–31.

Kristeva, J. 1977. 'D'une identité l'autre.' *Polylogue*, 149–72. Editions Seuil, Paris.

——1979. 'Le temps des femmes.' *Cahiers de recherche de S. T. D. Paris VII* 5: 5–18.

Kroll, W. 1923. *C. Valerius Catullus Herausgegeben und Erklärt*. Teubner, Leipzig.

——1924. *Studium zur Verständnis der römischen Literatur*. J. B. Metzler, Stuttgart.

Kühner, R. and C. Stegmann. 1955. *Ausführliche Grammatik der lateinsichen Sprache Satzlehre*. Vol. 1. Hahnsche Buchhandlung, Hannover.

Kuinoel, C. T. 1805. *Propertii carmina rec. et illust*. Fritisch, Leipzig.

La Penna, A. 1950/1951. 'Properzio e i poeti latini dell' età aurea.' *Maia* 3: 209–36; 4: 43–69.
——1951a. 'Studi sulla tradizione di Properzio I'. *SIFC* 25: 199–238.
——1951b. *Properzio. Saggio critico seguito da due ricerche filologiche.* La Nuova Italia, Florence.
——1977. *L'integrazione difficile. Un profilo di Properzio.* Einaudi, Torino.
Labate, M. 1984. *L'arte di farsi amare.* Giardini, Pisa.
Lacan, J. 1975. *Le séminaire livre XX: Encore.* Ed. Jacques-Alain Miller. Paris.
——1982. 'Seminar of 21 January 1975.' In J. Mitchell and J. Rose, eds. Trans. J. Rose. *Feminine Sexuality: Jacques Lacan and the école freudienne*, 162–71. W.W, Norton, New York.
——1986. *Le séminaire VII: L'éthique de la psychanalyse.* Ed. Jacques-Alain Miller. Paris.
——1991. *Le séminaire VIII: Le transfert.* Ed. Jacques-Alain Miller. Paris.
Lachmann, K. 1816 (1973). *Sexti Aurelii Propertii Carmina.* Gerhard Fleischer, Leipzig (Reprinted Hildesheim).
Langen, P. 1896–7. *C. Valeri Flacci Setini Balbi Argonavticon libri octo.* S. Calvary, Berlin.
Last, H. 1934. 'The social policy of Augustus.' In *Cambridge Ancient History Volume 10*, 425–64. Cambridge University Press, Cambridge.
Latte, K. 1960. *Romische Religionsgeschichte.* Beck, Munich.
Leach, E. W. 1997. 'Horace and the material culture of Augustan Rome: a revisionary reading.' In T. Habinek and A. Schiesaro, eds. *The Roman Cultural Revolution*, 105–21. Cambridge University Press, Cambridge.
Lee, G. 1980. 'The Gallan Elegiacs.' *LCM* 5: 45–6.
LeFèvre, E. 1966. *Propertius Ludibundus. Elemente des Humors in seinen Elegien.* Winter, Heidelberg.
Lefkowitz, M. R. 1981. *Heroines and Hysterics.* Duckworth, London.
——and Fant, M. B. 1982. *Women's Life in Greece and Rome.* Johns Hopkins University Press, Baltimore.
Lemaire, N.E. 1832. *Sexti Aurelii Propertii Elegiarum Libri Quattuor.* Julius Didot, Paris.
Leo, F. 1889. 'Vindiciae Propertianae.' *RhM* 35: 431–47.
——1898a. 'Das Schlussgedicht der ersten Buches des Properz.' In *Nachrichten Gesselschaft der Wissenschaften zu Göttingen. Philologisch Historische Klasse.* 468–78.
——1898b. 'Rezension Propertius Elegien, erklärt von Max Rothstein.' *GGA* 160: 722–50.
Levi, M. A. 1989. 'Ercole e Semo Sanco. Properzio 4.9.77ff.' *PP* 44: 341–60.

Liberman, G. 1995. 'En Lisant Properce.' *Mélanges de l'Ecole française de Rome, Italie et Méditerranée* 107: 315–34.
Lilja, S. 1965 (1978). *The Roman Elegists' Attitude to Women.* Suomalainen Tiedeakatemia, Helsinki. Reprinted New York.
Lipparini, G. 1970. *Sesto Properzio, Elegie.* Nichola Zanichelli, Bologna.
Lissarague, F. 1990. 'The Sexual Life of Satyrs.' In David M. Halperin, John J. Winkler, and Froma I. Zeitlin, eds., *Before Sexuality: The Construction of Erotic Experience in the Ancient Greek World*, 53–81. Princeton University Press, Princeton.
Littlewood, R. J. 1983. 'Humour in Tibullus.' *ANRW* 2.30.3: 2128–58.
Lloyd, G. 1984. *The Man of Reason: 'Male' and 'Female' in Western Philosophy.* University of Minnesota Press, Minneapolis.
Lloyd-Jones, H. 1984. 'A Hellenistic Miscellany.' *SIFC* 77 (= 3rd Series 2): 52–72.
——and P. J., Parsons, eds. 1983. *Supplementum Hellenisticum.* W. De Gruyter, Berlin.
Löfstedt, E. 1933 (1942). *Syntactica. Studien und Beitrage zur historischen Syntax des Lateins.* Gleerup, Lund.
Lovibond, Sabina. 1994. 'An Ancient Theory of Gender. Plato and the Pythagorean Table.' In L. J. Archer, S. Fischer, and M. Wyke, eds. *Women in Ancient Societies: An Illusion of the Night*, 88–101. Routledge, New York.
Luck, G. 1957. 'The Cave and the Source. On the Imagery of Propertius III 1.1–6.' *CQ* 51: 175–9.
——1959. *Latin Love Elegy.* Methuen, London.
——1960. *The Latin Love Elegy.* Barnes & Noble, New York.
——1961. *Römische Liebeselegie.* C. Winter, Heidelberg.
——1962. *Hexen und Zauberei in der römischen Dichtung.* Artemis, Zurich.
——1974. 'The woman's role in Latin love poetry.' In G. K. Galinsky (ed.), *Perspectives of Roman Poetry*, 15–31. University of Texas Press, Austin.
——1979. 'Notes on Propertius.' *AJP* 100: 79–93.
Lucot, R. 1953. 'Vertumne et Mécène.' *Pallas* 1: 65–80.
Lyne, R. O. A. M. 1970. 'Propertius and Cynthia: Elegy 1.3.' *PCPS* 196: 60–78.
——1974. 'Propertius I,5.' *Mnemosyne* 27: 262–9.
——1979. '*Servitium Amoris*.' *CQ* 29: 117–30.
——1980 (1996, 2000). *The Latin Love Poets. From Catullus to Horace.* Clarendon Press, Oxford.
——1998a. 'Propertius and Tibullus. Early Exchanges.' *CQ* 48: 519–44.

———1998b. 'Propertius 2.10 and 2.11 and the Structure of Books "2A" and "2B."' *JRS* 38: 21–36.
Macherey, P. 1978 (1985). *A Theory of Literary Production*. Trans. G. Wall. Routledge, Boston.
Mack, S. 1988. *Ovid*. Yale University Press, New Haven.
Macleod, C. W. 1973. 'Parodies and Personalities in Catullus.' *CQ* 23: 294–303.
———1976. 'Propertius 4,1.' *PLLS* 1: 141–53.
———1977. 'The Poet, the Critic and the Moralist: Horace, Epistles 1.19.' *CQ* 27: 359–76.
Maleuvre, J. Y. 1998. *Jeux de masques dans l'élégie latine: Tibulle, Properce, Ovide*. Editions Peeters, Louvain.
Maltby, R. 1980. *Latin Love Elegy*. Bristol Classical Press, Waucunda, IL.
Marioni, G. D. 1979. 'Aspetti dell' espressività properziana nel IV libro.' *SIFC* 51: 103–30.
Marouzeau, J. 1935 (1970). *Traité de stylistique latine*. Les Belles Lettres, Paris.
Marr, J. L. 1970. 'Notes on Propertius 4.1 and 4.4.' *CQ* 20: 160–73.
Martindale, C. A. 1993. 'Introduction,' in C. A. Martindale and D. Hopkins, eds. *Horace Made New: Horation Influences on British Writing from the Renaissance to the Twentieth Century*, 1–26. Cambridge University Press, Cambridge.
Maxfield, V. A. 1981. *The Military Decorations of the Roman Army*. Batsford, London.
McCarthy, K. 1998. '*Servitium amoris: amor servitii*.' In S. Joshel and S. Murnaghan, eds. *Women and Slaves in Greco-Roman Culture*, 174–92. Routledge, New York.
McCoskey, D. E. 1999. 'Reading Cynthia and Sexual Difference in the Poems of Propertius.' *Ramus* 28: 16–39.
McCrone, K. 1988. 'Silence: A Puzzle.' *Friends Journal* 44: 7.
McGann, M. J. 1983. 'The Marathus Elegies of Tibullus.' *ANRW* 2.30.3: 1976–1999.
McGinn, T. A. J. 1998. *Prostitution, Sexuality, and the Law in Ancient Rome*. Oxford University Press, New York.
McKeown, J. C. 1979. 'Augustan Elegy and Mime.' *PCPS* 205: 71–84.
———1987. *Ovid: Amores, Text, Prolegomena and Commentary in Four Volumes*. Vol. 1. Francis Cairns, Leeds.
———1989. *Ovid: Amores, Text, Prolegomena and Commentary in Four Volumes*. Vol. 2. Francis Cairns, Leeds.
McManus, B. F. 1997. *Classics and Feminism: Gendering the Classics*. Twayne. New York.

McNally, S. 1978. 'The Maenad in Early Greek Art.' *Arethusa* 11: 101–35.
McNamee, K. 1993. 'Propertius, poetry, and love.' In M. DeForest, ed. *Woman's Power, Man's Game: Essays in Honor of Joy King*, 215–48. Bolchazy-Carducci, Wauconda, IL.
Mendez, C. W. 1980. 'Virginia Woolf and the Voices of Silence.' *Language and Style* 13: 94–112.
Menes, E. P. 1983. 'The External Evidence for Division of Propertius, Book 2.' *CP* 78: 136–43.
Merguet, H. 1877–84. *Lexicon zu den Reden des Cicero*. H. Dufft, Jena.
——1887–94. *Lexicon zu den philosophischen Schriften des Cicero*. H. Dufft, Jena.
——1905–6. *Handlexicon zu Cicero*. Leipzig. repr. 1964. Dieterich, Hildesheim.
Meyer, H. D. 1961. *Die Aussenpolitik des Augustus und die augusteische Dichtung*. Böhlau Verlag, Cologne.
Miles, G. B. 1992. 'The First Roman Marriage and the Theft of the Sabine Women.' In Ralph Hexter and Daniel Selden, eds., *Innovations of Antiquity*, 161–96. Routledge, New York.
Miller, P. A. 1994. *Lyric Texts and Lyric Consciousness: The Birth of a Genre From Archaic Greece to Augustan Rome*. Routledge, London.
——1995. 'The Minotaur Within: Fire, the Labyrinth, and Strategies of Containment in *Aeneid* 5 and 6.' *CP* 90: 225–40.
——1998a. 'Images of Sterility: The Bodily Grotesque in Roman Satire.' *Arethusa* 31: 257–83.
——1998b. 'Why Propertius is a Woman.' Paper delivered at the meeting of the *Classical Association of the Middle West and South*, Charlottesville, VA.
——2004. *Subjecting Verses. Latin Love Elegy and the Emergence of the Real*. Princeton University Press: Princeton, NJ.
——2010. 'What is a Propertian poem?' Paper presented at the annual meeting of the American Philological Association, Anaheim.
——and C. Platter, 1999a. 'Introduction to special issue, "Power, politics, & discourse in Augustan elegy,"' *CW* 92.5: 403–7.
—— ——1999b. 'The Crux as Symptom: Augustan Elegy and Beyond.' *CW* 92: 445–54.
Moi, T. 1985. *Sexual/Textual Politics: Feminist Literary Theory*. Methuen, London.
Monteleone, C. 1979. 'Cornelio Gallo tra Ila e le Driadi (Virgilio, Properzio e una controversia letteraria).' *Latomus* 38: 28–53.

Montiglio, S. 2000. *Silence in the Land of Logos*. Princeton University Press, Princeton.

Morgan, K. 1977. *Ovid's Art of Imitation: Propertius in the Amores*. Brill, Leiden.

Moritz, L. A. 1967. 'Well-matched Lovers (Propertius I.5).' *CP* 62: 106–8.

Morson, G. S. 1989. 'Parody, History, and Metaparody.' In G. S. Morson and C. Emerson, eds. *Rethinking Bakhtin: Extensions and Challenges*, 63–86. Northwestern University Press, Evanston.

Munari, F. 1951. P. *Ovidi Nasonis Amores. Testo, introduzione, traduzione e note*. La Nuova Italia, Firenze.

Murgatroyd, P. 1975. '*Militia Amoris* and the Roman Elegists.' *Latomus* 34: 59–79.

——— 1981. 'Servitium Amoris and the Roman Elegists.' *Latomus* 40: 589–606.

Murgia, C. E. 2000. 'The Division of Propertius 2.' *MD* 45: 145–242.

Myers, K. S. 1996. 'The poet and the procuress: the *lena* in Latin love elegy.' *JRS* 86: 1–21.

Nagore, J. and E. Perez. 1981. 'El Episodio de Hercules y Caco en Cuatro Autores Latinos.' *Argos* 5: 35–51.

Nell, V. 1988. *Lost in a Book. The Psychology of Reading for Pleasure*. Yale University Press, New Haven.

Nethercut, W. R. 1961. '*Ille parum cauti pectoris egit opus*.' *TAPA* 92: 389–407.

——— 1963. *Propertius and Augustus*. Diss. Columbia University.

——— 1968. 'Notes on the Structure of Propertius, Book IV.' *AJP* 89: 449–64.

——— 1970. 'The ironic priest: Propertius' 'Roman Elegies' iii, 1–5: imitations of Horace and Vergil.' *AJP* 91: 385–407.

——— 1983. 'Recent Scholarship on Propertius.' *ANRW* 2.30.3. Berlin: 1813–57.

Newlands, C. E. 1995. *Playing with Time: Ovid and the Fasti*. Cornell University Press, Ithaca.

Newman, J. K. 1997. *Augustan Propertius: The Recapitulation of a Genre*. Olms, Hildesheim.

Nicolet, C. 1966. *L'ordre équestre à l'époque républicaine*, Vol 1. Editions de Boccard, Paris.

Nisbet, R. G. M. and M. Hubbard. 1970. *A Commentary on Horace, Odes Book I*. Clarendon Press, Oxford.

——— ——— 1978. *A Commentary on Horace Odes Book II*. Clarendon Press, Oxford.

Nock, A. D. 1972. 'Greek Magical Papyri.' In Z. Stewart, ed. *Essays on Religion and the Ancient World by Arthur Darby Nock*, Vol. 1, 176–94. Clarendon Press, Oxford.

Norden, E. 1903 (1927, 1981). *P. Vergilius Maro. Aeneis Buch VI.* Teubner, Stuttgart.

——1913 (1956). *Agnostos Theos: Untersuchungen zur Formengeschichte religiöser Rede*, 2nd ed. Wissenschaftliche Buchgesellschaft, Darmstadt.

Noreña, C. F. 2007. 'Pliny's Correspondence with Trajan.' *AJP* 128: 239–77.

Nosarti, L. 1976. 'Note acciane, esegetiche e testuali.' *QIFL* 4: 53ff.

Nugent, G. 1990. 'This Sex Which is not One: De-Constructing Ovid's Hermaphrodite.' *differences* 2: 160–85.

Nussbaum, M. 1989. 'Beyond Obsession and Disgust: Lucretius' Genealogy of Love.' *Apeiron* 22: 1–59.

Ogilvie, R. M. 1965. *A Commentary on Livy, Books 1–5*. Oxford University Press, Oxford.

Oliensis, E. 1997. 'The Erotics of *Amicitia*: Readings in Tibullus, Propertius, and Horace.' In J. Hallett and M. Skinner, eds., *Roman Sexualities*, 151–71. Princeton University Press, Princeton.

Olsen, T. 1978. *Silences*. Delacorte Press, New York.

O'Neil, E. N. 1967. 'Tibullus 2.6: A New Interpretation.' *CP* 62: 163–8.

O'Neill, K. 2000. 'Slumming with Vertumnus.' *AJP* 121: 259–77.

Oniana, R. B. 1951. *The Origins of European Thought*. Cambridge University Press, Cambridge.

Otis, B. 1965. 'Propertius' Single Book.' *HSCP* 70: 1–44.

——1966. *Ovid as an Epic Poet*. Cambridge University Press, Cambridge.

Packman, Z. M. 1993. 'Call It Rape: A Motif in Roman Comedy and Its Suppression in English-Speaking Publications.' *Helios* 20: 42–55.

Paganelli, D. 1964. *Properce: Elégies*. Les Belles Lettres, Paris.

Paley, F. A. 1853. *The Elegies of Propertius with English Notes*. John W. Parker & Son, London.

Papanghelis, T. 1987. *Propertius: A Hellenistic Poet on Love and Death*. Cambridge University Press, Cambridge.

Paratore, E. 1936. *L'elegia III.11 e gli atteggiamenti politici di Properzio*. F. Ciuni, Palermo.

——1976. *Romanae litterae*. Bardi, Rome.

——1985. "Gli atteggiamente politici di Properzio." In F. Santucci and P. Catanzaro, eds. *Bimillennano della Morte di Properzio*, 75–94. Accademia Properziana del Subasio. Assisi.

Parker, H. 2009. 'Books and Reading Latin Poetry.' In W. A. Johnson and H. Parker, eds. *Ancient Literacies. The Culture of Reading in Greece and Rome*, 186–232. Oxford University Press, Oxford.

Parsons, P. 1977. 'Callimachus: Victoria Berenices.' *ZPE* 25: 1–50.
Pasoli, E. 1957. *Propertii Monobiblon commentationes*. Pàtron, Bologna.
—— 1974. *Sesto Properzio. Il libro IV delle elegie*. Sansoni, Bologna.
Pasquali, G. 1920 (1964). *Orazio lirico*. (reprint ed. A. LaPenna). Felice le Monnier, Florence.
—— 1942 (1968). *Arte Allusiva*. In *Pagine stravaganti* Vol. II. Felice le Monnier, Florence.
Paul, G. M. 1966. 'Sallust.' In T. A. Dorey, ed. *Latin Historians*, 85–113. Routledge, London.
Pease, A. S. 1920. *M. Tulli Ciceronis De Divinatione*. University of Illinois, Urbana.
—— 1935. *Aeneid IV*. Harvard University Press, Cambridge.
Perkell, C. G. 1981. 'On Creusa, Dido, and the Quality of Victory in Virgil's *Aeneid*.' In H. Foley, ed. *Reflections of Women in Antiquity*. Gordon & Breach, New York: 355–77.
Petersmann, G. 1980. 'Themenführung und Motiventfaltung in der Monobiblos des Properz.' *Grazer Beiträge Supplementband* 1. Berger & Söhne, Horn-Graz.
Pfeiffer, R. 1949 (1965). *Callimachus Vol. 1 Fragmenta*. Clarendon Press, Oxford.
—— 1953. *Callimachus Vol. 2. Hymni et Epigrammata*. Clarendon Press, Oxford.
Phillimore, J. S. 1901. *Sexti Properti Carmina*. Clarendon Press, Oxford.
Pillinger, H. E. 1969. 'Callimachean Influences on Propertius Book IV.' *HSCP* 73: 171–99.
Pinchon, R. 1902 (1966). *Index verborum amatoriorum*. Olms, Hildesheim.
Pinotti, P. 1974. 'Sulle fonti e le intenzioni di Properzio IV 4.' *GIF* 5 (26): 18–32.
—— 1977. 'Properz. IV.9: Alessandrinismo e Arte Allusiva.' *GIF* 29: 50–71.
—— 1983. 'Properzio e Vertumno: anticonformismo e restaurazione augustea.' In G. Catanzaro and F. Santucci, eds. *Colloquium Propertianum III*. Accademia properziana del Subasio, Assisi: 75–96.
—— 2004. *Primus Ingredior. Studi su Properzio*. Pàtron, Bologna.
Platner, S. B. and T. Ashby. 1929. *A Topographical Dictionary of Rome*. Oxford University Press, London.
Platter, C. 1995. '*Officium* in Catullus and Propertius: A Foucauldian Reading.' *CP* 90: 211–24.
Pomeroy, S. B. 1975. *Goddesses, Whores, Wives and Slaves*. Schocken Books, New York.
Postgate, J. P. 1881 (1884). *Select Elegies of Propertius*. Macmillan, London.
—— 1893. *Corpus Poetarum Latinorum*. G. Bell, London.

Postgate, J. P. 1894. *Sexti Properti Carmina*. G. Bell, London.
——1915 (1963). *Tibullus carmina*. Oxford University, Oxford.
Puccioni, G. 1970. 'Herkules Trikaranos nell *Origo gentis Romanae*.' In G. Lanata, ed. *Mythos. Scripta in honorem Marii Untersteiner*, 235–9. Inst di Filologia Classica, Genoa.
Puelma Piwonka, M. 1949. *Lucilius und Kallimachos*. V. Klostermann, Frankfurt.
Putnam, M. C. J. 1979. 'Propertius 3.22: Tullus' Return.' *ICS* 2: 240–54.
Quadlbauer, F. 1968. '*Non tutior ibis*. Zu Poperz II 34, 35.' In *Hans Gerstinger— Festgabe zum 80. Geburtstag. Arbeiten aus dem Grazer Schulerkreis*, 53–68. Akademische Druck- und Verlaganstalt, Graz.
——1970. '*Non humilem . . . poetam*: zur literargeschichtlichen Stellung von Prop. 1,7,21.' *Hermes* 98: 331–9.
Quinn, K. 1970. *Catullus. The Poems*. Macmillan, London.
Rabinowitz, N. S. 1993. *Anxiety Unveiled: Euripides and the Traffic in Women*. Cornell University Press, Ithaca.
Raditsa, L. 1980. 'Augustus' legislation concerning marriage, procreation, love affairs, and adultery.' *ANRW* 2.13: 278–339.
Ramminger, A. 1937. *Motivgeschichtliche Studien zu Catulls Basiagedichten*. Triltisch, Würzburg.
Ramsby, T. 2007. *Textual Permanence*. Duckworth, London.
Rawson, E. 1978. 'Caesar, Etruria and the *Disciplina Etrusca*.' *JRS* 68: 132–52.
Reeve, M. 2000. '*Cuius in usum*? Recent and Future Editing.' *JRS* 90: 196–206.
Reitzenstein, E. 1931. *Festschrift R. Reitzenstein*. Teubner, Leipzig.
Ribbeck, O. 1885. 'Zur Erklärung und Kritik des Properz.' *RhM* 40: 481–505.
Rich, A. 1978. 'Cartographies of Silence.' In A. Rich, *The Dream of a Common Language, Poems 1974–1977*, 16–20. W.W. Norton, New York.
Richardson, L. 1977. *Propertius: Elegies I–IV*. University of Oklahoma Press, Norman.
——1992. *A New Topographical Dictionary of Ancient Rome*. Johns Hopkins University Press, Baltimore.
Richardson, N. J. 1974. *The Homeric Hymn to Demeter*. Clarendon Press, Oxford.
Richlin, A. 1981. 'Approaches to the sources on adultery at Rome.' In *Reflections on Women in Antiquity*, Ed. H. Foley: 379–404. Routledge, New York.
——1983 (1992). *The Garden of Priapus: Sexuality and Aggression in Roman Humour*. New Haven, reprinted Oxford University Press, Oxford.
——1984. 'Invective Against Women in Roman Satire.' *Arethusa* 17: 67–80.
Richmond, L. O. 1928. *Sex. Propertii quae supersunt opera edidit novoque apparatu critico instruxit*. Cambridge University Press, Cambridge.

Ringeltaube, H. 1913. *Quaestiones ad veterum philosophorum de affectibus doctrinam pertinentes.* Officina academica Huthiana, Göttingen.

Robertson, F. 1969. 'Lament for Paetus. Propertius 3.7.' *TAPA* 100: 377–86.

Rose, P. W. 1993. 'The Case for Not Ignoring Marx in the Study of Women in Antiquity.' In N. S. Rabinowitz and A. Richlin, eds. *Feminist Theory and the Classics*, 211–37. Routledge, New York.

Ross, D. O. 1969. *Style and Tradition in Catullus.* Harvard Univesity Press, Cambridge.

——1975a. *Backgrounds to Augustan Poetry. Gallus, elegy, and Rome.* Cambridge University Press, Cambridge.

——1975b. 'The *Culex* and *Moretum* as Post-Augustan Literary Parodies.' *HSCP* 79: 235–63.

Rossi, N.E. 1971. 'I generi letterari e le loro leggi scritte e non scritte nelle letterature classische.' *BICS* 18: 83–6.

Rothstein, M. 1898 (1920, 1966, 1979). *Die Elegien des Sextus Propertius.* Weidmann, Berlin. Reprinted in Dublin and New York.

Russell, D.A. 1981. 'Longinus Revisited.' *Mnemosyne* 34: 72–86.

Rutledge, H. C. 1964. 'Propertius' Tarpeia: The Poem Itself.' *CJ* 60: 68–73.

Rykwert, J. 1976. *The Idea of a Town.* Princeton University Press, Princeton.

Salvatore, A. 1956. 'Review of Schuster's *Sexti Propertii elegiarum libri IV* and Shackleton Bailey's *Propertiana*.' *Athenaeum* 34: 184–213.

Sandbach, F. H. 1962. 'Some Problems in Propertius.' *CQ* 12: 263–76.

Sandys, J. E. 1885. *Cicero Orator.* Cambridge University Press, Cambridge.

Santirocco, M. 1986. *Unity and Design in Horace's Odes.* University of North Carolina Press, Chapel Hill.

——1995. 'Horace and Augustan Ideology.' *Arethusa* 28: 225–43.

Saylor, C. 1967. '*Querelae*: Propertius' Distinctive Technical Name for his Elegy.' *Agon* 1:142–9.

Schuster, M. 1954 (1958). *Sexti Propertii Elegiarum Libri IV.* Tuebner, Leipzig. (1958 edition edited by F. Dornseiff).

Schwab, G. M. 1991. 'Irigarayan Dialogism: Play and Powerplay.' In D. M. Bauer and S. J. Mckinstry, eds. *Feminism, Bakhtin, and the Dialogic*, 57–72. State University of New York Press, Albany.

Scivoletto, N. 1961. *Aulus Perseus Flaccus. Saturae.* La Nuova Italia, Florence.

——1976. *Musa Iocosa. Studia sulla poesia giovanile di Ovidio.* Editrice Elia, Rome.

——1981. 'La città di Roma nella poesia di Properzio.' *Colloquium Propertianum* Accademia properziana del Subasio, Assisi: 27–38.

Sedgwick, E. K. 1985. 'Gender Asymmetry and Erotic Triangles.' In *Between Men: English Literature and Male Homosocial Desire*, 21–7. Columbia University Press, New York.

Serrao, G. 1971. *Problemi di poesia allesandrina. I. Studi su Teocrito*. Edizioni del Ateneo, Rome.
Shackleton Bailey, D. R. 1947. 'Interpretations of Propertius.' *CQ* 41: 89–92.
——1949. 'Propertiana.' *CQ* 43: 22–9.
——1956 (1967). *Propertiana*. A.M. Hakkert, Cambridge.
——1980. *Cicero Epistulae ad Quintum Fratrem et M. Brutum*. Cambridge University Press, Cambridge.
Sharrock, A. R. 1991a. 'Womanufacture.' *JRS* 81: 36–49.
——1991b. 'The Love of Creation.' *Ramus* 20: 169–82.
——1994a. *Seduction and Repetition in Ovid's Ars Amatoria II*. Clarendon Press, Oxford.
——1994b. 'Ovid and the Politics of Reading.' *MD* 33: 97–122.
——1995. 'The Drooping Rose: Elegiac Failure in *Amores* 3.7.' *Ramus* 24: 152–80.
——2000. 'Constructing Characters in Propertius.' *Arethusa* 33: 263–84.
Sissa, G. 1990. *Greek Virginity*. Trans. by Arthur Goldhammer. Harvard University Press, Cambridge.
Skinner, M. 1983. 'Clodia Metelli.' *TAPA* 113: 273–87.
——1986. 'Rescuing Creusa: new approaches to women in antiquity.' *Helios* 13.2: 1–8.
——1997. 'Introduction: *Quod multo fit aliter in Graecia*....' In J. Hallett and M. Skinner, eds. *Roman Sexualities*, 3–25. Princeton University Press, Princeton.
Skutsch, F. 1901. *Aus Vergils Frühzeit*. Teubner, Leipzig.
——1906. *Gallus und Vergil*. Tuebner, Leipzig.
Skutsch, O. 1963. 'The Structure of the Propertian Monobiblos.' *CP* 58: 238–9.
——1973. 'Readings in Propertius.' *CQ* 23: 316–23.
——1975. 'The Second Book of Propertius.' *HSCP* 79: 229–33.
Smith, B. H. 1977. *On the Margins of Discourse: the Relation of Literature to Language*. University of Chicago Press, Chicago.
Smith, K. F. 1913 (1971). *The Elegies of Albius Tibulus*. Wissenschaftliche Buchgesellschaft, Darmstadt.
Smith, L. P. 1994. 'Audience Response to Rape: Chaerea in Terence's *Eunuchus*.' *Helios* 21: 21–38.
Smyth, W. R. 1970. *Thesaurus Criticus ad Sexti Properti Textum*. Mnemosyne Supplement 12. Brill, Leiden.
Solmsen, F. 1948. 'Propertius and Horace.' *CP* 43: 105–9.

───1961. 'Propertius and his Literary Relations with Tibullus and Vergil.' *Philol.* 105: 273–89.

Spencer, D. 2001. 'Propertius, Hercules, and the Dynamics of Roman Mythic Space in Elegy 4.9.' *Arethusa* 34: 259–84.

Spies, A., 1930 (1978). *Militat omnis amans. Ein Beitrag zur Bildersprache der antiken Erotik.* Diss. Tübingen.

Staden, H. von. 1991. '*Apud nos foediora verba*: Celsus' reluctant construction of the female body.' In G. Sabbah, ed., *Le Latin médical: La constitution d'un langage scientifique. Réalités et langage de la médecine dans le monde romaine.* Actes du IIIe colloque international 'Textes medicaux latins antiques.' Saint-Etienne, 11–13 Septembre 1989, 271–96. Universitè de St. Etienne, Saint-Etienne.

Stahl, H. P. 1950. 'Properzio e i poeti latini dell' età aurea.' *Maia* 3: 209–36.

───1981. 'Aeneas—an "Unheroic" Hero?' *Arethusa* 14: 157–77.

───1985. *Propertius: 'love' and 'war': individual and state under Augustus.* University of California Press, Berkeley.

───1990. 'The Death of Turnus: Augustan Vergil and the Political Rival.' In Raaflaub, K. A., M. Toher, and G. W. Bowersock. *Between republic and empire: interpretations of Augustus and his principate,* 174–211. University of California Press, Berkeley.

Steele, M. 1997. *Theorizing Textual Subjects: Agency and Oppression.* Cambridge University Press, Cambridge.

Steidle, W. 1962. 'Das Motif der Lebenswahl bei Tibull und Properz.' *WS* 75: 100–40.

Strong, E. 1929. *L'arte in Roma antica.* Istituto Italiano d'Arti Grafiche, Bergamo.

Suits, T. A. 1976. 'The Iambic Character of Propertius 1.4.' *Philologus* 120: 86–91.

Sullivan, J. P. 1961. 'Two problems in Roman love elegy.' *TAPA* 92: 522–36.

───1964. *Ezra Pound and Sextus Propertius: A Study in Creative Translation.* University of Texas Press, Austin.

───1976. *Propertius. A Critical Introduction.* Cambridge University Press, Cambridge.

───1984. 'Propertius IV: Themes and Structure.' *ICS* 9: 30–4.

Swinburne, A. 1925. *The Complete Works of Algernon Charles Swinburne.* Edmund Gosse and Thomas James Wise, eds. W. Heinemann, London.

Syme, Ronald. 1938. 'The origin of Cornelius Gallus.' *CQ* 32: 39–44.

───1939. *The Roman Revolution.* Oxford University Press, Oxford.

───1978. *History in Ovid.* Oxford University Press, Oxford.

Taliercio, A. 1985. 'Alcuni aspetti dell'etiologia in età Augustea.' *RCCM* 21: 13–21.

Tanselle, G. Thomas. 1990. *Textual Criticism and Scholarly Editing*. University Press of Virginia, Charlottesville.

Tarrant, R. J. 1979. 'Review of K. Morgan, *Ovid's Art of Imitation: Propertius in the Amores* (Leiden).' *Phoenix* 33: 92–3.

——1987. 'Toward a Typology of Interpolation in Latin Poetry.' *TAPA* 117: 281–98.

——1989. 'The Reader as Author. Collaborative Interpolation in Latin Poetry.' In J. N. Grant, ed. *Editing Greek and Latin Texts*, 121–62. AMS Press, New York.

——2006. 'Propertian textual criticism and editing.' In H. C. Günther, ed. *Brill's Companion to Propertius*, 45–65. Brill, Leiden.

Taylor, G. 1989. *Reinventing Shakespeare: A Cultural History from the Restoration to the Present*. Weidenfeld & Nicholson, New York.

Thomas, E. 1964. 'Variations on a Military Theme in Ovid's *Amores*.' *G&R* n.s. 11: 151–65.

Thomas, R. 1979. 'New Comedy, Callimachus, and Roman Poetry.' *HSCP* 83: 179–206.

——1983. 'Callimachus, the Victoria Berenices, and Roman Poetry.' *CQ* 33: 92–113.

——1996. 'Genre through intertextuality. Theocritus to Vergil and Propertius.' In M. A. Harder, R. F. Regtuit, and G. C. Wakker, eds. *Theocritus*. Forsten, (Hellenistica Groningana 2), Groningen: 227–46.

——1998. 'Melodious Tears. Sepulchral epigram and generic mobility.' *Hellenistica Groningana* 3: 205–23.

——2004. '"Drownded in the Tide": The *Nauagika* and some problems in Augustan poetry.' In B. Acosta-Hughes, E. Kosmetatou, and M. Baumbach, eds. *Labored in Papyrus Leaves: Perspectives on an Epigram Collection Attributed to Posidippus*, 258–75. Center for Hellenic Studies, Trustees for Harvard University, Washington, DC.

Tracy, V. A. 1979. 'One aspect of *nequitia* in Ovid's *Amores*.' In Carl Deroux, ed. *Studies in Latin Literature and Roman History* I. *Collection Latomus* 164: 343–8.

Tränkle, H. 1960. *Die Sprachkunst des Properz und die Tradition der lateinischen Dichtersprache*. F. Steiner, Wiesbaden.

——1968. 'Beiträge zur Textkritik und Erklärung des Properz.' *Hermes* 96: 559–82.

——1983. 'Properzio poeta dell' opposizione politica?' *Colloquium Propertianum (tertium): Atti*, 149–62. Accademia Properziana del Subasio, Assisi.

——1985. 'Die Sprache des Properz und die stilistischen Tendenzen der augusteischen Dichtung.' In G. Catanzaro and F. Santucci, eds. *Bimillenario della morte di Properzio.*, 155–73. Accademia Properziana del Subasio, Assisi.

Treggiari, S. 1991. *Roman marriage: iusti coniuges from the time of Cicero to the time of Ulpian.* Clarendon Press, Oxford.

Tupet, A. M. 1976. *La magie dans la poésie latine.* Les Belles Lettres, Paris.

Tyrrell, W. B. 1984. *Amazons: A Study in Athenian Mythmaking.* Johns Hopkins University Press, Baltimore.

Van Sickle, John. 1978. *The Design of Virgil's Bucolics.* Edizioni dell'Ateneo & Bizzarri, Rome.

Veyne, P. 1983. *L'Élégie érotique romaine: l'amour, la poésie et l'occident.* Paris: Éditions du Seuil.

——1988. *Roman erotic elegy: love, poetry, and the West.* Trans. by D. Pellauer. University of Chicago Press, Chicago.

Viarre, S. 2005. *Properce: Élégies.* Les Belles Lettres, Paris.

Viparelli Santangelo, V. 1984. 'La Teoria del Neologismo in Orazio.' *BStudLat.* 14: 39–63.

Walde, A. and J. B. Hofmann. 1938 (1954). *Lateinisches etymologisches Wörterbuch* 3. C. Winter, Heidelberg.

Wallace-Hadrill, A. 1985. 'Propaganda and Dissent? Augustan Moral Legislation and the Love-Poets.' *Klio* 67: 180–4.

Walsh, T. J. R. 1983. 'Propertius' Tarpeia Elegy (4.4).' *LCM* 8.5: 75–6.

Walter, H. 1999. 'Zum Gedichtschluss von Ovid, Am. 1,2.' In Werner Schubert, ed. *Ovid: Werk und Wirkung, Festgabe für Michael von Albrecht zum 65 Geburtstag*, vol. 1. Peter Lang, Frankfurt: 87–98.

Warden, J. 1978. 'Another Would-Be Amazon: Propertius 4, 4, 72–72.' *Hermes* 106: 177–87.

——1980. *Fallax Opus: Poet and Reader in the Elegies of Propertius.* University of Toronto Press, Toronto.

——1982. 'Epic into Elegy: Propertius 4.9.70ff.' *Hermes* 110: 228–42.

Weeber, K. H. 1977. *Das 4. Properz-Buch: Interpretationen zu seiner Eigenart und seiner Stellung im Gesamtwerk.* Diss. Ruhr-Universität Bochum.

——1978. 'Prop. 4.1.1–70 und das 8. Buch der Aeneis.' *Latomus* 37: 489–506.

Weed, E. 1994. 'The Question of Style.' In C. Burke, N. Schor, and M. Whitford, eds. *Engaging with Irigaray*, 79–109. Columbia University Press, New York.

Welch, T. S. 2005a. *The Elegiac Cityscape: Propertius and the Meaning of Roman Monuments.* Ohio State University Press, Columbus.

Welch, T. S. 2005b. '*Amor* vs. *Roma*: Gender and Landscape in Propertius' Tarpeia Poem.' In E. Greene and R. Ancona, eds. *Gendered Dynamics in Latin Love Elegy.* 296–317. Johns Hopkins University Press, Baltimore.
Wellesley, K. 1969. '*Propertius' Tarpeia Poem (IV 4).*' *Acta Classica Univ. Scient. Debrecen.* 5: 93–103.
West, D. 1983. '*Pauca meo Gallo.*' *LCM* 8.6: 92–3.
Whitaker, R. 1983. *Myth and Personal Experience in Roman Love-Elegy: A Study in Poetic Technique.* Vandenhoeck & Ruprecht, Göttingen.
White, P. 1993. *Promised verse. Poets in the Society of Augustan Rome.* Harvard University Press, Cambridge.
Whitford, M. 1991. *Luce Irigaray: Philosophy in the Feminine.* Routledge, London.
Wiggers, N. 1977. 'Reconsideration of Propertius 2.1.' *CJ* 72: 334–41.
Wilamowitz, U. 1935–72. *Kleine Schriften* Vols. I–IV. Ed. P. Maas. Weidmann, Berlin.
Wilkinson, L. P. 1960. 'Propertius III 4.' In *Studi in onore di Luigi Castiglioni*, vol. 2, 1091–103. G.C. Sansoni, Florence.
——1966. 'The continuity of Propertius ii.13.' *CR* 16: 141–4.
Wille, G. 1983. 'Der Aufbau des dritten Elegienbuches des Properz.' In P. Händel and W. Meid, eds. *Festschrift für Robert Muth. Innsbrucker Beitrager zur Kulturwissenschaft* 22: 597–611.
Williams, C. 1999. *Roman Homosexuality: Ideologies of Masculinity in Classical Antiquity.* Oxford University Press, New York.
Williams, G. 1958. 'Some aspects of marriage ceremonies and ideals.' *JRS* 48: 16–29.
——1968. *Tradition and Originality in Roman Poetry.* Clarendon Press, Oxford.
——1969. *The Third Book of Horace's Odes.* Clarendon Press, Oxford.
Williams, P. 1991. *The Alchemy of Race and Rights.* Harvard University Press, Cambridge.
Wilson, M. F. 2006. 'The new Posidippus Papyri and Propertius' Shipwreck Odes (Prop. 1.17 and 3.7).' *Classica et Mediaevalia* 57: 103–24.
Wimmel, W. 1960. *Kallimachos in Rom: Die Nachfolge seines apologetischen Dichtens in der Augusteerzeit.* Steiner, Wiesbaden.
——1973. *Hirtenkrieg und arkadisches Rom. Reduktionsmedien in Vergils Aeneis.* W. Fink, Munich.
——1976. *Tibull und Delia. 1. Teil: Tibulls Elegie 1, 1. Hermes Einzelschriften* 37. Franz Steiner, Wiesbaden.
Wiseman, T. P. 1969. *Catullan Questions.* Leicester University Press, Leicester.

———1971. *New Men in the Roman Senate. 139 B.C.–A.D. 14*. Oxford University Press, Oxford.
———1978. 'Flavians on the Capitol.' *AJAH* 3: 163–78.
———1979. *Clio's Cosmetics*. Leicester University Press, Leicester.
———1985. *Catullus and his World: A Reappraisal*. Cambridge University Press, Cambridge.
Wistrand, E. 1977. *Miscellanea Propertiana. Studia Graeca et Latina Gothoburg.* 38. Acta Universitatis, Goteborg.
Woodman, A. and J. Powell, (eds.) 1992. *Author and Audience in Latin Literature*. Cambridge University Press, Cambridge.
Woolley, A. 1967. 'The Structure of Propertius Book III.' *BICS* 14: 80–3.
Wyke, M. 1984. *The Elegiac Woman and her Male Creators: Propertius and the Written Cynthia*. Diss., University of Cambridge.
———1987a. 'The Elegiac Woman at Rome.' *PCPS* 33: 153–78.
———1987b. 'Written Women: Propertius' *Scripta Puella*.' *JRS* 77: 47–61.
———1989a. 'Mistress and Metaphor in Augustan Elegy.' *Helios* 16: 25–47.
———1989b. 'In Pursuit of Love, the Poetic Self, and a Process of Reading: Augustan Elegy in the 1980s.' *JRS* 79: 165–73.
———1995. 'Taking the Woman's Part: Engendering Roman Love Elegy.' In A. J. Boyle, ed. *Roman Literature and Ideology: Ramus Essays for J. P. Sullivan*, 110–28. Aureal Publications, Bendigo, Australia.
———2002. *The Roman Mistress. Ancient and Modern Representations*. Oxford University Press, Oxford.
Yardley, G. 1978. 'The Elegiac Paraklausithyron.' *Eranos* 75: 19–34.
Zanker, P. 1988. *The Power of Images in the Age of Augustus*. Trans. H. A. Shapiro. Ann University of Michigan Press, Arbor.
Zeitlin, F. 1996. 'Playing the Other: Theater, Theatricality, and the Feminine in Greek Drama.' In *Playing the Other: Gender and Society in Classical Greek Literature*, 341–74. University of Chicago Press, Chicago.
Zetzel, J. G. 1977. 'Review article: Gallus, Elegy, and Ross.' *CP* 72: 249–60.
———1980. 'Horace's *Liber Sermonum*: The Structure of Ambiguity.' *Arethusa* 13: 59–77.
———1983. 'Re-Creating the Canon: Augustan Literature and the Alexandrian Past.' *Criticial Inquiry* 10: 83–105.
———1992. 'Roman Romanticism and Other Fables.' In K. Galinsky, ed. *The Interpretation of Roman Poetry: Empiricism or Hermeneutics*, 41–57. Peter Lang, Frankfurt.

Zetzel, J. G. 1996. 'Poetic Baldness and its Cure.' *MD* 36: 73–100.
Zingerle, A. 1869. *Ovidius und sein Verhältnis zu den Vorgangern und gleichzeitigen römischen Dichter* I. Druck der Wagnerschen Buchdruckerei, Innsbruck.
Zizek, S. 1989. *The Sublime Object of Ideology.* Verso, London.
——1991. *Looking Awry: An Introduction to Jacques Lacan through Popular Culture.* MIT Press, Cambridge.
——1993. Tarrying with the Negative: Kant, Hegel, and the Critique of Ideology. Duke University Press, Durham.

# Index of Propertius Poems

1.1  212–13, 217–22, 228
1.2  205–7, 219–21
1.3  34–5, 213–21, 325, 418
1.4  140–74, 178–185
1.5  140–74, 178–85, 200, 223–6, 228, 230
1.6  257–8, 262, 280
1.7  187, 205, 228
1.8  228–230, 325–6, 334–5, 363–4
1.9  187
1.9  187, 205, 228–30
1.10  226–8, 230
1.13  199
1.15  37–9
1.17  196–8
1.18  197–8, 210–11
1.20  60–1, 107, 197–8, 200
1.21  39–40, 71–2, 196–9
1.22  71–2, 196–9

2.1  79, 281–2, 351–2, 373–5, 377, 379, 381, 442–9
2.3  79–81
2.5  51
2.7  273–5, 289–98, 339–40, 349, 449–54
2.8  285–6, 375–88
2.9  388–403
2.10  189
2.13  230, 287
2.14  7, 282–4
2.15  77, 282–3, 433–6
2.16  110, 283, 347, 433–5
2.18  365–6
2.19  335
2.22  367
2.30  287

2.31  308–10
2.33  76–7
2.34  81–6, 91–2, 237

3.1  236–40
3.2  56–7, 305, 363
3.3  36, 458
3.4  57, 187, 240–3, 457–62
3.5  187, 245–6, 249–57, 457, 462–8
3.6  63
3.7  62–3, 251
3.9  107, 247–8, 307–8
3.10  74–5
3.11  305–7, 311, 343, 455–7
3.12  251
3.13  57–8, 81, 86–8
3.14  54–6, 88–90
3.16  51–3
3.21  262
3.22  260–70, 418
3.23  366
3.25  336

4.1  192–5, 304–5, 310–13, 315–16, 318, 344
4.2  313
4.3  191–3, 313
4.4  118, 192, 311, 313, 318, 404–8, 411–29
4.5  51, 313
4.6  58–9, 193, 313–14
4.7  194–5, 313, 337
4.8  109, 313, 337
4.9  118–37, 314, 318
4.10  314–15
4.11  193, 315, 355–6, 367–9

# General Index

Achilles 285–6, 383–8, 391–2, 395–7, 399, 401
Actium 17, 21, 58–9, 84–5, 190–1, 193, 237, 239, 242, 282–3, 302–6 *passim*, 313–4, 431–5, 437
*Aition*/aetion/aetiological 12, 116–20, 124–6, 135, 190–2, 194, 268, 313–4, 334, 336, 412
Alexandrian tradition 12, 14, 33, 113, 116–37 *passim*, 208, 210, 220–1, 229, 237, 240, 467
Amazons 88–90, 417–20, 423, 425
*Amicus/amicitia* 294, 376–7, 385, 389, 395, 397, 402
Antigone 381–4, 391
Antony, Marc 8, 124, 175, 248, 255, 283, 348, 433–5, 445, 455–6
Apollo 17, 36, 58–9, 83–4, 117, 190, 193–4, 207, 209, 219, 229, 237, 240, 307–9, 313, 338, 366, 434, 442, 447
Apollonius Rhodius 116, 188–9, 197
Apuleius 331, 340
Archaism 4, 6, 33, 104–6, 121, 218
Asinius Pollio 168, 177, 340
Augustus 15–18, 58–9, 124, 126, 172, 178, 193, 195–6, 199, 235–6, 238, 242, 247–58, 265, 274, 288, 290, 303, 304–5, 310, 315–17, 406, 436, 449–50, 452–3, 456–7, 461, 469–70 *see also* Octavian
  Marriage legislation 283–301 *passim*, 349–50, 449–51
  propaganda 124–5, 265, 348, 433, 459, 469
  pro, anti–Augustanism 15–22, 75, 235–72 *passim*, 290, 405, 432–7, 451–3, 460–1

Bassus 13, 141–2, 147–68 *passim*, 162–7, 182–5, 199, 221, 284, 367
Briseis 383–4, 387–8, 391–2, 395, 401

*Callida iunctura* 14, 104–13 *passim*
Callimachus 12–14, 100, 164, 166, 208–9, 237, 239, 247, 266, 333, 338–9
Callimacheanism 4, 12, 117–20, 123, 125, 130, 137, 184, 191, 208–9, 211–12, 220–2, 228, 231, 333, 432, 455, 458
  *Aitia* 117, 136–7, 139, 188, 210, 239
  *Epigrams* 144–5, 219
  *Hymns* 119, 136, 188
  *Iambi* 13, 164, 166
Calvus 83–5, 100–1
*Captatio benevolentiae* 130, 133
Catullus 64, 84–5, 101, 197–208, 139, 189, 198, 214–20, 224
Cicero 100, 173–4, 409–10
Cleopatra 111, 242, 304–6, 348, 362, 433–5, 455–6
Clodia Metelli 278, 345–7
Cornelia 21, 26, 190, 193, 195, 355–7, 367–70, 413, 415

Dating of the collection 176, 178–9, 457–8
*Deducere* 208, 228
*Domina* 102, 343, 347, 352, 371, 394, 399, 441

*Ekphrasis* 22, 412
Erotodidaxis 13, 142, 145–7
*Exclusus amator* 125–37, 142, 144, 161, 295
Ezra Pound 7, 44, 49, 137

*Fama* 82, 181, 375, 378, 381
Foucault 350, 358

Gallus 8, 11, 13, 39–40, 48, 50, 72, 84, 101–2, 138–185 *passim*, 195–200 *passim*, 206, 210, 218–26, 230, 335, 337, 349, 358, 364, 470
Graffiti 16, 50–3, 63, 93
Grecisms 10, 102, 103–8

## General Index

Haemon 381, 383, 391–92
Hair 14–5, 34, 55, 64, 74, 79,
  203–11, 231, 255, 330, 332,
  392, 416
Hellenistic poetry 4, 6, 10, 12, 33, 45, 58,
  100–1, 105, 107, 136, 139–40, 164,
  166–7, 178, 188, 218, 237, 274–5,
  279, 326–7, 338, 343, 442
Hercules 12, 17, 116–37 *passim*, 314,
  318, 333
Horace 97, 99, 103–14 *passim*, 256, 265,
  276, 288
  *Ars Poetica* 103–4, 129
  *Epistles* 14, 103, 112–14, 180–2
  *Epodes* 112–13
  *Odes* 112–13, 139, 144, 147, 164, 173,
    181–2, 252, 305, 317, 456
  *Satires* 112–14
Hostia 331, 334, 338, 340–41

Iambic poetry 163–8, 178, 184, 221
*Iliad* 201, 279, 281, 285–8, 296, 293,
  304, 336–7, 384, 392
Imaginary 17, 346–7, 406, 430–2,
  444–5, 471
Irigaray, Luce 405–9, 427, 438–41

*Jouissance* 437, 441

*Komos/komastes* 17, 126–7, 136,
  143, 294

Lacan, Jacques 370, 405–6, 430–1,
  437–41
Livia 21, 126, 135
Livy 100, 123, 243, 304, 312–14,
  415, 427

Maecenas 16, 19, 82, 126, 178, 192, 242,
  247–8, 256, 272, 281, 290, 294, 307,
  334, 376, 386, 431, 433, 436, 442–5,
  449, 455, 458, 469
Magic 212, 218, 221–230, 266, 400
*Magister amoris*, see *erotodidaxis*
Manuscript tradition (general) 4, 6,
  32–33, 45–8, 53–5, 58–61, 63–4, 68,
  72–3, 120, 193, 468
*Materia* 381–2, 387, 400
Meleager 12, 14, 100

Milanion 217–20, 266
*Militia amoris* 255, 275–8, 279–81, 284,
  286–9, 293–4, 299–300, 343–4,
  351–2, 354, 443, 453, 462, 464, 466
*Monobiblos* 25, 140, 146, 168, 174–7,
  179, 182, 203, 205, 212, 22–3, 230,
  236, 261–2, 333, 362, 367–8, 383–4,
  431–2, 468, 480

Neologism 4, 6, 33, 36, 103–106, 362
*Negotium* 284, 460, 470
Neoteric 10–11, 211, 215, 219–20,
  229–30

Octavian 175, 195, 199, 235, 243–4, 246,
  260, 263, 264, 308, 348, 432 *see also*
  Augustus
*Odyssey* 286, 337, 137, 304, 336
Odysseus 337, 391, 396
*Otium* 276–8, 282, 300, 444, 460, 470
Ovid 53, 103, 107, 109, 113, 358–9, 363
  *Amores* 14, 171–2, 203–13, 221, 223,
    231–2, 324, 352–3
  *Ars amatoria* 75, 204, 216, 406
  *Metamorphoses* 139–140, 208–9

*Paraklausithyron* 125–37
Parthians 201, 238, 240–58 *passim*, 279,
  282, 459, 461–2
*Pax* 238–40, 247, 249–50, 264, 461
Penelope 216, 285–6, 337, 390–91, 397
Perugia 39, 43, 177, 195–6, 199–200,
  205, 229, 238, 397
Philitas 220, 237, 247, 266
Pindar 140, 157
Ponticus 162–3, 165–6, 199–200, 205,
  221, 229, 228

Quintilian 48, 50, 53

*Recusatio* 244, 256, 281, 288, 292, 304,
  307, 355, 374, 376, 431–3, 439, 442,
  448, 451
Rome, city of 21, 191, 197–8, 416,
  302–22 *passim*, 405, 410, 414,
  416, 422
  Ara Maxima 2, 116–25 *passim*, 314
  Bona Dea, shrine 120, 124–37
    *passim*

Rome, city of (*Cont.*)
  *Forum Boarium* 116–18, 120, 125, 314
  Palatine 117–16, 120
  urban life 136, 191, 302–22 *passim*
  *Velabrum* 117, 120, 312–14

Sabines 404–6, 415–16, 420, 426, 429
Sallust 100, 345, 348
*Servitium amoris* 27, 150–2, 156, 279, 343, 352, 354, 361, 375, 441, 454
Sparta 54–5, 88–90, 157, 162
Symbolic 431–2, 437–8, 440–1, 450, 452, 455, 461, 466, 470

Tarpeia 21, 26–7, 118, 121, 126, 192–3, 311–12, 318, 355, 370, 414–29 *passim*
Tatius 414–17, 421–3, 425–6, 428

Theocritus 12, 21, 100, 112, 128–9, 136, 144, 148–9, 157–8
Tibullus 48, 103, 105–15 *passim*, 180–2, 222, 271, 276–8, 332, 335
Tullus 147, 174, 176–9, 183, 199, 255, 257, 260–3, 266–70, 272

Varro Reatinus 117, 125, 304, 311–13
Varro Atacinus 83–5, 101, 108
Vergil 80–6, 101–15 *passim*, 118, 168, 177, 235–8, 242
  *Aeneid* 21, 81–6, 120–4, 210, 243n 245, 264, 268, 291, 303–6, 316, 318, 337, 382–3, 429, 457–9, 461
  *Eclogues* 82–5, 112, 179–80, 189, 197, 208–11, 219, 230
  *Georgics* 82–6, 113, 189